CLASSICAL

P9-AFC-318

A08943961001

DATE DUE

NO 8 '91			
JA 8 '93			
SE 2 9 '98			
AP 1 30			
DE 1 9 01			
OC 1 5 09			

DEMCO 38-296

CLASSICAL POLITICAL THEORIES

SOURCEBOOKS IN PHILOSOPHY
Paul Edwards, General Editor

CLASSICAL

 POLITICAL

THEORIES

FROM
PLATO
TO
MARX

EDITED, WITH INTRODUCTION, NOTES,
AND BIBLIOGRAPHY BY

Robert Brown
THE AUSTRALIAN NATIONAL UNIVERSITY

MACMILLAN   PUBLISHING   COMPANY
NEW YORK
COLLIER   MACMILLAN   PUBLISHERS
LONDON

Editor: Helen McInnis
Production Supervisor: John Sollami
Production Manager: Nick Sklitsis
Text Designer: Folio Graphics Company, Inc.
Cover Designer: Carol Russo Design, Inc.

This book was set in Cheltenham Light by Digitype, and printed and bound by Hamilton Printing Company. The cover was printed by Phoenix Color Corporation.

Macmillan Publishing Company
866 Third Avenue, New York, New York 10022

Collier Macmillan Canada, Inc.

Library of Congress Cataloging-in-Publication Data
Classical political theories: from Plato to Marx / edited with
  introduction, notes, and bibliography by Robert Brown.
    p.   cm. — (Sourcebooks in philosophy)
  ISBN 0-02-315591-4
  1. Political science — History. I. Brown, Robert, 1920- .
II. Series.
JA81.C56 1990
320'.01'1 — dc20   89-12848
                CIP

Printing: 1 2 3 4 5 6 7   Year: 0 1 2 3 4 5 6

Acknowledgments

A volume of this size and scope is bound to have required the labor of many people who have contributed to its better features and are innocent of its faults. This anthology owes its initial outline, and much else besides, to Professor James Moore of Concordia University, Montreal. It has been aided in many ways by my colleagues Dr. Knud Haakonssen and Professor Eugene Kamenka, and has certainly benefited from the research efforts of Elizabeth Short. I thank Dr. Nicholas Phillipson of Edinburgh University for useful bibliographical suggestions. The large burden of clerical work has been greatly lessened for me by the help of Wendie Hare, Margaret Tyrie, and Vibeke Wetselaar, and I am heavily indebted to them.

I am most grateful for permission to reprint selections from books whose copyright is held by Associated Book Publishers (U.K.) Ltd., Basil Blackwell, Oxford, J.M. Dent & Sons, Ltd., London, and International Publishers, New York. The details of each of these permissions are given at the beginning of the relevant sections in the text.

In the Contents I have abbreviated chapter titles in the selections from Machiavelli and Hobbes and shortened book titles for Pufendorf and Locke. I have also supplied various titles in the selections from Plato, Aristotle, Cicero, Hume, and Mill. In the case of Pufendorf his own book and section titles have been given in the Contents, but not in the text itself.

R. B.

Contents

St. Thomas Aquinas
(1225–1274)

Niccolò Machiavelli
(1469–1527)

Jean Bodin
(1530–1596)

Thomas Hobbes
(1588–1679)

Samuel von Pufendorf
(1632–1694)

John Locke
(1632–1704)

Baron de Montesquieu
(1689–1755)

David Hume
(1711–1776)

Jean-Jacques Rousseau
(1712-1778)

Edmund Burke
(1729-1797)

Thomas Paine
(1737-1809)

Georg W. F. Hegel
(1770-1831)

John Stuart Mill
(1806-1873)

Karl Marx
(1818-1883)

CLASSICAL POLITICAL THEORIES

INTRODUCTION

I

The phrase "political theory" has several different senses and should be treated with caution even though it has been used in the title of this book. The phrase sometimes is used, for example, to refer to the structure, efficiency, and social consequences of different sorts of political systems. At other times the phrase refers to something quite different—to the moral worthiness of the judgments and principles that are expressed in those systems. The first usage asks us to consider questions such as how certain political institutions —for example, the judicial system of the legislature—can be more efficiently organized to carry out their intended work, or how a particular form of authoritarian regime compares with its rivals in controlling political dissidents. The second usage, in leading us to examine the philosophical—usually moral—foundations of political arrangements, gives rise to queries such as "What is an unjust action?" "Should people treat each other as political equals?" and "Should there be limits on freedom of expression?" Thus, each of the two usages raises distinctive types of questions, and correspondingly different methods are required to obtain answers to them. The methods are different because questions about the character of a particular kind of organization are largely questions of fact. They may be very complicated, or perhaps unanswerable with the information at our disposal, but the only rational way to approach the problem is to examine the ways in which the organization actually works. We must seek evidence in experience and draw conclusions from it.

In contrast, questions about the moral value of a political practice or institution demand that we utilize our ethical principles and moral beliefs not as fact but as supporting evidence. We can try to show, for example, that our political practices reflect our principles because the former are concrete manifestations of the latter or in some other way follow from them. But we can also try to show that our principles express, or lead to, moral valuations that we are prepared to defend — that our moral rules and basic valuations are more worthwhile than competing ones. One common way in which we try to do this is to begin by arguing that the results of adopting our rules of behavior are more acceptable, desirable, or valuable than results produced by the adoption of a different set of rules. If, for instance, promise-keeping and truth-telling must be widely practiced in order for society to function appropriately — or perhaps function at all — then they are necessary rules, and components, of social life. If we value social life for the sorts of human qualities and relationships that it makes possible, then we must value these rules for their part in the process. Hence we must keep promises and tell the truth. The question then becomes what sort of value we are placing upon these rules: Is it moral value in whole or part? Or is it merely their usefulness as means to valuable goals? Or is some other kind of valuation present?

Under the category of "political theory" there is, then, a basic distinction between interest in the actual operations of political systems, institutions, and offices and interest in the moral principles, rules, and judgments that are incorporated in those political arrangements. The first interest is that of the modern political scientist or student of government. It is well represented in the writings of some of the authors assembled here. Machiavelli is an outstanding example of someone whose interest in political life is almost entirely of this kind, or at least of someone who does not explicitly discuss the moral problems that are generated by political actions. For this reason he is not really a political philosopher and fits oddly into any group of them. Yet it is almost impossible to omit him from a history of political philosophy. Why is this? It is impossible because Machiavelli's ideas have become an important part of the discussions carried on by political philosophers. Some of his views have often been misunderstood and even more often criticized. But his views are important because they express permanent problems in the use and maintenance of political power, and hence in the functioning of any complex society. Machiavelli has come, therefore, to serve both as an indispensable target for critics of power politics and as an equally indispensable authority for its supporters. Since the argument between these two schools of thought is a moral one — whether moral considerations ought to be subordinated to political benefits — the issue cannot be avoided by political philosophers.

The second interest, that of the moral problems raised by political institutions and behavior, is displayed in explicit form in all the texts in this volume except those by Machiavelli. Two particularly clear examples are the selections from Plato's *Republic* and Aquinas's *Summa Theologiae*. Both are concerned with the nature of justice or morally right conduct. Aquinas begins by discussing, and approving of, Aristotle's definition of justice as the rendering to each person that which is his or hers by right — that which is due to the person. Aquinas then goes on to describe, and argue for, various features of justice and the relationship of justice to other virtues. Plato, by contrast, begins at the other end by considering some common definitions of justice such as reciprocity: that is, harming enemies and helping friends. After exposing the inadequacy of these definitions, Plato takes up the question of whether justice is desirable simply because it is useful or because it is good in itself. He concludes by comparing justice as a quality of government and justice as a quality of an individual person's actions. The two sorts of justice turn out to be very similar for Plato and yield the definition for which he has been searching.

Most of the texts included here — and large parts of political theory in general — are not, however, pure examples of either political philosophy or the discussion of different political institutions and types of government. They are mixtures of both. For instance, in Book III of the *Politics* Aristotle remarks that where the wealthy rule that is an oligarchy "and where the poor rule, that is a democracy." In support of this, he points out that because the poor are everywhere numerous and the wealthy few, it is sometimes thought, mistakenly, that an oligarchy is to be defined as the rule of the few and a democracy as the rule of the many. This is a mistake, Aristotle says, because even if the wealthy were numerous their rule would be an oligarchy since the government would be exercised in the interests of the rich alone. Their claim to power is based on the size of their possessions and not on their numbers. The democrats reject this claim and base their own claims for the poor on the freedom produced by political equality. At this point Aristotle expands his topic from that of distinguishing between two forms of government to that of describing, and criticizing, the two different views of justice held by the oligarchs and the democrats. For these two views are employed by their supporters to justify the establishment of their preferred form of government. Thus, Aristotle's discussion begins with the different forms of government and develops into a piece of philosophical analysis concerned with justice. Later in Book III Aristotle applies the results of that second investigation to actual Greek practices such as legal ostracism — the banishment from the city for a time of people who are excessively rich or influential. This sort of interchange between the two kinds of analysis is characteristic of the classical tradition of political theory.

Moreover, each of the two sorts of analysis can be usefully subdivided — usefully because otherwise we shall neglect a pair of important activities carried on by political thinkers. Analysis of different forms of government, once we recall examples of it, is of two types. First, there is the description and practical criticism of organizational practices and of administrative institutions and systems, either current or historical. Machiavelli's remarks, in *The Discourses*, Book I, Chapters 4, 5, and 6, on the quarrels between the people and the senate in ancient Rome are a good example of this sort of description and criticism. Another example is Mill's discussion, in *The Subjection of Women*, of why women have so commonly failed to rebel against their subjection to the power of men. The reasons he gives are sociological and historical rather than moral. Women, he reminds us, "are brought up from the very earliest years in the belief that their ideal of character is the very opposite to that of men"; they are entirely dependent on their husbands for "every privilege or pleasure"; and women are taught that it is an essential part of their attractiveness that they be submissive and meek. In addition, if a woman complains of being badly treated by her husband the law simply returns her to the household, and hence the power, of the man who ill-used her.

Much of what is called "political theory" has always been of this practical kind: the scrutiny of existing practices with a view to improving them. The lengthy, and, in the case of some authors, interminable, discussions of the differences between the "true" forms of the state—monarchy, aristocracy, and constitutional government—and "perverted" forms—tyranny, oligarchy, and democracy—owe their original popularity to the fact that they dealt with important practical issues of the period, namely, which social groups were to hold power. It mattered greatly to Hobbes where the line was drawn between the monarch's power and the liberties of his subjects. For Hobbes wrote the *Leviathan* in the midst of the English civil war when the two opposing sides, the Royalists and the Puritans, held very different views, for which they took up arms, as to what the powers of the king and the rights of his people should be. Questions such as under what conditions mercenary troops—hired foreign soldiers—could be safely used by a government, or how a ruler should choose his personal assistants and advisors, were of widespread interest in the days before there was either a compulsory military service or a national bureaucracy of civil servants that provided expert advice.

The second type of administrative analysis is the description and advocacy of some ideal form of political organization, institution, or practice— ideal not in the sense of being unobtainable in principle because of human limitations, but ideal in the sense of being the best that human beings will be able to obtain in their present life or in the foreseeable future. Ideal forms of political organization have been advocated by political thinkers on the assumption that these ideal forms, taking human nature as we now find it, can actually be brought into existence if people are willing to use the available means to do so. Typical cases are Plato's republic, Cicero's mixed commonwealth, and various conceptions of complete sovereignty, or ruling power, such as those put forward by Bodin, Hobbes, and Rousseau. Ideal cases of this kind are at best only approximated by existing political forms. It is the intention of their authors that we use these ideal cases as standards by which to judge our prevailing practices. True, Cicero does say through his character Scipio that the constitution of the Roman republic is better than all others "for organization, distribution of power, and respect for authority." It is a mixed commonwealth: although royalty is dominant, the aristocrats have power and influence, and some matters are "reserved to the people for decision and judgment." Although it is not the perfect state, it is the best, according to Cicero, that has yet existed. Similarly, when we look at Bodin's list of the essential features of sovereignty—the ruler's absolute power to make and nullify laws while not being bound by them, to govern as the ruler thinks fit, "to determine war and peace," to appoint all senior officials, to be the final court of legal appeal — it is clear that most rulers have not held complete sovereignty. Most rulers have had their powers constrained by the political power of other social groups, and some of the states in which these rulers held power have approximated mixed commonwealths. But Bodin's ideal is the completely sovereign ruler, however uncommon such rulers might be. They would, he believed, ensure political equilibrium in the social turmoil of the sixteenth-century Europe in which he lived.

Just as there are two types of administrative analysis used by political thinkers, so there are two types of moral or philosophical analysis used by them. One is the critical examination of the moral views that underlie and justify the two kinds of administrative scrutiny. The other is the consideration of the more general relations that connect moral problems and political practices. The first concentrates on the particular moral issues that are raised by specific political institutions and arrangements. The second deals with the wider and more abstract connections or bonds that exist between moral issues and topics, on the one hand, and political action or social conditions on the other. In considering examples of these two types, we must bear in mind that often the boundary between them is indistinct, for there is no reason to expect that in all instances concrete moral issues and more abstract ones either can or should be separate.

Pufendorf's procedure in advocating political equality is a case in point. As a lawyer interested in making the international legal system an orderly one, Pufendorf prefers to discuss individual instances under general headings. Thus, he claims that "those who excell in the goods of the mind, of the body, or of fortune, ought not to treat men of lower condition with haughtiness and insolence; so neither ought these to envy or rifle their superiors." But why not? Because, he says, "the obligation to a social life equally binds all men, inasmuch as it is the inseparable companion of human nature." The most "properly sociable" people are those "who grant the same privilege to others, which they desire should be allowed themselves." Anyone who demands more goods and privileges than other people must be able to support a claim for special treatment, and Pufendorf then discusses both the reasons in favor of the natural equality of human beings and the results of applying that principle to specific cases such as arbitration, division of goods, and generosity. Having begun with a particular sort of action — that of haughty and envious behavior — Pufendorf treats it as a violation of the principle of equality. That is, he discusses the specific moral principle he takes to underline a particular form of social behavior. It is a case of a specific practice raising a specific moral issue.

Another example is displayed in Mill's defense of the Mormons' right to practice polygamy. It is a practice of which he deeply disapproves, he says, because it is a voluntary submission by women to a relationship in which they are disadvantaged. Nevertheless, the Mormons, having separated themselves from other nations, are entitled to live under their own laws "provided they commit no aggression on other nations, and allow perfect freedom of departure" to the dissatisfied. Polygamy is a social practice whose spread ought to be resisted. But there is no moral principle, Mill thinks, that allows non-Mormons to eliminate polygamy among Mormons simply on the grounds that their form of marriage is a return to barbarism. Whatever moral issues are raised by polygamy, they do not justify its forcible suppression.

The second type of philosophical analysis to be found in the work of political thinkers is more general. A representative instance is Hume's argument that the sole origin of justice is public utility. One of his claims is that if every person were provided fully with all the goods that he wanted, questions of justice—of equal distribution of benefits and burdens, and of fair exchange—would not arise. "Let us suppose," he says, that "without any care or industry on our part, every individual finds himself fully provided with whatever his most voracious appetites can want, or luxurious imagination wish or desire." Under these circumstances "every other social virtue would flourish," but justice, not being required, would not exist. It would be "totally useless" since there would be no disputes about who was entitled to what. Another of Hume's claims is that even if the supply of goods and services remained as it now is, an increase in human benevolence, in which each person cared as much for everyone else's interests as for his or her own, would similarly abolish the need for justice. Whatever was due to each person as a fair share or fair exchange would be supplied by other people as a matter of course. The "whole human race would form only one family." Between close friends and within some present families we already find this sort of shared interest. Hume concludes that such examples demonstrate that the existence of justice depends entirely on the presence of certain other conditions in a society: scarce resources and inadequate benevolence, for example. His argument is an attempt to reveal a general connection—in this case that of cause and effect—between a social condition and a moral practice, that of justice in the sharing and exchange of goods and services. Hence, "the rules of equity or justice depend entirely on the particular state and condition in which men are placed, and owe their origin and existence to that utility which results to the public" from the observance of those rules.

A general connection of a different kind between ethics and politics is that put forward by Marx in the *Economic and Philosophical Manuscripts.* What gives the highest value to human existence, according to Marx, is the human capacity to determine or create a social life that fully expresses the needs and potentialities of all men and women. So freedom from domination by nature or by social institutions is necessary for genuine human development. Anything that interferes with such development, anything that subordinates people against their will to the forces of the natural or social environment, is inimical to the existence of a truly human social life and is therefore to be resisted. One especially ugly form of interference with self-development is that of the dehumanization, or self-alienation, produced by people subjecting themselves to the economic arrangements that they themselves have created: the demands made upon them by social institutions such as economic profits, rent, and capital. By enslaving themselves to these forces of economic production, human beings become less human, for they prostrate themselves before idols whose human origin they do not recognize. They come to believe that the hierarchical social and economic system of capitalism, for example, is as natural and unchangeable as the physical and biological processes that determine the environment. They forget that what people have made of social life they can also change, that their political actions can and should aim at exemplifying a certain moral view. This view, says Marx, is that social life must be arranged so as to give each person the fullest scope for the free development of his or her own capacities in an attempt to satisfy the great range of human needs, desires, and interests. For Marx, organized political action and protest have a moral basis in the principle that everyone should be able to participate in social life free from economic and social domination by other people. It is this moral principle that both motivates and justifies revolutionary political activity. This, then, is a very general connection between a specific moral valuation and a broad program of political action.

II

Of course, there is an indefinite number of ways in which the history of political theories can be interpreted and organized. But one basic and useful way to do this is by topics. Obviously there is a set of topics that appears repeatedly in the writings of the political thinkers represented here, which is not surprising, since all of them are known to have been familiar with at least some of the work of their contemporaries or predecessors, and therefore could have been influenced, either positively or negatively, by them. Plato and Aristotle were teacher and student. In Book II of *Politics* Aristotle examines Plato's advocacy in the *Republic* of communal property and community of women; in Book IV, he criticizes Plato's scheme, described in the *Laws*, for elections to the council of a possible state; and in Book V he tries to show the inadequacy of Plato's discussion of the necessary parts of a state. Cicero knew Plato's *Republic* and *Laws* and, in addition, Aristotle's *Politics*, and used these books as sources for his own remarks on justice and on the mixed constitution. Aquinas's treatise on justice is a commentary on Aristotle's views as put forward in the *Ethics*. Machiavelli read Plato, Aristotle, and Cicero. These four authors' political writings were known to Bodin, and all the works so far mentioned were familiar to Hobbes. The other writers in this volume, with the exception of Paine, were extremely well read in political philosophy and its history. Pufendorf's criticism of Hobbes, for instance, was well known to Locke and Hume. The latter knew Rousseau only too well — for their close friendship ended badly because of Rosseau's paranoia — and Rousseau, himself an omnivorous reader, was quite familiar with the writings of the other two men. Both Hegel and Marx were noted for the scope and depth of their knowledge of political theory, and Mill, a child prodigy, was steeped in this literature from his childhood onward. The history of political theories is thus, in part, a chain of linked commentaries on shared topics that connects later political thinkers quite closely with their intellectual ancestors.

However, not all topics in the works of the classical political thinkers are widely shared. For example, among these authors Machiavelli is alone in writing so extensively on soldiers, fortifications, and warfare, as is Marx in his treatment of the worker's self-alienation or the revolutionary role of the proletariat. In any case, we must distinguish between the existence of a set of persisting, widely shared topics and a set of persisting, widely shared problems. One topic can give rise to innumerable problems and one problem can be related to many different topics. The status of women is a topic that includes problems such as whether the wages of women should be equal to those of men and whether the children of career women must suffer psychologically. These, in turn, bear on other topics, such as the economic effects of equal wages or the physical health of working mothers. Therefore, the frequent claim that there are no persisting intellectual problems in the history of political philosophy — that major thinkers change the nature of the intellectual problems that they inherit and with which they deal — even if correct, does not rule out the existence of persisting topics. What should decide our selection is what we wish to do with the topics that we select. In the present case this is not difficult. As part of their philosophical task, our authors have identified and characterized their own topics and, in many cases, what they take to be the topics of their predecessors and contemporaries. By using some of the topics the authors have chosen, we can begin to understand what they thought they were doing, and by examining the topics these authors shared, we can discover how far they are, or are not, thinking along the same lines to some common goals.

Consider the following topics, and the passages in which they are treated by our authors, from the selections given in this volume:

THE SEARCH FOR JUSTICE

PLATO: *Republic,* Books I, II, IV, IX (588–592).

ARISTOTLE: *Politics,* Book III, Chapters 6–13; Book V, Chapter 1, Book VII, Chapters 1–3.

CICERO: *On the Commonwealth,* Book III, Sections XI–XVI, XIX–XX, XXIV.

AQUINAS: *Summa Theologiae,* Questions 58, 61.

HOBBES: *Leviathan,* Part I, Chapter XV.

PUFENDORF: *The Law of Nature and Nations,* Book I, Chapter VII.

HUME: *An Enquiry Concerning the Principles of Morals*, Section III, Parts one and two.

THE NATURE OF SOVEREIGNTY

ARISTOTLE: *Politics*, Book III, Chapters 6 – 13.

CICERO: *On the Commonwealth*, Book II, Sections XXV – XXXV.

BODIN: *Six Books of the Commonwealth*, Book I, Chapters VIII, X.

HOBBES: *Leviathan*, Part II, Chapters XVII, XVIII.

ROUSSEAU: *The Social Contract*, Book I, Chapters VI, VII; Book II, Chapters I, II.

THE STATE OF NATURE AND EARLY POLITICAL SOCIETY

ARISTOTLE: *Politics*, Book I, Sections 1, 2.

CICERO: *On the Commonwealth*, Book I, Section XXV.

HOBBES: *Leviathan*, Part I, Chapter XIII; Part II, Chapters XVII, XVIII.

PUFENDORF: *The Law of Nature and Nations*, Book II, Chapter II.

LOCKE: *The Second Treatise of Government*, Chapters II, VIII.

ROUSSEAU: *A Dissertation on the Origin and Foundation of the Inequality of Mankind; The Social Contract*, Chapters VI, VIII.

THE ORIGIN AND ROLE OF PROPERTY

ARISTOTLE: *Politics*, Book I, Chapters 4, 7 – 9; Book II, Chapters 5 – 7.

BODIN: *Six Books of the Commonwealth*, Book V, Chapter II.

PUFENDORF: *The Law of Nature and Nations*, Book III, Chapter II, Section V.

LOCKE: *The Second Treatise of Government*, Chapter V, Sections 26 – 51.

HUME: *An Enquiry Concerning the Principles of Morals*, Parts 1, 2.

ROUSSEAU: *The Social Contract*, Book I, Chapter IX.

MARX AND ENGELS: *Economic and Philosophic Manuscripts of 1844, Private Property and Communism; Manifesto of the Communist Party*, Parts I, II.

These topics are only a few of the many possible ones that could be extracted from our selections. There is, for example, the question of the status of women, a topic dealt with by Plato, Aristotle, and Mill. There is also the topic of political revolution and seizure of power discussed by Aristotle, Machiavelli, Bodin, Locke, Hegel, and Marx and Engels. More interesting than the number of possible topics, however, is the fact that these topics are all phrased in terms that are familiar to our authors. They are not terms imposed on these thinkers, but are the terms in which they themselves thought and wrote. The significance of this is that it allows us reasonably to ask several different questions. One is why these particular topics have interested so many political thinkers over such a long period of time. Is it because the same political conditions, and hence the same political problems, have reappeared over and over again? Is it because the same ideas and views have been passed down without careful scrutiny, through generations of commentators who have simply applied them to very different political circumstances? Or is it that these topics embody categories and beliefs that are linked together in some way so that anyone thinking about one of them, say justice, is bound to be led to another, equality for example, and from there to still another, such as property? Is it possible, for instance, to discuss the search for justice without also discussing questions of liberty and equality — and if not, why not?

Another question closely connected with the first concerns individual political thinkers rather than political thinkers as a group. Why, we may ask, was Aristotle or Cicero or Bodin so concerned with the nature of sovereign rule, with the qualifications that political leaders should meet in order to be called "genuine sovereigns"? To try to answer such a question is to enter the distinctive intellectual and political realm in which each of these authors worked, and we have no reason to expect that the results will be the same for each of them. In trying to determine why a specific topic attracted a particular thinker, do we wish to know what it was in his personal background, or in his political circumstances, or in the intellectual controversies of his period, that made him interested in the problem of political leadership? These are three different questions and the answers to them are likely to be correspondingly dissimilar. It is well known, for example, that Mill's interest in improving the status of women dated from his early years, and that Harriet Taylor, later his wife, held firm views on the subject thirty years before Mill wrote *The Subjection of Women* in 1861. She had written: "Women are educated for one single object, to gain their living by marrying . . . to be married is the object of their existence and that being gained they do really cease to exist to anything worth calling life or any useful purpose." So if we ask why Mill was attracted to the topic, the answer we receive could take two forms. One is that the policy of equal rights for women had fitted in with, and been demanded by, some of Mill's ethical beliefs for all of his adult life. This answer is in terms of the coherence of Mill's ideas. The other answer is that the same was true of Harriet Taylor, and that, in addition, their long association with each other and their many discussions of the problem powerfully reinforced Mill's convictions and stimulated him to put these ideas into written form not long after his wife's death. Thus, the two answers differ, in part, in that the latter refers to specific stimuli and the first does not; but of course we might wish to have both.

There is also a third query that is suggested by our list of topics and would be suggested by almost any list that we drew up. This is directed at the changes that occur in the treatment of the same topic by different thinkers, sometimes by thinkers who belong to the same time and place, and some-times by thinkers who are widely separated. One topic, such as political liberty and equality, can engender quite distinct treatments. In *The Discourses*, Chapters 5 and 7, under the heading "liberty," Machiavelli discusses, first, the need for citizens to have legal means of expressing and correcting their grievances and, second, the use of public indictments to prevent power-ful citizens from encroaching on the freedom of the less powerful. Hobbes, somewhat similarly, treats liberty as a person's ability "to do what he has a will to," and considers what actions a person may justly refuse to do when commanded by his or her political ruler. Mill extends the question beyond that of how people can be protected against the tyranny of their rulers. He takes up the problem of how the individual citizen can be protected against various other forms of social authority, including that of restriction of freedom of thought and public expression of opinion, especially unpopular opinion. So if we traced the changes in the problems concerning liberty dealt with by generations of political thinkers, we should find that as old liberties were secured, new ones were demanded and fought for, not always successfully, and that the gains of earlier victories often slipped away. As a result, the topic of liberty would be found to have grown greatly in content over time, even though some of the original problems were no longer live issues. Hence many questions would present themselves, concerned with what produced these changes from writer to writer or what factors produced a certain trend.

Finally, there are the many problems raised when critics organize the work of political thinkers not by the authors' topics but by their own. This procedure is extremely common and there is no general reason why it should not be practiced. However, the critic must make clear that the topics — the headings under which the work is being divided — are those of the critic and not of the author. Otherwise, the critic may replace topics that are a useful sign as to what the author was trying to accomplish with others that may shed much light on the critic's intentions but little on those of the author. Sometimes, of course, this does not matter, since the critic's may intend to show how the author could, or should, have done his work differently. However, that intention of the critic needs to be made plain and not be confused with what the author was actually trying to do. Someone might, for example, have an interest in the ideal of a classless society, and hence try to interpret the history of political thought as providing evidence of a constant desire by all the major thinkers to show that it either was being, or should be, achieved. This would seriously distort the views of most of the authors whose work is displayed here, Rousseau and Marx and Engels being the exceptions. Similarly, it would be a misrepresentation to impose on our authors the topic of a democratic world state or that of anarchism — the abolition of state authority. These topics belong to political traditions not represented by the work collected here.

III

Several decades ago Isaiah Berlin, in a paper entitled "Does Political Theory Still Exist?," remarked that it is absurd to believe that there ever were, or could be, periods in which there was no political philosophy. "There is," he wrote, "no human activity without some kind of general outlook: scepticism, cynicism, refusal to dabble in abstract issues or to question values, hard boiled opportunism, contempt for theorizing, all the varieties of nihilism, are, of course, themselves metaphysical and ethical positions, commital attitudes." Now it is true that if any general political outlook is to be considered political philosophy, then political philosophy has certainly existed as long as there have been human societies. But there is no good reason to make this identification. Living a political life, as all people do, is not the same as critically examining its concepts, principles, presuppositions, and consistency, as only philosophers do. Because philosophy consists of a critical scrutiny of various kinds of human activity, we can date the origins of philosophic investigation to a particular time and place — to the Milesian school of Ionia, Asia Minor, in the sixth century B.C. A man can be a successful politician and yet never give any attention to the general ideas embodied in his party's opinions. He can be a mere vote counter and an expert at manipulating other people's attitudes. Political philosophy emerges only when practitioners try to explain why their policies are morally sound: why the practice of slavery is evil or why civil liberties should be protected. Political philosophy becomes a developed discipline when different moral judgments are brought into opposition with one another and are organized into competing systems. General political outlooks or attitudes have a much longer history, and a much wider distribution, than has political philosophy proper.

Nevertheless, it is impossible for someone — even a politician — to avoid all connection with political philosophy, anymore than it is possible for someone to be completely insulated from moral problems, and hence from their philosophical bases. A politician who begins a speech with the words "The people have a right to know where the governor was last night" has already taken for granted the soundness of a set of moral views: that the public should have legal access to certain kinds of information about its elected representative because that is its "right"; that a "right" is a justifiable claim whose supporting reasons include moral ones; that the public should possess this particular "right" because the moral grounds in favor of possession outweigh those against it. Each of these views can be challenged because it conflicts with other moral views — the right to privacy, for example. But once a politician begins to answer these challenges he must do so both in terms of more general moral principles, and the content of notions such as freedom, happiness, right and wrong, interests, duties, and rationality. In addition, of course, he must work out the various relationships among these concepts. To embark on all this is to engage in political philosophy and not merely in the discussion of political actions and behavior. It is certainly possible for people to avoid explicit philosophical debate or argument; however, it is not always possible for them to avoid assuming political principles, presupposing certain value judgments, or making use of morally controversial ideas. That they do not realize that they are doing so, or that they claim to have no interest in theories and principles, does not mean that these moral issues are not present. It simply means that they exist in subterranean form and thus escape critical examination by people who must nevertheless act on them.

Until very recently the study of political theories has often been a dangerous practice. It is still so in many parts of the world. The lives of Socrates, Aristotle, Cicero, Machiavelli, Hobbes, Pufendorf, Locke, Hume, Rousseau, Paine, and Marx all testify to the suspicion and dislike that the politically powerful experience when the moral basis of their rule is criticized, or even examined. This suspicion is well founded. It is based on the correct common sense belief that political action is intimately connected with — in fact is supported by — moral principles, and that to critically scrutinize the latter is to increase the likelihood of rejecting the former. If the moral basis of a political party, program, or administration is found unacceptable, then its superstructure of practical politics cannot remain unchallenged for long. That is why the practice of political philosophy has so often been a dangerous one. It is also the reason why the activity is inescapable, why it cannot be avoided permanently. So asking the question "Why should I, or anyone else, be interested in the problems of political theory and philosophy?" is predicated on the assumption that we have a choice about being concerned with these matters. But there is no such choice. The only options we have are either to take up these issues thoughtfully and critically, as the thinkers of the classical tradition tried to do, or to pretend that the questions do not exist and so will not, from their intellectual hiding places, direct and control our political behavior.

PLATO

INTRODUCTION

Disappointingly little is known about Plato's life. In the 27 dialogues that are commonly taken to be by Plato, he refers to himself only in relation to the trial in 399 B.C. of his teacher Socrates, who was charged with intellectually corrupting the youth of Athens and not believing in Athenian gods. What information we have comes from four sources: references in the dialogues to Plato's relatives, acquaintances, and other historical figures and events, his public letters known as the *Epistles*, scattered remarks about him by his contemporaries, such as Aristotle, and authors such as Plutarch and Diogenes Laertius, who lived hundreds of years later. It is known that Plato was born either in or near Athens, that his family was politically distinguished, and that since he sometimes used the names and characters of his well-known relatives in his dialogues, he must have taken pride in his social position. As a young man he joined the circle of Socrates, and it was the trial and execution of Socrates that disillusioned Plato with political life and made him, at the age of 28, reluctant to enter into a public career. Instead, he left Athens with some friends, and after the group had established itself at the nearby city of Megara to carry on the philosophical investigations that Socrates had begun, Plato seems to have written the earliest of his "imaginary dialogues."

At the age of 40 Plato was persuaded to visit and tutor Dionysius I, the despotic ruler of Sicily. The visit seems to have been a failure, since he soon left the court to return to Athens. There, in 388 B.C., he established the Academy, an advanced school that was intended to train future statesmen in the proper philosophical exercise of their art. Aristotle entered when he was a young man and remained there as a student, and then teacher, until the death of Plato two decades later. Instruction by the staff was given in mathematics, astronomy, law, political theory, biology, science, music, and philosophy through tutorials and lectures. A number of students returned to their own cities as political advisers and legislators. Plato himself made two more futile trips to Sicily in an effort to educate the new ruler, Dionysius II, in philosophy, and each time he managed to leave the court only with difficulty after good relations between him and Dionysius had ceased.

In the last decade of Plato's life he was, he wrote, sick of his Sicilian political adventures, and it is thought that he must have devoted much of his remaining years to the writing of the *Laws*, the last and by far the longest of his dialogues. It is not known whether in the end Plato concluded, as so many of his commentators have, that even though all good statesmen must be philosophically trained, very few eminent philosophers, including Plato himself, have made, or would make, good statesmen.

The full Greek title of *The Republic* is *The State or On the Just Man*, and this indicates the subject of the dialogue. It was probably written about 374 B.C., although the conversation is supposed to take place about 50 years earlier. The present selection is taken from Benjamin Jowett's translation of *The Dialogues of Plato*, 3rd edition, London: Macmillan Company, 1894.

SELECTIONS FROM

The Republic

Book I   Common Ideas of Justice

PERSONS OF THE DIALOGUE

SOCRATES, *who is the narrator*   CEPHALUS
GLAUCON   THRASYMACHUS
ADEIMANTUS   CLEITOPHON
POLEMARCHUS

And others who are mute auditors

The Scene *is laid in the house of Cephalus at the Piraeus; and the whole dialogue is narrated by Socrates the day after it actually took place to Timaeus, Hermocrates, Critias, and a nameless person, who are introduced in the Timaeus.*

I went down yesterday to the Piraeus with Glaucon the son of Ariston, that I might offer up my prayers to the goddess; and also because I wanted to see in what manner they would celebrate the festival, which was a new thing. I was delighted with the procession of the inhabitants; but that of the Thracians was equally, if not more, beautiful. When we had finished our prayers and viewed the spectacle, we turned in the direction of the city; and at that instant Polemarchus the son of Cephalus chanced to catch sight of us from a distance as we were starting on our way home, and told his servant to run and bid us wait for him. The servant took hold of me by the cloak behind, and said: Polemarchus desires you to wait.

SOCRATES,
POLEMARCHUS,
GLAUCON,
ADEIMANTUS,
CEPHALUS.

Meeting of
Socrates and
Glaucon with
Polemarchus at
the Bendidean
festival.

I turned round, and asked him where his master was.

There he is, said the youth, coming after you, if you will only wait.

Certainly we will, said Glaucon; and in a few minutes Polemarchus appeared, and with him Adeimantus, Glaucon's brother, Niceratus the son of Nicias, and several others who had been at the procession.

Polemarchus said to me: I perceive, Socrates, that you and your companion are already on your way to the city.

You are not far wrong, I said.

But do you see, he rejoined, how many we are?

Of course.

And are you stronger than all these? for if not, you will have to remain where you are.

SOCRATES,
POLEMARCHUS,
GLAUCON,
ADEIMANTUS,
CEPHALUS.

May there not be the alternative, I said, that we may persuade you to let us go?

But can you persuade us, if we refuse to listen to you? he said.

Certainly not, replied Glaucon.

Then we are not going to listen; of that you may be assured.

Adeimantus added: Has no one told you of the torch-race on horseback in honour of the goddess which will take place in the evening?

The equestrian
torchrace.

With horses! I replied: That is a novelty. Will horsemen carry torches and pass them one to another during the race?

Yes, said Polemarchus, and not only so, but a festival will be celebrated at night, which you certainly ought to see. Let us rise soon after supper and see this festival; there will be a gathering of young men, and we will have a good talk. Stay then, and do not be perverse.

Glaucon said: I suppose, since you insist, that we must.

Very good, I replied.

The gathering
of friends at the
house of
Cephalus

Accordingly we went with Polemarchus to his house; and there we found his brothers Lysias and Euthydemus, and with them Thrasymachus the Chalcedonian, Charmantides the Paeanian, and Cleitophon the son of Aristonymus. There too was Cephalus the father of Polemarchus, whom I had not seen for a long time, and I thought him very much aged. He was seated on a cushioned chair, and had a garland on his head, for he had been sacrificing in the court; and there were some other chairs in the room arranged in a semicircle, upon which we sat down by him. He saluted me eagerly, and then he said: —

You don't come to see me, Socrates, as often as you ought: If I were still able to go and see you I would not ask you to come to me. But at my age I can hardly get to the city, and therefore you should come oftener to the Piraeus. For let me tell you, that the more the pleasures of the body fade away, the greater to me is the pleasure and charm of conversation. Do not then deny my request, but make our house your resort and keep company with these young men; we are old friends, and you will be quite at home with us.

CEPHALUS,
SOCRATES.

I replied: There is nothing which for my part I like better, Cephalus, than conversing with aged men; for I regard them as travellers who have gone a journey which I too may have to go, and of whom I ought to enquire, whether the way is smooth and easy, or rugged and difficult. And this is a question which I should like to ask of you who have arrived at that time which the poets call the 'threshold of old age' — Is life harder towards the end, or what report do you give of it?

I will tell you, Socrates, he said, what my own feeling is. Men of my age flock together; we are birds of a feather, as the old proverb says; and at our meetings the tale of my acquaintance commonly is — I cannot eat, I cannot drink; the pleasures of youth and love are fled away: there was a good time once, but now that is gone, and life is no longer life. Some complain of the slights which are put upon them by relations, and they will tell you sadly of how many evils their old age is the cause. But to me, Socrates, these complainers seem to blame that which is not really in fault. For if old age were the cause, I too being old, and every other old man, would have felt as they do. But this is not my own experience, nor that of others whom I have known. How well I remember the aged poet Sophocles, when in answer to the question, How does love suit with age, Sophocles, — are you still the man you were? Peace, he replied; most gladly have I escaped the thing of which you speak; I feel as if I had escaped from a mad and furious master. His words have often occurred to my mind since, and they seem as good to me now as at the time when he uttered them. For certainly old age has a great sense of calm and freedom; when the passions relax their hold, then, as Sophocles says, we are freed from the grasp not of one mad master only, but of many. The truth is, Socrates, that these regrets, and also the complaints about relations, are to be attributed to the same cause, which is not old age, but men's characters and tempers; for he who is of a calm and happy nature will hardly feel the pressure of age, but to him who is of an opposite disposition youth and age are equally a burden.

I listened in admiration, and wanting to draw him out, that he might go on — Yes, Cephalus, I said; but I rather suspect that people in general are not convinced by you when you speak thus; they think that old age sits lightly upon you, not because of your happy disposition, but because you are rich, and wealth is well known to be a great comforter.

You are right, he replied; they are not convinced: and there is something in what they say; not, however, so much as they imagine. I might answer them as Themistocles answered the Seriphian who was abusing him and saying that he was famous, not for his own merits but because he was an Athenian: 'If you had been a native of my country or I of yours, neither of us would have been famous.' And to those

Old age is not to blame for the troubles of old men.

The excellent saying of Sophocles.

It is admitted that the old, if they are to be comfortable,

must have a fair share of external goods; neither virtue alone nor riches alone can make an old man happy.

who are not rich and are impatient of old age, the same reply may be made; for to the good poor man old age cannot be a light burden, nor can a bad rich man ever have peace with himself.

May I ask, Cephalus, whether your fortune was for the most part inherited or acquired by you?

Acquired! Socrates; do you want to know how much I acquired? In the art of making money I have been midway between my father and grandfather: for my grandfather, whose name I bear, doubled and trebled the value of his patrimony, that which he inherited being much what I possess now; but my father Lysanias reduced the property below what it is at present: and I shall be satisfied if I leave to these my sons not less but a little more than I received.

That was why I asked you the question, I replied, because I see that you are indifferent about money, which is a characteristic rather of those who have inherited their fortunes than of those who have acquired them; the makers of fortunes have a second love of money as a creation of their own, resembling the affection of authors for their own poems, or of parents for their children, besides that natural love of it for the sake of use and profit which is common to them and all men. And hence they are very bad company, for they can talk about nothing but the praises of wealth.

That is true, he said.

Yes, that is very true, but may I ask another question? —What do you consider to be the greatest blessing which you have reaped from your wealth?

One, he said, of which I could not expect easily to convince others. For let me tell you, Socrates, that when a man thinks himself to be near death, fears and cares enter into his mind which he never had before; the tales of a world below and the punishment which is exacted there of deeds done here were once a laughing matter to him, but now he is tormented with the thought that they may be true: either from the weakness of age, or because he is now drawing nearer to that other place, he has a clearer view of these things; suspicions and alarms crowd thickly upon him, and he begins to reflect and consider what wrongs he has done to others. And when he finds that the sum of his transgressions is great he will many a time like a child start up in his sleep for fear, and he is filled with dark forebodings. But to him who is conscious of no sin, sweet hope, as Pindar charmingly says, is the kind nurse of his age:

Cephalus has inherited rather than made a fortune; he is therefore indifferent to money.

The advantages of wealth.

The fear of death and the consciousness of sin become more vivid in old age; and to be rich frees a man from many temptations.

'Hope,' he says, 'cherishes the soul of him who lives in justice and holiness, and is the nurse of his age and the companion of his journey; — hope which is mightiest to sway the restless soul of man.'

How admirable are his words! And the great blessing of riches, I do not say to every man, but to a good man, is, that he has had no occasion to deceive or to defraud others, either intentionally or unintentionally; and when he departs to the world below he is not in any apprehension about offerings due to the gods or debts which he owes to men. Now to this peace of mind the possession of wealth greatly contributes; and therefore I say, that, setting one thing against another, of the many advantages which wealth has to give, to a man of sense this is in my opinion the greatest.

Well said, Cephalus, I replied; but as concerning justice, what is it? — to speak the truth and to pay your debts — no more than this? And even to this are there not exceptions? Suppose that a friend when in his right mind has deposited arms with me and he asks for them when he is not in his right mind, ought I to give them back to him? No one would say that I ought or that I should be right in doing so, any more than they would say that I ought always to speak the truth to one who is in his condition.

You are quite right, he replied.

But then, I said, speaking the truth and paying your debts is not a correct definition of justice.

Quite correct, Socrates, if Simonides is to be believed, said Polemarchus interposing.

I fear, said Cephalus, that I must go now, for I have to look after the sacrifices, and I hand over the argument to Polemarchus and the company.

Is not Polemarchus your heir? I said.

To be sure, he answered, and went away laughing to the sacrifices.

Tell me then, O thou heir of the argument, what did Simonides say, and according to you truly say, about justice?

He said that the re-payment of a debt is just, and in saying so he appears to me to be right.

I should be sorry to doubt the word of such a wise and inspired man, but his meaning, though probably clear to you, is the reverse of clear to me. For he certainly does not mean, as we were just now saying, that I ought to return a deposit of arms or of anything else to one who asks for it when he is not in his right senses; and yet a deposit cannot be denied to be a debt.

True.

Then when the person who asks me is not in his right mind I am by no means to make the return?

Certainly not.

When Simonides said that the repayment of a debt was justice, he did not mean to include that case?

Certainly not; for he thinks that a friend ought always to do good to a friend and never evil.

You mean that the return of a deposit of gold which is to the injury of the receiver, if the two parties are friends, is not the repayment of a debt, — that is what you would imagine him to say?

Yes.

And are enemies also to receive what we owe to them?

To be sure, he said, they are to receive what we owe them, and an enemy, as I take it, owes to an enemy that which is due or proper to him — that is to say, evil.

Simonides, then, after the manner of poets, would seem to have spoken darkly of the nature of justice; for he really meant to say that justice is the giving to each man what is proper to him, and this he termed a debt.

That must have been his meaning, he said.

By heaven! I replied; and if we asked him what due or proper thing is given by medicine, and to whom, what answer do you think that he would make to us?

He would surely reply that medicine gives drugs and meat and drink to human bodies.

And what due or proper thing is given by cookery, and to what?

Seasoning to food.

And what is that which justice gives, and to whom?

If, Socrates, we are to be guided at all by the analogy of the preceding instances, then justice is the art which gives good to friends and evil to enemies.

That is his meaning then?

I think so.

And who is best able to do good to his friends and evil to his enemies in time of sickness?

The physician.

Or when they are on a voyage, amid the perils of the sea?

The pilot.

And in what sort of actions or with a view to what result

is the just man most able to do harm to his enemy and good to his friend?

In going to war against the one and in making alliances with the other.

But when a man is well, my dear Polemarchus, there is no need of a physician?

No.

And he who is not on a voyage has no need of a pilot?

No.

Then in time of peace justice will be of no use?

I am very far from thinking so.

You think that justice may be of use in peace as well as in war?

Yes.

Like husbandry for the acquisition of corn?

Yes.

Or like shoemaking for the acquisition of shoes, — that is what you mean?

Yes.

And what similar use or power of acquisition has justice in time of peace?

In contracts, Socrates, justice is of use.

And by contracts you mean partnerships?

Exactly.

But is the just man or the skilful player a more useful and better partner at a game of draughts?

The skilful player.

And in the laying of bricks and stones is the just man a more useful or better partner than the builder?

Quite the reverse.

Then in what sort of partnership is the just man a better partner than the harp-player, as in playing the harp the harp-player is certainly a better partner than the just man?

In a money partnership.

Yes, Polemarchus, but surely not in the use of money; for you do not want a just man to be your counsellor in the purchase or sale of a horse; a man who is knowing about horses would be better for that, would he not?

Certainly.

And when you want to buy a ship, the shipwright or the pilot would be better?

True.

Then what is that joint use of silver or gold in which the just man is to be preferred?

When you want a deposit to be kept safely.

You mean when money is not wanted, but allowed to lie?

Precisely.

That is to say, justice is useful when money is useless?

That is the inference.

And when you want to keep a pruning-hook safe, then justice is useful to the individual and to the state; but when you want to use it, then the art of the vine-dresser?

Clearly.

And when you want to keep a shield or a lyre, and not to use them, you would say that justice is useful; but when you want to use them, then the art of the soldier or of the musician?

Certainly.

And so of all the other things; — justice is useful when they are useless, and useless when they are useful?

That is the inference.

Then justice is not good for much. But let us consider this further point: Is not he who can best strike a blow in a boxing match or in any kind of fighting best able to ward off a blow?

Certainly.

And he who is most skilful in preventing or escaping from a disease is best able to create one?

True.

And he is the best guard of a camp who is best able to steal a march upon the enemy?

Certainly.

Then he who is a good keeper of anything is also a good thief?

That, I suppose, is to be inferred.

Then if the just man is good at keeping money, he is good at stealing it.

That is implied in the argument.

Then after all the just man has turned out to be a thief. And this is a lesson which I suspect you must have learnt out of Homer; for he, speaking of Autolycus, the maternal grandfather of Odysseus, who is a favourite of his, affirms that

He was excellent above all men in theft and perjury.

And so, you and Homer and Simonides are agreed that justice is an art of theft; to be practised however 'for the good of friends and for the harm of enemies,' — that was what you were saying?

But not in the
use of money;
and if so,
justice is only
useful when
money or
anything else is
useless.

A new point of
view: Is not he
who is best
able to do
good best able
to do evil?

No, certainly not that, though I do not now know what I did say; but I still stand by the latter words.

Well, there is another question: By friends and enemies do we mean those who are so really, or only in seeming?

Surely, he said, a man may be expected to love those whom he thinks good, and to hate those whom he thinks evil.

Yes, but do not persons often err about good and evil: many who are not good seem to be so, and conversely?

That is true.

Then to them the good will be enemies and the evil will be their friends?

True.

And in that case they will be right in doing good to the evil and evil to the good?

Clearly.

But the good are just and would not do an injustice?

True.

Then according to your argument it is just to injure those who do no wrong?

Nay, Socrates; the doctrine is immoral.

Then I suppose that we ought to do good to the just and harm to the unjust?

I like that better.

But see the consequence: — Many a man who is ignorant of human nature has friends who are bad friends, and in that case he ought to do harm to them; and he has good enemies whom he ought to benefit; but, if so, we shall be saying the very opposite of that which we affirmed to be the meaning of Simonides.

Very true, he said; and I think that we had better correct an error into which we seem to have fallen in the use of the words 'friend' and 'enemy.'

What was the error, Polemarchus? I asked.

We assumed that he is a friend who seems to be or who is thought good.

And how is the error to be corrected?

We should rather say that he is a friend who is, as well as seems, good; and that he who seems only, and is not good, only seems to be and is not a friend; and of an enemy the same may be said.

You would argue that the good are our friends and the bad our enemies?

Yes.

And instead of saying simply as we did at first, that it is just to do good to our friends and harm to our enemies, we

Justice an art of theft to be practised for the good of friends and the harm of enemies. But who are friends and enemies?

Mistakes will sometimes happen.

Correction of the definition.

To appearance we must add reality. He is a friend who 'is' as well as 'seems' good. And we should do

SOCRATES,
POLEMARCHUS.

should further say: It is just to do good to our friends when they are good and harm to our enemies when they are evil?

Yes, that appears to me to be the truth.

But ought the just to injure any one at all?

Undoubtedly he ought to injure those who are both wicked and his enemies.

When horses are injured, are they improved or deteriorated?

The latter.

Deteriorated, that is to say, in the good qualities of horses, not of dogs?

good to our
good friends
and harm to
our bad
enemies.

Yes, of horses.

And dogs are deteriorated in the good qualities of dogs, and not of horses?

Of course.

And will not men who are injured be deteriorated in that which is the proper virtue of man?

To harm men
is to injure
them; and to
injure them is
to make them
unjust. But
justice cannot
produce
injustice.

Certainly.

And that human virtue is justice?

To be sure.

Then men who are injured are of necessity made unjust?

That is the result.

But can the musician by his art make men unmusical?

Certainly not.

Or the horseman by his art make them bad horsemen?

Impossible.

Illustrations.

And can the just by justice make men unjust, or speaking generally, can the good by virtue make them bad?

Assuredly not.

Any more than heat can produce cold?

It cannot.

Or drought moisture?

Clearly not.

Nor can the good harm any one?

Impossible,

And the just is the good?

Certainly.

Then to injure a friend or anyone else is not the act of a just man, but of the opposite, who is the unjust?

I think that what you say is quite true, Socrates.

Then if a man says that justice consists in the repayment of debts, and that good is the debt which a man owes to his friends, and evil the debt which he owes to his enemies, — to say this is not wise; for it is not true, if, as has been clearly shown, the injuring of another can be in no case just.

I agree with you, said Polemarchus.

Then you and I are prepared to take up arms against any one who attributes such a saying to Simonides or Bias or Pittacus, or any other wise man or seer?

I am quite ready to do battle at your side, he said.

Shall I tell you whose I believe the saying to be?

Whose?

I believe that Periander or Perdiccas or Xerxes or Ismenias the Theban, or some other rich and mighty man, who had a great opinion of his own power, was the first to say that justice is 'doing good to your friends and harm to your enemies.'

Most true, he said.

Yes, I said; but if this definition of justice also breaks down, what other can be offered?

The saying however explained is not to be attributed to any good or wise man.

Several times in the course of the discussion Thrasymachus had made an attempt to get the argument into his own hands, and had been put down by the rest of the company, who wanted to hear the end. But when Polemarchus and I had done speaking and there was a pause, he could no longer hold his peace; and, gathering himself up, he came at us like a wild beast, seeking to devour us. We were quite panic-stricken at the sight of him.

The brutality of Thrasymachus.

He roared out to the whole company: What folly, Socrates, has taken possession of you all? And why, sillybillies, do you knock under to one another? I say that if you want really to know what justice is, you should not only ask but answer, and you should not seek honour to yourself from the refutation of an opponent, but have your own answer; for there is many a one who can ask and cannot answer. And now I will not have you say that justice is duty or advantage or profit or gain or interest, for this sort of nonsense will not do for me; I must have clearness and accuracy.

I was panic-stricken at his words, and could not look at him without trembling. Indeed I believe that if I had not fixed my eye upon him, I should have been struck dumb: but when I saw his fury rising, I looked at him first, and was therefore able to reply to him.

Thrasymachus, I said, with a quiver, don't be hard upon us. Polemarchus and I may have been guilty of a little mistake in the argument, but I can assure you that the error was not intentional. If we were seeking for a piece of gold, you would not imagine that we were 'knocking under to one another,' and so losing our chance of finding it. And why, when we are seeking for justice, a thing more precious than

SOCRATES,
THRASYMACHUS,
GLAUCON.

many pieces of gold, do you say that we are weakly yielding
to one another and not doing our utmost to get at the truth?
Nay, my good friend, we are most willing and anxious to do
so, but the fact is that we cannot. And if so, you people who
know all things should pity us and not be angry with us.

How characteristic of Socrates! he replied, with a bitter
laugh; — that's your ironical style! Did I not forsee — have I
not already told you, that whatever he was asked he would
refuse to answer, and try irony or any other shuffle, in order
that he might avoid answering?

Socrates
cannot give
any answer if
all true answers
are excluded.

You are a philosopher, Thrasymachus, I replied, and
well know that if you ask a person what numbers make up
twelve, taking care to prohibit him whom you ask from
answering twice six, or three times four, or six times two, or
four times three, 'for this sort of nonsense will not do for
me,' — then obviously, if that is your way of putting the
question, no one can answer you. But suppose that he were
to retort, Thrasymachus, what do you mean? If one of these
numbers which you interdict be the true answer to the
question, am I falsely to say some other number which is not
the right one? — is that your meaning?' — How would you
answer him?

Thrasymachus
is assailed with
his own
weapons.

Just as if the two cases were at all alike! he said.

Why should they not be? I replied; and even if they are
not, but only appear to be so to the person who is asked,
ought he not to say what he thinks, whether you and I forbid
him or not?

I presume then that you are going to make one of the
interdicted answers?

I dare say that I may, notwithstanding the danger, if
upon reflection I approve of any of them.

But what if I give you an answer about justice other and
better, he said, than any of these? What do you deserve to
have done to you?

Done to me! — as becomes the ignorant, I must learn
from the wise — that is what I deserve to have done to me.

The Sophist
demands
payment for his
instructions.
The company
are very willing
to contribute.

What, and no payment! a pleasant notion!

I will pay when I have the money, I replied.

But you have, Socrates, said Glaucon: and you, Thrasymachus, need be under no anxiety about money, for we will
all make a contribution for Socrates.

Yes, he replied, and then Socrates will do as he always
does — refuse to answer himself, but take and pull to pieces
the answer of some one else.

Why, my good friend, I said, how can any one answer

SOCRATES,
THRASYMACHUS,
GLAUCON.

who knows, and says that he knows, just nothing; and who, even if he has some faint notions of his own, is told by a man of authority not to utter them? The natural thing is, that the speaker should be some one like yourself who professes to know and can tell what he knows. Will you then kindly answer, for the edification of the company and of myself?

Socrates knows little or nothing: how can he answer? And he is deterred by the interdict of Thrasymachus.

Glaucon and the rest of the company joined in my request and Thrasymachus, as any one might see, was in reality eager to speak; for he thought that he had an excellent answer, and would distinguish himself. But at first he affected to insist on my answering; at length he consented to begin. Behold, he said, the wisdom of Socrates; he refuses to teach himself, and goes about learning of others, to whom he never even says Thank you.

That I learn of others, I replied, is quite true; but that I am ungrateful I wholly deny. Money I have none, and therefore I pay in praise, which is all I have; and how ready I am to praise any one who appears to me to speak well you will very soon find out when you answer; for I expect that you will answer well.

Listen, then, he said; I proclaim that justice is nothing else than the interest of the stronger. And now why do you not praise me? But of course you won't.

The definition of Thrasymachus: 'Justice is the interest of the stronger or ruler.'

Let me first understand you, I replied. Justice, as you say, is the interest of the stronger. What, Thrasymachus, is the meaning of this? You cannot mean to say that because Polydamas, the pancratiast, is stronger than we are, and finds the eating of beef conducive to his bodily strength, that to eat beef is therefore equally for our good who are weaker than he is, and right and just for us?

That's abominable of you, Socrates; you take the words in the sense which is most damaging to the argument.

Not at all, my good sir, I said; I am trying to understand them; and I wish that you would be a little clearer.

Well, he said, have you never heard that forms of government differ; there are tyrannies, and there are democracies, and there are aristocracies?

Yes, I know.

And the government is the ruling power in each state?

Certainly.

And the different forms of government make laws democratical, aristocratical, tyrannical, with a view to their several interests; and these laws, which are made by them for their own interests, are the justice which they deliver to their subjects, and him who transgresses them they punish as a

Socrates compels Thrasymachus to explain his meaning.

breaker of the law, and unjust. And that is what I mean when I say that in all states there is the same principle of justice, which is the interest of the government; and as the government must be supposed to have power, the only reasonable conclusion is, that everywhere there is one principle of justice, which is the interest of the stronger.

Now I understand you, I said; and whether you are right or not I will try to discover. But let me remark, that in defining justice you have yourself used the word 'interest' which you forbade me to use. It is true, however, that in your definition the words 'of the stronger' are added.

A small addition, you must allow, he said.

Great or small, never mind about that: we must first enquire whether what you are saying is the truth. Now we are both agreed that justice is interest of some sort, but you go on to say 'of the stronger'; about this addition I am not so sure, and must therefore consider further.

Proceed.

I will; and first tell me, Do you admit that it is just for subjects to obey their rulers?

I do.

But are the rulers of states absolutely infallible, or are they sometimes liable to err?

To be sure, he replied, they are liable to err.

Then in making their laws they may sometimes make them rightly, and sometimes not?

True.

When they make them rightly, they make them agreeably to their interest; when they are mistaken, contrary to their interest; you admit that?

Yes.

And the laws which they make must be obeyed by their subjects, — and that is what you call justice?

Doubtless.

Then justice, according to your argument, is not only obedience to the interest of the stronger but the reverse?

What is that you are saying? he asked.

I am only repeating what you are saying, I believe. But let us consider: Have we not admitted that the rulers may be mistaken about their own interest in what they command, and also that to obey them is justice? Has not that been admitted?

Yes.

Then you must also have acknowledged justice not to be for the interest of the stronger, when the rulers unintentionally command things to be done which are to their own injury. For if, as you say, justice is the obedience which the subject renders to their commands, in that case, O wisest of men, is there any escape from the conclusion that the weaker are commanded to do; not what is for the interest, but what is for the injury of the stronger?

Nothing can be clearer, Socrates, said Polemarchus.

Yes, said Cleitophon, interposing, if you are allowed to be his witness.

But there is no need of any witness, said Polemarchus, for Thrasymachus himself acknowledges that rulers may sometimes command what is not for their own interest, and that for subjects to obey them is justice.

Yes, Polemarchus, — Thrasymachus said that for subjects to do what was commanded by their rulers is just.

Yes, Cleitophon, but he also said that justice is the interest of the stronger, and, while admitting both these propositions, he further acknowledged that the stronger may command the weaker who are his subjects to do what is not for his own interest; whence follows that justice is the injury quite as much as the interest of the stronger.

But, said Cleitophon, he meant by the interest of the stronger what the stronger thought to be his interest, — this was what the weaker had to do; and this was affirmed by him to be justice.

Those were not his words, rejoined Polemarchus.

Never mind, I replied, if he now says that they are, let us accept his statement. Tell me, Thrasymachus, I said, did you mean by justice what the stronger thought to be his interest, whether really so or not?

Certainly not, he said. Do you suppose that I call him who is mistaken the stronger at the time when he is mistaken?

Yes, I said, my impression was that you did so, when you admitted that the ruler was not infallible but might be sometimes mistaken.

You argue like an informer, Socrates. Do you mean, for example, that he who is mistaken about the sick is a physician in that he is mistaken? or that he who errs in arithmetic or grammar is an arithmetician or grammarian at the time when he is making the mistake, in respect of the mistake? True, we say that the physician or arithmetician or grammarian has made a mistake, but this is only a way of speaking; for the fact is that neither the grammarian nor any other person of skill ever makes a mistake in so far as he is what

SOCRATES,
CLEITOPHON,
POLEMARCUS,
THRASYMACHUS.

Cleitophon tries to make a way of escape for Thrasymachus by inserting the words 'thought to be.'

This evasion is repudiated by Thrasymachus;

who adopts another line of defence: 'No artist or ruler is ever mistaken *quâ* artist or ruler.'

SOCRATES,
THRASYMACHUS.

his name implies; they none of them err unless their skill fails them, and then they cease to be skilled artists. No artist or sage or ruler errs at the time when he is what his name implies; though he is commonly said to err, and I adopted the common mode of speaking. But to be perfectly accurate, since you are such a lover of accuracy, we should say that the ruler, in so far as he is a ruler, is unerring, and, being unerring, always commands that which is for his own interest; and the subject is required to execute his commands; and therefore, as I said at first and now repeat, justice is the interest of the stronger.

Indeed, Thrasymachus, and do I really appear to you to argue like an informer?

Certainly, he replied.

And do you suppose that I ask these questions with any design of injuring you in the argument?

Nay, he replied, 'suppose' is not the word — I know it; but you will be found out, and by sheer force of argument you will never prevail.

I shall not make the attempt, my dear man; but to avoid any misunderstanding occurring between us in future, let me ask, in what sense do you speak of a ruler or stronger whose interest, as you were saying, he being the superior, it is just that the inferior should execute — is he a ruler in the popular or in the strict sense of the term?

In the strictest of all senses, he said. And now cheat and play the informer if you can; I ask no quarter at your hands. but you never will be able, never.

And do you imagine, I said, that I am such a madman as to try and cheat Thrasymachus? I might as well shave a lion.

Why, he said, you made the attempt a minute ago, and you failed.

Enough, I said, of these civilities. It will be better that I should ask you a question: Is the physician, taken in that strict sense of which you are speaking, a healer of the sick or a maker of money? And remember that I am now speaking of the true physician.

A healer of the sick, he replied.

And the pilot — that is to say, the true pilot — is he a captain of sailors or a mere sailor?

A captain of sailors.

The circumstance that he sails in the ship is not to be taken into account; neither is he to be called a sailor; the name pilot by which he is distinguished has nothing to do

The essential meaning of words distinguished from their attributes.

with sailing, but is significant of his skill and of his authority over the sailors.

Very true, he said.

Now, I said, every art has an interest?

Certainly.

For which the art has to consider and provide?

Yes, that is the aim of art.

And the interest of any art is the perfection of it — this and nothing else?

What do you mean?

I mean what I may illustrate negatively by the example of the body. Suppose you were to ask me whether the body is self-sufficing or has wants, I should reply: Certainly the body has wants; for the body may be ill and require to be cured, and has therefore interests to which the art of medicine ministers; and this is the origin and intention of medicine, as you will acknowledge. Am I not right?

Quite right, he replied.

But is the art of medicine or any other art faulty or deficient in any quality in the same way that the eye may be deficient in sight or the ear fail of hearing, and therefore requires another art to provide for the interests of seeing and hearing — has art in itself, I say, any similar liability to fault or defect, and does every art require another supplementary art to provide for its interests, and that another and another without end? Or have the arts to look only after their own interests? Or have they no need either of themselves or of another? — having no faults or defects, they have no need to correct them, either by the exercise of their own art or of any other; they have only to consider the interest of their subject-matter. For every art remains pure and faultless while remaining true — that is to say, while perfect and unimpaired. Take the words in your precise sense, and tell me whether I am not right.

Art has no imperfection to be corrected, and therefore no extraneous interest.

Yes, clearly.

Then medicine does not consider the interest of medicine, but the interest of the body?

Illustrations.

True, he said.

Nor does the art of horsemanship consider the interests of the art of horsemanship, but the interests of the horse; neither do any other arts care for themselves, for they have no needs; they care only for that which is the subject of their art?

True, he said.

SOCRATES,
THRASYMACHUS.

But surely, Thrasymachus, the arts are the superiors and rulers of their own subjects?

To this he assented with a good deal of reluctance.

Then, I said, no science or art considers or enjoins the interest of the stronger or superior, but only the interest of the subject and weaker?

He made an attempt to contest this proposition also, but finally acquiesced.

Then, I continued, no physician, in so far as he is a physician, considers his own good in what he prescribes, but the good of his patient; for the true physician is also a ruler having the human body as a subject, and is not a mere money-maker; that has been admitted?

Yes.

And the pilot likewise, in the strict sense of the term, is a ruler of sailors and not a mere sailor?

That has been admitted.

And such a pilot and ruler will provide and prescribe for the interest of the sailor who is under him, and not for his own or the ruler's interest?

He gave a reluctant 'Yes.'

The disinterestedness of rulers.

Then, I said, Thrasymachus, there is no one in any rule who, in so far as he is a ruler, considers or enjoins what is for his own interest, but always what is for the interest of his subject or suitable to his art; to that he looks, and that alone he considers in everything which he says and does.

When we had got to this point in the argument, and every one saw that the definition of justice had been completely upset, Thrasymachus, instead of replying to me, said: Tell me, Socrates, have you got a nurse?

The impudence of Thrasymachus.

Why do you ask such a question, I said, when you ought rather to be answering?

Because she leaves you to snivel, and never wipes your nose: she has not even taught you to know the shepherd from the sheep.

What makes you say that? I replied.

Thrasymachus dilates upon the advantages of injustice,

Because you fancy that the shepherd or neatherd fattens or tends the sheep or oxen with a view to their own good and not to the good of himself or his master; and you further imagine that the rulers of states, if they are true rulers, never think of their subjects as sheep, and that they are not studying their own advantage day and night. Oh, no; and so entirely astray are you in your ideas about the just and unjust as not even to know that justice and the just are in reality another's good; that is to say, the interest of the ruler and stronger, and the loss of the subject and servant; and injustice the opposite; for the unjust is lord over the truly simple and just: he is the stronger, and his subjects do what is for his interest, and minister to his happiness, which is very far from being their own. Consider further, most foolish Socrates, that the just is always a loser in comparison with the unjust. First of all, in private contracts: wherever the unjust is the partner of the just you will find that, when the partnership is dissolved, the unjust man has always more and the just less. Secondly, in their dealings with the State: when there is an income-tax, the just man will pay more and the unjust less on the same amount of income; and when there is anything to be received the one gains nothing and the other much. Observe also what happens when they take an office; there is the just man neglecting his affairs and perhaps suffering other losses, and getting nothing out of the public, because he is just; moreover he is hated by his friends and acquaintance for refusing to serve them in un-lawful ways. But all this is reversed in the case of the unjust man. I am speaking, as before, of injustice on a large scale in which the advantage of the unjust is more apparent; and my meaning will be most clearly seen if we turn to that highest form of injustice in which the criminal is the happiest of men, and the sufferers or those who refuse to do injustice are the most miserable — that is to say tyranny, which by fraud and force takes away the property of others, not little by little but wholesale; comprehending in one, things sacred as well as profane, private and public; for which acts of wrong, if he were detected perpetrating any one of them singly, he would be punished and incur great disgrace — they who do such wrong in particular cases are called rob-bers of temples, and man-stealers and burglars and swin-dlers and thieves. But when a man besides taking away the money of the citizens has made slaves of them, then, instead of these names of reproach, he is termed happy and blessed, not only by the citizens but by all who hear of his having achieved the consummation of injustice. For man-kind censure injustice, fearing that they may be the victims of it and not because they shrink from committing it. And thus, as I have shown, Socrates, injustice, when on a suffi-cient scale, has more strength and freedom and mastery than justice; and, as I said at first, justice is the interest of the stronger, whereas injustice is a man's own profit and interest.

Thrasymachus, when he had thus spoken, having, like a

Thrasymachus
having made
his speech
wants to run
away, but is
detained by the
company.

bathman, deluged our ears with his words, had a mind to go away. But the company would not let him; they insisted that he should remain and defend his position; and I myself added my own humble request that he would not leave us. Thrasymachus, I said to him, excellent man, how suggestive are your remarks! And are you going to run away before you have fairly taught or learned whether they are true or not? Is the attempt to determine the way of man's life so small a matter in your eyes — to determine how life may be passed by each one of us to the greatest advantage?

And do I differ from you, he said, as to the importance of the enquiry?

You appear rather, I replied, to have no care or thought about us, Thrasymachus — whether we live better or worse from not knowing what you say you know, is to you a matter of indifference. Prithee, friend, do not keep your knowledge to yourself; we are a large party; and any benefit which you confer upon us will be amply rewarded. For my own part I openly declare that I am not convinced, and that I do not believe injustice to be more gainful than justice, even if uncontrolled and allowed to have free play. For, granting that there may be an unjust man who is able to commit injustice either by fraud or force, still this does not convince me of the superior advantage of injustice, and there may be others who are in the same predicament with myself. Perhaps we may be wrong; if so, you in your wisdom should convince us that we are mistaken in preferring justice to injustice.

The swagger of
Thrasymachus.

And how am I to convince you, he said, if you are not already convinced by what I have just said; what more can I do for you? Would you have me put the proof bodily into your souls?

Heaven forbid! I said; I would only ask you to be consistent; or, if you change, change openly and let there be no deception. For I must remark, Thrasymachus, if you will recall what was previously said, that although you began by defining the true physician in an exact sense, you did not observe a like exactness when speaking of the shepherd; you thought that the shepherd as a shepherd tends the sheep not with a view to their own good, but like a mere diner or banquetter with a view to the pleasures of the table; or, again, as a trader for sale in the market, and not as a shepherd. Yet surely the art of the shepherd is concerned only with the good of his subjects; he has only to provide the best for them, since the perfection of the art is already ensured whenever all the requirements of it are satisfied. And that was what I was saying just now about the ruler. I conceived that the art of the ruler, considered as ruler, whether in a state or in private life, could only regard the good of his flock or subjects; whereas you seem to think that the rulers in states, that is to say, the true rulers, like being in authority.

Think! Nay, I am sure of it.

Then why in the case of lesser offices do men never take them willingly without payment, unless under the idea that they govern for the advantage not of themselves but of others? Let me ask you a question: Are not the several arts different, by reason of their each having a separate function? And, my dear illustrious friend, do say what you think, that we may make a little progress.

The arts have different functions and are not to be confounded with the art of payment which is common to them all.

Yes, that is the difference, he replied.

And each art gives us a particular good and not merely a general one — medicine, for example, gives us health; navigation, safety at sea, and so on?

Yes, he said.

And the art of payment has the special function of giving pay: but we do not confuse this with other arts, any more than the art of the pilot is to be confused with the art of medicine, because the health of the pilot may be improved by a sea voyage. You would not be inclined to say, would you, that navigation is the art of medicine, at least if we are to adopt your exact use of language?

Certainly not.

Or because a man is in good health when he receives pay you would not say that the art of payment is medicine?

I should say not.

Nor would you say that medicine is the art of receiving pay because a man takes fees when he is engaged in healing?

Certainly not.

And we have admitted, I said, that the good of each art is specially confined to the art?

Yes.

Then, if there be any good which all artists have in common, that is to be attributed to something of which they all have the common use?

True, he replied.

And when the artist is benefited by receiving pay the advantage is gained by an additional use of the art of pay, which is not the art professed by him?

SOCRATES, GLAUCON.

He gave a reluctant assent to this.

Then the pay is not derived by the several artists from their respective arts. But the truth is, that while the art of medicine gives health, and the art of the builder builds a house, another art attends them which is the art of pay. The various arts may be doing their own business and benefiting that over which they preside, but would the artist receive any benefit from his art unless he were paid as well?

I suppose not.

But does he therefore confer no benefit when he works for nothing?

Certainly, he confers a benefit.

The true ruler or artist seeks, not his own advantage, but the perfection of his art; and therefore he must be paid.

Then now, Thrasymachus, there is no longer any doubt that neither arts nor governments provide for their own interests; but, as we were before saying, they rule and provide for the interests of their subjects who are the weaker and not the stronger—to their good they attend and not to the good of the superior. And this is the reason, my dear Thrasymachus, why, as I was just now saying, no one is willing to govern; because no one likes to take in hand the reformation of evils which are not his concern without remuneration. For, in the execution of his work, and in giving his orders to another, the true artist does not regard his own interest, but always that of his subjects; and therefore in order that rulers may be willing to rule, they must be paid in one of three modes of payment, money, or honour, or a penalty for refusing.

What do you mean, Socrates? said Glaucon. The first two modes of payment are intelligible enough, but what the penalty is I do not understand, or how a penalty can be a payment.

Three modes of paying rulers, money, honour, and a penalty for refusing to rule.

You mean that you do not understand the nature of this payment which to the best men is the great inducement to rule? Of course you know that ambition and avarice are held to be, as indeed they are, a disgrace?

Very true.

The penalty is the evil of being ruled by an inferior.

And for this reason, I said, money and honour have no attraction for them; good men do not wish to be openly demanding payment for governing and so to get the name of hirelings, nor by secretly helping themselves out of the public revenues to get the name of thieves. And not being ambitious they do not care about honour. Wherefore necessity must be laid upon them, and they must be induced to serve from the fear of punishment. And this, as I imagine, is the reason why the forwardness to take office, instead of waiting to be compelled, has been deemed dishonourable. Now the worst part of the punishment is that he who refuses to rule is liable to be ruled by one who is worse than himself. And the fear of this, as I conceive, induces the good to take office, not because they would, but because they cannot help — not under the idea that they are going to have any benefit or enjoyment themselves, but as a necessity, and because they are not able to commit the task of ruling to any one who is better than themselves, or indeed as good. For there is reason to think that if a city were composed entirely of good men, then to avoid office would be as much an object of contention as to obtain office is at present; then we should have plain proof that the true ruler is not meant by nature to regard his own interest, but that of his subjects; and every one who knew this would choose rather to receive a benefit from another than to have the trouble of conferring one. So far am I from agreeing with Thrasymachus that justice is the interest of the stronger. This latter question need not be further discussed at present; but when Thrasymachus says that the life of the unjust is more advantageous than that of the just, his new statement appears to me to be of a far more serious character. Which of us has spoken truly? And which sort of life, Glaucon, do you prefer?

I for my part deem the life of the just to be the more advantageous, he answered.

Did you hear all the advantages of the unjust which Thrasymachus was rehearsing?

Yes, I heard him, he replied, but he has not convinced me.

Then shall we try to find some way of convincing him, if we can, that he is saying what is not true?

Most certainly, he replied.

If, I said, he makes a set speech and we make another recounting all the advantages of being just, and he answers and we rejoin, there must be a numbering and measuring of the goods which are claimed on either side, and in the end we shall want judges to decide; but if we proceed in our enquiry as we lately did, by making admissions to one another, we shall unite the offices of judge and advocate in our own persons.

Very good, he said.

And which method do I understand you to prefer? I said.

That which you propose.

Well, then, Thrasymachus, I said, suppose you begin at the beginning and answer me. You say that perfect injustice is more gainful than perfect justice?

Yes, that is what I say, and I have given you my reasons.

And what is your view about them? Would you call one of them virtue and the other vice?

Certainly.

I suppose that you would call justice virtue and injustice vice?

What else then would you say?

The opposite, he replied.

And would you call justice vice?

No, I would rather say sublime simplicity.

Then would you call injustice malignity?

No; I would rather say discretion.

And do the unjust appear to you to be wise and good?

Yes, he said; at any rate those of them who are able to be perfectly unjust, and who have the power of subduing states and nations; but perhaps you imagine me to be talking of cutpurses. Even this profession if undetected has advantages, though they are not to be compared with those of which I was just now speaking.

I do not think that I misapprehend your meaning, Thrasymachus, I replied; but still I cannot hear without amazement that you class injustice with wisdom and virtue, and justice with the opposite.

Certainly I do so class them.

Now, I said, you are on more substantial and almost unanswerable ground; for if the injustice which you were maintaining to be profitable had been admitted by you as by others to be vice and deformity, an answer might have been

given to you on received principles; but now I perceive that you will call injustice honourable and strong, and to the unjust you will attribute all the qualities which were attributed by us before to the just, seeing that you do not hesitate to rank injustice with wisdom and virtue.

You have guessed most infallibly, he replied.

Then I certainly ought not to shrink from going through with the argument so long as I have reason to think that you, Thrasymachus, are speaking your real mind; for I do believe that you are now in earnest and are not amusing yourself at our expense.

I may be in earnest or not, but what is that to you? — to refute the argument is your business.

Very true, I said; that is what I have to do: But will you be so good as answer yet one more question? Does the just man try to gain any advantage over the just?

Far otherwise; if he did he would not be the simple amusing creature which he is.

And would he try to go beyond just action?

He would not.

And how would he regard the attempt to gain an advantage over the unjust; would that be considered by him as just or unjust?

He would think it just, and would try to gain the advantage; but he would not be able.

The just tries to obtain an advantage over the unjust, but not over the just; the unjust over both just and unjust.

Whether he would or would not be able, I said, is not to the point. My question is only whether the just man, while refusing to have more than another just man, would wish and claim to have more than the unjust?

Yes, he would.

And what of the unjust — does he claim to have more than the just man and to do more than is just?

Of course, he said, for he claims to have more than all men.

And the unjust man will strive and struggle to obtain more than the unjust man or action, in order that he may have more than all?

True.

We may put the matter thus, I said — the just does not desire more than his like but more than his unlike, whereas the unjust desires more than both his like and his unlike?

Nothing, he said, can be better than that statement.

And the unjust is good and wise, and the just is neither?

Good again, he said.

And is not the unjust like the wise and good and the just unlike them?

Of course, he said, he who is of a certain nature, is like those who are of a certain nature; he who is not, not.

Each of them, I said, is such as his like is?

Certainly, he replied.

Very good, Thrasymachus, I said; and now to take the case of the arts: you would admit that one man is a musician and another not a musician?

Illustrations.

Yes.

And which is wise and which is foolish?

Clearly the musician is wise, and he who is not a musician is foolish.

And he is good in as far as he is wise, and bad in as far as he is foolish?

Yes.

And you would say the same sort of thing of the physician?

Yes.

And do you think, my excellent friend, that a musician when he adjusts the lyre would desire or claim to exceed or go beyond a musician in the tightening and loosening the strings?

I do not think that he would.

But he would claim to exceed the non-musician?

Of course.

And what would you say of the physician? In prescribing meats and drinks would he wish to go beyond another physician or beyond the practice of medicine?

He would not.

But he would wish to go beyond the non-physician?

Yes.

The artist remains within the limits of his art;

And about knowledge and ignorance in general; see whether you think that any man who has knowledge ever would wish to have the choice of saying or doing more than another man who has knowledge. Would he not rather say or do the same as his like in the same case?

That, I suppose, can hardly be denied.

And what of the ignorant? would he not desire to have more than either the knowing or the ignorant?

I dare say.

And the knowing is wise?

Yes.

And the wise is good?

True.

Then the wise and good will not desire to gain more than his like, but more than his unlike and opposite?

I suppose so.

Whereas the bad and ignorant will desire to gain more than both?

Yes.

But did we not say, Thrasymachus, that the unjust goes beyond both his like and unlike? Were not these your words?

They were.

and similarly the just man does not exceed the limits of other just men.

And you also said that the just will not go beyond his like but his unlike?

Yes.

Then the just is like the wise and good, and the unjust like the evil and ignorant?

That is the inference.

And each of them is such as his like is?

That was admitted.

Then the just has turned out to be wise and good and the unjust evil and ignorant.

Thrasymachus made all these admissions, not fluently, as I repeat them, but with extreme reluctance; it was a hot summer's day, and the perspiration poured from him in torrents; and then I saw what I had never seen before, Thrasymachus blushing. As we were now agreed that justice was virtue and wisdom, and injustice vice and ignorance, I proceeded to another point:

Well, I said, Thrasymachus, that matter is now settled; but were we not also saying that injustice had strength; do you remember?

Yes, I remember, he said, but do not suppose that I approve of what you are saying or have no answer; if however I were to answer, you would be quite certain to accuse me of haranguing; therefore either permit me to have my say out, or if you would rather ask, do so, and I will answer 'Very good,' as they say to story-telling old women, and will nod 'Yes' and 'No.'

Certainly not, I said, if contrary to your real opinion.

Yes, he said, I will, to please you, since you will not let me speak. What else would you have?

Nothing in the world, I said; and if you are so disposed I will ask and you shall answer.

Proceed.

Then I will repeat the question which I asked before, in order that our examination of the relative nature of justice and injustice may be carried on regularly. A statement was made that injustice is stronger and more powerful than justice, but now justice, having been identified with wisdom and virtue, is easily shown to be stronger than injustice, if injustice is ignorance; this can no longer be questioned by any one. But I want to view the matter, Thrasymachus, in a different way: You would not deny that a state may be unjust and may be unjustly attempting to enslave other states or may have already enslaved them, and may be holding many of them in subjection?

True, he replied; and I will add that the best and most perfectly unjust state will be most likely to do so.

I know, I said, that such was your position; but what I

would further consider is, whether this power which is possessed by the superior state can exist or be exercised without justice or only with justice.

If you are right in your view, and justice is wisdom, then
only with justice; but if I am right, then without justice.

I am delighted, Thrasymachus, to see you not only
nodding assent and dissent, but making answers which are
quite excellent.

That is out of civility to you, he replied.

You are very kind, I said; and would you have the
goodness also to inform me, whether you think that a state,
or an army, or a band of robbers and thieves, or any other
gang of evil-doers could act at all if they injured one
another?

No indeed, he said, they could not.

But if they abstained from injuring one another, then
they might act together better?

Yes.

And this is because injustice creates divisions and
hatreds and fighting, and justice imparts harmony and
friendship; is not that true, Thrasymachus?

I agree, he said, because I do not wish to quarrel with
you.

How good of you, I said; but I should like to know also
whether injustice, having this tendency to arouse hatred,
wherever existing, among slaves or among freemen, will not
make them hate one another and set them at variance and
render them incapable of common action?

Certainly.

And even if injustice be found in two only, will they not
quarrel and fight, and become enemies to one another and
to the just?

They will.

And suppose injustice abiding in a single person, would
your wisdom say that she loses or that she retains her natural
power?

Let us assume that she retains her power.

Yet is not the power which injustice exercises of such a
nature that wherever she takes up her abode, whether in a
city, in an army, in a family, or in any other body, that body
is, to begin with, rendered incapable of united action by
reason of sedition and distraction; and does it not become
its own enemy and at variance with all that opposes it, and
with the just? Is not this the case?

Yes, certainly.

And is not injustice equally fatal when existing in a single person; in the first place rendering him incapable of action because he is not at unity with himself, and in the second place making him an enemy to himself and the just? Is not that true, Thrasymachus?

Yes.

And O my friend, I said, surely the gods are just?

Granted that they are.

But if so, the unjust will be the enemy of the gods, and the just will be their friend?

Feast away in triumph, and take your fill of the argument; I will not oppose you, lest I should displease the company.

Recapitulation.

Well then, proceed with your answers, and let me have the remainder of my repast. For we have already shown that the just are clearly wiser and better and abler than the unjust, and that the unjust are incapable of common action; nay more, that to speak as we did of men who are evil acting at any time vigorously together, is not strictly true, for if they had been perfectly evil, they would have laid hands upon one another; but it is evident that there must have been some remnant of justice in them, which enabled them to combine; if there had not been they would have injured one another as well as their victims; they were but half-villains in their enterprises; for had they been whole villains, and utterly unjust, they would have been utterly incapable of action. That, as I believe, is the truth of the matter, and not what you said at first. But whether the just have a better and happier life than the unjust is a further question which we also proposed to consider. I think that they have, and for the reasons which I have given; but still I should like to examine further, for no light matter is at stake, nothing less than the rule of human life.

Illustrations of ends and excellences preparatory to the enquiry into the end and excellence of the soul.

Proceed.

I will proceed by asking a question: Would you not say that a horse has some end?

I should.

And the end or use of a horse or of anything would be that which could not be accomplished, or not so well accomplished, by any other thing?

I do not understand, he said.

Let me explain: Can you see, except with the eye?

Certainly not.

Or hear, except with the ear?

No.

These then may be truly said to be the ends of these organs?

They may.

But you can cut off a vine-branch with a dagger or with a chisel, and in many other ways?

Of course.

And yet not so well as with a pruning-hook made for the purpose?

True.

May we not say that this is the end of a pruning-hook?

We may.

Then now I think you will have no difficulty in understanding my meaning when I asked the question whether the end of anything would be that which could not be accomplished, or not so well accomplished by any other thing?

I understand your meaning, he said, and assent.

All things which have ends have also virtues and excellences by which they fulfil those ends.

And that to which an end is appointed has also an excellence? Need I ask again whether the eye has an end?

It has.

And has not the eye an excellence?

Yes.

And the ear has an end and an excellence also?

True.

And the same is true of all other things; they have each of them an end and a special excellence?

That is so.

Well, and can the eyes fulfil their end if they are wanting in their own proper excellence and have a defect instead?

How can they, he said, if they are blind and cannot see?

You mean to say, if they have lost their proper excellence, which is sight; but I have not arrived at that point yet. I would rather ask the question more generally, and only enquire whether the things which fulfil their ends fulfil them by their own proper excellence, and fail of fulfilling them by their own defect?

Certainly, he replied.

I might say the same of the ears; when deprived of their own proper excellence they cannot fulfil their end?

True.

And the same observation will apply to all other things?

I agree.

Well; and has not the soul an end which nothing else can fulfil? for example, to superintend and command and deliberate and the like. Are not these functions proper to the soul, and can they rightly be assigned to any other?

To no other.

And is not life to be reckoned among the ends of the soul?

Assuredly, he said.

And has not the soul an excellence also?

Yes.

And can she or can she not fulfil her own ends when deprived of that excellence?

She cannot.

Then an evil soul must necessarily be an evil ruler and superintendent, and the good soul a good ruler?

Yes, necessarily.

And we have admitted that justice is the excellence of the soul, and injustice the defect of the soul?

That has been admitted.

Then the just soul and the just man will live well, and the unjust man will live ill?

That is what your argument proves.

And he who lives well is blessed and happy, and he who lives ill the reverse of happy?

Certainly.

Then the just is happy, and the unjust miserable?

So be it.

But happiness and not misery is profitable.

Of course.

Then, my blessed Thrasymachus, injustice can never be more profitable than justice.

Let this, Socrates, he said, be your entertainment at the Bendidea.

For which I am indebted to you, I said, now that you have grown gentle towards me and have left off scolding. Nevertheless, I have not been well entertained; but that was my own fault and not yours. As an epicure snatches a taste of every dish which is successively brought to table, he not having allowed himself time to enjoy the one before, so have I gone from one subject to another without having discovered what I sought at first, the nature of justice. I left that enquiry and turned away to consider whether justice is virtue and wisdom or evil and folly; and when there arose a further question about the comparative advantages of justice and injustice, I could not refrain from passing on to that. And the result of the whole discussion has been that I know

[margin notes:]

And the soul has a virtue and an end — the virtue justice, the end happiness.

Hence justice and happiness are necessarily connected.

Socrates is displeased with himself and with the argument.

SOCRATES.

nothing at all. For I know not what justice is, and therefore I am not likely to know whether it is or is not a virtue, nor can I say whether the just man is happy or unhappy.

Book II   Is Justice Better Than Injustice?

SOCRATES,
GLAUCON.

With these words I was thinking that I had made an end of the discussion; but the end, in truth, proved to be only a beginning. For Glaucon, who is always the most pugnacious of men, was dissatisfied at Thrasymachus' retirement; he wanted to have the battle out. So he said to me: Socrates, do you wish really to persuade us, or only to seem to have persuaded us, that to be just is always better than to be unjust?

I should wish really to persuade you, I replied, if I could.

The three-fold
division of
goods.

Then you certainly have not succeeded. Let me ask you now: — How would you arrange goods — are there not some which we welcome for their own sakes, and independently of their consequences, as, for example, harmless pleasures and enjoyments, which delight us at the time, although nothing follows from them?

I agree in thinking that there is such a class, I replied.

Is there not also a second class of goods, such as knowledge, sight, health, which are desirable not only in themselves, but also for their results?

Certainly, I said.

And would you not recognize a third class, such as gymnastic, and the care of the sick, and the physician's art; also the various ways of money-making — these do us good but we regard them as disagreeable; and no one would choose them for their own sakes, but only for the sake of some reward or result which flows from them?

There is, I said, this third class also. But why do you ask?

Because I want to know in which of the three classes you would place justice?

In the highest class, I replied, — among those goods which he who would be happy desires both for their own sake and for the sake of their results.

Then the many are of another mind; they think that justice is to be reckoned in the troublesome class, among goods which are to be pursued for the sake of rewards and of reputation, but in themselves are disagreeable and rather to be avoided.

SOCRATES,
GLAUCON.

I know, I said, that this is their manner of thinking, and that this was the thesis which Thrasymachus was maintaining just now, when he censured justice and praised injustice. But I am too stupid to be convinced by him.

I wish, he said, that you would hear me as well as him, and then I shall see whether you and I agree. For Thrasymachus seems to me, like a snake, to have been charmed by your voice sooner than he ought to have been; but to my mind the nature of justice and injustice have not yet been made clear. Setting aside their rewards and results, I want to know what they are in themselves, and how they inwardly work in the soul. If you please, then, I will revive the argument of Thrasymachus. And first I will speak of the nature and origin of justice according to the common view of them. Secondly, I will show that all men who practise justice do so against their will, of necessity, but not as a good. And thirdly, I will argue that there is reason in this view, for the life of the unjust is after all better far than the life of the just — if what they say is true, Socrates, since I myself am not of their opinion. But still I acknowledge that I am perplexed when I hear the voices of Thrasymachus and myriads of others dinning in my ears; and, on the other hand, I have never yet heard the superiority of justice to injustice maintained by any one in a satisfactory way. I want to hear justice praised in respect of itself; then I shall be satisfied, and you are the person from whom I think that I am most likely to hear this; and therefore I will praise the unjust life to the utmost of my power, and my manner of speaking will indicate the manner in which I desire to hear you too praising justice and censuring injustice. Will you say whether you approve of my proposal?

Three heads of the argument:
— 1. The nature of justice:
2. Justice a necessity, but not a good:
3. The reasonableness of this notion.

Indeed I do; nor can I imagine any theme about which a man of sense would oftener wish to converse.

I am delighted, he replied, to hear you say so, and shall begin by speaking, as I proposed, of the nature and origin of justice.

They say that to do injustice is, by nature, good; to suffer injustice, evil; but that the evil is greater than the good. And so when men have both done and suffered injustice and have had experience of both, not being able to avoid the one and obtain the other, they think that they had better agree among themselves to have neither; hence there arise laws and mutual convenants; and that which is ordained by

Justice a compromise between doing and suffering evil.

GLAUCON.

law is termed by them lawful and just. This they affirm to be the origin and nature of justice;—it is a mean or compromise, between the best of all, which is to do injustice and not be punished, and worst of all, which is to suffer injustice without the power of retaliation; and justice, being at a middle point between the two, is tolerated not as a good, but as the lesser evil, and honoured by reason of the inability of men to do injustice. For no man who is worthy to be called a man would ever submit to such an agreement if he were able to resist; he would be mad if he did. Such is the received account, Socrates, of the nature and origin of justice.

Now that those who practise justice do so involuntarily and because they have not the power to be unjust will best appear if we imagine something of this kind: having given both to the just and the unjust power to do what they will, let us watch and see whither desire will lead them; then we shall discover in the very act the just and unjust man to be proceeding along the same road, following their interest, which all natures deem to be their good, and are only diverted into the path of justice by the force of law. The liberty which we are supposing may be most completely given to them in the form of such a power as is said to have been possessed by Gyges the ancestor of Croesus the Ly-

The story of Gyges.

dian. According to the tradition, Gyges was a shepherd in the service of the king of Lydia; there was a great storm, and an earthquake made an opening in the earth at the place where he was feeding his flock. Amazed at the sight, he descended into the opening, where, among other marvels, he beheld a hollow brazen horse, having doors, at which he stooping and looking in saw a dead body of stature, as appeared to him, more than human, and having nothing on but a gold ring; this he took from the finger of the dead and reascended. Now the shepherds met together, according to custom, that they might send their monthly report about the flocks to the king; into their assembly he came having the ring on his finger, and as he was sitting among them he chanced to turn the collet of the ring inside his hand, when instantly he became invisible to the rest of the company and they began to speak of him as if he were no longer present. He was astonished at this, and again touching the ring he turned the collet outwards and reappeared; he made several trials of the ring, and always with the same result—when he turned the collet inwards he became invisible, when outwards he reappeared. Whereupon he contrived to be chosen one of the messengers who were sent to the court; where as soon as he arrived he seduced the queen, and with her help conspired against the king and slew him, and took the kingdom. Suppose now that there were two such magic rings, and the just put on one of them and the unjust the other; no man can be imagined to be of such an iron nature that he would stand fast in justice. No man would keep his hands off what was not his own when he could safely take what he liked out of the market, or go into houses and lie with any one at his pleasure, or kill or release from prison whom he would, and in all respects be like a God among men. Then the actions of the just would be as the actions of the unjust; they would both come at last to the same point. And this we may truly affirm to be a great proof that a man is just, not willingly or because he thinks that justice is any good to him individually, but of necessity, for wherever any one thinks that he can safely be unjust, there he is unjust. For all men believe in their hearts that injustice is far more profitable to the individual than justice, and he who argues as I have been supposing, will say that they are right. If you could imagine any one obtaining this power of becoming invisible, and never doing any wrong or touching what was another's, he would be thought by the lookers-on to be a most wretched idiot, although they would praise him to one another's faces, and keep up appearances with one another from a fear that they too might suffer injustice. Enough of this.

Now, if we are to form a real judgment of the life of the just and unjust, we must isolate them; there is no other way; and how is the isolation to be effected? I answer: Let the unjust man be entirely unjust, and the just man entirely just; nothing is to be taken away from either of them, and both are to be perfectly furnished for the work of their respective lives. First, let the unjust be like other distinguished masters of craft; like the skilful pilot or physician, who knows intuitively his own powers and keeps within their limits, and who, if he fails at any point, is able to recover himself. So let the unjust make his unjust attempts in the right way, and lie hidden if he means to be great in his injustice (he who is found out is nobody): for the highest reach of injustice is, to be deemed just when you are not. Therefore I say that in the perfectly unjust man we must assume the most perfect injustice; there is to be no deduction, but we must allow him, while doing the most unjust acts, to have acquired the greatest reputation for justice. If he have taken a false step he

GLAUCON.

The application of the story of Gyges.

The unjust to be clothed with power and reputation.

SOCRATES,
GLAUCON.

The just to be
unclothed of
all but his
virtue.

must be able to recover himself; he must be one who can
speak with effect, if any of his deeds come to light, and who
can force his way where force is required by his courage and
strength, and command of money and friends. And at his
side let us place the just man in his nobleness and simplicity,
wishing, as Aeschylus says, to be and not to seem good.
There must be no seeming, for if he seem to be just he will
be honoured and rewarded, and then we shall not know
whether he is just for the sake of justice or for the sake of
honours and rewards; therefore, let him be clothed in justice
only, and have no other covering; and he must be imagined
in a state of life the opposite of the former. Let him be the
best of men, and let him be thought the worst; then he will
have been put to the proof; and we shall see whether he will
be affected by the fear of infamy and its consequences. And
let him continue thus to the hour of death; being just and
seeming to be unjust. When both have reached the uttermost extreme, the one of justice and the other of injustice,
let judgment be given which of them is the happier of the
two.

Heavens! my dear Glaucon, I said, how energetically
you polish them up for the decision, first one and then the
other, as if they were two statues.

I do my best, he said. And now that we know what they
are like there is no difficulty in tracing out the sort of life
which awaits either of them. This I will proceed to describe;
but as you may think the description a little too coarse, I ask
you to suppose, Socrates, that the words which follow are
not mine. — Let me put them into the mouths of the eulo-
gists of injustice: They will tell you that the just man who is
thought unjust will be scourged, racked, bound — will have
his eyes burnt out; and, at last, after suffering every kind of
evil, he will be impaled: Then he will understand that he
ought to seem only, and not to be, just; the words of Aeschylus may be more truly spoken of the unjust than of the
just. For the unjust is pursuing a reality; he does not live with
a view to appearances — he wants to be really unjust and
not to seem only: —

The just man
will learn by
each experi-
ence that he
ought to seem
and not to be
just.

'His mind has a soil deep and fertile,
Out of which spring his prudent counsels.'

In the first place, he is thought just, and therefore bears rule
in the city; he can marry whom he will, and give in marriage
to whom he will; also he can trade and deal where he likes,

and always to his own advantage, because he has no misgivings about injustice; and at every contest, whether in public or private, he gets the better of his antagonists, and gains at their expense, and is rich, and out of his gains he can benefit his friends, and harm his enemies; moreover, he can offer sacrifices, and dedicate gifts to the gods abundantly and magnificently, and can honour the gods or any man whom he wants to honour in a far better style than the just, and therefore he is likely to be dearer than they are to the gods. And thus, Socrates, gods and men are said to unite in making the life of the unjust better than the life of the just.

SOCRATES, GLAUCON, ADIEMANTUS.

The unjust who appears just will attain every sort of prosperity.

I was going to say something in answer to Glaucon, when Adeimantus, his brother, interposed: Socrates, he said, you do not suppose that there is nothing more to be urged?

Why, what else is there? I answered.

The strongest point of all has not been even mentioned, he replied.

Well, then, according to the proverb, 'Let brother help brother' — if he fails in any part do you assist him; although I must confess that Glaucon has already said quite enough to lay me in the dust, and take from me the power of helping justice.

Nonsense, he replied. But let me add something more: There is another side to Glaucon's argument about the praise and censure of justice and injustice, which is equally required in order to bring out what I believe to be his meaning. Parents and tutors are always telling their sons and their wards that they are to be just; but why? not for the sake of justice, but for the sake of character and reputation; in the hope of obtaining for him who is reputed just some of those offices, marriages, and the like which Glaucon has enumerated among the advantages accruing to the unjust from the reputation of justice. More, however, is made of appearances by this class of persons than by the others; for they throw in the good opinion of the gods, and will tell you of a shower of benefits which the heavens, as they say, rain upon the pious; and this accords with the testimony of the noble Hesiod and Homer, the first of whom says, that the gods make the oaks of the just —

Adiemantus takes up the argument.

Justice is praised and injustice blamed, but only out of regard to their consequences.

'To bear acorns at their summit, and bees in the middle;
And the sheep are bowed down with the weight of their fleeces,'

ADEIMANTUS.

and many other blessings of a like kind are provided for them. And Homer has a very similar strain; for he speaks of one whose fame is —

'As the fame of some blameless king who, like a god,
Maintains justice; to whom the black earth brings forth
Wheat and barley, whose trees are bowed with fruit,
And his sheep never fail to bear, and the sea gives him
fish.'

The rewards
and punish-
ments of
another life.

Still grander are the gifts of heaven which Musaeus and his son vouchsafe to the just; they take them down into the world below, where they have the saints lying on couches at a feast, everlastingly drunk, crowned with garlands; their idea seems to be that an immortality of drunkenness is the highest meed of virtue. Some extend their rewards yet further; the posterity, as they say, of the faithful and just shall survive to the third and fourth generation. This is the style in which they praise justice. But about the wicked there is another strain; they bury them in a slough in Hades, and make them carry water in a sieve; also while they are yet living they bring them to infamy, and inflict upon them the punishments which Glaucon described as the portion of the just who are reputed to be unjust; nothing else does their invention supply. Such is their manner of praising the one and censuring the other.

Men are always
repeating that
virtue is painful
and vice
pleasant.

Once more, Socrates, I will ask you to consider another way of speaking about justice and injustice, which is not confined to the poets, but is found in prose writers. The universal voice of mankind is always declaring that justice and virtue are honourable, but grievous and toilsome; and that the pleasures of vice and injustice are easy of attainment, and are only censured by law and opinion. They say also that honesty is for the most part less profitable than dishonesty; and they are quite ready to call wicked men happy, and to honour them both in public and private when they are rich or in any other way influential, while they despise and overlook those who may be weak and poor, even though acknowledging them to be better than the others. But most extraordinary of all is their mode of speaking about virtue and the gods: they say that the gods apportion calamity and misery to many good men, and good and happiness to the wicked. And mendicant prophets go to rich men's doors and persuade them that they have a power committed to them by the gods of making an atonement for a man's own or his ancestor's sins by sacrifices or charms, with rejoicings and feasts; and they promise to harm an enemy, whether just or unjust, at a small cost; with magic arts and incantations binding heaven, as they say, to execute their will. And the poets are the authorities to whom they appeal, now smoothing the path of vice with the words of Hesiod: —

'Vice may be had in abundance without trouble; the way is smooth and her dwelling-place is near. But before virtue the gods have set toil.'

and a tedious and uphill road: then citing Homer as a witness that the gods may be influenced by men; for he also says: —

'The gods, too, may be turned from their purpose; and men pray to them and avert their wrath by sacrifices and soothing entreaties, and by libations and the odour of fat, when they have sinned and transgressed.'

And they produce a host of books written by Musaeus and Orpheus, who were children of the Moon and the Muses — that is what they say — according to which they perform their ritual, and persuade not only individuals, but whole cities, that expiations and atonements for sin may be made by sacrifices and amusements which fill a vacant hour, and are equally at the service of the living and the dead; the latter sort they call mysteries, and they redeem us from the pains of hell, but if we neglect them no one knows what awaits us.

He proceeded: And now when the young hear all this said about virtue and vice, and the way in which gods and men regard them, how are their minds likely to be affected, my dear Socrates, — those of them, I mean, who are quick-witted, and, like bees on the wing, light on every flower, and from all that they hear are prone to draw conclusions as to what manner of persons they should be and in what way they should walk if they would make the best of life? Probably the youth will say to himself in the words of Pindar—

'Can I by justice or by crooked ways of deceit ascend a loftier tower which may be a fortress to me all my days?'

For what men say is that, if I am really just and am not also

Margin notes:

ADEIMANTUS.

They are taught that sins may be easily expiated.

The effects of all this upon the youthful mind.

ADEIMANTUS.

thought just, profit there is none, but the pain and loss on the other hand are unmistakeable. But if, though unjust, I acquire the reputation of justice, a heavenly life is promised to me. Since then, as philosophers prove, appearance tyrannizes over truth and is lord of happiness, to appearance I must devote myself. I will describe around me a picture and shadow of virtue to be the vestibule and exterior of my house; behind I will trail the subtle and crafty fox, as Archilochus, greatest of sages, recommends. But I hear some one exclaiming that the concealment of wickedness is often difficult: to which I answer, Nothing great is easy. Nevertheless, the argument indicates this, if we would be happy, to be the path along which we should proceed. With a view to

The existence of the gods is only known to us through the poets, who likewise assure us that they may be bribed and that they are very ready to forgive.

concealment we will establish secret brotherhoods and political clubs. And there are professors of rhetoric who teach the art of persuading courts and assemblies; and so, partly by persuasion and partly by force, I shall make unlawful gains and not be punished. Still I hear a voice saying that the gods cannot be deceived, neither can they be compelled. But what if there are no gods? or, suppose them to have no care of human things — why in either case should we mind about concealment? And even if there are gods, and they do care about us, yet we know of them only from tradition and the genealogies of the poets; and these are the very persons who say that they may be influenced and turned by 'sacrifices and soothing entreaties and by offerings.' Let us be consistent then, and believe both or neither. If the poets speak truly, why then we had better be unjust, and offer of the fruits of injustice; for if we are just, although we may escape the vengeance of heaven, we shall lose the gains of injustice; but, if we are unjust, we shall keep the gains, and by our sinning and praying, and praying and sinning, the gods will be propitiated, and we shall not be punished. 'But there is a world below in which either we or our posterity will suffer for our unjust deeds.' Yes, my friend, will be the reflection, but there are mysteries and atoning deities, and these have great power. That is what mighty cities declare; and the children of the gods, who were their poets and prophets, bear a like testimony.

All this, even if not absolutely true, affords great excuse for doing wrong.

On what principle, then, shall we any longer choose justice rather than the worst injustice? when, if we only unite the latter with a deceitful regard to appearances, we shall fare to our mind both with gods and men, in life and after death, as the most numerous and the highest authorities tell us. Knowing all this, Socrates, how can a man who has any

superiority of mind or person or rank or wealth, be willing to
honour justice; or indeed to refrain from laughing when he
hears justice praised? And even if there should be some one
who is able to disprove the truth of my words, and who is
satisfied that justice is best, still he is not angry with the
unjust, but is very ready to forgive them, because he also
knows that men are not just of their own free will; unless,
peradventure, there be some one whom the divinity within
him may have inspired with a hatred of injustice, or who has
attained knowledge of the truth—but no other man. He
only blames injustice who, owing to cowardice or age or
some weakness, has not the power of being unjust. And this
is proved by the fact that when he obtains the power, he
immediately becomes unjust as far as he can be.

The cause of all this, Socrates, was indicated by us at
the beginning of the argument, when my brother and I told
you how astonished we were to find that of all the professing panegyrists of justice—beginning with the ancient
heroes of whom any memorial has been preserved to us,
and ending with the men of our own time—no one has ever
blamed injustice or praised justice except with a view to the
glories, honours, and benefits which flow from them. No
one has ever adequately described either in verse or prose
the true essential nature of either of them abiding in the soul,
and invisible to any human or divine eyes; or shown that of
all the things of a man's soul which he has within him, justice
is the greatest good, and injustice the greatest evil. Had this
been the universal strain, had you sought to persuade us of
this from our youth upwards, we should not have been on
the watch to keep one another from doing wrong, but every
one would have been his own watchman, because afraid, if
he did wrong, of harbouring in himself the greatest of evils. I
dare say that Thrasymachus and others would seriously hold
the language which I have been merely repeating, and
words even stronger than these about justice and injustice,
grossly, as I conceive, perverting their true nature. but I
speak in this vehement manner, as I must frankly confess to
you, because I want to hear from you the opposite side; and
I would ask you to show not only the superiority which
justice has over injustice, but what effect they have on the
possessor of them which makes the one to be a good and
the other an evil to him. And please, as Glaucon requested
of you, to exclude reputations; for unless you take away
from each of them his true reputation and add on the false,
we shall say that you do not praise justice, but the appear-

ADEIMANTUS.

Men should be
taught that
justice is in it-
self the greatest
good and
injustice the
greatest evil.

ADEIMANTUS, ance of it; we shall think that you are only exhorting us to
SOCRATES.   keep injustice dark, and that you really agree with Thrasymachus in thinking that justice is another's good and the
interest of the stronger, and that injustice is a man's own
profit and interest, though injurious to the weaker. Now as
you have admitted that justice is one of that highest class of
goods which are desired indeed for their results, but in a far
greater degree for their own sakes — like sight or hearing or
knowledge or health, or any other real and natural and not
merely conventional good — I would ask you in your praise
of justice to regard one point only: I mean the essential good
and evil which justice and injustice work in the possessors of
them. Let others praise justice and censure injustice, magni-
fying the rewards and honours of the one and abusing the
other; that is a manner of arguing which, coming from them,
I am ready to tolerate, but from you who have spent your
whole life in the consideration of this question, unless I hear
the contrary from your own lips, I expect something better.
And therefore, I say, not only prove to us that justice is
better than injustice, but show what they either of them do
to the possessor of them, which makes the one to be a good
and the other an evil, whether seen or unseen by gods and
men. . . .

Book IV   Virtues in the State
Justice in the Individual

SOCRATES,   But where, amid all this, is justice? son of Ariston, tell
GLAUCON.   me where. Now that our city has been made habitable, light
a candle and search, and get your brother and Polemarchus
and the rest of our friends to help, and let us see where in it
we can discover justice and where injustice, and in what
they differ from one another, and which of them the man
who would be happy should have for his portion, whether
seen or unseen by gods and men.

Nonsense, said Glaucon: did you not promise to search
yourself, saying that for you not to help justice in her need
would be an impiety?

I do not deny that I said so; and as you remind me, I will
be as good as my word; but you must join.

We will, he replied.

Well, then, I hope to make the discovery in this way: I

mean to begin with the assumption that our State, if rightly
ordered, is perfect.

That is most certain.

And being perfect, is therefore wise and valiant and
temperate and just.

That is likewise clear.

And whichever of these qualities we find in the State,
the one which is not found will be the residue?

Very good.

If there were four things, and we were searching for
one of them, wherever it might be, the one sought for might
be known to us from the first, and there would be no further
trouble; or we might know the other three first, and then the
fourth would clearly be the one left.

Very true, he said.

And is not a similar method to be pursued about the
virtues, which are also four in number?

Clearly.

First among the virtues found in the State, wisdom
comes into view, and in this I detect a certain peculiarity.

What is that?

The State which we have been describing is said to be
wise as being good in counsel?

Very true.

And good counsel is clearly a kind of knowledge, for
not by ignorance, but by knowledge, do men counsel well?

Clearly.

And the kinds of knowledge in a State are many and
diverse?

Of course.

There is the knowledge of the carpenter; but is that the
sort of knowledge which gives a city the title of wise and
good in counsel?

Certainly not; that would only give a city the reputation
of skill in carpentering.

Then a city is not to be called wise because possessing
a knowledge which counsels for the best about wooden
implements?

Certainly not.

Nor by reason of a knowledge which advises about
brazen pots, I said, nor as possessing any other similar
knowledge?

Not by reason of any of them, he said.

Nor yet by reason of a knowledge which cultivates the
earth; that would give the city the name of agricultural?

The place of
the virtues in
the State:(1)
The wisdom of
the statesman
advises, not
about particular
arts or pursuits,
but about the
whole State.

SOCRATES,
GLAUCON.

Yes.

Well, I said, and is there any knowledge in our recently-founded State among any of the citizens which advises, not about any particular thing in the State, but about the whole, and considers how a State can best deal with itself and with other States?

There certainly is.

And what is this knowledge, and among whom is it found? I asked.

It is the knowledge of the guardians, he replied, and is found among those whom we were just now describing as perfect guardians.

And what is the name which the city derives from the possession of this sort of knowledge?

The name of good in counsel and truly wise.

The statesmen or guardians are the smallest of all classes in the State.

And will there be in our city more of these true guardians or more smiths?

The smiths, he replied, will be far more numerous.

Will not the guardians be the smallest of all the classes who receive a name from the profession of some kind of knowledge?

Much the smallest.

And so by reason of the smallest part or class, and of the knowledge which resides in this presiding and ruling part of itself, the whole State, being thus constituted according to nature, will be wise; and this, which has the only knowledge worthy to be called wisdom, has been ordained by nature to be of all classes the least.

Most true.

Thus, then, I said, the nature and place in the State of one of the four virtues has somehow or other been discovered.

And, in my humble opinion, very satisfactorily discovered, he replied.

Again, I said, there is no difficulty in seeing the nature of courage, and in what part that quality resides which gives the name of courageous to the State.

How do you mean?

(2) The courage which makes the city courageous is found chiefly in the soldier.

Why, I said, every one who calls any State courageous or cowardly, will be thinking of the part which fights and goes out to war on the State's behalf.

No one, he replied, would ever think of any other.

The rest of the citizens may be courageous or may be cowardly, but their courage or cowardice will not, as I conceive, have the effect of making the city either the one or the other.

Certainly not.

The city will be courageous in virtue of a portion of herself which preserves under all circumstances that opinion about the nature of things to be feared and not to be feared in which our legislator educated them; and this is what you term courage.

Socrates, Glaucon. It is the quality which preserves right opinion about things to be feared and not to be feared.

I should like to hear what you are saying once more, for I do not think that I perfectly understand you.

I mean that courage is a kind of salvation.

Salvation of what?

Of the opinion respecting things to be feared, what they are and of what nature, which the law implants through education; and I mean by the words 'under all circumstances' to intimate that in pleasure or in pain, or under the influence of desire or fear, a man preserves, and does not lose this opinion. Shall I give you an illustration?

If you please.

You know, I said, that dyers, when they want to dye wool for making the true sea-purple, begin by selecting their white colour first; this they prepare and dress with much care and pains, in order that the white ground may take the purple hue in full perfection. The dyeing then proceeds; and whatever is dyed in this manner becomes a fast colour, and no washing either with lyes or without them can take away the bloom. But, when the ground has not been duly prepared, you will have noticed how poor is the look either of purple or of any other colour.

Illustration from the art of dyeing.

Yes, he said; I know that they have a washed-out and ridiculous appearance.

Then now, I said, you will understand what our object was in selecting our soldiers, and educating them in music and gymnastic; we were contriving influences which would prepare them to take the dye of the laws in perfection, and the colour of their opinion about dangers and of every other opinion was to be indelibly fixed by their nurture and training, not to be washed away by such potent lyes as pleasure —mightier agent far in washing the soul than any soda or lye; or by sorrow, fear, and desire, the mightiest of all other solvents. And this sort of universal saving power of true opinion in conformity with law about real and false dangers I call and maintain to be courage, unless you disagree.

Our soldiers must take the dye of the laws.

But I agree, he replied; for I suppose that you mean to exclude mere uninstructed courage, such as that of a wild beast or of a slave—this, in your opinion, is not the courage which the law ordains, and ought to have another name.

Most certainly.

Then I may infer courage to be such as you describe?

Why, yes, said I, you may, and if you add the words 'of a citizen,' you will not be far wrong; — hereafter, if you like, we will carry the examination further, but at present we are seeking not for courage but justice; and for the purpose of our enquiry we have said enough.

You are right, he replied.

Two other virtues, temperance and justice, which must be considered in their proper order.

Two virtues remain to be discovered in the State — first temperance, and then justice which is the end of our search.

Very true.

Now, can we find justice without troubling ourselves about temperance?

I do not know how that can be accomplished, he said, nor do I desire that justice should be brought to light and temperance lost sight of; and therefore I wish that you would do me the favour of considering temperance first.

Certainly, I replied, I should not be justified in refusing your request.

Then, consider, he said.

Yes, I replied; I will; and as far as I can at present see, the virtue of temperance has more of the nature of harmony and symphony than the preceding.

How so? he asked.

Temperance, I replied, is the ordering or controlling of certain pleasures and desires; this is curiously enough implied in the saying of 'a man being his own master;' and other traces of the same notion may be found in language.

No doubt, he said.

There is something ridiculous in the expression 'master of himself;' for the master is also the servant and the servant the master; and in all these modes of speaking the same person is denoted.

The temperate is master of himself but the same person, when intemperate, is also the slave of himself.

Certainly.

The meaning is, I believe, that in the human soul there is a better and also a worse principle; and when the better has the worse under control, then a man is said to be master of himself; and this is a term of praise: but when, owing to evil education or association, the better principle, which is also the smaller, is overwhelmed by the greater mass of the worse — in this case he is blamed and is called the slave of self and unprincipled.

Yes, there is reason in that.

And now, I said, look at our newly-created State, and there you will find one of these two conditions realized; for the State, as you will acknowledge, may be justly called master of itself, if the words 'temperance' and 'self-mastery' truly express the rule of the better part over the worse.

Yes, he said, I see that what you say is true.

Let me further note that the manifold and complex pleasures and desires and pains are generally found in children and women and servants, and in the freemen so called who are of the lowest and more numerous class.

Certainly, he said.

Whereas the simple and moderate desires which follow reason, and are under the guidance of mind and true opinion, are to be found only in a few, and those the best born and best educated.

Very true.

These two, as you may perceive, have a place in our State; and the meaner desires of the many are held down by the virtuous desires and wisdom of the few.

The State which has the passions and desires of the many controlled by the few may be rightly called temperate.

That I perceive, he said.

Then if there be any city which may be described as master of its own pleasures and desires, and master of itself, ours may claim such a designation?

Certainly, he replied.

It may also be called temperate, and for the same reasons?

Yes.

And if there be any State in which rulers and subjects will be agreed as to the question who are to rule, that again will be our State?

Undoubtedly.

And the citizens being thus agreed among themselves, in which class will temperance be found — in the rulers or in the subjects?

In both, as I should imagine, he replied.

Do you observe that we were not far wrong in our guess that temperance was a sort of harmony?

Why so?

Why, because temperance is unlike courage and wisdom, each of which resides in a part only, the one making the State wise and the other valiant; not so temperance, which extends to the whole, and runs through all the notes of the scale, and produces a harmony of the weaker and the stronger and the middle class, whether you suppose them to be stronger or weaker in wisdom or power or numbers or wealth, or anything else. Most truly then may we deem

Temperance resides in the whole State.

SOCRATES, GLAUCON.

SOCRATES,
GLAUCON.
temperance to be the agreement of the naturally superior and inferior, as to the right to rule of either, both in states and individuals.

I entirely agree with you.

And so, I said, we may consider three out of the four virtues to have been discovered in our State. The last of those qualities which make a state virtuous must be justice, if we only knew what that was.

The inference is obvious.

Justice is not
far off.
The time then has arrived, Glaucon, when, like huntsmen, we should surround the cover, and look sharp that justice does not steal away, and pass out of sight and escape us; for beyond a doubt she is somewhere in this country: watch therefore and strive to catch a sight of her, and if you see her first, let me know.

Would that I could! but you should regard me rather as a follower who has just eyes enough to see what you show him — that is about as much as I am good for.

Offer up a prayer with me and follow.

I will, but you must show me the way.

Here is no path, I said, and the wood is dark and perplexing; still we must push on.

Let us push on.

Here I saw something: Halloo! I said, I begin to perceive a track, and I believe that the quarry will not escape.

Good news, he said.

Truly, I said, we are stupid fellows.

Why so?

Why, my good sir, at the beginning of our enquiry, ages ago, there was justice tumbling out at our feet, and we never saw her; nothing could be more ridiculous. Like people who go about looking for what they have in their hands — that was the way with us — we looked not at what we were seeking, but at what was far off in the distance; and therefore, I suppose, we missed her.

What do you mean?

I mean to say that in reality for a long time past we have been talking of justice, and have failed to recognise her.

I grow impatient at the length of your exordium.

We had already
found her
when we spoke
of one man
doing one thing
only.
Well then, tell me, I said, whether I am right or not: You remember the original principle which we were always laying down at the foundation of the State, that one man should practise one thing only, the thing to which his nature was best adapted; — now justice is this principle or a part of it.

Yes, we often said that one man should do one thing only.

Further, we affirmed that justice was doing one's own business, and not being a busybody; we said so again and again, and many others have said the same to us.

Yes, we said so.

Then to do one's own business in a certain way may be assumed to be justice. Can you tell me whence I derive this inference?

I cannot, but I should like to be told.

Because I think that this is the only virtue which remains in the State when the other virtues of temperance and courage and wisdom are abstracted; and, that this is the ultimate cause and condition of the existence of all of them, and while remaining in them is also their preservative; and we were saying that if the three were discovered by us, justice would be the fourth or remaining one.

From another
point of view
Justice is the
residue of the
three others.

That follows of necessity.

If we are asked to determine which of these four qualities by its presence contributes most to the excellence of the State, whether the agreement of rulers and subjects, or the preservation in the soldiers of the opinion which the law ordains about the true nature of dangers, or wisdom and watchfulness in the rulers, or whether this other which I am mentioning, and which is found in children and women, slave and freeman, artisan, ruler, subject, — the quality, I mean, of every one doing his own work and not being a busybody, would claim the palm — the question is not so easily answered.

Certainly, he replied, there would be a difficulty in saying which.

Then the power of each individual in the State to do his own work appears to compete with the other political virtues, wisdom, temperance, courage.

Yes, he said.

And the virtue which enters into this competition is justice?

Exactly.

Let us look at the question from another point of view: Are not the rulers in a State those to whom you would entrust the office of determining suits at law?

Our idea is
confirmed by
the administra-
tion of justice
in lawsuits. No
man is to have
what is not his
own.

Certainly.

And are suits decided on any other ground but that a man may neither take what is another's, nor be deprived of what is his own?

SOCRATES,
GLAUCON.

Yes; that is their principle.

Which is a just principle?

Yes.

Then on this view also justice will be admitted to be the having and doing what is a man's own, and belongs to him?

Very true.

Illustration:
Classes, like in-
dividuals,
should not
meddle with
one another's
occupations.

Think, now, and say whether you agree with me or not. Suppose a carpenter to be doing the business of a cobbler, or a cobbler of a carpenter; and suppose them to exchange their implements or their duties, or the same person to be doing the work of both, or whatever be the change; do you think that any great harm would result to the State?

Not much.

But when the cobbler or any other man whom nature designed to be a trader, having his heart lifted up by wealth or strength or the number of his followers, or any like advantage, attempts to force his way into the class of war-riors, or a warrior into that of legislators and guardians, for which he is unfitted, and either to take the implements or the duties of the other; or when one man is trader, legislator, and warrior all in one, then I think you will agree with me in saying that this interchange and this meddling of one with another is the ruin of the State.

Most true.

Seeing then, I said, that there are three distinct classes, any meddling of one with another, or the change of one into another, is the greatest harm to the State, and may be most justly termed evil-doing?

Precisely.

And the greatest degree of evil-doing to one's own city would be termed by you injustice?

Certainly.

This then is injustice; and on the other hand when the trader, the auxiliary, and the guardian each do their own business, that is justice, and will make the city just.

I agree with you.

From the larger example of the State we will now return to the individual.

We will not, I said, be over-positive as yet; but if, on trial, this conception of justice be verified in the individual as well as in the State, there will be no longer any room for doubt; if it be not verified, we must have a fresh enquiry. First let us complete the old investigation, which we began, as you remember, under the impression that, if we could previously examine justice on the larger scale, there would be less difficulty in discerning her in the individual. That larger example appeared to be the State, and accordingly we constructed as good a one as we could, knowing well that in the good State justice would be found. Let the discovery which we made be now applied to the individual—if they agree, we shall be satisfied; or, if there be a difference in the individual, we will come back to the State and have another trial of the theory. The friction of the two when rubbed together may possibly strike a light in which justice will shine forth, and the vision which is then revealed we will fix in our souls.

SOCRATES, GLAUCON.

That will be in regular course; let us do as you say.

I proceeded to ask: When two things, a greater and less, are called by the same name, are they like or unlike in so far as they are called the same?

Like, he replied.

The just man then, if we regard the idea of justice only, will be like the just State?

He will.

And a State was thought by us to be just when the three classes in the State severally did their own business; and also thought to be temperate and valiant and wise by reason of certain other affections and qualities of these same classes?

True, he said.

And so of the individual; we may assume that he has the same three principles in his own soul which are found in the State; and he may be rightly described in the same terms, because he is affected in the same manner?

Certainly, he said. . . .

. . . And so, after much tossing, we have reached land, and are fairly agreed that the same principles which exist in the State exist also in the individual, and that they are three in number.

Exactly.

Must we not then infer that the individual is wise in the same way, and in virtue of the same quality which makes the State wise?

The conclusion that the same three principles exist both in the State and in the individual applied to each of them.

Certainly.

Also that the same quality which constitutes courage in the State constitutes courage in the individual, and that both the State and the individual bear the same relation to all the other virtues?

Assuredly.

And the individual will be acknowledged by us to be just in the same way in which the State is just?

That follows of course.

We cannot but remember that the justice of the State

SOCRATES,   consisted in each of the three classes doing the work of its
GLAUCON.   own class?

We are not very likely to have forgotten, he said.

We must recollect that the individual in whom the several qualities of his nature do their own work will be just, and will do his own work?

Yes, he said, we must remember that too.

And ought not the rational principle, which is wise, and has the care of the whole soul, to rule, and the passionate or spirited principle to be the subject and ally?

Certainly.

Music and   And, as we were saying, the united influence of music
gymnastic will   and gymnastic will bring them into accord, nerving and
harmonize   sustaining the reason with noble words and lessons, and
passion and   moderating and soothing and civilizing the wildness of pas-
reason. These   sion by harmony and rhythm?
two combined
will control   Quite true, he said.
desire, and will
be the best   And these two, thus nurtured and educated, and having
defenders both   learned truly to know their own functions, will rule over the
of body and   concupiscent, which in each of us is the largest part of the
soul.   soul and by nature most insatiable of gain; over this they will
keep guard, lest, waxing great and strong with the fulness of bodily pleasures, as they are termed, the consupiscent soul, no longer confined to her own sphere, should attempt to enslave and rule those who are not her natural-born subjects, and overturn the whole life of man?

Very true, he said.

Both together will they not be the best defenders of the whole soul and the whole body against attacks from without; the one counselling, and the other fighting under his leader, and courageously executing his commands, and counsels?

True.

And he is to be deemed courageous whose spirit re-
The   tains in pleasure and in pain the commands of reason about
courageous.   what he ought or ought not to fear?

Right, he replied.

The wise.   And him we call wise who has in him that little part which rules, and which proclaims these commands; that part too being supposed to have a knowledge of what is for the interest of each of the three parts and of the whole?

Assuredly.

The temperate.   And would you not say that he is temperate who has these same elements in friendly harmony, in whom the one ruling principle of reason, and the two subject ones of spirit and desire are equally agreed that reason ought to rule, and do not rebel?

Certainly, he said, that is the true account of temperance whether in the State or individual.

And surely, I said, we have explained again and again how and by virtue of what quality a man will be just.

The just.

That is very certain.

And is justice dimmer in the individual, and is her form different, or is she the same which we found her to be in the State?

There is no difference in my opinion, he said.

Because, if any doubt is still lingering in our minds, a few commonplace instances will satisfy us of the truth of what I am saying.

What sort of instances do you mean?

If the case is put to us, must we not admit that the just State, or the man who is trained in the principles of such a State, will be less likely than the unjust to make away with a deposit of gold or silver? Would any one deny this?

The nature of justice illustrated by commonplace instances.

No one, he replied.

Will the just man or citizen ever be guilty of sacrilege or theft, or treachery either to his friends or to his country?

Never.

Neither will he ever break faith where there have been oaths or agreements?

Impossible.

No one will be less likely to commit adultery, or to dishonour his father and mother, or to fail in his religious duties?

No one.

And the reason is that each part of him is doing its own business, whether in ruling or being ruled?

Exactly so.

Are you satisfied then that the quality which makes such men and such states is justice, or do you hope to discover some other?

Not I, indeed.

Then our dream has been realized; and the suspicion which we entertained at the beginning of our work of construction, that some divine power must have conducted us to a primary form of justice, has now been verified?

We have realized the hope entertained in the first construction of the State.

Yes, certainly.

And the division of labour which required the carpenter

SOCRATES,
GLAUCON.

and the shoemaker and the rest of the citizens to be doing each his own business, and not another's, was a shadow of justice, and for that reason it was of use?

Clearly.

The three principles harmonize in one.

But in reality justice was such as we were describing, being concerned however, not with the outward man, but with the inward, which is the true self and concernment of man: for the just man does not permit the several elements within him to interfere with one another, or any of them to do the work of others, — he sets in order his own inner life, and is his own master and his own law, and at peace with himself; and when he has bound together the three principles within him, which may be compared to the higher, lower and middle notes of the scale, and the intermediate intervals — when he has bound all these together, and is no longer many, but has become one entirely temperate and perfectly adjusted nature, then he proceeds to act, if he has to act, whether in a matter of property, or in the treatment of the body, or in some affair of politics or private business; always thinking and calling that which preserves and co-operates with this harmonious condition, just and good action, and the knowledge which presides over it, wisdom, and that which at any time impairs this condition, he will call unjust action, and the opinion which presides over it ignorance.

The harmony of human life.

You have said the exact truth, Socrates.

Very good; and if we were to affirm that we had discovered the just man and the just State, and the nature of justice in each of them, we should not be telling a falsehood?

Most certainly not.

May we say so, then?

Let us say so.

And now, I said, injustice has to be considered.

Clearly.

Injustice the opposite of justice.

Must not injustice be a strife which arises among the three principles — a meddlesomeness, and interference, and rising up of a part of the soul against the whole, an assertion of unlawful authority, which is made by a rebellious subject against a true prince, of whom he is the natural vassal, — what is all this confusion and delusion but injustice, and intemperance and cowardice and ignorance, and every form of vice?

Exactly so.

And if the nature of justice and injustice be known, then

the meaning of acting unjustly and being unjust, or, again, of
acting justly, will also be perfectly clear?

What do you mean? he said.

Why, I said, they are like disease and health; being in
the soul just what disease and health are in the body.

How so? he said.

Why, I said, that which is healthy causes health, and
that which is unhealthy causes disease.

Analogy of
body and soul.

Yes.

Health: disease:
justice:
injustice.

And just actions cause justice, and unjust actions cause
injustice?

That is certain.

And the creation of health is the institution of a natural
order and government of one by another in the parts of the
body; and the creation of disease is the production of a state
of things at variance with this natural order?

True.

And is not the creation of justice the institution of a
natural order and government of one by another in the parts
of the soul, and the creation of injustice the production of a
state of things at variance with the natural order?

Exactly so, he said.

Then virtue is the health and beauty and well-being of
the soul, and vice the disease and weakness and deformity
of the same?

True.

And do not good practices lead to virtue, and evil
practices to vice?

Assuredly.

Still our old question of the comparative advantage of
justice and injustice has not been answered: Which is the
more profitable, to be just and act justly and practise virtue,
whether seen or unseen of gods and men, or to be unjust
and act unjustly, if only unpunished and unreformed?

The old
question,
whether the
just or the
unjust is the
happier, has
become
ridiculous.

In my judgment, Socrates, the question has now become ridiculous. We know that, when the bodily constitution is gone, life is no longer endurable, though pampered
with all kinds of meats and drinks, and having all wealth and
all power; and shall we be told that when the very essence
of the vital principle is undermined and corrupted, life is still
worth having to a man, if only he be allowed to do whatever
he likes with the single exception that he is not to acquire
justice and virtue, or to escape from injustice and vice;
assuming them both to be such as we have described?

Socrates,   Yes, I said, the question is, as you say, ridiculous. . . .
Glaucon.

Book V   The Status of Women

. . . For men born and educated like our citizens, the only way, in my opinion, of arriving at a right conclusion about the possession and use of women and children is to follow the path on which we originally started, when we said that the men were to be the guardians and watchdogs of the herd.

True.

Let us further suppose the birth and education of our women to be subject to similar or nearly similar regulations; then we shall see whether the result accords with our design.

What do you mean?

No distinction among the animals such as is made between men and women.

What I mean may be put into the form of a question, I said: Are dogs divided into hes and shes, or do they both share equally in hunting and in keeping watch and in the other duties of dogs? or do we entrust to the males the entire and exclusive care of the flocks, while we leave the females at home, under the idea that the bearing and suckling their puppies is labour enough for them?

No, he said, they share alike; the only difference between them is that the males are stronger and the females weaker.

But can you use different animals for the same purpose, unless they are bred and fed in the same way?

You cannot.

Then, if women are to have the same duties as men, they must have the same nurture and education?

Yes.

The education which was assigned to the men was music and gymnastic.

Yes.

Women must be taught music, gymnastic, and military exercises equally with men.

Then women must be taught music and gymnastic and also the art of war, which they must practise like the men?

That is the inference, I suppose.

I should rather expect, I said, that several of our proposals, if they are carried out, being unusual, may appear ridiculous.

No doubt of it.

Yes, and the most ridiculous thing of all will be the sight

of women naked in the palaestra, exercising with the men, especially when they are no longer young; they certainly will not be a vision of beauty, any more than the enthusiastic old men who in spite of wrinkles and ugliness continue to frequent the gymnasia.

Yes, indeed, he said: according to present notions the proposal would be thought ridiculous.

But then, I said, as we have determined to speak our minds, we must not fear the jests of the wits which will be directed against this sort of innovation; how they will talk of women's attainments both in music and gymnastic, and above all about their wearing armour and riding upon horseback!

Very true, he replied.

Yet having begun we must go forward to the rough places of the law; at the same time begging of these gentlemen for once in their life to be serious. Not long ago, as we shall remind them, the Hellenes were of the opinion, which is still generally received among the barbarians, that the sight of a naked man was ridiculous and improper; and when first the Cretans and then the Lacedaemonians introduced the custom, the wits of that day might equally have ridiculed the innovation.

No doubt.

But when experience showed that to let all things be uncovered was far better than to cover them up, and the ludicrous effect to the outward eye vanished before the better principle which reason asserted, then the man was perceived to be a fool who directs the shafts of his ridicule at any other sight but that of folly and vice, or seriously inclines to weigh the beautiful by any other standard but that of the good.

Very true, he replied.

First, then, whether the question is to be put in jest or in earnest, let us come to an understanding about the nature of woman: Is she capable of sharing either wholly or partially in the actions of men, or not at all? And is the art of war one of those arts in which she can or can not share? That will be the best way of commencing the enquiry, and will probably lead to the fairest conclusion.

That will be much the best way.

Shall we take the other side first and begin by arguing against ourselves; in this manner the adversary's position will not be undefended.

Why not? he said.

Convention should not be permitted to stand in the way of a higher good.

SOCRATES,
GLAUCON.

Objection: We
were saying
that every one
should do his
own work:
Have not
women and
men severally a
work of their
own?

Then let us put a speech into the mouths of our opponents. They will say: 'Socrates and Glaucon, no adversary
need convict you, for you yourselves, at the first foundation
of the State, admitted the principle that everybody was to do
the one work suited to his own nature.' And certainly, if I am
not mistaken, such an admission was made by us. 'And do
not the natures of men and women differ very much indeed?' And we shall reply: Of course they do. Then we shall
be asked, 'Whether the tasks assigned to men and to women
should not be different, and such as are agreeable to their
different natures?' Certainly they should. But if so, have you
not fallen into a serious inconsistency in saying that men and
women, whose natures are so entirely different, ought to
perform the same actions?' — What defence will you make
for us, my good Sir, against any one who offers these
objections?

That is not an easy question to answer when asked
suddenly; and I shall and I do beg of you to draw out the
case on our side.

These are the objections, Glaucon, and there are many
others of a like kind, which I foresaw long ago; they made
me afraid and reluctant to take in hand any law about the
possession and nurture of women and children.

By Zeus, he said, the problem to be solved is anything
but easy.

Why yes, I said, but the fact is that when a man is out of
his depth, whether he has fallen into a little swimming bath
or into mid ocean, he has to swim all the same.

Very true.

And must not we swim and try to reach the shore: we
will hope that Arion's dolphin or some other miraculous
help may save us?

I suppose so, he said.

Well then, let us see if any way of escape can be found.
We acknowledged — did we not? That different natures
ought to have different pursuits, and that men's and
women's natures are different. And now what are we
saying? — that different natures ought to have the same
pursuits, — this is the inconsistency which is charged upon
us.

Precisely.

Verily, Glaucon, I said, glorious is the power of the art
of contradiction!

Why do you say so?

Because I think that many a man falls into the practice

against his will. When he thinks that he is reasoning he is really disputing, just because he cannot define and divide, and so know that of which he is speaking; and he will pursue a merely verbal opposition in the spirit of contention and not of fair discussion.

SOCRATES,
GLAUCON.

The seeming
inconsistency
arises out of a
verbal
opposition.

Yes, he replied, such is very often the case; but what has that to do with us and our argument?

A great deal; for there is certainly a danger of our getting unintentionally into a verbal opposition.

In what way?

Why we valiantly and pugnaciously insist upon the verbal truth, that different natures ought to have different pursuits, but we never considered at all what was the meaning of sameness or difference of nature, or why we distinguished them when we assigned different pursuits to different natures and the same to the same natures.

When we as-
signed to
different na-
tures different
pursuits, we
meant only
those
differences of
nature which
affected the
pursuits.

Why, no, he said, that was never considered by us.

I said: Suppose that by way of illustration we were to ask the question whether there is not an opposition in nature between bald men and hairy men; and if this is admitted by us, then, if bald men are cobblers, we should forbid the hairy men to be cobblers, and conversely?

That would be a jest, he said.

Yes, I said, a jest; and why? Because we never meant when we constructed the State, that the opposition of natures should extend to every difference, but only to those differences which affected the pursuit in which the individual is engaged; we should have argued, for example, that a physician and one who is in mind a physician may be said to have the same nature.

True.

Whereas the physician and the carpenter have different natures?

Certainly.

And if, I said, the male and female sex appear to differ in their fitness for any art or pursuit, we should say that such pursuit or art ought to be assigned to one or the other of them; but if the difference consists only in women bearing and men begetting children, this does not amount to a proof that a woman differs from a man in respect of the sort of education she should receive; and we shall therefore continue to maintain that our guardians and their wives ought to have the same pursuits.

Very true, he said.

Next, we shall ask our opponent how, in reference to

any of the pursuits or arts of civic life, the nature of a woman differs from that of a man?

That will be quite fair.

And perhaps he, like yourself, will reply that to give a sufficient answer on the instant is not easy; but after a little reflection there is no difficulty.

Yes, perhaps.

Suppose then that we invite him to accompany us in the argument, and then we may hope to show him that there is nothing peculiar in the constitution of women which would affect them in the administration of the State.

By all means.

The same
natural gifts are
found in both
sexes, but they
are possessed
in a higher
degree by men
than women.

Let us say to him: Come now, and we will ask you a question: — when you spoke of a nature gifted or not gifted in any respect, did you mean to say that one man will acquire a thing easily, another with difficulty; a little learning will lead the one to discover a great deal; whereas the other, after much study and application, no sooner learns than he forgets; or again, did you mean, that the one has a body which is a good servant to his mind, while the body of the other is a hindrance to him? — would not these be the sort of differences which distinguish the man gifted by nature from the one who is ungifted?

No one will deny that.

And can you mention any pursuit of mankind in which the male sex has not all these gifts and qualities in a higher degree than the female? Need I waste time in speaking of the art of weaving, and the management of pancakes and preserves, in which womankind does really appear to be great, and in which for her to be beaten by a man is of all things the most absurd?

You are quite right, he replied, in maintaining the general inferiority of the female sex: although many women are in many things superior to many men, yet on the whole what you say is true.

And if so, my friend, I said, there is no special faculty of administration in a state which a woman has because she is a woman, or which a man has by virtue of his sex, but the gifts of nature are alike diffused in both; all the pursuits of men are the pursuits of women also, but in all of them a woman is inferior to a man.

Men and
women are to
be governed by
the same laws
and to have the
same pursuits.

Very true.

Then are we to impose all our enactments on men and none of them on women?

That will never do.

One woman has a gift of healing, another not; one is a musician, and another has no music in her nature?

Very true.

And one woman has a turn for gymnastic and military exercises, and another is unwarlike and hates gymnastics?

Certainly.

And one woman is a philosopher, and another is an enemy of philosophy; one has spirit, and another is without spirit?

That is also true.

Then one woman will have the temper of a guardian, and another not. Was not the selection of the male guardians determined by differences of this sort?

Yes.

Men and women alike possess the qualities which make a guardian; they differ only in their comparative strength or weakness.

Obviously.

And those women who have such qualities are to be selected as the companions and colleagues of men who have similar qualities and whom they resemble in capacity and in character?

Very true.

And ought not the same natures to have the same pursuits?

They ought.

Then, as we were saying before, there is nothing unnatural in assigning music and gymnastic to the wives of the guardians — to that point we come round again.

Certainly not.

The law which we then enacted was agreeable to nature, and therefore not an impossibility or mere aspiration; and the contrary practice, which prevails at present, is in reality a violation of nature.

That appears to be true.

We had to consider, first, whether our proposals were possible, and secondly whether they were the most beneficial?

Yes.

And the possibility has been acknowledged?

Yes.

The very great benefit has next to be established?

Quite so.

SOCRATES,
GLAUCON.

There are
different de-
grees of
goodness both
in women and
men.

You will admit that the same education which makes a man a good guardian will make a woman a good guardian; for their original nature is the same?

Yes.

I should like to ask you a question.

What is it?

Would you say that all men are equal in excellence, or is one man better than another?

The latter.

And in the commonwealth which we were founding do you conceive the guardians who have been brought up on our model system to be more perfect men, or the cobblers whose education has been cobbling?

What a ridiculous question!

You have answered me, I replied: Well, and may we not further say that our guardians are the best of our citizens?

By far the best.

And will not their wives be the best women?

Yes, by far the best.

And can there be anything better for the interests of the State than that the men and women of a State should be as good as possible?

There can be nothing better.

And this is what the arts of music and gymnastic, when present in such manner as we have described, will accomplish?

Certainly.

Then we have made an enactment not only possible but in the highest degree beneficial to the State?

True.

Then let the wives of our guardians strip, for their virtue will be their robe, and let them share in the toils of war and the defence of their country; only in the distribution of labours the lighter are to be assigned to the women, who are the weaker natures, but in other respects their duties are to be the same. And as for the man who laughs at naked women exercising their bodies from the best of his motives, in his laughter he is plucking

'A fruit of unripe wisdom,'

and he himself is ignorant of what he is laughing at, or what he is about; — for that is, and ever will be, the best of sayings, *That the useful is the noble and the hurtful is the base.*

The noble
saying.

Very true. . . .

Book IX The Unhappiness of the Tyrant and the Happiness of the Just Person

. . . these things, in the misery and evil which they inflict upon a State, do not come within a thousand miles of the tyrant; when this noxious class and their followers grow numerous and become conscious of their strength assisted by the infatuation of the people, they choose from among themselves the one who has most of the tyrant in his own soul, and him they create their tyrant.

Yes, he said, and he will be the most fit to be a tyrant.

If the people yield, well and good; but if they resist him, as he began by beating his own father and mother, so now, if he has the power, he beats them, and will keep his dear old fatherland or motherland, as the Cretans say, in subjection to his young retainers whom he has introduced to be their rulers and masters. This is the end of his passions and desires.

Exactly.

When such men are only private individuals and before they get power, this is their character; they associate entirely with their own flatterers or ready tools; or if they want anything from anybody, they in their turn are equally ready to bow down before them: they profess every sort of affection for them; but when they have gained their point they know them no more.

Yes, truly.

They are always either the masters or servants and never the friends of anybody; the tyrant never tastes of true freedom or friendship.

Certainly not.

And may we not rightly call such men treacherous?

No question.

Also they are utterly unjust, if we were right in our notion of justice?

Yes, he said, and we were perfectly right.

Let us then sum up in a word, I said, the character of the worst man: he is the waking reality of what we dreamed.

Most true.

And this is he who being by nature most of a tyrant bears rule, and the longer he lives the more of a tyrant he becomes.

That is certain, said Glaucon, taking his turn to answer.

And will not he who has been shown to be the wickedest, be also the most miserable? And he who has tyran-

SOCRATES,
ADEIMANTUS,
GLAUCON.

A private person can do but little harm in comparison to the tyrant.

The behaviour of the tyrant to his early supporters.

He is always either master or servant, always treacherous, unjust, the waking reality of our dream, a tyrant by nature, a tyrant in fact. The wicked are also the most miserable.

nized longest and most, most continually and truly miserable; although this may not be the opinion of men in general?

Yes, he said, inevitably.

And must not the tyrannical man be like the tyrannical
State, and the democratical man like the democratical State;
and the same of the others?

Certainly.

And as State is to State in virtue and happiness, so is
man in relation to man?

To be sure.

Then comparing our original city, which was under a
king, and the city which is under a tyrant, how do they stand
as to virtue?

They are the opposite extremes, he said, for one is the
very best and the other is the very worst.

There can be no mistake, I said, as to which is which,
and therefore I will at once enquire whether you would
arrive at a similar decision about their relative happiness and
misery. And here we must not allow ourselves to be panic-
stricken at the apparition of the tyrant, who is only a unit and
may perhaps have a few retainers about him; but let us go as
we ought into every corner of the city and look all about,
and then we will give our opinion.

A fair invitation, he replied; and I see, as every one
must, that a tyranny is the wretchedest form of government,
and the rule of a king the happiest.

And in estimating the men too, may I not fairly make a
like request, that I should have a judge whose mind can
enter into and see through human nature? He must not be
like a child who looks at the outside and is dazzled at the
pompous aspect which the tyranical nature assumes to the
beholder, but let him be one who has a clear insight. May I
suppose that the judgment is given in the hearing of us all by
one who is able to judge, and has dwelt in the same place
with him, and been present at his daily life and known him in
his family relations, where he may be seen stripped of his
tragedy attire, and again in the hour of public danger — he
shall tell us about the happiness and misery of the tyrant
when compared with other men?

That again, he said, is a very fair proposal.

Shall I assume that we ourselves are able and experienced judges and have before now met with such a person?
We shall then have some one who will answer our enquiries.

By all means.

Let me ask you not to forget the parallel of the individual and the State; bearing this in mind, and glancing in turn from one to the other of them, will you tell me their respective conditions?

What do you mean? he asked.

Beginning with the State, I replied, would you say that a city which is governed by a tyrant is free or enslaved?

No city, he said, can be more completely enslaved.

And yet, as you see, there are freemen as well as masters in such a State?

Yes, he said, I see that there are — a few; but the people, speaking generally, and the best of them are miserably degraded and enslaved.

Then if the man is like the State, I said, must not the same rule prevail? His soul is full of meanness and vulgarity —the best elements in him are enslaved; and there is a small ruling part, which is also the worst and maddest.

Inevitably.

And would you say that the soul of such an one is the soul of a freeman, or of a slave?

He has the soul of a slave, in my opinion.

And the State which is enslaved under a tyrant is utterly incapable of acting voluntarily?

Utterly incapable.

And also the soul which is under a tyrant (I am speaking of the soul taken as a whole) is least capable of doing what she desires; there is a gadfly which goads her, and she is full of trouble and remorse?

Certainly.

And is the city which is under a tyrant rich or poor?

Poor.

And the tyrannical soul must be always poor and insatiable?

True.

And must not such a State and such a man be always full of fear?

Yes, indeed.

Is there any State in which you will find more of lamentation and sorrow and groaning and pain?

Certainly not.

And is there any man in whom you will find more of this sort of misery than in the tyrannical man, who is in a fury of passions and desires?

Impossible.

Reflecting upon these and similar evils, you held the tyrannical State to be the most miserable of States?

SOCRATES,
GLAUCON.

Also the
tyrannical man
is most
miserable.

Yet there is a
still more
miserable
being, the ty-
rannical man
who is a public
tyrant.

And I was right, he said.

Certainly, I said. And when you see the same evils in the tyrannical man, what do you say of him?

I say that he is by far the most miserable of all men.

There, I said, I think that you are beginning to go wrong.

What do you mean?

I do not think that he has as yet reached the utmost extreme of misery.

Then who is more miserable?

One of whom I am about to speak.

Who is that?

He who is of a tyrannical nature, and instead of leading a private life has been cursed with the further misfortune of being a public tyrant.

From what has been said, I gather that you are right.

Yes, I replied, but in this high argument you should be a little more certain, and should not conjecture only; for of all questions, this respecting good and evil is the greatest.

Very true, he said.

Let me then offer you an illustration, which may, I think, throw a light upon this subject.

What is your illustration?

In cities there
are many great
slave-owners,
and they help
to protect one
another.

The case of rich individuals in cities who possess many slaves, from them you may form an idea of the tyrant's condition, for they both have slaves; the only difference is that he has more slaves.

Yes, that is the difference.

You know that they live securely and have nothing to apprehend from their servants?

What should they fear?

Nothing. But do you observe the reason of this?

Yes; the reason is, that the whole city is leagued together for the protection of each individual.

Very true, I said. But imagine one of these owners, the master say of some fifty slaves, together with his family and property and slaves, carried off by a god into the wilderness, where there are no freemen to help him — will he not be in an agony of fear lest he and his wife and children should be put to death by his slaves?

Yes, he said, he will be in the utmost fear.

But suppose a
slaveowner and
his slaves
carried off into
the wilderness,
what will
happen then?
Such is the
condition of
the tyrant.

The time has arrived when he will be compelled to flatter divers of his slaves, and make many promises to them of freedom and other things, much against his will — he will have to cajole his own servants.

Yes, he said, that will be the only way of saving himself.

And suppose the same god, who carried him away, to surround him with neighbours who will not suffer one man to be the master of another, and who, if they could catch the offender, would take his life?

His case will be still worse, if you suppose him to be everywhere surrounded and watched by enemies.

And is not this the sort of prison in which the tyrant will be bound—he who being by nature such as we have described, is full of all sorts of fears and lusts? His soul is dainty and greedy, and yet alone, of all men in the city, he is never allowed to go on a journey, or to see the things which other freemen desire to see, but he lives in his hole like a woman hidden in the house, and is jealous of any other citizen who goes into foreign parts and sees anything of interest.

SOCRATES, GLAUCON.

He is the daintiest of all men and has to endure the hardships of a prison;

Very true, he said.

And amid evils such as these will not he who is ill-governed in his own person—the tyrannical man, I mean—whom you just now decided to be the most miserable of all—will not he be yet more miserable when, instead of leading a private life, he is constrained by fortune to be a public tyrant? He has to be master of others when he is not master of himself: he is like a diseased or paralytic man who is compelled to pass his life, not in retirement, but fighting and combating with other men.

Miserable in himself, he is still more miserable if he be in a public station.

Yes, he said, the similitude is most exact.

Is not his case utterly miserable? And does not the actual tyrant lead a worse life than he whose life you determined to be the worst?

Certainly.

He who is the real tyrant, whatever men may think, is the real slave, and is obliged to practise the greatest adulation and servility, and to be the flatterer of the vilest of mankind. He has desires which he is utterly unable to satisfy, and has more wants than any one, and is truly poor, if you know how to inspect the whole soul of him: all his life long he is beset with fear and is full of convulsions, and distractions, even as the State which he resembles: and surely the resemblance holds?

He then leads a life worse than the worst, in unhappiness,

Very true, he said.

Moreover, as we were saying before, he grows worse from having power: he becomes and is of necessity more jealous, more faithless, more unjust, more friendless, more impious, than he was at first; he is the purveyor and cherisher of every sort of vice, and the consequence is that he is

and in wickedness.

The umpire
decides that

supremely miserable, and that he makes everybody else as miserable as himself.

No man of any sense will dispute your words.

Come then, I said, and as the general umpire in theatrical contests proclaims the result, do you also decide who in your opinion is first in the scale of happiness, and who second, and in what order the others follow: there are five of them in all — they are the royal, timocratical, oligarchical, democratical, tyrannical.

The decision will be easily given, he replied; they shall be choruses coming on the stage, and I must judge them in the order in which they enter, by the criterion of virtue and vice, happiness and misery.

the best is the
happiest and
the worst is the
most miserable.
This is the
proclamation
of the son of
Ariston.

Need we hire a herald, or shall I announce, that the son of Ariston [the best] has decided that the best and justest is also the happiest, and that this is he who is the most royal man and king over himself; and that the worst and most unjust man is also the most miserable, and that this is he who being the greatest tyrant of himself is also the greatest tyrant of his State?

Make the proclamation yourself, he said.

And shall I add, 'whether seen or unseen by gods and men'?

Let the words be added.

Then this, I said, will be our first proof; and there is another, which may also have some weight.

What is that?

Proof, derived
from the three
principles of
the soul.

The second proof is derived from the nature of the soul: seeing that the individual soul, like the State, has been divided by us into three principles, the division may, I think, furnish a new demonstration.

Of what nature?

It seems to me that to these three principles three pleasures correspond; also three desires and governing powers.

How do you mean? he said.

There is one principle with which, as we were saying, a man learns, another with which he is angry; the third, having many forms, has no special name, but is denoted by the general term appetitive, from the extraordinary strength and vehemence of the desires of eating and drinking and the other sensual appetites which are the main elements of it; also money-loving, because such desires are generally satisfied by the help of money.

That is true, he said.

If we were to say that the loves and pleasures of this third part were concerned with gain, we should then be able to fall back on a single notion; and might truly and intelligibly describe this part of the soul as loving gain or money.

SOCRATES, GLAUCON.

(1) The appetitive:

I agree with you.

Again, is not the passionate element wholly set on ruling and conquering and getting fame?

True.

Suppose we call it the contentious or ambitious — would the term be suitable?

(2) The ambitious:

Extremely suitable.

On the other hand, every one sees that the principle of knowledge is wholly directed to the truth, and cares less than either of the others for gain or fame.

(3) The principle of knowledge and truth.

Far less.

'Lover of wisdom,' 'lover of knowledge,' are titles which we may fitly apply to that part of the soul?

Certainly.

One principle prevails in the souls of one class of men, another in others, as may happen?

Yes.

Then we may begin by assuming that there are three classes of men — lovers of wisdom, lovers of honour, lovers of gain?

Exactly.

And there are three kinds of pleasure, which are their several objects?

Very true.

Now, if you examine the three classes of men, and ask of them in turn which of their lives is pleasantest, each will be found praising his own and depreciating that of others: the money-maker will contrast the vanity of honour or of learning if they bring no money with the solid advantages of gold and silver?

Each will depreciate the others, but only the philosopher has the power to judge, because he alone has experience of the highest pleasures and is also acquainted with the lower.

True, he said.

And the lover of honour — what will be his opinion? Will he not think that the pleasure of riches is vulgar, while the pleasure of learning, if it brings no distinction, is all smoke and nonsense to him?

Very true.

And are we to suppose, I said, that the philosopher sets any value on other pleasures in comparison with the pleasure of knowing the truth, and in that pursuit abiding, ever learning, not so far indeed from the heaven of pleasure? Does he not call the other pleasures necessary, under the idea that if there were no necessity for them, he would rather not have them?

There can be no doubt of that, he replied.

Since, then, the pleasures of each class and the life of each are in dispute, and the question is not which life is more or less honourable, or better or worse, but which is the more pleasant or painless—how shall we know who speaks truly?

I cannot myself tell, he said.

Well, but what ought to be the criterion? Is any better than experience and wisdom and reason?

There cannot be a better, he said.

Then, I said, reflect. Of the three individuals, which has the greatest experience of all the pleasures which we enumerated? Has the lover of gain, in learning the nature of essential truth, greater experience of the pleasure of knowledge than the philosopher has of the pleasure of gain?

The philosopher, he replied, has greatly the advantage; for he has of necessity always known the taste of the other pleasures from his childhood upwards: but the lover of gain in all his experience has not of necessity tasted—or, I should rather say, even had he desired, could hardly have tasted—the sweetness of learning and knowing truth.

Then the lover of wisdom has a great advantage over the lover of gain, for he has a double experience?

Yes, very great.

Again, has he greater experience of the pleasures of honour, or the lover of honour or the pleasures of wisdom?

Nay, he said, all three are honoured in proportion as they attain their object; for the rich man and the brave man and the wise man alike have their crowd of admirers, and as they all receive honour they all have experience of the pleasures of honour; but the delight which is to be found in the knowledge of true being is known to the philosopher only.

His experience, then, will enable him to judge better than any one?

Far better.

And he is the only one who has wisdom as well as experience?

Certainly.

Further, the very faculty which is the instrument of judgment is not possessed by the covetous or ambitious man, but only by the philosopher?

What faculty?

Reason, with whom, as we were saying, the decision ought to rest.

Yes.

And reasoning is peculiarly his instrument?

Certainly.

If wealth and gain were the criterion, then the praise or blame of the lover of gain would surely be the most trustworthy?

Assuredly.

Or if honour or victory or courage, in that case the judgment of the ambitious or pugnacious would be the truest?

Clearly.

But since experience and wisdom and reason are the judges—

the pleasures which he approves are the true pleasures: he places (1) the love of wisdom, (2) the love of honour, (3) and lowest the love of gain.

The only inference possible, he replied, is that pleasures which are approved by the lover of wisdom and reason are the truest.

And so we arrive at the result, that the pleasure of the intelligent part of the soul is the pleasantest of the three, and that he of us in whom this is the ruling principle has the pleasantest life.

Unquestionably, he said, the wise man speaks with authority when he approves of his own life.

And what does the judge affirm to be the life which is next, and the pleasure which is next?

Clearly that of the soldier and lover of honour; who is nearer to himself than the money-maker.

Last comes the lover of gain?

Very true, he said.

Twice in succession, then, has the just man overthrown the unjust in this conflict; and now comes the third trial, which is dedicated to Olympian Zeus the saviour: a sage whispers in my ear that no pleasure except that of the wise is quite true and pure—all others are a shadow only; and surely this will prove the greatest and most decisive of falls?

True pleasure is not relative but absolute.

Yes, the greatest; but will you explain yourself?

I will work out the subject and you shall answer my questions.

Proceed.

Say, then, is not pleasure opposed to pain?

True.

And there is a neutral state which is neither pleasure nor pain?

There is.

A state which is intermediate, and a sort of repose of the soul about either — that is what you mean?

Yes.

You remember what people say when they are sick?

What do they say?

That after all nothing is pleasanter than health. But then they never knew this to be the greatest of pleasures until they were ill.

Yes, I know, he said.

The states intermediate between pleasure and pain are termed pleasures or pains only in relation to their opposites.

And when persons are suffering from acute pain, you must have heard them say that there is nothing pleasanter than to get rid of their pain?

I have.

And there are many other cases of suffering in which the mere rest and cessation of pain, and not any positive enjoyment, is extolled by them as the greatest pleasure?

Yes, he said; at the time they are pleased and well content to be at rest.

Again, when pleasure ceases, that sort of rest or cessation will be painful?

Doubtless, he said.

Then the intermediate state of rest will be pleasure and will also be pain?

So it would seem.

But can that which is neither become both?

I should say not.

And both pleasure and pain are motions of the soul, are they not?

Yes.

Pleasure and pain are said to be states of rest, but they are really motions.

But that which is neither was just now shown to be rest and not motion, and in a mean between them?

Yes.

How, then, can we be right in supposing that the absence of pain is pleasure, or that the absence of pleasure is pain?

Impossible.

This then is an appearance only and not a reality; that is to say, the rest is pleasure at the moment and in comparison of what is painful, and painful in comparison of what is pleasant; but all these representations, when tried by the test of true pleasure, are not real but a sort of imposition?

That is the inference.

Look at the other class of pleasures which have no antecedent pains and you will no longer suppose, as you perhaps may at present, that pleasure is only the cessation of pain, or pain of pleasure.

What are they, he said, and where shall I find them?

There are many of them: take as an example the pleasures of smell, which are very great and have no antecedent pains; they come in a moment, and when they depart leave no pain behind them.

All pleasures are not merely cessations of pains, or pains of pleasures; e.g. the pleasures of smell are not.

Most true, he said.

Let us not, then, be induced to believe that pure pleasure is the cessation of pain, or pain of pleasure.

No.

Still, the more numerous and violent pleasures which reach the soul through the body are generally of this sort — they are reliefs of pain.

That is true.

And the anticipations of future pleasures and pains are of a like nature?

Yes.

Shall I give you an illustration of them?

Let me hear.

You would allow, I said, that there is in nature an upper and lower and middle region?

Illustrations of the unreality of certain pleasures.

I should.

And if a person were to go from the lower to the middle region, would he not imagine that he is going up; and he who is standing in the middle and sees whence he has come, would imagine that he is already in the upper region, if he has never seen the true upper world?

To be sure, he said; how can he think otherwise?

But if he were taken back again he would imagine, and truly imagine, that he was descending?

No doubt.

All that would arise out of his ignorance of the true upper and middle and lower regions?

Yes.

Then can you wonder that persons who are inexperienced in the truth, as they have wrong ideas about many other things, should also have wrong ideas about pleasure and pain and the intermediate state; so that when they are only being drawn towards the painful they feel pain and think the pain which they experience to be real, and in like manner, when drawn away from pain to the neutral or intermediate state, they firmly believe that they have reached the goal of satiety and pleasure; they, not knowing

SOCRATES,
GLAUCON.
pleasure, err in contrasting pain with the absence of pain, which is like contrasting black with grey instead of white — can you wonder, I say, at this?

No, indeed; I should be much more disposed to wonder at the opposite.

Look at the matter thus: — Hunger, thirst, and the like, are inanitions of the bodily state?

Yes.

And ignorance and folly are inanitions of the soul?

True.

And food and wisdom are the corresponding satisfactions of either?

Certainly.

The intellectual more real than the sensual.

And is the satisfaction derived from that which has less or from that which has more existence the truer?

Clearly, from that which has more.

What classes of things have a greater share of pure existence in your judgment — those of which food and drink and condiments and all kinds of sustenance are examples, or the class which contains true opinion and knowledge and mind and all the different kinds of virtue? Put the question in this way: — Which has a more pure being — that which is concerned with the invariable, the immortal, and the true, and is of such a nature, and is found in such natures; or that which is concerned with and found in the variable and mortal, and is itself variable and mortal?

Far purer, he replied, is the being of that which is concerned with the invariable.

And does the essence of the invariable partake of knowledge in the same degree as of essence?

Yes, of knowledge in the same degree.

And of truth in the same degree?

Yes.

And, conversely, that which has less of truth will also have less of essence?

Necessarily.

Then, in general, those kinds of things which are in the service of the body have less of truth and essence than those which are in the service of the soul?

Far less.

And has not the body itself less of truth and essence than the soul?

Yes.

What is filled with more real existence, and actually has

a more real existence, is more really filled than that which is filled with less real existence and is less real?

Of course.

And if there be a pleasure in being filled with that which is according to nature, that which is more really filled with more real being will more really and truly enjoy true pleasure; whereas that which participates in less real being will be less truly and surely satisfied, and will participate in an illusory and less real pleasure?

SOCRATES,
GLAUCON.

The pleasures
of the sensual
and also of the
passionate
element are
unreal and
mixed.

Unquestionably.

Those then who know not wisdom and virtue, and are always busy with gluttony and sensuality, go down and up again as far as the mean; and in this region they move at random throughout life, but they never pass into the true upper world; thither they neither look, nor do they ever find their way, neither are they truly filled with true being, nor do they taste of pure and abiding pleasure. Like cattle, with their eyes always looking down and their heads stooping to the earth, that is, to the dining-table, they fatten and feed and breed, and, in their excessive love of these delights, they kick and butt at one another with horns and hoofs which are made of iron; and they kill one another by reason of their insatiable lust. For they fill themselves with that which is not substantial, and the part of themselves which they fill is also unsubstantial and incontinent.

Verily, Socrates, said Glaucon, you describe the life of the many like an oracle.

Their pleasures are mixed with pains — how can they be otherwise? For they are mere shadows and pictures of the true, and are coloured by contrast, which exaggerates both light and shade, and so they implant in the minds of fools insane desires of themselves; and they are fought about as Stesichorus says that the Greeks fought about the shadow of Helen at Troy in ignorance of the truth.

Something of that sort must inevitably happen.

And must not the like happen with the spirited or passionate element of the soul? Will not the passionate man who carries his passion into action, be in the like case, whether he is envious and ambitious, or violent and contentious, or angry and discontented, if he be seeking to attain honour and victory and the satisfaction of his anger without reason or sense?

Yes, he said, the same will happen with the spirited element also.

SOCRATES,
GLAUCON.
Both kinds of
pleasures are
attained in the
highest degree
when the
desires which
seek them are
under the
guidance of
reason.

Then may we not confidently assert that the lovers of money and honour, when they seek their pleasures under the guidance and in the company of reason and knowledge, and pursue after and win the pleasures which wisdom shows them, will also have the truest pleasures in the highest degree which is attainable to them, inasmuch as they follow truth; and they will have the pleasures which are natural to them, if that which is best for each one is also most natural to him?

Yes, certainly; the best is the most natural.

And when the whole soul follows the philosophical principle, and there is no division, the several parts are just, and do each of them their own business, and enjoy severally the best and truest pleasures of which they are capable?

Exactly.

But when either of the two other principles prevails, it fails in attaining its own pleasure, and compels the rest to pursue after a pleasure which is a shadow only and which is not their own?

True.

And the greater the interval which separates them from philosophy and reason, the more strange and illusive will be the pleasure?

Yes.

And is not that farthest from reason which is at the greatest distance from law and order?

Clearly.

And the lustful and tyrannical desires are, as we saw, at the greatest distance?

Yes.

And the royal and orderly desires are nearest?

Yes.

Then the tyrant will live at the greatest distance from true or natural pleasure, and the king at the least?

Certainly.

But if so, the tyrant will live most unpleasantly, and the king most pleasantly?

Inevitably . . . Well, I said, and now having arrived at this stage of the argument, we may revert to the words which brought us hither: Was not some one saying that injustice was a gain to the perfectly unjust who was reputed to be just?

Yes, that was said.

Refutation of
Thrasymachus.

Now then, having determined the power and quality of

justice and injustice, let us have a little conversation with him.

What shall we say to him?

Let us make an image of the soul, that he may have his own words presented before his eyes.

Of what sort?

An ideal image of the soul, like the composite creations of ancient mythology, such as the Chimera or Scylla or Cerberus, and there are many others in which two or more different natures are said to grow into one.

The triple animal who has outwardly the image of a man.

There are said to have been such unions.

Then do you now model the form of a multitudinous, many-headed monster, having a ring of heads of all manner of beasts, tame and wild, which he is able to generate and metamorphose at will.

You suppose marvellous powers in the artist; but, as language is more pliable than wax or any similar substance, let there be such a model as you propose.

Suppose now that you make a second form as of a lion, and a third of a man, the second smaller than the first, and the third smaller than the second.

That, he said, is an easier task; and I have made them as you say.

And now join them, and let the three grow into one.

That has been accomplished.

Next fashion the outside of them into a single image, as of a man, so that he who is not able to look within, and sees only the outer hull, may believe the beast to be a single human creature.

I have done so, he said.

And now, to him who maintains that it is profitable for the human creature to be unjust, and unprofitable to be just, let us reply that, if he be right, it is profitable for this creature to feast the multitudinous monster and strengthen the lion and the lion-like qualities, but to starve and weaken the man, who is consequently liable to be dragged about at the mercy of either of the other two; and he is not to attempt to familiarize or harmonize them with one another—he ought rather to suffer them to fight and bite and devour one another.

Will any one say that we should strengthen the monster and the lion at the expense of the man?

Certainly, he said; that is what the approver of injustice says.

To him the supporter of justice makes answer that he should ever so speak and act as to give the man within him in some way or other the most complete mastery over the entire human creature. He should watch over the many-headed monster like a good husbandman, fostering and cultivating the gentle qualities, and preventing the wild ones from growing; he should be making the lion-heart his ally, and in common care of them all should be uniting the several parts with one another and with himself.

Yes, he said, that is quite what the maintainer of justice will say.

And so from every point of view, whether of pleasure, honour, or advantage, the approver of justice is right and speaks the truth, and the disapprover is wrong and false and ignorant?

Yes, from every point of view.

For the noble principle subjects the beast to the man, the ignoble the man to the beast.

Come, now, and let us gently reason with the unjust, who is not intentionally in error. 'Sweet Sir,' we will say to him, 'what think you of things esteemed noble and ignoble? Is not the noble that which subjects the beast to the man, or rather to the god in man; and the ignoble that which subjects the man to the beast?' He can hardly avoid saying Yes—can he now?

Not if he has any regard for my opinion.

A man would not be the gainer if he sold his child: how much worse to sell his soul!

But, if he agrees so far, we may ask him to answer another question; 'Then how would a man profit if he received gold and silver on the condition that he was to enslave the noblest part of him to the worst? Who can imagine that a man who sold his son or daughter into slavery for money, especially if he sold them into the hands of fierce and evil men, would be the gainer, however large might be the sum which he received? And will any one say that he is not a miserable caitiff who remorselessly sells his own divine being to that which is most godless and detestable? Eriphyle took the necklace as the price of her husband's life, but he is taking a bribe in order to compass a worse ruin.'

Yes, said Glaucon, far worse—I will answer for him.

Proofs: (1) Men are blamed for the predominance of the lower nature, as well as for the meanness of their employ-ments and character:

Has not the intemperate been censured of old, because in him the huge multiform monster is allowed to be too much at large?

Clearly.

And men are blamed for pride and bad temper when the lion and serpent element in them disproportionately grows and gains strength?

Yes.

And luxury and softness are blamed, because they relax and weaken this same creature, and make a coward of him?

Very true.

And is not a man reproached for flattery and meanness who subordinates the spirited animal to the unruly monster, and, for the sake of money, of which he can never have enough, habituates him in the days of his youth to be trampled in the mire, and from being a lion to become a monkey?

True, he said.

And why are mean employments and manual arts a reproach? Only because they imply a natural weakness of the higher principle; the individual is unable to control the creatures within him, but has to court them, and his great study is how to flatter them.

Such appears to be the reason.

And therefore, being desirous of placing him under a rule like that of the best, we say that he ought to be the servant of the best, in whom the Divine rules; not, as Thrasymachus supposed, to the injury of the servant, but because every one had better be ruled by divine wisdom dwelling within him; or, if this be impossible, then by an external authority, in order that we may be all, as far as possible, under the same government, friends and equals.

(2) It is admitted that every one should be the servant of a divine rule, or at any rate be kept under control by an external authority:

True, he said.

And this is clearly seen to be the intention of the law, which is the ally of the whole city; and is seen also in the authority which we exercise over children, and the refusal to let them be free until we have established in them a principle analogous to the constitution of a state, and by cultivation of this higher element have set up in their hearts a guardian and ruler like our own, and when this is done they may go their ways.

Yes, he said, the purpose of the law is manifest.

From what point of view, then, and on what ground can we say that a man is profited by injustice or intemperance or other baseness, which will make him a worse man, even though he acquire money or power by his wickedness?

(3) The care taken of children shows that we seek to establish in them a higher principle.

From no point of view at all.

What shall he profit, if his injustice be undetected and unpunished? He who is undetected only gets worse, whereas he who is detected and punished has the brutal part of his nature silenced and humanized; the gentler element in him is liberated, and his whole soul is perfected and ennobled by the acquirement of justice and temperance and wisdom, more than the body ever is by receiving gifts of

The wise man will employ his energies in freeing and harmonizing the nobler elements of his nature and in regulating his bodily habits.

beauty, strength and health, in proportion as the soul is more honourable than the body.

Certainly, he said.

To this nobler purpose the man of understanding will devote the energies of his life. And in the first place, he will honour studies which impress these qualities on his soul, and will disregard others?

Clearly, he said.

In the next place, he will regulate his bodily habit and training, and so far will he be from yielding to brutal and irrational pleasures, that he will regard even health as quite a secondary matter; his first object will be not that he may be fair or strong or well, unless he is likely thereby to gain temperance, but he will always desire so to attemper the body as to preserve the harmony of the soul?

Certainly he will, if he has true music in him.

His first aim not health but harmony of soul.

And in the acquisition of wealth there is a principle of order and harmony which he will also observe; he will not allow himself to be dazzled by the foolish applause of the world, and heap up riches to his own infinite harm?

Certainly not, he said.

He will not heap up riches,

He will look at the city which is within him, and take heed that no disorder occur in it, such as might arise either from superfluity or from want; and upon this principle he will regulate his property and gain or spend according to his means.

Very true.

and he will only accept such political honours as will not deteriorate his character. He has a city of his own, and the ideal pattern of this will be the law of his life.

And, for the same reason, he will gladly accept and enjoy such honours as he deems likely to make him a better man; but those, whether private or public, which are likely to disorder his life, he will avoid?

Then, if that is his motive, he will not be a statesman.

By the dog of Egypt, he will! In the city which is his own he certainly will, though in the land of his birth perhaps not, unless he have a divine call.

I understand; you mean that he will be a ruler in the city of which we are the founders, and which exists in idea only; for I do not believe that there is such an one anywhere on earth?

In heaven, I replied, there is laid up a pattern of it, methinks, which he who desires may behold, and beholding, may set his own house in order. But whether such an one exists, or ever will exist in fact, is no matter; for he will live after the manner of that city, having nothing to do with any other.

I think so, he said.

ARISTOTLE

384 – 322 B.C.

INTRODUCTION

ARISTOTLE'S father was court physician to the king of Macedonia in Northern Greece, and Aristotle was born and reared in Stagira, close to the present city of Thessalonika. Some time after the death of his parents, Aristotle, then aged 17, was sent by his guardian to Athens in order to complete his education. Three years later he joined the Academy of Plato, a center already famous for its scientific and philosophical work. Little is known of the 20 years that Aristotle spent at the Academy except that Plato is said to have regarded him highly. The many dialogues that Aristotle wrote during this period were aimed at a wider audience, but none of these writings has survived.

With the death of Plato in 347 B.C. and the appointment of a new director unacceptable to Aristotle, he joined a group of friends in establishing an academy in the town of Assus on what is now the Turkish coast. Under the patronage of the local ruler, a man who was to become not only a close friend of Aristotle but his father-in-law, Aristotle remained there for 3 years before moving to the neighboring island of Lesbos. Two years later he accepted an invitation from Philip II, King of Macedonia, to tutor his 13-year-old son, Alexander, who later became the greatest military conqueror of the ancient world. Although Aristotle remained at this court for 7 years until Philip was assassinated in 336 B.C., Alexander could not have spent much time with him after the first few years, and there is no evidence that Aristotle's teaching had much effect on his busy pupil. By the age of 16 Alexander was ruling the kingdom in his father's absence and 2 years later he was an army commander in the field.

In 335 B.C. Aristotle returned to Athens, by then under the control of Macedonia, and rented premises for his new academy, which became known as the Lyceum, named after the grove of trees in which it was situated. For the next 7 years Aristotle wrote and taught from here. It is apparently from this period that his existing works date. We know that although Aristotle was on good and close terms with Antipater, the chief administrator of Greek affairs in Alexander's empire, he was also sympathetic to the opposition's efforts to resurrect Athenian democracy. But on the sudden death of Alexander at Babylon in 323 B.C., the Athenians rose up against the Macedonians, charged Aristotle, as they had Socrates, with irreverence toward the Athenian gods, and forced him to flee the city before he was put on trial. He died the next year, leaving behind him a will in which he provided carefully for his son and daughter, and for the emancipation of his four slaves and their children. The executor of his will was Antipater, his Macedonian friend, protector, and enemy of Athenian home rule.

Since the *Politics* is composed, apparently, of half a dozen separate essays, the question of their proper sequence and dates of composition has long been at issue. One common view is that the essays were written in the period between 335 and 322 B.C. when Aristotle was teaching at the Lyceum. The selections printed here are from Benjamin Jowett's translation, first published in 1885 and reprinted as *Aristotle's Politics*, Oxford: Clarendon Press, 1905.

SELECTIONS FROM
The Politics

Book I The Structure of the State and Household

Every state is a community of some kind, and every community is established with a view to some good; for mankind always act in order to obtain that which they think good. But, if all communities aim at some good, the state or political community, which is the highest of all, and which embraces all the rest, aims, and in a greater degree than any other, at the highest good.

Now there is an erroneous opinion that a statesman, king, householder, and master are the same, and that they differ, not in kind, but only in the number of their subjects. For example, the ruler over a few is called a master; over more, the manager of a household; over a still larger number, a statesman or king, as if there were no difference between a great household and a small state. The distinction which is made between the king and the statesman is as follows: When the government is personal, the ruler is a king; when, according to the principles of the political science, the citizens rule and are ruled in turn, then he is called a statesman.

But all this is a mistake; for governments differ in kind, as will be evident to any one who considers the matter according to the method which has hitherto guided us. As in other departments of science, so in politics, the compound should always be resolved into the simple elements or least parts of the whole. We must therefore look at the elements of which the state is composed, in order that we may see in what they differ from one another, and whether any scientific distinction can be drawn between the different kinds of rule.

He who thus considers things in their first growth and origin, whether a state or anything else, will obtain the clearest view of them. In the first place (1) there must be a union of those who cannot exist without each other; for example, of male and female, that the race may continue; and this is a union which is formed, not of deliberate purpose, but because, in common with other animals and with plants, mankind have a natural desire to leave behind them an image of themselves. And (2) there must be a union of natural ruler and subject, that both may be preserved. For he who can foresee with his mind is by nature intended to be lord and master, and he who can work with his body is a subject, and by nature a slave; hence master and slave have the same interest. Nature, however, has distinguished between the female and the slave. For she is not niggardly, like the smith who fashions the Delphian knife for many uses; she makes each thing for a single use, and every instrument is best made when intended for one and not for many uses. But among barbarians no distinction is made between women and slaves, because there is no natural ruler among them: they are a community of slaves, male and female. Wherefore the poets say, —

'It is meet that Hellenes should rule over barbarians;'

as if they thought that the barbarian and the slave were by nature one.

Out of these two relationships between man and woman, master and slave, the family first arises, and Hesiod is right when he says, —

'First house and wife and an ox for the plough,'

for the ox is the poor man's slave. The family is the association established by nature for the supply of men's every-day wants, and members of it are called by Charondas 'companions of the cupboard' and by Epimenides the Cretan, 'companions of the manger.' But when several families are united, and the association aims at something more than the supply of daily needs, then comes into existence the village. And the most natural form of the village appears to be that of a colony from the family, composed of the children and grandchildren, who are said to be 'suckled with the same milk.' And this is the reason why Hellenic states were originally governed by kings; because the Hellenes were under royal rule before they came together, as the barbarians still are. Every family is ruled by the eldest, and therefore in the colonies of the family the kingly form of government prevailed because they were of the same blood. As Homer says [of the Cyclopes]: —

'Each one gives law to his children and to his wives.'

For they lived dispersedly, as was the manner in ancient times. Wherefore men say that the Gods have a king, because they themselves either are or were in ancient times under the rule of a king. For they imagine, not only the forms of the Gods, but their ways of life to be like their own.

When several villages are united in a single community, perfect and large enough to be nearly or quite self-sufficing, the state comes into existence, originating in the bare needs of life, and continuing in existence for the sake of a good life. And therefore, if the earlier forms of society are natural, so is the state, for it is the end of them, and the [completed] nature is the end. For what each thing is when fully developed, we call its nature, whether we are speaking of a man, a horse, or a family. Besides, the final cause and end of a thing is the best, and to be self-sufficing is the end and the best.

Hence it is evident that the state is a creation of nature, and that man is by nature a political animal. And he who by nature and not by mere accident is without a state, is either above humanity, or below it; he is the

'Tribeless, lawless, heartless one,'

whom Homer denounces — the outcast who is a lover of war; he may be compared to an unprotected piece in the game of draughts.

Now the reason why man is more of a political animal than bees or any other gregarious animals is evident. Nature, as we often say, makes nothing in vain, and man is the only animal whom she has endowed with the gift of speech. And whereas mere sound is but an indication of pleasure or pain, and is therefore found in other animals (for their nature attains to the perception of pleasure and pain and the intimation of them to one another, and no further), the power of speech is intended to set forth the expedient and inexpedient, and likewise the just and the unjust. And it is a characteristic of man that he alone has any sense of good and evil, of just and unjust, and the association of living beings who have this sense makes a family and a state.

Thus the state is by nature clearly prior to the family and to the individual, since the whole is of necessity prior to the part; for example, if the whole body be destroyed, there will be no foot or hand, except in an equivocal sense, as we might speak of a stone hand; for when destroyed the hand will be no better. But things are defined by their working and power; and we ought not to say that they are the same when they are no longer the same, but only that they have the same name. The proof that the state is a creation of nature and prior to the individual is that the individual, when isolated, is not self-sufficing; and therefore he is like a part in relation to the whole. But he who is unable to live in society, or who has no need because he is sufficient for himself, must be either a beast or a god: he is no part of a state. A social instinct is implanted in all men by nature, and yet he who first founded the state was the greatest of benefactors. For man, when perfected, is the best of animals, but, when separated from law and justice, he is the worst of all; since armed injustice is the more dangerous, and he is equipped at birth with the arms of intelligence and with moral qualities which he may use for the worst ends. Wherefore, if he have not virtue, he is the most unholy and the most savage of animals, and the most full of lust and gluttony. But justice is the bond of men in states, and the administration of justice, which is the determination of what is just, is the principle of order in political society.

Seeing then that the state is made up of households, before speaking of the state we must speak of the management of the household. The parts of the household are the persons who compose it, and a complete household consists of slaves and freemen. Now we should begin by examining everything in its least elements; and the first and least parts of a family are master and slave, husband and wife, father and children. We have therefore to consider what each of these three relations is and ought to be: — I mean the relation of master and servant, of husband and wife, and thirdly of parent and child. And there is another element of a household, the so-called art of money-making, which, according to some, is identical with household management, according to others, a principal part of it; the nature of this art will also have to be considered by us.

Let us first speak of master and slave, looking to the needs of practical life and also seeking to attain some better theory of their relation than exists at present. For some are of opinion that the rule of a master is a science, and that the management of a household, and the mastership of slaves, and the political and royal rule, as I was saying at the outset, are all the same. Others affirm that the rule of a master over slaves is contrary to nature, and that the distinction between slave and freeman exists by law only, and not by nature; and being an interference with nature is therefore unjust.

Property is a part of the household, and therefore the art of acquiring property is a part of the art of managing the household; for no man can live well, or indeed live at all, unless he be provided with necessaries. And as in the arts which have a definite sphere the workers must have their own proper instruments for the accomplishment of their work, so it is in the management of a household. Now, instruments are of various sorts; some are living, others lifeless; in the rudder, the pilot of a ship has a lifeless, in the look-out man, a living instrument; for in the arts the servant is a kind of instrument. Thus, too, a possession is an instrument for maintaining life. And so, in the arrangement of the family, a slave is a living possession, and property a number of such instruments; and the servant is himself an instrument, which takes precedence of all other instruments. For if every instrument could accomplish its own work, obeying or anticipating the will of others, like the statues of Daedalus, or the tripods of Hephaestus, which, says the poet,

'of their own accord entered the assembly of the Gods';

if, in like manner, the shuttle would weave and the plectrum touch the lyre without a hand to guide them, chief workmen would not want servants, nor masters slaves. Here, however, another distinction must be drawn: the instruments commonly so called are instruments of production, whilst a possession is an instrument of action. The shuttle, for example, is not only of use, but something else is made by it, whereas of a garment or of a bed there is only the use. Further, as production and action are different in kind, and both require instruments, the instruments which they employ must likewise differ in kind. But life is action and not production, and therefore the slave is the minister of action [for he ministers to his master's life]. Again, a possession is spoken of as a part is spoken of; for the part is not only a part of something else, but wholly belongs to it; and this is also true of a possession. The master is only the master of the slave; he does not belong to him, whereas the slave is not only the slave of his master, but wholly belongs to him. Hence we see what is the nature and office of a slave; he who is by nature not his own but another's and yet a man, is by nature a slave; and he may be said to belong to another who, being a human being, is also a possession. And a possession may be defined as an instrument of action, separable from the possessor.

But is there any one thus intended by nature to be a slave, and for whom such a condition is expedient and right, or rather is not all slavery a violation of nature?

There is no difficulty in answering this question, on grounds both of reason and of fact. For that some should rule and others be ruled is a thing, not only necessary, but expedient; from the hour of their birth, some are marked out for subjection, others for rule.

And whereas there are many kinds both of rulers and subjects, that rule is the better which is exercised over better subjects — for example, to rule over men is better than to rule over wild beasts. The work is better which is executed by better workmen; and where one man rules and another is ruled, they may be said to have a work. In all things which form a composite whole and which are made up of parts, whether continuous or discrete, a distinction between the ruling and the subject element comes to light. Such a duality exists in living creatures, but not in them only; it originates in the constitution of the universe; even in things which have no life, there is a ruling principle, as in musical harmony. But we are wandering from the subject. We will, therefore, restrict ourselves to the living creature which, in the first place, consists of soul and body: and of these two, the one is by nature the ruler, and the other the subject. But then we must look for the intentions of nature in things which retain their nature, and not in things which are corrupted. And therefore we must study the man who is in the most perfect state both of body and soul, for in him we shall see the true relation of the two; although in bad or corrupted natures the body will often appear to rule over the soul, because they are in an evil and unnatural condition. First then we may observe in living creatures both a despotical and a constitutional rule; for the soul rules the body with a despotical rule, whereas the intellect rules the appetites with a constitutional and royal rule. And it is clear that the rule of the soul over the body, and of the mind and the rational element over the passionate is natural and expedient; whereas the equality of the two or the rule of the inferior is always hurtful. The same holds good of animals as well as of men; for tame animals have a better nature than wild, and all tame animals are better off when they are ruled by man; for then they are preserved. Again, the male is by nature superior, and the female inferior; and the one rules, and the other is ruled; this principle, of necessity, extends to all mankind. Where then there is such a difference as that between soul and body, or between men and animals (as in the case of those whose business is to use their body, and who can do nothing better), the lower sort are by nature slaves, and it is better for them as for all inferiors that they should be under the rule of a master. For he who can be, and therefore is another's, and he who participates in reason enough to apprehend, but not to have, reason, is a slave by nature. Whereas the lower animals cannot even apprehend reason; they obey their instincts. And indeed the use made of slaves and of tame animals is not very different; for both with their bodies minister to the needs of life. Nature would like to distinguish between the bodies of freemen and slaves, making the one strong for servile labour, the other upright, and although useless for such services, useful for political life in the arts both of war and peace. But this does not hold universally: for some slaves have the souls and others have the bodies of freemen. And doubtless if men differed from one another in the mere forms of their bodies as much as the statues of the Gods do from men, all would acknowledge that the inferior class should be slaves of the superior. And if there is a difference in the body, how much more in the soul! But the beauty of the body is seen, whereas the beauty of the soul is not seen. It is clear, then, that some men are by nature free, and others slaves, and that for these latter slavery is both expedient and right.

But that those who take the opposite view have in a certain way right on their side, may be easily seen. For the words slavery and slave are used in two senses. There is a slave or slavery by law as well as by nature. The law of which I speak is a sort of convention, according to which whatever is taken in war is supposed to belong to the victors. But this right many jurists impeach, as they would an orator who brought forward an unconstitutional measure: they detest the notion that, because one man has the power of doing violence and is superior in brute strength, another shall be his slave and subject. Even among philosophers there is a difference of opinion. The origin of the dispute, and the reason why the arguments cross, is as follows: Virtue, when furnished with means, may be deemed to have the greatest power of doing violence; and as superior power is only found where there is superior excellence of some kind, power is thought to imply virtue. But does it likewise imply justice? — that is the question. And, in order to make a distinction between them, some assert that justice is benevolence: to which others reply that justice is nothing more than the rule of a superior. If the two views are regarded as antagonistic and exclusive [i.e. if the notion that justice is benevolence excludes the idea of a just rule of a superior], the alternative [viz. that no one should rule over others] has no force or plausibility, because it implies that not even the superior in virtue ought to rule, or be master. Some, clinging, as they think, to a principle of justice (for law and custom are a sort of justice), assume that slavery in war is justified by law, but they are not consistent. For what if the cause of the war be unjust? No one would ever say that he is a slave who is unworthy to be a slave. Were this the case, men of the highest rank would be slaves and the children of slaves if they or their parents chance to have been taken captive and sold. Wherefore Hellenes do not like to call themselves slaves, but confine the term to barbarians. Yet, in using this language, they really mean the natural slave of whom we spoke at first; for it must be admitted that some are slaves everywhere, others nowhere. The same principle applies to nobility. Hellenes regard themselves as noble everywhere, and not only in their own country, but they deem the barbarians noble only when at home, thereby implying that there are two sorts of nobility and freedom, the one absolute, the other relative. The Helen of Theodectes says: —

'Who would presume to call me servant who am on both sides sprung from the stem of the Gods?'

What does this mean but that they distinguish freedom and slavery, noble and humble birth, by the two principles of good and evil? They think that as men and animals beget men and animals, so from good men a good man springs. But this is what nature, though she may intend it, often fails to accomplish.

We see then that there is some foundation for this difference of opinion, and that some actual slaves and freemen are not so by nature, and also that there is in some cases a marked distinction between the two classes, rendering it expedient and right for the one to be slaves and the others to be masters: the one practising obedience, the others exercising the authority which nature intended them to have. The abuse of this authority is injurious to both; for the interests of part and whole, of body and soul, are the same, and the slave is a part of the master, a living but separated part of his bodily frame. Where the relation between them is natural they are friends and have a common interest, but where it rests merely on law and force the reverse is true.

The previous remarks are quite enough to show that the rule of a master is not a constitutional rule, and therefore that all the different kinds of rule are not, as some affirm, the same with each other. For there is one rule exercised over subjects who are by nature free, another over subjects who are by nature slaves. The rule of a household is a monarchy, for every house is under one head: whereas constitutional rule is a government of freemen and equals. The master is not called a master because he has science, but because he is of a certain character, and the same remark applies to the slave and the freeman. Still there may be a science for the master and a science for the slave. The science of the slave would be such as the man of Syracuse taught, who made money by instructing slaves in their ordinary duties. And such a knowledge may be carried further, so as to include cookery and similar menial arts. For some duties are of the more necessary, others of the more honourable sort; as the proverb says, 'slave before slave, master before master.' But all such branches of knowledge are servile. There is likewise a science of the master, which teaches the use of slaves; for the master as such is concerned, not with the acquisition, but with the use of them. Yet this so-called science is not anything great or wonderful; for the master need only know how to order that which the slave must know how to execute. Hence those who are in a position which places them above toil, have stewards who attend to their households while they occupy themselves with philosophy or with politics. But the art of acquiring slaves, I mean of justly acquiring them, differs both from the art of the master and the art of the slave, being a species of hunting or war. Enough of the distinction between master and slave.

Let us now enquire into property generally, and into the art of money-making, in accordance with our usual method [of resolving a whole into its parts], for a slave has been shown to be a part of property. The first question is whether the art of money-making is the same with the art of managing a household or a part of it, or instrumental to it; and if the last, whether in the way that the art of making shuttles is instrumental to the art of weaving, or in the way that the casting of bronze is instrumental to the art of the statuary, for they are not instrumental in the same way, but the one provides tools and the other material; and by material I mean the substratum out of which any work is made; thus wool is the material of the weaver, bronze of the statuary. Now it is easy to see that the art of household management is not identical with the art of money-making, for the one uses the material which the other provides. And the art which uses household stores can be no other than the art of household management. There is, however, a doubt whether the art of money-making is a part of household management or a distinct art. [They appear to be connected]; for the money-maker has to consider whence money and property can be procured, but there are many sorts of property and wealth: — there is husbandry and the care and provision of food in general; are these parts of the money-making art or distinct arts? Again, there are many sorts of food, and therefore there are many kinds of lives both of animals and men; they must all have food, and the differences in their food have made differences in their ways of life. For of beasts, some are gregarious, others are solitary; they live in the way which is best adapted to sustain them, accordingly as they are carnivorous or herbivorous or omnivorous: and their habits are determined for them by nature in such a manner that they may obtain with greater facility the food of their choice. But, as different individuals have different tastes, the same things are not naturally pleasant to all of them; and therefore the lives of carnivorous or herbivorous animals further differ among themselves. In the lives of men too there is a great difference. The laziest are shepherds, who lead an idle life, and get their subsistence without trouble from tame animals; their flocks having to wander from place to place in search of pasture, they are compelled to follow them, cultivating a sort of living farm. Others support themselves by hunting, which is of different kinds. Some, for example, are pirates, others who dwell near lakes or marshes or rivers or a sea in which there are fish, are fishermen, and others live by the pursuit of birds or wild beasts. The greater number obtain a living from the fruits of the soil. Such are the modes of subsistence which prevail among those whose industry is employed immediately upon the products of nature, and whose food is not acquired by exchange and retail trade — there is the shepherd, the husbandman, the pirate, the fisherman, the hunter. Some gain a comfortable maintenance out of two employments, eking out the deficiencies of one of them by another: thus the life of a shepherd may be combined with that of a brigand, the life of a farmer with that of a hunter. Other modes of life are similarly combined in any way which the needs of men may require. Property, in the sense of a bare livelihood, seems to be given by nature herself to all, both when they are first born, and when they are grown up. For some animals bring forth, together with their offspring, so much food as will last until they are able to supply themselves; of this the vermiparous or oviparous animals are an instance; and the viviparous animals have up to a certain time a supply of food for their young in themselves, which is called milk. In like manner we may infer that, after the birth of animals, plants exist for their sake, and that the other animals exist for the sake of man, the tame for use and food, the wild, if not all, at least the greater part of them, for food, and for the provision of clothing and various instruments. Now if nature makes nothing incomplete, and nothing in vain, the inference must be that she has made all animals and plants for the sake of man. And so, in one point of view, the art of war is a natural art of acquisition, for it includes hunting, an art which we ought to practise against wild beasts, and against men who, though intended by nature to be governed, will not submit; for war of such a kind is naturally just.

Of the art of acquisition then there is one kind which is natural and is a part of the management of a household. Either we must suppose the necessaries of life to exist previously, or the art of household management must provide a store of them for the common use of the family or state. They are the elements of true wealth; for the amount of property which is needed for a good life is not unlimited, although Solon in one of his poems says that,

'No bound to riches has been fixed for man.'

But there is a boundary fixed, just as there is in the arts; for the instruments of any art are never unlimited, either in number or size, and wealth may be defined as a number of instruments to be used in a household or in a state. And so we see that there is a natural art of acquisition which is practised by managers of households and by statesmen, and what is the reason of this.

There is another variety of the art of acquisition which is commonly and rightly called the art of making money, and has in fact suggested the notion that wealth and property have no limit. Being nearly connected with the preceding, it is often identified with it. But though they are not very different, neither are they the same. The kind already described is given by nature, the other is gained by experience and art.

Let us begin our discussion of the question with the following considerations: —

Of everything which we possess there are two uses: both belong to the thing as such, but not in the same manner, for one is the proper, and the other the improper or secondary use of it. For example, a shoe is used for wear, and is used for exchange; both are uses of the shoe. He who gives a shoe in exchange for money or food to him who wants one, does indeed use the shoe as a shoe, but this is not its proper or primary purpose, for a shoe is not made to be an object of barter. The same may be said of all possessions, for the art of exchange extends to all of them, and it arises at first in a natural manner from the circumstance that some have too little, others too much. Hence we may infer that retail trade is not a natural part of the art of money-making; had it been so, men would have ceased to exchange when they had enough. And in the first community, which is the family, this art is obviously of no use, but only begins to be useful when the society increases. For the members of the family originally had all things in common; in a more divided state of society they still shared in many things, but they were different things which they had to give in exchange for what they wanted, a kind of barter which is still practised among barbarous nations who exchange with one another the necessaries of life and nothing more; giving and receiving wine, for example, in exchange for corn and the like. This sort of barter is not part of the money-making art and is not contrary to nature, but is needed for the satisfaction of men's natural wants. The other or more complex form of exchange grew out of the simpler. When the inhabitants of one country became more dependent on those of another, and they imported what they needed, and exported the surplus, money necessarily came into use. For the various necessaries of life are not easily carried about, and hence men agreed to employ in their dealings with each other something which was intrinsically useful and easily applicable to the purposes of life, for example, iron, silver, and the like. Of this the value was at first measured by size and weight, but in process of time they put a stamp upon it, to save the trouble of weighing and to mark the value.

When the use of coin had once been discovered, out of the barter of necessary articles arose the other art of money-making, namely, retail trade; which was at first probably a simple matter, but became more complicated as soon as men learned by experience whence and by what exchanges the greatest profit might be made. Originating in the use of coin, the art of money-making is generally thought to be chiefly concerned with it, and to be the art which produces wealth and money; having to consider how they may be accumulated. Indeed, wealth is assumed by many to be only a quantity of coin, because the art of money-making and retail trade are concerned with coin. Others maintain that coined money is a mere sham, a thing not natural, but conventional only, which would have no value or use for any of the purposes of daily life if another commodity were substituted by the users. And, indeed, he who is rich in coin may often be in want of necessary food. But how can that be wealth of which a man may have a great abundance and yet perish with hunger, like Midas in the fable, whose insatiable prayer turned everything that was set before him into gold?

Men seek after a better notion of wealth and of the art of making money than the mere acquisition of coin, and they are right. For natural wealth and the natural art of money-making are a different thing; in their true form they are part of the management of a household; whereas retail trade is the art of producing wealth, not in every way, but by exchange. And it seems to be concerned with coin; for coin is the starting-point and the goal of exchange. And there is no bound to the wealth which springs from this art of money-making. As in the art of medicine there is no limit to the pursuit of health, and as in the other arts there is no limit to the pursuit of their several ends, for they aim at accomplishing their ends to the uttermost; (but of the means there is a limit, for the end is always the limit), so, too, in this art of money-making there is no limit of the end, which is wealth of the spurious kind, and the acquisition of money. But the art of household management has a limit; the unlimited acquisition of money is not its business. And, therefore, in one point of view, all wealth must have a limit; nevertheless, as a matter of fact, we find the opposite to be the case; for all money-makers increase their hoard of coin without limit. The course of the confusion is the near connexion between the two kinds of money-making; in either, the instrument [i.e. wealth] is the same, although the use is different, and so they pass into one another; for each is a use of the same property, but with a difference: accumulation is the end in the one case, but there is a further end in the other. Hence some persons are led to believe that making money is the object of household management, and the whole idea of their lives is that they ought either to increase their money without limit, or at any rate not to lose it. The origin of this disposition in men is that they are intent upon living only, and not upon living well; and, as their desires are unlimited, they also desire that the means of gratifying them should be without limit. Even those who aim at a good life seek the means of obtaining bodily pleasures; and, since the enjoyment of these appears to depend on property, they are absorbed in making money: and so there arises the second species of money-making. For, as their enjoyment is in excess, they seek an art which produces the excess of enjoyment; and, if they are not able to supply their pleasures by the art of money-making, they try other arts, using in turn every faculty in a manner contrary to nature. The quality of courage, for example, is not intended to make money, but to inspire confidence; neither is this the aim of the general's or of the physician's art; but the one aims at victory and the other at health. Nevertheless, some men turn every quality or art into a means of making money; this they conceive to be the end, and to the promotion of the end all things must contribute.

Thus, then, we have considered the art of money-making, which is unnecessary, and why men want it; and also the necessary art of money-making, which we have seen to be different from the other, and to be a natural part of the art of managing a household, concerned with the provision of food, not, however, like the former kind, unlimited, but having a limit.

And we have found the answer to our original question, Whether the art of money-making is the business of the manager of a household and of the statesman or not their business? — viz. that it is an art which is presupposed by them. For political science does not make men, but takes them from nature and uses them; and nature provides them with food from the element of earth, air, or sea. At this stage begins the duty of the manager of a household, who has to order the things which nature supplies; — he may be compared to the weaver who has not to make but to use wool, and to know what sort of wool is good and serviceable or bad and unserviceable. Were this otherwise, it would be difficult to see why the art of money-making is a part of the management of a household and the art of medicine not; for surely the members of a household must have health just as they must have life or any other necessary. And as from one point of view the master of the house and the ruler of the state have to consider about health, from another point of view not they but the physician; so in one way the art of household management, in another way the subordinate art, has to consider about money. But, strictly speaking, as I have already said, the means of life must be provided beforehand by nature; for the business of nature is to furnish food to that which is born, and the food of the offspring always remains over in the parent. Wherefore the art of making money out of fruits and animals is always natural.

Of the two sorts of money-making one, as I have just said, is a part of household management, the other is retail trade: the former necessary and honourable, the latter a kind of exchange which is justly censured; for it is unnatural, and a mode by which men gain from one another. The most hated sort, and with the greatest reason, is usury, which makes a gain out of money itself, and not from the natural use of it. For money was intended to be used in exchange, but not to increase at interest. And this term usury, which means the birth of money from money, is applied to the breeding of money because the offspring resembles the parent. Wherefore of all modes of making money this is the most unnatural.

Book II   Plato on the State, Family, and Property

Our purpose is to consider what form of political community is best of all for those who are most able to realize their ideal of life. We must therefore examine not only this but other constitutions, both such as actually exist in well-governed states, and any theoretical forms which are held in esteem; that what is good and useful may be brought to light. And let no one suppose that in seeking for something beyond them we at all want to philosophize at the expense of truth; we only undertake this enquiry because all the constitutions with which we are acquainted are faulty.

We will begin with the natural beginning of the subject. Three alternatives are conceivable: The members of a state must either have (1) all things or (2) nothing in common, or (3) some things in common and some not. That they should have nothing in common is clearly impossible, for the state is a community, and must at any rate have a common place — one city will be in one place, and the citizens are those who share in that one city. But should a well-ordered state have all things, as far as may be, in common, or some only and not others? For the citizens might conceivably have wives and children and property in common, as Socrates proposes in the Republic of Plato. Which is better, our present condition, or the proposed new order of society?

There are many difficulties in the community of women. The principle on which Socrates rests the necessity of such an institution does not appear to be established by his arguments; and then again as a means to the end which he ascribes to the state, taken literally, it is impossible, and how we are to limit and qualify it is nowhere precisely stated. I am speaking of the premiss from which the argument of Socrates proceeds, that the greater the unity of the state the better. Is it not obvious that a state may at length attain such a degree of unity as to be no longer a state? — since the nature of a state is to be a plurality, and in tending to greater unity, from being a state, it becomes a family, and from being a family, an individual; for the family may be said to be more one than the state, and the individual than the family. So that we ought not to attain this greatest unity even if we could, for it would be the destruction of the state. Again, a state is not made up only of so many men, but of different kinds of men; for similars do not constitute a state. It is not like a military alliance, of which the usefulness depends upon its quantity even where there is no difference in quality. For in that mutual protection is the end aimed at; and the question is the same as about the scales of a balance: which is the heavier?

In like manner, a state differs from a nation, whenever in a nation the people are not dispersed in villages, but are in the condition of the Arcadians; in a state the elements out of which the unity is to be formed differ in kind. Wherefore the principle of reciprocity, as I have already remarked in the Ethics, is the salvation of states. And among freemen and equals this is a principle which must be maintained, for they cannot all rule together, but must change at the end of a year or some other period of time or in some order of succession. The result is that upon this plan they all govern; [but the manner of government is] just as if shoemakers and carpenters were to exchange their occupations, and the same persons did not always continue shoemakers and carpenters. And it is clearly better that, as in business, so also in politics there should be continuance of the same persons where this is possible. But where this is not possible by reason of the natural equality of the citizens, and it would be unjust that any one should be excluded from the government (whether to govern be a good thing or a bad), then it is better, instead of all holding power, to adopt a principle of rotation, equals giving place to equals, as the original rulers gave place them. Thus the one party rule and the others are ruled in turn, as if they were no longer the same persons. In like manner there is a variety in the offices held by them. Hence it is evident that a city is not by nature one in that sense which some persons affirm; and that what is said to be the greatest good of cities is in reality their destruction; but surely the good of things must be that which preserves them. Again, in another point of view, this extreme unification of the state is clearly not good; for a family is more self-sufficing than an individual, and a city than a family, and a city only comes into being when the community is large enough to be self-sufficing. If then self-sufficiency is to be desired, the lesser degree of unity is more desirable than the greater.

But, even supposing that it were best for the community to have the greatest degree of unity, this unity is by no means indicated by the fact 'of all men saying 'mine' and 'not mine' at the same instant of time,' which, according to Socrates, is the sign of perfect unity in a state. For the word 'all' is ambiguous. If the meaning be that every individual says 'mine' and 'not mine' at the same time, then perhaps the result at which Socrates aims may be in some degree accomplished; each man will call the same person his own son and his own wife, and so of his property and of all that belongs to him. This, however, is not the way in which people would speak who had their wives and children in common; they would say 'all' but not 'each.' In like manner their property would be described as belonging to them, not severally but collectively. There is an obvious fallacy in the term 'all': like some other words, 'both,' 'odd,' 'even,' it is ambiguous, and in argument becomes a source of logical puzzles. That all persons call the same thing mine in the sense in which each does so may be a fine thing, but it is impracticable; or if the words are taken in the other sense [i.e. the sense which distinguishes 'all' from 'each'], such a unity in no way conduces to harmony. And there is another objection to the proposal. For that which is common to the greatest number has the least care bestowed upon it. Every one thinks chiefly of his own, hardly at all of the common interest; and only when he is himself concerned as an individual. For besides other considerations, everybody is more inclined to neglect the duty which he expects another to fulfil; as in families many attendants are often less useful than a few. Each citizen will have a thousand sons who will not be his sons individually, but anybody will be equally the son of anybody, and will therefore be neglected by all alike. Further, upon this principle, every one will call another 'mine' or 'not mine' according as he is prosperous or the reverse;—however small a fraction he may be of the whole number, he will say of every individual of the thousand, or whatever be the number of the city, 'such a one is mine,' 'such a one his'; and even about this he will not be positive; for it is impossible to know who chanced to have a child, or whether, if one came into existence, it has survived. But which is better—to be able to say 'mine' about every one of the two thousand or the ten thousand citizens, or to use the word 'mine' in the ordinary and more restricted sense? For usually the same person is called by one man his son whom another calls his brother or cousin or kinsman or blood-relation or connexion by marriage either of himself or of some relation of his, and these relationships he distinguishes from the tie which binds him to his tribe or ward; and how much better is it to be the real cousin of somebody than to be a son after Plato's fashion! Nor is there any way of preventing brothers and children and fathers and mothers from sometimes recognizing one another; for children are born like their parents, and they will necessarily be finding indications of their relationship to one another. Geographers declare such to be the fact; they say that in Upper Libya, where the women are common, nevertheless the children who are born are assigned to their respective fathers on the grounds of their likeness. And some women, like the females of other animals—for example mares and cows—have a strong tendency to produce offspring resembling their parents, as was the case with the Pharsalian mare called Dicaea (the Just).

Other evils, against which it is not easy for the authors of such a community to guard, will be assaults and homicides, voluntary as well as involuntary, quarrels and slanders, all which are most unholy acts when committed against fathers and mothers and near relations, but not equally unholy when there is no relationship. Moreover, they are much more likely to occur if the relationship is unknown, and, when they have occurred, the customary expiations of them cannot be made. Again, how strange it is that Socrates, after having made the children common, should hinder lovers from carnal intercourse only, but should permit familiarities between father and son or between brother and brother, than which nothing can be more unseemly, since even without them, love of this sort is improper. How strange, too, to forbid intercourse for no other reason than the violence of the pleasure, as though the relationship of father and son or of brothers with one another made no difference.

This community of wives and children seems better suited to the husbandmen than to the guardians, for if they have wives and children in common, they will be bound to one another by weaker ties, as a subject class should be, and they will remain obedient and not rebel. In a word, the result of such a law would be just the opposite of that which good laws ought to have, and the intention of Socrates in making these regulations about women and children would defeat itself. For friendship we believe to be the greatest good of states and the preservative of them against revolutions; neither is there anything which Socrates so greatly lauds as the unity of the state which he and all the world declare to be created by friendship. But the unity which he commends would be like that of the lovers in the Symposium, who, as Aristophanes says, desire to grow together in the excess of their affection, and from being two to become one, in which case one or both would certainly perish. Whereas [the very opposite will really happen;] in a state having women and children common, love will be watery; and the father will certainly not say 'my son,' or the son 'my father.' As a little sweet wine mingled with a great deal of water is imperceptible in the mixture, so, in this sort of community, the idea of relationship which is based upon these names will be lost; there is no reason why the so-called father should care about the son, or the son about the father, or brothers about one another. Of the two qualities which chiefly inspire regard and affection — that a thing is your own and that you love it — neither can exist in such a state as this.

Again, the transfer of children as soon as they are born from the rank of husbandmen or of artisans to that of guardians, and from the rank of guardians into a lower rank, will be very difficult to arrange; the givers or transferrers cannot but know whom they are giving and transferring, and to whom. And the previously mentioned evils, such as assaults, unlawful loves, homicides, will happen more often amongst those who are transferred to the lower classes, or who have a place assigned to them among the guardians; for they will no longer call the members of any other class brothers, and children, and fathers, and mothers, and will not, therefore, be afraid of committing any crimes by reason of consanguinity. Touching the community of wives and children; let this be our conclusion.

Next let us consider what should be our arrangements about property: should the citizens of the perfect state have their possessions in common or not? This question may be discussed separately from the enactments about women and children. Even supposing that the women and children belong to individuals, according to the custom which is at present universal, may there not be an advantage in having and using possessions in common? Three cases are possible: (1) the soil may be appropriated, but the produce may be thrown for consumption into the common stock; and this is the practice of some nations. Or (2), the soil may be common, and may be cultivated in common, but the produce divided among individuals for their private use; this is a form of common property which is said to exist among certain barbarians. Or (3), the soil and the produce may be alike common.

When the husbandmen are not the citizens, the case will be different and easier to deal with; but when the citizens till the ground themselves the question of ownership will give a world of trouble. If they do not share equally in enjoyments and toils, those who labour much and get little will necessarily complain of those who labour little and receive or consume much. There is always a difficulty in men living together and having things in common, but especially in their having common property. The partnerships of fellow-travellers are an example to the point; for they generally fall out by the way and quarrel about any trifle which turns up. So with servants: we are most liable to take offence at those with whom we most frequently come into contact in daily life.

These are only some of the disadvantages which attend the community of property; the present arrangement, if improved as it might be by good customs and laws, would be far better, and would have the advantages of both systems. Property should be in a certain sense common, but, as a general rule, private; for, when every one has a distinct interest, men will not complain of one another, and they will make more progress, because every one will be attending to his own business. And yet among the good, and in respect of use, 'Friends,' as the proverb says, 'will have all things common.' Even now there are traces of such a principle, showing that it is not impracticable, but, in well-ordered states, exists already to a certain extent and may be carried further. For, although every man has his own property, some things he will place at the disposal of his friends, while of others he shares the use with them. The Lacedaemonians, for example, use one another's slaves, and horses and dogs, as if they were their own; and when they happen to be in the country, they appropriate in the fields whatever provisions they want. It is clearly better that property should be private, but the use of it common; and the special business of the legislator is to create in men this benevolent disposition. Again, how immeasurably greater is the pleasure, when a man feels a thing to be his own; for the love of self is a feeling implanted by nature and not given in vain, although selfishness is rightly censured; this, however, is not the mere love of self, but the love of self in excess, like the miser's love of money; for all, or almost all, men love money, and other such objects in a measure. And further, there is the greatest pleasure in doing a kindness or service to friends or guests or companions, which can only be rendered when a man has private property. The advantage is lost by the excessive unification of the state. Two virtues are annihilated in such a state: first, temperance towards women (for it is an honourable action to abstain from another's wife for temperance sake); secondly, liberality in the matter of property. No one, when men have all things in common, will any longer set an example of liberality or do any liberal action; for liberality consists in the use which is made of property.

Such legislation may have a specious appearance of benevolence; men readily listen to it, and are easily induced to believe that in some wonderful manner everybody will become everybody's friend, especially when some one is heard denouncing the evils now existing in states, suits about contracts, convictions for perjury, flatteries of rich men and the like, which are said to arise out of the possession of private property. These evils, however, are due to a very different cause—the wickedness of human nature. Indeed, we see that there is much more quarrelling among those who have all things in common, though there are not many of them when compared with the vast numbers who have private property.

Again, we ought to reckon, not only the evils from which the citizens will be saved, but also the advantages which they will lose. The life which they are to lead appears to be quite impracticable. The error of Socrates must be attributed to the false notion of unity from which he starts. Unity there should be, both of the family and of the state, but in some respects only. For there is a point at which a state may attain such a degree of unity as to be no longer a state, or at which, without actually ceasing to exist, it will become an inferior state, like harmony passing into unison, or rhythm which has been reduced to a single foot. The state, as I was saying, is a plurality, which should be united and made into a community by education; and it is strange that the author of a system of education, which he thinks will make the state virtuous, should expect to improve his citizens by regulations of this sort, and not by philosophy or by customs and laws, like those which prevail at Sparta and Crete respecting common meals, whereby the legislator has [to a certain degree] made property common. Let us remember that we should not disregard the experience of ages; in the multitude of years these things, if they were good, would certainly not have been unknown; for almost everything has been found out, although sometimes they are not put together; in other cases men do not use the knowledge which they have. Great light would be thrown on this subject if we could see such a form of government in the actual process of construction; for the legislator could not form a state at all without distributing and dividing the citizens into associations for common meals, and into phratries and tribes. But all this legislation ends only in forbidding agriculture to the guardians, a prohibition which the Lacedaemonians try to enforce already.

Again, Socrates has not said, nor is it easy to decide, what in such a community will be the general form of the state. The citizens who are not guardians are the majority, and about them nothing has been determined: are the husbandmen, too, to have their property in common? Or, besides the common land which he tills, is each individual to have his own? And are their wives and children to be individual or common? If, like the guardians, they are to have all things in common, in what do they differ from them, or what will they gain by submitting to their government? Or, upon what principle would they submit, unless indeed the governing class adopt the ingenious policy of the Cretans, who give their slaves the same institutions as their own, but forbid them gymnastic exercises and the possession of arms. If, on the other hand, the inferior classes are too like other cities in respect of marriage and property, what will be the form of the community? Must it not contain two states in one, each hostile to the other? One class will consist of the guardians, who are a sort of watchmen; another, of the husbandmen, and there will be the artisans and the other citizens. But [if so] the suits and quarrels, and all the evils which Socrates affirms to exist in other states, will exist equally among them. He says indeed that, having so good an education, the citizens will not need many laws, for example, laws about the city or about the markets; but then he confines his education to the guardians. Again, he makes the husbandmen owners of the land upon condition of their paying a tribute. But in that case they are likely to be much more unmanageable and conceited than the Helots, or Penestae, or slaves in general. And whether community of wives and property be necessary for the lower equally with the higher class or not, and the questions akin to this, what will be the education, form of government, laws of the lower class, Socrates has nowhere determined: neither is it easy, though very important, to discover what should be the character of the inferior classes, if the common life of the guardians is to be maintained.

Again, if Socrates makes the women common, and retains private property, the men will see to the fields, but who will see to the house? And what will happen if the agricultural class have both their property and their wives in common? Once more; it is absurd to argue, from the analogy of the animals, that men and women should follow the same pursuits; for animals have not to manage a household. The government, too, as constituted by Socrates, contains elements of danger; for he makes the same persons always rule. And if this is often a cause of disturbance among the meaner sort, how much more among high-spirited warriors? But that the persons whom he makes rulers must be the same is evident; for the gold which the God mingles in the souls of men is not at one time given to one, at another time to another, but always to the same: as he says, 'God mingles gold in some, and silver in others, from their very birth; but brass and iron in those who are meant to be artisans and husbandmen.' Again, he deprives the guardians of happiness, and says that the legislator ought to make the whole state happy. But the whole cannot be happy unless most, or all, or some of its parts enjoy happiness. In this respect happiness is not like the even principle in numbers, which may exist only in the whole, but in none of the parts; not so happiness. And if the guardians are not happy, who are? Surely not the artisans, or the common people. The Republic of which Socrates discourses has all these difficulties, and others quite as great.

Book III   The Different Forms of Government

. . . There is no difficulty in distinguishing the various kinds of authority; they have been often defined already in popular works. The rule of a master, although the slave by nature and the master by nature have in reality the same interests, is nevertheless exercised primarily with a view to the interest of the master, but accidentally considers the slave, since, if the slave perish, the rule of the master perishes with him. On the other hand, the government of a wife and children and of a household, which we have called household-management, is exercised in the first instance for the good of the governed or for the common good of both parties, but essentially for the good of the governed, as we see to be the case in medicine, gymnastics, and the arts in general, which are only accidentally concerned with the good of the artists themselves. (For there is no reason why the trainer may not sometimes practise gymnastics, and the pilot is always one of the crew.) The trainer or pilot considers the good of those committed to his care. But, when he is one of the persons taken care of, he accidentally participates in the advantage, for the pilot is also a sailor, and the trainer becomes one of those in training. And so in politics: when the state is framed upon the principle of equality and likeness, the citizens think that they ought to hold office by turns. In the order of nature every one would take his turn of service; and then again, somebody else would look after his interest, just as he, while in office, had looked after theirs. [That was originally the way.] But nowadays, for the sake of the advantage which is to be gained from the public revenues and from office, men want to be always in office. One might imagine that the rulers, being sickly, were only kept in health while they continued in office; in that case we may be sure that they would be hunting after places. The conclusion is evident: that governments, which have a regard to the common interest, are constituted in accordance with strict principles of justice, and therefore true forms; but those which regard only the interest of the rulers are all defective and perverted forms, for they are despotic, whereas a state is a community of freemen.

Having determined these points, we have next to consider how many forms of government there are, and what they are; and in the first place what are the true forms, for when they are determined the perversions of them will at once be apparent. The words constitution and government have the same meaning, and the government, which is the supreme authority in states, must be in the hands of one, or of a few, or of many. The true forms of government, therefore, are those in which the one, or the few, or the many, govern with a view to the common interest; but governments which rule with a view to the private interest, whether of the one, or of the few, or of the many, are perversions. For citizens, if they are truly citizens, ought to participate in the advantages of a state. Of forms of government in which one rules, we call that which regards the common interests, kingship or royalty; that in which more than one, but not many, rule, aristocracy [the rule of the best]; and it is so called, either because the rulers are the best men, or because they have at heart the best interests of the state and of the citizens. But when the citizens at large administer the state for the common interest, the government is called by the generic name — a constitution. And there is a reason for this use of language. One man or a few may excel in virtue; but of virtue there are many kinds: and as the number increases it becomes more difficult for them to attain perfection in every kind, though they may in military virtue, for this is found in the masses. Hence, in a constitutional government the fighting-men have the supreme power, and those who possess arms are the citizens.

Of the above-mentioned forms, the perversions are as follows: — of royalty, tyranny; of aristocracy, oligarchy; of constitutional government, democracy. For tyranny is a kind of monarchy which has in view the interest of the monarch only; oligarchy has in view the interest of the wealthy; democracy, of the needy: none of them the common good of all.

But there are difficulties about these forms of government, and it will therefore be necessary to state a little more at length the nature of each of them. For he who would make a philosophical study of the various sciences, and does not regard practice only, ought not to overlook or omit anything, but to set forth the truth in every particular. Tyranny, as I was saying, is monarchy exercising the rule of a master over political society; oligarchy is when men of property have the government in their hands; democracy, the opposite, when the indigent, and not the men of property, are the rulers. And here arises the first of our difficulties, and it relates to the definition just given. For democracy is said to be the government of the many. But what if the many are men of property and have the power in their hands? In like manner oligarchy is said to be the government of the few; but what if the poor are fewer than the rich, and have the power in their hands because they are stronger? In these cases the distinction which we have drawn between these different forms of government would no longer hold good.

Suppose, once more, that we add wealth to the few and poverty to the many, and name the governments accordingly — an oligarchy is said to be that in which the few and the wealthy, and a democracy that in which the many and the poor are the rulers — there will still be a difficulty. For, if the only forms of government are the ones already mentioned, how shall we describe those other governments also just mentioned by us, in which the rich are the more numerous and the poor are the fewer, and both govern in their respective states?

The argument seems to show that, whether in oligarchies or in democracies, the number of the governing body, whether the greater number, as in a democracy, or the smaller number, as in an oligarchy, is an accident due to the fact that the rich everywhere are few, and the poor numerous. But if so, there is a misapprehension of the causes of the difference between them. For the real difference between democracy and oligarchy is poverty and wealth. Wherever men rule by reason of their wealth, whether they be few or many, that is an oligarchy, and where the poor rule, that is a democracy. But as a fact the rich are few and the poor many: for few are well-to-do, whereas freedom is enjoyed by all, and wealth and freedom are the grounds on which the oligarchical and democratical parties respectively claim power in the state.

Let us begin by considering the common definitions of oligarchy and democracy, and what is justice oligarchical and democratical. For all men cling to justice of some kind, but their conceptions are imperfect and they do not express the whole idea. For example, justice is thought by them to be, and is, equality, not, however, for all, but only for equals. And inequality is thought to be, and is, justice; neither is this for all, but only for unequals. When the persons are omitted, then men judge erroneously. The reason is that they are passing judgment on themselves, and most people are bad judges in their own case. And whereas justice implies a relation to persons as well as to things, and a just distribution, as I have already said in the Ethics, embraces alike persons and things, they acknowledge the equality of the things, but dispute about the merit of the persons, chiefly for the reason which I have just given—because they are bad judges in their own affairs; and secondly, because both the parties to the argument are speaking of a limited and partial justice, but imagine themselves to be speaking of absolute justice. For those who are unequal in one respect, for example wealth, consider themselves to be unequal in all; and any who are equal in one respect, for example freedom, consider themselves to be equal in all. But they leave out the capital point. For if men met and associated out of regard to wealth only, their share in the state would be proportioned to their property, and the oligarchical doctrine would then seem to carry the day. It would not be just that he who paid one mina should have the same share of a hundred minae, whether of the principal or of the profits, as he who paid the remaining ninety-nine. But a state exists for the sake of a good life, and not for the sake of life only: if life only were the object, slaves and brute animals might form a state, but they cannot, for they have no share in happiness or in a life of free choice. Nor does a state exist for the sake of alliance and security from injustice, nor yet for the sake of exchange and mutual intercourse; for then the Tyrrhenians and the Carthaginians, and all who have commercial treaties with one another, would be the citizens of one state. True, they have agreements about imports, and engagements that they will do no wrong to one another, and written articles of alliance. But there are no magistracies common to the contracting parties who will enforce their engagements; different states have each their own magistracies. Nor does one state take care that the citizens of the other are such as they ought to be, nor see that those who come under the terms of the treaty do no wrong or wickedness at all, but only that they do no injustice to one another. Whereas, those who care for good government take into consideration [the larger question of] virtue and vice in states. Whence it may be further inferred that virtue must be the serious care of a state which truly deserves the name: for [without this ethical end] the community becomes a mere alliance which differs only in place from alliances of which the members live apart; and law is only a convention, 'a surety to one another of justice,' as the sophist Lycophron says, and has no real power to make the citizens good and just.

This is obvious; for suppose distinct places, such as Corinth and Megara, to be united by a wall, still they would not be one city, not even if the citizens had the right to intermarry, which is one of the rights peculiarly characteristic of states. Again, if men dwelt at a distance from one another, but not so far off as to have no intercourse, and there were laws among them that they should not wrong each other in their exchanges, neither would this be a state. Let us suppose that one man is a carpenter, another a husbandman, another a shoemaker, and so on, and that their number is ten thousand: nevertheless, if they have nothing in common but exchange, alliance, and the like, that would not constitute a state. Why is this? Surely not because they are at a distance from one another: for even supposing that such a community were to meet in one place, and that each man had a house of his own, which was in a manner his state, and that they made alliance with one another, but only against evil-doers; still an accurate thinker would not deem this to be a state, if their intercourse with one another was of the same character after as before their union. It is clear then that a state is not a mere society, having a common place, established for the prevention of crime and for the sake of exchange. These are conditions without which a state cannot exist; but all of them together do not constitute a state, which is a community of well-being in families and aggregations of families, for the sake of a perfect and self-sufficing life. Such a community can only be established among those who live in the same place and intermarry. Hence arise in cities family connexions, brotherhoods, common sacrifices, amusements which draw men together. They are created by friendship, for friendship is the motive of society. The end is the good life, and these are the means towards it. And the state is the union of families and villages having for an end a perfect and self-sufficing life, by which we mean a happy and honourable life.

Our conclusion, then, is that political society exists for the sake of noble actions, and not of mere companionship. And they who contribute most to such a society have a greater share in it than those who have the same or a greater freedom or nobility of birth but are inferior to them in political virtue; or than those who exceed them in wealth but are surpassed by them in virtue.

From what has been said it will be clearly seen that all the partisans of different forms of government speak of a part of justice only.

There is also a doubt as to what is to be the supreme power in the state: — Is it the multitude? Or the wealthy? Or the good? Or the one best man? Or a tyrant? Any of these alternatives seems to involve disagreeable consequences. If the poor, for example, because they are more in number, divide among themselves the property of the rich, is not this unjust? No, by heaven (will be the reply), for the lawful authority [i.e. the people] willed it. But if this is not injustice, pray what is? Again, when [in the first division] all has been taken, and the majority divide anew the property of the minority, is it not evident, if this goes on, that they will ruin the state? Yet surely, virtue is not the ruin of those who possess her, nor is justice destructive of a state; and therefore this law of confiscation clearly cannot be just. If it were, all the acts of a tyrant must of necessity be just; for he only coerces other men by superior power, just as the multitude coerce the rich. But is it just, then, that the few and the wealthy should be the rulers? And what if they, in like manner, rob and plunder the people — is this just? If so, the other case [i.e. the case of the majority plundering the minority] will likewise be just. But there can be no doubt that all these things are wrong and unjust.

Then ought the good to rule and have supreme power? But in that case everybody else, being excluded from power, will be dishonoured. For the offices of a state are posts of honour; and if one set of men always hold them, the rest must be deprived of them. Then will it be well that the one best man should rule? Nay, that is still more oligarchical, for the number of those who are dishonoured is thereby increased. Some one may say that it is bad for a man, subject as he is to all the accidents of human passion, to have the supreme power, rather than the law. But what if the law itself be democratical or oligarchical, how will that help us out of our difficulties? Not at all; the same consequences will follow.

Most of these questions may be reserved for another occasion. The principle that the multitude ought to be supreme rather than the few best is capable of a satisfactory explanation, and, though not free from difficulty, yet seems to contain an element of truth. For the many, of whom each individual is but an ordinary person, when they meet together may very likely be better than the few good, if regarded not individually but collectively, just as a feast to which many contribute is better than a dinner provided out of a single purse. For each individual among the many has a share of virtue and prudence, and when they meet together they become in a manner one man, who has many feet, and hands, and senses; that is a figure of their mind and disposition. Hence the many are better judges than a single man of music and poetry; for some understand one part, and some another, among them, they understand the whole. There is a similar combination of qualities in good men, who differ from any individual of the many, as the beautiful are said to differ from those who are not beautiful, and works of art from realities, because in them the scattered elements are combined, although, if taken separately, the eye of one person or some other feature in another person would be fairer than in the picture. Whether this principle can apply to every democracy, and to all bodies of men, is not clear. Or rather, by heaven, in some cases it is impossible of application; for the argument would equally hold about brutes; and wherein, it will be asked, do some men differ from brutes? But there may be bodies of men about whom our statement is nevertheless true. And if so, the difficulty which has been already raised, and also another which is akin to it — viz. what power should be assigned to the mass of freemen and citizens, who are not rich and have no personal merit — are both solved. There is still a danger in allowing them to share the great offices of state, for their folly will lead them into error, and their dishonesty into crime. But there is a danger also in not letting them share, for a state in which many poor men are excluded from office will necessarily be full of enemies. The only way of escape is to assign to them some deliberative and judicial functions. For this Solon and certain other legislators give them the power of electing to offices, and of calling the magistrates to account, but they do not allow them to hold office singly. When they meet together their perceptions are quite good enough, and combined with the better class they are useful to the state (just as impure food when mixed with what is pure sometimes makes the entire mass more wholesome than a small quantity of the pure would be), but each individual, left to himself, forms an imperfect judgment. On the other hand, the popular form of government involves certain difficulties. In the first place, it might be objected that he who can judge of the healing of a sick man would be one who could himself heal his disease, and make him whole — that is, in other words, the physician; and so in all professions and arts. As, then, the physician ought to be called to account by physicians, so ought men in general to be called to account by their peers. But physicians are of three kinds: — there is the apothecary, and there is the physician of the higher class, and thirdly the intelligent man who has studied the art: in all arts there is such a class; and we attribute the power of judging to them quite as much as to professors of the art. Now, does not the same principle apply to elections? For a right election can only be made by those who have knowledge; a geometrician, for example, will choose rightly in matters of geometry, or a pilot in matters of steering; and, even if there be some occupations and arts with which private persons are familiar, they certainly cannot judge better than those who know. So that, according to this argument, neither the election of magistrates, nor the calling of them to account, should be entrusted to the many. Yet possibly these objections are to a great extent met by our old answer, that if the people are not utterly degraded, although individually they may be worse judges than those who have special knowledge — as a body they are as good or better. Moreover, there are some artists whose works are judged of solely, or in the best manner, not by themselves, but by those who do not possess the art; for example, the knowledge of the house is not limited to the builder only; the user, or, in other words, the master, of the house will even be a better judge than the builder, just as the pilot will judge better of a rudder than the carpenter, and the guest will judge better of a feast than the cook.

This difficulty seems now to be sufficiently answered, but there is another akin to it. That inferior persons should have authority in greater matters than the good would appear to be a strange thing, yet the election and calling to account of the magistrates is the greatest of all. And these, as I was saying, are functions which in some states are assigned to the people, for the assembly is supreme in all such matters. Yet persons of any age, and having but a small property qualification, sit in the assembly and deliberate and judge, although for the great officers of state, such as controllers and generals, a high qualification is required. This difficulty may be solved in the same manner as the preceding, and the present practice of democracies may be really defensible. For the power does not reside in the dicast, or senator, or ecclesiast, but in the court and the senate, and the assembly, of which individual senators, or ecclesiasts, or dicasts, are only parts or members. And for this reason the many may claim to have a higher authority than the few; for the people, and the senate, and the courts consist of many persons, and their property collectively is greater than the property of one or of a few individuals holding great offices. But enough of this.

The discussion of the first question shows nothing so clearly as that laws, when good, should be supreme; and that the magistrate or magistrates should regulate those matters only on which the laws are unable to speak with precision owing to the difficulty of any general principle embracing all particulars. But what are good laws has not yet been clearly explained; the old difficulty remains. The goodness or badness, justice or injustice, of laws is of necessity relative to the constitutions of states. But if so, true forms of government will of necessity have just laws, and perverted forms of government will have unjust laws.

In all sciences and arts the end is a good, and especially and above all in the highest of all — this is the political science of which the good is justice, in other words, the common interest. All men think justice to be a sort of equality; and to a certain extent they agree in the philosophical distinctions which have been laid down by us about Ethics. For they admit that justice is a thing having relation to persons, and that equals ought to have equality. But there still remains a question — equality or inequality of what? Here is a difficulty which the political philosopher has to resolve. For very likely some persons will say that offices of state ought to be unequally distributed according to superior excellence, in whatever respect, of the citizen, although there is no other difference between him and the rest of the community; for that those who differ in any one respect have different rights and claims. But, surely, if this is true, the complexion or height of a man, or any other advantage, will be a reason for his obtaining a greater share of political rights. The error here lies upon the surface, and may be illustrated from the other arts and sciences. When a number of flute-players are equal in their art, there is no reason why those of them who are better born should have better flutes given to them; for they will not play any better on the flute, and the superior instrument should be reserved for him who is the superior artist. If what I am saying is still obscure, it will be made clearer as we proceed. For if there were a superior flute-player who was far inferior in birth and beauty, although either of these may be a greater good than the art of flute-playing, and persons gifted with these qualities may excel the flute-player in a greater ratio than he excels them in his art, still he ought to have the best flutes given to him, unless the advantages of wealth and birth contribute to excellence in flute-playing, which they do not. Moreover upon this principle any good may be compared with any other. For if a given height, then height in general may be measured either against height or against freedom. Thus if A excels in height more than B in virtue, and height in general is more excellent than virtue, all things will be commensurable [which is absurd]; for if a certain magnitude is greater than some other, it is clear that some other will be equal. But since no such comparison can be made, it is evident that there is good reason why in politics men do not ground their claim to office on every sort of inequality any more than in the arts. For if some be slow, and others swift, that is no reason why the one should have little and the others much; it is in gymnastic contests that such excellence is rewarded. Whereas the rival claims of candidates for office can only be based on the possession of elements which enter into the composition of a state, [such as wealth, virtue, etc.]. And therefore the noble, or freeborn, or rich, may with good reason claim office; for holders of offices must be freemen and tax-payers: a state can be no more composed entirely of poor men than entirely of slaves. But if wealth and freedom are necessary elements, justice and valour are equally so; for without the former a state cannot exist at all, without the latter not well.

If the existence of the state is alone to be considered, then it would seem that all, or some at least, of these claims are just; but, if we take into account a good life, as I have already said, education and virtue have superior claims. As, however, those who are equal in one thing ought not to be equal in all, nor those who are unequal in one thing to be unequal in all, it is certain that all forms of government which rest on either of these principles are perversions. All men have a claim in a certain sense, as I have already admitted, but they have not an absolute claim. The rich claim because they have a greater share in the land, and land is the common element of the state; also they are generally more trustworthy in contracts. The free claim under the same title as the noble; for they are nearly akin. And the noble are citizens in a truer sense than the ignoble, since good birth is always valued in a man's own home and country. Another reason is, that those who are sprung from better ancestors are likely to be better men, for nobility is excellence of race. Virtue, too, may be truly said to have a claim, for justice has been acknowledged by us to be a social virtue, and it implies all others. Again, the many may urge their claim against the few; for, when taken collectively, and compared with the few, they are stronger and richer and better. But, what if the good, the rich, the noble, and the other classes who make up a state, are all living together in the same city; will there, or will there not, be any doubt who shall rule? — No doubt at all in determining who ought to rule in each of the above-mentioned forms of government. For states are characterized by differences in their governing bodies — one of them has a government of the rich, another of the virtuous, and so on. But a difficulty arises when all these elements coexist. How are we to decide? Suppose the virtuous to be very few in number: may we consider their numbers in relation to their duties, and ask whether they are enough to administer the state, or must they be so many as will make up a state?

Objections may be urged against all the aspirants to political power. For those who found their claims on wealth or family have no basis of justice; on this principle, if any one person were richer than all the rest, it is clear that he ought to be the ruler of them. In like manner he who is very distinguished by his birth ought to have the superiority over all those who claim on the ground that they are freeborn. In an aristocracy, or government of the best, a like difficulty occurs about virtue; for if one citizen be better than the other members of the government, however good they may be, he too, upon the same principle of justice, should rule over them. And if the people are to be supreme because they are stronger than the few, then if one man, or more than one, but not a majority, is stronger than the many, they ought to rule, and not the many.

All these considerations appear to show that none of the principles on which men claim to rule, and hold all other men in subjection to them, are strictly right. To those who claim to be the masters of state on the ground of their virtue or their wealth, the many might fairly answer that they themselves are often better and richer than the few — I do not say individually, but collectively. And another ingenious objection which is sometimes put forward may be met in a similar manner. Some persons doubt whether the legislator who desires to make the justest laws ought to legislate with a view to the good of the higher classes or of the many, when the case which we have mentioned occurs [i.e. when all the elements coexist]. Now what is just or right is to be interpreted in the sense of 'what is equal'; and that which is right in the sense of being equal is to be considered with reference to the advantage of the state, and the common good of the citizens. And a citizen is one who shares in governing and being governed. He differs under different forms of government, but in the best state he is one who is able and willing to be governed and to govern with a view to the life of virtue.

If, however, there be some one person, or more than one, although not enough to make up the full complement of a state, whose virtue is so pre-eminent that the virtues or the political capacity of all the rest admit of no comparison with his or theirs, he or they can be no longer regarded as part of a state; for justice will not be done to the superior, if he is reckoned only as the equal of those who are so far inferior to him in virtue and in political capacity. Such an one may truly be deemed a God among men. Hence we see that legislation is necessarily concerned only with those who are equal in birth and in power; and that for men of pre-eminent virtue there is no law — they are themselves a law. Any one would be ridiculous who attempted to make laws for them: they would probably retort what, in the fable of Antisthenes, the lions said to the hares ['where are your claws?'], when in the council of the beasts the latter began haranguing and claiming equality for all. And for this reason democratic states have instituted ostracism; equality is above all things their aim, and therefore they ostracise and banish from the city for a time those who seem to predominate too much through their wealth, or the number of their friends, or through any other political influence. Mythology tells us that the Argonauts left Heracles behind for a similar reason; the ship Argo would not take him because she feared that he would have been too much for the rest of the crew. Wherefore those who denounce tyranny and blame the counsel which Periander gave to Thrasybulus cannot be held altogether just in their censure. The story is that Periander, when the herald was sent to ask counsel of him, said nothing, but only cut off the tallest ears of corn till he had brought the field to a level. The herald did not know the meaning of the action, but came and reported what he had seen to Thrasybulus, who understood that he was to cut off the principal men in the state; and this is a policy not only expedient for tyrants or in practice confined to them, but equally necessary in oligarchies and democracies. Ostracism is a measure of the same kind, which acts by disabling and banishing the most prominent citizens. Great powers do the same to whole cities and nations, as the Athenians did to the Samians, Chians, and Lesbians; no sooner had they obtained a firm grasp of the empire, than they humbled their allies contrary to treaty; and the Persian king has repeatedly crushed the Medes, Babylonians, and other nations, when their spirit has been stirred by the recollection of their former greatness.

The problem is a universal one, and equally concerns all forms of government, true as well as false; for, although perverted forms with a view to their own interests may adopt this policy, those which seek the common interest do so likewise. The same thing may be observed in the arts and sciences; for the painter will not allow the figure to have a foot which, however beautiful, is not in proportion, nor will the ship-builder allow the stern or any other part of the vessel to be unduly large, any more than the chorus-master will allow any one who sings louder or better than all the rest to sing in the choir. Monarchs, too, may practise compulsion and still live in harmony with their cities, if their government is for the interest of the state. Hence where there is an acknowledged superiority the argument in favour of ostracism is based upon a kind of political justice. It would certainly be better that the legislator should from the first so order his state as to have no need of such a remedy. But if the need arises, the next best thing is that he should endeavour to correct the evil by this or some similar measure. The principle, however, has not been fairly applied in states; for, instead of looking to the public good, they have used ostracism for factious purposes. It is true that under perverted forms of government, and from their special point of view, such a measure is just and expedient, but it is also clear that it is not absolutely just. In the perfect state there would be great doubts about the use of it, not when applied to excess in strength, wealth, popularity , or the like, but when used against some one who is pre-eminent in virtue, — what is to be done with him? Mankind will not say that such an one is to be expelled and exiled; on the other hand, he ought not to be a subject — that would be as if men should claim to rule over Zeus on the principle of rotation of office. The only alternative is that all should joyfully obey such a ruler, according to what seems to be the order of nature, and that men like him should be kings in their state for life.

Book V   Revolutions and Their Causes

The design which we proposed to ourselves is now nearly completed. Next in order follow the causes of revolution in states, how many, and of what nature they are; what elements work ruin in particular states, and out of what, and into what they mostly change; also what are the elements of preservation in states generally, or in a particular state, and by what means each state may be best preserved: these questions remain to be considered.

In the first place we must assume as our starting-point that in the many forms of government which have sprung up there has always been an acknowledgement of justice and proportionate equality, although mankind fail in attaining them, as indeed I have already explained. Democracy, for example, arises out of the notion that those who are equal in any respect are equal in all respects; because men are equally free, they claim to be absolutely equal. Oligarchy is based on the notion that those who are unequal in one respect are in all respects unequal; being unequal, that is, in property, they suppose themselves to be unequal absolutely. The democrats think that as they are equal they ought to be equal in all things; while the oligarchs, under the idea that they are unequal, claim too much, which is one form of inequality. All these forms of government have a kind of justice, but, tried by an absolute standard, they are faulty; and, therefore, both parties, whenever their share in the government does not accord with their preconceived ideas, stir up revolution. Those who excel in virtue have the best right of all to rebel (for they alone can with reason be deemed absolutely unequal), but then they are of all men the least inclined to do so. There is also a superiority which is claimed by men of rank; for they are thought noble because they spring from wealthy and virtuous ancestors. Here then, so to speak, are opened the very springs and fountains of revolution; and hence arise two sorts of changes in governments; the one affecting the constitution, when men seek to change from an existing form into some other, for example, from democracy into oligarchy, and from oligarchy into democracy, or from either of them into constitutional government or aristocracy, and conversely; the other not affecting the constitution, when, without disturbing the form of government, whether oligarchy, or monarchy, or any other, they try to get the administration into their own hands. Further, there is a question of degree; an oligarchy, for example, may become more or less oligarchical, and a democracy more or less democratical; and in like manner the characteristics of the other forms of government may be more or less strictly maintained. Or, the revolution may be directed against a portion of the constitution only, e.g. the establishment or overthrow of a particular office: as at Sparta it is said that Lysander attempted to overthrow the monarchy, and king Pausanias the ephoralty. At Epidamnus, too, the change was partial. For instead of phylarchs or heads of tribes, a council was appointed; but to this day the magistrates are the only members of the ruling class who are compelled to go to the Heliaea when an election takes place, and the office of the single archon [survives, which] is another oligarchical feature. Everywhere inequality is a cause of revolution, but an inequality in which there is no proportion, for instance, a perpetual monarchy among equals; and always it is the desire of equality which rises in rebellion.

Now equality is of two kinds, numerical and proportional; by the first I mean sameness or equality in number or size; by the second, equality of ratios. For example, the excess of three over two is equal to the excess of two over one; whereas four exceeds two in the same ratio in which two exceeds one, for two is the same part of four that one is of two, namely, the half. As I was saying before, men agree about justice in the abstract, that it is treating others according to their deserts, but there is a difference of opinion about the application of the principle; some think that if they are equal in any respect they are equal absolutely, others that if they are unequal in any respect they are unequal in all. Hence there are two principal forms of government, democracy and oligarchy; for good birth and virtue are rare, but wealth and numbers are more common. In what city shall we find a hundred persons of good birth and of virtue? whereas the poor everywhere abound. That a state should be ordered, simply and wholly, according to either kind of equality, is not a good thing; the proof is the fact that such forms of government never last. They are originally based on a mistake, and, as they begin badly, cannot fail to end badly. The inference is that both kinds of equality should be employed; numerical in some cases, and proportionate in others.

Still democracy appears to be safer and less liable to revolution than oligarchy. For in oligarchies there is the double danger of the oligarchs falling out among themselves and also with the people; but in democracies there is only the danger of a quarrel with the oligarchs. No dissension worth mentioning arises among the people themselves. And we may further remark that a government which is composed of the middle class more nearly approximates to democracy than to oligarchy, and is the safest of the imperfect forms of government.

In considering how dissensions and political revolutions arise, we must first of all ascertain the beginnings and causes of them which affect constitutions generally. They may be said to be three in number; and we have now to give an outline of each. We want to know (1) what is the feeling? and (2) what are the motives of those who make them? (3) whence arise political disturbances and quarrels? The universal and chief cause of this revolutionary feeling has been already mentioned; viz. the desire of equality, when men think that they are equal to others who have more than themselves; or, again, the desire of inequality and superiority, when conceiving themselves to be superior they think that they have not more but the same or less than their inferiors; pretensions which may and may not be just. Inferiors revolt in order that they may be equal, and equals that they may be superior. Such is the state of mind which creates revolutions. The motives for making them are the desire of gain and honour, or the fear of dishonour and loss; the authors of them want to divert punishment or dishonour from themselves or their friends. The causes and reasons of these motives and dispositions which are excited in men, about the things which I have mentioned, viewed in one way, may be regarded as seven, and in another as more than seven. Two of them have been already noticed; but they act in a different manner, for men are excited against one another by the love of gain and honour—not, as in the case which I have just supposed, in order to obtain them for themselves, but at seeing others, justly or unjustly, engrossing them. Other causes are insolence, fear, love of superiority, contempt, disproportionate increase in some part of the state; causes of another sort are election intrigues, carelessness, neglect about trifles, dissimilarity of elements.

What share insolence and avarice have in creating revolutions, and how they work, is plain enough. When the magistrates are insolent and grasping they conspire against one another and also against the constitution from which they derive their power, making their gains either at the expense of individuals or of the public. It is evident, again, what an influence honour exerts and how it is a cause of revolution. Men who are themselves dishonoured and who see others obtaining honours rise in rebellion; the honour or dishonour when undeserved is unjust, and just when awarded according to merit. Again, superiority is a cause of revolution when one or more persons have a power which is too much for the state and the power of the government; this is a condition of affairs out of which there arises a monarchy, or a family oligarchy. And, therefore, in some places, as at Athens and Argos, they have recourse to ostracism. But how much better to provide from the first that there should be no such pre-eminent individuals instead of letting them come into existence and then finding a remedy.

Another cause of revolution is fear. Either men have committed wrong, and are afraid of punishment, or they are expecting to suffer wrong and are desirous of anticipating their enemy. Thus at Rhodes the notables conspired against the people through fear of the suits that were brought against them. Contempt is also a cause of insurrection and revolution; for example, in oligarchies—when those who have no share in the state are the majority, they revolt, because they think that they are the stronger. Or, again, in democracies, the rich despise the disorder and anarchy of the state; at Thebes, for example, where, after the battle of Oenophyta, the bad administration of the democracy led to its ruin. At Megara the fall of the democracy was due to a defeat occasioned by disorder and anarchy. And at Syracuse the democracy was overthrown before the tyranny of Gelo arose; at Rhodes before the insurrection.

Political revolutions also spring from a disproportionate increase in any part of the state. For as a body is made up of many members, and every member ought to grow in proportion, that symmetry may be preserved, but loses its nature if the foot be four cubits long and the rest of the body two spans; and, should the abnormal increase be one of quality as well as of quantity, may even take the form of another animal: even so a state has many parts, of which some one may often grow imperceptibly; for example, the number of poor in democracies and in constitutional states. And this disproportion may sometimes happen by an accident, as at Tarentum, from a defeat in which many of the notables were slain in a battle with the Iapygians just after the Persian War, the constitutional government in consequence becoming a democracy; or, as was the case at Argos, where after the losses inflicted in 'the Battle of the Seventh Day' by Cleomenes the Lacedaemonian, the Argives were compelled to admit to citizenship some of their perioeci: and at Athens, when, after frequent defeats of their infantry in the times of the Peloponnesian War, the notables were reduced in number, because the soldiers had to be taken from the roll of citizens. Revolutions arise from this cause in democracies as well as in other forms of government, but not to so great an extent. When the rich grow numerous or properties increase, the form of government changes into an oligarchy or a government of families. Forms of government also change—sometimes even without revolution, owing to election contests, as at Heraea (where, instead of electing their magistrates, they took them by lot, because the electors were in the habit of choosing their own partisans); or owing to carelessness, when disloyal persons are allowed to find their way into the highest offices, as at Oreum, where, upon the accession of Heracleodorus to office, the oligarchy was overthrown, and changed by him into a constitutional and democratical government.

Again, the revolution may be accomplished by small degrees; I mean that a great change may sometimes slip into the constitution through neglect of a small matter; at Ambracia, for instance, the qualification for office, small at first, was eventually reduced to nothing. For the Ambraciots thought that a small qualification was much the same as none at all.

Another cause of revolution is difference of races which do not at once acquire a common spirit; for a state is not the growth of a day, neither is it a multitude brought together by accident. Hence the reception of strangers in colonies, either at the time of their foundation or afterwards, has generally produced revolution; for example, the Achaeans who joined the Troezenians in the foundation of Sybaris, being the more numerous, afterwards expelled them; hence the curse fell upon Sybaris. At Thurii the Sybarites quarrelled with their fellow-colonists; thinking that the land belonged to them, they wanted too much of it and were driven out. At Byzantium the new colonists were detected in a conspiracy, and were expelled by force of arms; the people of Antissa, who had received the Chian exiles, fought with them, and drove them out; and the Zancleans, after having received the Samians, were driven by them out of their own city. The citizens of Apollonia on the Euxine, after the introduction of a fresh body of colonists, had a revolution; the Syracusans, after the expulsion of their tyrants, having admitted strangers and mercenaries to the rights of citizenship, quarrelled and came to blows; the people of Amphipolis, having received Chalcidian colonists, were nearly all expelled by them.

Now, in oligarchies the masses make revolution under the idea that they are unjustly treated, because, as I said before, they are equals, and have not an equal share, and in democracies the notables revolt, because they are not equals, and yet have only an equal share.

Again, the situation of cities is a cause of revolution when the country is not naturally adapted to preserve the unity of the state. For example, the Chytrians at Clazomenae did not agree with the people of the island; and the people of Colophon quarrelled with the Notians; at Athens, too, the inhabitants of the Piraeus are more democratic than those who live in the city. For just as in war, the impediment of a ditch, though ever so small, may break a regiment, so every cause of difference, however slight, makes a breach in a city. The greatest opposition is confessedly that of virtue and vice; next comes that of wealth and poverty; and there are other antagonistic elements, greater or less, of which one is this difference of place.

In revolutions the occasions may be trifling, but great interests are at stake. Trifles are most important when they concern the rulers, as was the case of old at Syracuse; for the Syracusan constitution was once changed by a love-quarrel of two young men, who were in the government. The story is that while one of them was away from home his beloved was gained over by his companion, and he to revenge himself seduced the other's wife. They then drew all the members of the ruling class into their quarrel and made a revolution. We learn from this story that we should be on our guard against the beginnings of such evils, and should put an end to the quarrels of chiefs and mighty men. The mistake lies in the beginning — as the proverb says, 'Well begun is half done' — so an error at the beginning, though quite small, has the proportion of a half to the whole matter. In general, when the notables quarrel, the whole city is involved, as happened in Hestiaea after the Persian War. The occasion was the division of an inheritance; one of two brothers refused to give an account of their father's property and the treasure which he had found: so the poorer of the two quarrelled with him and enlisted in his cause the popular party, the other, who was very rich, the wealthy classes.

At Delphi, again, a quarrel about a marriage was the beginning of all the troubles which followed. In this case the bridegroom, fancying some occurrence to be of evil omen, came to the bride, and went away without taking her. Whereupon her relations, thinking that they were insulted by him, put some of the sacred treasure [among his offerings] while he was sacrificing, and then slew him, pretending that he had been robbing the temple. At Mitylene, too, a dispute about heiresses was the beginning of many misfortunes, and led to the war with the Athenians in which Paches took their city. A wealthy citizen, named Timophanes, left two daughters; Doxander, another citizen, wanted to obtain them for his sons, but he was rejected in his suit, whereupon he stirred up a revolution, and instigated the Athenians (of whom he was proxenus) to interfere. A similar quarrel about an heiress arose at Phocis between Mnaseas the father of Mnason, and Euthycrates the father of Onomarchus; this was the beginning of the Sacred War. A marriage-quarrel was also the cause of a change in the government of Epidamnus. A certain man betrothed his daughter secretly to a person whose father, having been made a magistrate, fined the father of the girl, and the latter, stung by the insult, conspired with the unenfranchised classes to overthrow the state.

Governments also change into oligarchy or into democracy or into a constitutional government because the magistrates, or some other section of the state, increase in power or renown. Thus at Athens the reputation gained by the court of the Areopagus, in the Persian War, seemed to tighten the reins of government. On the other hand, the victory of Salamis, which was gained by the common people who served in the fleet, and won for the Athenians the empire of the sea, strengthened the democracy. At Argos, the notables, having distinguished themselves against the Lacedaemonians in the battle of Mantinea, attempted to put down the democracy. At Syracuse, the people having been the chief authors of the victory in the war with the Athenians, changed the constitutional government into democracy. At Chalcis, the people, uniting with the notables, killed Phoxus the tyrant, and then seized the government. At Ambracia, the people, in like manner, having joined with the conspirators in expelling the tyrant Periander, transferred the government to themselves. And generally, it should be remembered that those who have secured power to the state, whether private citizens, or magistrates, or tribes, or any other part or section of the state, are apt to cause revolutions. For either envy of their greatness draws others into rebellion, or they themselves, in their pride of superiority, are unwilling to remain on a level with others.

Revolutions break out when opposite parties, e.g. the rich and the poor, are equally balanced, and there is little or nothing between them; for, if either party were manifestly superior, the other would not risk an attack upon them. And, for this reason, those who are eminent in virtue do not stir up insurrections, being always a minority. Such are the beginnings and causes of the disturbances and revolutions to which every form of government is liable.

Revolutions are effected in two ways, by force and by fraud. Force may be applied either at the time of making the revolution or afterwards. Fraud, again, is off two kinds; for (1) sometimes the citizens are deceived into a change of government, and afterwards they are held in subjection against their will. This was what happened in the case of the Four Hundred, who deceived the people by telling them that the king would provide money for the war against the Lacedaemonians, and when the deception was over, still endeavoured to retain the government. (2) In other cases the people are persuaded at first, and afterwards, by a repetition of the persuasion, their goodwill and allegiance are retained. The revolutions which affect constitutions generally spring from the above-mentioned causes.

Book VII   Basic Features of the Ideal State

He who would duly enquire about the best form of a state ought first to determine which is the most eligible life; while this remains uncertain the best form of the state must also be uncertain; for, in the natural order of things, those may be expected to lead the best life who are governed in the best manner of which their circumstances admit. We ought therefore to ascertain, first of all, which is the most generally eligible life, and then whether the same life is or is not best for the state and for individuals.

Assuming that enough has been already said in exoteric discourses concerning the best life, we will now only repeat the statements contained in them. Certainly no one will dispute the propriety of that partition of goods which separates them into three classes, viz. external goods, goods of the body, and goods of the soul, or deny that the happy man must have all three. For no one would maintain that he is happy who has not in him a particle of courage or temperance or justice or prudence, who is afraid of every insect which flutters past him, and will commit any crime, however great, in order to gratify his lust of meat or drink, who will sacrifice his dearest friend for the sake of half a farthing, and is as feeble and false in mind as a child or a madman. These propositions are universally acknowledged as soon as they are uttered, but men differ about the quantity which is desirable or the relative superiority of this or that good. Some think that a very moderate amount of virtue is enough, but set no limit to their desires of wealth, property, power, reputation, and the like. To whom we reply by an appeal to facts, which easily prove that mankind do not acquire or preserve virtue by the help of external goods, but external goods by the help of virtue, and that happiness, whether consisting in pleasure or virtue, or both, is more often found with those who are most highly cultivated in their mind and in their character, and have only a moderate share of external goods, than among those who possess external goods to a useless extent but are deficient in higher qualities; and this is not only matter of experience, but, if reflected upon, will easily appear to be in accordance with reason. For, whereas external goods have a limit, like any other instrument, and all things useful are of such a nature that where there is too much of them they must either do harm, or at any rate be of no use, to their possessors, every good of the soul, the greater it is, is also of greater use, if the epithet 'useful' as well as 'noble' is appropriate to such subjects. No proof is required to show that the best state of one thing in relation to another is proportioned to the degree of excellence by which the natures corresponding to those states are separated from each other: so that, if the soul is more noble than our possessions or our bodies, both absolutely and in relation to us, it must be admitted that the best state of either has a similar ratio to the other. Again, it is for the sake of the soul that goods external and goods of the body are eligible at all, and all wise men ought to choose them for the sake of the soul, and not the soul for the sake of them.

Let us acknowledge then that each one has just so much of happiness as he has of virtue and wisdom, and of virtuous and wise action. God is a witness to us of this truth; for he is happy and blessed, not by reason of any external good, but in himself and by reason of his own nature. And herein of necessity lies the difference between good fortune and happiness; for external goods come of themselves, and chance is the author of them, but no one is just or temperate by or through chance. In like manner, and by a similar train of argument, the happy state may be shown to be that which is [morally] best and which acts rightly; and rightly it cannot act without doing right actions, and neither individual nor state can do right actions without virtue and wisdom. Thus the courage, justice, and wisdom of a state have the same form and nature as the qualities which give the individual who possesses them the name of just, wise, or temperate.

Thus much may suffice by way of preface: for I could not avoid touching upon these questions, neither could I go through all the arguments affecting them; these must be reserved for another discussion.

Let us assume then that the best life, both for individuals and states, is the life of virtue, having external goods enough for the performance of good actions. If there are any who controvert our assertion, we will in this treatise pass them over, and consider their objections hereafter.

There remains to be discussed the question, Whether the happiness of the individual is the same as that of the state, or different? Here again there can be no doubt—no one denies that they are the same. For those who hold that the well-being of the individual consists in his wealth, also think that riches make the happiness of the whole state, and those who value most highly the life of a tyrant deem that city the happiest which rules over the greatest number; while they who approve an individual for his virtue say that the more virtuous a city is, the happier it is. Two points here present themselves for consideration: first (1), which is the more eligible life, that of a citizen who is a member of a state, or that of an alien who has no political ties; and again (2), which is the best form of constitution or the best condition of a state, either on the supposition that political privileges are given to all, or that they are given to a majority only? Since the good of the state and not of the individual is the proper subject of political thought and speculation, and we are engaged in a political discussion, while the first of these two points has a secondary interest for us, the latter will be the main subject of our enquiry.

Now it is evident that the form of government is best in which every man, whoever he is, can act for the best and live happily. But even those who agree in thinking that the life of virtue is the most eligible raise a question, whether the life of business and politics is or is not more eligible than one which is wholly independent of external goods, I mean than a contemplative life, which by some is maintained to be the only one worthy of a philosopher. For these two lives—the life of the philosopher and the life of the statesman—appear to have been preferred by those who have been most keen in the pursuit of virtue, both in our own and in other ages. Which is the better is a question of no small moment; for the wise man, like the wise state, will necessarily regulate his life according to the best end. There are some who think that while a despotic rule over others is the greatest injustice, to exercise a constitutional rule over them, even though not unjust, is a great impediment to a man's individual well-being. Others take an opposite view; they maintain that the true life of man is the practical and political, and that every virtue admits of being practised, quite as much by statesmen and rulers as by private individuals. Others, again, are of opinion that arbitrary and tyrannical rule alone consists with happiness; indeed, in some states the entire aim of the laws is to give men despotic power over their neighbours. And, therefore, although in most cities the laws may be said generally to be in a chaotic state, still, if they aim at anything, they aim at the maintenance of power: thus in Lacedaemon and Crete the system of education and the greater part of the laws are framed with a view to war. And in all nations which are able to gratify their ambition military power is held in esteem, for example among the Scythians and Persians and Thracians and Celts. In some nations there are even laws tending to stimulate the warlike virtues, as at Carthage, where we are told that men obtain the honour of wearing as many armlets as they have served campaigns. There was once a law in Macedonia that he who had not killed an enemy should wear a halter, and among the Scythians no one who had not slain his man was allowed to drink out of the cup which was handed round at a certain feast. Among the Iberians, a warlike nation, the number of enemies whom a man has slain is indicated by the number of spits which are fixed in the earth round his tomb; and there are numerous practices among other nations of a like kind, some of them established by law and others by custom. Yet to a reflecting mind it must appear very strange that the statesman should be always considering how he can dominate and tyrannize over others, whether they will or not. How can that which is not even lawful be the business of the statesman or the legislator? Unlawful it certainly is to rule without regard to justice, for there may be might where there is no right. The other arts and sciences offer no parallel; a physician is not expected to persuade or coerce his patients, nor a pilot the passengers in his ship. Yet many appear to think that a despotic government is a true political form, and what men affirm to be unjust and inexpedient in their own case they are not ashamed of practising towards others; they demand justice for themselves, but where other men are concerned they care nothing about it. Such behaviour is irrational; unless the one party is born to command, and the other born to serve, in which case men have a right to command, not indeed all their fellows, but only those who are intended to be subjects; just as we ought not to hunt mankind, whether for food or sacrifice, but only the animals which are intended for food or sacrifice, that is to say, such wild animals as are eatable. And surely there may be a city happy in isolation, which we will assume to be well-governed (for it is quite possible that a city thus isolated might be well-administered and have good laws); but such a city would not be constituted with any view to war or the conquest of enemies—all that sort of thing must be excluded. Hence we see very plainly that warlike pursuits, although generally to be deemed honourable, are not the supreme end of all things, but only means. And the good lawgiver should enquire how states and races of men and communities may participate in a good life, and in the happiness which is attainable by them. His enactments will not be always the same; and where there are neighbours he will have to deal with them according to their characters, and to see what duties are to be performed towards each. The end at which the best form of government should aim may be properly made a matter of future consideration.

Let us now address those who, while they agree that the life of virtue is the most eligible, differ about the manner of practising it. For some renounce political power, and think that the life of the freeman is different from the life of the statesman and the best of all; but others think the life of the statesman best. The argument of the latter is that he who does nothing cannot do well, and that virtuous activity is identical with happiness. To both we say: 'you are partly right and partly wrong.' The first class are right in affirming that the life of the freeman is better than the life of the despot; for there is nothing grand or noble in having the use of a slave, in so far as he is a slave; or in issuing commands about necessary things. But it is an error to suppose that every sort of rule is despotic like that of a master over slaves, for there is as great a difference between the rule over freemen and the rule over slaves as there is between slavery by nature and freedom by nature, about which I have said enough at the commencement of this treatise. And it is equally a mistake to place inactivity above action, for happiness is activity, and the actions of the just and wise are the realization of much that is noble.

But perhaps some one, accepting these premisses, may still maintain that supreme power is the best of all things, because the possessors of it are able to perform the greatest number of noble actions. If so, the man who is able to rule, instead of giving up anything to his neighbour, ought rather to take away his power; and the father should make no account of his son, nor the son of his father, nor friend of friend; they should not bestow a thought on one another in comparison with this higher object, for the best is the most eligible and 'doing well ' is the best. There might be some truth in such a view if we assume that robbers and plunderers attain the chief good. But this can never be; and hence we infer the view to be false. For the actions of a ruler cannot really be honourable, unless he is as much superior to other men as a husband is to a wife, or a father to his children, or a master to his slaves. And therefore he who violates the law can never recover by any success, however great, what he has already lost in departing from virtue. For equals share alike in the honourable and the just, as is just and equal. But that the unequal should be given to equals, and the unlike to those who are like, is contrary to nature, and nothing which is contrary to nature is good. If, therefore, there is any one superior in virtue and in the power of performing the best actions, him we ought to follow and obey, but he must have the capacity for action as well as virtue.

If we are right in our view, and happiness is assumed to be virtuous activity, the active life will be the best, both for the city collectively, and for individuals. Not that a life of action must necessarily have relations to others, as some persons think, nor are those ideas only to be regarded as practical which are pursued for the sake of practical results, but much more the thoughts and contemplations which are independent and complete in themselves; since virtuous activity, and therefore action, is an end, and even in the case of external actions the directing mind is most truly said to act. Neither, again, is it necessary that states which are cut off from others and choose to live alone should be inactive; for there may be activity also in the parts; there are many ways in which the members of a state act upon one another. The same thing is equally true of every individual. If this were otherwise, God and the universe, who have no external actions over and above their own energies, would be far enough from perfection. Hence it is evident that the same life is best for each individual, and for states, and for mankind collectively.

MARCUS TULLIUS CICERO

106 – 42 B.C.

INTRODUCTION

We have much more biographical information about Cicero, one of the most admired lawyers, statesmen, orators, and philosophical authors of ancient Rome, than we have about either Plato or Aristotle, the two Greek authors whom Cicero called "the princes of philosophy." Cicero's father, a prosperous country gentleman, sent his two sons to Rome to be well educated for public office and Marcus Tullius showed himself to be an exceptionally able student, not only of law and rhetoric, but of Greek and philosophy. His unusual command of Greek enabled him later to introduce the chief Greek philosophers to his Latin audience, and his command of Latin was so complete that his writings still retain a dominating position in classical literature.

Cicero rapidly established himself as a successful lawyer, and after spending 2 years in Athens and Rhodes for further study returned to Rome and immersed himself in political life. During the next decade he was successful in being elected to various administrative and judicial offices of increasing seniority. By the age of 43 he had reached the highest public office of the Roman republic, that of Consul, despite the considerable handicap of not being a noble. He gained immense popularity by suppressing the dangerous conspiracy of Catiline against the government, although a few years later he was exiled briefly on his enemies' complaint that the conspirators had been executed without trial. When he returned, the long struggle between Pompey and Caesar for control of Rome had begun, and although Cicero supported first one side and then the other, his influence was not great. By the time Caesar had become uncrowned dictator in 46 B.C., Cicero, who hated him, had retired from politics. In the following year and a half Cicero, writing at great speed during the political turmoil that preceded and followed the assassination of Caesar, produced more than a dozen philosophical books on topics such as fate, immortality, friendship, and morality. It was these works, in addition to earlier writings such as *On the Commonwealth*, that made Latin, for the first time, a language in which serious philosophy could be written.

Cicero then came out of retirement and began attacking, in a series of famous speeches, the tyrannical government of Marc Antony. This powerful opponent shortly after made peace with his chief rival, Caesar's adopted son, Octavian, the man on whose support Cicero and his fellow senators had counted for protection against Antony. Many of them were immediately listed as public outlaws and Antony's soldiers were sent out to kill them. The soldiers found Cicero as he was about to board ship, killed him, and cut off his head and hands to be hung up for public display in Rome.

Our Latin text of Cicero's *De Re Publica* comes largely from a fourth- or fifth-century manuscript discovered in the Vatican library and first published in 1822. The manuscript seems to contain only about 30% of the original text and is thus seriously incomplete. It is given here in the translation by George Holland Sabine and Stanley Barney Smith, published in 1929 by the Ohio State University Press in Columbus, Ohio. The translators have used Roman type for printing Cicero's own words, and italics for "all passages, whether derived from other works of Cicero or from later writers, which reproduce the sense but not the actual words of Cicero's *Commonwealth*."

SELECTIONS FROM
On the Commonwealth

Book I The Three Basic Forms of Government

XXV. SCIPIO: The commonwealth, then, is the people's affair; and the people is not every group of men, associated in any manner, but is the coming together of a considerable number of men who are united by a common agreement about law and rights and by the desire to participate in mutual advantages. The original cause of this coming together is not so much weakness as a kind of social instinct natural to man. For the human kind is not solitary, nor do its members live lives of isolated roving; but it is so constituted that, even if it possessed the greatest plenty of material comforts, [it would nevertheless be impelled by its nature to live in social groups. . . .]

(The second leaf of the ninth quaternion is missing)

For what is the commonwealth except the people's affair? Hence, it is a common affair, that is, an affair belonging to a state. And what is a state except a considerable number of men brought together in a certain bond of harmony? The view that we meet in the Roman authors is as follows: In a short time a scattered and wandering aggregate of men became a state through harmony.

Scholars have not attributed the founding of cities to a single first principle. For some hold that, when men first sprang up from the soil, they lived a roving life in the forests and plains, and were united by no bonds either of speech or of law, but made their beds in the leaves and grass and had caves and crevices in the rocks for houses, and were a prey to the more powerful wild beasts and animals. Later, they say, those men who had been torn by wild beasts or had seen their comrades torn, and had made their escape, were driven by consciousness of their danger to ally themselves with other men. From them they sought aid, at first making their wants known by signs and gestures. Afterwards they experimented with the beginnings of speech and, by giving names to things, gradually developed a system of language. These scholars believe, further, that, when men perceived that even in large numbers they needed to be protected against animals, they began to build towns, either with a view to making themselves safe at night, or for the purpose of warding off the attacks of animals, not by fighting them hand to hand, but by interposing barriers for their own protection . . . To other scholars, on the other hand, these views have appeared little better than madness, as in fact they were. These scholars held that the reason why men came together in groups is not to be found in the depredations of wild beasts, but rather in the social nature of mankind. Consequently, they said, men formed societies because it is their nature to shun solitude and to seek the relationships of social intercourse.

XXVI. SCIPIO: . . . [These gregarious impulses] are, so to speak, the seeds [of social virtues]; nor can any other source be found for the remaining virtues or, indeed, for the commonwealth itself. Such groups, therefore, brought into being for the reason I have mentioned, first settled themselves in a fixed abode that they might have dwellings. And when they had fortified this abode, either by taking advantage of the natural features of the land or by building artificial works, they called such a group of buildings, with the places set aside for shrines and for common use, either a town or a city. Consequently, every people, which is a number of men united in the way I have explained, every state, which is an organization of the people, every commonwealth, which, as I have said, is the people's affair, needs to be ruled by some sort of deliberating authority in order that it may endure. This authority, in the first place, must always be relative to the peculiar grounds which have brought the particular state into being. It must, in the second place, be delegated either to a single man, or to certain selected persons, or it must be retained by all the members of the group.

When, therefore, the supreme power is in the hands of one man, we call that man a king and that form of government a monarchy. When it is in the hands of certain selected persons, that state is said to be ruled by the will of an aristocracy. And a state is democratic — for that is the term used — when all authority is in the hands of the people themselves. Any one of these three forms of government, while not, of course, perfect nor in my judgment the best, is nevertheless a passable form of government, if the bond holds which originally united its members in the social order of the commonwealth; and one may be better than another. For either a just and wise king, or an aristocracy of leading citizens, or even the people themselves — though this last is the least desirable form of the three — appears capable of carrying on a stable government so long as injustice and greed have not crept into the state.

XXVII. Nevertheless, in a monarchy all except the king are too much excluded from the protection of the law and from participation in deliberative functions, though these rights belong to the whole people. In a government dominated by an aristocracy the mass of the people have hardly any share in freedom, since they have no part in common deliberative and executive powers. And when the state is governed by the people, even though they be just and self-disciplined, yet their very equality is inequitable in that it does not recognize degrees of merit. Therefore, even if Cyrus the Persian was a perfectly just and wise king, nevertheless the condition of the commons — that is, the commonwealth, as I have said above — does not seem to have been one which we should particularly covet, since it was subject to the caprice of a single man. Similarly, even if our clients, the Massilians, are governed with the greatest justice by their oligarchy of nobles, still in a people so situated there exists something like slavery. And even if the Athenians at certain periods after the fall of the Areopagus conducted all public business through enactments and decrees of the people, still their state did not preserve its glory, since it failed to regard differences of worth.

XXVIII. I am speaking of the three types of government, not as they are when they have become disordered and deranged, but as they are when they maintain their true character. In this condition, each type is subject, first, to the defects which I have mentioned, and in addition has other faults likely to be fatal to its permanence. For each of these types of commonwealth has a tendency to slip headlong into that form of evil government which is most closely related to it. Take, for example, a king at his best, a Cyrus, who was an endurable or, if you like, even a lovable ruler. Nevertheless, his character may change, for there lurks in him the utterly inhuman Phalaris into whose likeness arbitrary power in the hands of one man readily and easily degenerates. Furthermore, the government of the Massilian state by a few chief men is closely approximated by the oligarchical conspiracy of the Thirty Tyrants which once ruled Athens. And finally, at Athens the Athenians themselves—to seek no other [authority—admit] that the absolute power of the people degenerated into the irresponsible madness of a mob. . . .

(The seventh leaf of the ninth quaternion is missing)

XXIX. SCIPIO: . . . a veritable scoundrel [comes to the front;] and from this condition of the state there may arise an aristocracy or a tyrannical government by a party or a monarchy or, quite frequently, even a democracy. And likewise it often happens that from this last type there grows up one of those forms of state which I have noted before. For there is a remarkable rotation and, if I may say so, cycle of changes in the life of states. It is the business of a philosopher to understand the order in which these changes occur; but to foresee impending modifications, and at the same time to pilot the state, to direct its course, and to keep it under control, is the part of a great statesman and a man of all but godlike powers. There is, accordingly, a fourth kind of commonwealth which, in my opinion, should receive the highest approval, since it is formed by the combination, in due measure, of the three forms of state which I described as original.

XXX. LAELIUS: I know, Africanus, that you prefer this composite type of state, for I have often heard you say so. But still, if there is no objection, I should like to know which of the three unmixed kinds of state you consider the best. For it will be of some use to know. . . .

(The first leaf of the tenth quaternion is missing)

XXXI. SCIPIO: . . . and every state varies according to the character and inclination of its sovereign. Consequently, no state except one in which the people have supreme power provides a habitation for liberty, than which surely nothing can be sweeter. But if liberty is not equally enjoyed by all the citizens, it is not liberty at all. And yet, how can all citizens have an equal share in liberty—I pass over the citizens in a monarchy, for there, of course, the subjection of the people is neither concealed nor questionable—but even in those states in which all men are nominally free? They do, of course, cast their votes; they elect the civil and military officials; their suffrages are solicited for purposes of election and legislation. Nevertheless, the powers which they bestow they would have to bestow, even against their will; and they do not possess the powers which others seek to obtain from them. For they have no share in military commands, or in advisory councils, or in special jury panels. These offices are in fact reserved to men of ancient family or to men of wealth. But in a free people, as at Rhodes or at Athens, there is no citizen who [is not eligible to all the offices of state]. . . .

(The third leaf of the tenth quaternion is missing)

XXXII. SCIPIO: [The advocates of democracy] affirm that, [when] one man or a few men become wealthier and more powerful than the other citizens, their pride and arrogance give rise [to special privileges], because the inactive and the weak give way and submit to the pretensions of the rich. So long, however, as the people actually retain their power, these thinkers hold that no form of government is better, more liberal, or more prosperous, since the people have control over legislation, the administration of justice, the making of war and peace, the concluding of treaties, and over the civil status and property of each individual citizen. This, according to their view, is the only form of government which can properly be called a commonwealth, that is, the people's affair; and therefore, while there are many instances where the people's affair is freed from the yoke of kings and patricians, there is none of a free people's demanding a king or an aristocratic form of government. They assert, moreover, that it is not right for democracy in general to be condemned because an uncontrolled populace has defects; that, so long as a people is harmonious and subordinates everything to its safety and freedom, there is no form of government less subject to revolution or more stable; and that the kind of state in which harmony is most easily attained is one in which the interests of all the citizens are the same. Dissension, as they hold, arises from diversity of interests, whenever the well-being of some is contrary to the well-being of others. Consequently, when the government was in the hands of aristocrats, the form of the state has never remained stable. Still less has this been the case with monarchies, for, in Ennius' words,

In a kingdom there is no sacred fellowship or trust.

Since, then, law is the bond that holds political society together, and since equality of rights is a part of law, by what principle of right can an association of citizens be held together, when the status of these citizens is not equal? For, if it is not thought desirable that property should be equally distributed, and if the natural capacities of all men cannot possibly be equal, yet certainly all who are citizens of the same commonwealth ought to enjoy equal rights in their mutual relations. What, indeed, is a state, if it is not an association of citizens united by law? . . .

(The sixth leaf of the tenth quaternion is missing)

XXXIV. SCIPIO: . . . . if a state [chooses its rulers] at haphazard, it will be overthrown as quickly as a ship will founder if its pilot is chosen by lot from among the passengers. But if a free people chooses those to whose guidance it will submit itself, and if it chooses for this purpose all its best citizens — provided, of course, that the people wish to be secure — surely, then, the safety of the state has been founded upon the wisdom of its ablest members. This is particularly true since nature has contrived to make the men who are superior in courage and ability rule over the weak, and the weak willing to submit themselves to the best. This perfect relationship between men has been overthrown, according to the partizans of aristocracy, by the false notions that prevail about human excellence. For, as few men possess excellence, so few are able to recognize and judge it. Thus, being ignorant of its nature, the masses suppose that men of wealth, influence, and important family connections are the best. When, as a result of this error on the part of the commons, the wealth rather than the excellence of a few men has come to control the state, these leaders cling stubbornly to the title of aristocrats, utterly lacking though they may be in the substance of excellence. For riches and reputation and power, if devoid of wisdom and of moderation in conduct and in the exercise of authority, are characterized by shamelessness and insufferable arrogance. There is, indeed, no uglier kind of state than one in which the richest men are thought to be the best.

On the other hand, when excellence governs the commonwealth, what can be more glorious? For then he who rules over others is not himself the slave of any base desire; the requirements which he lays upon his fellow-citizens he has fulfilled himself; he does not impose upon the people laws which he does not himself obey; he holds up his own life before his fellow-citizens as the law by which they may guide their lives. If one such man were able to accomplish effectively all the business of the state, there would be no need for others; and if the body of citizens could always discover this perfect ruler and agree in regard to him, no one would demand specially chosen leaders. The difficulty of determining policy wisely has caused the transfer of authority from the king to several persons; and, conversely, the ignorance and reck-lessness of the commons have caused it to pass from the many to the few. Thus, between the weakness inherent in a single ruler and the recklessness inherent in the many, aristocracy has come to hold a middle place. Nothing, in fact, can be more perfectly balanced; and as long as an aristocracy guards the state, the people are necessarily in the happiest condition, since they are free from all care and anxiety. Their ease has been put into the safe-keeping of others, who must protect it and take care that nothing arises to make the people believe that their interests are being neglected by their leaders.

Now the equal rights of which democracies are so fond cannot be maintained. Indeed, no matter how free and untrammeled popular governments may be, they are still exceptionally prone to confer many favors on many men, and show decided preferences in the matter of individuals and in the matter of high rank. And what is called equality is, in reality, extremely unequal. For when the same importance is attached to the high and the low — and in every community these two classes necessarily exist — that very equality is most unequal. Such a condition cannot arise in states that are governed by aristocracies.

Arguments of much this character, Laelius, and others of the same kind, are usually put forward by those who praise most highly the aristocratic form of government.

XXXV.   LAELIUS: But of the three simple forms of state, Scipio, which do you especially approve?

SCIPIO: You frame your question well when you ask, "Which of the three" I especially approve, because I do not approve any one of them considered separately and by itself. I prefer rather the mixed form, which is a combination of all three, to any one taken by itself. Still, if I had to express preference for one of the unmixed forms, I should choose monarchy [and accord it first place. In this kind of state] we find that the king is described as if he were a father, planning for his subjects as if they were his children, and zealously protecting them [but never reducing them to subjection. Thus it is much better for the weak and ignorant] to be guarded by the care of one man, who is at once the strongest and the best man in the state. There are, to be sure, the aristocrats, who claim that they do this better than the king, and assert that there would be greater wisdom in a number of men than in one, and withal the same justice and good faith. Finally, the people themselves declare loudly that they do not wish to obey either one man or several. Nothing, they say, is sweeter than freedom, even to wild beasts; and no citizen possesses freedom when he is subject either to a king or to an aristocracy.

Thus I prefer monarchy for the love which the king bears to his subjects; aristocracy for its wisdom in counsel; and democracy for its freedom. When I compare them, I find it hard to decide which feature we desire the most. . . .

Book III   Should People Pursue Justice?

X. Now if I cared to enumerate the different kinds of laws, institutions, customs, and practices, I might show not only that they differ in different races, but that even in a single city — our own, for example — they have undergone a thousand changes. Thus our friend Manilius here, in his capacity of jurisconsult, advises those who ask his opinion that the law governing legacies and inheritances by women is different now from what it was when he gave his opinion as a younger man, before the Voconian Law was passed. This is a statute enacted in the interests of men but fraught with injustice toward women. For why should a woman not have money [on the same terms as a man]? Why may a Vestal bequeath property and her mother not? Or again, granting that the amount of property which a woman can receive must be limited, why should the daughter of Publius Crassus, if she be his only child, be permitted to inherit a hundred million sesterces without violating the law, while my daughter cannot inherit three million? . . .

(The seventh leaf of the twenty-ninth quaternion is missing)

XI. PHILUS: [If justice were natural, then nature] would have laid down our laws; all peoples would be subject to the same laws; and the same people would not be subject to different laws at different times. Now I put the question to you: If it be the duty of a just man and a good citizen to obey the laws, what laws should he obey? Shall he obey any laws that happen to prevail? But surely rectitude does not admit of inconsistency, and nature does not permit different standards of conduct. Laws, therefore, are obeyed because of the penalties they may inflict and not because of our sense of justice. Consequently, the law has no sanction in nature. It follows, then, that men are not just by nature. Or do they mean that, while there is diversity in human legislation, good men follow true justice rather than that which is merely thought to be just? For rendering unto everything its deserts is said to be the mark of a good and just man. But in the first place, then, what shall we render to dumb animals? Thus, Pythagoras and Empedocles, men of no ordinary attainments but scholars of the first rank, assert that there is a single legal status belonging to all living creatures. They proclaim, moreover, that everlasting punishment awaits those who have wronged anything that lives. It is a crime, accordingly, to injure an animal, and he who presumes to commit this offense. . . .

(Of the next eighty leaves, composing quaternions thirty to thirty-nine, all but four are missing and these four cannot be precisely placed)

XII. *If a man wishes to act in accordance with justice, and yet is ignorant of the divine law, he will honor the enactments of his own people as if they were the true law, although they are in general the product, not of justice, but of self-interest. Why indeed have diverse and unlike codes of law been established among all peoples? Is it not because each people has enacted for itself such provisions as it thought to be useful in its own conditions of life? But how wide is the divergence between justice and utility may be learned from the case of the Roman people itself. By using the Fetial College in their declarations of war, they gave acts of aggression the color of law.*

Thus, they constantly coveted and seized the possessions of others and so made themselves the masters of the whole world.

For unless I am mistaken, every kingdom or empire is acquired by war and extended by victory, and furthermore, the chief element in war and victory is the capture and overthrow of cities. Such acts are impossible without doing injury to the gods, for the destruction of the city's walls is likewise the destruction of its temples; the murder of its citizens involves likewise the murder of its priests; and the plundering of secular wealth includes also the plunder of sacred treasures. Hence, the irreligious acts of the Roman people equal the number of its trophies; every triumph over a people is a triumph over its gods; the collections of booty equal in number the surviving images of captive gods.

Therefore, since the arguments of the philosophers were weak, Carneades made bold to refute them because he knew that they could be refuted. The heads of his discourse were as follows. Men have established laws to serve their own advantages. These laws, of course, were different to suit the different characters of peoples, and even in the same people they were often modified to accord with changing conditions. On the other hand, there is no natural law. All human beings as well as all other living creatures are led by nature to consult their own self-interest. Hence, either there is no such thing as justice, or, if there is, it is the height of folly, since a person would do injury to himself by consulting the interests of others. And Carneades brought forward the following proof. All peoples who built up empires — including the Romans themselves, who became masters of the world — would be obliged to return to huts and live in wretched poverty if they wished to be just, that is, if they should restore all that is not their own.

> *Ever to count your country's welfare first*

is an utterly meaningless verse if you banish the discord that prevails among men. What, I ask, are the advantages of your country if they be not the disadvantages of another state or race? For it is to the advantage of your country to extend its boundaries by forcibly appropriating the territories of others, to enlarge the sphere of its power, and to increase its revenues. . . . When, therefore, a man has won for his country these goods, as his countrymen call them; that is, when he has overthrown states, destroyed peoples, filled the exchequer with their wealth, taken their territory, and enriched his fellow-citizens, he is extolled to the skies. In him a consummate and perfect excellence is supposed to reside. This is a mistake not only of the common people and the ignorant, but of philosophers as well, for the latter also supply lessons in injustice, that folly and wrong-doing may not lack the authority that comes from education.

XIII. PHILUS: . . . for all those who have the power of life and death over a people are tyrants, but they prefer to take the name which belongs to Jupiter the Most High and to call themselves kings. And when a group of men controls the commonwealth by virtue of their wealth, their birth, or any advantages they happen to possess, they form an oligarchy, but they call themselves leading citizens. And again, if the people have the supreme power and if all public business is carried on at their pleasure, we have what is called liberty, but what in fact is license. Now when the citizens fear each other, when man fears man and class fears class, no one feels secure; and as a result, a contract, as we may call it, is made by the commons and those who have power. From this agreement there arises the composite form of state which Scipio was praising. Thus, neither nature nor deliberate choice but weakness is the mother of justice. For since a man must choose one of three possibilities — either to act unjustly without suffering injustice, or both to act unjustly and to suffer injustice, or neither to act unjustly nor to suffer injustice — the best choice is to act unjustly without suffering the consequences, if you can. The second choice is neither to act unjustly nor to suffer injustice. But the most wretched condition of all is an incessant warfare in which men both do and suffer injustice. Consequently, he who [cannot] attain the first choice [mentioned above, of doing without suffering injustice, must take the second choice, viz., neither doing nor suffering injustice].

(Either two or four leaves are missing)

XIV. For when [a pirate] was asked what criminal impulse had led him to make the sea unsafe with a single little ship, he replied, "The same impulse which has led you, [Alexander], to make the whole world unsafe."

XV. PHILUS: . . . prudence bids you to use every means to expand your influence, to increase your wealth, and to extend your boundaries. For how could the eulogy, "He extended the frontiers of the empire," have been inscribed upon the monuments of famous generals, if they had not added some territory which belonged to another people? Prudence also bids you to govern as many as you can, to enjoy pleasures, to have power, to rule, and to be the master of men. Justice, on the other hand, teaches you to spare all men, to consider the interests of the human race, to render to each his own, and not to tamper with that which is sacred, that which is public, and that which belongs to another. What is gained, then, if we obey prudence? Both individuals and peoples gain wealth, power, influence, repute, dominion, and rule. But seeing that the commonwealth forms the topic of our discussion, we find these results more clearly illustrated in the activities of states. And since the principle of justice is the same for both persons and states, I feel that I must discuss prudence as the rule of a people's conduct. Our own nation, whose history Africanus traced from its beginnings in yesterday's discourse, now holds sway over the whole world. Saying nothing of other peoples, I ask you: Was it by justice or by prudence that our nation rose from the least among states [to be the greatest of all]?

(At least two leaves are missing)

PHILUS: . . . except the Arcadians and Athenians, who, I presume, feared that justice might sometime interpose her decree [against their further occupancy of land they had taken by force], and pretended, accordingly, that they had sprung from the earth, like the field mice we see here before us.

XVI.   Against these arguments the following answers are usually advanced, in the first place, by [the Epicureans], for they are least disingenuous in presenting their case. Their reasoning on the present question has the more weight because, in their inquiry about the good man, whom we would have to be a person of transparent genuineness of character, they are neither tricky, deceitful, nor insincere. Now [the Epicureans] assert that the wise man is good, not because he is pleased with goodness and justice in and for themselves, but because the lives of good men are free from fear, worry, anxiety, and danger. Wicked men, on the other hand, always have a certain uneasiness at the bottom of their hearts, and always have before their eyes the penalties of the law. But according to [the Epicureans], there is no profit and no reward gained by injustice great enough to repay a man for being always in fear, or for believing that some punishment is always at hand and hanging over him. . . . .

(Either two or four leaves are missing)

XVII.   PHILUS: I put the question to you: Let us suppose that there are two men, one of whom is thoroughly upright and honorable, a man of consummate justice and unique integrity, while the other is a man of extraordinary depravity and shamelessness. And let us assume that the state in which they live is so misguided as to believe the good man a monster of unspeakable criminality, while, on the other hand, it considers the scoundrel to be a model of uprightness and good faith. Let us suppose further that, in conformity with this error on the part of all the citizens, the good man is persecuted, harassed, has his hands cut off and his eyes gouged out, is condemned, cast into chains, tortured by fire, exiled, and reduced to destitution. Finally, let us assume that he is universally regarded as justly meriting his wretched condition. On the other hand, let us suppose that the evil man is praised, honored, and esteemed by all; that all sorts of offices, civil and military, and every form of influence and wealth are conferred upon him; and that he is universally held to be an excellent man, fully deserving the best gifts fortune can bestow. I ask you then: Who under these circumstances will be so mad as to doubt which of the two lots he would prefer?

XVIII.   What is true of individuals is true also of states. There is no country so stupid as not to prefer unjust dominion to just subjection. I shall not adduce remote examples. In my consulate, I presided over an inquiry into the treaty with Numantia, and you were members of my council. Every one knew that Quintus Pompey and Mancinus had both concluded treaties under similar circumstances. The latter of these men was of sterling character and even urged the passage of the law which I proposed in accordance with the senate's decree, while Pompey defended himself most stubbornly. If you wish an example of conscientiousness, integrity, and good faith, Mancinus displayed these qualities; if, on the other hand, you desire shrewdness, penetration, and prudence, Pompey carries off the prize. Whether. . . .

XIX.   *Then Carneades abandoned the general question [of justice as against injustice] and went on to specific examples. Let us suppose, he said, that a good man possesses a runaway slave or an insanitary and unhealthful house, and that he alone is aware of these defects. If, on this account, he offers the slave or the house for sale, will he declare that he is putting on the market a runaway slave or an unhealthful house, or will he conceal these defects from a purchaser? If he admits them, he will be considered honest in that he will not deceive, but he will also be regarded as a fool, for he will either sell at a low price or he will not sell at all. If he conceals the defects, he will be prudent in that he considers his own interest, but he will be dishonest in that he deceives. Again let us suppose that a man finds a dealer who thinks he is selling copper, though it is really gold, or who thinks he is selling lead, when it is really silver. Will an honorable man keep silence in order to buy at a low price, or will he disclose the truth and pay a high price? Only a fool, it appears, would choose the latter course. By such examples Carneades would have it understood that the just and good man is a fool and that the prudent man is wicked, and yet that men may be content with poverty without being ruined.*

XX.   *Carneades accordingly passed on to more important cases in which a man could not be just without endangering his life. For he said: Certainly justice requires us not to kill human beings and not in any way to touch another's property. What, then, will the just man do if he is in a shipwreck and someone weaker than himself has found a plank [on which to keep afloat]? Will he not push the weaker man off the plank, that he may get on it himself and thus make his escape, especially when there is no one in the middle of the sea to bear witness against him? If he is prudent he will do this, for he will inevitably lose his own life if he does not. If, however, he would rather die than raise his hand against another man, he is indeed just but he is a fool, because in sparing another's life he fails to spare his own. Similarly, when the army in which he is fighting has been routed, and the enemy begin pursuit, if a man finds a wounded soldier mounted on a horse, will he spare the wounded man and be killed himself, or will he throw the other from the horse in order that he may himself escape the enemy? If he follows the latter course, he is prudent but also wicked; if he takes the former course, it necessarily follows that, though just, he is a fool. Accordingly, after Carneades had distinguished two kinds of justice, political and natural, he overthrew both, for political justice is in fact prudence and not justice, while natural justice, though it is really justice, is not prudence.*

Clearly these arguments are subtle and ensnaring; indeed, Cicero could not refute them. For though he makes Laelius answer Philus and present the case for justice, Cicero left all these objections unrefuted, as if they were mere traps. The result is that Laelius appears as the defender not of natural justice, which had been subjected to the charge of being mere stupidity, but rather of political justice, which Philus had admitted to be prudent, though it was not just.

XXI. PHILUS: I should not feel it burdensome [to continue the subject], Laelius, if I did not think that our friends here wished that you too should take some part in this discussion of ours, and if I myself did not desire it also, especially since you said yesterday that you would have even more to say than we should care to hear. But, of course, that is impossible, and we all beg you not to disappoint us.

LAELIUS: But our youth ought not to listen to [Carneades] at all. For in fact, if he meant what he says, he is a scoundrel; if he believed otherwise, as I prefer to think, his discourse is nevertheless monstrous.

XXII. LAELIUS: There is in fact a true law — namely, right reason — which is in accordance with nature, applies to all men, and is unchangeable and eternal. By its commands this law summons men to the performance of their duties; by its prohibitions it restrains them from doing wrong. Its commands and prohibitions always influence good men, but are without effect upon the bad. To invalidate this law by human legislation is never morally right, nor is it permissible ever to restrict its operation, and to annul it wholly is impossible. Neither the senate nor the people can absolve us from our obligation to obey this law, and it requires no Sextus Aelius to expound and interpret it. It will not lay down one rule at Rome and another at Athens, nor will it be one rule today and another tomorrow. But there will be one law, eternal and unchangeable, binding at all times upon all peoples; and there will be, as it were, one common master and ruler of men, namely God, who is the author of this law, its interpreter, and its sponsor. The man who will not obey it will abandon his better self, and, in denying the true nature of a man, will thereby suffer the severest of penalties, though he has escaped all the other consequences which men call punishment.

XXIII. *I know that in Cicero's work on the Commonwealth — in the third book, unless I am mistaken — there is a discussion of the proposition that* no war is undertaken by a well-conducted state except in defense of its honor or for its security. *What he means by security, or what he would have his reader understand by a state that is secure, he shows in another passage:* From those penalties of which even the stupidest men are sensible — such as destitution, exile, chains, and stripes — private individuals often escape by adopting the proffered alternative of a speedy death. But for states death is itself a punishment, though for individual men it seems to be a deliverance from punishment. For the state ought to be so organized that it will endure forever. Hence, death is not a natural end for the commonwealth as it is for a human being, whose death is not only necessary but frequently even desirable. But when a state is destroyed and wiped out and annihilated, it is somewhat as if — to compare small things with great — this whole world should perish and collapse.

There are four kinds of wars, the lawful, the unlawful, civil wars, and foreign wars. A lawful war is one which is formally declared and which is waged either to secure restitution of property for which a claim has been made, or to repel an invader. An unlawful war is one that is begun from a mad impulse and without a legitimate cause. Of this kind of war Cicero says in his work on the Commonwealth: Wars are unlawful which are undertaken without a reason. For no war can be justly waged except for the purpose of redressing an injury or of driving out an invader. *And a little farther on Cicero adds:* No war is held to be lawful unless it is officially announced, unless it is declared, and unless a formal claim for satisfaction has been made.

Our people, on the other hand, were by this time masters of the whole world because they defended their allies.

XXIV. *To be sure, many spirited and powerful arguments are advanced in the same work on the commonwealth against injustice and in favor of justice. In the earlier part of the discussion, when the case for injustice and against justice was presented, and when it was urged that the commonwealth could not exist or expand without injustice, it was laid down as an irrefutable principle that it was always unjust for human beings to be the subjects and chattels of other human beings; and yet, unless an imperial state — to which class the great commonwealth belongs — should practice this kind of injustice, it could not rule dependencies. In the argument on behalf of justice the answer was accordingly made that subjection is just because it is advantageous for a certain kind of men, and that it serves the advantage of such men when it is brought about in the right way — that is, when the power of doing wrong is taken from wicked men, and when those who have been conquered will be better off, inasmuch as they were worse off when unconquered. In support of this reasoning a notable illustration was adduced, drawn as it were from nature, and the following argument was advanced:* Do we not perceive that the dominion which nature herself has given to the best conduces in a high degree to the interests of the weak? Is it not for this reason that God rules man, that the soul commands the body, and that reason governs desire, anger, and all the other defective elements of the soul?

XXV. We must recognize, however that there are different kinds of rulership and subjection. Thus, the soul is said to rule the body and also the desires. But whereas it rules the former as a king governs his subjects or a father his children, it rules the desires as a master drives his slaves, since in this case its rule is repressive and crushing. Similarly, the authority which kings, generals, magistrates, senates, and peoples exert over citizens and allies resembles the rule of the soul over the body. On the other hand, masters discipline their slaves as the soul's best element, wisdom, disciplines the defective and weaker elements of the same soul, such as the lusts, the passions, and all other emotions.

For there is a kind of subjection that is not just. It exists when those who might be their own masters are subject to another; but when those are slaves [who cannot rule themselves, no injustice is done.]

ST. THOMAS AQUINAS

1 2 2 5 – 1 2 7 4

INTRODUCTION

Aquinas, a central figure in European theology and philosophy, was the son of the Count of Aquino, whose castle was located between Naples and Rome at a town of that name. At the age of 6 Aquinas went to school at the Benedictine abbey of Monte Casino, and at the age of 14 to the University of Naples, which had been founded by the Emperor a few years earlier. Aquinas's decision in 1244 to enter the Dominican order displeased his family and they confined him under guard for some months. Once released, he went first to Paris and then to Cologne to continue his studies as a Dominican under Albertus Magnus, a noted scientist and Aristotelian scholar. Four years later Aquinas returned to Paris to lecture on scripture and philosophy at the University. By 1256 he had been made a professor of theology in Paris, and he spent the next 3 years teaching and writing at a Dominican convent there. For most of the following decade he was a teacher of theology attached to the papal court as it took up residence in various Italian cities. During this period the Pope was still concerned, as his predecessor had been, at the influence that Aristotle's teachings, interpreted and transmitted by the Arabs, was exerting on Catholic teachers. So William of Moerbeke, a Dominican, undertook to retranslate most of Aristotle's works from Greek into Latin in order that Aquinas, who could not read Greek, could provide detailed commentaries on each of them from a suitably Catholic point of view. In this way Aristotle's *Politics* was first translated in 1260, to be followed later by a commentary that Aquinas left unfinished at his death.

For the 3 years from 1269 to 1271 Aquinas was in Paris, engaged in the Church's internal organizational struggles and attempting to combat Arabic Aristotelianism within the University. In 1272 he was sent to Naples to organize a House of Studies for the Dominican order. While doing this and teaching at the University he fell ill, underwent what seems to have been a mystical experience, and reported that his writings, including the immensely long and unfinished *Summa Theologiae* on which he was then working, were "so much straw compared with what I have seen and with what has been revealed to me." He died of fever the following year when he was traveling to France to participate in the Council of Lyons, leaving to us a great mass of interrelated works dealing with every branch of philosophy and theology, almost all of it written in the last 20 years of his life when he was deeply engaged in the administrative service of his order.

The book entitled *Justice* from which these selections are taken is the thirty-seventh of the many volumes that make up the *Summa Theologiae*, the comprehensive system of theology that Aquinas produced for the Catholic Church in the last 6 years of his life, 1268–1274. The English translation used is by Thomas Gilby, published by Eyre and Spottiswoode, London, 1975, and reprinted here with their permission.

SELECTIONS FROM
Summa Theologiae

Question 58: Justice

In discussing justice itself there are twelve points of inquiry:

1. what justice is;
2. whether it is always towards another;
3. whether it is a virtue;
4. whether it is seated in the will;
5. whether it is a general virtue;
6. whether as a general virtue it is essentially the same as every virtue;
7. whether there is a particular justice;
8. whether particular justice has its own proper matter;
9. whether it is about emotions or only about deeds;
10. whether the virtuous mean of justice is objectively real and impersonal;
11. whether the activity of justice is to render to each his own;
12. whether justice is the chief of the moral virtues.

ARTICLE 1. IS JUSTICE WELL DEFINED AS THE LASTING AND CONSTANT WILL OF RENDERING TO EACH ONE HIS RIGHT?

THE FIRST POINT: 1. It seems that the jurists have unfittingly so defined it. For, according to Aristotle, *justice is the habit which makes a man capable of doing what is just and of being just in resolve and action.* But *will* denotes a faculty, and also an act. Justice, then, is unsuitably defined as a will.

2. Besides, the will's rightness is not the will itself, for if it were no will would be perverse. Now, according to Anselm, *justice is rightness.* Therefore it is not will.

3. Also, God's will alone is lasting. Were justice a lasting will it would be solely in God, which is not true.

4. Moreover, whatever is lasting is constant because immutable. Redundant, then, to include both adjectives in the definition.

5. Again, to render right to each and everyone is for a ruler. If that is what justice does then it is only in a ruler. Which is awkward.

6. Further, Augustine writes that *justice is love serving God alone.* Consequently it does not render to each his due.

REPLY: The definition given is fitting if understood aright. Since every virtue is a principle of good activity, it has to be defined by that in a specific field of virtue. Now with respect to justice this is made up of deeds that bear on another, as will be shown later. So then the activity of justice in relation to its proper field and objective is touched on in the phrase, *rendering to each his right*; as Isidore remarks, *A man is called just because he safeguards right.*

Then for an act to be virtuous in any field whatever it has to be voluntary and to spring from a stable and firm disposition; Aristotle teaches that the requirements of a virtuous act are that it is done, first, knowingly, second, from choice and for a fitting end, and third, unwaveringly. The first is included in the second, since, as Aristotle says, *what is done in ignorance is involuntary.* Hence the definition starts with the *will* in order to show that the act of justice has to be voluntary, and qualifies this as *lasting and constant* in order to indicate the firmness of the act.

Accordingly it is a complete definition, even though it refers to the activity of justice rather than the habitual disposition; this last, however, is relative to the activity which specifically shapes it. If you want to cast it into the proper form of a definition, you can say that justice is the habit whereby a person with a lasting and constant will renders to each his due. This is much the same definition as that given by Aristotle, *Justice is a habit according to which a person is said to be active by choosing that which is right.*

Hence: 1. *Will* here refers to the activity, not the power. It is customary for an author to define habits by their activities; for instance Augustine writes that *faith is to believe what you do not see.*

2. Justice is not essentially identical with uprightness or righteousness; the two are related causally. We are treating it as a habit according to which a person wills and does aright.

3. A will may be called lasting in two ways. One with respect to the activity, and thus God's will alone is perpetual. The other with respect to its object, as when a man wills to do something always. And this is required for the quality of justice. It is not enough to wish to observe justice for the time being in some particular affair; indeed scarcely anybody could be found who willed to act unjustly in every case. What is required, however, is that a man has the will to preserve justice permanently and in all cases.

4. Since *lasting* is not understood to mean an everlasting duration of the will's activity, the addition of *constant* is not superfluous. A lasting will designates the purpose of keeping justice always, a constant will the firm perseverance in this resolve.

5. A judge renders a person his due by way of command and direction. According to the *Ethics* he is *living justice*, and a ruler is *the guardian of right.* Subjects, however, render this due by carrying it out.

6. As loving our neighbour is comprised in loving God, as we have explained, so rendering to each his due is comprised in serving God.

ARTICLE 2. IS JUSTICE ALWAYS TOWARDS ANOTHER?

THE SECOND POINT: 1. It seems not. St Paul says that the *justice of God is by faith in Jesus Christ.* Now the dealing of one man with another does not define faith. Nor, then, justice.

2. Further, because it serves God, Augustine writes that it is *for justice to command other things subject to man*. But the emotional appetite is subject to man, according to *Genesis, The lust thereof*, namely of sin, *shall be under you, and you shall have dominion over it*. To be master of one's own emotions, then, is a matter of justice. And so justice will operate towards oneself.

3. Besides, God's justice is eternal. But who other than God is co-eternal with him? Therefore it is not of the essence of justice to be relative to another.

4. Moreover, what a man does with himself needs to be straightened out as well as his dealings with another. This is through justice; *The justice of the upright shall straighten his path*. Therefore justice is about our doings in relation to ourselves as well as to others.

ON THE OTHER HAND, there is Cicero holding that the purpose of justice is to hold men together in companionable living in common. This implies a social relationship. Therefore justice is occupied only with our dealings with others.

REPLY: Since its very name spells an equalization, as we have noted, justice of its nature bears a relationship to another, for something is equal to another, not to itself. And since it is for justice to straighten human acts, as we have also taught, it must needs be that the otherness required is that between diverse beings capable of acting for themselves. Acts are done by whole and complete substances, not, properly speaking, by parts and forms and powers; except by analogy we do not speak of a hand striking or of heat making hot, but of a man striking with his hand or of fire making hot through its heat. So then justice requires a diversity of persons, and accordingly it is only of one man towards another. Nevertheless in one single man by analogy we can treat various principles of activity as though they were so many diverse agents, such as his reason and his emotional powers of desiring and of coping with difficulties. And so by a figure of speech justice is said to operate within one and the same man in that his reason commands his desirous and spirited emotions and these obey, and also in general that each of his parts is fittingly composed. Aristotle entitles this justice in the metaphorical sense of the term.

Hence: 1. The justice that works in us by faith is that through which the ungodly are justified; it lies, as we have seen when treating of justification, in the due order of the parts of the soul. This belongs to justice in its metaphorical sense, and it can be found even in a man who lives all by himself.

2. And so the reply to the second objection is clear.

3. God's justice is everlasting on the part of his eternal will and purpose; in this justice chiefly consists. Yet on the part of its effect, it is not everlasting, since nothing is co-eternal with God.

4. A man's actions with regard to himself are sufficiently straightened out when his emotions are ruled aright by the other moral virtues. His actions with regard to another, however, call for a special rightfulness in relation to the

other on which they bear, not only to his acting self. And so for such actions there is a special virtue, and this is justice.

ARTICLE 3. IS JUSTICE A VIRTUE?

THE THIRD POINT: 1. Apparently not. For it is written, *When you have done all that is commanded you, say, We are unworthy servants; we have only done what was our duty.* Now to do a virtuous deed is not unprofitable; Ambrose writes, *We look for a profit estimated not by pecuniary gain, but by reaching godliness.* Hence to do what we are bound to do is not virtuous. Yet such is a work of justice. Which, accordingly, is not virtue.

2. Further, that which is done under necessity is not meritorious. But to render a man his due, as justice requires, is of necessity. Therefore it is not meritorious. Yet it is by acts of virtue that we merit. Consequently, justice is not a virtue.

3. Besides, every moral virtue concerns our doings. But externally constituted things are not deeds we do but works we make, as is clear from Aristotle. Since then it is for justice to produce an external work that is just in itself, it seems that it is not a moral virtue.

ON THE OTHER HAND, there is Gregory holding that *the entire structure of morality rises from the four virtues*, namely prudence, justice, fortitude, and temperance.

REPLY: Human and moral virtue is that which makes a human act and the man himself good. And this applies to justice. For men's acts are good inasmuch as they reach the measure of reason, which is the norm of their rightness. Now since justice makes human acts right, it is clear that it makes them good. Cicero declares that *men are called good chiefly because of their justice*, and that *in justice above all shines the lustre of virtue.*

Hence: 1. When a man does his bounden duty he brings no profit to the person to whom it is owed, but only abstains from doing him a wrong. All the same he does profit himself in that he fulfils his duty with a spontaneous and ready will. Accordingly it is written that God's *wisdom teaches temperance and prudence and justice and fortitude, than which nothing is more profitable to men*, that is virtuous men.

2. There are two sorts of necessity: one, of force or constraint, and this, because it conflicts with voluntariness, takes away the quality of merit; the other is the obligation resulting from a command or of an indispensable means to an end, as when someone cannot achieve virtue without some particular deed. Such necessity does not rule out the quality of merit, inasmuch as a man does voluntarily what he is bound to do, though this rules out the credit of supererogation, according to St Paul, *If I preach the Gospel, that gives me no ground for glory, for a necessity is laid upon me.*

3. Justice is not engaged with the making precisely of external things, for

that is the function of art, but with how we use them in our dealings with others.

ARTICLE 4. IS JUSTICE SEATED IN THE WILL?

THE FOURTH POINT: 1. It would seem not. For being just is sometimes called being a truthful character. Now this lies in the mind, not the will. Therefore justice is not seated in the will.

2. Further, justice is about matters relative to another. Now to relate and order one to another is an act of reason. It is there that justice lies, rather than in the will.

3. Besides, since it is not designed for knowing, justice is not an intellectual virtue. We are left with it then as a moral virtue. Now moral virtue is located in those powers which share in the life of reason, namely in those of desirous and of spirited feeling, as appears from Aristotle. Therefore justice is located there, rather than in our will.

ON THE OTHER HAND, Anselm writes that *justice is rightness of will preserved for its own sake.*

REPLY: The seat of a virtue is that psychological faculty the activity of which the virtue aims to set right. Now justice is not set on directing any cognitive power; we are not said to be just because we know something correctly. Accordingly the seat of justice is not the intelligence or reason, which is a cognitive power. Well then, since we are called just in that we do something rightly, and since the immediate principle of doing is a conative or appetitive power, it must needs be that justice is seated in some power of that sort.

That power is twofold, namely of will, which is in the reason, and of feeling, which follows sense perception, and is divided into the emotive of desire and that of tackling the difficult, as we have explained in the *Prima Pars.* The act of rendering each his due cannot spring from the emotional appetite, because sense perception does not go so far as to look into the relationship of one thing to another; this is proper to reason. Therefore justice cannot be seated in the desirous or the spirited emotional powers, but only in the will. Accordingly Aristotle defines it, as we have seen, by an act of will.

Hence: 1. Since the will is the rational appetite, when the rightness of reason, which is said to be truth, is imprinted on it by its closeness to reason, it keeps the name of truth. And so justice sometimes is called truthfulness.

2. The will is borne towards its object after it is grasped by the reason. So then because the reason relates one thing to another, the will can bid something that serves another, which is the function of justice.

3. To share in the life of reason is not only for the conative or appetitive powers of desirous or spirited emotion but for our appetitive power entirely, as noted in the *Ethics*, since mind charges it all. Appetitive power includes the will, which, therefore, can be the seat of moral virtue.

ARTICLE 5. IS JUSTICE A GENERAL VIRTUE?

THE FIFTH POINT: 1. It would seem not. For justice is condivided with other species of virtue, as when Scripture says that wisdom *teaches temperance and prudence, justice and fortitude.* Now the general or generic is not classed together with or numbered among the species contained under it. Therefore justice is not a general virtue.

2. Again, as justice is counted a cardinal virtue, so also are fortitude and temperance. Yet they are not held to be general virtues. Neither, then, should justice be set down as a general virtue in any way.

3. Besides, we have agreed that justice is always towards another. Yet a sin against our neighbour is not a general sin, since it is condivided with a sin against oneself. It follows that justice also is not a general virtue.

ON THE OTHER HAND, Aristotle holds that *justice is all virtue.*

REPLY: As we have seen, justice directs a man in his relations with others. These fall under two heads, those with others considered as individuals and those with others as belonging to the community, inasmuch as he who serves the community serves all who come within it. Consequently justice in its proper meaning can cover both. Now clearly all who are contained in a community are related to it as parts to a whole. A part as such belongs to the whole, so that any good of the part can be subordinate to the good of the whole. Accordingly the value in each and every virtue, whether it composes a man in himself or whether it disposes him in relation to others, may be referred to the common good, to which justice orders us. In this way the acts of all the virtues can belong to justice in that it orders a man to the common good. It is in this sense that justice is called a general virtue. And since it is for law to regulate for the common good, as we have seen, such general justice is called legal justice, for thereby a person accords with law which directs acts of all the virtues to the common good.

Hence: 1. As grouped yet contrasted with the other virtues, justice is a special virtue, not a general virtue, as we shall see later on.

2. Fortitude and temperance are in the emotional appetite, that is in our spirited and desirous propensities respectively. These are affective or conative with respect to certain particular goods, and correspond to sensation which is cognitive of particulars. Whereas justice is in the rational appetite, which is able to love good as a universal or unrestricted value, which the mind apprehends. Consequently justice, rather than fortitude or temperance, can be a general virtue.

3. Matters which relate to oneself can be ordered to another, especially as regards the common good. Accordingly general or legal justice, as directing to the common good, may be called a general virtue. For the same reason so may injustice be called a general sin, according to the words, *All sin is lawlessness.*

ARTICLE 6: IS JUSTICE AS A GENERAL VIRTUE ESSENTIALLY THE SAME AS EVERY VIRTUE?

THE SIXTH POINT: 1. So it would seem. For Aristotle regards virtue and legal justice as identical with all virtue, though notionally different. Now a merely logical distinction does not constitute an essential difference. Therefore justice is essentially identical with every virtue.

2. Further, a virtue which is not essentially the same as all virtue is a section of virtue. How the justice we are talking about, according to Aristotle, is not a section but the whole of virtue. Hence it is essentially the same as every virtue.

3. Moreover, the nature of the habit does not change by the virtue being directed to a higher end; the specific character of the habit of temperance remains the same even though its activity be directed to a divine good. Now it is the function of general or legal justice to dispose the activities of all the moral virtues to a higher end, that is to the common good of the people, which transcends the good of one individual person. Therefore it is essentially the same as all virtue.

4. Also, any good of a part should be subordinate to the good of the whole, otherwise it would seem without point or purpose. This a virtuous deed cannot be. Apparently, then, you cannot have a virtuous deed that does not come under general justice, which sets it towards the common good. So then it seems that general justice is essentially identical with all virtue.

ON THE OTHER HAND, Aristotle observes that many are able to be virtuous in matters affecting themselves though not in matters relating to others. And again, that the virtue of a good man is not simply the same as that of a good citizen. This last is general justice, which governs our acts for the common good. Therefore it is not the same as ordinary personal virtue, indeed one can be possessed without the other.

REPLY: There are two manners in which something is said to be general, by predication and by power. First, by predication as a genus, thus *animal* is general or generic with respect to man and horse and the like; in this manner the general enters the essence of the subjects that come under the classification, since its genus is part of the essence of a species and falls within its definition. Second, by power or virtually, thus a universal cause is general to all its effects; the sun's energy, for instance, spreads to all bodies lit and transformed by it. The general in this manner does not have to enter the essence of its subjects, since cause and effect are not essentially identical.

To apply the distinction. It is in the second manner that we have spoken of justice as a general virtue, inasmuch as it orders the activities of other virtues to its own end by moving them by its command. For as charity may be called a general virtue because it sets the activities of all the virtues towards the divine good, so it is with legal or general justice which sets them towards the common good. And, to continue the comparison, as charity, which is centred on God's goodness as its proper object, is of its essence a special virtue, so general or legal justice, which regards the common good as its proper object, yet remains a special virtue in essence. As such it resides in the sovereign ruler chiefly and after the fashion of a master-art, and in subjects secondarily and as it were administratively.

All the same, though legal justice, if general by power, is a special virtue in essence, any virtue may be called by its name when ordered to the common good. And to speak in this sense, as Aristotle does, legal justice is one in essence with all virtue though notionally distinct.

Hence: 1 & 2. The replies to the first and second objections are clear.

3. This argument again takes legal justice for the virtue it commands.

4. Each virtue, considered in its own specific meaning, directs its activity to its own proper end. That it be directed to a further end, whether always or sometimes, comes from some superior virtue, not from its own special character. Hence the need for one sovereign moral virtue, essentially distinct from the rest of the moral virtues, which orders them to the common good: this is legal justice.

ARTICLE 7. BESIDES GENERAL JUSTICE IS THERE A PARTICULAR JUSTICE?

THE SEVENTH POINT: 1. It would seem not. For with the virtues, as with nature, there is nothing superfluous. Now general justice is enough to direct a man in his dealings with others. Needless, then, to postulate some particular justice.

2. Besides, the species of a virtue does not vary whether or not it engages one or many objects in number. Now, as we have agreed, legal justice orders a man to others in that they make up the many. Accordingly there is not another specific kind of justice relating to others as single individuals.

3. Again, between the individual and the political group comes the domestic group. If, then, in addition to general justice there be a particular justice respecting the individual, with equal reason there should be a domestic justice respecting the common welfare of one family. Yet this is not advanced. No more, then, should a particular justice apart from legal or general justice.

ON THE OTHER HAND, on the words, *Blessed are they that hunger and thirst after justice*, Chrysostom comments, *By justice the Lord signifies either the general virtue or the particular virtue opposed to the greed for possessions.*

REPLY: We have seen that legal justice, which directly charges a man with the common good, is not essentially identical with all virtue, and that there are other virtues which bear him directly to particular goods. These may relate either to himself or to another individual person. Accordingly, as besides legal justice other particular virtues are called for, which compose a man in himself, namely fortitude and temperance, so also is a particular justice, which orders his dealings with another individual person.

Hence: 1. Legal justice is indeed sufficient to govern us in our dealings with others, immediately when they comprise the common good, yet mediately in the case of the good of one individual person. Hence the need of a particular justice immediately engaged with this.

2. The common good of the State and the particular good of the individual person differ, not just quantitatively as the large and the little, but in kind; the meaning of the common good is other than that of an individual good, as the meaning of a whole is not that of a part. Accordingly Aristotle remarks that *they speak not well who maintain that the State and the home and like communities differ only as the many and the few and not in kind.*

3. In the *Politics* Aristotle distinguishes three ties in the household community, namely of husband and wife, father and son, and master and slave, in which one person belongs as it were to another. Consequently in this respect justice pure and simple does not obtain, but a kind of justice, namely domestic justice, as stated in the *Ethics.*

ARTICLE 8. HAS PARTICULAR JUSTICE A SPECIFIC SUBJECT-MATTER?

THE EIGHTH POINT: 1. Apparently not. *The fourth river is Euphrates*, on these words the Gloss comments, *Euphrates is translated 'fruitful', though it is not stated through which region it flows, because justice goes to all parts of the soul.* This would not be so were justice to have a specific subject-matter, confined to one special faculty. Hence particular justice has no special subject-matter.

2. Further, Augustine writes that *there are four virtues of the soul whereby it lives spiritually in this life, namely prudence, temperance, fortitude, and justice*, and he adds that *the fourth pervades them all.* Therefore particular justice, which is one of the four cardinal virtues, has no special subject-matter.

3. Besides, justice sufficiently directs a man in matters relating to others. They cover everything in our present social life. Therefore the subject-matter of justice is general, not special.

ON THE OTHER HAND, there is Aristotle postulating a particular justice engaged with our dealings in social intercourse.

REPLY: All whatsoever that can be ruled aright by reason are matters for moral virtue, which is defined by right reason, as Aristotle makes clear. The soul's inner feelings, its outward actions, and the outside things it makes use of, all can be ruled aright by reason. All the same it is through external actions and things, through which men mutually communicate, that the order of one to another is observed, whereas in a man's interior feelings you take note of his uprightness within himself. Since it is directed to others, justice consequently is not about the whole field of moral virtue, but only about external deeds and things, and these under a certain specific aspect, namely of the due co-ordination of one person with another.

Hence: 1. Of its nature justice belongs to one part of the soul, namely to the will where it is located. Yet the will sets in motion the other parts of the soul by its command. And so justice affects them, not directly, but by a kind of overflowing.

2. We have already seen how the cardinal virtues are taken in two senses. First, as special virtues having determinate subject-matters. Second, as signifying certain general modes of virtue. In this second sense Augustine speaks in the passage quoted; he goes on to say that *prudence is knowledge of what we should seek or avoid, temperance the curbing of lust for fleeting pleasure, fortitude the firmness of spirit against passing trials, and justice the love of God and our neighbour pervading the rest*, which, indeed, is the common root of our whole bearing towards others.

3. Our inner feelings, which are part of the matter of morality, of themselves are not directed on others. To ensure this is the special function of justice. Their effects, namely outer actions, are ordainable to others. Yet it does not follow thereby that the subject-matter of justice is general.

ARTICLE 9. IS JUSTICE ABOUT FEELINGS?

THE NINTH POINT: 1. So it would seem. For Aristotle regards moral virtue as being about pleasure and pain. Now we have agreed that both these are feelings. Since it is a moral virtue, justice is accordingly about our feelings.

2. Further, our dealings with others are put straight by justice. But this cannot be done unless our feelings are right, for if they are in disorder so also will be our dealings; sexual lust leads to adultery and excessive love of money to theft. Therefore justice must needs be about our feelings.

3. Again, particular justice is like legal justice in being engaged with others. Now legal justice is about our feelings, otherwise it would not cover all the virtues, some of which are clearly about our feelings. Therefore particular justice is about them too.

ON THE OTHER HAND, there is Aristotle, who holds that justice is about what we do.

REPLY: The truth of the matter appears on two counts. First, because the seat of justice is the will, the motions or acts of which are not emotions, feelings, or passions, as we have seen; it is only the motions of sensitive appetite that are called such. And so justice, unlike fortitude and temperance, which are of our spirited and desirous feelings, is not emotional. Second, to take the subject-matter of justice, namely our dealings with others; our feelings do not immediately relate to our being well-ordered here. And so justice is not about our feelings.

Hence: 1. Not every moral virtue is engaged with pleasures and pains as its subject-matter; fortitude, for instance, is about feelings of fear and aggression. Yet every moral virtue involves them as consequences or adjuncts, and, as Aristotle says in effect, they play a large part in telling us what is bad and what is good. In this way, too, they come into justice, for, as he also says, *there is not a just man who does not rejoice in just actions.*

2. External actions come midway as it were between external things, which are their material, and internal feelings or emotions, which are their sources. Sometimes it happens that there is a flaw in one but not in the other, as when a man steals another's property from the will to hurt him, not the greed to possess it, or conversely, when he covets it yet without the will to steal it. Accordingly our actions as bearing on external things are put right by justice, but as originating in our feelings they are put right by other moral virtues, which are about our emotions. And so justice stops the theft of another's property as upsetting the proper balance which should be maintained among external things, while liberality stops it as springing from immoderate greed for wealth. Yet since external actions get their specific character from the external things which are their objective interest rather than from the internal feelings with which they are performed, it follows that, to speak exactly, they are the subject-matter more of justice than of the other moral virtues.

3. The common good is the end or purpose of individual persons living in the community as the good of the whole is that of each part. Yet the good of one individual person is not the end or purpose of another. That is why general or legal justice, which is ordered to the common good, is more capable than particular justice, which is ordered to the good of another individual person, of extending to inner feelings affecting a man in himself. General and legal justice, all the same, covers the other virtues chiefly in respect of their outward deeds, in that, as noted in the *Ethics, the law commands the performance of works of a brave, or of a temperate, or of a gentle person.*

ARTICLE 10. IS THE VIRTUOUS MEAN OF JUSTICE OBJECTIVE AND OUTSIDE US?

THE TENTH POINT: 1. It seems not. For the meaning in a genus is preserved in a species. And a moral virtue is defined by Aristotle as a habit of choice which observes the mean determined by reason with respect to us. Therefore in justice also the mean is that of our reason, not of objective reality.

2. Besides, things quite simply good offer nothing that is too much or too little, and consequently there is nothing middling about them, as appears in the virtues, according to the *Ethics.* But justice is with things that are simply good, so it is taught in the *Ethics.* For justice, consequently, there is no objective middling course.

3. Also, why the other virtues are said to strike a mean of inner reason and not of outer reality is because the mean for them varies from person to

person; as Aristotle remarks, *too much for one is not enough for another.* This applies to justice as well, for the same penalty is not incurred by striking a ruler and by striking a private person. Therefore justice has a mean of reason, not an objective mean outside us.

ON THE OTHER HAND, Aristotle fixed the mean for justice according to arithmetical proportion, which strikes an objective mean in outside reality.

REPLY: As we have said the other moral virtues are engaged chiefly with our feelings, and their rightness is not gauged save in reference to the man who has them, namely according as he desires or reacts spiritedly as he should in the circumstances in which he finds himself. Hence the virtuous mean in their case is taken only with reference to the man of virtue himself, not by the proportion of one thing to another. On this account the mean for them is only a mean of reason relative to the psychology of the person acting.

The subject-matter of justice, however, is an external deed in so far as the doing or employing something is duly proportionate to another person. So therefore the mean of justice lies in a certain proportion matching or equalizing the external work to an external person. As stated in the *Metaphysics*, the equal is really the mean between the plus and the minus. Therefore justice strikes a mean in objective reality.

Hence: 1. The objectively real mean of justice is also the mean of reason, and so justice keeps the character of a moral virtue.

2. We speak of the simply good in two senses. First, to mean what is good all round; thus the virtues are good. And taken so there is middling and extremes with these values. Second, to mean what is good in the abstract, namely considered in its general nature, though in fact it may become evil by being abused; thus riches and honours as such. With these you can strike a mean between excess and defect with reference to the men who can use them either well or ill. And in this second sense justice is said to be about things which are simply good.

3. Inflicting an injury is differently proportioned to a ruler and to a private person. Consequently the equalization by retribution is different for the two cases. This implies a difference in the objective scale, not merely in subjective standards of reason.

ARTICLE 11. IS THE ACT OF JUSTICE TO RENDER EACH HIS DUE?

THE ELEVENTH POINT: 1. It seems not. For Augustine ascribes to justice *succouring the needy.* But we do this to others by giving them what is ours, not theirs. Therefore the act of justice is not rendering to each his due.

2. Again, Cicero says that *beneficence, which may be called benignity or liberality, belongs to justice.* Now it is for liberality to give what is our own, not another's. And so the act of justice is not to render to each his own.

3. Also, it is for justice, not only duly to dispense things, but also to

repress injurious actions, such as murder, adultery and the like. But rendering to each what is his own seems to relate only to the dispensing of things, and therefore does not adequately expose the characteristic activity of justice.

ON THE OTHER HAND, there is Ambrose, *It is justice that renders to each what is his and claims not what is another's; it disregards one's own profit in order to maintain a common equity.*

REPLY: As we have said, the subject-matter of justice is what we outwardly do, according as the doing or the thing we employ is proportionate to the other person who lays claim to our justice. Now each person's own is that which is due to him in proportion to making things even. That is why the proper activity of justice is none other than to render to each his own.

Hence: 1. Since justice is a cardinal virtue, other secondary virtues hinge on it, such as mercy, liberality, and the like, as we shall see later. And therefore to succour the needy, which is a work of mercy or compassion, and to be open-handedly beneficent, which is a work of liberality, come back in a sense to justice, which is the main virtue.

2. And so the reply to the second objection is clear.

3. As Aristotle says, the terms 'loss' and 'gain' are borrowed from dealings of voluntary exchange: there, to have more than one's own is called gain or profit, and to have less than one had at the outset is called loss, thus in buying and selling. The reason for this is that justice was first and is more commonly exercised in such exchanges, where 'loss' and 'gain' are properly employed, and are thence derived to all matters involving justice. The same applies to the phrase, 'rendering to each his due'.

ARTICLE 12. IS JUSTICE PRE-EMINENT AMONG THE MORAL VIRTUES?

THE TWELFTH POINT: 1. It would seem not. Because justice renders to another what belongs to him, whereas liberality gives of one's own, which is more virtuous. Therefore liberality is a higher virtue than justice.

2. Besides, nothing is adorned save by something worthier than itself. But Aristotle speaks of magnanimity as the adornment of justice and all the virtues. Therefore it is worthier than justice.

3. Also, virtue is engaged with the good and the difficult, as stated in the *Ethics.* Now fortitude, more than justice, is engaged with things difficult, that is with mortal dangers, according to the *Ethics.* Therefore it is more excellent than justice.

ON THE OTHER HAND, Cicero says that *justice is the most resplendent of the virtues, and gives its name to an upright man.*

REPLY: If we are speaking of general or legal justice, it is evident that justice outshines the other moral virtues, because the common good surpasses the individual good of one person. Accordingly Aristotle declares that justice is the most splendid virtue, and Morning or Evening Star are not so wonderful.

If we are speaking of particular justice, then it is distinguished among the other moral virtues on two counts. First, as regards its seat; it is in the nobler part of the soul, namely the rational appetite or will, whereas other moral virtues are in the sensitive appetite, the principle of the emotions which are the field of other moral virtues. Second, as regards its objective interest. The other virtues are commended only for the good they do their possessor, justice, however, for the good it does to another; Aristotle remarks how in a sense justice is another's good. And he also declares that *the greatest virtues must needs be the most decent to others, for virtue is a beneficent power. On this account the greatest honours are accorded the brave and the just; courage serves others in war, yet justice serves others in both war and peace.*

Hence: 1. Though by liberality one gives from one's own, the emphasis there is on the good of the giver's own virtue, whereas with the justice of rendering to another that which is his, it is on the social good. And furthermore justice is observed towards all, whereas liberality cannot be extended to all. Again, liberality, which gives of one's own, is based on justice, which safeguards the rights of each.

2. When magnanimity is added to justice the goodness of justice is increased. Yet without justice it would not have the character of virtue.

3. The more difficult and the better — fortitude is about the first, not the second. It serves only where there is conflict, whereas justice serves also in peace, as we have mentioned.

Question 61: Commutative and Distributive Justice

Here there are four points of inquiry:

1. whether there are two kinds of justice, commutative and distributive;
2. whether each strikes the virtuous mean in the same manner;
3. whether their subject-matter is uniform or manifold;
4. whether in each the just is identified with reciprocal give-and-take.

ARTICLE 1. ARE THE SPECIES OF JUSTICE WELL DIVIDED INTO COMMUTATIVE AND DISTRIBUTIVE?

THE FIRST POINT: 1. It would seem not. For that which is harmful to the many cannot be a species of justice, which serves the common good. Now it is harmful to the common good for the goods of the community to be distributed among the many, both because it would exhaust the common resources and because it would corrupt men's morals. Cicero says that *he who receives becomes worse, and ever more ready to receive more.* So therefore distribution is no part of any kind of justice.

2. Besides, we have agreed that the act of justice is to render to each what is his. But in distributing he does not receive what was his, instead there is newly appropriated to him something which belonged to the community. This is not a work of justice.

3. Again, we have agreed that justice is in subjects as well as in rulers. Yet distribution is the office always of a ruler. Therefore to be distributive is not part of justice.

4. Also, according to the *Ethics*, distributive justice is of community goods. These, however, are the concern of general or legal justice. Consequently distributive justice is a species of that, not of particular justice.

5. Further, being engaged with one or many does not make for a difference of kind in a virtue. Now commutative justice lies in rendering one person his due, distributive in giving something to the many. Therefore they are not different kinds or species of justice.

ON THE OTHER HAND, Aristotle assigns two parts to justice, and says that *one governs distributions and the other exchanges.*

REPLY: As we have seen, particular justice is directed towards the private person, who may be compared to the community as a part to a whole. Now with a part we may note a twofold relationship. First, that of one part to another, and this corresponds to the ordering of private persons among themselves. This is governed by commutative justice, which is engaged with their mutual dealings one with another. Second, that of the whole to a part, which goes with the bearing of the community on individual persons. This is governed by distributive justice which apportions proportionately to each his share from the common stock. And so there are two species of justice, namely commutative and distributive justice.

Hence: 1. A private person is commended for due moderation in his bountifulness, and blamed for squandering it in waste. So likewise should moderation be showed in dispensing community goods, and this is governed by distributive justice.

2. As a part and the whole are identical in a sense, so too in a sense that which is of the whole is also of a part. Accordingly when something is given to each from the goods of the community each in a way receives what is his own.

3. The act of distributing common goods is the office of him who is their guardian. Nevertheless distributive justice is also in subjects in that they are content with the fair sharing out. Yet note that distributive justice may be from the common goods of the family, not the State, and this dispensing can be done by the authority of a private person.

4. A movement gets its character from the term it arrives at. Accordingly general or legal justice aims to conduct the dealings of private persons to the

good of the community, whereas the reverse holds when that is brought to private persons; such distribution is a function of particular justice.

5. It is not merely the one and the many that gives rise to the distinction between commutative and distributive justice, it is also the difference between types or kinds of what is due, for somebody is entitled in one manner to what is his own, but in another to what is the community's.

ARTICLE 2. DO COMMUTATIVE AND DISTRIBUTIVE JUSTICE STRIKE THE JUST MEAN IN THE SAME FASHION?

THE SECOND POINT: 1. So it would seem. For we have agreed that both are contained under particular justice. Now all the specific parts of the moral virtues of fortitude and temperance take the virtuous mean in the same manner. So then also the commutative and distributive parts of justice.

2. Again, the shaping principle or form of a moral virtue consists in observing a mean determined by reason. Since, then, there is one and the same form in one virtue, it would seem that the virtuous mean is struck in the same manner by commutative and distributive justice alike.

3. Further, in distributive justice the mean is struck when attention is paid to differences of personal rank. But this is attended to in commutative justice, for instance, in imposing penalties, for a heavier sentence is incurred for offering violence to a ruler than to a private person. Both kinds of justice, then, are alike in taking the virtuous mean.

ON THE OTHER HAND, Aristotle holds that the mean is taken *in distributive justice according to geometrical proportion and in commutative justice according to arithmetical proportion.*

REPLY: We have said that distributive justice gives something to a private person in so far as something belonging to the community is due to a part. This is so much the more considerable in correspondence with the greater importance of the part in the whole. Consequently so much the more is given from the common stock as the recipient holds more responsibility in the community. Importance is assessed in an aristocracy by virtue, in an oligarchy by wealth, in a democracy by liberty, and in other régimes variously. So then the virtuous mean is taken in distributive justice, not according to an equality between thing and thing, but according to a proportion between things and persons, and in such a way that even as one person exceeds another so also that which is meted out to him exceeds that which is meted out to the other. Accordingly Aristotle describes the mean here as being *according to geometric proportionality*, in which the even balance or equality lies in a comparative relation, not in a fixed quantity. Thus we reckon that 6 is to 4 as 3 is to 2; in each case the proportion is 1 · 5, since the greater number is the sum of the smaller plus a half. The excess is not, however, of simple quantity, since 6 exceeds 4 by 2, whereas 3 exceeds 2 by 1.

It is otherwise in exchanges between persons. There something is rendered to an individual person in return for something of his that has been received: this most evidently appears in buying and selling, from which originates the notion of an exchange. There the balance or equilization of thing with thing is called for, so that a man should repay the other as much as he gains in acquiring the thing which belonged to the other. Here the equality will be according to arithmetical mean, which lies between an equal plus and minus of quantities. Thus 5 is the mean between 6 and 4, since it exceeds the first and is exceeded by the second by 1. If each has 5 to start with, and one receives 1 from what belongs to the other, he will have 6 and the other will be left with 4. Justice will be served when both are brought back to the mean, by 1 being taken from the one who has 6 and given to the other who has 4. Then both will have 5, which is the mean.

Hence: 1. With the other moral virtues the mean is taken according to right reason with respect to the doer, not to outside things. Justice, however, strikes this latter objective medium, and, consequently, in diverse fashions corresponds to the diversity in social reality.

2. Equality is the general shaping form of justice, and here both distributive and commutative justice agree, but in the first it is taken according to geometrical proportionality, while in the second according to arithmetical.

3. In the give-and-take of action and passion among men the quality of a person involved affects the quantity or size of the thing done; striking a ruler offers greater injury than striking a private person. Yet with distributive justice what counts is the quality or station of a person considered in itself, whereas with commutative justice it lies in a diversification arising from the objective condition of that which is owing.

ARTICLE 3. IS THE SUBJECT-MATTER DIVERSE FOR EACH KIND OF JUSTICE?

THE THIRD POINT: 1. Apparently not. For a diversity of matter makes a diversity of virtue, as is clear in the case of fortitude and temperance. Were distributive justice and commutative justice to have diverse subject-matters, they would not be contained under one virtue, namely justice.

2. Further, the dispensing, with which distributive justice is engaged, according to the *Ethics* is of money or honours or whatever can be apportioned to members of the community. These also are matters of exchanges between persons, and thus are the concern of commutative justice. Therefore the matters of distributive and commutative justice are not diverse.

3. Again, if the reason alleged for the difference of their subject-matters is the specific difference between distributive and commutative justice, then if there is no such specific difference the need for a difference of subject-matters will not arise. Now, though holding that commutative justice is one species of virtue, Aristotle admits that its subject-matter is manifold. It would not seem, then, that the two kinds of justice have different subject-matters.

ON THE CONTRARY, it is stated in the *Ethics that one kind of justice is the governing virtue in distributions and another kind in exchanges.*

REPLY: We have said that justice is engaged with certain external activities concerning distributions and exchanges. These consist in the application or use of what is outside us, whether things or persons or works we do. Things, as when we take from or restore to another his property; persons, as when we strike or insult another or, alternatively, treat him with respect; works, as when we justly claim another's labour or do a job for him. Now if we take as subject-matter what each kind of justice employs, then there is no difference between them, for things of the same sort can be apportioned out of the common stock and be also exchanged between individuals, and likewise hard work can be a matter both of allotment by the community and also of repayment according to private contract. If, however, in the subject-matter of the two kinds of justice we stress the dominant for each in dealing with persons, using things, and performing works, then there is a difference on either side. For distributive justice governs the apportioning of community goods, whereas commutative governs the exchanging that may take place between two persons.

Of these exchanges some are involuntary, some voluntary. They are involuntary when somebody employs another's thing, person, or work without his consent. This may be done secretly by deceit or openly by violence. In either way injury may be committed against another's property or person or against the person of one close to him. Against his property: if taken secretly it is called theft, if openly it is called robbery. Against his person, if his life and health be attacked, and also his good-name and dignity: the first may be done secretly, as when he is treacherously slain, struck, or poisoned, or openly, as when he is publicly executed, struck, maimed, or sent to prison. His dignity is injured secretly by false witness, detraction, and the like, whereby he is robbed of his good name; it is done openly by accusation in a court of law or public insult. Against the person of a connection of his, as when he is injured by adultery with his wife, which is usually secret, or by the enticement of a servant; it can also be done openly. Whatever injury may be done to the principal victim under the headings outlined above may also be done to persons connected with him. Yet adultery and enticement are injuries properly against him, and the latter, since a servant in a sense is his belonging, comes back to theft.

Exchanges are called voluntary when a person willingly transfers something he owns to another. If he simply passes it to another in such wise that the recipient incurs no strict debt, as when he makes a gift, this is an act of liberality, not of justice. A voluntary transfer comes under justice in so far as it involves the notion of something due. This can enter in several ways. First, when somebody simply transfers what is his in payment for something else, as happens in buying and selling. Second, when somebody transfers a thing he owns that another may have the use of it with the obligation of returning it later: if the use is granted without charge, then for things that bear fruit it is called usufruct, and for things that do not, such as cash, crockery, and so forth, it is called borrowing or lending. If there is a charge on the use, it is called renting or hiring. Third, when somebody hands over his property for safekeeping, not for use, and means to recover it, as with a deposit, or because of an obligation, as when he pledges a piece of property or stands surety for another.

In all dealings of this sort, whether involuntary or voluntary, the just mean is taken in the same sense according to a balance or equality in requital. Accordingly they all come under the same species of justice, namely commutative justice.

Hence: The reply to the objections is clear.

ARTICLE 4. IS THE JUST SIMPLY THE SAME AS THE RECIPROCAL?

THE FOURTH POINT: 1. So it would seem. For the divine judgment is purely and simply just, and this is the form it follows, that as a person does so shall he suffer; *With the judgment you pronounce you will be judged, and the measure you give will be the measure you get.* Therefore the just simply is the same as the reciprocal.

2. Further, in either kind of justice something is rendered to a person according to a certain equivalence. With distributive justice this regards his worth, which is weighed by his works in the service of the community; with commutative justice this regards the thing in which he has suffered loss. Both demand requital for what has been done. So then it seems that the just simply is the same as the reciprocal.

3. Besides, the chief reason why a man should not get what he gives seems to lie with the difference between involuntary and voluntary action; he who does an injury involuntarily suffers the lighter penalty. But voluntary and involuntary are terms qualifying what is done on our side, and do not affect the just mean, which is a measure in reality, not merely according to our frame of mind. Consequently the just simply seems the same as the reciprocal.

ON THE OTHER HAND, there is Aristotle proving that the just does not always coincide with the reciprocal.

REPLY: The term *contrapassum*, literally 'counter-suffered', spells an exact concordance of a reaction with the antecedent action. Such a tit-for-tat most properly applies when injury is undergone caused by a man harming the person of his neighbour, for instance if he strike him let him be struck in return. The Old Law determines such a just requital; *If any harm follows, you shall give life for life, eye for eye, tooth for tooth,* and so forth. In the second place, because to take from another his property is a thing unjust, the notion of retaliation also applies there, so that one who inflicts loss on another should also suffer loss in his belongings. This, too, is contained in the Old Law; *If a man steals an ox or a sheep, and kills it or sells it, he shall pay five oxen for an ox, and four sheep for a sheep.* Finally, the notion is extended to voluntary exchanges, where there is something done and undergone on either side. Remember, however, that the passive character of undergoing something is lessened by its voluntariness. In all such cases the nature of commutative justice demands that equivalent recompense be made, namely that the reaction as repayment matches the action.

This would not always be the case were the doer to undergo the same in kind to that which he caused. Take the case, to begin with, of a subordinate who injures his superior; his action is more serious than a like action done on him in return. And so he who strikes a ruler is not only struck back, but also much more severely punished. Then take the case of one who unjustly takes another's property without the owner's consent; his action would exceed his undergoing the consequences were only that property to be taken away from him, for he who inflicted loss on another would suffer no loss of property in return. In consequence he is punished by a fine heavier than the simple disgorgement of his gain, for he did an injury, not only to a private person, but also to the commonwealth by breaking the security which is in its charge. So too neither in voluntary exchanges is requital always the give and return of things of the same sort, for sometimes they are unequal. Consequently in exchanges the equalization of what is done and what is undergone in return requires a certain proportionate standard of measurement: for this purpose was money invented. It is in this sense that a *quid pro quo* is what is right and just for commutative justice.

Note, however, that in distributive justice such reciprocity has no place, for the equalization is not taken there according to the proportion of thing to thing, or of doing an action to undergoing the reaction (whence the term *contrapassum*), but according to the proportionality of things to persons, as already explained.

Hence: 1. Divine judgment follows the form of commutative justice in that reward is the recompense of merit, and punishment that of sin.

2. When a man who has served the community is requited for his services, that is an act of commutative, not distributive justice. For distributive justice considers the correspondence, not between that which is spent and that which is received, but between that which is received by one and by another in accordance with their respective degrees.

3. The injury is augmented when the injurious action is voluntary, and is treated accordingly as a more important thing. Hence it calls for greater punishment in recompense. The difference is not in our thinking merely, but also in objective reality.

NICCOLÒ MACHIAVELLI

1 4 6 9 – 1 5 2 7

INTRODUCTION

Machiavelli, whose name has been used for hundreds of years to refer to the approval of unscrupulous political action, was a highly honorable man who was himself the victim of the sort of political deceit, corruption, and violence that his writings have often been thought to advocate. His father, a lawyer in Florence, came from an old and noble family, and since the mother of Niccolò also seems to have been educated, it is likely that he was well taught in literature, philosophy, Latin, and law. From the age of 20–29 he worked in Rome, employed in the banking business of a fellow Florentine. A few years after the death of his former employer, Machiavelli succeeded in becoming administrative secretary to the governing council of Florence and held the post until the Spanish army overthrew the republic some 14 years later. Since he had been on many diplomatic missions for the republic, had given its governor, a close friend of his, much political advice, and was thought by the conquerors to be a possible conspirator against them, Machiavelli was dismissed from his post, arrested, and tortured, but released shortly afterward. He then retired from public life to his modest family property for the next 6 years in an effort to provide for his wife and six children.

By 1518 Machiavelli was giving public readings of his written work, especially the *Discourses* and the *Art of War*. The latter was the only one of Machiavelli's four important books on politics to be published during his lifetime. *The Prince*, the *History of Florence*, and *Discourses* were published a few years after his death. In the last period of his life he was given an annual grant by the Pope to write the history of Florence and was also given the task of improving the fortification of that city. Unfortunately, in 1527 the army of the Holy Roman Empire captured and pillaged Rome, and the Pope, Machiavelli's benefactor, was taken prisoner. At the same time, the papal government of Florence was overthrown and Florence was once again proclaimed a republic. Although Machiavelli had long been known as a republican, he gained nothing by the change of government since he had carried out work for the previous, and much disliked, rulers.

Shortly after the coup, Machiavelli became ill with a stomach complaint and died, leaving his family in poverty. Although he had been constantly disappointed and frustrated in his life-long ambition to play an important political role in his native city, the commentaries and analyses he produced as a substitute have long made his readers grateful that he was forced to write about politics rather than simply engage in it.

The Discourses on the First Ten Books of Titus Livius is Machiavelli's fullest discussion of his views on the practice of politics and government, and on the theories that should guide that practice. It was written, apparently, in much the same period as *The Prince*, 1513–1519. But whereas the latter is a brief handbook for the use of rulers, the former is an extended commentary on the first 10 of the 35 books that remain to us of Livy's history of Rome, the other 107 books having been lost some time after his death in 17 A.D. The present translation of *The Discourses* is by L. J. Walker, published by Routledge & Kegan Paul, London, 1950, and used here by their permission. The translation of *The Prince* is by W. K. Marriott, published by J. M. Dent & Sons, London, 1908, and the selections reprinted here are used with their permission.

SELECTIONS FROM
The Discourses of the First Ten Books of Titus Livius

Book I The Best Form of Government

3
WHAT KIND OF EVENTS GAVE RISE IN ROME TO THE CREATION OF TRIBUNES OF THE PLEBS, WHEREBY THAT REPUBLIC WAS MADE MORE PERFECT

All writers on politics have pointed out, and throughout history there are plenty of examples which indicate, that in constituting and legislating for a commonwealth it must needs be taken for granted that all men are wicked and that they will always give vent to the malignity that is in their minds when opportunity offers. That their evil dispositions often do not show themselves for a time is due to a hidden cause which those fail to perceive who have had no experience of such contrariness; but in time — which is said to be the father of all truth — it reveals itself.

After the expulsion of the Tarquins there appeared to be in Rome the utmost harmony between the plebs and the senate. The nobles seemed to have set aside their pride, to have become imbued with the same spirit as the populace, and to be bearable by all, even by the meanest. In this neither their deception nor the cause of it was apparent so long as the Tarquins lived; for the nobility were afraid of them and feared that, if they treated the plebs badly, it would not be friendly towards them, but would make common cause with the Tarquins, so they treated the plebs with consideration. But, no sooner were the Tarquins dead and the fears of the nobility removed, than they began to vomit forth against the plebs the poison hid in their hearts and to oppress them in every way they could.

This bears out what has been said above, namely, that men never do good unless necessity drives them to it; but when they are free to choose and can do just as they please, confusion and disorder become everywhere rampant. Hence it is said that hunger and poverty make men industrious, and that laws make them good. There is no need of legislation so long as things work well without it, but, when such good customs break down, legislation forthwith becomes necessary. Hence when the regime of the Tarquins collapsed and the nobility were no longer kept in check by the fear of them, it became necessary to devise some new institution which should produce the same effect as the Tarquins had done in their time. Wherefore, after many disturbances, rumours, and dangers of scandal had been occasioned by the squabbles between the plebs and the nobility, for the security of the former tribunes came to be appointed, and were invested with such prerogatives and standing that henceforth they could always mediate between the plebs and the senate and curb the arrogance of the nobility.

4

That Discord between the Plebs and the Senate of Rome Made This Republic Both Free and Powerful

I must not fail to discuss the tumults that broke out in Rome between the death of the Tarquins and the creation of the tribunes, nor yet to mention certain facts which militate against the view of those who allege that the republic of Rome was so tumultuous and so full of confusion that, had not good fortune and military virtue counterbalanced these defects, its condition would have been worse than that of any other republic. I by no means deny that fortune and military organisation had a good deal to do with Rome's empire, but it seems to me that this view fails to take account of the fact that where military organisation is good there must needs be good order, and that rarely does it happen that good fortune does not also accompany it.

There are also other points to be observed in connection with this city. To me those who condemn the quarrels between the nobles and the plebs, seem to be cavilling at the very things that were the primary cause of Rome's retaining her freedom, and that they pay more attention to the noise and clamour resulting from such commotions than to what resulted from them, i.e. to the good effects which they produced. Nor do they realise that in every republic there are two different dispositions, that of the populace and that of the upper class and that all legislation favourable to liberty is brought about by the clash between them.

It is easy to see that this was the consequence in Rome; for from the days of the Tarquins to those of the Gracchi, which was more than three hundred years in Rome very seldom led to banishment, and still more seldom to bloodshed. One cannot, therefore, regard such tumults as harmful, nor such a republic as divided, seeing that during so long a period it did not on account of its discords send into exile more than eight or ten citizens, put very few to death, and did not on many impose fines. Nor can a republic reasonably be stigmatised in any way as disordered in which there occur such striking examples of virtue, since good examples proceed from good education, good education from good laws, and good laws in this case from those very tumults which many so inconsiderately condemn; for anyone who studies carefully their result, will not find that they occasioned any banishment or act of violence inimical to the common good, but that they led to laws and institutions whereby the liberties of the public benefited.

But, someone may object, the means used were extraordinary and almost barbaric. Look how people used to assemble and clamour against the senate, and how the senate decried the people who ran helter-skelter about the streets, how the shops were closed and how the plebs *en masse* would troop out of Rome—events which terrify all who read about them, not to mention others. To which I answer that every city should provide ways and means whereby the ambitions of the populace may find an outlet, especially a city which proposes to avail itself of the populace in important undertakings. The city of Rome was one of those which did provide such ways and means in that, when the populace wanted a law passed, it either behaved in some such way as we have described or it refused to enlist for the wars, so that, to placate it, it had to some extent to be satisfied.

The demands of a free populace, too, are very seldom harmful to liberty, for they are due either to the populace being oppressed or to the suspicion that it is going to be oppressed, and, should these impressions be false, a remedy is provided in the public platform on which some man of standing can get up, appeal to the crowd, and show that it is mistaken. And though, as Tully remarks, the populace may be ignorant, it is capable of grasping the truth and readily yields when a man, worthy of confidence, lays the truth before it.

Critics, therefore, should be more sparing in finding fault with the government of Rome, and should reflect that the excellent results which this republic obtained could have been brought about only by excellent causes. Hence if tumults led to the creation of the tribunes, tumults deserve the highest praise, since, besides giving the populace a share in the administration, they served as the guardian of Roman liberties, as we shall show in the next chapter.

5
WHETHER THE SAFEGUARDING OF LIBERTY CAN BE MORE SAFELY ENTRUSTED TO THE POPULACE OR TO THE UPPER CLASS; AND WHICH HAS THE STRONGER REASON FOR CREATING DISTURBANCES, THE 'HAVE-NOTS' OR THE 'HAVES'

Those who have displayed prudence in constituting a republic have looked upon the safeguarding of liberty as one of the most essential things for which they had to provide, and according to the efficiency with which this has been done liberty has been enjoyed for a longer or a shorter time. And, since in every republic there is an upper and a lower class, it may be asked into whose hands it is best to place the guardianship of liberty. By the Lacaedemonians, and in our day by Venice, it was entrusted to the nobles, but by the Romans it was entrusted to the plebs.

It is necessary, therefore, to enquire which of these republics made the better choice. If we appeal to reason arguments may be adduced in support of either thesis; but, if we ask what the result was, the answer will favour the nobility, for the freedom of Sparta and of Venice lasted longer than did that of Rome.

Let us deal first with the appeal to reason. It may be urged in support of the Roman view that the guardianship of anything should be placed in the hands of those who are less desirous of appropriating it to their own use. And unquestionably if we ask what it is the nobility are after and what it is the common people are after, it will be seen that in the former there is a great desire to dominate and in the latter merely the desire not to be dominated. Consequently the latter will be more keen on liberty since their hope of usurping dominion over others will be less than in the case of the upper class.

So that if the populace be made the guardians of liberty, it is reasonable to suppose that they will take more care of it, and that, since it is impossible for them to usurp power, they will not permit others to do so.

On the other hand, the defenders of the Spartan and Venetian systems say that to place the guardianship in the hands of the powerful has two good results. First, it satisfies their ambition more, since with this stick in their hands, they play a more important part in the republic, and so should be more contented. Secondly, it prevents the restless minds of the plebs from acquiring a sense of power, which is the cause of endless squabbles and trouble in a republic, and is enough to drive the nobility to despair which in course of time has disastrous results. They cite as an instance Rome itself, where, when the plebs through their tribunes got this power into their hands, they were not content with one plebeian consul, but wanted to have both. After which they demanded the censorship, the praetorship, and all the other great offices in the city. Nor did this satisfy them, but, impelled by the same mad desire,they began later on to worship any men they saw were strong enough to get the better of the nobility. Whence arose the power of Marius and Rome's undoing. It must be confessed, then, if due weight be given to both sides, that it still remains doubtful which to select as the guardians of liberty, for it is impossible to tell which of the two dispositions we find in men is more harmful in a republic, that which seeks to maintain an established position or that which has none but seeks to acquire it.

All things considered, however, and due distinctions being made, we shall arrive in the end at this conclusion. Either you have in mind a republic that looks to founding an empire, as Rome did; or one that is content to maintain the *status quo*. In the first case it is necessary to do in all things as Rome did. In the second case it is possible to imitate Venice and Sparta, as will be explained in the next chapter.

Turning now to the question as to which are more harmful in a republic, the 'have-nots' who wish to have or the 'haves' who are afraid of losing what they have, I would point out that when Marcus Menenius was appointed dictator and Marcus Fulvius master of horse, both of them plebeians, in order to investigate certain conspiracies formed in Capua against Rome, the people empowered them to enquire also about those in Rome who, moved by ambition, had sought to obtain the consulship and other posts in the city by other than the accepted methods. To the nobility it looked as if the authority thus vested in the dictator was a hit at them, so they spread it about in Rome that it was not the nobles who had ambitioned these positions and used out of the way means to get them, but commoners who, having neither blood nor virtue on which to rely, sought to obtain these posts by roundabout methods, and in particular they accused the dictator of this. So much weight was attached to this accusation that Menenius, having made a speech in which he refuted the calumnies spread by the nobles, resigned the dictatorship, and submitted his actions to the judgment of the people. He defended his own case and was acquitted.

At the trial there arose considerable discussion as to whether the 'haves' or the 'have-nots' were the more ambitious, for the appetites of both might easily become the cause of no small disturbance. Actually, however, such disturbances are more often caused by the 'haves', since the fear of losing what they have arouses in them the same inclination we find in those who want to get more, for men are inclined to think that they cannot hold securely what they possess unless they get more at others' expense. Furthermore, those who have great possessions can bring about changes with greater effect and greater speed. And yet again their corrupt and grasping deportment arouses in the minds of the 'have-nots' the desire to have, either to revenge themselves on those who have despoiled them, or that they may again share in those riches and honours in regard to which they deem themselves to have been badly used by the other party.

6

WHETHER IN ROME SUCH A FORM OF GOVERNMENT COULD HAVE BEEN SET UP AS WOULD HAVE REMOVED THE HOSTILITY BETWEEN THE POPULACE AND THE SENATE

We have just been discussing the effects produced by the controversies between the populace and the senate. Now, since these controversies went on until the time of the Gracchi when they became the causes which led to the destruction of liberty, it may occur to some to ask whether Rome could have done the great things she did without the existence of such animosities. Hence it seems to me worth while to enquire whether it would have been possible to set up in Rome a form of government which would have prevented these controversies. In order to discuss this question it is necessary to consider those republics which have been free from such animosities and tumults and yet have enjoyed a long spell of liberty, to look at their governments, and to ask whether they could have been introduced into Rome.

Amongst ancient states Sparta is a case in point, and amongst modern states Venice, as I have already pointed out. Sparta set up a king and a small senate to govern it. Venice did not distinguish by different names those who took part in its government, but all who were eligible for administrative posts were classed under one head and called gentry. This was due to chance rather than to the prudence of its legislators; for many people having retired to those sandbanks on which the city now stands and taken up their abode there for the reasons already assigned, when their numbers grew to such an extent that it became necessary for them to make laws if they were to live together, they devised a form of government. They had frequently met together to discuss the city's affairs, so, when it seemed to them that the population was sufficient to form a body politic, they decided that all new-comers who meant to reside there, should not take part in the government. Then, when in course of time they found that there were quite a number of inhabitants in the place who were disbarred from government, with an eye to the reputation of those who governed they called them gentlefolk and the rest commoners.

Such a form of government could arise and be maintained without tumult because, when it came into being, whoever then dwelt in Venice was admitted to the government, so that no one could complain. Nor had those who came to dwell there later on and found the form of government firmly established, either cause or opportunity to make a commotion. They had no cause because they had been deprived of nothing. They had no opportunity because the government had the whip-hand and did not employ them in matters which would enable them to acquire authority. Besides, there were not many who came later to dwell in Venice, nor were they so numerous as to upset the balance between rulers and ruled; for the number of gentlefolk was either equal to, or greater than, that of the newcomers. These, then, were the causes which enabled Venice to set up this form of government and to maintain it without disruption.

Sparta, as I have said, was governed by a king and by a small senate. It was able to maintain itself in this way for a long time, because in Sparta there were few inhabitants and access to outsiders desirous of coming to dwell there was forbidden. Moreover, it had adopted the laws of Lycurgus and shared in his repute, and, as these laws were observed, they removed all occasion for tumult, so that the Spartans were able to live united for a long time. The reason was that the laws of Lycurgus prescribed equality of property and insisted less on equality of rank. Poverty was shared by all alike, and the plebeians were without ambition, since offices in the city were open but to few citizens and from them the plebs were kept out; nor did it desire to have them since the nobles never ill treated the plebs. This was due to the position assigned to the Spartan kings, for, since in this principality they were surrounded by nobles, the best way of maintaining their position was to protect the plebs from injustice. It thus came about that the plebs neither feared authority nor desired to have it, and, since they neither feared it nor desired it, there was no chance of rivalry between them and the nobility, nor any ground for disturbances, and they could live united for a long time. It was, however, mainly two things which brought this union about: (i) the smallness of Sparta's population, which made it possible for a few to rule, and (ii) the exclusion of foreigners from the state, which gave it no chance either to become corrupt or to become so unwieldy that it could no longer be managed by the few who governed it.

All things considered, therefore, it is clear that it was necessary for Rome's legislators to do one of two things if Rome was to remain tranquil like the aforesaid states: either to emulate the Venetians and not employ its plebs in wars, or, like the Spartans, not to admit foreigners. Rome did both these things, and, by doing so, gave to its plebs alike strength, increase, and endless opportunities for commotion. On the other hand, had the government of Rome been such as to bring greater tranquility, there would have ensued this inconvenience, that it would have been weaker, owing to its having cut off the source of supply which enabled it to acquire the greatness at which it arrived, so that, in seeking to remove the causes of tumults, Rome would have removed also the causes of expansion.

So in all human affairs one notices, if one examines them closely, that it is impossible to remove one inconvenience without another emerging. If, then, you want to have a large population and to provide it with arms so as to establish a great empire, you will have made your population such that you cannot now handle it as you please. While, if you keep it either small or unarmed so as to be able to manage it, and then acquire dominions, either you will lose your hold on it or it will become so debased that you will be at the mercy of anyone who attacks you. Hence in all discussions one should consider which alternative involves fewer inconveniences and should adopt this as the better course; for one never finds any issue that is clear cut and not open to question. Rome might indeed have emulated Sparta, have appointed a prince for life, and have made its senate small; but it would not in that case have been able to avoid increasing its population with a view to establishing a great empire; nor would the appointment of a king for life and of a small number of senators have been of much help in the matter of unity.

Should, then, anyone be about to set up a republic, he should first enquire whether it is to expand, as Rome did, both in dominion and in power, or is to be confined to narrow limits. In the first case it is essential to constitute it as Rome was constituted and to expect commotions and disputes of all kinds which must be dealt with as best they can, because without a large population, and this well armed, such a republic will never be able to grow, or to hold its own should it grow. In the second case it might be constituted as Sparta and Venice were, but, since expansion is poison to republics of this type, it should use every endeavour to prevent it from expanding, for expansion, when based on a weak republic, simply means ruin. This happened both in Sparta's case and in that of Venice. For of these republics the first, after having subjugated almost the whole of Greece, revealed, on an occasion of slight importance in itself, how weak its foundation was, since, when Thebes revolted at the instigation of Pelopidas and other cities followed suit, this republic entirely collapsed. In like manner Venice, having occupied a large part of Italy, most of it not by dint of arms, but of money and astute diplomacy, when its strength was put to the test, lost everything in a single battle.

I am firmly convinced, therefore, that to set up a republic which is to last a long time, the way to set about it is to constitute it as Sparta and Venice were constituted; to place it in a strong position, and so to fortify it that no one will dream of taking it by a sudden assault; and, on the other hand, not to make it so large as to appear formidable to its neighbours. It should in this way be able to enjoy its form of government for a long time. For war is made on a commonwealth for two reasons: (i) to subjugate it, and (ii) for fear of being subjugated by it. Both these reasons are almost entirely removed by the aforesaid precautions; for, if it be difficult to take by assault owing to its being well organised for defence, as I am presupposing, rarely or never will it occur to anyone to seize it. And, if it be content with its own territory, and it becomes clear by experience that it has no ambitions, it will never occur to anyone to attack it for fear it may make war on them, especially if by its constitution or by its laws expansion is prohibited. Nor have I the least doubt that, if this balance could be maintained, there would be genuine political life and real tranquility in such a city.

Since, however, all human affairs are ever in a state of flux and cannot stand still, either there will be improvement or decline, and necessity will lead you to do many things which reason does not recommend. Hence if a commonwealth be constituted with a view to its maintaining the *status quo*, but not with a view to expansion, and by necessity it be led to expand, its basic principles will be subverted and it will soon be faced with ruin. So, too, should heaven, on the other hand, be so kind to it that it has no need to go to war, it will then come about that idleness will either render it effeminate or give rise to factions; and these two things, either in conjunction or separately, will bring about its downfall.

Wherefore, since it is impossible, so I hold, to adjust the balance so nicely as to keep things exactly to this middle course, one ought, in constituting a republic, to consider the possibility of its playing a more honourable role, and so to constitute it that, should necessity actually force it to expand, it may be able to retain possession of what it has acquired. Coming back, then, to the first point we raised, I am convinced that the Roman type of constitution should be adopted, not that of any other republic, for to find a middle way between the two extremes I do not think possible. Squabbles between the populace and the senate should, therefore, be looked upon as an inconvenience which it is necessary to put up with in order to arrive at the greatness of Rome. For, besides the reasons already adduced to show that the authority of the tribunes was essential to the preservation of liberty, it is easy to see what benefit a republic derives when there is an authority that can bring charges in court, which was amongst the powers vested in the tribunes, as will be shown in the following chapter.

7

How Necessary Public Indictments Are for the Maintenance of Liberty in a Republic

No authority more useful and necessary can be granted to those appointed to look after the liberties of a state than that of being able to indict before the people or some magistrate or court such citizens as have committed any offence prejudicial to the freedom of the state. Such an institution has two consequences most useful in a republic. First, for fear of being prosecuted, its citizens attempt nothing prejudicial to the state, and, if they do attempt anything, are suppressed forthwith without respect to persons. Secondly, an outlet is provided for that ill feeling which is apt to grow up in cities against some particular citizen, however it comes about; and, when for such ill feeling there is no normal outlet, recourse is had to abnormal methods likely to bring disaster on the republic as a whole. Hence nothing does so much to stabilise and strengthen a republic as some institution whereby the changeful humours which agitate it are afforded a proper outlet by way of the laws.

This can be shown by numerous examples, and especially by one that Titus Livy adduces, namely, that of Coriolanus. Livy tells us that, when the nobility were annoyed with the plebs because it seemed to them that the plebs had too much authority owing to the appointment of tribunes to protect them, and when, besides this, there was a great scarcity of provisions in Rome and the senate had to send to Sicily for corn, Coriolanus, who was hostile to the popular faction, suggested that the time had come to punish the plebs and to deprive them of the authority they had assumed to the prejudice of the nobility. Hence he advised that they should be kept hungry and that the corn should not be distributed amongst them. When this came to the ears of the populace, indignation against Coriolanus grew so intense that, as he was leaving the senate, he would have been killed in the tumult if the tribunes had not cited him to appear in his own defence. One notes in this incident what has been said above, namely, how useful and necessary it is for republics to provide a legal outlet for the anger which the general public has conceived against a particular citizen, because when no such normal means are available, recourse is had to abnormal means, which unquestionably have a worse effect than does the normal method.

The reason is that, though wrong may be done when a citizen is punished in the normal way, scarce any disorder, or none at all, is brought about in the republic; for in carrying out the sentence no appeal is made either to private or to foreign forces, and it is these that entail the downfall of civic liberties. On the contrary, such force as is employed, is employed by public authority which functions within specified limits, and does not, overstepping them, go on to do things which ruin the republic.

There is no need to corroborate this view by citing further examples from olden times in addition to that of Coriolanus. In his regard, however, all should reflect on the evils that might have ensued in the Roman republic had he been tumultuously put to death, for this would have been an act of private vengeance, which would have aroused fear; and fear would have led to defensive action; this to the procuring of partisans; partisans would have meant the formation of factions in the city; and factions would have brought about its downfall. As, however, the matter was settled by persons vested with the requisite authority, no opening was provided for the evils that might have resulted had the matter been settled by private authority.

In our own times we have seen innovations introduced into the republic of Florence owing to the inability of the masses to find a normal outlet for the animus aroused by one of its citizens. This happened at the time when Francesco Valori's standing in the city was akin to that of a prince. He was regarded by many as an ambitious man, likely, owing to his audacity and high spirits, to resort to unconstitutional methods. As there was no way of resisting him save by forming a rival party, it came about that he began to collect supporters to defend himself since he had nothing to be afraid of unless extraordinary steps were taken. On the other hand, since to his opponents no ordinary means of suppressing him were available, they made up their minds to use other means, and eventually took up arms. Had it in this case been possible to oppose Valori by constitutional methods, an end would have been put to his authority without harm to anybody but himself; but since it had to be done by unconstitutional methods, harm resulted not only to him, but to many other noble citizens.

One might also cite in support of the conclusion just reached an incident that actually happened in Florence shortly after this. It concerns Piero Soderini, and was entirely due to the absence in this republic of any means whereby legal action might be taken against the ambition displayed by powerful citizens. For to indict a powerful citizen before eight judges was inadequate. There should have been plenty of judges, for the few always act as the few are wont to act. Had this been the case, the citizens would either have indicted him, if his conduct had been bad, and in this way would have found an outlet for the animosity without getting a Spanish army to intervene; or, if his conduct had not been bad, would not have dared to take action against him for fear that they themselves should be indicted. Thus in either case the appetite which occasioned the scandal would have ceased to operate.

We thus reach the conclusion that, whenever one finds outside forces called in by a party of men residing in a city, it may be taken for granted that this is due to a defect in its constitution in that it comprises no institution which provides an outlet for the malignant humours to which men are prone, without their taking unconstitutional action. Adequate provision for this is made when there is a sufficiency of judges before whom indictments may be made, and when judgeship is looked on as an honourable post.

Such matters were so well provided for in Rome that in the great disputes which arose between the senate and the plebs, never did either the senate, the plebs, or any private citizen, contemplate the calling in of outside forces, because, there being a remedy at home, there was no need to seek one abroad. And, though the examples already cited should suffice to prove my case, I am going to give you yet another, taken from Titus Livy's history. In it he relates how in Clusium — in those days the most noble city in Tuscany — a sister of Aruns had been violated by Lucumon, and how Aruns, unable to obtain justice owing to the power of her betrayer, went to the Gauls who then controlled the province we now call Lombardy, and besought them to bring armed forces to Clusium, pointing out that it would be to their own advantage to avenge the injustice done to him; and how if Aruns had seen how to obtain justice by appeal to the city's laws he would not have invoked barbarian forces. But if such indictments are of advantage to a republic, calumny is not only useless, but harmful, as we shall show in the next chapter.

SELECTIONS FROM
The Prince

Chapter Fifteen

CONCERNING THINGS FOR WHICH MEN, AND ESPECIALLY PRINCES, ARE PRAISED
OR BLAMED

It remains now to see what ought to be the rules of conduct for a prince towards subject and friends. And as I know that many have written on this point, I expect I shall be considered presumptuous in mentioning it again, especially as in discussing it I shall depart from the methods of other people. But, it being my intention to write a thing which shall be useful to him who apprehends it, it appears to me more appropriate to follow up the real truth of a matter than the imagination of it; for many have pictured republics and principalities which in fact have never been known or seen, because how one lives is so far distant from how one ought to live, that he who neglects what is done for what ought to be done, sooner effects his ruin than his preservation; for a man who wishes to act entirely up to his professions of virtue soon meets with what destroys him among so much that is evil.

Hence it is necessary for a prince wishing to hold his own to know how to do wrong, and to make use of it or not according to necessity. Therefore, putting on one side imaginary things concerning a prince, and discussing those which are real, I say that all men when they are spoken of, and chiefly princes for being more highly placed, are remarkable for some of those qualities which bring them either blame or praise; and thus it is that one is reputed liberal, another miserly, using a Tuscan term (because an avaricious person in our language is still he who desires to possess by robbery, whilst we call one miserly who deprives himself too much of the use of his own); one is reputed generous, one rapacious; one cruel, one compassionate; one faithless, another faithful; one effeminate and cowardly, another bold and brave; one affable, another haughty; one lascivious, another chaste; one sincere, another cunning; one hard, another easy; one grave, another frivolous; one religious, another unbelieving, and the like. And I know that every one will confess that it would be most praiseworthy in a prince to exhibit all the above qualities that are considered good; but because they can neither be entirely possessed nor observed, for human conditions do not permit it, it is necessary for him to be sufficiently prudent that he may know how to avoid the reproach of those vices which would lose him his state; and also to keep himself, if it be possible, from those which would not lose him it; but this not being possible, he may with less hesitation abandon himself to them. And again, he need not make himself uneasy at incurring a reproach for those vices without which the state can only be saved with difficulty, for if every-thing is considered carefully, it will be found that something which looks like virtue, if followed, would be his ruin; whilst something else, which looks like vice, yet followed brings him security and prosperity.

Chapter Sixteen

CONCERNING LIBERALITY AND MEANNESS

Commencing then with the first of the above-named characteristics, I say that it would be well to be reputed liberal. Nevertheless, liberality exercised in a way that does not bring you the reputation for it, injures you; for if one exercises it honestly and as it should be exercised, it may not become known, and you will not avoid the reproach of its opposite. Therefore, any one wishing to maintain among men the name of liberal is obliged to avoid no attribute of magnificence; so that a prince thus inclined will consume in such acts all his property, and will be compelled in the end, if he wish to maintain the name of liberal, to unduly weigh down his people, and tax them, and do everything he can to get money. This will soon make him odious to his subjects, and becoming poor he will be little valued by any one; thus, with his liberality, having offended many and rewarded few, he is affected by the very first trouble and imperilled by whatever may be the first danger; recognising this himself, and wishing to draw back from it, he runs at once into the reproach of being miserly.

Therefore, a prince, not being able to exercise this virtue of liberality in such a way that it is recognised, except to his cost, if he is wise he ought not to fear the reputation of being mean, for in time he will come to be more considered than if liberal, seeing that with his economy his revenues are enough, that he can defend himself against all attacks, and is able to engage in enterprises without burdening his people; thus it comes to pass that he exercises liberality towards all from whom he does not take, who are number-less, and meanness towards those to whom he does not give, who are few.

We have not seen great things done in our time except by those who have been considered mean; the rest have failed. Pope Julius the Second was assisted in reaching the papacy by a reputation for liberality, yet he did not strive afterwards to keep it up, when he made war on the King of France; and he made many wars without imposing any extraordinary tax on his subjects, for he supplied his additional expenses out of his long thriftiness. The present King of Spain would not have undertaken or conquered in so many enter-prises if he had been reputed liberal. A prince, therefore, provided that he has not to rob his subjects, that he can defend himself, that he does not become poor and abject, that he is not forced to become rapacious, ought to hold of little account a reputation for being mean, for it is one of those vices which will enable him to govern.

And if any one should say: Caesar obtained empire by liberality, and many others have reached the highest positions by having been liberal, and by being considered so, I answer: Either you are a prince in fact, or in a way to become one. In the first case this liberality is dangerous, in the second it is very necessary to be considered liberal; and Caesar was one of those who wished to become pre-eminent in Rome; but if he had survived after becoming so, and had not moderated his expenses, he would have destroyed his government. And if any one should reply: Many have been princes, and have done great things with armies, who have been considered very liberal, I reply: Either a prince spends that which is his own or his subjects' or else that of others. In the first case he ought to be sparing, in the second he ought not to neglect any opportunity for liberality. And to the prince who goes forth with his army, supporting it by pillage, sack, and extortion, handling that which belongs to others, this liberality is necessary, otherwise he would not be followed by soldiers. And of that which is neither yours nor your subjects' you can be a ready giver, as were Cyrus, Caesar, and Alexander; because it does not take away your reputation if you squander that of others, but adds to it; it is only squandering your own that injures you.

And there is nothing wastes so rapidly as liberality, for even whilst you exercise it you lose the power to do so, and so become either poor or despised, or else, in avoiding poverty, rapacious and hated. And a prince should guard himself, above all things, against being despised and hated; and liberality leads you to both. Therefore it is wiser to have a reputation for meanness which brings reproach without hatred, than to be compelled through seeking a reputation for liberality to incur a name for rapacity which begets reproach with hatred.

Chapter Seventeen

CONCERNING CRUELTY AND CLEMENCY, AND WHETHER IT IS BETTER TO BE LOVED THAN FEARED

Coming now to the other qualities mentioned above, I say that every prince ought to desire to be considered clement and not cruel. Nevertheless he ought to take care not to misuse this clemency. Cesare Borgia was considered cruel; notwithstanding, his cruelty reconciled the Romagna, unified it, and restored it to peace and loyalty. And if this be rightly considered, he will be seen to have been much more merciful than the Florentine people, who, to avoid a reputation for cruelty, permitted Pistoia to be destroyed. Therefore a prince, so long as he keeps his subjects united and loyal, ought not to mind the reproach of cruelty; because with a few examples he will be more merciful than those who, through too much mercy, allow disorders to arise, from which follow murder or robbery; for these are wont to injure the whole people, whilst those executions which originate with a prince offend the individual only.

And of all princes, it is impossible for the new prince to avoid the imputation of cruelty, owing to new states being full of dangers. Hence Virgil, through the mouth of Dido, excuses the inhumanity of her reign owing to its being new. . . . Nevertheless he ought to be slow to believe and to act, nor should he himself show fear, but proceed in a temperate manner with prudence and humanity, so that too much confidence may not make him incautious and too much distrust render him intolerable.

Upon this a question arises: whether it be better to be loved than feared or feared than loved? It may be answered that one should wish to be both, but, because it is difficult to unite them in one person, it is much safer to be feared than loved, when, of the two, either must be dispensed with. Because this is to be asserted in general of men, that they are ungrateful, fickle, false, cowards, covetous, and as long as you succeed they are yours entirely; they will offer you their blood, property, life, and children, as is said above, when the need is far distant; but when it approaches they turn against you. And that prince who, relying entirely on their promises, has neglected other precautions, is ruined; because friendships that are obtained by payments, and not by greatness or nobility of mind, may indeed be earned, but they are not secured, and in time of need cannot be relied upon; and men have less scruple in offending one who is beloved than one who is feared, for love is preserved by the link of obligation which, owing to the baseness of men, is broken at every opportunity for their advantage; but fear preserves you by a dread of punishment which never fails.

Nevertheless a prince ought to inspire fear in such a way that, if he does not win love, he avoids hatred; because he can endure very well being feared whilst he is not hated, which will always be as long as he abstains from the property of his citizens and subjects and from their women. But when it is necessary for him to proceed against the life of some one, he must do it on proper justification and for manifest cause, but above all things he must keep his hands off the property of others, because men more quickly forget the death of their father than the loss of their patrimony. Besides, pretexts for taking away the property are never wanting; for he who has once begun to live by robbery will always find pretexts for seizing what belongs to others; but reasons for taking life, on the contrary, are more difficult to find and sooner lapse. But when a prince is with his army, and has under control a multitude of soldiers, then it is quite necessary for him to disregard the reputation of cruelty, for without it he would never hold his army united or disposed to its duties.

Among the wonderful deeds of Hannibal this one is enumerated: that having led an enormous army, composed of many various races of men, to fight in foreign lands, no dissensions arose either among them or against the prince, whether in his bad or in his good fortune. This arose from nothing else than his inhuman cruelty, which, with his boundless valour, made him revered and terrible in the sight of his soldiers, but without that cruelty, his other virtues were not sufficient to produce this effect. And short-sighted writers admire his deeds from one point of view and from another condemn the principal cause of them. That it is true his other virtues would not have been sufficient for him may be proved by the case of Scipio, that most excellent man, not only of his own times but within the memory of man, against whom, nevertheless, his army rebelled in Spain; this arose from nothing but his too great forbearance, which gave his soldiers more licence than is consistent with military discipline. For this he was upbraided in the Senate by Fabius Maximus, and called the corruptor of Roman soldiery. The Locrians were laid waste by a legate of Scipio, yet they were not avenged by him, nor was the insolence of the legate punished, owing entirely to his easy nature. Insomuch that some one in the Senate, wishing to excuse him, said there were many men who knew much better how not to err than to correct the errors of others. This disposition, if he had been continued in the command, would have destroyed in time the fame and glory of Scipio; but, he being under the control of the Senate, this injurious characteristic not only concealed itself, but contributed to his glory.

Returning to the question of being feared or loved, I come to the conclusion that, men loving according to their own will and fearing according to that of the prince, a wise prince should establish himself on that which is in his own control and not in that of others; he must endeavour only to avoid hatred, as is noted.

Chapter Eighteen

CONCERNING THE WAY IN WHICH PRINCES SHOULD KEEP FAITH

Every one admits how praiseworthy it is in a prince to keep faith, and to live with integrity and not with craft. Nevertheless our experience has been that those princes who have done great things have held good faith of little account, and have known how to circumvent the intellect of men by craft, and in the end have overcome those who have relied on their word. You must know there are two ways of contesting, the one by the law, the other by force; the first method is proper to men, the second to beasts; but because the first is frequently not sufficient, it is necessary to have recourse to the second. Therefore it is necessary for a prince to understand how to avail himself of the beast and the man. This has been figuratively taught to princes by ancient writers, who describe how Achilles and many other princes of old were given to the Centaur Chiron to nurse, who brought them up in his discipline; which means solely that, as they had for a teacher one who was half beast and half man, so it is necessary for a prince to know how to make use of both natures, and that one without the other is not durable. A prince, therefore, being compelled knowingly to adopt the beast, ought to choose the fox and the lion; because the lion cannot defend himself against snares and the fox cannot defend himself against wolves. Therefore, it is necessary to be a fox to discover the snares and a lion to terrify the wolves. Those who rely simply on the lion do not understand what they are about. Therefore a wise lord cannot, nor ought he to, keep faith when such observance may be turned against him, and when the reasons that caused him to pledge it exist no longer. If men were entirely good this precept would not hold, but because they are bad, and will not keep faith with you, you too are not bound to observe it with them. Nor will there ever be wanting to a prince legitimate reasons to excuse this non-observance. Of this endless modern examples could be given, showing how many treaties and engagements have been made void and of no effect through the faithlessness of princes; and he who has known best how to employ the fox has succeeded best.

But it is necessary to know well how to disguise this characteristic, and to be a great pretender and dissembler; and men are so simple, and so subject to present necessities, that he who seeks to deceive will always find some one who will allow himself to be deceived. One recent example I cannot pass over in silence. Alexander the Sixth did nothing else but deceive men, nor ever thought of doing otherwise, and he always found victims; for there never was a man who had greater power in asserting, or who with greater oaths would affirm a thing, yet would observe it less; nevertheless his deceits always succeeded according to his wishes, because he well understood this side of mankind.

Therefore it is unnecessary for a prince to have all the good qualities I have enumerated, but it is very necessary to appear to have them. And I shall dare to say this also, that to have them and always to observe them is injurious, and that to appear to have them is useful; to appear merciful, faithful, humane, religious, upright, and to be so, but with a mind so framed that should you require not to be so, you may be able to know how to change to the opposite.

And you have to understand this, that a prince, especially a new one, cannot observe all those things for which men are esteemed, being often forced, in order to maintain the state, to act contrary to fidelity, friendship, humanity, and religion. Therefore it is necessary for him to have a mind ready to turn itself accordingly as the winds and variations of fortune force it, yet, as I have said above, not to diverge from the good if he can avoid doing so, but, if compelled, then to know how to set about it.

For this reason a prince ought to take care that he never lets anything slip from his lips that is not replete with the above-named five qualities, that he may appear to him who sees and hears him altogether merciful, faithful, humane, upright, and religious. There is nothing more necessary to appear to have than this last quality, inasmuch as men judge generally more by the eye than by the hand, because it belongs to everybody to see you, to few to come in touch with you. Every one sees what you appear to be, few really know what you are, and those few dare not oppose themselves to the opinion of the many, who have the majesty of the state to defend them; and in the actions of all men, and especially of princes, which it is not prudent to challenge, one judges by the result.

For that reason, let a prince have the credit of conquering and holding his state, the means will always be considered honest, and he will be praised by everybody; because the vulgar are always taken by what a thing seems to be and by what comes of it; and in the world there are only the vulgar, for the few find a place there only when the many have no ground to rest on.

One prince of the present time, whom it is not well to name, never preaches anything else but peace and good faith, and to both he is most hostile, and either, if he had kept it, would have deprived him of reputation and kingdom many a time.

Chapter Twenty-Five

What Fortune Can Effect in Human Affairs, and How to Withstand Her

It is not unknown to me how many men have had, and still have, the opinion that the affairs of the world are in such wise governed by fortune and by God that men with their wisdom cannot direct them and that no one can even help them; and because of this they would have us believe that it is not necessary to labour much in affairs, but to let chance govern them. This opinion has been more credited in our times because of the great changes in affairs which have been seen, and may still be seen, every day, beyond all human conjecture. Sometimes pondering over this, I am in some degree inclined to their opinion. Nevertheless, not to extinguish our free will, I hold it to be true that fortune is the arbiter of one half of our actions, but that she still leaves us to direct the other half, or perhaps a little less.

I compare her to one of those raging rivers, which when in flood overflows the plains, sweeping away trees and buildings, bearing away the soil from place to place; everything flies before it, all yield to its violence, without being able in any way to withstand it; and yet, though its nature be such, it does not follow therefore that men, when the weather becomes fair, shall not make provision, both with defences and barriers, in such a manner that, rising again, the waters may pass away by canal, and their force be neither so unrestrained nor so dangerous. So it happens with fortune, who shows her power where valour has not prepared to resist her, and thither she turns her forces where she knows that barriers and defences have not been raised to constrain her.

And if you will consider Italy, which is the seat of these changes, and which has given to them their impulse, you will see it to be an open country without barriers and without any defence. For if it had been defended by proper valour, as are Germany, Spain, and France, either this invasion would not have made the great changes it has made or it would not have come at all. And this I consider enough to say concerning resistance to fortune in general.

But confining myself more to the particular, I say that a prince may be seen happy to-day and ruined to-morrow without having shown any change of disposition or character. This, I believe, arises firstly from causes that have already been discussed at length, namely, that the prince who relies entirely upon fortune is lost when it changes. I believe also that he will be successful who directs his actions according to the spirit of the times, and that he whose actions do not accord with the times will not be successful. Because men are seen, in affairs that lead to the end which every man has before him, namely, glory and riches, to get there by various methods; one with caution, another with haste; one by force, another by skill; one by patience, another by its opposite; and each one succeeds in reaching the goal by a different method. One can also see of two cautious men the one attain his end, the other fail; and similarly, two men by different observances are equally successful, the one being cautious, the other impetuous; all this arises from nothing else than whether or not they conform in their methods to the spirit of the times. This follows from what I have said, that two men working differently bring about the same effect, and of two working similarly, one attains his object and the other does not.

Changes in estate also issue from this, for if, to one who governs himself with caution and patience, times and affairs converge in such a way that his administration is successful, his fortune is made; but if times and affairs change, he is ruined if he does not change his course of action. But a man is not often found sufficiently circumspect to know how to accommodate himself to the change, both because he cannot deviate from what nature inclines him to, and also because, having always prospered by acting in one way, he cannot be persuaded that it is well to leave it; and, therefore, the cautious man, when it is time to turn adventurous, does not know how to do it, hence he is ruined; but had he changed his conduct with the times fortune would not have changed.

Pope Julius the Second went to work impetuously in all his affairs, and found the times and circumstances conform so well to that line of action that he always met with success. Consider his first enterprise against Bologna, Messer Giovanni Bentivogli being still alive. The Venetians were not agreeable to it, not was the King of Spain, and he had the enterprise still under discussion with the King of France; nevertheless he personally entered upon the expedition with his accustomed boldness and energy, a move which made Spain and the Venetians stand irresolute and passive, the latter from fear, the former from desire to recover all the kingdom of Naples; on the other hand, he drew after him the King of France, because that king, having observed the movement, and desiring to make the Pope his friend so as to humble the Venetians, found it impossible to refuse him soldiers without manifestly offending him. Therefore Julius with his impetuous action accomplished what no other pontiff with simple human wisdom could have done; for if he had waited in Rome until he could get away, with his plans arranged and everything fixed, as any other pontiff would have done, he would never have succeeded. Because the King of France would have made a thousand excuses, and the others would have raised a thousand fears.

I will leave his other actions alone, as they were all alike, and they all succeeded, for the shortness of his life did not let him experience the contrary; but if circumstances had arisen which required him to go cautiously, his ruin would have followed, because he would never have deviated from those ways to which nature inclined him.

I conclude therefore that, fortune being changeful and mankind steadfast in their ways, so long as the two are in agreement men are successful, but unsuccessful when they fall out. For my part I consider that it is better to be adventurous than cautious, because fortune is a woman, and if you wish to keep her under it is necessary to beat and ill-use her; and it is seen that she allows herself to be mastered by the adventurous rather than by those who go to work more coldly. She is, therefore, always, woman-like, a lover of young men, because they are less cautious, more violent, and with more audacity command her.

JEAN BODIN

1530 – 1596

INTRODUCTION

Bodin's father was a prosperous tailor in Angers, a small city in the northwest of France, and sent his son to be educated at the local Carmelite order as a priest in training. At the age of 16, Bodin was transferred to Paris for further preparation. There he acquired some knowledge of Greek philosophy, especially that of Aristotle and Plato. In addition, he read widely in Hebrew literature and thus laid the foundations for the extraordinary range of sources referred to in his books. At some point in his early 20s Bodin gave up the priesthood and returned to Angers. By 1556 he was at the University of Toulouse enrolled, first, as a student of civil law, and then, later, as a teacher of it. Six years later he was in Paris practicing as a lawyer. During this period he wrote three books, one of which — *The Method for the Easy Comprehension of History* — brought him widespread recognition. Another book gave the first correct explanation of the price-inflation then prevalent.

However, Bodin's growing success was checked in 1569 by a royal order dismissing all Protestants from government positions and universities. Bodin was imprisoned for more than a year on suspicion of being a Protestant and thus an enemy of the Catholic Church. The royal amnesty of 1570 reinstated the Protestants and freed Bodin. In the following year he was appointed, as a diplomatic counselor, to the staff of the King's younger brothers, only to lose the post a few years later when his employer was discovered, perhaps with Bodin's help, to be conspiring against the heir to the throne. Nevertheless, Bodin reappeared as a delegate to the national assembly in 1576, the same year in which his most important work, *Six Books of the Commonwealth*, was published as a defense of the King's authority over Protestant resisters. But this defense was nullified in the King's view by Bodin's opposition in the assembly to the royal proposals for once again dealing with the Protestants by force. Bodin favored negotiation.

The King's brother died in 1583 and Bodin took up a legal post that he had inherited in Lâon, north of Paris. He was still there in 1588 when the Catholic League began both a campaign against the Protestants and a rebellion against the King for tolerating them. Bodin, a secret sympathizer with toleration for Protestants, but also a supporter of the King's authority, was put in an impossible position in Lâon, a stronghold of the Catholic extremists. For his own safety he was forced to join with the Catholic rebels, although they mistrusted him. But when the King's troops finally won possession of Lâon in 1594, Bodin found that his collaboration with the King's enemies had cost him any hope of reward for his intellectual support of royal political power. Like Machiavelli, he gained nothing from the triumph of the policies that he helped to produce. He died of plague 2 years later.

The *Six Books*, modeled in part on Aristotle's *Politics*, was first published, in French, in 1576 and 10 years later in Latin, the two versions differing somewhat. The only complete translation into English of this huge work dates from 1606. The present selections are drawn from M. J. Tooley's abridged translation entitled *Six Books of the Commonwealth by Jean Bodin*, first published by Basil Blackwell, Oxford, 1955, and used here with their permission.

SELECTIONS FROM
Six Books of the Commonwealth

Book I

CONCERNING SOVEREIGNTY [CHAPTER VIII]

Sovereignty is that absolute and perpetual power vested in a commonwealth which in Latin is termed *majestas* . . . The term needs careful definition, because although it is the distinguishing mark of a commonwealth, and an understanding of its nature fundamental to any treatment of politics, no jurist or political philosopher has in fact attempted to define it. . . .

I have described it as *perpetual* because one can give absolute power to a person or group of persons for a period of time, but that time expired they become subjects once more. Therefore even while they enjoy power, they cannot properly be regarded as sovereign rulers, but only as the lieutenants and agents of the sovereign ruler, till the moment comes when it pleases the prince or the people to revoke the gift. The true sovereign remains always seized of his power. Just as a feudal lord who grants lands to another retains his eminent domain over them, so the ruler who delegates authority to judge and command, whether it be for a short period, or during pleasure, remains seized of those rights of jurisdiction actually exercised by another in the form of a revocable grant, or precarious tenancy. For this reason the law requires the governor of a province, or the prince's lieutenant, to make a formal surrender of the authority committed to him, at the expiration of his term of office. In this respect there is no difference between the highest officer of state and his humblest subordinate. If it were otherwise, and the absolute authority delegated by the prince to a lieutenant was regarded as itself sovereign power, the latter could use it against his prince who would thereby forfeit his eminence, and the subject could command his lord, the servant his master. This is a manifest absurdity, considering that the sovereign is always excepted personally, as a matter of right, in all delegations of authority, however extensive. However much he gives there always remains a reserve of right in his own person, whereby he may command, or intervene by way of prevention, confirmation, evocation, or any other way he thinks fit, in all matters delegated to a subject, whether in virtue of an office or a commission. Any authority exercised in virtue of an office or a commission can be re-voked, or made tenable for as long or short a period as the sovereign wills.

These principles accepted as the foundations of sovereignty, it follows that neither the Roman Dictator, the Harmost of Sparta, the Esymnete of Salonika, the Archus of Malta, nor the ancient Balia of Florence (who has the same sort of authority), nor regents of kingdoms, nor holders of any other sort of commission, nor magistrates whatsoever, who have absolute power to govern the commonwealth for a certain term only, are possessed of sovereign authority. . . .

But supposing the king grants absolute power to a lieutenant for the term of his life, is not that a perpetual sovereign power? For if one confines *perpetual* to that which has no termination whatever, then sovereignty cannot subsist save in aristocracies and popular states, which never die. If one is to include monarchy too, sovereignty must be vested not in the king alone, but in the king and the heirs of his body, which supposes a strictly hereditary monarchy. In that case there can be very few sovereign kings, since there are only a very few strictly hereditary monarchies. Those especially who come to the throne by election could not be included.

A perpetual authority therefore must be understood to mean one that lasts for the lifetime of him who exercises it. If a sovereign magistrate is given office for one year, or for any other predetermined period, and continues to exercise the authority bestowed on him after the conclusion of his term, he does so either by consent or by force and violence. If he does so by force, it is manifest tyranny. The tyrant is a true sovereign for all that. The robber's possession by violence is true and natural possession although contrary to the law, for those who were formerly in possession have been disseized. But if the magistrate continues in office by consent, he is not a sovereign prince, seeing that he only exercises power on sufferance. Still less is he a sovereign if the term of his office is not fixed, for in that case he has no more than a precarious commission. . . .

What bearing have these considerations on the case of the man to whom the people has given absolute power for the term of his natural life? One must distinguish. If such absolute power is given him simply and unconditionally, and not in virtue of some office or commission, nor in the form of a revocable grant, the recipient certainly is, and should be acknowledged to be, a sovereign. The people has renounced and alienated its sovereign power in order to invest him with it and put him in possession, and it thereby transfers to him all its powers, authority, and sovereign rights, just as does the man who gives to another possessory and proprietary rights over what he formerly owned. The civil law expresses this in the phrase 'all power is conveyed to him and vested in him'.

But if the people give such power for the term of his natural life to anyone as its official or lieutenant, or only gives the exercise of such power, in such a case he is not a sovereign, but simply an officer, lieutenant, regent, governor, or agent, and as such has the exercise only of a power inhering in another. When a magistrate institutes a perpetual lieutenant, even if he abandons all his rights of jurisdiction and leaves their exercise entirely to his lieutenant, the authority to command and to judge nevertheless does not reside in the lieutenant, nor the action and force of the law derive from him. If he exceeds his authority his acts have no validity, unless approved and confirmed by him from whom he draws his authority. For this reason King

John, after his return from captivity in England, solemnly ratified all the acts of his son Charles, who had acted in his name as regent, in order, as was necessary, to regularize the position.

Whether then one exercises the power of another by commission, by institution, or by delegation, or whether such exercise is for a set term, or in perpetuity, such a power is not a sovereign power, even if there is no mention of such words as representative, lieutenant, governor, or regent, in the letters of appointment, or even if such powers are a consequence of the normal working of the laws of the country. In ancient times in Scotland, for instance, the law vested the entire governance of the realm in the next of kin, if the king should be a minor, on condition that everything that was done, was done in the king's name. But this law was later altered because of its inconvenient consequences.

Let us now turn to the other term of our definition and consider the force of the word *absolute*. The people or the magnates of a commonwealth can bestow simply and unconditionally upon someone of their choice a sovereign and perpetual power to dispose of their property and persons, to govern the state as he thinks fit, and to order the succession, in the same way that any proprietor, out of his liberality, can freely and unconditionally make a gift of his property to another. Such a form of gift, not being qualified in any way, is the only true gift, being at once unconditional and irrevocable. Gifts burdened with obligations and hedged with conditions are not true gifts. Similarly sovereign power given to a prince charged with conditions is neither properly sovereign, nor absolute, unless the conditions of appointment are only such as are inherent in the laws of God and of nature. . . .

If we insist however that absolute power means exemption from all law whatsoever, there is no prince in the world who can be regarded as sovereign, since all the princes of the earth are subject to the laws of God and of nature, and even to certain human laws common to all nations. On the other hand, it is possible for a subject who is neither a prince nor a ruler, to be exempted from all the laws, ordinances, and customs of the commonwealth. We have an example in Pompey the Great who was dispensed from the laws for five years, by express enactment of the Roman people, at the instance of the Tribune Gabinius . . . But notwithstanding such exemptions from the operations of the law, the subject remains under the authority of him who exercises sovereign power, and owes him obedience.

On the other hand it is the distinguishing mark of the sovereign that he cannot in any way be subject to the commands of another, for it is he who makes law for the subject, abrogates law already made, and amends obsolete law. No one who is subject either to the law or to some other person can do this. That is why it is laid down in the civil law that the prince is above the law, for the word *law* in Latin implies the command of him who is invested with sovereign power. Therefore we find in all statutes the phrase 'notwithstanding all edicts and ordinances to the contrary that we have infringed, or do infringe by these present'. This clause applies both to former acts of the prince himself, and to those of his predecessors. For all laws, ordinances, letters patent, privileges, and grants whatsoever issued by the prince, have force only during his own lifetime, and must be expressly, or at least tacitly, confirmed by the reigning prince who has cognizance of them . . . In proof of which, it is the custom of this realm for all corporations and corporate bodies to ask for the confirmation of their privileges, rights, and jurisdictions, on the accession of a new king. Even Parlements and high courts do this, as well as individual officers of the crown.

If the prince is not bound by the laws of his predecessors, still less can he be bound by his own laws. One may be subject to laws made by another, but it is impossible to bind oneself in any matter which is the subject of one's own free exercise of will. As the law says, 'there can be no obligation in any matter which proceeds from the free will of the undertaker'. It follows of necessity that the king cannot be subject to his own laws. Just as, according to the canonists, the Pope can never tie his own hands, so the sovereign prince cannot bind himself, even if he wishes. For this reason edicts and ordinances conclude with the formula 'for such is our good pleasure', thus intimating that the laws of a sovereign prince, even when founded on truth and right reason, proceed simply from his own free will.

It is far otherwise with divine and natural laws. All the princes of the earth are subject to them, and cannot contravene them without treason and rebellion against God. His yoke is upon them, and they must bow their heads in fear and reverence before His divine majesty. The absolute power of princes and sovereign lords does not extend to the laws of God and of nature. He who best understood the meaning of absolute power, and made kings and emperors submit to his will, defined his sovereignty as a power to override positive law; he did not claim power to set aside divine and natural law.

But supposing the prince should swear to keep the laws and customs of his country, is he not bound by that oath? One must distinguish. If a prince promises in his own heart to obey his own laws, he is nevertheless not bound to do so, any more than anyone is bound by an oath taken to himself. Even private citizens are not bound by private oaths to keep agreements. The law permits them to cancel them, even if the agreements are in themselves reasonable and good. But if one sovereign prince promises another sovereign prince to keep the agreements entered into by his predecessors, he is bound to do so even if not under oath, if that other prince's interests are involved. If they are not, he is not bound either by a promise, or even by an oath.

The same holds good of promises made by the sovereign to the subject, even if the promises were made prior to his election (for this does not make the difference that many suppose). It is not that the prince is bound either by his own laws or those of his predecessors. But he is bound by the just covenants and promises he has made, whether under oath to do so or not, to exactly the same extent that a private individual is bound in like case. A private individual can be released from a promise that was unjust or unreasonable, or beyond his competence to fulfil, or extracted from him by misrepresentations or fraud, or made in error, or under restraint and by intimidation, because of the injury the keeping of it does him. In the same way a sovereign prince can make good any invasion of his sovereign rights, and for the same reasons. So the principle stands, that the prince is not subject to his own laws, or those of his predecessors, but is bound by the just and reasonable engagements which touch the interests of his subjects individually or collectively.

Many have been led astray by confusing the laws of the prince with covenants entered into by him. This confusion has led some to call these covenants contractual laws. This is the term used in Aragon when the king issues an ordinance upon the petition of the Estates, and in return receives some aid or subsidy. It is claimed that he is strictly bound by these laws, even though he is not by any of his other enactments. It is however admitted that he may override even these when the purpose of their enactment no longer holds. All this is true enough, and well-founded in reason and authority. But no bribe or oath is required to bind a sovereign prince to keep a law which is in the interests of his subjects. The bare word of a prince should be as sacred as a divine pronouncement. It loses its force if he is ill-thought of as one who cannot be trusted except under oath, nor relied on to keep a promise unless paid to do so. Nevertheless it remains true in principle that the sovereign prince can set aside the laws which he has promised or sworn to observe, if they no longer satisfy the requirements of justice, and he may do this without the consent of his subjects. It should however be added that the abrogation must be express and explicit in its reference, and not just in the form of a general repudiation. But if on the other hand there is no just cause for breaking a law which the prince has promised to keep, the prince ought not to do so, and indeed cannot contravene it, though he is not bound to the same extent by the promises and covenants of his predecessors unless he succeeds by strict hereditary right.

A law and a covenant must therefore not be confused. A law proceeds from him who has sovereign power, and by it he binds the subject to obedience, but cannot bind himself. A covenant is a mutual undertaking between a prince and his subjects, equally binding on both parties, and neither can contravene it to the prejudice of the other, without his consent. The prince has no greater privilege than the subject in this matter. But in the case of laws, a prince is no longer bound by his promise to keep them when they cease to satisfy the claims of justice. Subjects however must keep their engagements to one another in all circumstances, unless the prince releases them from such obligations. Sovereign princes are not bound by oath to keep the laws of their predecessors. If they are so bound, they are not properly speaking sovereign. . . .

The constitutional laws of the realm, especially those that concern the king's estate being, like the salic law, annexed and united to the Crown, cannot be infringed by the prince. Should he do so, his successor can always annul any act prejudicial to the traditional form of the monarchy, since on this is founded and sustained his very claim to sovereign majesty. . . .

As for laws relating to the subject, whether general or particular, which do not involve any question of the constitution, it has always been usual only to change them with the concurrence of the three estates, either assembled in the States-General of the whole of France, or in each bailliwick separately. Not that the king is bound to take their advice, or debarred from acting in a way quite contrary to what they wish, if his acts are based on justice and natural reason. At the same time the majesty of the prince is most fully manifested in the assembly of the three estates of the whole realm, humbly petitioning and supplicating him, without any power of commanding or determining, or any right to a deliberative voice. Only that which it pleases the prince to assent to or dissent from, to command or to forbid, has the force of law and is embodied in his edict or ordinance.

Those who have written books about the duties of magistrates and such like matters are in error in maintaining that the authority of the Estates is superior to that of the prince. Such doctrines serve only to encourage subjects to resist their sovereign rulers. Besides, such views bear no relation to the facts, except when the king is in captivity, lunatic or a minor. If he were normally subject to the Estates, he would be neither a prince nor a sovereign, and the commonwealth would not be a kingdom or a monarchy, but a pure aristocracy where authority is shared equally between the members of the ruling class. . . .

Although in the Parliaments of the kingdom of England, which meet every three years, all three orders use great freedom of speech, as is characteristic of northern peoples, they still must proceed by petitions and supplications . . . Moreover Parliaments in England can only assemble, as in this kingdom and in Spain, under letters patent expressly summoning them in the king's name. This is sufficient proof that Parliaments have no independent power of considering, commanding or determining, seeing that they can neither assemble nor adjourn without express royal command . . . It may be objected that no extraordinary taxes or subsidies can be imposed without the agreement and consent of Parliament. King Edward I agreed to this principle in the Great Charter, which is always appealed to by the people against the claims of the king. But I hold that in this matter no other king has any more right than has the King of England, since it is not within the competence of any prince in the world to levy taxes at will on his people, or seize the goods of another arbitrarily, as Philippe de Comines very wisely argued at the Estates at Tours, as we may read in his *Memoirs*.

We must agree then that the sovereignty of the king is in no wise qualified or diminished by the existence of Estates. On the contrary his majesty appears more illustrious when formally recognized by his assembled subjects, even though in such assemblies princes, not wishing to fall out with their people, agree to many things which they would not have consented to, unless urged by the petitions, prayers, and just complaints of a people burdened by grievances unknown to the prince. After all, he depends for his information on the eyes and ears and reports of others.

From all this it is clear that the principal mark of sovereign majesty and absolute power is the right to impose laws generally on all subjects regardless of their consent . . . And if it is expedient that if he is to govern his state well, a sovereign prince must be above the law, it is even more expedient that the ruling class in an aristocracy should be so, and inevitable in a popular state. A monarch in a kingdom is set apart from his subjects, and the ruling class from the people in an aristocracy. There are therefore in each case two parties, those that rule on the one hand, and those that are ruled on the other. This is the cause of the disputes about sovereignty that arise in them, but cannot in a popular state . . . There the people, rulers and ruled, form a single body and so cannot bind themselves by their own laws. . . .

When edicts are ratified by Estates or Parlements, it is for the purpose of securing obedience to them, and not because otherwise a sovereign prince could not validly make law. As Theodosius said with reference to the consent of the Senate, 'it is not a matter of necessity but of expediency'. He also remarked that it was most becoming in a sovereign prince to keep his own laws, for this is what makes him feared and respected by his subjects, whereas nothing so undermines his authority as contempt for them. As a Roman Senator observed 'it is more foolish and ill-judged to break your own laws than those of another'.

But may it not be objected that if the prince forbids a sin, such as homicide, on pain of death, he is in this case bound to keep his own law? The answer is that this is not properly the prince's own law, but a law of God and nature, to which he is more strictly bound than any of his subjects. Neither his council, nor the whole body of the people, can exempt him from his perpetual responsibility before the judgement-seat of God, as Solomon said in unequivocal terms. Marcus Aurelius also observed that the magistrate is the judge of persons, the prince of the magistrates, and God of the prince. Such was the opinion of the two wisest rulers the world has ever known. Those who say without qualification that the prince is bound neither by any law whatsoever, nor by his own express engagements, insult the majesty of God, unless they intend to except the laws of God and of nature, and all just convenants and solemn agreements. Even Dionysius, tyrant of Syracuse, said to his mother that he could exempt her from the laws and customs of Syracuse, but not from the laws of God and of nature. For just as contracts and deeds of gift of private individuals must not derogate from the ordinances of the magistrate, nor his ordinances from the law of the land, nor the law of the land from the enactments of a sovereign prince, so the laws of a sovereign prince cannot override or modify the laws of God and of nature. . . .

There is one other point. If the prince is bound by the laws of nature, and the civil law is reasonable and equitable, it would seem to follow that the prince is also bound by the civil law. As Pacatius said to the Emperor Theodosius 'as much is permitted to you as is permitted by the laws'. In answer to this I would point out that the laws of a sovereign prince concern either public or private interests or both together. All laws moreover can be either profitable at the expense of honour, or profitable without involving honour at all, or honourable without profit, and neither honourable nor profitable. When I say 'honour' I mean that which conforms with what is natural and right, and it has already been shown that the prince is bound in such cases. Laws of this kind, though published by the prince's authority, are properly natural laws. Laws which are profitable as well as just are even more binding on him. One need hardly concern oneself about the sanctity of laws which involve neither profit nor honour. But if it is a question of weighing honour against profit, honour should always be preferred. Aristides the Just said of Themistocles that his advice was always very useful to the people, but shameful and dishonourable.

But if a law is simply useful and does not involve any principle of natural justice, the prince is not bound by it, but can amend it or annul it altogether as he chooses, provided that with the alteration of the law the profit to some does not do damage to others without just cause. The prince then can annul an ordinance which is merely useful in order to substitute one more or less advantageous, for profit, honour, and justice all have degrees of more and less. And just as the prince can choose the most useful among profitable laws, so he can choose the most just among equitable laws, even though while some profit by them others suffer, provided it is the public that profits, and only the private individual that suffers. It is however never proper for the subject to disobey the laws of the prince under the pretext that honour and justice require it. . . .

Edicts and ordinances therefore do not bind the ruler except in so far as they embody the principles of natural justice; that ceasing, the obligation ceases. But subjects are bound till the ruler has expressly abrogated the law, for it is a law both divine and natural that we should obey the edicts and ordinances of him whom God has set in authority over us, providing his edicts are not contrary to God's law. For just as the rear-vassal owes an oath of fealty in respect of and against all others, saving his sovereign prince, so the subject owes allegiance to his sovereign prince in respect of and against all others, saving the majesty of God, who is lord of all the princes of this world. From this principle we can deduce that other rule, that the sovereign prince is bound by the covenants he makes either with his subjects, or some other prince. Just because he enforces the covenants and mutual engagements entered into by his subjects among themselves, he must be the mirror of justice in all his own acts . . . He has a double obligation in this case. He is bound in the first place by the principles of natural equity, which require that conventions and solemn promises should be kept, and in the second place in the interests of his own good faith, which he ought to preserve even to his own disadvantage, because he is the formal guarantor to all his subjects of the mutual faith they owe one another. . . .

A distinction must therefore be made between right and law, for one implies what is equitable and the other what is commanded. Law is nothing else than the command of the sovereign in the exercise of his sovereign power. A sovereign prince is not subject to the laws of the Greeks, or any other alien power, or even those of the Romans, much less to his own laws, except in so far as they embody the law of nature which, according to Pindar, is the law to which all kings and princes are subject. Neither Pope nor Emperor is exempt from this law, though certain flatterers say they can take the goods of their subjects at will. But both civilians and canonists have repudiated this opinion as contrary to the law of God. They err who assert that in virtue of their sovereign power princes can do this. It is rather the law of the jungle, an act of force and violence. For as we have shown above, absolute power only implies freedom in relation to positive laws, and not in relation to the law of God. God has declared explicitly in His Law that it is not just to take, or even to covet, the goods of another. Those who defend such opinions are even more dangerous than those who act on them. They show the lion his claws, and arm princes under a cover of just claims. The evil will of a tyrant, drunk with such flatteries, urges him to an abuse of absolute power and excites his violent passions to the pitch where avarice issues in confiscations, desire in adultery, and anger in murder. . . .

Since then the prince has no power to exceed the laws of nature which God Himself, whose image he is, has decreed, he cannot take his subjects' property without just and reasonable cause, that is to say by purchase, exchange, legitimate confiscation, or to secure peace with the enemy when it cannot be otherwise achieved. Natural reason instructs us that the public good must be preferred to the particular, and that subjects should give up not only their mutual antagonisms and animosities, but also their possessions, for the safety of the commonwealth. . . .

It remains to be determined whether the prince is bound by the covenants of his predecessors, and whether, if so, it is a derogation to his sovereign power . . . A distinction must be made between the ruler who succeeds because he is the natural heir of his predecessor, and the ruler who succeeds in virtue of the laws and customs of the realm. In the first case the heir is bound by the oaths and promises of his predecessors just as is any ordinary heir. In the second case he is not so bound even if he is sworn, for the oath of the predecessor does not bind the successor. He is bound however in all that tends to the benefit of the kingdom.

There are those who will say that there is no need of such distinctions since the prince is bound in any case by the law of nations, under which covenants are guaranteed. But I consider that these distinctions are necessary nevertheless, since the prince is bound as much by the law of nations, but no more, than by any of his own enactments. If the law of nations is iniquitous in any respect, he can disallow it within his own kingdom, and forbid his subjects to observe it, as was done in France in regard to slavery. He can do the same in relation to any other of its provisions, so long as he does nothing against the law of God. If justice is the end of the law, the law the work of the prince, and the prince the image of God, it follows of necessity that the law of the prince should be modelled on the law of God.

The True Attributes of Sovereignty [chapter x]

. . . Aristotle, Polybius, and Dionysius Halicarnassus alone among the Greeks discussed the attributes of sovereignty. But they treated the subject so briefly that one can see at a glance that they did not really understand the principles involved. I quote Aristotle. 'There are', he says, 'three parts of a commonwealth. There must be provision for the taking and giving of counsel, for appointing to office and assigning to each citizen his duties, for the administration of justice.' If he did not mean by *parts* attributes of sovereignty, he never treated of the subject at all, since this is the only passage which has any bearing. Polybius does not define the rights and duties of sovereignty either, but he says of the Romans that their constitution was a mixture of monarchy, aristocracy, and popular government, since the people made law and appointed to office, the Senate administered the provinces and conducted great affairs of state, the consuls enjoyed the pre-eminence of honour accorded to kings, especially in the field, where they exercised supreme command. This passage appears to imply a treatment of sovereign rights, since he says that those who enjoyed those rights had sovereign power. Dionysius Halicarnassus however had a clearer and better understanding of the matter than the others. When he was explaining how the King Servius deprived the Senate of authority, he observed that he transferred to the people the power to make and unmake law, to determine war and peace, to institute and deprive magistrates, and the right of hearing appeals from all courts whatsoever. In another passage, when describing the third conflict between the nobles and the people, he reported how the Consul Marcus Valerius rebuked the people and said that they should be content with the powers of making law, appointing to office and hearing appeals. Other matters should be left to the Senate.

Since ancient times civilians, and especially those of more recent years, have elaborated these rights, especially in their treatises on what they call regalian rights. Under this heading they have collected an immense number of particular rights and privileges enjoyed by dukes, counts, bishops, and various officials, and even subjects of sovereign princes. As a result they describe dukes, such as those of Milan, Mantua, Ferrara, and Savoy, and even counts, as sovereign princes. However reasonable it may appear, this is an error. How can these rulers be regarded as anything but sovereign, they argue, when they make law for their subjects, levy war and conclude peace, appoint to all office in their dominions, levy taxes, make a free man of whom they please, pardon those who have forfeited their lives. What other powers has any sovereign prince?

But we have already shown above that the Dukes of Milan, Mantua, Ferrara, Florence, and Savoy hold of the Empire. Their most honourable title is that of Imperial Vicar and Prince of the Empire . . . We have also pointed out the absurdities that ensue if one makes sovereigns of vassals, since the lord and his subject, the master and his servant, the man who makes the law and the man on whom it is imposed, the man who issues orders and the man who obeys them, are thereby placed on an equal footing. Since this cannot be, it follows that dukes, counts, and all those who hold of another, or are bound by his laws and subject to his commands, whether of right or by constraint, are not sovereign. The same holds good of the highest officers of state, lieutenant-generals of the king, governors, regents, dictators, whatever the extent of their powers. They are not sovereigns since they are subject to the laws and commands of another and may be appealed against.

The attributes of sovereignty are therefore peculiar to the sovereign prince, for if communicable to the subject, they cannot be called attributes of sovereignty . . . Just as Almighty God cannot create another God equal with Himself, since He is infinite and two infinities cannot co-exist, so the sovereign prince, who is the image of God, cannot make a subject equal with himself without self-destruction.

If this is so, it follows that rights of jurisdiction are not attributes of sovereignty since they are exercised by subjects as well as the prince. The same is true of the appointment and dismissal of officials, for this power also the prince shares with the subject, not only in regard to the lesser offices of justice, of police, of the armed forces, or of the revenues, but also in regard to responsible commanders in peace and war . . . The infliction of penalties and the bestowing of awards is not an attribute of sovereignty either, for the magistrate has this power, though it is true he derives it from the sovereign. Nor is taking counsel about affairs of state an attribute of sovereignty, for such is the proper function of the privy council or senate in the commonwealth, a body always distinct from that in which sovereignty is vested. Even in the popular state, where sovereignty lies in the assembly of the people, so far from it being the function of the assembly to take counsel, it ought never be permitted to do so, as I shall show later.

It is clear therefore that none of the three functions of the state that Aristotle distinguishes are properly attributes of sovereignty. As for what Halicarnassus says about Marcus Valerius' speech to the people of Rome, when trying to pacify them, that they should be content with the prerogatives of making law and appointing magistrates, he does not make the point sufficiently clear. As I have already said, appointing to office is not an attribute of sovereignty. Moreover some further explanation is necessary of the nature of the law-making power. A magistrate can make laws binding on those subject to his jurisdiction, provided such laws do not conflict with the edicts and ordinances of his sovereign prince.

Before going any further, one must consider what is meant by *law*. The word law signifies the right command of that person, or those persons, who have absolute authority over all the rest without exception, saving only the law-giver himself, whether the command touches all subjects in general or only some in particular. To put it another way, the law is the rightful command of the sovereign touching all his subjects in general, or matters of general application . . . As to the commands of the magistrate, they are not properly speaking laws but only edicts. 'An edict', says Varro, 'is an order issued by a magistrate.' Such orders are only binding on those subject to his jurisdiction, and are only in force for his term of office.

The first attribute of the sovereign prince therefore is the power to make law binding on all his subjects in general and on each in particular. But to avoid any ambiguity one must add that he does so without the consent of any superior, equal, or inferior being necessary. If the prince can only make law with the consent of a superior he is a subject; if of an equal he shares his sovereignty; if of an inferior, whether it be a council of magnates or the people, it is not he who is sovereign. The names of the magnates that one finds appended to a royal edict are not there to give force to the law, but as witnesses, and to make it more acceptable . . . When I say that the first attribute of sovereignty is to give law to all in general and each in particular, I mean by this last phrase the grant of privileges. I mean by a privilege a concession to one or a small group of individuals which concerns the profit or loss of those persons only. . . .

It may be objected however that not only have magistrates the power of issuing edicts and ordinances, each according to his competence and within his own sphere of jurisdiction, but private citizens can make law in the form of general or local custom. It is agreed that customary law is as binding as statute law. But if the sovereign prince is author of the law, his subjects are the authors of custom. But there is a difference between law and custom. Custom establishes itself gradually over a long period of years, and by common consent, or at any rate the consent of the greater part. Law is made on the instant and draws its force from him who has the right to bind all the rest. Custom is established imperceptibly and without any exercise of compulsion. Law is promulgated and imposed by authority, and often against the wishes of the subject. For this reason Dion Chrysostom compared custom to the king and law to the tyrant. Moreover law can break custom, but custom cannot derogate from the law, nor can the magistrate, or any other responsible for the administration of law, use his discretion about the enforcement of law as he can about custom. Law, unless it is permissive and relaxes the severity of another law, always carries penalties for its breach. Custom only has binding force by the sufferance and during the good pleasure of the sovereign prince, and so far as he is willing to authorize it. Thus the force of both statutes and customary law derives from the authorization of the prince . . . Included in the power of making and unmaking law is that of promulgating it and amending it when it is obscure, or when the magistrates find contradictions and absurdities. . . .

All the other attributes and rights of sovereignty are included in this power of making and unmaking law, so that strictly speaking this is the unique attribute of sovereign power. It includes all other rights of sovereignty, that is to say of making peace and war, of hearing appeals from the sentences of all courts whatsoever, of appointing and dismissing the great officers of state; of taxing, or granting privileges of exemption to all subjects, of appreciating or depreciating the value and weight of the coinage, of receiving oaths of fidelity from subjects and liege-vassals alike, without exception of any other to whom faith is due. . . .

But because *law* is an unprecise and general term, it is as well to specify the other attributes of sovereignty comprised in it, such as the making of war and peace. This is one of the most important rights of sovereignty, since it brings in its train either the ruin or the salvation of the state. This was a right of sovereignty not only among the ancient Romans, but has always been so among all other peoples . . . Sovereign princes are therefore accustomed to keep themselves informed of the smallest accidents and undertakings connected with warfare. Whatever latitude they may give to their representatives to negotiate peace or an alliance, they never grant the authority to conclude without their own express consent. This was illustrated in the negotiations leading up to the recent treaty of Câteaux-Cambrésis, when the king's envoys kept him almost hourly informed of all proposals and counter-proposals . . . In popular states and aristocracies the difficulty of assembling the people, and the danger of making public all the secrets of diplomacy has meant that the people have generally handed responsibility over to the council. Nevertheless it remains true that the commissions and the orders that it issues in discharge of this function proceed from the authority of the people, and are despatched by the council in the name of the people. . . .

The third attribute of sovereignty is the power to institute the great officers of state. It has never been questioned that the right is an attribute of sovereignty, at any rate as far as the great officers are concerned. I confine it however to high officials, for there is no commonwealth in which these officers, and many guilds and corporate bodies besides, have not some power of appointing their subordinate officials. They do this in virtue of their office, which carries with it the power to delegate. For instance, those who hold feudal rights of jurisdiction of their sovereign prince in faith and homage have the power to appoint the judges in their courts, and their assistants. But this power is devolved upon them by the prince . . . It is therefore not the mere appointment of officials that implies sovereign right, but the authorization and confirmation of such appointments. It is true however that in so far as the exercise of this right is delegated, the sovereignty of the prince is to that extent qualified, unless his concurrence and express consent is required.

The fourth attribute of sovereignty, and one which has always been among its principal rights, is that the prince should be the final resort of appeal from all other courts . . . Even though the prince may have published a law, as did Caligula, forbidding any appeal or petition against the sentences of his officers, nevertheless the subject cannot be deprived of the right to make an appeal, or present a petition, to the prince in person. For the prince cannot tie his own hands in this respect, nor take from his subjects the means of redress, supplication, and petition, notwithstanding the fact that all rules governing appeals and jurisdictions are matters of positive law, which we have shown does not bind the prince. This is why the Privy

Council, including the Chancellor de l'Hôpital, considered the action of the commissioners deputed to hold an enquiry into the conduct of the President l'Alemant irregular and unprecedented. They had forbidden him to approach within twenty leagues of the court, with the intention of denying him any opportunity of appeal. The king himself could not deny this right to the subject, though he is free to make whatsoever reply to the appeal, favourable or unfavourable, that he pleases . . . Were it otherwise, and the prince could acquit his subjects or his vassals from the obligation to submit their causes to him in the last instance, he would make of them sovereigns equal with himself . . . But if he would preserve his authority, the surest way of doing so is to avoid ever devolving any of the attributes of sovereignty upon a subject. . . .

With this right is coupled the right of pardoning convicted persons, and so of overruling the sentences of his own courts, in mitigation of the severity of the law, whether touching life, property, honour, or domicile. It is not in the power of any magistrate, whatever his station, to do any of these things, or to make any revision of the judgement he has once given . . . In a well-ordered commonwealth the right should never be delegated either to a special commission, or to any high officer of state, save in those circumstances where it is necessary to establish a regency, either because the king is abroad in some distant place, or in captivity, or incapable, or under age. For instance, during the minority of Louis IX, the authority of the Crown was vested in his mother Blanche of Castile as his guardian . . . Princes however tend to abuse this right, thinking that to pardon is pleasing to God, whereas to exact the utmost punishment is displeasing to Him. But I hold, subject to correction, that the sovereign prince cannot remit any penalty imposed by the law of God, any more than he can dispense any one from the operation of the law of God, to which he himself is subject. If the magistrate who dispenses anyone from obedience to the ordinance of his king merits death, how much more unwarrantable is it for the prince to acquit a man of the punishment ordained by God's law? If a sovereign prince cannot deny a subject his civil rights, how can he acquit him of the penalties imposed by God, such as the death penalty exacted by divine law for treacherous murder?

It may be objected that the prince can never show the quality of mercy if he cannot remit punishments prescribed by divine law. But in my opinion there are other means of showing clemency, such as pardoning breaches of positive laws. For instance, if the prince forbids the carrying of arms, or the selling of foodstuffs to the enemy in time of war, on pain of death, he can very properly pardon the offence of carrying arms if it was done in self-defence, or the selling of provisions if done under the pressure of extreme poverty. Again, the penalty for larceny under the civil law is death. A merciful prince can reduce this to fourfold restitution, which is what is required by divine law. It has always been the custom among Christian kings to pardon unpardonable offences on Good Friday. But pardons of this kind bring in their train pestilences, famine, war, and the downfall of states. That is why it is said in the law of God that in punishing those who have merited death one averts the curse on the whole people. Of a hundred criminals only two are brought to justice, and of those brought to justice only one half are proved guilty. If the few proven cases of guilt are pardoned, how can punishment act as a deterrent to evil-doers? . . . The best way for a prince to exercise his prerogative of mercy is to pardon offences against his own person. Of all exercises of mercy none is more pleasing to God. But what can one hope of the prince who cruelly avenges all injuries to himself, but pardons those inflicted on others? . . .

Faith and homage are also among the most important attributes of sovereignty, as was made clear when the prince was described as the one to whom obedience was due without exception. . . .

Book 5

HOW TO PREVENT THOSE DISORDERS WHICH SPRING FROM EXCESSIVE WEALTH AND EXCESSIVE POVERTY [CHAPTER II]

The commonest cause of disorders and revolutions in commonwealths has always been the too great wealth of a handful of citizens, and the too great poverty of the rest. The histories are full of occasions on which those who have given all sorts of reasons for their discontents have taken the first opportunity that offered of dispoiling the rich of their possessions . . . For this reason Plato called riches and poverty the two original plagues of the commonwealth, not only because of the misery that hunger occasions, but the shame, and shame is a very evil and dangerous malady. To remedy this condition of things, it has been suggested that there should be an equality of possessions. This suggestion has been strongly supported, and it has been claimed that it would prove a source of peace and amity among subjects, whereas inequality is the source of enmity, faction, hatred, and prejudice. He who has more than another, and is conscious of being richer in possessions, thinks he should also enjoy a greater measure of honour, luxury, pleasure, have more food and more clothes. He thinks he should be looked up to by the poor whom he despises and treads underfoot. The poor, for their part, suffer acute envy and jealousy in considering themselves just as worthy or even more worthy of riches, yet oppressed by hunger, poverty, misery, and contempt. Therefore many architects of republics in the ancient world advocated an equal division of property among all subjects. Even within living memory Thomas More, the Chancellor of England, in his *Republic* laid down that a necessary condition of general well-being was that men should enjoy a community of goods, which is not possible where there are private property rights . . . Lycurgus accomplished this at the risk of his life, for after having prohibited the circulation of gold and silver, he made an equal division of all lands . . . The Romans as a people were more equitable and had more understanding of the principles of justice than any other. They often decreed a general remission of debts, sometimes to the amount of one quarter, or one third, sometimes even the whole amount. This was the best and quickest way they found of composing disorders and discontents. . . .

On the other side it can be argued that equality of possessions is subversive of the commonwealth. The surest foundation of a commonwealth is public confidence, for without it neither justice, nor any sort of lasting association is possible. Confidence only arises where promises and legal obligations are honoured. If these obligations are cancelled, contracts annulled, debts abolished, what else can one expect but the total subversion of the state, for none would any longer have any confidence in his fellows . . . But if the inconveniences of such abolitions are obvious, still more unfortunate is the equal division of lands and possessions which are either rightful inheritances, or justly acquired. In the case of debts, one can make the excuse of usury. But this cannot be alleged against lands legitimately inherited. Such partitions of the goods of another is robbery in the name of equality. Moreover to say that equality is the mother of amity is to abuse the ignorant, for there is no hatred so bitter, or enmity so deadly as that between equals. Jealousy of equals one of another is the source of unrest, disorder, and civil war. On the other hand the poor, the weak, and the unprotected defer to and obey their betters, the rich and the powerful, most willingly, with a view to their assistance, and the advantages they hope will accrue. . . .

Besides, what Lycurgus intended in dividing up property among individuals to preserve equality of heritages in perpetuity was a thing impossible of achievement. He could see for himself that the original equality between individuals was almost immediately upset by the fact that some parents had twelve or fifteen children, and others one or two, or even none at all . . . Some, like Hippodamus the Milesian lawgiver, have tried to solve this difficulty by limiting the citizen body to ten thousand . . . Sir Thomas More, the English Chancellor, thought that no family should consist of less than ten or more than sixteen children, as if he could command nature . . . But one should never be afraid of having too many subjects or too many citizens, for the strength of the commonwealth consists in men. Moreover the greater the multitude of citizens, the greater check there is on factious seditions. For there will be many in an intermediate position between the rich and the poor, the good and the bad, the wise and the foolish. There is nothing more dangerous to the commonwealth than that its subjects should be divided into two factions, with none to mediate between them. This is the normal situation in a small commonwealth of few citizens. Let us therefore reject the schemes of those who wish to introduce equality of property in commonwealths already founded, by taking a man's property from him, instead of securing to each that which belongs to him, for this is the only way of establishing natural justice. Let us also reject the idea of limiting the number of citizens, and conclude that there should be no partition of inheritances except on the foundation of a new commonwealth in a conquered country. In such case the division should be by families and not by individuals, and a certain pre-eminence should be accorded to one particular family, and an order of priority established within each family. . . .

THOMAS HOBBES

1 5 8 8 – 1 6 7 9

INTRODUCTION

Britain's greatest political philosopher began writing on politics and philosophy only in middle age. Before then he was a scholar and tutor in Latin and Greek, having been educated at grammar school in the west of England and later at Oxford. After graduation Hobbes became a tutor and companion to the first Earl of Devonshire, then only 17, and thus was given the use of a large private library and the company of the many eminent noblemen, writers, and amateur scientists who were friendly with his patron's family, the Cavendishes. It was with this family that Hobbes, who never married, lived for the greater part of his long life.

In 1610 the young Earl and Hobbes toured France and Italy together to learn foreign languages, and on this trip Hobbes learned something of the new astronomy being developed by Kepler and Galileo. On his return to England Hobbes settled down to his classical studies in the Earl's household until the latter's death in 1625. During this period Hobbes was becoming known for his abilities as a classicist, and for a few years acted as secretary and translator for Francis Bacon. In 1629 Hobbes accompanied the son of another nobleman to the continent and, chancing to read a copy of Euclid's *Elements* in Geneva, became fascinated with both geometry and the idea of applying the method of geometry—the deduction of absolutely certain conclusions from self-evident premises—to a new science of human nature and society. In the following years Hobbes became interested in Galileo's theory of motion as the natural state of bodies, and in his first book used this theory to explain human sensation and thought.

For most of the period between 1634 and 1650 Hobbes lived in Paris so as to avoid his religious enemies and the civil war in England, serving for some years as mathematics tutor to another English refugee, the future King

Charles II. There Hobbes was an active member of a circle of scientifically minded and anti-Aristotelian philosophers that included Descartes, a philosopher with whose views Hobbes was in fundamental disagreement. During these years he published his chief political works, *The Elements of Law, The Citizen*, and in 1651 *Leviathan*. They brought him notoriety as being anticlerical and insufficiently in favor of the English monarchy. Banished from the Paris court of Charles II, Hobbes returned to England, made peace with Cromwell who was then in power, and retired to the Cavendish estate. When Charles gained the throne in 1660 Hobbes once again became a court favorite. He spent the remainder of his life in controversy with the Oxford mathematician, Wallis, and in the company of some of the most distinguished people of the day. He still had energy and wit enough at the age of 80 to translate the *Iliad* and *Odyssey* from Greek into English verse because, he said, "I had nothing else to do."

The full title of Hobbes's chief work is *Leviathan or the Matter, Forme and Power of a Commonwealth Ecclesiastical and Civil*. First published in English in 1651, the *Leviathan* was later translated by Hobbes into Latin and published in 1670. The present selections are from the *English Works of Thomas Hobbes*, edited by Sir William Molesworth in 11 volumes, 1839.

SELECTIONS FROM
Leviathian

PART I Of Man

Chapter XIII.   Of the Natural Condition of Mankind as Concerning Their Felicity, and Misery

Men by nature equal.

Nature hath made men so equal, in the faculties of the body, and mind; as that though there be found one man sometimes manifestly stronger in body, or of quicker mind than another; yet when all is reckoned together, the difference between man, and man, is not so considerable, as that one man can thereupon claim to himself any benefit, to which another may not pretend, as well as he. For as to the strength of body, the weakest has strength enough to kill the strongest, either by secret machination, or by confederacy with others, that are in the same danger with himself.

And as to the faculties of the mind, setting aside the arts grounded upon words, and especially that skill of proceeding upon general, and infallible rules, called science; which very few have, and but in few things; as being not a native faculty, born with us; nor attained, as prudence, while we look after somewhat else, I find yet a greater equality amongst men, than that of strength. For prudence, is but experience; which equal time, equally bestows on all men, in those things they equally apply themselves unto. That which may perhaps make such equality incredible, is but a vain conceit of one's own wisdom, which almost all men think they have in a greater degree, than the vulgar; that is, than all men but themselves, and a few others, whom by fame, or for concurring with themselves, they approve. For such is the nature of men, that howsoever they may acknowledge many others to be more witty, or more eloquent, or more learned; yet they will hardly believe there be many so wise as themselves; for they see their own wit at hand, and other men's at a distance. But this proveth rather that men are in that point equal, that unequal. For there is not ordinarily a greater sign of the equal distribution of any thing, than that every man is contented with his share.

From this equality of ability, ariseth equality of hope in the attaining of our ends. And therefore if any two men desire the same thing, which nevertheless they cannot both enjoy, they become enemies; and in the way to their end, which is principally their own conservation, and sometimes their delectation only, endeavour to destroy, or subdue one another. And from hence it comes to pass, that where an invader hath no more to fear, than another man's single power; if one plant, sow, build, or possess a convenient seat, others may probably be expected to come prepared with forces united, to dispossess, and deprive him, not only of the fruit of his labour, but also of his life, or liberty. And the invader again is in the like danger of another.

From equality proceeds diffidence.

And from this diffidence of one another, there is no way for any man to secure himself, so reasonable, as anticipation; that is, by force, or wiles, to master the persons of all men he can, so long, till he see no other power great enough to endanger him: and this is no more than his own conservation requireth, and is generally allowed. Also because there be some, that taking pleasure in contemplating their own power in the acts of conquest, which they pursue farther than their security requires; if others, that otherwise would be glad to be at ease within modest bounds, should not by invasion increase their power, they would not be able, long time, by standing only on their defence, to subsist. And by consequence, such augmentation of dominion over men being necessary to a man's conservation, it ought to be allowed him.

From diffi-dence war.

Again, men have no pleasure, but on the contrary a great deal of grief, in keeping company, when there is no power able to over-awe them all. For every man looketh that his companion should value him, at the same rate he sets upon himself: and upon all signs of contempt, or undervaluing, naturally endeavours, as far as he dares, (which amongst them that have no common power to keep them in quiet, is far enough to make them destroy each other), to extort a greater value from his contemners, by damage; and from others, by the example.

So that in the nature of man, we find three principal causes of quarrel. First, competition; secondly, diffidence; thirdly, glory.

The first, maketh men invade for gain; the second, for

safety; and the third, for reputation. The first use violence, to make themselves masters of other men's persons, wives, children, and cattle; the second, to defend them; the third, for trifles, as a word, a smile, a different opinion, and any other sign of undervalue, either direct in their persons, or by reflection in their kindred, their friends, their nation, their profession, or their name.

Hereby it is manifest, that during the time men live without a common power to keep them all in awe, they are in that condition which is called war; and such a war, as if of every man, against every man. For WAR, consisteth not in battle only, or the act of fighting; but in a tract of time, wherein the will to contend by battle is sufficiently known: and therefore the notion of *time*, is to be considered in the nature of war; as it is in the nature of weather. For as the nature of foul weather, lieth not in a shower or two of rain; but in an inclination thereto of many days together: so the nature of war, consisteth not in actual fighting; but in the known disposition thereto, during all the time there is no assurance to the contrary. All other time is PEACE.

Whatsoever therefore is consequent to a time of war, where every man is enemy to every man; the same is consequent to the time, wherein men live without other security, than what their own strength, and their own invention shall furnish them withal. In such condition, there is no place for industry; because the fruit thereof is uncertain: and consequently no culture of the earth; no navigation, nor use of the commodities that may be imported by sea; no commodious building; no instruments of moving, and removing, such things as require much force; no knowledge of the face of the earth; no account of time; no arts; no letters; no society; and which is worst of all, continual fear, and danger of violent death; and the life of man, solitary, poor, nasty, brutish, and short.

It may seem strange to some man, that has not well weighed these things; that nature should thus dissociate, and render men apt to invade, and destroy one another: and he may therefore, not trusting to this inference, made from the passions, desire perhaps to have the same confirmed by experience. Let him therefore consider with himself, when taking a journey, he arms himself, and seeks to go well accompanied; when going to sleep, he locks his doors; when even in his house he locks his chests; and this when he knows there be laws, and public officers, armed, to revenge all injuries shall be done him; what opinion he has of his

Out of civil states, there is always war of every one against every one.

The incommodities of such a war.

fellow-subjects, when he rides armed; of his fellow citizens, when he locks his doors; and of his children, and servants, when he locks his chests. Does he not there as much accuse mankind by his actions, as I do by my words? But neither of us accuse man's nature in it. The desires, and other passions of man, are in themselves no sin. No more are the actions, that proceed from those passions, till they know a law that forbids them: which till laws be made they cannot know: nor can any law be made, till they have agreed upon the person that shall make it.

It may peradventure be thought, there was never such a time, nor condition of war as this; and I believe it was never generally so, over all the world: but there are many places, where they live so now. For the savage people in many places of America, except the government of small families, the concord whereof dependeth on natural lust, have no government at all; and live at this day in that brutish manner, as I said before. Howsoever, it may be perceived what manner of life there would be, where there were no common power to fear, by the manner of life, which men that have formerly lived under a peaceful government, use to degenerate into, in a civil war.

But though there had never been any time, wherein particular men were in a condition of war one against another; yet in all times, kings, and persons of sovereign authority, because of their independency, are in continual jealousies, and in the state and posture of gladiators; having their weapons pointing, and their eyes fixed on one another; that is, their forts, garrisons, and guns upon the frontiers of their kingdoms; and continual spies upon their neighbours; which is a posture of war. But because they uphold thereby, the industry of their subjects; there does not follow from it, that misery, which accompanies the liberty of particular men.

To this war of every man, against every man, this also is consequent; that nothing can be unjust. The notions of right and wrong, justice and injustice have there no place. When there is no common power, there is no law: where no law, no injustice. Force, and fraud, are in war the two cardinal virtues. Justice, and injustice are none of the faculties neither of the body, nor mind. If they were, they might be in a man that were alone in the world, as well as his senses, and passions. They are qualities, that relate to men in society, not in solitude. It is consequent also to the same condition, that there be no propriety, no dominion, no *mine* and *thine*

In such a war nothing is unjust.

distinct; but only that to be every man's, that he can get; and for so long, as he can keep it. And thus much for the ill condition, which man by mere nature is actually placed in; though with a possibility to come out of it, consisting partly in the passions, partly in his reason.

The passions that incline men to peace.

The passions that incline men to peace, are fear of death; desire of such things as are necessary to commodious living; and a hope by their industry to obtain them. And reason suggesteth convenient articles of peace, upon which men may be drawn to agreement. These articles, are they, which otherwise are called the Laws of Nature: whereof I shall speak more particularly, in the two following chapters.

Chapter XV.   Of Other Laws of Nature

The third law of nature, justice.

From that law of nature, by which we are obliged to transfer to another, such rights, as being retained, hinder the peace of mankind, there followeth a third; which is this, *that men perform their covenants made:* without which, covenants are in vain, and but empty words; and the right of all men to all things remaining, we are still in the condition of war.

Justice and injustice what.

And in this law of nature, consisteth the fountain and original of JUSTICE. For where no covenant hath preceded, there hath no right been transferred, and every man has right to every thing; and consequently, no action can be unjust. But when a covenant is made, then to break it is *unjust:* and the definition of INJUSTICE, is no other than *the not performance of covenant.* And whatsoever is not unjust, is *just.*

Justice and propriety begin with the constitution of commonwealth.

But because covenants of mutual trust, where there is a fear of not performance on either part, as hath been said in the former chapter, are invalid; though the original of justice be the making of covenants; yet injustice actually there can be none, till the cause of such fear be taken away; which while men are in the natural condition of war, cannot be done. Therefore before the names of just, and unjust can have place, there must be some coercive power, to compel men equally to the performance of their covenants, by the terror of some punishment, greater than the benefit they expect by the breach of their covenant; and to make good that propriety, which by mutual contract men acquire, in recompense of the universal right they abandon: and such power there is none before the erection of a commonwealth. And this is also to be gathered out of the ordinary definition of justice in the Schools: for they say, that *justice is the constant will of giving to every man his own.* And therefore where there is no *own*, that is no propriety, there is no injustice; and where there is no coercive power erected, that is, where there is no commonwealth, there is no propriety; all men having right to all things: therefore where there is no commonwealth, there nothing is unjust. So that the nature of justice, consisteth in keeping of valid covenants: but the validity of covenants begins not but with the constitution of a civil power, sufficient to compel men to keep them: and then it is also that propriety begins.

The fool hath said in his heart, there is no such thing as justice; and sometimes also with his tongue; seriously alleging, that every man's conservation, and contentment, being committed to his own care, there could be no reason, why every man might not do what he thought conduced thereunto: and therefore also to make, or not make; keep, or not keep covenants, was not against reason, when it conduced to one's benefit. He does not therein deny, that there be covenants; and that they are sometimes broken, sometimes kept; and that such breach of them may be called injustice, and the observance of them justice: but he questioneth, whether injustice, taking away the fear of God, for the same fool hath said in his heart there is no God, may not sometimes stand with that reason, which dictateth to every man his own good; and particularly then, when it conduceth to such a benefit, as shall put a man in a condition, to neglect not only the dispraise, and revilings, but also the power of other men. The kingdom of God is gotten by violence: but what if it could be gotten by unjust violence? were it against reason so to get it, when it is impossible to receive hurt by it? and if it be not against reason, it is not against justice; or else justice is not to be approved for good. From such reasoning as this, successful wickedness hath obtained the name of virtue: and some that in all other things have disallowed the violation of faith; yet have allowed it, when it is for the getting of a kingdom. And the heathen that believed, that Saturn was deposed by his son Jupiter, believed nevertheless the same Jupiter to be the avenger of injustice: somewhat like to a piece of law in Coke's *Commentaries on Littleton*; where he says, if the right heir of the crown be attainted of treason; yet the crown shall descend to him, and *eo instante* the attainder be void: from which instances a man will be very prone to infer; that when the heir apparent of a kingdom, shall kill him that is in possession, though his father; you may call it injustice, or by what other name you

Justice not
contrary to
reason.

Justice not contrary to reason.

will; yet it can never be against reason, seeing all the voluntary actions of men tend to the benefit of themselves; and those actions are most reasonable, that conduce most to their ends. This specious reasoning is nevertheless false.

For the question is not of promises mutual, where there is no security of performance on either side; as when there is no civil power erected over the parties promising; for such promises are no covenants: but either where one of the parties has performed already; or where there is a power to make him perform; there is the question whether it be against reason, that is, against the benefit of the other to perform, or not. And I say it is not against reason. For the manifestation whereof, we are to consider; first, that when a man doth a thing, which notwithstanding any thing can be foreseen, and reckoned on, tendeth to his own destruction, howsoever some accident which he could not expect, arriving may turn it to his benefit; yet such events do not make it reasonably or wisely done. Secondly, that in a condition of war, wherein every man to every man, for want of a common power to keep them all in awe, is an enemy, there is no man who can hope by his own strength, or wit, to defend himself from destruction, without the help of confederates; where every one expects the same defence by the confederation, that any one else does: and therefore he which declares he thinks it reason to deceive those that help him, can in reason expect no other means of safety, than what can be had from his own single power. He therefore that breaketh his covenant, and consequently declareth that he thinks he may with reason do so, cannot be received into any society, that unite themselves for peace and defence, but by the error of them that receive him; nor when he is received, be retained in it, without seeing the danger of their error; which errors a man cannot reasonably reckon upon as the means of his security: and therefore if he be left, or cast out of society, he perisheth; and if he live in society, it is by the errors of other men, which he could not foresee, nor reckon upon; and consequently against the reason of his preservation; and so, as all men that contribute not to his destruction, forbear him only out of ignorance of what is good for themselves.

As for the instance of gaining the secure and perpetual felicity of heaven, by any way; it is frivolous: there being but one way imaginable; and that is not breaking, but keeping of covenant.

And for the other instance of attaining sovereignty by

rebellion; it is manifest, that though the event follow, yet because it cannot reasonably be expected, but rather the contrary; and because by gaining it so, others are taught to gain the same in like manner, the attempt thereof is against reason. Justice therefore, that is to say, keeping of covenant, is a rule of reason, by which we are forbidden to do any thing destructive to our life; and consequently a law of nature.

There be some that proceed further; and will not have the law of nature, to be those rules which conduce to the preservation of man's life on earth; but to the attaining of an eternal felicity after death; to which they think the breach of covenant may conduce; and consequently be just and reasonable; such are they that think it a work of merit to kill, or depose, or rebel against, the sovereign power constituted over them by their own consent. But because there is no natural knowledge of man's estate after death; much less of the reward that is then to be given to breach of faith; but only a belief grounded upon other men's saying, that they know it supernaturally, or that they know those, that knew them, that knew others, that knew it supernaturally; breach of faith cannot be called a precept of reason, or nature.

Others, that allow for a law of nature, the keeping of faith, do nevertheless make exception of certain persons; as heretics, and such as use not to perform their covenant to others: and this also is against reason. For if any fault of a man, be sufficient to discharge our covenant made; the same ought in reason to have been sufficient to have hindered the making of it.

Covenants not discharged by the vice of the person to whom they are made.

The names of just, and injust, when they are attributed to men, signify one thing; and when they are attributed to actions, another. When they are attributed to men, they signify conformity, or inconformity of manners, to reason. But when they are attributed to actions, they signify the conformity, or inconformity to reason, not of manners, or manner of life, but of particular actions. A just man therefore, is he that taketh all the care he can, that his actions may be all just: and an unjust man, is he that neglecteth it. And such men are more often in our language styled by the names of righteous, and unrighteous; than just, and unjust; though the meaning be the same. Therefore a righteous man, does not lose that title, by one, or a few unjust actions, that proceed from sudden passion, or mistake of things, or persons: nor does an unrighteous man, lose his character, for such actions, as he does, or forbears to do, for fear:

Justice of men and justice of actions what.

because his will is not framed by the justice, but by the apparent benefit of what he is to do. That which gives to human actions the relish of justice, is a certain nobleness or gallantness of courage, rarely found, by which a man scorns to be beholden for the contentment of his life, to fraud, or breach of promise. This justice of the manners, is that which is meant, where justice is called a virtue; and injustice a vice.

But the justice of actions denominates men, not just, but *guiltless*: and the injustice of the same, which is also called injury, gives them but the name of *guilty*.

Justice of manners, and justice of actions.

Again, the injustice of manners, is the disposition, or aptitude to do injury; and is injustice before it proceed to act; and without supposing any individual person injured. But the injustice of an action, that is to say injury, supposeth an individual person injured; namely him, to whom the covenant was made: and therefore many times the injury is received by one man, when the damage redoundeth to another. As when the master commandeth his servant to give money to a stranger; if it be not done, the injury is done to the master; whom he had before covenanted to obey; but the damage redoundeth to the stranger, to whom he had no obligation; and therefore could not injure him. And so also in commonwealths, private men may remit to one another their debts; but not robberies or other violences, whereby they are endamaged; because the detaining of debt, is an injury to themselves; but robbery and violence, are injuries to the person of the commonwealth.

Nothing done to a man by his own consent can be injury.

Whatsoever is done to a man, conformable to his own will signified to the doer, is no injury to him. For if he that doeth it, hath not passed away his original right to do what he please, by some antecedent covenant, there is no breach of covenant; and therefore no injury done him. And if he have; then his will to have it done being signified, is a release of that covenant: and so again there is no injury done him.

Justice commutative and distributive.

Justice of actions, is by writers divided into *commutative*, and *distributive:* and the former they say consisteth in proportion arithmetical; the latter in proportion geometrical. Commutative therefore, they place in the equality of value of the things contracted for; and distributive, in the distribution of equal benefit, to men of equal merit. As if it were injustice to sell dearer than we buy; or to give more to a man than he merits. The value of all things contracted for, is measured by the appetite of the contractors: and therefore the just value, is that which they be contented to give. And merit, besides that which is by covenant, where the performance on one part, meriteth the performance of the other part, and falls under justice commutative, not distributive, is not due by justice; but is rewarded of grace only. And therefore this distinction, in the sense wherein it useth to be expounded, is not right. To speak properly, commutative justice, is the justice, of a contractor; that is, a performance of covenant, in buying, and selling; hiring, and letting to hire; lending, and borrowing; exchanging, bartering, and other acts of contract.

And distributive justice, the justice of an arbitrator; that is to say, the act of defining what is just. Wherein, being trusted by them that make him arbitrator, if he perform his trust, he is said to distribute to every man his own: and this is indeed just distribution, and may be called, though improperly, distributive justice; but more properly equity; which also is a law of nature, as shall be shown in due place. . . .

PART II Of Commonwealth

Chapter XVII.   Of the Causes, Generation, and Definition of a Commonwealth

The end of common-wealth, particular security:

The final cause, end, or design of men, who naturally love liberty, in the dominion over others, in the introduction of that restraint upon themselves, in which we see them live in commonwealths, is the foresight of their own preservation, and of a more contented life thereby; that is to say, of getting themselves out from that miserable condition of war, which is necessarily consequent, as hath been shown in chapter XIII, to the natural passions of men, when there is no visible power to keep them in awe, and tie them by fear of punishment to the performance of their covenants, and observation of those laws of nature set down in the fourteenth and fifteenth chapters.

Which is not to be had from the law of nature:

For the laws of nature, as *justice, equity, modesty, mercy,* and, in sum, *doing to others, as we would be done to,* of themselves, without the terror of some power, to cause them to be observed, are contrary to our natural passions, that carry us to partiality, pride, revenge, and the like. And covenants, without the sword, are but words, and of no strength to secure a man at all. Therefore notwithstanding the laws of nature, which every one hath then kept, when he has the will to keep them, when he can do it safely, if there be no power erected, or not great enough for our security; every man will, and may lawfully rely on his own strength and art, for caution against all other men. And in all places, where men have lived by small families, to rob and spoil one another, has been a trade, and so far from being reputed against the law of nature, that the greater spoils they gained, the greater was their honour; and men observed no other laws therein, but the laws of honour; that is, to abstain from cruelty, leaving to men their lives, and instruments of husbandry. And as small families did then; so now do cities and kingdoms which are but greater families, for their own security, enlarge their dominions, upon all pretences of danger, and fear of invasion, or assistance that may be given to invaders, and endeavour as much as they can, to subdue, or weaken their neighbours, by open force, and secret arts, for want of other caution, justly; and are remembered for it in after ages with honour.

Nor is it the joining together of a small number of men, that gives them this security; because in small numbers, small additions on the one side or the other, make the advantage of strength so great, as is sufficient to carry the victory; and therefore gives encouragement to an invasion. The multitude sufficient to confide in for our security, is not determined by any certain number, but by comparison with the enemy we fear; and is then sufficient, when the odds of the enemy is not of so visible and conspicuous moment, to determine the event of war, as to move him to attempt.

Nor from the conjunction of a few men or families:

And be there never so great a multitude; yet if their actions be directed according to their particular judgments, and particular appetites, they can expect thereby no defence, nor protection, neither against a common enemy, nor against the injuries of one another. For being distracted in opinions concerning the best use and application of their strength, they do not help but hinder one another; and reduce their strength by mutual opposition to nothing: whereby they are easily, not only subdued by a very few that agree together; but also when there is no common enemy, they make war upon each other, for their particular interests. For if we could suppose a great multitude of men to consent in the observation of justice, and other laws of nature, without a common power to keep them all in awe; we might as well suppose all mankind to do the same; and then there neither would be, nor need to be any civil government, or commonwealth at all; because there would be peace without subjection.

Nor from a great multitude, unless directed by one judgment:

Nor is it enough for the security, which men desire should last all the time of their life, that they be governed, and directed by one judgment, for a limited time; as in one battle, or one war. For though they obtain a victory by their unanimous endeavour against a foreign enemy; yet afterwards, when either they have no common enemy, or he that by one part is held for an enemy, is by another part held for a friend, they must needs by the difference of their interests dissolve, and fall again into a war amongst themselves.

And that continually.

It is true, that certain living creatures, as bees, and ants, live sociably one with another, which are therefore by Aristotle numbered amongst political creatures; and yet have no other direction, than their particular judgments and appe-

Why certain creatures without reason, or speech, do nevertheless live in society, without any coercive power.

tites; nor speech, whereby one of them can signify to another, what he thinks expedient for the common benefit: and therefore some man may perhaps desire to know, why mankind cannot do the same. To which I answer,

First, that men are continually in competition for honour and dignity, which these creatures are not; and consequently amongst men there ariseth on that ground, envy and hatred, and finally war; but amongst these not so.

Secondly, that amongst these creatures, the common good differeth not from the private; and being by nature inclined to their private, they procure thereby the common benefit. But man, whose joy consisteth in comparing himself with other men, can relish nothing but what is eminent.

Thirdly, that these creatures, having not, as man, the use of reason, do not see, nor think they see any fault, in the administration of their common business; whereas amongst men, there are very many, that think themselves wiser, and abler to govern the public, better than the rest; and these strive to reform and innovate, one this way, another that way; and thereby bring it into distraction and civil war.

Fourthly, that these creatures, though they have some use of voice, in making known to one another their desires, and other affections; yet they want that art of words, by which some men can represent to others, that which is good, in the likeness of evil; and evil, in the likeness of good; and augment, or diminish the apparent greatness of good and evil; discontenting men, and troubling their peace at their pleasure.

Fifthly, irrational creatures cannot distinguish between *injury*, and *damage;* and therefore as long as they be at ease, they are not offended with their fellows: whereas man is then most troublesome, when he is most at ease: for then it is that he loves to shew his wisdom, and control the actions of them that govern the commonwealth.

Lastly, the agreement of these creatures is natural; that of men, is by covenant only, which is artificial: and therefore it is no wonder if there be somewhat else required, besides covenant, to make their agreement constant and lasting; which is a common power, to keep them in awe, and to direct their actions to the common benefit.

The generation of a commonwealth.

The only way to erect such a common power, as may be able to defend them from the invasion of foreigners, and the injuries of one another, and thereby to secure them in such sort, as that by their own industry, and by the fruits of

the earth, they may nourish themselves and live contentedly;
is, to confer all their power and strength upon one man, or
upon one assembly of men, that may reduce all their wills,
by plurality of voices, unto one will: which is as much as to
say, to appoint one man, or assembly of men, to bear their
person; and every one to own, and acknowledge himself to
be author of whatsoever he that so beareth their person,
shall act, or cause to be acted, in those things which concern the common peace and safety; and therein to submit
their wills, every one to his will, and their judgments, to his
judgment. This is more than consent, or concord; it is a real
unity of them all, in one and the same person, made by
covenant of every man with every man, in such manner, as if
every man should say to every man, *I authorise and give up
my right of governing myself, to this man, or to this assembly of men, on this condition, that thou give up thy right to
him, and authorize all his actions in like manner.* This
done, the multitude so united in one person, is called a
COMMONWEALTH, in Latin CIVITAS. This is the generation of
that great LEVIATHAN, or rather, to speak more reverently, of
that *mortal god,* to which we owe under the *immortal God,*
our peace and defence. For by this authority, given him by
every particular man in the commonwealth, he hath the use
of so much power and strength conferred on him, that by
terror thereof, he is enabled to perform the wills of them all,
to peace at home, and mutual aid against their enemies
abroad, And in him consisteth the essence of the commonwealth; which, to define it, is *one person, of whose acts a
great multitude, by mutual covenants one with another,
have made themselves every one the author, to the end he
may use the strength and means of them all, as he shall
think expedient, for their peace and common defence.*

The definition
of a common-
wealth.

And he that carrieth this person, is called SOVEREIGN,
and said to have *sovereign power,* and every one besides,
his SUBJECT.

Sovereign, and
subject, what.

The attaining to this sovereign power, is by two ways.
One, by natural force; as when a man maketh his children,
to submit themselves, and their children to his government,
as being able to destroy them if they refuse; or by war
subdueth his enemies to his will, giving them their lives on
that condition. The other, is when men agree amongst
themselves, to submit to some man, or assembly of men,
voluntarily, on confidence to be protected by him against all
others. This latter, may be called a political commonwealth,

or commonwealth by *institution;* and the former, a commonwealth by *acquisition.* And first, I shall speak of a commonwealth by institution.

Chapter XVIII.   Of the Rights of Sovereigns by Institution

The act of instituting a commonwealth, what.

A *commonwealth* is said to be *instituted,* when a *multitude* of men do agree, and *covenant, every one, with every one,* that to whatsoever *man,* or *assembly of men,* shall be given by the major part, the *right* to *present* the person of them all, that is to say, to be their *representative;* every one, as well he that *voted for it,* as he that *voted against it,* shall *authorize* all the actions and judgments, of that man, or assembly of men, in the same manner, as if they were his own, to the end, to live peaceably amongst themselves, and be protected against other men.

The consequences to such institution, are.

From this institution of a commonwealth are derived all the *rights,* and *faculties* of him, or them, on whom sovereign power is conferred by the consent of the people assembled.

1. The subjects cannot change the form of government.

First, because they covenant, it is to be understood, they are not obliged by former covenant to anything repugnant hereunto. And consequently they that have already instituted a commonwealth, being thereby bound by covenant, to own the actions, and judgments of one, cannot lawfully make a new covenant, amongst themselves, to be obedient to any other, in any thing whatsoever, without his permission. And therefore, they that are subjects to a monarch, cannot without his leave cast off monarchy, and return to the confusion of a disunited multitude; nor transfer their person from him that beareth it, to another man, or other assembly of men: for they are bound, every man to every man, to own, and be reputed author of all, that he that already is their sovereign, shall do, and judge fit to be done: so that any one man dissenting, all the rest should break their covenant made to that man, which is injustice: and they have also every man given the sovereignty to him that beareth their person; and therefore if they depose him, they take from him that which is his own, and so again it is injustice. Besides, if he that attempteth to depose his sovereign, be killed, or punished by him for such attempt, he is author of his own punishment, as being by the institution, author of all his sovereign shall do: and because it is injustice for a man to do anything, for which he may be punished by his own authority, he is also upon that title, unjust. And whereas some men have pretended for their disobedience to their sovereign, a new covenant, made, not with men, but with God; this also is unjust: for there is no covenant with God, but by mediation of somebody that representeth God's person; which none doth but God's lieutenant, who hath the sovereignty under God. But this pretence of covenant with God, is so evident a lie, even in the pretenders' own consciences, that it is not only an act of an unjust, but also of a vile, and unmanly disposition.

Secondly, because the right of bearing the person of them all, is given to him they make sovereign, by covenant only of one to another, and not of him to any of them; there can happen no breach of covenant on the part of the sovereign; and consequently none of his subjects, by any pretence of forfeiture, can be freed from his subjection. That he which is made sovereign maketh no covenant with his subjects beforehand, is manifest; because either he must make it with the whole multitude, as one party to the covenant; or he must make a several covenant with every man. With the whole, as one party, it is impossible; because as yet they are not one person: and if he make so many several covenants as there be men, those covenants after he hath the sovereignty are void; because what act soever can be pretended by any one of them for breach thereof, is the act both of himself, and of all the rest, because done in the person, and by the right of every one of them in particular. Besides, if any one, or more of them, pretend a breach of the covenant made by the sovereign at his institution; and others, or one other of his subjects, or, himself alone, pretend there was no such breach, there is in this case, no judge to decide the controversy; it returns therefore to the sword again; and every man recovereth the right of protecting himself by his own strength, contrary to the design they had in the institution. It is therefore in vain to grant sovereignty by way of precedent covenant. The opinion that any monarch receiveth his power by covenant, that is to say, on condition, proceedeth from want of understanding this easy truth, that covenants being but words and breath, have no force to oblige, contain, constrain, or protect any man, but what it has from the public sword; that is, from the untied hands of that man, or assembly of men that hath the sovereignty, and whose actions are avouched by them all, and performed by

2. Sovereign power cannot be forfeited.

the strength of them all, in him united. But when an assembly of men is made sovereign; then no man imagineth any such covenant to have passed in the institution; for no man is so dull as to say, for example, the people of Rome made a covenant with the Romans, to hold the sovereignty on such or such conditions; which not performed, the Romans might lawfully depose the Roman people. That men see not the reason to be alike in a monarchy, and in a popular government, proceedeth from the ambition of some, that are kinder to the government of an assembly, whereof they may hope to participate, than of monarchy, which they despair to enjoy.

3. No man can without injustice protest against the institution of the sovereign declared by the major part.

Thirdly, because the major part hath by consenting voices declared a sovereign; he that dissented must now consent with the rest; that is, be contented to avow all the actions he shall do, or else justly be destroyed by the rest. For if he voluntarily entered into the congregation of them that were assembled, he sufficiently declared thereby his will, and therefore tacitly covenanted, to stand to what the major part should ordain: and therefore if he refuse to stand thereto, or make protestation against any of their decrees, he does contrary to his covenant, and therefore unjustly. And whether he be of the congregation, or not; and whether his consent be asked, or not, he must either submit to their decrees, or be left in the condition of war he was in before; wherein he might without injustice be destroyed by any man whatsoever.

4. The sovereign's actions cannot be justly accused by the subject.

Fourthly, because every subject is by this institution author of all the actions, and judgments of the sovereign instituted; it follows, that whatsoever he doth, it can be no injury to any of his subjects; nor ought he to be by any of them accused of injustice. For he that doth anything by authority from another, doth therein no injury to him by whose authority he acteth: but by this institution of a commonwealth, every particular man is author of all the sovereign doth: and consequently he that complaineth of injury from his sovereign, complaineth of that whereof he himself is author; and therefore ought not to accuse any man but himself; no nor himself of injury; because to do injury to one's self, is impossible. It is true that they that have sovereign power may commit iniquity; but not injustice, or injury in the proper signification.

5. Whatsoever the sovereign doth is unpunishable by the subject.

Fifthly, and consequently to that which was said last, no man that hath sovereign power can justly be put to death, or otherwise in any manner by his subjects punished. For seeing every subject is author of the actions of his sovereign; he punisheth another for the actions committed by himself.

And because the end of this institution, is the peace and defence of them all; and whosoever has right to the end, has right to the means; it belongeth of right, to whatsoever man, or assembly that hath the sovereignty, to be judge both of the means of peace and defence, and also of the hindrances, and disturbances of the same; and to do whatsoever he shall think necessary to be done, both beforehand, for the preserving of peace and security, by prevention of discord at home, and hostility from abroad; and, when peace and security are lost, for the recovery of the same. And therefore,

6. The sovereign is judge of what is necessary for the peace and defence of his subjects.

Sixthly, it is annexed to the sovereignty, to be judge of what opinions and doctrines are averse, and what conducing to peace; and consequently, on what occasions, how far, and what men are to be trusted withal, in speaking to multitudes of people; and who shall examine the doctrines of all books before they be published. For the actions of men proceed from their opinions; and in the well-governing of opinions, consisteth the well-governing of men's actions; in order to their peace, and concord. And though in matter of doctrine, nothing ought to be regarded but the truth; yet this is not repugnant to regulating the same by peace. For doctrine repugnant to peace, can no more be true, than peace and concord can be against the law of nature. It is true, that in a commonwealth, where by the negligence, or unskilfulness of governors, and teachers, false doctrines are by time generally received; the contrary truths may be generally offensive. Yet the most sudden, and rough bursting in of a new truth, that can be, does never break the peace, but only sometimes awake the war. For those men that are so remissly governed, that they dare take up arms to defend, or introduce an opinion, are still in war; and their condition not peace, but only a cessation of arms for fear of one another; and they live, as it were, in the precincts of battle continually. It belongeth therefore to him that hath the sovereign power, to be judge, or constitute all judges of opinions and doctrines, as a thing necessary to peace; thereby to prevent discord and civil war.

And judge of what doctrines are fit to be taught them.

Seventhly, is annexed to the sovereignty, the whole power of prescribing the rules, whereby every man may know, what goods he may enjoy, and what actions he may do, without being molested by any of his fellow-subjects; and this is it men call *propriety.* For before constitution of

7. The right of making rules; whereby the subjects may every man know what is so his own, as no other subject can without injustice take it from him.

sovereign power, as hath already been shown, all men had right to all things; which necessarily causeth war: and therefore this propriety, being necessary to peace, and depending on sovereign power, is the act of that power, in order to the public peace. These rules of propriety, or *meum* and *tuum*, and of *good, evil, lawful,* and *unlawful* in the actions of subjects, are the civil laws; that is to say, the laws of each commonwealth in particular; though the name of civil law be now restrained to the ancient civil laws of the city of Rome; which being the head of a great part of the world, her laws at that time were in these parts the civil law.

8. To him also belongeth the right of judicature and decision of controversy.

Eighthly, is annexed to the sovereignty, the right of judicature; that is to say, of hearing and deciding all controversies, which may arise concerning law, either civil, or natural; or concerning fact. For without the decision of controversies, there is no protection of one subject, against the injuries of another; the laws concerning *meum* and *tuum* are in vain; and to every man remaineth, from the natural and necessary appetite of his own conservation, the right of protecting himself by his private strength, which is the condition of war, and contrary to the end for which every commonwealth is instituted.

9. And of making war, and peace, as he shall think best.

Ninthly, is annexed to the sovereignty, the right of making war and peace with other nations, and commonwealths; that is to say, of judging when it is for the public good, and how great forces are to be assembled, armed, and paid for that end; and to levy money upon the subjects, to defray the expenses thereof. For the power by which the people are to be defended, consisteth in their armies; and the strength of an army, in the union of their strength under one command; which command the sovereign instituted, therefore hath; because the command of the *militia*, without other institution, maketh him that hath it sovereign. And therefore whosoever is made general of an army, he that hath the sovereign power is always generalissimo.

10. And of choosing all counsellors and ministers, both of peace & war.

Tenthly, is annexed to the sovereignty, the choosing of all counsellors, ministers, magistrates, and officers, both in peace, and war. For seeing the sovereign is charged with the end, which is the common peace and defence, he is understood to have power to use such means, as he shall think most fit for his discharge.

11. And of rewarding and punishing, and that (where no former law hath determined the measure of it) arbitrarily.

Eleventhly, to the sovereign is committed the power of rewarding with riches, or honour, and of punishing with corporal or pecuniary punishment, or with ignominy, every subject according to the law he hath formerly made; or if there be no law made, according as he shall judge most to conduce to the encouraging of men to serve the commonwealth, or deterring of them from doing disservice to the same.

Lastly, considering what value men are naturally apt to set upon themselves; what respect they look for from others; and how little they value other men; from whence continually arise amongst them, emulation, quarrels, factions, and at last war, to the destroying of one another, and diminution of their strength against a common enemy; it is necessary that there be laws of honour, and a public rate of the worth of such men as have deserved, or are able to deserve well of the commonwealth; and that there be force in the hands of some or other, to put those laws in execution. But it hath already been shown, that not only the whole *militia*, or forces of the commonwealth; but also the judicature of all controversies, is annexed to the sovereignty. To the sovereign therefore it belongeth also to give titles of honour; and to appoint what order of place, and dignity, each man shall hold; and what signs of respect, in public or private meetings, they shall give to one another.

12. And of honour and order.

These are the rights, which make the essence of sovereignty; and which are the marks, whereby a man may discern in what man, or assembly of men, the sovereign power is placed, and resideth. For these are incommunicable, and inseparable. The power to coin money; to dispose of the estate and persons of infant heirs; to have praeemption in markets; and all other statute prerogatives, may be transferred by the sovereign; and yet the power to protect his subjects be retained. But if he transfer the *militia*, he retains the judicature in vain, for want of execution of the laws: or if he grant away the power of raising money; the *militia* is in vain; or if he give away the government of doctrines, men will be frighted into rebellion with the fear of spirits. And so if we consider any one of the said rights, we shall presently see, that the holding of all the rest will produce no effect, in the conservation of peace and justice, the end for which all commonwealths are instituted. And this division is it, whereof it is said, *a kingdom divided in itself cannot stand:* for unless this division precede, division into opposite armies can never happen. If there had not first been an opinion received of the greatest part of England, that these powers were divided between the King, and the Lords, and the House of Commons, the people had never been divided and fallen into this civil war; first between those that disagreed in

These rights are indivisible.

politics; and after between the dissenters about the liberty of religion; which have so instructed men in this point of sovereign right, that there be few now in England that do not see, that these rights are inseparable, and will be so generally acknowledged at the next return of peace; and so continue, till their miseries are forgotten; and no longer, except the vulgar be better taught than they have hitherto been.

And can by no grant pass away without direct renouncing of the sovereign power.

And because they are essential and inseparable rights, it follows necessarily, that in whatsoever words any of them seem to be granted away, yet if the sovereign power itself be not in direct terms renounced, and the name of sovereign no more given by the grantees to him that grants them, the grant is void: for when he has granted all he can, if we grant back the sovereignty, all is restored, as inseparably annexed thereunto.

This great authority being indivisible, and inseparably annexed to the sovereignty, there is little ground for the opinion of them, that say of sovereign kings, though they be *singulis majores*, of greater power than every one of their

The power and honour of subjects vanisheth in the presence of the power sovereign.

subjects, yet they be *universis minores*, of less power than them all together. For if by *all together*, they mean not the collective body as one person, then *all together*, and *every one*, signify the same; and the speech is absurd. But if by *all together*, they understand them as one person, which person the sovereign bears, then the power of all together, is the same with the sovereign's power; and so again the speech is absurd: which absurdity they see well enough, when the sovereignty is in an assembly of the people; but in a monarch they see it not; and yet the power of sovereignty is the same in whomsoever it be placed.

And as the power, so also the honour of the sovereign, ought to be greater, than that of any, or all the subjects. For in the sovereignty is the fountain of honour. The dignities of lord, earl, duke, and prince are his creatures. As in the presence of the master, the servants are equal, and without any honour at all; so are the subjects, in the presence of the sovereign. And though they shine some more, some less, when they are out of his sight; yet in his presence, they shine no more than the stars in the presence of the sun.

Sovereign power not so hurtful as the want of it, and the hurt proceeds for the greatest part from not submitting readily to a less.

But a man may here object, that the condition of subjects is very miserable; as being obnoxious to the lusts, and other irregular passions of him, or them that have so unlimited a power in their hands. And commonly they that live under a monarch, think it the fault of the monarchy; and they that live under the government of democracy, or other sovereign assembly, attribute all the inconvenience to that form of commonwealth; whereas the power in all forms, if they be perfect enough to protect them, is the same: not considering that the state of man can never be without some incommodity or other; and that the greatest, that in any form of government can possibly happen to the people in general, is scarce sensible, in respect of the miseries, and horrible calamities, that accompany a civil war, or that dissolute condition of masterless men, without subjection to laws, and a coercive power to tie their hands from rapine and revenge: nor considering that the greatest pressure of sovereign governors, proceedeth not from any delight, or profit they can expect in the damage or weakening of their subjects, in whose vigour, consisteth their own strength and glory; but in the restiveness of themselves, that unwillingly contributing to their own defence, make it necessary for their governors to draw from them what they can in time of peace, that they may have means on any emergent occasion, or sudden need, to resist, or take advantage on their enemies. For all men are by nature provided of notable multiplying glasses, that is their passions and self-love, through which, every little payment appeareth a great grievance; but are destitute of those prospective glasses, namely moral and civil science, to see afar off the miseries that hang over them, and cannot without such payments be avoided.

Chapter XXI.   Of the Liberty of Subjects

Liberty, or FREEDOM, signifieth, properly, the absence of opposition; by opposition, I mean external impediments of motion; and may be applied no less to irrational, and inanimate creatures, than to rational. For whatsoever is so tied, or environed, as it cannot move but within a certain space, which space is determined by the opposition of some external body, we say it hath not liberty to go further. And so of all living creatures, whilst they are imprisoned, or restrained, with walls, or chains; and of the water whilst it is kept in by banks, or vessels, that otherwise would spread itself into a larger space, we use to say, they are not at liberty, to move in such manner, as without those external impediments they would. But when the impediment of motion, is in the constitution of the thing itself, we use not to say; it wants the

Liberty what.

liberty; but the power to move; as when a stone lieth still, or a man is fastened to his bed by sickness.

And according to this proper, and generally received meaning of the word, a FREEMAN, *is he, that in those things, which by his strength and wit he is able to do, is not hindered to do what he has a will to.* But when the words *free,* and *liberty,* are applied to any thing but *bodies,* they are abused; for that which is not subject to motion, is not subject to impediment: and therefore, when it is said, for example, the way is free, no liberty of the way is signified, but of those that walk in it without stop. And when we say a gift is free, there is not meant any liberty of the gift, but of the giver, that was not bound by any law or covenant to give it. So when we *speak freely,* it is not the liberty of voice, or pronunciation, but of the man, whom no law hath obliged to speak otherwise than he did. Lastly, from the use of the word *free-will,* no liberty can be inferred of the will, desire, or inclination, but the liberty of the man; which consisteth in this, that he finds no stop, in doing what he has the will, desire, or inclination to do.

Fear and liberty are consistent; as when a man throweth his goods into the sea for *fear* the ship should sink, he doth it nevertheless very willingly, and may refuse to do it if he will: it is therefore the action of one that was *free:* so a man sometimes pays his debt, only for *fear* of imprisonment, which because nobody hindered him from detaining, was the action of a man at *liberty.* And generally all actions which men do in commonwealths, for *fear* of the law, are actions, which the doers had *liberty* to omit.

Liberty, and *necessity* are consistent: as in the water, that hath not only *liberty,* but a *necessity* of descending by the channel; so likewise in the actions which men voluntarily do: which, because they proceed from their will, proceed from *liberty;* and yet, because every act of man's will, and every desire, and inclination proceedeth from some cause, and that from another cause, in a continual chain, whose first link is in the hand of God the first of all causes, proceed from *necessity.* So that to him that could see the connexion of those causes, the *necessity* of all men's voluntary actions, would appear manifest. And therefore God, that seeth, and disposeth all things, seeth also that the *liberty* of man in doing what he will, is accompanied with the *necessity* of doing that which God will, and no more, nor less. For though men may do many things, which God does not command, nor is therefore author of them; yet they can have no passion, nor appetite to anything, of which appetite God's will is not the cause. And did not his will assure the *necessity* of man's will, and consequently of all that on man's will dependeth, the *liberty* of men would be a contradiction, and impediment to the omnipotence and *liberty* of God. And this shall suffice, as to the matter in hand, of that natural *liberty*, which only is properly called *liberty*.

But as men, for the attaining of peace, and conservation of themselves thereby, have made an artificial man, which we call a commonwealth; so also have they made artificial chains, called *civil laws*, which they themselves, by mutual covenants, have fastened at one end, to the lips of that man, or assembly, to whom they have given the sovereign power; and at the other end to their own ears. These bonds, in their own nature but weak, may nevertheless be made to hold, by the danger, though not by the difficulty of breaking them.

Artificial bonds, or covenants.

In relation to these bonds only it is, that I am to speak now, of the *liberty* of *subjects*. For seeing there is no commonwealth in the world, wherein there be rules enough set down, for the regulating of all the actions, and words of men; as being a thing impossible: it followeth necessarily, that in all kinds of actions by the laws praetermitted, men have the liberty, of doing what their own reasons shall suggest, for the most profitable to themselves. For if we take liberty in the proper sense, for corporal liberty; that is to say, freedom from chains and prison; it were very absurd for men to clamour as they do, for the liberty they so manifestly enjoy. Again, if we take liberty, for an exemption from laws, it is it no less absurd, for men to demand as they do, that liberty, by which all other men may be masters of their lives. And yet, as absurd as it is, this is it they demand; not knowing that the laws are of no power to protect them, without a sword in the hands of a man, or men, to cause those laws to be put in execution. The liberty of a subject, lieth therefore only in those things, which in regulating their actions, the sovereign hath praetermitted: such as is the liberty to buy, and sell, and otherwise contract with one another; to choose their own abode, their own diet, their own trade of life, and institute their children as they themselves think fit; and the like.

Liberty of subjects consisteth in liberty from covenants.

Nevertheless we are not to understand, that by such liberty, the sovereign power of life and death, is either abolished, or limited. For it has been already shown, that nothing the sovereign representative can do to a subject, on what pretence soever, can properly be called injustice, or

Liberty of the subject consistent with the unlimited power of the sovereign.

Liberty of the
subject
consistent with
the unlimited
power of the
sovereign.

injury; because every subject is author of every act the
sovereign doth; so that he never wanteth right to anything,
otherwise, than as he himself is the subject of God, and
bound thereby to observe the laws of nature. And therefore
it may, and doth often happen in commonwealths, that a
subject may be put to death, by the command of the sovereign power; and yet neither do the other wrong: as when
Jephtha caused his daughter to be sacrificed: in which, and
the like cases, he that so dieth, had liberty to do the action,
for which he is nevertheless, without injury put to death. And
the same holdeth also in a sovereign prince, that putteth to
death an innocent subject. For though the action be against
the law of nature, as being contrary to equity, as was the
killing of Uriah, by David; yet it was not an injury to Uriah,
but to God. Not to Uriah, because the right to do what he
pleased was given him by Uriah himself: and yet to God,
because David was God's subject, and prohibited all iniquity
by the law of nature: which distinction, David himself, when
he repented the fact, evidently confirmed, saying, *To thee
only have I sinned*. In the same manner, the people of
Athens, when they banished the most potent of their commonwealth for ten years, thought they committed no injustice; and yet they never questioned what crime he had done;
but what hurt he would do: nay they commanded the banishment of they knew not whom; and every citizen bringing
his oystershell into the market place, written with the name
of him he desired should be banished, without actually
accusing him, sometimes banished an Aristides, for his reputation of justice; and sometimes a scurrilous jester, as Hy-
perbolus, to make a jest of it. And yet a man cannot say,
the sovereign people of Athens wanted right to banish them;
or an Athenian the liberty to jest, or to be just.

The liberty
which writers
praise, is the
liberty of
sovereigns; not
of private men.

The liberty, whereof there is so frequent and honourable mention, in the histories, and philosophy of the ancient
Greeks, and Romans, and in the writings, and discourse of
those that from them have received all their learning in the
politics, is not the liberty of particular men; but the liberty of
the commonwealth: which is the same with that which every
man then should have, if there were no civil laws, nor
commonwealth at all. And the effects of it also be the same.
For as amongst masterless men, there is perpetual war, of
every man against his neighbour; no inheritance, to transmit
to the son, nor to expect from the father; no propriety of
goods, or lands; no security; but a full and absolute liberty in
every particular man: so in states, and commonwealths not

dependent on one another, every commonwealth, not every man, has an absolute liberty, to do what it shall judge, that is to say, what that man, or assembly that representeth it, shall judge most conducing to their benefit. But withal, they live in the condition of a perpetual war, and upon the confines of battle, with their frontiers armed, and cannons planted against their neighbours round about. The Athenians, and Romans were free; that is, free commonwealths: not that any particular men had the liberty to resist their own representative; but that their representative had the liberty to resist, or invade other people. There is written on the turrets of the city of Lucca in great characters at this day, the word LIBERTAS; yet no man can thence infer, that a particular man has more liberty, or immunity from the service of the commonwealth there, than in Constantinople. Whether a commonwealth be monarchical, or popular, the freedom is still the same.

The liberty which writers praise, is the liberty of sovereigns; not of private men.

But it is an easy thing, for men to be deceived, by the specious name of liberty; and for want of judgment to distinguish, mistake that for their private inheritance, and birthright, which is the right of the public only. And when the same error is confirmed by the authority of men in reputation for their writings on this subject, it is no wonder if it produce sedition, and change of government. In these western parts of the world, we are made to receive our opinions concerning the institution, and rights of commonwealths, from Aristotle, Cicero, and other men, Greeks and Romans, that living under popular states, derived those rights, not from the principles of nature, but transcribed them into their books, out of the practice of their own commonwealths, which were popular; as the grammarians describe the rules of language, out of the practice of the time; or the rules of poetry, out of the poems of Homer and Virgil. And because the Athenians were taught, to keep them from desire of changing their government, that they were freemen, and all that lived under monarchy were slaves; therefore Aristotle puts it down in his *Politics, (lib. 6. cap. ii.) In democracy, LIBERTY is to be supposed: for it is commonly held, that no man is FREE in any other government.* And as Aristotle; so Cicero, and other writers have grounded their civil doctrine, on the opinions of the Romans, who were taught to hate monarchy, at first, by them that having deposed their sovereign, shared amongst them the sovereignty of Rome; and afterwards by their successors. And by reading of these Greek, and Latin authors, men from their childhood have gotten a habit, under a false show of liberty, of favouring tumults, and of licentious controlling the actions of their sovereigns, and again of controlling those controllers; with the effusion of so much blood, as I think I may truly say, there was never any thing so dearly bought, as these western parts have bought the learning of the Greek and Latin tongues.

Liberty of subjects how to be measured.

To come now to the particulars of the true liberty of a subject; that is to say, what are the things, which though commanded by the sovereign, he may nevertheless, without injustice, refuse to do; we are to consider, what rights we pass away, when we make a commonwealth; or, which is all one, what liberty we deny ourselves, by owning all the actions, without exception, of the man, or assembly we make our sovereign. For in the act of our *submission*, consisteth both our *obligation*, and our *liberty*; which must therefore be inferred by arguments taken from thence; there being no obligation on any man, which ariseth not from some act of his own; for all men equally, are by nature free. And because such arguments, must either be drawn from the express words, *I authorize all his actions*, or from the intention of him that submitteth himself to his power, which intention is to be understood by the end for which he so submitteth; the obligation, and liberty of the subject, is to be derived, either from those words, or others equivalent; or else from the end of the institution of sovereignty, namely, the peace of the subjects within themselves, and their defence against a common enemy.

Subjects have liberty to defend their own bodies, even against them that lawfully invade them.

First therefore, seeing sovereignty by institution, is by covenant of every one to every one; and sovereignty by acquisition, by covenants of the vanquished to the victor, or child to the parent; it is manifest, that every subject has liberty in all those things, the right whereof cannot by covenant be transferred. I have shewn before in the 14th chapter, that covenants, not to defend a man's own body, are void. Therefore,

Are not bound to hurt themselves.

If the sovereign command a man, though justly condemned, to kill, wound, or maim himself; or not to resist those that assault him; or to abstain from the use of food, air, medicine, or any other thing, without which he cannot live; yet hath that man the liberty to disobey.

If a man be interrogated by the sovereign, or his authority, concerning a crime done by himself, he is not bound, without assurance of pardon, to confess it; because no man, as I have shown in the same chapter, can be obliged by covenant to accuse himself.

Again, the consent of a subject to sovereign power, is contained in these words, *I authorize, or take upon me, all his actions*; in which there is no restriction at all, of his own former natural liberty; for by allowing him to *kill me*, I am not bound to kill myself when he commands me. It is one thing to say, *kill me, or my fellow, if you please*; another thing to say, *I will kill myself, or my fellow*. It followeth therefore, that

No man is bound by the words themselves, either to kill himself, or any other man; and consequently, that the obligation a man may sometimes have, upon the command of the sovereign to execute any dangerous, or dishonourable office, dependeth not on the words of our submission; but on the intention, which is to be understood by the end thereof. When therefore our refusal to obey, frustrates the end for which the sovereignty was ordained; then there is no liberty to refuse; otherwise there is.

Upon this ground, a man that is commanded as a soldier to fight against the enemy, though his sovereign have right enough to punish his refusal with death, may nevertheless in many cases refuse, without injustice; as when he substituteth a sufficient soldier in his place: for in this case he deserteth not the service of the commonwealth. And there is allowance to be made for natural timorousness; not only to women, of whom no such dangerous duty is expected, but also to men of feminine courage. When armies fight, there is on one side, or both, a running away; yet when they do it not out of treachery, but fear, they are not esteemed to do it unjustly, but dishonourably. For the same reason, to avoid battle, is not injustice, but cowardice. But he that inrolleth himself a soldier, or taketh imprest money, taketh away the excuse of a timorous nature; and is obliged, not only to go to the battle, but also not to run from it, without his captain's leave. And when the defence of the commonwealth, requireth at once the help of all that are able to bear arms, every one is obliged; because otherwise the institution of the commonwealth, which they have not the purpose, or courage to preserve, was in vain.

Nor to warfare, unless they voluntarily undertake it.

To resist the sword of the commonwealth, in defence of another man, guilty, or innocent, no man hath liberty; because such liberty, takes away from the sovereign, the means of protecting us; and is therefore destructive of the very essence of government. But in case a great many men together, have already resisted the sovereign power unjustly, or committed some capital crime, for which every one of them expecteth death, whether have they not the liberty then to join together, and assist, and defend one another? Certainly they have: for they but defend their lives, which the guilty man may as well do, as the innocent. There was indeed injustice in the first breach of their duty; their bearing of arms subsequent to it, though it be to maintain what they have done, is no new unjust act. And if it be only to defend their persons, it is not unjust at all. But the offer of pardon taketh from them, to whom it is offered, the plea of self-defence, and maketh their perseverance in assisting, or defending the rest, unlawful.

The greatest liberty of subjects, dependeth on the silence of the law.

As for other liberties, they depend on the silence of the law. In cases where the sovereign has prescribed no rule, there the subject hath the liberty to do, or forbear, according to his own discretion. And therefore such liberty is in some places more, and in some less; and in some times more, in other times less, according as they that have the sovereignty shall think most convenient. As for example, there was a time, when in England a man might enter into his own land, and dispossess such as wrongfully possessed it, by force. But in aftertimes, that liberty of forcible entry, was taken away by a statute made, by the king, in parliament. And in some places of the world, men have the liberty of many wives: in other places, such liberty is not allowed.

If a subject have a controversy with his sovereign, of debt, or of right of possession of lands or goods, or concerning any service required at his hands, or concerning any penalty, corporal, or pecuniary, grounded on a precedent law; he hath the same liberty to sue for his right, as if it were against a subject; and before such judges, as are appointed by the sovereign. For seeing the sovereign demandeth by force of a former law, and not by virtue of his power; he declareth thereby, that he requireth no more, than shall appear to be due by that law. The suit therefore is not contrary to the will of the sovereign; and consequently the subject hath the liberty to demand the hearing of his cause; and sentence, according to that law. But if he demand, or take anything by pretence of his power; there lieth, in that case, no action of law; for all that is done by him in virtue of his power, is done by the authority of every subject, and consequently he that brings an action against the sovereign, brings it against himself.

If a monarch, or sovereign assembly, grant a liberty to all, or any of his subjects, which grant standing, he is disabled to provide for their safety, the grant is void; unless he directly renounce, or transfer the sovereignty to another. For in that he might openly, if it had been his will, and in plain terms, have renounced, or transferred it, and did not; it is to be understood it was not his will, but that the grant proceeded from ignorance of the repugnancy between such a liberty and the sovereign power; and therefore the sovereignty is still retained; and consequently all those powers, which are necessary to the exercising thereof; such as are the power of war, and peace, of judicature, of appointing officers, and councillors, of levying money, and the rest named in the 18th chapter.

The obligation of subjects to the sovereign, is understood to last as long, and no longer, than the power lasteth, by which he is able to protect them. For the right men have by nature to protect themselves, when none else can protect them, can by no covenant be relinquished. The sovereignty is the soul of the commonwealth; which once departed from the body, the members do no more receive their motion from it. The end of obedience is protection; which, wheresoever a man seeth it, either in his own, or in another's sword, nature applieth his obedience to it, and his endeavour to maintain it. And though sovereignty, in the intention of them that make it, be immortal; yet is it in its own nature, not only subject to violent death, by foreign war; but also through the ignorance, and passions of men, it hath in it, from the very institution, many seeds of a natural mortality, by intestine discord. *In what cases subjects are absolved of their obedience to their sovereign.*

If a subject be taken prisoner in war; or his person, or his means of life be within the guards of the enemy, and hath his life and corporal liberty given him, on condition to be subject to the victor, he hath liberty to accept the condition; and having accepted it, is the subject of him that took him; because he had no other way to preserve himself. The case is the same, if he be detained on the same terms, in a foreign country. But if a man be held in prison, or bonds, or is not trusted with the liberty of his body; he cannot be understood to be bound by covenant to subjection; and therefore may, if he can, make his escape by any means whatsoever. *In case of captivity.*

If a monarch shall relinquish the sovereignty, both for himself, and his heirs; his subjects return to the absolute liberty of nature; because, though nature may declare who are his sons, and who are the nearest of his kin; yet it dependeth on his own will, as hath been said in the precedent chapter, who shall be his heir. If therefore he will have no heir, there is no sovereignty, nor subjection. The case is the same, if he die without known kindred, and without *In case the sovereign cast off the government from himself and his heirs.*

declaration of his heir. For then there can no heir be known, and consequently no subjection be due.

In case of banishment.

If the sovereign banish his subject; during the banishment, he is not subject. But he that is sent on a message, or hath leave to travel, is still subject; but it is, by contract between sovereigns, not by virtue of the covenant of subjection. For whosoever entereth into another's dominion, is subject to all the laws thereof; unless he have a privilege by the amity of the sovereigns, or by special licence.

In case the sovereign render himself subject to another.

If a monarch subdued by war, render himself subject to the victor; his subjects are delivered from their former obligation, and become obliged to the victor. But if he be held prisoner, or have not the liberty of his own body; he is not understood to have given away the right of sovereignty; and therefore his subjects are obliged to yield obedience to the magistrates formerly placed, governing not in their own name, but in his. For, his right remaining, the question is only of the administration; that is to say, of the magistrates and officers; which, if he have not means to name, he is supposed to approve those, which he himself had formerly appointed.

SAMUEL von PUFENDORF

1 6 3 2 – 1 6 9 4

INTRODUCTION

One of the great jurists and social philosophers of the seventeenth century, Pufendorf was the son of a poor Lutheran minister in rural Saxony. Sent by his father to study theology at the University of Leipzig, Pufendorf soon rejected the dogmatism and conservatism of his teachers in favor of a broader education at Leipzig and later at the University of Jena. He then became a tutor in the family of the Swedish ambassador in Copenhagen, only to be imprisoned for 8 months with the family when the Swedes unexpectedly resumed war against the Danes. Pufendorf used the time to write his first book, *Elements of Universal Jurisprudence*, published when he and the family were free to move to the Netherlands. Two years later, in 1662, he obtained a recommendation that led to his becoming the professor of natural and international law at the University of Heidelberg, where he remained for 8 years, publishing under a pseudonym a notorious attack on the administration of the Holy Roman, or German, Empire to which Heidelberg belonged.

In 1670 Pufendorf accepted the offer of a chair in international law in the new university at Lund in Sweden, and *The Law of Nature and Nations*, the immensely long work for which he is now chiefly remembered, was published there in 1672 under the protection of his Lutheran patron, King Charles XI, who defended him against his Lutheran critics. In the 7 years that Pufendorf remained at Lund he wrote a legal textbook that, in combination with *The Law of Nature*, during the next century went through more than a hundred editions in the chief European languages. His earlier book on the German empire was also widely read into the early years of the eighteenth century.

Pufendorf's career as a lawyer and political thinker underwent a sudden change in 1676 when Lund was captured by the Danes and Pufendorf, having lost his university post, became Sweden's Royal Historian. In the next decade he wrote a political history of Sweden in 33 volumes and a number of shorter works, including the influential *Of the Relation Between Church and State.* From 1688 until his death 6 years later, Pufendorf was Court Historian at Berlin in Prussia, writing a history of the reign of his employer and ruler, Frederick William, and, after this patron's death, an unfinished diplomatic history of the new ruler, Frederick III. Pufendorf then had the difficult problem of reconciling these accounts with the somewhat different one that he had already written on the same topics for the Swedish king. In 1694 Pufendorf went to Sweden, obtained permission to publish unchanged his Swedish manuscript then held in Stockholm, received a knighthood, and set sail for Germany. He died of an embolism shortly after his return, leaving unanswered the question of how to provide a consistent historical justification of the competing policies of the two rulers who employed him.

Written in Latin, and first published in Lund, Sweden, in 1672, Pufendorf's *De Jure Naturae et Gentium* was first translated into English by Basil Kennet and published in London, 1710. The selections given here are from the fifth edition of that translation, London, 1749. The complete title is *The Law of Nature and Nations: or, A General System of the Most Important Principles of Morality, Jurisprudence, and Politics. In Eight Books.*

SELECTIONS FROM
The Law of Nature and Nations

Book I, Chapter VII

XIII. Mr. Hobbes hath advanced one single notion of justice to comprehend every kind; making it nothing else but a keeping of faith, and fulfilling of covenants; which opinion he borrowed from Epicurus. Commutative justice, he says, takes place in contracts, as in buying and selling, hiring and letting to hire, lending and borrowing, exchanging, bartering, and the like. Distributive justice (tho' improperly so called) is, he says, the justice of an Arbitrator, when being trusted by them who make him arbitrator, if he perform his trust, he is said to distribute to every man his own. Nor will he allow any other equality to be observed but this, that since we are all equal by nature, one man ought not to arrogate to himself more right than he allows another, unless he hath obtained a greater right than ordinary, by the intervention of covenants. Farther, since, according to his sentiments, an injury, or an unjust action, or omission; is nothing else but the violation of a covenant; he hence infers, that we cannot offer an injury to a man, unless we have before covenanted with him. This assertion is founded on his old maxim, of the right of every man to all things, which he hath stretched far beyond its just limits; so that he imagines, before any covenant is made, by which one man might transfer his right to another, every man hath a right of doing to others what he pleaseth; and thus, only using his right, he cannot be said to commit an injury. But we shall by and by shew, that this right of every man to all things can be extended to no farther sense than this, that nature allows a man to use all such means as reason shall judge conducible to his firm and lasting preservation: As indeed, Mr. Hobbes himself, in his definition of right, inserts the use of reason. But now sound reason will never advise us, out of our own pleasure and humour, to put such affronts on another, as cannot but provoke him to war, or to a reciprocal desire of hurting us. Besides it implies a manifest contradiction to say, that upon the supposal of many men equal in rights, each of them hath a right to all things; since the right of one man to all things, if it hath any effect, must extinguish the rights of the rest; and if the right hath no effect upon the other, it is useless, absurd, and ridiculous: For, in moral account, not to be, and not to be effectual, are much the same. And indeed, how can we call that a right, which another may oppose with an equal right? Who would say, I had the right, of commanding a man, if he, by the same right, might despise my orders? Or, that I had a right of beating another, when he too had a right of returning my blows, and, if he pleased, with advantage and increase? 'Tis certain therefore, that he that doth these things to another, hath no right of doing them, and, consequently, is injurious. On the contrary, the other party hath a right that such things should not be put upon him, and is therefore injured. Thus we see, that such right as being violated produceth an injury, is not only acquired by covenant, but was given at first by nature, without the intervention of any human act: And so the assertion, that an injury can be done to no man, unless we have transferred something on him by covenant, or gift, is false and unreasonable.

The other position of Mr. Hobbes, that justice, as well as property, owes its original to civil constitutions, we shall hereafter consider and refute.

Indeed, so far is it from being rational to resolve all justice into performance of covenants, that, on the contrary, before we can know whether any covenant is to be performed, we ought to be certain that it was entered upon, either by the command, or with the permission of the laws of nature; that is, that it was justly made.

From what hath been here offered, it is farther evident, that although otherwise damage and injury are very different things, and though it be possible that the injury of any action may redound to the man, and the damage to another; yet the inference which Mr. Hobbes draws from this consideration will not hold, that a bare damage, and not an injury is done to him, who is either hurt, or hath something taken from him, by a man with whom he had passed no covenant. Nor do the instances which he brings to countenance this conjecture, make very much to the purpose. When the master, says he, commands his servant to give money, or to do a kindness to a third person; if it be omitted, the injury is done to the master, but the damage to the third person. But indeed, if the servant does not pay the money which is due, as he is ordered, the creditor shall suffer no damage, since his actions remains good against the master. Nor, if a servant, being commanded to do a kindness to another man, fails in performing it, shall the other man incur any damage. Though he is indeed guilty of theft, or otherlike crime, if he intercept and keep for his own use, what he ought, on his master's account, to have delivered to others. For, besides that from the not receiving of a kindness, which is not strictly due, damage, properly so called, cannot arise, the other person may complain to the master, who will be sure to compel the servant to his duty. And though we suppose the servant to have been never so far from doing an injury to the third person, yet, for all this, 'tis certain he did not what by right he ought to have done; because he affords the other man sufficient grounds of a complaint against him. His other instance Mr. Hobbes thus proposeth in his *Leviathan*, Chap. xv, p. 75. Private men may remit to one another their debts, but not robberies, or other violences whereby they are endamaged: Because the detaining of a debt is an injury only to themselves, but robbery and violence are injuries to the person of the commonwealth. Which we are willing enough to admit, provided he will not hence infer, that in crimes an injury is not, likewise, done to the particular person who is hurt. But as he proposeth the same in his book *De Cive*, cap. iii s. 4. it is by no means to be endured. He says, that in a state, if any one hurts another, with whom he hath not covenanted, he damageth the party on whom he brings the evil, but he doth an injury only to him who holds the sovereign power in the state. For, if one of my fellow-subjects hurts me by violence, doth he offer an injury to the king only, and not to me? Or suppose we should grant, as Mr. Hobbes desires, that when men live in a natural liberty, each of them hath a right to all things, yet will this hold good amongst the members of the same republick, who own one common master? As to what he subjoins, that if the person who received the damage, should accuse the other of injuring him, he would be answered in this manner. What are you to me? Why should I act according to your pleasure, rather than my own, since I don't hinder you from acting by your own will, rather than by mine? 'Tis so far from being true, that if no particular covenants have intervened, this way of speaking will not be free from reprehension, that we would rather imagine a man to be out of his senses, who should hope by such a way of arguing to satisfy the complaints of one whom he had hurt. Yet one thing Mr. Hobbes hath well remarked, that the term of injustice signifies with reference to the law, but the term of injury with reference both to the law, and to the particular person. For, when an unjust thing is done, all may call that unjust, or it is unjust to all. But an injury may have been done, not to me, or to him, but to a third person, and sometimes to no private subject, but to the state only; as when a man is killed in a duel, for instance, upon a fair challenge. For, in this case, the party who received the hurt, cannot complain of having an injury done him; since he himself agreed to the chance of the unlawful combat: But the legislator may, however, prosecute the survivor for transgressing his prohibition.

XIV. Having arrived to know what justice is, we may easily settle our notions of injustice, and of its several species. An action, then, is unjust, either when we apply it designedly, to a person to whom we owed a different action, or when we deny another somewhat which was really his due. That is, we are equally guilty of a breach of justice, by doing any evil to another which we had no right to do, and by taking from another, or denying him any good which he had a fair title to require. For good things are of that nature, that they may be given to any man without a reason, provided a third person is not defrauded thereby: And the evils, likewise, which a man hath merited, we may, without injury, with-hold from him, if, at the same time, we do not endamage others by our forbearance. An unjust action, therefore, either brings upon another man, what it ought not to bring upon him, or denies and with-holds what it ought to give him. For the denial or omission of an action, is, in moral account, itself an action.

Book II, Chapter II

VI. That the state of nature then is a state of war, Mr. Hobbes endeavours in this manner to demonstrate. The reason why man is continually in fear of man, and consequently in a state of war with him, he draws from this principle, that men have both the power and the will of hurting one another. That they have the power of hurting each other, he shews by observing that men of ripe and settled age are commonly equal in strength. For though one may frequently have the advantage of another in bodily force, yet, 'tis possible, that the weakest may kill the strongest, either by secret machination, or by confederacy with others; inasmuch as the stoutest mortal has his vital parts not better ensured from extreme violence, than the most puny and impotent wretch. Neither is it probable that the larger degree of natural cunning (in which, of two men, one commonly exceeds the other) should be able to secure a man's safety while he has no guard, and no protector but himself. Farther, since the greatest evil that men can bring upon one another is death, and since this may as well be brought on the stout by the weakly, as on the weakly by the stout, he says it follows, that those who can bring on each other the greatest evil, must, in effect, be of equal power and strength. As to the will of hurting others, this, he says, is, in some men, out of necessity, and in some out of lust and pleasure. For while some are for living as they list, for arrogating to themselves undue honours, and for petulantly setting on their quiet neighbours; it's impossible but that those neighbours, how modest soever they may be, and how willing soever to allow others an equal liberty with themselves, must necessarily defend themselves against the violence of their assailants: Besides, he tells us, that the will of hurting arises frequently from the contention of wit, while every man thinks himself wiser than his fellows, and yet at the same time cannot bear the same arrogance in others. Hence, he says, it comes to pass, that it is not only odious to contradict, but, likewise, not to consent: For not to consent to another in a thing, is tacitly to accuse him of error in that matter; and to dissent in very many things, is as much as to count him a fool, in not being able to apprehend such an evident truth, as every one takes his own opinion to be. Hence, since all pleasure and satisfaction of mind conflicts in this, that one be able to prefer one's self to others, 'tis impossible but that now and then some signs of contempt towards others will break out; than which no affront is more provoking to human minds. The last and most frequent cause of a mutual desire of hurting, arises, according to Hobbes, from hence, that many desire one and the same thing at once, which frequently they neither can, nor will, enjoy in common, nor yet divide. From whence it follows, that it must be given to the stronger; and who is the stronger, can only be known by fighting. Upon all these accounts, he declares it to be impossible but that men should live in perpetual fear and suspicion of one another. And that since not only natural passion, but reason too, recommends to every man his own safety in the highest manner, and indulges him in the use of all means for the attaining of that end, the fitness of which, no superior being yet admitted, is to be determined by each man's particular judgment; hence there must necessarily arise a desire rather of preventing others, than of yielding to their invasion: From whence there will, at last, result a state of infinite war, of all men against all; the consequence of which is, that it shall be lawful for any man to do to any man, either secretly or openly, whatever he shall think expedient for his own affairs: In doing which, although his reason should sometimes fail him, yet he would not offer an injury to any body, since justice and injustice have nothing to do but with societies and established corporations: Though a man may indeed sin against reason, by using unfit means for his own preservation.

VII. These notions are in some measure, tolerable, if proposed only by way of hypothesis. And that Hobbes designed them for nothing more, we may be apt to conclude from those words in the eighth chapter of his book, *De Cive*; but to return again to a natural state, and to consider men as if they were just now risen out of the earth like a mushroom, and of full stature, without any manner of obligation to each other. Yet in the thirteenth chapter of the same book, and frequently in other places, he calls the state of public bodies, not by way of supposition, but seriously and absolutely natural; that is, as he explains it, hostile. Which seeming contrariety we may do him the justice thus to reconcile; it shall be a pure hypothesis, that all men did at any time live together in such a state of nature, as they would have done if they had risen suddenly in a great multitude from the earth: but what he seriously maintains shall be only this, that such a natural state doth really exist amongst some men; that is, amongst such as are neither subject one to the other, nor to a common master, as is now the case of all established communities. And this indeed is his own judgment, as he has moderated it in his *Leviathan*. Though (says he) there never had been any time, wherein particular men were in a condition of war one against another; yet in all times, kings and persons of sovereign authority, because of their independency, are in continual jealousies, and in the state and posture of gladiators, etc.

But the contrary opinion seems more reasonable, as what is clearly favoured by the origin of mankind, as related in the infallible records of holy scripture; which represent the natural state of man, not hostile, but peaceful, and show that men in their true condition, are rather hearty friends than spiteful foes. From these sacred histories we learn, that the first man being, by divine power, produced out of the earth, a companion was soon joined to him different in sex, whose substance was therefore taken out of him, to engage him immediately in the deepest love and affection for her, as being bone of his bone, and flesh of his flesh. This primitive and original couple God Almighty was pleased to unite in the most solemn manner, and with the most sacred tie; and since from them all human race orderly descended, we may conceive mankind mutually engaged, not only by such a vulgar friendship as might result from similitude of nature, but also by such a tender affection as endears persons allied by a nearness of race and of blood: Although the sense of this kind passion may be almost worn off amongst the descendants, by reason of their great distance from the common stock. Now if any man should pretend to divest himself of this affection, and entertain a temper of hostility against all others, he ought to be censured as a revolter from the primitive and natural state of mankind. Nor will it signify much here to object, that, even from this account of matters, it follows, that the natural state of men is a state of war; inasmuch as if societies were therefore instituted at the beginning of the world to make men live peaceably together, it must be true on the contrary side, that without societies men would not have lived peaceably, and that hence arose the necessity of making societies be born with them. To which we reply, that our present enquiries are not made after such a natural state, as may be conceived by the help of abstraction, but after such an one as really has been, and is now, in the world. And that therefore, since the first mortals were placed in such a state as inspired them with love, and not with enmity, and since from this state all the rest of mankind descended, it is plain, if men were mindful of their first original, they might be rather accounted friends than foes. Nor were societies therefore established amongst men from the beginning, to hinder a natural state from taking place, but because human kind could not otherwise have been propagated and preserved. But a state of nature did then arise, when men being largely multiplied could no longer be contained in one society. Hence it is nonsense to say, that without the help of a social condition, mankind, at the beginning of their being, would have lived like enemies one to another, unless we first suppose, that in the beginning of things a multitude of men started up together, without being beholden to one another for their production. . . .

VIII. As to Mr. Hobbes's reasons, they are easily answered. In the first place, those cannot immediately hurt one another, who are divided by distance of place; for he who is not present cannot hurt me, except by somebody else who is present, and my possessions cannot be destroyed unless by one upon the spot: Therefore, since those who live separately, or at a distance from each other, can offer no mutual hurt so long as they continue thus distant, it doth not appear why such men should not rather be reckoned friends than enemies. For if any person is more inclined to call them neuters, he ought to understand, that the term of friendship may be there fairly applied, where there is neither will nor power to injure. And then, as for that equality of strength which Hobbes asserts, it is certainly more fit to restrain, than to provoke a desire of hurting. For no man in his wits is very fond of coming to an encounter with his equal, unless he is either driven upon it by necessity, or by the fairness of the opportunity put in hopes of success. Otherwise, to engage in an unnecessary fight, were the blows one gives will be returned with no less force, and where the event is merely dubious, is no better than foolhardiness. For when two equal combatants are so far engaged as to put both their lives in danger, neither of them can possibly gain so much by the victory, as he must lose who is killed in the fight; nor is it so much to have taken away another's life, as to have hazarded one's own. For the danger to which I expose my life, takes from me more good than can possibly accrue to me from my enemy's life being in the same danger; nor is his safety increased upon account of the uncertainty of mine: But each party is a loser, and yet the loss of neither turns to the advantage of the other.

Besides, the causes alledged by Mr. Hobbes, why men must have a mutual desire of hurting, are only particular, and therefore cannot infer a necessity of an universal war of all men against all, but only a war of some particular men against some others. And then it doth not always happen, as he would suppose, that modest and civil men should have a more fierce and insolent generation living near them; or, if the case be so, yet it is not necessary that the latter should be in a humour of invading the former. Contention of wit prevails only amongst men exalted above the ordinary level; the greater and vulgar part of mankind have none, or but very slight touches of that disease. Nor has the all-wise creator been so unkind, or so sparing in his provisions for human race, that two persons must always lay claim to the same thing. Farther, the general wickedness of men may have so much effect, as to hinder any one from rashly thrusting, or offering (as it were) his bare breast to another, especially if he has not a knowledge of him. But, that this suspicion or diffidence should proceed so far, as to the seizing, or the oppressing another, unless he hath declared a particular desire and design to hurt us, no man of sense will admit. Cicero (*Off.* i. 7.) [*De Officiis*] rightly calls it, an injury out of fear, when he that is contriving to do another man mischief, doth it by way of prevention, suspecting he should otherwise suffer hurt from the quarter where he now offers it. Hobbes is the more inexcusable for maintaining that his natural state cannot be removed and broken up, but by letting in the sovereignty of another, and by uniting in the same commonwealth: For that those commonwealths, how distinct soever, which are allied by friendship and by leagues, should still continue in a state of mutual war, is a contradiction evident to the common sense of mankind. Nor should we (as he would have us) discard all peace, as not deserving that name, which is not sufficiently firm and certain, any more than we should forbear saying, that such a man is in grace and favour with another, because the wills of men are subject to continual alterations.

IX. We must likewise take special care to observe, that we are not disputing about the natural state of a meer animal, governed by the sole impulse and inclination of the sensitive soul; but of an animal whose noblest and chiefest part is reason, the sovereign and controller of all other faculties; and which, even in a natural state, has a common, a firm, and an uniform measure to go by; namely, the nature of things, which, lastly, is very free and ready in offering itself, so far as to instruct us in the general precepts of living, and the dictates of natural law. And those who would rightly design and represent a state of nature, ought by no means to exclude the just use of this reason, but should join it with the operations of the other faculties. Forasmuch then as man has not only the rash cry of his lusts, but also the sober voice of reason (not measuring itself purely by private interest) to hearken to, if his wild affections incite him to a war, such as that extravagant one of all men against all, his reason will be more powerful in dissuading him from it; and that chiefly by giving him these two intimations, that a war undertaken without provocation from the other party, is both unseemly and unprofitable. For it is easy for any man to gather thus much, that he did not exist of himself, but was produced by some superior, who consequently retains a power and authority over him. And when he finds himself spurned on, as it were, by a double principle, of which one is wholly fixed on things present, the other can embrace in its thought what is absent or future; of which one drives him furiously on dangers, doubts, and disorders, the other conducts him to nothing but what is comely and safe; he will conclude, without any difficulty, that 'tis the pleasure of his creator, he should rather follow the latter guide than the former. And when to this consideration is added, the exceeding great benefit and advantage of that quiet condition which reason advises, a man cannot but naturally incline to peace. Especially, since, if at any time he should happen to neglect his reason, and follow his blind passions, he would find by the sad event that he took the wrong measures, and would be ready to wish those things to be undone, which were done against the orders and directions of his noblest faculty. From all which we conclude, that the natural state of men, although they be considered as not united in commonwealths, is not war, but peace. And this peace chiefly depends on the following laws and conditions; that no man hurt another, who doth not assault and provoke him; that every one allow others to enjoy their own goods and possessions; that he faithfully perform whatever shall be convenanted for, and voluntarily promote the interest and happiness of others, in all cases where a stricter obligation doth not interfere. For since the natural state of man includes the use of reason, we must by no means separate from it those obligations, which reason tells us we lie under. And because every man may discover it to be most for his interest and advantage, so to manage his behaviour, as to procure rather the benevolence, than the enmity of others; he may easily presume, from the likeness of nature, that other men have the same sentiments about the point as himself. Therefore it is very foul play, in describing this imaginary state, to suppose that all men, or however the greatest part of them, do act with disregard and defiance to reason, which is by nature constituted supreme directress of human proceedings; and such a state cannot, without the highest absurdity, be called natural, which owes its production to the neglect, or to the abuse of the natural principle in man.

Book III, Chapter II

I. Besides that affection which every man maintains for his own life, and body, and possessions, by which he cannot but resist and repel whatever threatens destruction to those dear concerns; we may discover, likewise, deeply rooted in his mind, a most tender esteem and value for himself; which, if any one endeavour to impair, he is seldom less (and sometimes much more) incensed, than if a mischief had been offered to this person, or to his estate. This passion, though it may be heightened and improved by various external causes, yet seems to lay its first foundations in the very constitution of human nature. The word man is thought to carry somewhat of dignity in its sound; and we commonly make use of this, as the last and the most prevailing argument against a rude insulter, I am not a beast, a dog, but I am a man as well as yourself. Since then human nature agrees equally to all persons, and since no one can live a sociable life with another, who does not own and respect him as a man; it follows as a command of the law of nature, that every man should esteem and treat another as one who is naturally his equal, of who is a man as well as he is.

II. For the better understanding this equality among men, we may observe, that Mr. Hobbes restrains it to a parity of strength, and of other human abilities which attend a ripe and perfect age; and would from hence infer, that all men have good cause naturally to fear each other. For he, indeed, can strike no terror in me, whose power reaches not far enough to hurt me. But now among men, he who is inferior to another in bodily strength, may either by treacherous contrivance, or by art and dexterity, take away the life of the stoutest mortal. Since, therefore, the greatest of natural evils which can proceed from human power, is death, which any grown person is able to bring upon another; since those may be termed equal, who can do equal mischief to each other, and since to kill is equally (because in the highest degree) mischievous, it follows hence that men are by nature equal. When he subjoins, that the present inequality has been introduced by civil law, he seems to me very much to have forgotten himself. For he had been speaking before of the natural equality of mens strength, to which it is a great impropriety to oppose the unequalness arising from politick institutions, which does not affect or regard the strength of men, but their state and condition; does not make one man stouter than another, but greater in quality and honour. Nor has the same author much better success, when he pretend to discover in the faculties of the mind a greater equality than that of strength. He says indeed, that all prudence is but experience, which nature in equal time equally bestows on all men, in those things they equally apply their minds unto. But do not we see one man piercing more deeply than another into the consequences of things, applying more dexterously what he observes, and distinguishing with more perspicacity the likeness or unlikeness of cases and circumstances? And hence it frequently comes to pass, that of two men who have been employed an equal time in the same business, one shall grow eminent for management and address, whilst the other's natural heaviness shall be little amended by so long a course and experience of affairs. Nor does the great disparity of man's prudence arise only from their own false and overweening conceit of their particular worth; every one thinking himself to have a higher degree of wisdom than the vulgar; that is, than all, except a few, whom by fame, or for concurring with himself, he is wont to approve and admire. For this disparity appears, not only when a man compares himself with others, but when he compares others amongst themselves, and is not concerned as to his own interest, which side carries the advantage. Nor do we always favour and commend him, who conspires with our own thoughts and designs; but whom the fair contrivance, and the good success of his project, entitles to our approbation. And although such is the natural temper of man, so greedy is he of esteem and applause, that every one disdains to be upbraided with folly or imprudence, and is exceedingly incensed against those who boast of much larger talents, much higher attainments than his neighbours, yet it does not follow from hence, that no one allows another to be wiser than himself. For what if we fancy two men falling together into the same danger, one of whom, by his dexterous management, comes cleanly off, whilst the other is basely hampered, and escapes not without considerable hurt or prejudice; will not the latter here acknowledge his fellow to have had a better head-piece than himself? This is indeed a part of that freedom which men equally enjoy, that a wiser person shall have no right to challenge the government of one more simple unless with his consent; especially if the latter profess himself to be contented with his own little sagacity, and not desirous of the control and the direction of others.

But although the consideration of equal strength is thus far serviceable to our present purpose, that it may restrain one man from rashly insulting over another, inasmuch as all contention with an equal is of dubious issue; and because it is extreme folly to desire the hurting another by undergoing ourselves the same proportion of mischief: Yet the equality which we are now treating of is of a different species, and the inviolable observation of it is, in the highest degree, conducible to the common benefit and interest of mankind. And here, as in all other things, may we justly admire the wise contrivance of nature, that whilst she distributes amongst men the goods of the body and of the mind, by unequal parcels and measures, she introduces this general equality, to form an agreeable harmony amongst all the other varieties and disproportions. For as in well-ordered commonwealths, one subject may exceed another in riches, or in honour, but all are equal sharers in the common liberty; so under this regulation of nature, how much soever a man may surpass his neighbours, as to bodily or intellectual endowments, he is still obliged to pay all natural duties, as readily and fully as he expects to receive them; nor, do those advantages give him the least power or privilege to oppress his fellows. Nor, on the other side, does the bare unkindness of nature, or of fortune, set a man in a worse condition than others, as to the enjoyment of common rights. But whatever one man requires or expects from others, the same may others (all circumstances being alike) demand from him; and the same judgment one decrees against another, he is obliged, in like case, to submit to himself. On this account we can by no means admit of Cicero's rule, which he lays down in his third book of *Offices*; lex ipsa naturae, etc. The law of nature itself, which preserves and holds together the common profit of mankind, does decree, that things necessary for life and sustenance may be transferred from an idle and useless person, to a man of wisdom, goodness, and valour, who, should he be suffered to perish, would exceedingly prejudice the publick by his death. Much more unworthy of approbation is that saying of the American, recorded by Montaign, who, coming to Roan in the Reign of Charles IX and being asked what he observed that was singular in France, answered, that, amongst other things, he could not but wonder to see some persons abounding in all manner of plenty, and others oppressed with the most grievous want, begging at their doors, and not rather choosing to invade and pillage them for their own support. For as those who excel in the goods of the mind, of the body, or of fortune, ought not to treat men of lower condition with haughtiness and insolence; so neither ought these to envy or rifle their superiors.

And this equality we may call an equality of right; the principle from which it springs is this, that the obligation to a social life equally binds all men, inasmuch as it is the inseparable companion of human nature, considered simply as such. Where we may observe farther, that between obligations enjoyed by a superior, and those which arise from mutual compact, there seems to be this difference, that the latter immediately cease to a man, when the other party hath broken the agreement; whereas the former may still engage us to some performances towards a person who is wanting in a natural return of duty. And the reason of this is, because the author and imposer of the obligation is able to make up to us some other way what we lose by being more just than our neighbours. But our obligation to the practice of natural duty and right, although imposed by the supreme lawgiver, does thus far agree with obligations of common bargains and covenants, that so soon as one person recedes from it, he can no longer require the same offices from another; and besides, the other party does hence acquire a right of compelling him by force to make satisfaction. Though the genius of civil society makes it necessary to abridge and allay this liberty adhering to a state of nature, for the support and maintenance of government and peace.

III. Other reasons there are popular and plausible, which might give us a little assistance in discovering, and in illustrating this equality. Amongst which this is not the least considerable, that we all derive our being from one stock, from the same common father of human race. . . .

Farther, that our bodies are all composed of the same matter, frail and brittle, liable to be destroyed by a thousand accidents of mischief. We all owe our existence to the same method of propagation, we are all by the same degrees fashioned and compacted in the womb of our mother; and the noblest mortal, in his entrance on the stage of life, is not distinguished by any difference of pomp, or of passage, from the lowest of mankind. Our growth and nourishment is performed alike, and the gross remainders of our food are carried into the same common sewer. Lastly, our life hastens to the same general mark; death observes no ceremony, but knocks as loud at the barriers of the court, as at the door of the cottage; and, after death, our bodies are resolved into the same dust and corruption. Besides, wise men are ever pressing it upon our consideration, that we are alike obnoxious to the sports of fortune, to the endless variety of dangers or mischances; or rather, that the divine disposer of all things ensures no man in his present state, or in the possession of unshaken felicity: But, according to the secret counsels of his providence, exposes divers men to various changes and troubles, as if he pleased himself in raising the poor out of the dust, and casting the high down to the ground. Our Christian profession suggests many motives to the same purpose; as that God does not esteem men according to their nobility, their power, or their wealth, but according to their sincere piety and goodness. And that at the last day of judgment, of the distribution of rewards and punishments in another life, no regard will be had to those who swell in port and figure, beyond their neighbours of this world.

IV. This equality being admitted, there flow from it several precepts, the observation of which bears a very great force in the maintaining of peace and friendship amongst men. And this, in the first place, is most manifest, that he who would use the assistance of others in promoting his own advantage, ought as freely to be at their service, when they want his help on the like occasions. One good turn requires another, is the common proverb. For he must certainly esteem others unequal to himself, who constantly demands their aid, and as constantly denies his own. And whoever is of this insolent temper, cannot but highly displease and provoke those about him, and soon give occasion to a breach of the common peace . . . And indeed, it as much implies a contradiction to determine differently in my own case, and another's, when they are exactly parallel, as to make contrary judgments on things really the same. Since then every man is well acquainted with his own nature, and as well, at least; as to general inclinations, with the nature of other men, it follows, that he who concludes one way as to his own right, and another way as to the same right of his neighbour, is guilty of a contradiction in the plainest matter; an argument of a mind unsound in no ordinary degree. For no good reason can be given, why what I esteem just for myself, I should reckon unjust for another in the same circumstances. Those, therefore, are most properly sociable creatures, who grant the same privilege to others, which they desire should be allowed themselves; and those who, on the other hand, are most unfit for society; who, imagining themselves a degree above vulgar mortals, would have a particular commission to do whatever they please; they give themselves a free pardon for all things, and vouchsafe not to others the least indulgence; they demand the principle share of common honours, and of common goods; though their right and title is not distinguished by any peculiar excellence or advantage. For as in raising an edifice, a stone, which by reason of its rough and angular figure, robs others of more room than it fills itself, and upon account of its exceeding hardness, cannot conveniently be cut into regularity, and so hinders the whole frame of building from closing together, is thrown aside by the workman, as unfit for all use and service; so those greedy churls, whose rough and savage temper inclines them to heap superfluities on themselves, and to deprive others of mere necessaries, and whose violence of passion makes them uncapable of being reclaimed, are indeed the great impediments of society, and the plagues of mankind. Hence it is a command of nature's law, that no man who has not obtained a particular and especial right, shall arrogate to himself a larger share than his fellows; but shall admit others to an enjoyment of equal privileges with himself. . . .

V. The same equality teaches a man how to carry himself, in case he be appointed arbitrator of any right betwixt others; namely, that he treat them as equals, and give no favour or indulgence to one above the rest, except such as can claim by virtue of some peculiar right. For he who, by a partial preference of one person to another, violates the rule of natural equality, is, at the same time, guilty of an injury, and of an affront, by denying a man what is his just due, and by detracting from that worthiness, which nature gives him in common with his fellow. It follows as a corollary from this doctrine, that if the thing which is to be distributed amongst many, admit not of a division, the persons who have an equal right to it, use it in common, and without restraint, if the quantity of the thing will allow it, if not, that they then use it in a certain and limited manner, and with proportion to their number. For it is not possible to find out any other way of observing an equality in these cases. But if the thing can neither be divided, nor possessed in common, then the use of it shall either be taken by turns; or, if this course too fail of success, and if, likewise, one of the contenders cannot give the others an equivalent to secure to himself the whole enjoyment of the thing desired, then one shall carry it from the rest, by the fair decision of a lot, which is the most proper remedy that can be applied to all differences of this kind, inasmuch as it takes away the notion of contempt, by setting all the parties on a level; and if it does not favour a man, yet does it not in the least disgrace him. Hobbes has divided lots into two sorts, arbitrary and natural. The former is such as the competitors agree upon, engaging to stand to the event, whilst they cannot, by any act, govern or foresee it; and, therefore, this kind of lot, with regard to men, depends entirely on meer chance and fortune. Natural lot, he says, is either first seizure, by which a thing, which can neither be enjoyed in common, nor divided, passes to him who shall first lay hands on it with a design to keep it; or primogeniture, by virtue of such paternal goods as can neither be divided nor possessed in common by many children, and are adjudged to the first-born. Yet, if we accurately consider things, there will appear to be no proper lot but what we call arbitrary. For 'tis not easy to assign a reason why such an event, as a man cannot procure by his own industry, should give him a right which should hold good against his equals, unless this right was assigned or adjudged to this particular event, by the arbitrary appointment and agreement of men. Thus a thing, which no one has a particular right to claim, belongs by compact to the first seizer; because when distinct proprieties were introduced, there seems to have passed this tacit agreement amongst men, that those things which were not peculiarly assigned to any owner, and yet could not, without a prejudice to mankind, be always left in common, should be the right of the first possessor. And thus too the right of primogeniture owes its original to human constitution and compact. For, otherwise, why should the younger brothers, born of the same parents, be placed in a worse condition than the eldest, barely upon account of an accident or circumstance, which it was not in their power to hinder? Now the reason why these two claims by promogeniture, and first seizure, are sometimes, though improperly, called lots, is this, because they cannot be foreseen, or directed by any power of human industry, and because it reflects no real disgrace on a man to lose the preference, for want of these advantages.

VI. This rule of equality is, likewise, transgressed by pride, when a man for no reason, or without sufficient reason, prefers himself to others, bearing a lofty carriage towards them, as base underlings, unworthy of his consideration or regard. How vastly distant this temper is from the virtue of generosity and true greatness of mind, Des Cartes has most elegantly shown in his *Treatise of the Passions*. He lays it down as a principle, that it is one of the chief parts of wisdom to know how and on what accounts every one ought to esteem or disesteem himself, and then he proves, that the only just cause of esteeming ourselves, arises from the lawful use of our power of free choice, and from the command and authority which we exercise over our wills; since besides the actions which depend on that faculty, there is nothing in us that can properly merit praise or dispraise. Hence he concludes, the true notion of generosity, which prompts a man to value himself as highly as in reason he ought, to consist in this, that he acknowledge nothing to be truly his own, but this free disposition of his will; that he be sensible he cannot purchase blame or commendation, otherwise than by the ill, or the good use of this power; and that, at the same time, he feel within himself a full purpose and resolution of using it well. He proceeds to observe, that those who have such a true sense of themselves, are easily inclined to think, that every man judges of his own worth in the same manner, since there is nothing in this notion, which hath any dependence on external things or persons. That for this reason they never despise others, but are ready to excuse their faults, as proceeding rather from mistake than design. That as they think themselves not much inferior to those who exceed them in wealth, honour, beauty, wit, or learning, knowing that these advantages ought not to come into the account; so when they find themselves possessed of the like goods, they do not fancy they are much superior to those who want them. Hence, he says, there is discoverable in the most generous spirits an honest humility; virtue consisting in the reflection which we make on the infirmity of our nature, and upon the miscarriages which we either have formerly been guilty of, or may be hereafter, these being no less than we see committed by others; whence it comes to pass, that we prefer not ourselves to any person living, wisely considering, that all men have the same faculty of free-will, and may all employ it to as good use. He remarks farther, that those who entertain a good opinion of themselves for any other cause, are not endued with real generosity, but puffed up with empty pride, which, as it is always vitious, so it is aggravated the more, the more unjust the cause is on which the self-conceit is founded. And the most unjust cause of pride is the being proud without cause; that is, when a man being conscious to himself, that he has no real merit which should entitle him to esteem, imagines glory to belong to every one who pleases to usurp it, and that the greater share a man claims of it, the greater he really enjoys. A vice so extremely absurd, that 'tis scarce credible any should prostitute themselves to such a baseness, were there not a pack of idle flatterers in the world, who, by their false praises, swell men of heavy parts into this most stupid degree of folly, which the poet calls a kind of madness. . . .

VII. A much heavier breach of this equality is it, for a man to show his contempt of others by outward and open signs, whether by actions or words, by a look or a laugh, or any such affront; one kind of which is often expressed by troubling another with a ridiculous or a disagreeable present. Which sin is to be reputed so much the more heinous, as it gives the highest provocation imaginable, and inflames the sufferer with the greatest violence of anger and revenge. For we find many persons who will expose their own life to present danger, and much more break the peace with others, rather than put up such a grating indignity: Inasmuch as every act of this nature is a wound to a man's glory or reputation, of which goods we are more proud, and more tenderly sensible than of any thing else we possess; and, in the safe and flourishing state of which, almost the whole pleasure of our mind consists.

VIII. From what has been offered on this head, it is easy to discover the absurdity of that opinion, derived from the ancient Greeks, of some mens being slaves by nature. Which, if taken in the same crudeness of sense, as it bears in the expression, is directly repugnant to that natural equality, which we have been endeavouring to establish. Thus much indeed is most evident, that some men are endued with such a happiness of wit and parts, as enables them not only to provide for themselves and their own affairs, but to direct and govern others. And that some again are so extremely stupid and heavy, as to be unfit to govern themselves, so that they either do mischief, or do nothing, unless others guide and compel them. And farther, that these last being commonly furnished by nature with strong and hardy bodies, are capable of bringing many notable advantages to others by their labour and service. Now when these have the fortune to live in subjection to a wise director, they are, without doubt, fixed in such a state, as is most agreeable to their genius and capacity. If therefore these two parties of men voluntarily consent to the establishing of some common government amongst them, it is consonant to nature, that the former be invested with the power of commanding, and the latter with the necessity of obeying, by which method the interest of both will be best promoted and secured. And, in this sense, we may without danger admit of Aristotle's aphorism, laid down in his first book of *Politicks*. Nothing is more suitable to nature, than that those who excel in understanding and prudence, and are able to judge of things at a distance, should rule and control those who are less happy in these advantages; on the other hand, those whose bodily strength and vigor enables them to put the commands of wiser men in execution, are by nature framed and designed for subjection and obedience. From this constitution of things the sovereign and the slave receive equal advantage, the benefits and the conveniences are alike on both sides. Yet it would be the greatest absurdity imaginable to believe, that nature actually invests the wise with the sovereignty over the weak and imprudent, or with a right of forcing them to submit and obey against their wills. For no sovereignty can be actually established, unless some human deed or covenant precede. Nor does a natural fitness for government presently make a man governor over another, who is as naturally adapted for subjection; nor, supposing a thing to be profitable for another, is it therefore lawful for me to force it upon him against his inclination. For all men enjoy a natural liberty in the same measure and degree, which, before they suffer to be impaired or diminished, there must intervene either their own consent, express, tacit, or interpretative, or some fact of theirs, by which others may obtain a right of abridging them of their liberty by force, in case they will not part with it by a voluntary submission. . . . The same truth may be thus explained in other words; since nature hath produced all men equal, and since servitude cannot be conceived without inequality, (for servitude necessarily brings in a distinction of superior and inferior; whereas in the notion of liberty, it is not requisite that we should have an inferior; but it is sufficient that we are subject to no superior) it follows that all men naturally, and antecedently to any human deed, are conceived to be free. But natural ability, or the possession of such qualities, as are requisite for any state, do not immediately set a man in that state. Every one who hath capacity enough to rule a people, or to command an army, is not without more ado a king or a general. . . .

Many other considerations there are of sufficient strength, to overthrow that vain and gross opinion of slaves by nature. For there is scarce any man so dull and stupid, but he fancies it will be more proper and convenient for him to live according to his own inclinations, than to submit himself to the command, and to the pleasure of another. This natural desire appears more evidently in whole nations, none of which are ever so low-spirited, as to prefer a foreign governor to a prince of their own country and race. Lastly, since nature does not actually constitute any superiority or government, and find those natural slaves, whom Aristotle speaks so much of, are commonly men of strong hands and able bodies, there would be a hard scuffle betwixt them and their wiser neighbours for the mastery; in which contention the latter party, with all their sagacity, could not promise themselves any infallible success. Aristotle's argument borrowed from the poets, deserves, likewise, to be thrown out as most arrogant and unreasonable. Therefore, says he, the poets tell us, it is just the Greeks should rule the barbarians; as if to be a barbarian, and to be a slave, were naturally the same thing. For, according to this doctrine, if we had a mind to destroy any nation differing from us in customs and manners, it were only to brand them with the reproachful name of barbarians, and then to invade them without farther colour or excuse. It is manifest, that this absurd notion of the Grecians arose chiefly from hence, that they were wholly inclined to a democratical government: whereas their mighty neighbours the Persians were constant maintainers of a monarchy, whom for this, and other reasons, they mortally hated beyond all bounds of justice or humanity. . . .

As for Aristotle's whole discourse on this subject, we shall put a more respectful, and a more favourable construction on his words, if we say that by making two kinds of servitude, natural and legal, he means the former to be when a man of more strength than wit, serves another, whose parts and genius dispose him for command, in which case both enjoy a condition most agreeable to their nature and their necessities. And that the legal servitude which he speaks of, is when a person of good endowments and abilities of mind, is, through the meanness of his birth, or the hardness of his fortune, compelled either by his own fear, or by public constitutions, to serve a master inferior to himself in those accomplishments of mind; and whenever this happens, it is feared possible but that the vasal should hate his lord; whereas, on the other hand, these relations produce a firm love and a kind of friendship, when each party bears that character which is most suitable to his disposition, and to his power. But still this must be fixed as a most undoubted principle, that the bare force of such a natural aptitude does neither give the one a right of imposing a condition of servitude, nor oblige the other to receive it.

IX. It will be proper to add somewhat in short, concerning the other kind of equality, which differs from the former in that it is rather a consequent, than an ingredient of the state of nature; we may call it an equality of power, or of liberty, by which all men are reckoned naturally equal in this respect, that antecedently to any deed or compact amongst them, no one hath power over another, but each is master of his own actions and abilities. This equality is taken away, when men enter into a civil state, where, whilst one or more are invested with the power of commanding, and all the rest enjoined the duty of obeying, there arises the greatest inequality imaginable between the sovereign and the subject. But since there still appears some inequality, even between the fellow-subjects, not only with regard to honour and esteem, but, likewise, as to the power which one obtained over another; we may observe that part of this inequality proceeds from the state of fathers of families; who being the chief ruler before the institution of public governments, brought into such governments the power which they before held over their wives, their children, and their servants. So that this inequality being more antient than the erection of civil states, can by no means owe its original to them; nor do they give this power to the fathers of families, but leave it in their hands as they found it; though, in some places, it is thought convenient very much to abridge, and to restrain it. If any further inequality, as to power, be discoverable amongst fellow-subjects, it is plain the fountain, and the occasion of it must be the supreme civil authority. For those whom we suppose to have passed into a public state, did, at their entrance on it, make over to their common sovereign, so much of the power which they before possessed, as was necessary to support this new constitution. And, therefore, in case any person had before this change transformed to another, any right over himself, that right would either cease, and be extinct in the present regulation, or it must submit to the pleasure and disposal of the superior authority. But after a man has once joined himself as a member to any civil community, he cannot, on any account, give another such power over himself, as shall hold valid against the right acquired by the chief ruler; since this would be to admit two independent masters, whom it is impossible to serve both at once. Whatever inequality, therefore, amongst fellow-subjects commences, after the settlement of the civil state, must take its rise, either from the public administration, on account of which the sovereign conveys by delegacy, to some of the subjects, a command over others; or from some certain privilege granted by the same supreme governing power. But disparity of riches does not of itself cause any inequality amongst fellow-subjects; only, as great wealth affords men matter of actual hurt or benefit to others, on which score the poorer sort are wont to seek the favour of the rich, by the most submissive methods of address, either to obtain advantage, or to secure themselves from injury. But there is nothing in this civil inequality any ways repugnant to those precepts, which we have before deduced from a natural equality.

JOHN LOCKE

1 6 3 2 – 1 7 0 4

INTRODUCTION

A man who wrote that he had "no other aims, than to pass silently through this world with the company of a few good friends and books," Locke was remarkably unsuccessful in achieving his aims. He became in his own lifetime one of England's greatest and most famous philosophers, the founder of a long line of British empiricist thinkers, the advisor and confidante of some of the most important political figures of his day, and an active, although hidden, participant in a number of crucial political events. Details of his political activities are still emerging from the study of the thousands of letters, and notes, drafts, lists, journals, and library books of his that have been preserved.

Locke was the son of an attorney who served as a legal clerk to Justices of the Peace in the county of Somerset. He went to Westminster School, then to Oxford for 6 years, first as a student and later as a lecturer in Greek and rhetoric. In 1665 he went briefly to Prussia on a diplomatic mission, and shortly after his return to Oxford met the rich, intelligent, and politically powerful Lord Ashley, whose life Locke, then studying medicine, proceeded to save by operating on him for an abscess on the liver. As a result of the friendship that developed between them, Locke became a member of the Ashley family in London and when Ashley, by then the Earl of Shaftesbury, became Lord Chancellor in 1672, Locke was given various administrative posts and acted both as a political secretary to Shaftesbury and as a tutor for his patron's son. Shaftesbury lost his position in the next year for opposing the king, and in 1675 Locke left for France to improve his poor health. He remained there 4 years and met some of the prominent followers of Descartes, but returned to England at Shaftesbury's request.

For the following 2 years Locke was engaged in highly secret intrigues, on Shaftesbury's behalf, against the future James II, a Catholic, succeeding to the throne. When these intrigues were discovered, Shaftesbury was arrested, tried, and acquitted, but fearing further prosecution fled to Holland, dying there in 1683. Later that same year Locke also fled to Holland, and when the English asked that he be extradited he hid for a period under an assumed name. However, he used these 5 years to work seriously on his major work, the *Essay Concerning Human Understanding*, and to add material to the *Two Treatises of Government* that he had begun several years before leaving England. Shortly after James II was driven from the throne in 1688, Locke returned to London, and from 1690 onward, in his late middle age, published most of the works on philosophy, education, and religion for which he is remembered. For the last 15 years of his life Locke lived at the country home of the Masham family outside London, dying while still at the center of a network of distinguished friends and admirers from all of Europe.

The *Second Treatise of Government*, subtitled *An Essay Concerning the True Original, Extent, and End of Civil Government*, was first published anonymously in London in 1690 as Book II of the volume *Two Treatises of Government*. Locke did not publicly claim authorship of this volume until he referred to it in his will in the year of his death, 1704. A satisfactory edition did not appear until 1764, and the selections given here are taken from one of the many reprintings of that edition. *A Letter Concerning Toleration* was first published anonymously in Latin in Holland in 1689, and published anonymously in London in an English translation by William Popple later that same year. The *Letter* was actually written 4 years earlier in Amsterdam. In later years Locke wrote two more works on the same subject in defense of the first letter. The selection here is drawn from the first 10 pages of the reprinting by J.W. Gough, Basil Blackwell, Oxford, 1948.

SELECTIONS FROM
The Second Treatise of Government and *A Letter Concerning Toleration*

Chapter II   Of the State of Nature

4. To understand political power right, and derive it from its original, we must consider what state all men are naturally in, and that is a state of perfect freedom to order their actions and dispose of their possessions and persons as they think fit, within the bounds of the law of nature, without asking leave or depending upon the will of any other man.

A state also of equality, wherein all the power and jurisdiction is reciprocal, no one having more than another; there being nothing more evident than that creatures of the same species and rank, promiscuously born to all the same advantages of nature and the use of the same faculties, should also be equal one amongst another without subordination or subjection; unless the lord and master of them all should, by any manifest declaration of his will, set one above another, and confer on him by an evident and clear appointment an undoubted right to dominion and sovereignty.

5. This equality of men by nature the judicious Hooker looks upon as so evident in itself and beyond all question that he makes it the foundation of that obligation to mutual love amongst men on which he builds the duties we owe one another, and from whence he derives the great maxims of justice and charity. His words are:

> The like natural inducement hath brought men to know that it is no less their duty to love others than themselves; for seeing those things which are equal must needs all have one measure; if I cannot but wish to receive good, even as much at every man's hands as any man can wish unto his own soul, how should I look to have any part of my desire herein satisfied unless myself be careful to satisfy the like desire, which is undoubtedly in other men, being of one and the same nature? To have anything offered them repugnant to this desire must needs in all respects grieve them as much as me; so that, if I do harm, I must look to suffer, there being no reason that others should show greater measure of love to me than they have by me showed unto them; my desire therefore to be loved of my equals in nature, as much as possibly may be, imposeth upon me a natural duty of bearing to them-ward fully the like affection; from which relation of equality between ourselves and them that are as ourselves, what several rules and canons natural reason hath drawn, for direction of life, no man is ignorant. (*Eccl. Pol.* lib. i.) [*Laws of Ecclesiastical Polity*, 1594]

6. But though this be a state of liberty, yet it is not a state of licence; though man in that state have an uncontrollable liberty to dispose of his person or possessions, yet he has not liberty to destroy himself, or so much as any creature in his possession, but where some nobler use than its bare preservation calls for it. The state of nature has a law of nature to govern it which obliges every one; and reason, which is that law, teaches all mankind who will but consult it that, being all equal and independent, no one ought to harm another in his life, health, liberty, or possessions; for men being all the workmanship of one omnipotent and infinitely wise Maker — all the servants of one sovereign master, sent into the world by his order, and about his business — they are his property whose workmanship they are, made to last during his, not one another's, pleasure; and being furnished with like faculties, sharing all in one community of nature, there cannot be supposed any such subordination among us that may authorize us to destroy another, as if we were made for one another's uses as the inferior ranks of creatures are for ours. Every one, as he is bound to preserve himself and not to quit his station wilfully, so by the like reason, when his own preservation comes not in competition, ought he, as much as he can, to preserve the rest of mankind, and may not, unless it be to do justice to an offender, take away or impair the life, or what tends to the preservation of life: the liberty, health, limb, or goods of another.

7. And that all men may be restrained from invading others' rights and from doing hurt to one another, and the law of nature be observed which willeth the peace and preservation of all mankind, the execution of the law of nature is, in that state, put into every man's hands, whereby everyone has a right to punish the transgressors of that law to such a degree as may hinder its violation; for the law of nature would, as all other laws that concern men in this world, be in vain, if there were nobody that in the state of nature had a power to execute that law and thereby preserve the innocent and restrain offenders. And if any one in the state of nature may punish another for any evil he has done, every one may do so; for in that state of perfect equality where naturally there is no superiority or jurisdiction of one over another, what any may do in prosecution of that law, every one must needs have a right to do.

8. And thus in the state of nature one man comes by a power over another; but yet no absolute or arbitrary power to use a criminal, when he has got him in his hands, according to the passionate heats or boundless extravagancy of his own will; but only to retribute to him, so far as calm reason and conscience dictate, what is proportionate to his transgression, which is so much as may serve for reparation and restraint; for these two are the only reasons why one man may lawfully do harm to another, which is that we call punishment. In transgressing the law of nature, the offender declares himself to live by another rule than that of reason and common equity, which is that measure God has set to the actions of men for their mutual security; and so he becomes dangerous to mankind, the tie which is to secure them from injury

and violence being slighted and broken by him. Which being a trespass against the whole species and the peace and safety of it provided for by the law of nature, every man upon this score, by the right he hath to preserve mankind in general, may restrain, or, where it is necessary, destroy things noxious to them, and so may bring such evil on any one who hath transgressed that law, as may make him repent the doing of it and thereby deter him, and by his example others, from doing the like mischief. And in this case, and upon this ground, *every man hath a right to punish the offender and be executioner of the law of nature.*

9. I doubt not but this will seem a very strange doctrine to some men; but before they condemn it, I desire them to resolve me by what right any prince or state can put to death or punish any alien for any crime he commits in their country. It is certain their laws, by virtue of any sanction they receive from the promulgated will of the legislative, reach not a stranger; they speak not to him, nor, if they did, is he bound to hearken to them. The legislative authority, by which they are in force over the subjects of that commonwealth, hath no power over him. Those who have the supreme power of making laws in England, France, or Holland, are to an Indian but like the rest of the world, men without authority; and therefore, if by the law of nature every man hath not a power to punish offences against it as he soberly judges the case to require, I see not how the magistrates of any community can punish an alien of another country, since, in reference to him, they can have no more power than what every man naturally may have over another.

10. Besides the crime which consists in violating the law and varying from the right rule of reason, whereby a man so far becomes degenerate and declares himself to quit the principles of human nature and to be a noxious creature, there is commonly injury done to some person or other, and some other man receives damage by his transgression; in which case he who hath received any damage has, besides the right of punishment common to him with other men, a particular right to seek reparation from him that has done it; and any other person, who finds it just, may also join with him that is injured and assist him in recovering from the offender so much as may make satisfaction for the harm he has suffered.

11. From these two distinct rights — the one of punishing the crime for restraint and preventing the like offence, which right of punishing is in everybody; the other of taking reparation, which belongs only to the injured party — comes it to pass that the magistrate, who by being magistrate hath the common right of punishing put into his hands, can often, where the public good demands not the execution of the law, remit the punishment of criminal offences by his own authority, but yet cannot remit the satisfaction due to any private man for the damage he has received. That he who has suffered the damage has a right to demand in his own name, and he alone can remit; the damnified person has this power of appropriating to himself the goods or service of the offender by right of self-preservation, as every man has a power to punish the crime to prevent its being committed again, by the right he has

of preserving all mankind, and doing all reasonable things he can in order to that end; and thus it is that every man, in the state of nature, has a power to kill a murderer, both to deter others from doing the like injury, which no reparation can compensate, by the example of the punishment that attends it from everybody, and also to secure men from the attempts of a criminal who, having renounced reason — the common rule and measure God hath given to mankind — hath, by the unjust violence and slaughter he hath committed upon one, declared war against all mankind; and therefore may be destroyed as a lion or a tiger, one of those wild savage beasts with whom men can have no society nor security. And upon this is grounded that great law of nature, "Whoso sheddeth man's blood, by man shall his blood be shed." And Cain was so fully convinced that every one had a right to destroy such a criminal that, after the murder of his brother, he cries out, "Every one that findeth me, shall slay me;" so plain was it writ in the hearts of mankind.

12. By the same reason may a man in the state of nature punish the lesser breaches of that law. It will perhaps be demanded: with death? I answer: Each transgression may be punished to that degree and with so much severity as will suffice to make it an ill bargain to the offender, give him cause to repent, and terrify others from doing the like. Every offence that can be committed in the state of nature may in the state of nature be also punished equally, and as far forth as it may in a commonwealth; for though it would be beside my present purpose to enter here into the particulars of the law of nature, or its measures of punishment, yet it is certain there is such a law, and that, too, as intelligible and plain to a rational creature and a studier of that law as the positive laws of commonwealths, nay, possibly plainer, as much as reason is easier to be understood than the fancies and intricate contrivances of men, following contrary and hidden interests put into words; for so truly are a great part of the municipal laws of countries, which are only so far right as they are founded on the law of nature, by which they are to be regulated and interpreted.

13. To this strange doctrine — viz., that in the state of nature every one has the executive power of the law of nature — I doubt not but it will be objected that it is unreasonable for men to be judges in their own cases, that self-love will make men partial to themselves and their friends, and, on the other side, that ill-nature, passion, and revenge will carry them too far in punishing others, and hence nothing but confusion and disorder will follow; and that therefore God hath certainly appointed government to restrain the partiality and violence of men. I easily grant that civil government is the proper remedy for the inconveniences of the state of nature, which must certainly be great where men may be judges in their own case; since it is easy to be imagined that he who was so unjust as to do his brother an injury will scarce be so just as to condemn himself for it; but I shall desire those who make this objection to remember that absolute monarchs are but men, and if government is to be the remedy of those evils which necessarily follow from

men's being judges in their own cases, and the state of nature is therefore not to be endured, I desire to know what kind of government that is, and how much better it is than the state of nature, where one man commanding a multitude has the liberty to be judge in his own case, and may do to all his subjects whatever he pleases, without the least liberty to any one to question or control those who execute his pleasure, and in whatsoever he doth, whether led by reason, mistake, or passion, must be submitted to? Much better it is in the state of nature, wherein men are not bound to submit to the unjust will of another; and if he that judges, judges amiss in his own or any other case, he is answerable for it to the rest of mankind.

14. It is often asked as a mighty objection, "Where are or ever were there any men in such a state of nature?" To which it may suffice as an answer at present that, since all princes and rulers of independent governments all through the world are in a state of nature, it is plain the world never was, nor ever will be, without numbers of men in that state. I have named all governors of independent communities, whether they are, or are not, in league with others; for it is not every compact that puts an end to the state of nature between men, but only this one of agreeing together mutually to enter into one community and make one body politic; other promises and compacts men may make one with another and yet still be in the state of nature. The promises and bargains for truck, etc., between the two men in the desert island, mentioned by Garcilasso de la Vega, in his *History of Peru*, or between a Swiss and an Indian, in the woods of America, are binding to them, though they are perfectly in a state of nature in reference to one another; for truth and keeping of faith belongs to men as men, and not as members of society.

15. To those that say there were never any men in the state of nature, I will not only oppose the authority of the judicious Hooker, *Eccl. Pol.*, lib. i., sect. 10, where he says,

> The laws which have been hitherto mentioned, (*i.e.*, the laws of nature) do bind men absolutely, even as they are men, although they have never any settled fellowship, never any solemn agreement amongst themselves what to do, or not to do; but forasmuch as we are not by ourselves sufficient to furnish ourselves with competent store of things needful for such a life as our nature doth desire, a life fit for the dignity of man; therefore to supply those defects and imperfections which are in us, as living singly and solely by ourselves, we are naturally induced to seek communion and fellowship with others. This was the cause of men's uniting themselves at first in politic societies.

But I, moreover, affirm that all men are naturally in that state and remain so till by their own consents they make themselves members of some politic society; and I doubt not in the sequel of this discourse to make it very clear.

Chapter V Of Property

26. God, who hath given the world to men in common, hath also given them reason to make use of it to the best advantage of life and convenience. The earth and all that is therein is given to men for the support and comfort of their being. And though all the fruits it naturally produces and beasts it feeds belong to mankind in common, as they are produced by the spontaneous hand of nature; and nobody has originally a private dominion exclusive of the rest of mankind in any of them, as they are thus in their natural state; yet, being given for the use of men, there must of necessity be a means to appropriate them some way or other before they can be of any use or at all beneficial to any particular man. The fruit or venison which nourishes the wild Indian, who knows no enclosure and is still a tenant in common, must be his, and so his, *i.e.*, a part of him, that another can no longer have any right to it before it can do him any good for the support of his life.

27. Though the earth and all inferior creatures be common to all men, yet every man has a property in his own person; this nobody has any right to but himself. The labour of his body and the work of his hands, we may say, are properly his. Whatsoever then he removes out of the state that nature hath provided and left it in, he hath mixed his labour with, and joined to it something that is his own, and thereby makes it his property. It being by him removed from the common state nature hath placed it in, it hath by this labour something annexed to it that excludes the common right of other men. For this labour being the unquestionable property of the labourer, no man but he can have a right to what that is once joined to, at least where there is enough and as good left in common for others.

28. He that is nourished by the acorns he picked up under an oak, or the apples he gathered from the trees in the wood, has certainly appropriated them to himself. Nobody can deny but the nourishment is his. I ask, then, when did they begin to be his? when he digested? or when he ate? or when he boiled? or when he brought them home? or when he picked them up? And it is plain, if the first gathering made them not his, nothing else could. That labour put a distinction between them and common; that added something to them more than nature, the common mother of all, had done; and so they became his private right. And will anyone say he had no right to those acorns or apples he thus appropriated, because he had not the consent of all mankind to make them his? Was it a robbery thus to assume to himself what belonged to all in common? If such a consent as that was necessary, man had starved, notwithstanding the plenty God had given him. We see in commons, which remain so by compact, that it is the taking any part of what is common and removing it out of the state nature leaves it in which begins the property, without which the common is of no use. And the taking of this or that part does not depend on the express consent of all the commoners. Thus the grass my horse has bit, the turfs my servant has cut, and the ore I have digged

in any place where I have a right to them in common with others, become my property without the assignation or consent of anybody. The labour that was mine, removing them out of that common state they were in, hath fixed my property in them.

29. By making an explicit consent of every commoner necessary to any one's appropriating to himself any part of what is given in common, children or servants could not cut the meat which their father or master had provided for them in common without assigning to every one his peculiar part. Though the water running in the fountain be every one's, yet who can doubt but that in the pitcher is his only who drew it out? His labour hath taken it out of the hands of nature, where it was common and belonged equally to all her children, and hath thereby appropriated it to himself.

30. Thus this law of reason makes the deer that Indian's who hath killed it; it is allowed to be his goods who hath bestowed his labour upon it, though before it was the common right of every one. And amongst those who are counted the civilized part of mankind, who have made and multiplied positive laws to determine property, this original law of nature, for the beginning of property in what was before common, still takes place; and by virtue thereof what fish any one catches in the ocean, that great and still remaining common of mankind, or what ambergris any one takes up here, is, by the labour that removes it out of that common state nature left it in, made his property who takes that pains about it. And even amongst us, the hare that anyone is hunting is thought his who pursues her during the chase; for, being a beast that is still looked upon as common and no man's private possession, who-ever has employed so much labour about any of that kind as to find and pursue her has thereby removed her from the state of nature wherein she was common, and hath begun a property.

31. It will perhaps be objected to this that "if gathering the acorns, or other fruits of the earth, etc., makes a right to them, then any one may engross as much as he will." To which I answer: not so. The same law of nature that does by this means give us property does also bound that property, too. "God has given us all things richly" (I Tim. vi. 17), is the voice of reason confirmed by inspiration. But how far has he given it us? To enjoy. As much as any one can make use of to any advantage of life before it spoils, so much he may by his labour fix a property in; whatever is beyond this is more than his share, and belongs to others. Nothing was made by God for man to spoil or destroy. And thus, considering the plenty of natural provisions there was a long time in the world, and the few spenders, and to how small a part of that provision the industry of one man could extend itself and engross it to the prejudice of others, especially keeping within the bounds set by reason of what might serve for his use, there could be then little room for quarrels or contentions about property so established.

32. But the chief matter of property being now not the fruits of the earth and the beasts that subsist on it, but the earth itself, as that which takes in and carries with it all the rest, I think it is plain that property in that, too, is

acquired as the former. As much land as a man tills, plants, improves, cultivates, and can use the product of, so much is his property. He by his labour does, as it were, enclose it from the common. Nor will it invalidate his right to say everybody else has an equal title to it, and therefore he cannot appropriate, he cannot enclose, without the consent of all his fellow commoners — all mankind. God, when he gave the world in common to all mankind, commanded man also to labour, and the penury of his condition required it of him. God and his reason commanded him to subdue the earth, *i.e.*, improve it for the benefit of life, and therein lay out something upon it that was his own, his labour. He that in obedience to this command of God subdued, tilled, and sowed any part of it, thereby annexed to it something that was his property, which another had no title to, nor could without injury take from him.

33. Nor was this appropriation of any parcel of land by improving it any prejudice to any other man, since there was still enough and as good left, and more than the yet unprovided could use. So that, in effect, there was never the less left for others because of his enclosure for himself; for he that leaves as much as another can make use of does as good as take nothing at all. Nobody could think himself injured by the drinking of another man, though he took a good draught, who had a whole river of the same water left him to quench his thirst; and the case of land and water, where there is enough for both, is perfectly the same.

34. God gave the world to men in common; but since he gave it them for their benefit and the greatest conveniences of life they were capable to draw from it, it cannot be supposed he meant it should always remain common and uncultivated. He gave it to the use of the industrious and rational — and labour was to be his title to it — not to the fancy or covetousness of the quarrelsome and contentious. He that had as good left for his improvement as was already taken up needed not complain, ought not to meddle with what was already improved by another's labour; if he did, it is plain he desired the benefit of another's pains which he had no right to, and not the ground which God had given him in common with others to labour on, and whereof there was as good left as that already possessed, and more than he knew what to do with, or his industry could reach to.

35. It is true, in land that is common in England or any other country where there is plenty of people under government who have money and commerce, no one can enclose or appropriate any part without the consent of all his fellow-commoners; because this is left common by compact, *i.e.*, by the law of the land, which is not to be violated. And though it be common in respect of some men, it is not so to all mankind, but is the joint property of this country or this parish. Besides, the remainder after such enclosure would not be as good to the rest of the commoners as the whole was when they could all make use of the whole; whereas in the beginning and first peopling of the great common of the world it was quite otherwise. The law man was under was rather for appropriating. God commanded, and his wants forced,

him to labour. That was his property which could not be taken from him wherever he had fixed it. And hence subduing or cultivating the earth and having dominion, we see, are joined together. The one gave title to the other. So that God; by commanding to subdue, gave authority so far to appropriates and the condition of human life which requires labour and material, to work on necessarily introduces private possessions.

36. The measure of property nature has well set by the extent of men's labour and the conveniences of life. No man's labour could subdue or appropriate all, nor could his enjoyment consume more than a small part; so that it was impossible for any man, this way, to entrench upon the right of another, or acquire to himself a property to the prejudice of his neighbour, who would still have room for as good and as large a possession — after the other had taken out his — as before it was appropriated. This measure did confine every man's possession to a very moderate proportion, and such as he might appropriate to himself without injury to anybody in the first ages of the world, when men were more in danger to be lost by wandering from their company in the then vast wilderness of the earth than to be straitened for want of room to plant in. And the same measure may be allowed still without prejudice to anybody, as full as the world seems; for supposing a man or family in the state they were at first peopling of the world by the children of Adam or Noah, let him plant in some inland, vacant places of America, we shall find that the possessions he could make himself, upon the measures we have given, would not be very large, nor, even to this day, prejudice the rest of mankind, or give them reason to complain or think themselves injured by this man's encroachment, though the race of men have now spread themselves to all the corners of the world and do infinitely exceed the small number which was at the beginning. Nay, the extent of ground is of so little value without labour that I have heard it affirmed that in Spain itself a man may be permitted to plough, sow, and reap, without being disturbed, upon land he has no other title to but only his making use of it. But, on the contrary, the inhabitants think themselves beholden to him who by his industry on neglected and, consequently, waste land has increased the stock of corn which they wanted. But be this as it will, which I lay no stress on, this I dare boldly affirm — that the same rule of propriety, viz., that every man should have as much as he could make use of, would hold still in the world without straitening anybody, since there is land enough in the world to suffice double the inhabitants, had not the invention of money and the tacit agreement of men to put a value on it introduced — by consent — larger possessions and a right to them; which, how it has done, I shall by-and-by show more at large.

37. This is certain, that in the beginning, before the desire of having more than man needed had altered the intrinsic value of things which depends only on their usefulness to the life of man, or had agreed that a little piece of yellow metal which would keep without wasting or decay should be worth a great piece of flesh or a whole heap of corn, though men had a right to appropriate, by their labour, each one to himself as much of the things of

nature as he could use, yet this could not be much, nor to the prejudice of others, where the same plenty was still left to those who would use the same industry. To which let me add that he who appropriates land to himself by his labour does not lessen but increase the common stock of mankind; for the provisions serving to the support of human life produced by one acre of enclosed and cultivated land are — to speak much within compass — ten times more than those which are yielded by an acre of land of an equal richness lying waste in common. And therefore he that encloses land, and has a greater plenty of the conveniences of life from ten acres than he could have from a hundred left to nature, may truly be said to give ninety acres to mankind; for his labour now supplies him with provisions out of ten acres which were by the product of a hundred lying in common. I have here rated the improved land very low in making its product but as ten to one, when it is much nearer a hundred to one; for I ask whether in the wild woods and uncultivated waste of America, left to nature, without any improvement, tillage, or husbandry, a thousand acres yield the needy and wretched inhabitants as many conveniences of life as ten acres equally fertile land do in Devonshire, where they are well cultivated.

Before the appropriation of land, he who gathered as much of the wild fruit, killed, caught, or tamed as many of the beasts as he could; he that so employed his pains about any of the spontaneous products of nature as any way to alter them from the state which nature put them in, by placing any of his labour on them, did thereby acquire a propriety in them; but, if they perished in his possession without their due use, if the fruits rotted or the venison putrified, before he could spend it, he offended against the common law of nature, and was liable to be punished; he invaded his neighbor's share, for he had no right farther than his use called for any of them, and they might serve to afford him conveniences of life.

38. The same measures governed the possession of land, too: whatsoever he tilled and reaped, laid up and made use of before it spoiled, that was his peculiar right; whatsoever he enclosed and could feed and make use of, the cattle and product was also his. But if either the grass of his enclosure rotted on the ground, or the fruit of his planting perished without gathering and laying up, this part of the earth, notwithstanding his enclosure, was still to be looked on as waste, and might be the possession of any other. Thus, at the beginning, Cain might take as much ground as he could till and make it his own land, and yet leave enough to Abel's sheep to feed on; a few acres would serve for both their possessions. But as families increased and industry enlarged their stocks, their possessions enlarged with the need of them; but yet it was commonly without any fixed property in the ground they made use of till they incorporated, settled themselves together, and built cities; and then, by consent, they came in time to set out the bounds of their distinct territories, and agree on limits between them and their neighbours, and by laws within themselves settled the properties of those of the same society; for we see that in that part of the world which was first inhabited, and therefore like

to be best peopled, even as low down as Abraham's time they wandered with their flocks and their herds, which was their substance, freely up and down; and this Abraham did in a country where he was a stranger. Whence it is plain that at least a great part of the land lay in common; that the inhabitants valued it not, nor claimed property in any more than they made use of. But when there was not room enough in the same place for their herds to feed together, they, by consent, as Abraham and Lot did (Gen. xiii. 5), separated and enlarged their pasture where it best liked them. And for the same reason Esau went from his father and his brother and planted in Mount Seir (Gen. xxxvi. 6).

39. And thus, without supposing any private dominion and property in Adam over all the world exclusive of all other men, which can no way be proved, nor any one's property be made out from it; but supposing the world given, as it was, to the children of men in common, we see how labour could make men distinct titles to several parcels of it for their private uses, wherein there could be no doubt of right, no room for quarrel.

40. Nor is it so strange, as perhaps before consideration it may appear, that the property of labour should be able to overbalance the community of land; for it is labour indeed that put the difference of value on everything; and let any one consider what the difference is between an acre of land planted with tobacco or sugar, sown with wheat or barley, and an acre of the same land lying in common, without any husbandry upon it, and he will find that the improvement of labour makes the far greater part of the value. I think it will be but a very modest computation to say that, of the products of the earth useful to the life of man, nine-tenths are the effects of labour; nay, if we will rightly estimate things as they come to our use and cast up the several expenses about them, what in them is purely owing to nature, and what to labour, we shall find that in most of them ninety-nine hundredths are wholly to be put on the account of labour.

41. There cannot be a clearer demonstration of anything than several nations of the Americans are of this, who are rich in land and poor in all the comforts of life; whom nature having furnished as liberally as any other people with the materials of plenty, *i.e.*, a fruitful soil, apt to produce in abundance what might serve for food, raiment, and delight, yet for want of improving it by labour have not one-hundredth part of the conveniences we enjoy. And a king of a large and fruitful territory there feeds, lodges, and is clad worse than a day-labourer in England.

42. To make this a little clear, let us but trace some of the ordinary provisions of life through their several progresses before they come to our use and see how much of their value they receive from human industry. Bread, wine, and cloth are things of daily use and great plenty; yet, notwithstanding, acorns, water, and leaves, or skins must be our bread, drink, and clothing, did not labour furnish us with these more useful commodities; for whatever bread is more worth than acorns, wine than water, and cloth or silk than leaves, skins, or moss, that is wholly owing to labour and industry: the one of these

being the food and raiment which unassisted nature furnishes us with; the other, provisions which our industry and pains prepare for us, which how much they exceed the other in value when any one hath computed, he will then see how much labour makes the far greatest part of the value of things we enjoy in this world. And the ground which produces the materials is scarce to be reckoned in as any, or at most but a very small, part of it; so little that even amongst us land that is left wholly to nature, that hath no improvement of pasturage, tillage, or planting, is called, as indeed it is, "waste"; and we shall find the benefit of it amount to little more than nothing.

This shows how much numbers of men are to be preferred to largeness of dominions; and that the increase of lands and the right of employing of them is the great art of government; and that prince who shall be so wise and godlike as by established laws of liberty to secure protection and encouragement to the honest industry of mankind, against the oppression of power and narrowness of party, will quickly be too hard for his neighbours; but this by the bye.

To return to the argument in hand.

43. An acre of land that bears here twenty bushels of wheat, and another in America which with the same husbandry would do the like, are, without doubt, of the same natural intrinsic value; but yet the benefit mankind receives from the one in a year is worth £5, and from the other possibly not worth a penny if all the profit an Indian received from it were to be valued and sold here; at least, I may truly say, not one-thousandth. It is labour, then, which puts the greatest part of the value upon land, without which it would scarcely be worth anything; it is to that we owe the greatest part of all its useful products; for all that the straw, bran, bread of that acre of wheat is more worth than the product of an acre of as good land which lies waste is all the effect of labour. For it is not barely the ploughman's pains, the reaper's and thresher's toil, and the baker's sweat is to be counted into the bread we eat; the labour of those who broke the oxen, who digged and wrought the iron and stones, who felled and framed the timber employed about the plough, mill, oven, or any other utensils, which are a vast number requisite to this corn, from its being seed to be sown to its being made bread, must all be charged on the account of labour, and received as an effect of that; nature and the earth furnished only the almost worthless materials as in themselves. It would be a strange "catalogue of things that industry provided and made use of about every loaf of bread," before it came to our use, if we could trace them: iron, wood, leather, bark, timber, stone, bricks, coals, lime, cloth, dyeing, drugs, pitch, tar, masts, ropes, and all the materials made use of in the ship that brought any of the commodities used by any of the workmen to any part of the work; all which it would be almost impossible, at least too long, to reckon up.

44. From all which it is evident that, though the things of nature are given in common, yet man, by being master of himself and proprietor of his own person and the actions or labour of it, had still in himself the great foundation

of property; and that which made up the greater part of what he applied to the support or comfort of his being, when invention and arts had improved the conveniences of life, was perfectly his own and did not belong in common to others.

45. Thus labour, in the beginning, gave a right of property wherever anyone was pleased to employ it upon what was common, which remained a long while the far greater part and is yet more than mankind makes use of. Men, at first, for the most part contented themselves with what unassisted nature offered to their necessities; and though afterwards, in some parts of the world—where the increase of people and stock, with the use of money, had made land scarce and so of some value—the several communities settled the bounds of their distinct territories and, by laws within themselves, regulated the properties of the private men of their society, and so, by compact and agreement, settled the property which labour and industry began. And the leagues that have been made between several states and kingdoms either expressly or tacitly disowning all claim and right to the land in the others' possession have, by common consent, given up their pretences to their natural common right which originally they had to those countries, and so have, by positive agreement, settled a property amongst themselves in distinct parts and parcels of the earth; yet there are still great tracts of ground to be found which—the inhabitants thereof not having joined with the rest of mankind in the consent of the use of their common money—lie waste, and are more than the people who dwell on it do or can make use of, and so still lie in common; though this can scarce happen amongst that part of mankind that have consented to the use of money.

46. The greatest part of things really useful to the life of man, and such as the necessity of subsisting made the first commoners of the world look after, as it doth the Americans now, are generally things of short duration, such as, if they are not consumed by use, will decay and perish of themselves; gold, silver, and diamonds are things that fancy or agreement hath put the value on, more than real use and the necessary support of life. Now of those good things which nature hath provided in common, every one had a right, as hath been said, to as much as he could use, and property in all that he could effect with his labour; all that his industry could extend to, to alter from the state nature had put it in, was his. He that gathered a hundred bushels of acorns or apples had thereby a property in them; they were his goods as soon as gathered. He was only to look that he used them before they spoiled, else he took more than his share and robbed others. And indeed it was a foolish thing, as well as dishonest, to hoard up more than he could make use of. If he gave away a part to anybody else so that it perished not uselessly in his possession, these he also made use of. And if he also bartered away plums that would have rotted in a week for nuts that would last good for his eating a whole year, he did no injury; he wasted not the common stock, destroyed no part of the portion of the goods that belonged to others, so long as nothing perished uselessly in his hands. Again, if he would give his nuts for a piece of

metal, pleased with its colour, or exchange his sheep for shells, or wool for a sparkling pebble or a diamond, and keep those by him all his life, he invaded not the right of others; he might heap as much of these durable things as he pleased; the exceeding of the bounds of his just property not lying in the largeness of his possession, but the perishing of anything uselessly in it.

47. And thus came in the use of money—some lasting thing that men might keep without spoiling, and that by mutual consent men would take in exchange for the truly useful but perishable supports of life.

48. And as different degrees of industry were apt to give men possessions in different proportions, so this invention of money gave them the opportunity to continue and enlarge them; for supposing an island, separate from all possible commerce with the rest of the world, wherein there were but a hundred families, but there were sheep, horses, and cows, with other useful animals, wholesome fruits, and land enough for corn for a hundred thousand times as many, but nothing in the island, either because of its commonness or perishableness, fit to supply the place of money; what reason could any one have there to enlarge his possessions beyond the use of his family and a plentiful supply to its consumption, either in what their own industry produced or they could barter for like perishable, useful commodities with others? Where there is not something both lasting and scarce, and so valuable to be hoarded up, there men will not be apt to enlarge their possessions of land were it ever so rich, ever so free for them to take. For, I ask, what would a man value ten thousand or a hundred thousand acres of excellent land, ready cultivated and well stocked, too, with cattle, in the middle of the inland parts of America where he had no hopes of commerce with other parts of the world to draw money to him by the sale of the product? It would not be worth the enclosing, and we should see him give up again to the wild common of nature whatever was more than would supply the conveniences of life to be had there for him and his family.

49. Thus in the beginning all the world was America, and more so than that is now; for no such thing as money was anywhere known. Find out something that hath the use and value of money amongst his neighbours, you shall see the same man will begin presently to enlarge his possessions.

50. But since gold and silver, being little useful to the life of man in proportion to food, raiment, and carriage, has its value only from the consent of men, whereof labour yet makes, in great part, the measure, it is plain that men have agreed to a disproportionate and unequal possession of the earth, they having, by a tacit and voluntary consent, found out a way how a man may fairly possess more land than he himself can use the product of, by receiving in exchange for the overplus gold and silver which may be hoarded up without injury to any one, these metals not spoiling or decaying in the hands of the possessor. This partage of things in an inequality of private possessions men have made practicable out of the bounds of society and without compact, only by putting a value on gold and silver, and tacitly agreeing in the use of money; for, in governments, the laws regulate the right

of property, and the possession of land is determined by positive constitutions.

51. And thus, I think, it is very easy to conceive how labour could at first begin a title of property in the common things of nature, and how the spending it upon our uses bounded it. So that there could then be no reason of quarrelling about title, nor any doubt about the largeness of possession it gave. Right and convenience went together; for as a man had a right to all he could employ his labour upon, so he had no temptation to labour for more than he could make use of. This left no room for controversy about the title, nor for encroachment on the right of others; what portion a man carved to himself was easily seen, and it was useless, as well as dishonest, to carve himself too much or take more than he needed.

Chapter VIII Of the Beginning of Political Societies

95. Men being, as has been said, by nature all free, equal, and independent, no one can be put out of this estate and subjected to the political power of another without his own consent. The only way whereby any one divests himself of his natural liberty, and puts on the bonds of civil society, is by agreeing with other men to join and unite into a community for their comfortable, safe, and peaceable living one amongst another, in a secure enjoyment of their properties and a greater security against any that are not of it. This any number of men may do, because it injures not the freedom of the rest; they are left as they were in the liberty of the state of nature. When any number of men have so consented to make one community or government, they are thereby presently incorporated and make one body politic wherein the majority have a right to act and conclude the rest.

96. For when any number of men have, by the consent of every individual, made a community, they have thereby made that community one body, with a power to act as one body, which is only by the will and determination of the majority; for that which acts any community being only the consent of the individuals of it, and it being necessary to that which is one body to move one way, it is necessary the body should move that way whither the greater force carries it, which is the consent of the majority; or else it is impossible it should act or continue one body, one community, which the consent of every individual that united into it agreed that it should; and so every one is bound by that consent to be concluded by the majority. And therefore we see that in assemblies impowered to act by positive laws, where no number is set by that positive law which impowers them, the act of the majority passes for the act of the whole, and, of course, determines, as having by the law of nature and reason the power of the whole.

97. And thus every man, by consenting with others to make one body politic under one government, puts himself under an obligation to every one

of that society to submit to the determination of the majority, and to be concluded by it; or else this original compact, whereby he with others incorporates into one society, would signify nothing, and be no compact, if he be left free and under no other ties than he was in before in the state of nature. For what appearance would there be of any compact? What new engagement if he were no farther tied by any decrees of the society than he himself thought fit and did actually consent to? This would be still as great a liberty as he himself had before his compact, or any one else in the state of nature hath who may submit himself and consent to any acts of it if he thinks fit.

98. For if the consent of the majority shall not in reason be received as the act of the whole and conclude every individual, nothing but the consent of every individual can make anything to be the act of the whole; but such a consent is next to impossible ever to be had if we consider the infirmities of health and avocations of business which in a number, though much less than that of a commonwealth, will necessarily keep many away from the public assembly. To which, if we add the variety of opinions and contrariety of interests which unavoidably happen in all collections of men, the coming into society upon such terms would be only like Cato's coming into the theatre only to go out again. Such a constitution as this would make the mighty leviathan of a shorter duration than the feeblest creatures, and not let it outlast the day it was born in; which cannot be supposed till we can think that rational creatures should desire and constitute societies only to be dissolved; for where the majority cannot conclude the rest, there they cannot act as one body, and consequently will be immediately dissolved again.

99. Whosoever, therefore, out of a state of nature unite into a community must be understood to give up all the power necessary to the ends for which they unite into society to the majority of the community, unless they expressly agreed in any number greater than the majority. And this is done by barely agreeing to unite into one political society, which is all the compact that is, or needs be, between the individuals that enter into or make up a commonwealth. And thus that which begins and actually constitutes any political society is nothing but the consent of any number of freemen capable of a majority to unite and incorporate into such a society. And this is that, and that only, which did or could give beginning to any lawful government in the world.

100. To this I find two objections made:

First, That there are no instances to be found in story of a company of men independent and equal one amongst another that met together and in this way began and set up a government.

Secondly, It is impossible of right that men should do so, because all men being born under government, they are to submit to that and are not at liberty to begin a new one.

101. To the first there is this to answer: that it is not at all to be wondered that history gives us but a very little account of men that lived together in the

state of nature. The inconveniences of that condition, and the love and want of society, no sooner brought any number of them together, but they presently united and incorporated if they designed to continue together. And if we may not suppose men ever to have been in the state of nature, because we hear not much of them in such a state, we may as well suppose the armies of Salmanasser or Xerxes were never children because we hear little of them till they were men and embodied in armies. Government is everywhere antecedent to records, and letters seldom come in amongst a people till a long continuation of civil society has, by other more necessary arts, provided for their safety, ease, and plenty; and then they begin to look after the history of their founders and search into their original, when they have outlived the memory of it; for it is with commonwealths as with particular persons, they are commonly ignorant of their own births and infancies; and if they know anything of their original, they are beholden for it to the accidental records that others have kept of it. And those that we have of the beginning of any politics in the world, excepting that of the Jews, where God himself immediately interposed, and which favours not at all paternal dominion, are all either plain instances of such a beginning as I have mentioned, or at least have manifest footsteps of it.

102. He must show a strange inclination to deny evident matter of fact when it agrees not with his hypothesis, who will not allow that the beginnings of Rome and Venice were by the uniting together of several men free and independent one of another, amongst whom there was no natural superiority or subjection. And if Josephus Acosta's word may be taken, he tells us that in many parts of America there was no government at all.

"There are great and apparent conjectures," says he, "that these men," speaking of those of Peru, "for a long time had neither kings nor commonwealths, but lived in troops, as they do this day in Florida, the Cheriquanas, those of Brasil, and many other nations which have no certain kings, but as occasion is offered, in peace or war, they choose their captains as they please."

If it be said that every man there was born subject to his father or the head of his family, that the subjection due from a child to a father took not away his freedom of uniting into what political society he thought fit, has been already proved. But be that as it will, these men, it is evident, were actually free; and whatever superiority some politicians now would place in any of them, they themselves claimed it not, but by consent were all equal till by the same consent they set rulers over themselves. So that their politic societies all began from a voluntary union and the mutual agreement of men freely acting in the choice of their governors and forms of government.

103. And I hope those who went away from Sparta with Palantus, mentioned by Justin, will be allowed to have been freemen, independent one of another, and to have set up a government over themselves by their own consent. Thus I have given several examples out of history of people free and in the state of nature that, being met together, incorporated and began a

commonwealth. And if the want of such instances be an argument to prove that governments were not nor could not be so begun, I suppose the contenders for paternal empire were better let it alone than urge it against natural liberty; for if they can give so many instances out of history of governments begun upon paternal right, I think — though at best an argument from what has been, to what should of right be, has no great force — one might, without any great danger, yield them the cause. But if I might advise them in the case, they would do well not to search too much into the original of governments as they have begun *de facto*, lest they should find at the foundation of most of them something very little favourable to the design they promote and such a power as they contend for.

104. But to conclude, reason being plain on our side that men are naturally free, and the examples of history showing that the governments of the world that were begun in peace had their beginning laid on that foundation, and were made by the consent of the people, there can be little room for doubt either where the right is, or what has been the opinion or practice of mankind about the first erecting of governments.

105. I will not deny that, if we look back as far as history will direct us towards the original of commonwealths, we shall generally find them under the government and administration of one man. And I am also apt to believe that where a family was numerous enough to subsist by itself, and continued entire together without mixing with others, as it often happens where there is much land and few people, the government commonly began in the father; for the father, having by the law of nature the same power with every man else to punish as he thought fit any offences against that law, might thereby punish his transgressing children even when they were men and out of their pupilage; and they were very likely to submit to his punishment and all join with him against the offender, in their turns, giving him thereby power to execute his sentence against any transgression, and so in effect make him the lawmaker and governour over all that remained in conjunction with his family. He was fittest to be trusted; paternal affection secured their property and interest under his care; and the custom of obeying him in their childhood made it easier to submit to him rather than to any other. If, therefore, they must have one to rule them, as government is hardly to be avoided amongst men that live together, who so likely to be the man as he that was their common father, unless negligence, cruelty, or any other defect of mind or body made him unfit for it? But when either the father died and left his next heir, for want of age, wisdom, courage, or any other qualities, less fit for rule, or where several families met and consented to continue together, there it is not to be doubted but they used their natural freedom to set up him whom they judged the ablest and most likely to rule well over them. Conformable hereunto we find the people of America, who — living out of the reach of the conquering swords and spreading domination of the two great empires of Peru and Mexico — enjoyed their own natural freedom, though, *cœteris paribus*, they commonly prefer the heir of their deceased king; yet, if they find him any way

weak or incapable, they pass him by and set up the stoutest and bravest man for their ruler.

106. Thus, though looking back as far as records give us any account of peopling the world and the history of nations, we commonly find the government to be in one hand; yet it destroys not that which I affirm — viz., that the beginning of politic society depends upon the consent of the individuals to join into and make one society; who, when they are thus incorporated, might set up what form of government they thought fit. But this having given occasion to men to mistake and think that by nature government was monarchical and belonged to the father, it may not be amiss here to consider why people in the beginning generally pitched upon this form, which though perhaps the father's pre-eminence might in the first institution of some commonwealth give rise to, and place in the beginning the power in one hand; yet it is plain that the reason that continued the form of government in a single person was not any regard or respect to paternal authority, since all petty monarchies, that is, almost all monarchies, near their original, have been commonly, at least upon occasion, elective.

107. First, then, in the beginning of things, the father's government of the childhood of those sprung from him having accustomed them to the rule of one man and taught them that where it was exercised with care and skill, with affection and love to those under it, it was sufficient to procure and preserve to men all the political happiness they sought for in society. It was no wonder that they should pitch upon and naturally run into that form of government which from their infancy they had been all accustomed to and which, by experience, they had found both easy and safe. To which, if we add that monarchy being simple and most obvious to men whom neither experience had instructed in forms of government, nor the ambition or insolence of empire had taught to beware of the encroachments of prerogative or the inconveniences of absolute power which monarchy in succession was apt to lay claim to and bring upon them, it was not at all strange that they should not much trouble themselves to think of methods of restraining any exorbitancies of those to whom they had given the authority over them, and of balancing the power of government by placing several parts of it in different hands. They had neither felt the oppression of tyrannical dominion, nor did the fashion of the age, nor their possessions, or way of living, which afforded little matter for covetousness or ambition, give them any reason to apprehend or provide against it; and therefore it is no wonder they put themselves into such a frame of government as was not only, as I said, most obvious and simple, but also best suited to their present state and condition, which stood more in need of defence against foreign invasions and injuries than of multiplicity of laws. The equality of a simple, poor way of living, confining their desires within the narrow bounds of each man's small property, made few controversies, and so no need of many laws to decide them or variety of officers to superintend the process or look after the execution of justice, where there were but few trespasses and offenders. Since, then, those who liked one

another so well as to join into society cannot but be supposed to have some acquaintance and friendship together and some trust one in another, they could not but have greater apprehensions of others than of one another; and therefore their first care and thought cannot but be supposed to be how to secure themselves against foreign force. It was natural for them to put themselves under a frame of government which might best serve to that end, and choose the wisest and bravest man to conduct them in their wars and lead them out against their enemies, and in this chiefly be their ruler.

108. Thus we see that the kings of the Indians in America, which is still a pattern of the first ages in Asia and Europe, whilst the inhabitants were too few for the country, and want of people and money gave men no temptation to enlarge their possessions of land or contest for wider extent of ground, are little more than generals of their armies; and though they command absolutely in war, yet at home and in time of peace they exercise very little dominion and have but a very moderate sovereignty, the resolutions of peace and war being ordinarily either in the people or in a council, though the war itself, which admits not of plurality of governors, naturally devolves the command into the king's sole authority.

110. Thus, whether a family by degrees grew up into a commonwealth and, the fatherly authority being continued on to the elder son, every one in his turn growing up under it tacitly submitted to it; and the easiness and equality of it not offending any one, every one acquiesced, till time seemed to have confirmed it and settled a right of succession by prescription; or whether several families, or the descendants of several families, whom chance, neighbourhood, or business brought together, uniting into society, the need of a general whose conduct might defend them against their enemies in war, and the great confidence the innocence and sincerity of that poor but virtuous age — such as are almost all those which begin governments that ever come to last in the world — gave men of one another, made the first beginners of commonwealths generally put the rule into one man's hand, without any other express limitation or restraint but what the nature of the thing and the end of government required. Whichever of those it was that at first put the rule into the hands of a single person, certain it is that nobody was intrusted with it but for the public good and safety, and to those ends, in the infancies of commonwealths, those who had it commonly used it. And unless they had done so, young societies could not have subsisted; without such nursing fathers, tender and careful of the public weal, all governments would have sunk under the weakness and infirmities of their infancy, and the prince and the people had soon perished together.

112. Thus we may see how probable it is that people that were naturally free, and by their own consent either submitted to the government of their father or united together out of different families to make a government, should generally put the rule into one man's hands and choose to be under the conduct of a single person, without so much as by express conditions limiting or regulating his power which they thought safe enough in his honesty

and prudence, though they never dreamed of monarchy being *jure divino*, which we never heard of among mankind till it was revealed to us by the divinity of this last age, nor ever allowed paternal power to have a right of dominion or to be the foundation of all government. And thus much may suffice to show that, as far as we have any light from history, we have reason to conclude that all peaceful beginnings of government have been laid in the consent of the people. I say peaceful, because I shall have occasion in another place to speak of conquest, which some esteem a way of beginning of governments.

The other objection I find urged against the beginning of politics, in the way I have mentioned, is this:

113. That all men being born under government, some or other, it is impossible any of them should ever be free, and at liberty to unite together and begin a new one, or ever be able to erect a lawful government.

If this argument be good, I ask, how came so many lawful monarchies into the world? For if anybody, upon this supposition, can show me any one man in any age of the world free to begin a lawful monarchy, I will be bound to show him ten other free men at liberty at the same time to unite and begin a new government under a regal or any other form, it being demonstration that if any one, born under the dominion of another, may be so free as to have a right to command others in a new and distinct empire, every one that is born under the dominion of another may be so free, too, and may become a ruler or subject of a distinct separate government. And so, by this their own principle, either all men, however born, are free, or else there is but one lawful prince, one lawful government in the world. And then they have nothing to do but barely to show us which that is; which, when they have done, I doubt not but all mankind will easily agree to pay obedience to him.

114. Though it be a sufficient answer to their objection to show that it involves them in the same difficulties that it doth those they use it against, yet I shall endeavour to discover the weakness of this argument a little farther. "All men," say they, "are born under government, and therefore they cannot be at liberty to begin a new one. Everyone is born a subject to his father, or his prince, and is therefore under the perpetual tie of subjection and allegiance." It is plain mankind never owned nor considered any such natural subjection that they were born in to one or to the other that tied them without their own consents to a subjection to them and their heirs.

115. For there are no examples so frequent in history, both sacred and profane, as those of men withdrawing themselves and their obedience from the jurisdiction they were born under, and the family or community they were bred up in, and setting up new governments in other places; from whence sprang all that number of petty commonwealths in the beginning of ages, and which always multiplied as long as there was room enough till the stronger or more fortunate swallowed the weaker, and those great ones again breaking to pieces dissolved into lesser dominions. All which are so many testimonies against paternal sovereignty, and plainly prove that it was not the natural right

of the father descending to his heirs that made governments in the beginning, since it was impossible, upon that ground, there should have been so many little kingdoms; all must have been but only one universal monarchy if men had not been at liberty to separate themselves from their families and the government, be it what it will, that was set up in it, and go and make distinct commonwealths and other governments as they thought fit.

116. This has been the practice of the world from its first beginning to this day; nor is it now any more hindrance to the freedom of mankind that they are born under constituted and ancient polities that have established laws and set forms of government, than if they were born in the woods, amongst the unconfined inhabitants that run loose in them; for those who would persuade us that "by being born under any government we are naturally subjects to it" and have no more any title or pretence to the freedom of the state of nature, have no other reason—bating that of paternal power, which we have already answered—to produce for it but only because our fathers or progenitors passed away their natural liberty, and thereby bound up themselves and their posterity to a perpetual subjection to the government which they themselves submitted to. It is true that, whatever engagement or promises any one has made for himself, he is under the obligation of them, but cannot by any compact whatsoever bind his children or posterity; for his son, when a man, being altogether as free as the father, any act of the father can no more give away the liberty of the son than it can of anybody else. He may indeed annex such conditions to the land he enjoyed as a subject of any commonwealth as may oblige his son to be of that community, if he will enjoy those possessions which were his father's, because that estate, being his father's property, he may dispose or settle it as he pleases.

117. And this has generally given the occasion to mistake in this matter; because commonwealths not permitting any part of their dominions to be dismembered, nor to be enjoyed by any but those of their community, the son cannot ordinarily enjoy the possessions of his father but under the same terms his father did, by becoming a member of the society; whereby he puts himself presently under the government he finds there established as much as any other subject of that commonwealth. And thus "the consent of freemen, born under government, which only makes them members of it," being given separately in their turns, as each comes to be of age, and not in a multitude together, people take no notice of it and, thinking it not done at all, or not necessary, conclude they are naturally subjects as they are men.

118. But, it is plain, governments themselves understand it otherwise; they claim no power over the son because of that they had over the father; nor look on children as being their subjects, by their father's being so. If a subject of England have a child by an English woman in France, whose subject is he? Not the King of England's, for he must have leave to be admitted to the privileges of it; nor the King of France's, for how then has his father a liberty to bring him away, and breed him as he pleases? And whoever was judged as a traitor or deserter, if he left or warred against a country, for

being barely born in it of parents that were aliens there? It is plain, then, by the practice of governments themselves as well as by the law of right reason, that "a child is born a subject of no country or government." He is under his father's tuition and authority till he comes to age of discretion; and then he is a freeman, at liberty what government he will put himself under, what body politic he will unite himself to; for if an Englishman's son, born in France, be at liberty, and may do so, it is evident there is no tie upon him by his father's being a subject of this kingdom, nor is he bound up by any compact of his ancestors. And why then hath not his son, by the same reason, the same liberty though he be born anywhere else? Since the power that a father hath naturally over his children is the same wherever they be born, and the ties of natural obligations are not bounded by the positive limits of kingdoms and commonwealths.

119. Every man being, as has been shown, naturally free, and nothing being able to put him into subjection to any earthly power but only his own consent, it is to be considered what shall be understood to be a sufficient declaration of a man's consent to make him subject to the laws of any government. There is a common distinction of an express and a tacit consent which will concern our present case. Nobody doubts but an express consent of any man entering into any society makes him a perfect member of that society, a subject of that government. The difficulty is, what ought to be looked upon as a tacit consent, and how far it binds, — *i.e.*, how far any one shall be looked upon to have consented and thereby submitted to any government, where he has made no expressions of it at all. And to this I say that every man that hath any possessions or enjoyment of any part of the dominions of any government doth thereby give his tacit consent and is as far forth obliged to obedience to the laws of that government, during such enjoyment, as anyone under it; whether this his possession be of land to him and his heirs for ever, or a lodging only for a week, or whether it be barely travelling freely on the highway; and, in effect, it reaches as far as the very being of anyone within the territories of that government.

120. To understand this the better, it is fit to consider that every man, when he at first incorporates himself into any commonwealth, he, by his uniting himself thereunto, annexes also, and submits to the community, those possessions which he has or shall acquire that do not already belong to any other government; for it would be a direct contradiction for any one to enter into society with others for the securing and regulating of property, and yet to suppose his land, whose property is to be regulated by the laws of the society, should be exempt from the jurisdiction of that government to which he himself, the proprietor of the land, is a subject. By the same act, therefore, whereby any one unites his person, which was before free, to any commonwealth, by the same he unites his possessions, which were before free, to it also; and they become, both of them, person and possession, subject to the government and dominion of that commonwealth as long as it hath a being. Whoever, therefore, from thenceforth by inheritance, purchase, permission,

or otherwise, enjoys any part of the land so annexed to, and under the government of that commonwealth, must take it with the condition it is under — that is, of submitting to the government of the commonwealth under whose jurisdiction it is as far forth as any subject of it.

121. But since the government has a direct jurisdiction only over the land, and reaches the possessor of it — before he has actually incorporated himself in the society — only as he dwells upon and enjoys that, the obligation any one is under by virtue of such enjoyment, to submit to the government, begins and ends with the enjoyment; so that whenever the owner, who has given nothing but such a tacit consent to the government, will, by donation, sale, or otherwise, quit the said possession, he is at liberty to go and incorporate himself into any other commonwealth, or to agree with others to begin a new one *in vacuis locis*, in any part of the world they can find free and unpossessed. Whereas he that has once, by actual agreement and any express declaration, given his consent to be of any commonwealth is perpetually and indispensably obliged to be and remain unalterably a subject to it, and can never be again in the liberty of the state of nature, unless by any calamity the government he was under comes to be dissolved, or else by some public act cuts him off from being any longer a member of it.

122. But submitting to the laws of any country, living quietly and enjoying privileges and protection under them, makes not a man a member of that society; this is only a local protection and homage due to and from all those who, not being in a state of war, come within the territories belonging to any government, to all parts whereof the force of its laws extends. But this no more makes a man a member of that society, a perpetual subject of that commonwealth, than it would make a man a subject to another in whose family he found it convenient to abide for some time, though, whilst he continued in it, he were obliged to comply with the laws, and submit to the government he found there. And thus we see that foreigners, by living all their lives under another government and enjoying the privileges and protection of it, though they are bound, even in conscience, to submit to its administration as far forth as any denizen, yet do not thereby come to be subjects or members of that commonwealth. Nothing can make any man so but his actually entering into it by positive engagement and express promise and compact. This is that which I think concerning the beginning of political societies and that consent which makes any one a member of any commonwealth.

Chapter XIX Of the Dissolution of Government

211. He that will with any clearness speak of the dissolution of government ought in the first place to distinguish between the dissolution of the society and the dissolution of the government. That which makes the community and

brings men out of the loose state of nature into one politic society is the agreement which everybody has with the rest to incorporate and act as one body, and so be one distinct commonwealth. The usual and almost only way whereby this union is dissolved is the inroad of foreign force making a conquest upon them; for in that case, not being able to maintain and support themselves as one entire and independent body, the union belonging to that body which consisted therein must necessarily cease, and so every one return to the state he was in before, with a liberty to shift for himself and provide for his own safety, as he thinks fit, in some other society. Whenever the society is dissolved, it is certain the government of that society cannot remain. Thus conquerors' swords often cut up governments by the roots and mangle societies to pieces, separating the subdued or scattered multitude from the protection of and dependence on that society which ought to have preserved them from violence. The world is too well instructed in, and too forward to allow of, this way of dissolving of governments to need any more to be said of it; and there wants not much argument to prove that where the society is dissolved, the government cannot remain — that being as impossible as for the frame of a house to subsist when the materials of it are scattered and dissipated by a whirlwind, or jumbled into a confused heap by an earthquake.

212. Besides this overturning from without, governments are dissolved from within.

First, When the legislative is altered. Civil society being a state of peace amongst those who are of it, from whom the state of war is excluded by the umpirage which they have provided in their legislative for the ending all differences that may arise amongst any of them, it is in their legislative that the members of a commonwealth are united and combined together into one coherent living body. This is the soul that gives form, life, and unity to the commonwealth; from hence the several members have their mutual influence, sympathy, and connexion; and, therefore, when the legislative is broken or dissolved, dissolution and death follows; for the essence and union of the society consisting in having one will, the legislative, when once established by the majority, has the declaring and, as it were, keeping of that will. The constitution of the legislative is the first and fundamental act of society, whereby provision is made for the continuation of their union under the direction of persons and bonds of laws made by persons authorized thereunto by the consent and appointment of the people, without which no one man or number of men amongst them can have authority of making laws that shall be binding to the rest. When any one or more shall take upon them to make laws, whom the people have not appointed so to do, they make laws without authority, which the people are not therefore bound to obey; by which means they come again to be out of subjection and may constitute to themselves a new legislative as they think best, being in full liberty to resist the force of those who without authority would impose anything upon them. Every one is at the disposure of his own will when those who had by the delegation of the society the declaring of the public will are excluded from it, and others usurp the place who have no such authority or delegation.

213. This being usually brought about by such in the commonwealth who misuse the power they have, it is hard to consider it aright, and know at whose door to lay it, without knowing the form of government in which it happens. Let us suppose then the legislative placed in the concurrence of three distinct persons:

(1) A single hereditary person having the constant supreme executive power, and with it the power of convoking and dissolving the other two within certain periods of time.
(2) An assembly of hereditary nobility.
(3) An assembly of representatives chosen *pro tempore* by the people. Such a form of government supposed, it is evident,

214. First, That when such a single person or prince sets up his own arbitrary will in place of the laws which are the will of the society declared by the legislative, then the legislative is changed; for that being in effect the legislative whose rules and laws are put in execution and required to be obeyed. When other laws are set up, and other rules pretended and enforced, than what the legislative constituted by the society have enacted, it is plain that the legislative is changed. Whoever introduces new laws, not being thereunto authorized by the fundamental appointment of the society, or subverts the old, disowns and overturns the power by which they were made, and so sets up a new legislative.

215. Secondly, When the prince hinders the legislative from assembling in its due time, or from acting freely pursuant to those ends for which it was constituted, the legislative is altered; for it is not a certain number of men, no, nor their meeting, unless they have also freedom of debating and leisure of perfecting what is for the good of the society, wherein the legislative consists. When these are taken away or altered so as to deprive the society of the due exercise of their power, the legislative is truly altered; for it is not names that constitute governments but the use and exercise of those powers that were intended to accompany them, so that he who takes away the freedom or hinders the acting of the legislative in its due seasons in effect takes away the legislative and puts an end to the government.

216. Thirdly, When, by the arbitrary power of the prince, the electors or ways of election are altered without the consent and contrary to the common interest of the people, there also the legislative is altered; for, if others than those whom the society hath authorized thereunto do choose, or in another way than what the society hath prescribed, those chosen are not the legislative appointed by the people.

217. Fourthly, The delivery also of the people into the subjection of a foreign power, either by the prince or by the legislative, is certainly a change of the legislative, and so a dissolution of the government; for the end why people entered into society being to be preserved one entire, free, independent society, to be governed by its own laws, this is lost whenever they are given up into the power of another.

218. Why in such a constitution as this the dissolution of the government in these cases is to be inputed to the prince is evident. Because he, having the force, treasure, and offices of the state to employ, and often persuading himself, or being flattered by others, that as supreme magistrate he is incapable of control—he alone is in a condition to make great advances toward such changes, under pretence of lawful authority, and has it in his hands to terrify or suppress opposers as factious, seditious, and enemies to the government. Whereas no other part of the legislative or people is capable by themselves to attempt any alteration of the legislative, without open and visible rebellion apt enough to be taken notice of, which, when it prevails, produces effects very little different from foreign conquest. Besides, the prince in such a form of government having the power of dissolving the other parts of the legislative, and thereby rendering them private persons, they can never in opposition to him or without his concurrence alter the legislative by a law, his consent being necessary to give any of their decrees that sanction. But yet, so far as the other parts of the legislative any way contribute to any attempt upon the government, and do either promote or not, what lies in them, hinder such designs, they are guilty, and partake in this, which is certainly the greatest crime men can be guilty of one towards another.

219. There is one way more whereby such a government may be dissolved, and that is when he who has the supreme executive power neglects and abandons that charge, so that the laws already made can no longer be put in execution. This is demonstratively to reduce all to anarchy, and so effectually to dissolve the government; for laws not being made for themselves, but to be by their execution the bonds of the society, to keep every part of the body politic in its due place and function. When that totally ceases, the government visibly ceases, and the people become a confused multitude, without order or connexion. Where there is no longer the administration of justice for the securing of men's rights, nor any remaining power within the community to direct the force or provide for the necessities of the public, there certainly is no government left. Where the laws cannot be executed, it is all one as if there were no laws; and a government without laws is, I suppose, a mystery in politics, inconceivable to human capacity and inconsistent with human society.

220. In these and the like cases, when the government is dissolved, the people are at liberty to provide for themselves by erecting a new legislative, differing from the other by the change of persons or form, or both, as they shall find it most for their safety and good; for the society can never by the fault of another lose the native and original right it has to preserve itself, which can only be done by a settled legislative, and a fair and impartial execution of the laws made by it. But the state of mankind is not so miserable that they are not capable of using this remedy till it be too late to look for any. To tell people they may provide for themselves by erecting a new legislative, when by oppression, artifice, or being delivered over to a foreign power, their old one is gone, is only to tell them they may expect relief when it is too late

and the evil is past cure. This is in effect no more than to bid them first be slaves, and then to take care of their liberty; and when their chains are on, tell them they may act like freemen. This, if barely so, is rather mockery than relief; and men can never be secure from tyranny if there be no means to escape it till they are perfectly under it; and therefore it is that they have not only a right to get out of it, but to prevent it.

221. There is, therefore, secondly, another way whereby governments are dissolved, and that is when the legislative or the prince, either of them, act contrary to their trust.

First, The legislative acts against the trust reposed in them when they endeavour to invade the property of the subject, and to make themselves or any part of the community masters or arbitrary disposers of the lives, liberties, or fortunes of the people.

222. The reason why men enter into society is the preservation of their property; and the end why they choose and authorize a legislative is that there may be laws made and rules set as guards and fences to the properties of all the members of the society, to limit the power and moderate the dominion of every part and member of the society; for since it can never be supposed to be the will of the society that the legislative should have a power to destroy that which every one designs to secure by entering into society, and for which the people submitted themselves to legislators of their own making. Whenever the legislators endeavour to take away and destroy the property of the people, or to reduce them to slavery under arbitrary power, they put themselves into a state of war with the people who are thereupon absolved from any further obedience, and are left to the common refuge which God hath provided for all men against force and violence. Whensoever, therefore, the legislative shall transgress this fundamental rule of society, and either by ambition, fear, folly, or corruption, endeavour to grasp themselves, or put into the hands of any other, an absolute power over the lives, liberties, and estates of the people, by this breach of trust they forfeit the power the people had put into their hands for quite contrary ends, and it devolves to the people who have a right to resume their original liberty, and by the establishment of a new legislative, such as they shall think fit, provide for their own safety and security, which is the end for which they are in society. What I have said here concerning the legislative in general holds true also concerning the supreme executor, who having a double trust put in him — both to have a part in the legislative and the supreme execution of the law — acts against both when he goes about to set up his own arbitrary will as the law of the society. He acts also contrary to his trust when he either employs the force, treasure, and offices of the society to corrupt the representatives and gain them to his purposes, or openly pre-engages the electors and prescribes to their choice such whom he has by solicitations, threats, promises, or otherwise won to his designs, and employs them to bring in such who have promised beforehand what to vote and what to enact. Thus to regulate candidates and electors, and new-model the ways of election, what is it but to cut up the government by

the roots, and poison the very fountain of public security? For the people, having reserved to themselves the choice of their representatives, as the fence to their properties, could do it for no other end but that they might always be freely chosen, and, so chosen, freely act and advise as the necessity of the commonwealth and the public good should upon examination and mature debate be judged to require. This, those who give their votes before they hear the debate, and have weighed the reasons on all sides, are not capable of doing. To prepare such an assembly as this, and endeavour to set up the declared abettors of his own will for the true representatives of the people and the lawmakers of the society, is certainly as great a breach of trust and as perfect a declaration of a design to subvert the government as is possible to be met with. To which if one shall add rewards and punishments visibly employed to the same end, and all the arts of perverted law made use of to take off and destroy all that stand in the way of such a design, and will not comply and consent to betray the liberties of their country, it will be past doubt what is doing. What power they ought to have in the society who thus employ it contrary to the trust that went along with it in its first institution is easy to determine; and one cannot but see that he who has once attempted any such thing as this cannot any longer be trusted.

223. To this perhaps it will be said that the people being ignorant and always discontented, to lay the foundation of government in the unsteady opinion and uncertain humour of the people is to expose it to certain ruin; and no government will be able long to subsist, if the people may set up a new legislative whenever they take offence at the old one. To this I answer: Quite the contrary. People are not so easily got out of their old forms as some are apt to suggest. They are hardly to be prevailed with to amend the acknowledged faults in the frame they have been accustomed to. And if there be any original defects, or adventitious ones introduced by time or corruption, it is not an easy thing to get them changed, even when all the world sees there is an opportunity for it. This slowness and aversion in the people to quit their old constitutions has in the many revolutions which have been seen in this kingdom, in this and former ages, still kept us to, or after some interval of fruitless attempts still brought us back again to, our old legislative of king, lords, and commons; and whatever provocations have made the crown be taken from some of our princes' heads, they never carried the people so far as to place it in another line.

224. But it will be said this hypothesis lays a ferment for frequent rebellion. To which I answer:

First, No more than any other hypothesis; for when the people are made miserable, and find themselves exposed to the ill-usage of arbitrary power, cry up their governors as much as you will for sons of Jupiter, let them be sacred or divine, descended, or authorized from heaven, give them out for whom or what you please, the same will happen. The people generally ill-treated, and contrary to right, will be ready upon any occasion to ease themselves of a burden that sits heavy upon them. They will wish and seek for the opportunity, which in the change, weakness, and accidents of human affairs seldom delays long to offer itself. He must have lived but a little while in the world who has not seen examples of this in his time, and he must have read very little who cannot produce examples of it in all sorts of governments in the world.

225. Secondly, I answer, such revolutions happen not upon every little mismanagement in public affairs. Great mistakes in the ruling part, many wrong and inconvenient laws, and all the slips of human frailty will be born by the people without mutiny or murmur. But if a long train of abuses, prevarications, and artifices, all tending the same way, make the design visible to the people, and they cannot but feel what they lie under and see whither they are going, it is not to be wondered that they should then rouse themselves and endeavour to put the rule into such hands which may secure to them the ends for which government was at first erected, and without which ancient names and specious forms are so far from being better that they are much worse than the state of nature or pure anarchy—the inconveniences being all as great and as near, but the remedy farther off and more difficult.

226. Thirdly, I answer that this doctrine of a power in the people of providing for their safety anew by a new legislative, when their legislators have acted contrary to their trust by invading their property, as the best fence against rebellion, and the probablest means to hinder it, for rebellion being an opposition, not to persons, but authority which is founded only in the constitutions and laws of the government those, whoever they be, who by force break through, and by force justify their violation of them, are truly and properly rebels; for when men, by entering into society and civil government, have excluded force and introduced laws for the preservation of property, peace, and unity amongst themselves, those who set up force again in opposition to the laws do *rebellare*—that is, bring back again the state of war— and are properly rebels; which they who are in power, by the pretence they have to authority, the temptation of force they have in their hands and the flattery of those about them, being likeliest to do, the properest way to prevent the evil is to show them the danger and injustice of it who are under the greatest temptation to run into it.

227. In both the forementioned cases, when either the legislative is changed or the legislators act contrary to the end for which they were constituted, those who are guilty are guilty of rebellion; for if any one by force takes away the established legislative of any society, and the laws of them made pursuant to their trust, he thereby takes away the umpirage which every one had consented to for a peaceable decision of all their controversies, and a bar to the state of war amongst them. They who remove or change the legislative take away this decisive power which nobody can have but by the appointment and consent of the people, and so destroying the authority which the people did, and nobody else can, set up, and introducing a power which the people hath not authorized, they actually introduce a state of war which is that of force without authority; and thus by removing the legislative

established by the society—in whose decisions the people acquiesced and united as to that of their own will—they untie the knot and expose the people anew to the state of war. And if those who by force take away the legislative are rebels, the legislators themselves, as has been shown, can be no less esteemed so, when they who were set up for the protection and preservation of the people, their liberties and properties, shall by force invade and endeavour to take them away; and so they putting themselves into a state of war with those who made them the protectors and guardians of their peace, are properly, and with the greatest aggravation, *rebellantes*, rebels.

228. But if they who say "it lays a foundation for rebellion" mean that it may occasion civil wars or intestine broils, to tell the people they are absolved from obedience when illegal attempts are made upon their liberties or properties, and may oppose the unlawful violence of those who were their magistrates when they invade their properties contrary to the trust put in them, and that therefore this doctrine is not to be allowed, being so destructive to the peace of the world: they may as well say, upon the same ground, that honest men may not oppose robbers or pirates, because this may occasion disorder or bloodshed. If any mischief come in such cases, it is not to be charged upon him who defends his own right, but on him that invades his neighbour's. If the innocent honest man must quietly quit all he has, for peace's sake, to him who will lay violent hands upon it, I desire it may be considered what a kind of peace there will be in the world, which consists only in violence and rapine, and which is to be maintained only for the benefit of robbers and oppressors. Who would not think it an admirable peace betwixt the mighty and the mean when the lamb without resistance yielded his throat to be torn by the imperious wolf? Polyphemus' den gives us a perfect pattern of such a peace and such a government, wherein Ulysses and his companions had nothing to do but quietly to suffer themselves to be devoured. And no doubt Ulysses, who was a prudent man, preached up passive obedience, and exhorted them to a quiet submission by representing to them of what concernment peace was to mankind, and by showing the inconveniences might happen, if they should offer to resist Polyphemus, who had now the power over them.

229. The end of government is the good of mankind. And which is best for mankind? That the people should be always exposed to the boundless will of tyranny, or that the rulers should be sometimes liable to be opposed when they grow exorbitant in the use of their power and employ it for the destruction and not the preservation of the properties of their people?

243. To conclude, the power that every individual gave the society when he entered into it can never revert to the individuals again as long as the society lasts, but will always remain in the community, because without this there can be no community, no commonwealth, which is contrary to the original agreement; so also when the society hath placed the legislative in any assembly of men, to continue in them and their successors with direction and authority for providing such successors, the legislative can never revert to the people whilst that government lasts, because having provided a legislative

with power to continue for ever, they have given up their political power to the legislative and cannot resume it. But if they have set limits to the duration of their legislative and made this supreme power in any person or assembly only temporary, or else when by the miscarriages of those in authority it is forfeited, upon the forfeiture, or at the determination of the time set, it reverts to the society, and the people have a right to act as supreme and continue the legislative in themselves, or erect a new form, or under the old form place it in new hands, as they think good.

SELECTIONS FROM
A Letter Concerning Toleration

Honoured sir,

Since you are pleased to inquire what are my thoughts about the mutual toleration of Christians in their different professions of religion, I must needs answer you freely, that I esteem that toleration to be the chief characteristic mark of the true church. For whatsoever some people boast of the antiquity of places and names, or of the pomp of their outward worship; others, of the reformation of their discipline; all, of the orthodoxy of their faith—for every one is orthodox to himself—these things, and all others of this nature, are much rather marks of men striving for power and empire over one another, than of the church of Christ. Let any one have never so true a claim to all these things, yet if he be destitute of charity, meekness, and good-will in general towards all mankind, even to those that are not Christians, he is certainly yet short of being a true Christian himself. "The kings of the Gentiles exercise lordship over them," said our Saviour to his disciples, "but ye shall not be so" (Luke xxii. 25). The business of true religion is quite another thing. It is not instituted in order to the erecting of an external pomp, nor to the obtaining of ecclesiastical dominion, nor to the exercising of compulsive force, but to the regulating of men's lives, according to the rules of virtue and piety. Whosoever will list himself under the banner of Christ, must in the first place, and above all things, make war upon his own lusts and vices. It is in vain for any man to usurp the name of Christian, without holiness of life, purity of manners, benignity and meekness of spirit. "Let every one that nameth the name of Christ, depart from iniquity" (2 Tim. ii. 19). "Thou, when thou art converted, strengthen thy brethren," said our Lord to Peter (Luke xxii. 32). It would, indeed, be very hard for one that appears careless about his own salvation to persuade me that he were extremely concerned for mine. For it is impossible that those should sincerely and heartily apply themselves to make other people Christians, who have not really embraced the Christian religion in their own hearts. If the Gospel and the apostles may be credited, no man can be a Christian without charity, and without that faith which works, not by force, but by love. Now, I appeal to the consciences of those that persecute, torment, destroy, and kill other men upon pretence of religion, whether they do it out of friendship and kindness towards them or no? And I shall then indeed, and not until then, believe they do so, when I shall see those fiery zealots correcting, in the same manner, their friends and familiar acquaintance for the manifest sins they commit against the precepts of the Gospel; when I shall see them persecute with fire and sword the members of their own communion that are tainted with enormous vices, and without amendment are in danger of eternal perdition; and when I shall see them thus express their love and desire of the salvation of their souls by the infliction of torments, and exercise of all manner of cruelties. For if it be out of a principle of charity, as they pretend, and love to men's souls, that they deprive them of their estates, maim them with corporal punishments, starve and torment them in noisome prisons, and in the end even take away their lives, — I say, if all this be done merely to make men Christians, and procure their salvation, why then do they suffer whoredom, fraud, malice, and such-like enormities, which (according to the apostle (Rom. i)) manifestly relish of heathenish corruption, to predominate so much and abound amongst their flocks and people? These, and such-like things, are certainly more contrary to the glory of God, to the purity of the church, and to the salvation of souls, than any conscientious dissent from ecclesiastical decisions, or separation from public worship, whilst accompanied with innocence of life. Why then does this burning zeal for God, for the church, and for the salvation of souls—burning, I say, literally, with fire and faggot—pass by those moral vices and wickednesses without any chastisement, which are acknowledged by all men to be diametrically opposite to the profession of Christianity, and bend all its nerves either to the introducing of ceremonies, or to the establishment of opinions, which for the most part are about nice and intricate matters, that exceed the capacity of ordinary understandings? Which of the parties contending about these things is in the right, which of them is guilty of schism or heresy, whether those that domineer or those that suffer, will then at last be manifest, when the causes of their separation comes to be judged of. He, certainly, that follows Christ, embraces his doctrine, and bears his yoke, though he forsake both father and mother, separate from the public assemblies and ceremonies of his country, or whomsoever or whatsoever else he relinquishes, will not then be judged a heretic.

Now, though the divisions that are amongst sects should be allowed to be never so obstructive of the salvation of souls; yet, nevertheless, adultery, fornication, uncleanliness, lasciviousness, idolatry, and suchlike things, cannot be denied to be works of the flesh, concerning which the apostle has expressly declared (Gal. v.) that "they who do them shall not inherit the kingdom of God". Whosoever, therefore, is sincerely solicitous about the kingdom of God, and thinks it his duty to endeavour the enlargement of it amongst men, ought to apply himself with no less care and industry to the rooting out of these immoralities than to the extirpation of sects. But if any one do otherwise, and whilst he is cruel and implacable towards those that differ from him in opinion, he be indulgent to such iniquities and immoralities as are unbecoming the name of a Christian, let such a one talk never so much of the church, he plainly demonstrates by his actions that it is another kingdom he aims it, and not the advancement of the kingdom of God.

That any man should think fit to cause another man — whose salvation he heartily desires — to expire in torments, and that even in an unconverted state, would, I confess, seem very strange to me, and, I think, to any other also. But nobody, surely, will ever believe that such a carriage can proceed from charity, love, or good-will. If any one maintain that men ought to be compelled by fire and sword to profess certain doctrines, and conform to this or that exterior worship, without any regard had unto their morals; if any one endeavour to convert those that are erroneous unto the faith, by forcing them to profess things that they do not believe, and allowing them to practise things that the Gospel does not permit, it cannot be doubted indeed but such a one is desirous to have a numerous assembly joined in the same profession with himself; but that he principally intends by those means to compose a truly Christian church, is altogether incredible. It is not, therefore, to be wondered at if those who do not really contend for the advancement of the true religion, and of the church of Christ, make use of arms that do not belong to the Christian warfare. If, like the Captain of our salvation, they sincerely desired the good of souls, they would tread in the steps and follow the perfect example of that Prince of peace, who sent out his soldiers to the subduing of nations, and gathering them into his church, not armed with the sword, or other instruments of force, but prepared with the Gospel of peace, and with the exemplary holiness of their conversation. This was his method. Though if infidels were to be converted by force, if those that are either blind or obstinate were to be drawn off from their errors by armed soldiers, we know very well that it was much more easy for him to do it with armies of heavenly legions, than for any son of the church, how potent soever, with all his dragoons.

The toleration of those that differ from others in matters of religion, is so agreeable to the Gospel of Jesus Christ, and to the genuine reason of mankind, that it seems monstrous for men to be so blind as not to perceive the necessity and advantage of it in so clear a light. I will not here tax the pride and ambition of some, the passion and uncharitable zeal of others. These are faults from which human affairs can perhaps scarce ever be perfectly freed; but yet such as nobody will bear the plain imputation of, without covering them with some specious colour; and so pretend to commendation, whilst they are carried away by their own irregular passions. But, however, that some may not colour their spirit of persecution and unchristian cruelty with a pretence of care of the public weal and observation of the laws; and that others, under pretence of religion, may not seek impunity for their libertinism and licentiousness; in a word, that none may impose either upon himself or others, by the pretences of loyalty and obedience to the prince, or of tenderness and sincerity in the worship of God, I esteem it above all things necessary to distinguish exactly the business of civil government from that of religion, and to settle the just bound that lie between the one and the other. If this be not done, there can be no end put to the controversies that will be always arising between those that have, or at least pretend to have, on the one side, a concernment for the interest of men's souls, and, on the other side, a care of the commonwealth.

The commonwealth seems to me to be a society of men constituted only for the procuring, preserving, and advancing their own civil interests.

Civil interests I call life, liberty, health, and indolency of body; and the possession of outward things, such as money, lands, houses, furniture, and the like.

It is the duty of the civil magistrate, by the impartial execution of equal laws, to secure unto all the people in general, and to every one of his subjects in particular, the just possession of these things belonging to this life. If any one presume to violate the laws of public justice and equity, established for the preservation of those things, his presumption is to be checked by the fear of punishment, consisting of the deprivation or diminution of those civil interests, or goods, which otherwise he might and ought to enjoy. But seeing no man does willingly suffer himself to be punished by the deprivation of any part of his goods, and much less of his liberty or life, therefore is the magistrate armed with the force and strength of all his subjects, in order to the punishment of those that violate any other man's rights.

Now that the whole jurisdiction of the magistrate reaches only to these civil concernments, and that all civil power, right, and dominion, is bounded and confined to the only care of promoting these things; and that it neither can nor ought in any manner to be extended to the salvation of souls, these following considerations seem unto me abundantly to demonstrate.

First, because the care of souls is not committed to the civil magistrate, any more than to other men. It is not committed unto him, I say, by God; because it appears not that God has ever given any such authority to one man over another, as to compel any one to his religion. Nor can any such power be vested in the magistrate by the consent of the people, because no man can so far abandon the care of his own salvation as blindly to leave to the choice of any other, whether prince or subject, to prescribe to him what faith or worship he shall embrace. For no man can, if he would, conform his faith to the dictates of another. All the life and power of true religion consist in the inward and full persuasion of the mind; and faith is not faith without believing. Whatever profession we make, to whatever outward worship we conform, if we are not fully satisfied in our own mind that the one is true, and the other well pleasing unto God, such profession and such practice, far from being any furtherance, are indeed great obstacles to our salvation. For in this manner, instead of expiating other sins by the exercise of religion, I say, in offering thus unto God Almighty such a worship as we esteem to be displeasing unto him, we add unto the number of our other sins those also of hypocrisy, and contempt of his Divine Majesty.

In the second place, the care of souls cannot belong to the civil magistrate, because his power consists only in outward force; but true and saving religion consists in the inward persuasion of the mind, without which nothing can be acceptable to God. And such is the nature of the understanding, that it cannot be compelled to the belief of anything by outward force. Confiscation of estate, imprisonment, torments, nothing of that nature can have any such efficacy as to make men change the inward judgment that they have framed of things.

It may indeed be alleged that the magistrate may make use of arguments, and thereby draw the heterodox into the way of truth, and procure their salvation. I grant it; but this is common to him with other men. In teaching, instructing, and redressing the erroneous by reason, he may certainly do what becomes any good man to do. Magistracy does not oblige him to put off either humanity or Christianity; but it is one thing to persuade, another to command; one thing to press with arguments, another with penalties. This civil power alone has a right to do; to the other good-will is authority enough. Every man has commission to admonish, exhort, convince another of error, and, by reasoning, to draw him into truth; but to give laws, receive obedience, and compel with the sword, belongs to none but the magistrate. And upon this ground, I affirm that the magistrate's power extends not to the establishing of any articles of faith, or forms of worship, by the force of his laws. For laws are of no force at all without penalties, and penalties in this case are absolutely impertinent, because they are not proper to convince the mind. Neither the profession of any articles of faith, nor the conformity to any outward form of worship (as has been already said), can be available to the salvation of souls, unless the truth of the one, and the acceptableness of the other unto God, be thoroughly believed by those that so profess and practise. But penalties are no way capable to produce such belief. It is only light and evidence that can work a change in men's opinions; which light can in no manner proceed from corporal sufferings, or any other outward penalties.

In the third place, the care of the salvation of men's souls cannot belong to the magistrate; because, though the rigour of laws and the force of penalties were capable to convince and change men's minds, yet would not that help at all to the salvation of their souls. For there being but one truth, one way to heaven, what hope is there that more men would be led into it if they had no rule but the religion of the court, and were put under the necessity to quit the light of their own reason, and oppose the dictates of their own consciences, and blindly to resign themselves up to the will of their governors, and to the religion which either ignorance, ambition, or superstition had chanced to establish in the countries where they were born? In the variety and contradiction of opinions in religion, wherein the princes of the world are as much divided as in their secular interests, the narrow way would be much straitened; one country alone would be in the right, and all the rest of the world put under an obligation of following their princes in the ways that lead to destruction; and that which heightens the absurdity, and very ill suits the notion of a Deity, men would owe their eternal happiness or misery to the places of their nativity.

These considerations, to omit many others that might have been urged to the same purpose, seem unto me sufficient to conclude that all the power of civil government relates only to men's civil interests, is confined to the care of the things of this world, and hath nothing to do with the world to come.

Let us now consider what a church is. A church, then, I take to be a voluntary society of men, joining themselves together of their own accord in order to the public worshipping of God in such manner as they judge acceptable to him, and effectual to the salvation of their souls.

I say it is a free and voluntary society. Nobody is born a member of any church; otherwise the religion of parents would descend unto children by the same right of inheritance as their temporal estates, and every one would hold his faith by the same tenure he does his lands, than which nothing can be imagined more absurd. Thus, therefore, that matter stands. No man by nature is bound unto any particular church or sect, but every one joins himself voluntarily to that society in which he believes he has found that profession and worship which is truly acceptable to God. The hope of salvation, as it was the only cause of his entrance into that communion, so it can be the only reason of his stay there. For if afterwards he discover anything either erroneous in the doctrine or incongruous in the worship of that society to which he has joined himself, why should it not be as free for him to go out as it was to enter? No member of a religious society can be tied with any other bonds but what proceed from the certain expectation of eternal life. A church, then, is a society of members voluntarily uniting to that end.

It follows now that we consider what is the power of this church, and unto what laws it is subject.

Forasmuch as no society, how free soever, or upon whatsoever slight occasion instituted, whether of philosophers for learning, of merchants for commerce, or of men of leisure for mutual conversation and discourse, no church or company, I say, can in the least subsist and hold together, but will presently dissolve and break in pieces, unless it be regulated by some laws, and the members all consent to observe some order. Place and time of meeting must be agreed on; rules for admitting and excluding members must be established; distinction of officers, and putting things into a regular course, and such-like, cannot be omitted. But since the joining together of several members into this church-society, as has already been demonstrated, is absolutely free and spontaneous, it necessarily follows that the right of making its laws can belong to none but the society itself; or, at least (which is the same thing), to those whom the society by common consent has authorised thereunto.

Some, perhaps, may object that no such society can be said to be a true church unless it have in it a bishop or presbyter, with ruling authority derived from the very apostles, and continued down to the present times by an uninterrupted succession.

To these I answer: In the first place, let them show me the edict by which Christ has imposed that law upon his church. And let not any man think me impertinent, if in a thing of this consequence I require that the terms of that edict be very express and positive; for the promise he has made us (Matt. xviii. 20), that wheresoever two or three are gathered together in his name, he will be in the midst of them, seems to imply the contrary. Whether such an assembly want anything necessary to a true church, pray do you consider. Certain I am that nothing can be there wanting unto the salvation of souls, which is sufficient to our purpose.

Next, pray observe how great have always been the divisions amongst even those who lay so much stress upon the divine institution and continued succession of a certain order of rulers in the church. Now, their very dissension unavoidably puts us upon a necessity of deliberating, and, consequently, allows a liberty of choosing that which upon consideration we prefer.

And, in the last place, I consent that these men have a ruler in their church, established by such a long series of succession as they judge necessary, provided I may have liberty at the same time to join myself to that society in which I am persuaded those things are to be found which are necessary to the salvation of my soul. In this manner ecclesiastical liberty will be preserved on all sides, and no man will have a legislator imposed upon him but whom himself has chosen.

But since men are so solicitous about the true church, I would only ask them here, by the way, if it be not more agreeable to the church of Christ to make the conditions of her communion consist in such things, and such things only, as the Holy Spirit has in the Holy Scriptures declared, in express words, to be necessary to salvation; I ask, I say, whether this be not more agreeable to the church of Christ than for men to impose their own inventions and interpretations upon others as if they were of divine authority, and to establish by ecclesiastical laws, as absolutely necessary to the profession of Christianity, such things as the Holy Scriptures do either not mention, or at least not expressly command? Whosoever requires those things in order to ecclesiastical communion, which Christ does not require in order to life eternal, he may, perhaps, indeed constitute a society accommodated to his own opinion and his own advantage; but how that can be called the church of Christ which is established upon laws that are not his, and which excludes such persons from its communion as he will one day receive into the kingdom of heaven, I understand not. But this being not a proper place to inquire into the marks of the true church, I will only mind those that contend so earnestly for the decrees of their own society, and that cry out continually, The church! the church! with as much noise, and perhaps upon the same principle, as the Ephesian silversmiths did for their Diana; this, I say, I desire to mind them of, that the Gospel frequently declares that the true disciples of Christ must suffer persecution; but that the church of Christ should persecute others, and force others by fire and sword to embrace her faith and doctrine, I could never yet find in any of the books of the New Testament.

The end of a religious society (as has already been said) is the public worship of God, and, by means thereof, the acquisition of eternal life. All discipline ought therefore to tend to that end, and all ecclesiastical laws to be thereunto confined. Nothing ought nor can be transacted in this society relating to the possession of civil and worldly goods. No force is here to be made use of upon any occasion whatsoever. For force belongs wholly to the civil magistrate, and the possession of all outward goods is subject to his jurisdiction.

But, it may be asked, by what means then shall ecclesiastical laws be established, if they must be thus destitute of all compulsive power? I answer:

They must be established by means suitable to the nature of such things, whereof the external profession and observation — if not proceeding from a thorough conviction and approbation of the mind — is altogether useless and unprofitable. The arms by which the members of this society are to be kept within their duty are exhortations, admonitions, and advices. If by these means the offenders will not be reclaimed, and the erroneous convinced, there remains nothing further to be done but that such stubborn and obstinate persons, who give no ground to hope for their reformation, should be cast out and separated from the society. This is the last and utmost force of ecclesiastical authority. No other punishment can thereby be inflicted than that, the relation ceasing between the body and the member which is cut off. The person so condemned ceases to be a part of that church.

These things being thus determined, let us inquire, in the next place: How far the duty of toleration extends, and what is required from every one by it?

And, first, I hold that no church is bound, by the duty of toleration, to retain any such person in her bosom as, after admonition, continues obstinately to offend against the laws of the society. For these being the condition of communion and the bond of the society, if the breach of them were permitted without any animadversion the society would immediately be thereby dissolved. But, nevertheless, in all such cases care is to be taken that the sentence of excommunication, and the execution thereof, carry with it no rough usage of word or action whereby the ejected person may any wise be damnified in body or estate. For all force (as has often been said) belongs only to the magistrate, nor ought any private persons at any time to use force, unless it be in self-defence against unjust violence. Excommunication neither does, nor can, deprive the excommunicated person of any of those civil goods that he formerly possessed. All those things belong to the civil government, and are under the magistrate's protection. The whole force of excommunication consists only in this: that the resolution of the society in that respect being declared, the union that was between the body and some member comes thereby to be dissolved; and that relation ceasing, the participation of some certain things which the society communicated to its members, and unto which no man has any civil right, comes also to cease. For there is no civil injury done unto the excommunicated person by the church minister's refusing him that bread and wine, in the celebration of the Lord's Supper, which was not bought with his but other men's money.

Secondly, no private person has any right in any manner to prejudice another person in his civil enjoyments because he is of another church or religion. All the rights and franchises that belong to him as a man, or as a denizen, are inviolably to be preserved to him. These are not the business of religion. No violence nor injury is to be offered him, whether he be Christian or Pagan. Nay, we must not content ourselves with the narrow measures of bare justice; charity, bounty, and liberality must be added to it. This the Gospel enjoins, this reason directs, and this that natural fellowship we are born into requires of us. If any man err from the right way, it is his own misfortune, no injury to thee; nor therefore art thou to punish him in the things of this life because thou supposest he will be miserable in that which is to come.

What I say concerning the mutual toleration of private persons differing from one another in religion, I understand also of particular churches which stand, as it were, in the same relation to each other as private persons among themselves: nor has any one of them any manner of jurisdiction over any other; no, not even when the civil magistrate (as it sometimes happens) comes to be of this or the other communion. For the civil government can give no new right to the church, nor the church to the civil government. So that whether the magistrate join himself to any church, or separate from it, the church remains always as it was before — a free and voluntary society. It neither requires the power of the sword by the magistrate's coming to it, nor does it lose the right of instruction and excommunication by his going from it. This is the fundamental and immutable right of a spontaneous society — that it has power to remove any of its members who transgress the rules of its institution; but it cannot, by the accession of any new members, acquire any right of jurisdiction over those that are not joined with it. And therefore peace, equity, and friendship are always mutually to be observed by particular churches, in the same manner as by private persons, without any pretence of superiority or jurisdiction over one another.

That the thing may be made clearer by an example, let us suppose two churches — the one of Arminians, the other of Calvinists — residing in the city of Constantinople. Will any one say that either of these churches has right to deprive the members of the other of their estates and liberty (as we see practised elsewhere), because of their differing from it in some doctrines and ceremonies, whilst the Turks in the meanwhile silently stand by, and laugh to see with what inhuman cruelty Christians thus rage against Christians? But if one of these churches hath this power to treating the other ill, I ask which of them it is to whom that power belongs, and by what right? It will be answered, undoubtedly, that it is the orthodox church which has the right of authority over the erroneous or heretical. This is, in great and specious words, to say just nothing at all. For every church is orthodox to itself; to others, erroneous or heretical. For whatsoever any church believes, it believes to be true; and the contrary unto those things, it pronounces to be error. So that the controversy between these churches about the truth of their doctrines, and the purity of their worship, is on both sides equal; nor is there any judge, either at Constantinople or elsewhere upon earth, by whose sentence it can be determined. The decision of that question belongs only to the Supreme Judge of all men, to whom also alone belongs the punishment of the erroneous. In the meanwhile, let those men consider how heinously they sin, who, adding injustice, if not to their error, yet certainly to their pride, do rashly and arrogantly take upon them to misuse the servants of another master, who are not at all accountable to them.

Nay, further: if it could be manifest which of these two dissenting churches were in the right, there would not accrue thereby unto the orthodox any right of destroying the other. For churches have neither any jurisdiction in worldly matters, nor are fire and sword any proper instruments wherewith to convince men's minds of error, and inform them of the truth. Let us suppose, nevertheless, that the civil magistrate inclined to favour one of them, and to put his sword into their hands, that (by his consent) they might chastise the dissenters as they pleased. Will any man say that any right can be derived unto a Christian church over its brethren from a Turkish emperor? An infidel, who has himself no authority to punish Christians for the articles of their faith, cannot confer such an authority upon any society of Christians, nor give unto them a right which he has not himself. This would be the case at Constantinople; and the reason of the thing is the same in any Christian kingdom. The civil power is the same in every place. Nor can that power, in the hands of a Christian prince, confer any greater authority upon the church than in the hands of a heathen; which is to say, just none at all.

Nevertheless, it is worthy to be observed and lamented that the most violent of these defenders of the truth, the opposers of errors, the exclaimers against schism, do hardly ever let loose this their zeal for God, with which they are so warmed and inflamed, unless where they have the civil magistrate on their side. But so soon as ever court favour has given them the better end of the staff, and they begin to feel themselves the stronger, then presently peace and charity are to be laid aside. Otherwise they are religiously to be observed. Where they have not the power to carry on persecution and to become masters, there they desire to live upon fair terms, and preach up toleration. When they are not strengthened with the civil power, then they can bear most patiently and unmovedly the contagion of idolatry, superstition, and heresy in their neighbourhood; of which on other occasions the interest of religion makes them to be extremely apprehensive. They do not forwardly attack those errors which are in fashion at court or are countenanced by the government. Here they can be content to spare their arguments; which yet (with their leave) is the only right method of propagating truth, which has no such way of prevailing as when strong arguments and good reason are joined with the softness of civility and good usage.

Nobody, therefore, in fine, neither single persons nor churches, nay, nor even commonwealths, have any just title to invade the civil rights and worldly goods of each other upon pretence of religion. Those that are of another opinion would do well to consider with themselves how pernicious a seed of discord and war, how powerful a provocation to endless hatreds, rapines, and slaughters they thereby furnish unto mankind. No peace and security, no, not so much as common friendship, can ever be established or preserved amongst men so long as this opinion prevails, that dominion is founded in grace and that religion is to be propagated by force of arms. . . .

BARON DE MONTESQUIEU

1 6 8 9 – 1 7 5 5

INTRODUCTION

Charles-Louis de Secondat, later to inherit his title and substantial estates at La Brède and Montesquieu in a wine-growing region near Bordeaux, was born in a fifteenth-century castle but, as was then a common practice for the French nobility, spent the first 3 years of his life being nursed by a village family. At age 11 he was sent hundreds of miles away to a well-known school outside Paris and received an excellent education there before returning to study law in the very poor department at the University of Bordeaux. From 1709 to 1713 he lived in Paris to learn legal practice and is known to have been active in various scientific academies and societies — an interest that he was to maintain throughout his life. On the death of his father, Charles-Louis inherited the family estate, married a local and well-to-do Protestant woman for whom he never showed much affection, and by inheritance from his uncle became both a large landholder and a senior officer in the provincial parliament. Somewhat bored by this life, Montesquieu spent the next few years writing a novel, *Persian Letters*, a satire on French life as observed by two Persian travelers. The book was an immediate and great success, and although it was published anonymously in Amsterdam in order to avoid French censorship, the author soon became known and famous.

Between 1721 and 1725 Montesquieu wrote a number of scientific and literary essays no longer read, made himself familiar in the literary salons of Paris, and sold his parliamentary office because of his debts. He then set out on a study tour of Italy and England that lasted 4 years. Because of his social rank and talents, he met and became friendly with many of the most eminent and distinguished political and literary figures of the period. By the time he returned home he had accumulated the knowledge and papers required to write his next two books. The first was *Considerations on the Causes of the Greatness of the Romans and Their Decline*, published anonymously in Holland in 1734. The second was the book that Montesquieu worked on until the end of the next decade, *The Spirit of Laws*, published in Geneva in 1748. This very long commentary on the role and effects of legal systems in different sorts of governments, and in various societies throughout the world, was immediately recognized as one of the major books of the period. Its discussion of topics such as political liberty, religious tolerance, the separation of powers in England, criminal law, the treatment of women, the effects of climate and soil, and the encouragement of commerce profoundly influenced the ideas and policies of the educated classes in Western Europe, and later North America, for many decades. Its author became revered, a symbol of political and religious tolerance, and of rational and well-informed thinking on social questions. Despite his partial blindness, the attacks made on him by the Jesuits and other religious groups for his views on toleration, divorce, and celibacy, and the placing of his book on the Vatican Index of Prohibited Books in company with one by Pufendorf, Montesquieu defended himself in print and enjoyed immense popularity, both in court circles and among critics of the government. While in Paris arranging his affairs so that he could retire permanently to his estate he fell seriously ill in an epidemic of influenza. Within a few days he was on his death bed, surrounded by eminent friends, and the center of a struggle between his Jesuit confessor and his friend, the Duchesse d'Aguillon, for possession of the corrected manuscript of the *Persian Letters*. The Duchesse won.

The *Spirit of Laws* was translated into English by Thomas Nugent soon after its original publication and appeared in London in 1751. Montesquieu read and approved the translation and no complete modern one has yet appeared. The Nugent translation has been often reprinted. The present selection is taken from one of these.

SELECTIONS FROM
The Spirit of Laws

BOOK XI
Of the Laws Which Establish Political Liberty with Regard to the Constitution.

1. — A GENERAL IDEA

I make a distinction between the laws that establish political liberty as it relates to the constitution, and those by which it is established as it relates to the citizen. The former shall be the subject of this book; the latter I shall examine in the next.

2. — DIFFERENT SIGNIFICATIONS OF THE WORD LIBERTY

There is no word that admits of more various significations, and has made more varied impressions on the human mind, than that of liberty. Some have taken it as a means of deposing a person on whom they had conferred a tyrannical authority; others for the power of choosing a superior whom they are obliged to obey; others for the right of bearing arms, and of being thereby enabled to use violence; others, in fine, for the privilege of being governed by a native of their own country, or by their own laws. A certain nation for a long time thought liberty consisted in the privilege of wearing a long beard. Some have annexed this name to one form of government exclusive of others: those who had a republican taste applied it to this species of polity; those who liked a monarchical state gave it to monarchy. Thus they have all applied the name of liberty to the government most suitable to their own customs and inclinations: and as in republics the people have not so constant and so present a view of the causes of their misery, and as the magistrates seem to act only in conformity to the laws, hence liberty is generally said to reside in republics, and to be banished from monarchies. In fine, as in democracies the people seem to act almost as they please, this sort of government has been deemed the most free, and the power of the people has been confounded with their liberty.

3. — IN WHAT LIBERTY CONSISTS

It is true that in democracies the people seem to act as they please; but political liberty does not consist in an unlimited freedom. In governments, that is, in societies directed by laws, liberty can consist only in the power of doing what we ought to will, and in not being constrained to do what we ought not to will.

We must have continually present to our minds the difference between independence and liberty. Liberty is a right of doing whatever the laws permit, and if a citizen could do what they forbid he would be no longer possessed of liberty, because all his fellow-citizens would have the same power.

4. — THE SAME SUBJECT CONTINUED

Democratic and aristocratic states are not in their own nature free. Political liberty is to be found only in moderate governments; and even in these it is not always found. It is there only when there is no abuse of power. But constant experience shows us that every man invested with power is apt to abuse it, and to carry his authority as far as it will go. Is it not strange, though true, to say that virtue itself has need of limits?

To prevent this abuse, it is necessary from the very nature of things that power should be a check to power. A government may be so constituted, as no man shall be compelled to do things to which the law does not oblige him, nor forced to abstain from things which the law permits.

5. — OF THE END OR VIEW OF DIFFERENT GOVERNMENTS

Though all governments have the same general end, which is that of preservation, yet each has another particular object. Increase of dominion was the object of Rome; war, that of Sparta; religion, that of the Jewish laws; commerce, that of Marseilles; public tranquillity, that of the laws of China; navigation, that of the laws of Rhodes; natural liberty, that of the policy of the Savages; in general, the pleasures of the prince, that of despotic states; that of monarchies, the prince's and the kingdom's glory; the independence of individuals is the end aimed at by the laws of Poland, thence results the oppression of the whole.

One nation there is also in the world that has for the direct end of its constitution political liberty. We shall presently examine the principles on which this liberty is founded; if they are sound, liberty will appear in its highest perfection.

To discover political liberty in a constitution, no great labor is requisite. If we are capable of seeing it where it exists, it is soon found, and we need not go far in search of it.

6. — OF THE CONSTITUTION OF ENGLAND

In every government there are three sorts of power: the legislative; the executive in respect to things dependent on the law of nations; and the executive in regard to matters that depend on the civil law.

By virtue of the first, the prince or magistrate enacts temporary or perpetual laws, and amends or abrogates those that have been already enacted. By the second, he makes peace or war, sends or receives embassies, establishes the public security, and provides against invasions. By the third, he punishes criminals, or determines the disputes that arise between individuals. The latter we shall call the judiciary power, and the other simply the executive power of the state.

The political liberty of the subject is a tranquillity of mind arising from the opinion each person has of his safety. In order to have this liberty, it is requisite the government be so constituted as one man need not be afraid of another.

When the legislative and executive powers are united in the same person, or in the same body of magistrates, there can be no liberty; because apprehensions may arise, lest the same monarch or senate should enact tyrannical laws, to execute them in a tyrannical manner.

Again, there is no liberty, if the judiciary power be not separated from the legislative and executive. Were it joined with the legislative, the life and liberty of the subject would be exposed to arbitrary control; for the judge would be then the legislator. Were it joined to the executive power, the judge might behave with violence and oppression.

There would be an end of everything, were the same man or the same body, whether of the nobles or of the people, to exercise those three powers, that of enacting laws, that of executing the public resolutions, and of trying the causes of individuals.

Most kingdoms in Europe enjoy a moderate government because the prince who is invested with the two first powers leaves the third to his subjects. In Turkey, where these three powers are united in the Sultan's person, the subjects groan under the most dreadful oppression.

In the republics of Italy, where these three powers are united, there is less liberty than in our monarchies. Hence their government is obliged to have recourse to as violent methods for its support as even that of the Turks; witness the state inquisitors, and the lion's mouth into which every informer may at all hours throw his written accusations.

In what a situation must the poor subject be in those republics! The same body of magistrates are possessed, as executors of the laws, of the whole power they have given themselves in quality of legislators. They may plunder the state by their general determinations; and as they have likewise the judiciary power in their hands, every private citizen may be ruined by their particular decisions.

The whole power is here united in one body; and though there is no external pomp that indicates a despotic sway, yet the people feel the effects of it every moment.

Hence it is that many of the princes of Europe, whose aim has been levelled at arbitrary power, have constantly set out with uniting in their own persons all the branches of magistracy, and all the great offices of state.

I allow indeed that the mere hereditary aristocracy of the Italian republics does not exactly answer to the despotic power of the Eastern princes. The number of magistrates sometimes moderate the power of the magistracy; the whole body of the nobles do not always concur in the same design; and different tribunals are erected, that temper each other. Thus at Venice the legislative power is in the council, the executive in the *pregadi*, and the judiciary in the *quarantia*. But the mischief is, that these different tribunals are composed of magistrates all belonging to the same body; which constitutes almost one and the same power.

The judiciary power ought not to be given to a standing senate; it should be exercised by persons taken from the body of the people at certain times of the year, and consistently with a form and manner prescribed by law, in order to erect a tribunal that should last only so long as necessity requires.

By this method the judicial power, so terrible to mankind, not being annexed by any particular state or profession, becomes, as it were, invisible. People have not then the judges continually present to their view; they fear the office, but not the magistrate.

In accusations of a deep and criminal nature, it is proper the person accused should have the privilege of choosing, in some measure, his judges, in concurrence with the law; or at least he should have a right to except against so great a number that the remaining part may be deemed his own choice.

The other two powers may be given rather to magistrates or permanent bodies, because they are not exercised on any private subject; one being no more than the general will of the state, and the other the execution of that general will.

But though the tribunals ought not to be fixed, the judgments ought; and to such a degree as to be ever conformable to the letter of the law. Were they to be the private opinion of the judge, people would then live in society, without exactly knowing the nature of their obligations.

The judges ought likewise to be of the same rank as the accused, or, in other words, his peers; to the end that he may not imagine he is fallen into the hands of persons inclined to treat him with rigor.

If the legislature leaves the executive power in possession of a right to imprison those subjects who can give security for their good behavior, there is an end of liberty; unless they are taken up, in order to answer without delay to a capital crime, in which case they are really free, being subject only to the power of the law.

But should the legislature think itself in danger by some secret conspiracy against the state, or by a correspondence with a foreign enemy, it might authorize the executive power, for a short and limited time, to imprison suspected persons, who in that case would lose their liberty only for a while, to preserve it forever.

And this is the only reasonable method that can be substituted to the tyrannical magistracy of the Ephori, and to the state inquisitors of Venice, who are also despotic.

As in a country of liberty, every man who is supposed a free agent ought to be his own governor; the legislative power should reside in the whole body of the people. But since this is impossible in large states, and in small ones is subject to many inconveniences, it is fit the people should transact by their representatives what they cannot transact by themselves.

The inhabitants of a particular town are much better acquainted with its wants and interests than with those of other places; and are better judges of the capacity of their neighbors than of that of the rest of their countrymen. The members, therefore, of the legislature should not be chosen from the general body of the nation; but it is proper that in every considerable place a representative should be elected by the inhabitants.

The great advantage of representatives is, their capacity of discussing public affairs. For this the people collectively are extremely unfit, which is one of the chief inconveniences of a democracy.

It is not at all necessary that the representatives who have received a general instruction from their constituents should wait to be directed on each particular affair, as is practised in the diets of Germany. True it is that by this way of proceeding the speeches of the deputies might with greater propriety be called the voice of the nation; but, on the other hand, this would occasion infinite delays; would give each deputy a power of controlling the assembly; and, on the most urgent and pressing occasions, the wheels of government might be stopped by the caprice of a single person.

When the deputies, as Mr. Sidney well observes, represent a body of people, as in Holland, they ought to be accountable to their constituents; but it is a different thing in England, where they are deputed by boroughs.

All the inhabitants of the several districts ought to have a right of voting at the election of a representative, except such as are in so mean a situation as to be deemed to have no will of their own.

One great fault there was in most of the ancient republics, that the people had a right to active resolutions, such as require some execution, a thing of which they are absolutely incapable. They ought to have no share in the government but for the choosing of representatives, which is within their reach. For though few can tell the exact degree of men's capacities, yet there are none but are capable of knowing in general whether the person they choose is better qualified than most of his neighbors.

Neither ought the representative body to be chosen for the executive part of government, for which it is not so fit; but for the enacting of laws, or to see whether the laws in being are duly executed, a thing suited to their abilities, and which none indeed but themselves can properly perform.

In such a state there are always persons distinguished by their birth, riches, or honors: but were they to be confounded with the common people, and to have only the weight of a single vote like the rest, the common liberty would be their slavery, and they would have no interest in supporting it, as most of the popular resolutions would be against them. The share they have, therefore, in the legislature ought to be proportioned to their other advantages in the state; which happens only when they form a body that has a right to check the licentiousness of the people, as the people have a right to oppose any encroachment of theirs.

The legislative power is therefore committed to the body of the nobles, and to that which represents the people, each having their assemblies and deliberations apart, each their separate views and interests.

Of the three powers above mentioned, the judiciary is in some measure next to nothing: there remain, therefore, only two; and as these have need of a regulating power to moderate them, the part of the legislative body composed of the nobility is extremely proper for this purpose.

The body of the nobility ought to be hereditary. In the first place it is so in its own nature; and in the next there must be a considerable interest to preserve its privileges — privileges that in themselves are obnoxious to popular envy, and of course in a free state are always in danger.

But as a hereditary power might be tempted to pursue its own particular interests, and forget those of the people, it is proper that where a singular advantage may be gained by corrupting the nobility, as in the laws relating to the supplies, they should have no other share in the legislation than the power of rejecting, and not that of resolving.

By the power of resolving I mean the right of ordaining by their own authority, or of amending what has been ordained by others. By the power of rejecting I would be understood to mean the right of annulling a resolution taken by another; which was the power of the tribunes at Rome. And though the person possessed of the privilege of rejecting may likewise have the right of approving, yet this approbation passes for no more than a declaration, that he intends to make no use of his privilege of rejecting, and is derived from that very privilege.

The executive power ought to be in the hands of a monarch, because this branch of government, having need of despatch, is better administered by one than by many: on the other hand, whatever depends on the legislative power is oftentimes better regulated by many than by a single person.

But if there were no monarch, and the executive power should be committed to a certain number of persons selected from the legislative body, there would be an end then of liberty; by reason the two powers would be united, as the same persons would sometimes possess, and would be always able to possess, a share in both.

Were the legislative body to be a considerable time without meeting, this would likewise put an end to liberty. For of two things one would naturally follow: either that there would be no longer any legislative resolutions, and then the state would fall into anarchy; or that these resolutions would be taken by the executive power, which would render it absolute.

It would be needless for the legislative body to continue always assembled. This would be troublesome to the representatives, and, moreover, would cut out too much work for the executive power, so as to take off its attention to its office, and oblige it to think only of defending its own prerogatives, and the right it has to execute.

Again, were the legislative body to be always assembled, it might happen to be kept up only by filling the places of the deceased members with new representatives; and in that case, if the legislative body were once corrupted, the evil would be past all remedy. When different legislative bodies succeed one another, the people who have a bad opinion of that which is actually sitting may reasonably entertain some hopes of the next: but were it to be always the same body, the people upon seeing it once corrupted would no longer expect any good from its laws; and of course they would either become desperate or fall into a state of indolence.

The legislative body should not meet of itself. For a body is supposed to have no will but when it is met; and besides, were it not to meet unanimously, it would be impossible to determine which was really the legislative body; the part assembled, or the other. And if it had a right to prorogue itself, it might happen never to be prorogued; which would be extremely dangerous, in case it should ever attempt to encroach on the executive power. Besides, there are seasons, some more proper than others, for assembling the legislative body: it is fit, therefore, that the executive power should regulate the time of meeting, as well as the duration of those assemblies, according to the circumstances and exigencies of a state known to itself.

Were the executive power not to have a right of restraining the encroachments of the legislative body, the latter would become despotic; for as it might arrogate to itself what authority it pleased, it would soon destroy all the other powers.

But it is not proper, on the other hand, that the legislative power should have a right to stay the executive. For as the execution has its natural limits, it is useless to confine it; besides, the executive power is generally employed in momentary operations. The power, therefore, of the Roman tribunes was faulty, as it put a stop not only to the legislation, but likewise to the executive part of government; which was attended with infinite mischief.

But if the legislative power in a free state has no right to stay the executive, it has a right and ought to have the means of examining in what manner its laws have been executed; an advantage which this government has over that of Crete and Sparta, where the Cosmi and the Ephori gave no account of their administration.

But whatever may be the issue of that examination, the legislative body ought not to have a power of arraigning the person, nor, of course, the conduct, of him who is intrusted with the executive power. His person should be sacred, because as it is necessary for the good of the state to prevent the legislative body from rendering themselves arbitrary, the moment he is accused or tried there is an end of liberty.

In this case the state would be no longer a monarchy, but a kind of republic, though not a free government. But as the person intrusted with the executive power cannot abuse it without bad counsellors, and such as have the laws as ministers, though the laws protect them as subjects, these men may be examined and punished — an advantage which this government has over that of Gnidus, where the law allowed of no such thing as calling the Amymones to an account, even after their administration, and therefore the people could never obtain any satisfaction for the injuries done them.

Though, in general, the judiciary power ought not to be united with any part of the legislative, yet this is liable to three exceptions, founded on the particular interest of the party accused.

The great are always obnoxious to popular envy; and were they to be judged by the people, they might be in danger from their judges, and would, moreover, be deprived of the privilege which the meanest subject is possessed of in a free state, of being tried by his peers. The nobility, for this reason, ought not to be cited before the ordinary courts of judicature, but before that part of the legislature which is composed of their own body.

It is possible that the law, which is clear sighted in one sense, and blind in another, might, in some cases, be too severe. But as we have already observed, the national judges are no more than the mouth that pronounces the words of the law, mere passive beings, incapable of moderating either its force or rigor. That part, therefore, of the legislative body, which we have just now observed to be a necessary tribunal on another occasion, also is a necessary tribunal in this; it belongs to its supreme authority to moderate the law in favor of the law itself, by mitigating the sentence.

It might also happen that a subject intrusted with the administration of public affairs may infringe the rights of the people, and be guilty of crimes which the ordinary magistrates either could not or would not punish. But, in general, the legislative power cannot try causes: and much less can it try this particular case, where it represents the party aggrieved, which is the people. It can only, therefore, impeach. But before what court shall it bring its impeachment? Must it go and demean itself before the ordinary tribunals, which are its inferiors, and, being composed, moreover, of men who are chosen from the people as well as itself, will naturally be swayed by the authority of so powerful an accuser? No: in order to preserve the dignity of the people and the security of the subject, the legislative part which represents the people must being in its charge before the legislative part which represents the nobility, who have neither the same interests nor the same passions.

Here is an advantage which this government has over most of the ancient republics, where this abuse prevailed, that the people were at the same time both judge and accuser.

The executive power, pursuant to what has been already said, ought to have a share in the legislature by the power of rejecting; otherwise it would soon be stripped of its prerogative. But should the legislative power usurp a share of the executive, the latter would be equally undone.

If the prince were to have a part in the legislature by the power of resolving, liberty would be lost. But as it is necessary he should have a share in the legislature for the support of his own prerogative, this share must consist in the power of rejecting.

The change of government at Rome was owing to this, that neither the senate, who had one part of the executive power, nor the magistrates, who were intrusted with the other, had the right of rejecting, which was entirely lodged in the people.

Here, then, is the fundamental constitution of the government we are treating of. The legislative body being composed of two parts, they check one another by the mutual privilege of rejecting. They are both restrained by the executive power, as the executive is by the legislative.

These three powers should naturally form a state of repose or inaction. But as there is a necessity for movement in the course of human affairs, they are forced to move, but still in concert.

As the executive power has no other part in the legislative than the privilege of rejecting, it can have no share in the public debates. It is not even necessary that it should propose, because as it may always disapprove of the resolutions that shall be taken, it may likewise reject the decisions on those proposals which were made against its will.

In some ancient commonwealths, where public debates were carried on by the people in a body, it was natural for the executive power to propose and debate in conjunction with the people, otherwise their resolutions must have been attended with a strange confusion.

Were the executive power to determine the raising of public money, otherwise than by giving its consent, liberty would be at an end; because it would become legislative in the most important point of legislation.

If the legislative power was to settle the subsidies, not from year to year, but forever, it would run the risk of losing its liberty, because the executive power would be no longer dependent; and when once it was possessed of such a perpetual right, it would be a matter of indifference whether it held it of itself or of another. The same may be said if it should come to a resolution of intrusting, not an annual, but a perpetual command of the fleets and armies to the executive power.

To prevent the executive power from being able to oppress, it is requisite that the armies with which it is intrusted should consist of the people, and have the same spirit as the people, as was the case at Rome till the time of Marius. To obtain this end, there are only two ways, either that the persons employed in the army should have sufficient property to answer for their conduct to their fellow-subjects, and be enlisted only for a year, as was customary at Rome; or if there should be a standing army, composed chiefly of the most despicable part of the nation, the legislative power should have a right to disband them as soon as it pleased; the soldiers should live in common with the rest of the people; and no separate camp, barracks, or fortress should be suffered.

When once an army is established, it ought not to depend immediately on the legislative, but on the executive power; and this from the very nature of the thing, its business consisting more in action than in deliberation.

It is natural for mankind to set a higher value upon courage than timidity, on activity than prudence, on strength than counsel. Hence the army will ever despise a senate, and respect their own officers. They will naturally slight the orders sent them by a body of men whom they look upon as cowards, and therefore unworthy to command them. So that as soon as the troops depend entirely on the legislative body, it becomes a military government; and if the contrary has ever happened, it has been owing to some extraordinary circumstances. It is because the army was always kept divided; it is because it was composed of several bodies that depended each on a particular province: it is because the capital towns were strong places, defended by their natural situation, and not garrisoned with regular troops. Holland, for instance, is still safer than Venice; she might drown or starve the revolted troops; for as they are not quartered in towns capable of furnishing them with necessary subsistence, this subsistence is of course precarious.

In perusing the admirable treatise of Tacitus "On the Manners of the Germans," we find it is from that nation the English have borrowed the idea of their political government. This beautiful system was invented first in the woods.

As all human things have an end, the state we are speaking of will lose its liberty, will perish. Have not Rome, Sparta, and Carthage perished? It will perish when the legislative power shall be more corrupt than the executive.

It is not my business to examine whether the English actually enjoy this liberty or not. Sufficient it is for my purpose to observe that it is established by their laws; and I inquire no further.

Neither do I pretend by this to undervalue other governments, nor to say that this extreme political liberty ought to give uneasiness to those who have only a moderate share of it. How should I have any such design, I who think that even the highest refinement of reason is not always desirable, and that mankind generally find their account better in mediums than in extremes?

Harrington, in his "Oceana," has also inquired into the utmost degree of liberty to which the constitution of a state may be carried. But of him, indeed, it may be said that for want of knowing the nature of real liberty he busied himself in pursuit of an imaginary one; and that he built a Chalcedon, though he had a Byzantium before his eyes.

7. — OF THE MONARCHIES WE ARE ACQUAINTED WITH

The monarchies we are acquainted with have not, like that we have been speaking of, liberty for their direct view: the only aim is the glory of the subject, of the state, and of the sovereign. But hence there results a spirit of liberty, which in those states is capable of achieving as great things, and of contributing as much, perhaps, to happiness, as liberty itself.

Here the three powers are not distributed and founded on the model of the constitution above mentioned; they have each a particular distribution, according to which they border more or less on political liberty; and if they did not border upon it, monarchy would degenerate into despotic government.

8. — WHY THE ANCIENTS HAD NOT A CLEAR IDEA OF MONARCHY

The ancients had no notion of a government founded on a body of nobles, and much less on a legislative body composed of the representatives of the people. The republics of Greece and Italy were cities that had each their own form of government, and convened their subjects within their walls. Before Rome had swallowed up all the other republics, there was scarcely anywhere a king to be found, no, not in Italy, Gaul, Spain, or Germany; they were all petty states or republics. Even Africa itself was subject to a great commonwealth: and Asia Minor was occupied by Greek colonies. There was, therefore, no instance of deputies of towns or assemblies of the states; one must have gone as far as Persia to find a monarchy.

I am not ignorant that there were confederate republics; in which several towns sent deputies to an assembly. But I affirm there was no monarchy on that model.

The first plan, therefore, of the monarchies we are acquainted with was thus formed. The German nations that conquered the Roman Empire were certainly a free people. Of this we may be convinced only by reading Tacitus "On the Manners of the Germans." The conquerors spread themselves over all the country; living mostly in the fields, and very little in towns. When they were in Germany, the whole nation was able to assemble. This they could no longer do, when dispersed through the conquered provinces. And yet as it was necessary that the nation should deliberate on public affairs, pursuant to their usual method before the conquest, they had recourse to representatives. Such is the origin of the Gothic government amongst us. At first it was mixed with aristocracy and monarchy — a mixture attended with this inconvenience, that the common people were bondmen. The custom afterwards succeeded of granting letters of enfranchisement, and was soon followed by so perfect a harmony between the civil liberty of the people, the privileges of the nobility and clergy, and the prince's prerogative, that I really think there never was in the world a government so well tempered as that of each part of Europe, so long as it lasted. Surprising that the corruption of the government of a conquering nation should have given birth to the best species of constitution that could possibly be imagined by man!

DAVID HUME

1 7 1 1 – 1 7 7 6

INTRODUCTION

Hume, a man judged by the economist Adam Smith, who knew him well, to be as near "to the idea of a perfectly wise and virtuous man, as perhaps the nature of human frailty will admit," was in his own lifetime often accused of being a liar, a rogue, a blockhead, hardhearted, oblivious to the truth, and bent on public mischief. No better example can be found of an author's moral character being attacked because of the intense discomfort produced by his ideas.

David Hume was the second son of a middle-class country family who lived in the south of Scotland. He went to the University of Edinburgh for 3 or 4 years, left at the age of 16 to prepare himself to be a lawyer, but soon gave it up. Two years later he had something like a nervous breakdown from his uninterrupted and passionate study of philosophy, and after slowly recovering went to France for 3 years to write a work that he published anonymously, on his return to London, under the title *A Treatise of Human Nature*. Its reception was discouraging and Hume, having failed to make his name in London, retired to the family home for the next 8 years, producing during that time the first volume of his *Essays*. These were well received, but Hume's reputation as a critic of religion prevented him, in 1744, from obtaining the professorship of philosophy in Edinburgh, as it did in Glasgow some years later.

In the following year Hume spent an unhappy period as tutor to a nobleman who was soon certified insane. However, Hume's prospects rapidly improved. He became secretary to a general who led a brief military expedition to the French coast and shortly after a secret mission to Vienna and Turin. These posts improved Hume's finances considerably and he returned to Scotland, living comfortably first with his brother and then, in

Edinburgh, with his sister. During the next 15 years he wrote all the other works that we still value — the two *Enquiries*, the remainder of the *Essays*, the two books on religion, and the six volumes of the *History of England.*

From 1763 to 1766 Hume served as secretary to the British ambassador in Paris, and for a few months after that as chargé d'affaires. Returning to London, he was appointed as an Undersecretary of State. He resigned 2 years later on grounds of poor health and lived the remainder of his life in Edinburgh, revising his essays, conducting a large correspondence with many distinguished friends, and becoming increasingly famous as an essayist and historian rather than, as we now think of him, as a philosopher. He died of cancer of the bowel, maintaining to the end his independence of all the comforts of religion.

An Enquiry Concerning the Principles of Morals first appeared in London, 1751, and was in Hume's opinion, of all his "writings, historical, philosophical, or literary, incomparably the best." The standard text is that of the posthumous edition of 1777, and the present selections are taken from one of the reprintings of that edition.

SELECTIONS FROM
An Enquiry Concerning the Principles of Morals

Section III. Of Justice.

PART I. THE ORIGIN OF JUSTICE IS PUBLIC UTILITY

That justice is useful to society, and consequently that *part* of its merit, at least, must arise from that consideration, it would be a superfluous undertaking to prove. That public utility is the *sole* origin of justice, and that reflections on the beneficial consequences of this virtue are the *sole* foundation of its merit; this proposition, being more curious and important, will better deserve our examination and enquiry.

Let us suppose that nature has bestowed on the human race such profuse *abundance* of all *external* conveniences, that, without any uncertainty in the event, without any care or industry on our part, every individual finds himself fully provided with whatever his most voracious appetites can want, or luxurious imagination wish or desire. His natural beauty, we shall suppose, surpasses all acquired ornaments: the perpetual clemency of the seasons renders useless all clothes or covering: the raw herbage affords him the most delicious fare; the clear fountain, the richest beverage. No laborious occupation required: no tillage: no navigation. Music, poetry, and contemplation form his sole business: conversation, mirth, and friendship his sole amusement.

It seems evident that, in such a happy state, every other social virtue would flourish, and receive tenfold increase; but the cautious, jealous virtue of justice would never once have been dreamed of. For what purpose make a partition of goods, where every one has already more than enough? Why give rise to property, where there cannot possibly be any injury? Why call this object *mine*, when upon the seizing of it by another, I need but stretch out my hand to possess myself of what is equally valuable? Justice, in that case, being totally useless, would be an idle ceremonial, and could never possibly have place in the catalogue of virtues.

We see, even in the present necessitous condition of mankind, that, wherever any benefit is bestowed by nature in an unlimited abundance, we leave it always in common among the whole human race, and make no subdivisions of right and property. Water and air, though the most necessary of all objects, are not challenged as the property of individuals; nor can any man commit injustice by the most lavish use and enjoyment of these blessings. In fertile extensive countries, with few inhabitants, land is regarded on the same footing. And no topic is so much insisted on by those, who defend the liberty of the seas, as the unexhausted use of them in navigation. Were the advantages, procured by navigation, as inexhaustible, these reasoners had never had any adversaries to refute; nor had any claims ever been advanced of a separate, exclusive dominion over the ocean.

It may happen, in some countries, at some periods, that there be established a property in water, none in land; if the latter be in greater abundance than can be used by the inhabitants, and the former be found, with difficulty, and in very small quantities.

Again; suppose, that, though the necessities of human race continue the same as at present, yet the mind is so enlarged, and so replete with friendship and generosity, that every man has the utmost tenderness for every man, and feels no more concern for his own interest than for that of his fellows; it seems evident, that the use of justice would, in this case, be suspended by such an extensive benevolence, nor would the divisions and barriers of property and obligation have ever been thought of. Why should I bind another, by a deed or promise, to do me any good office, when I know that he is already prompted, by the strongest inclination, to seek my happiness, and would, of himself, perform the desired service; except the hurt, he thereby receives, be greater than the benefit accruing to me? in which case, he knows, that, from my innate humanity and friendship, I should be the first to oppose myself to his imprudent generosity. Why raise land-marks between my neighbour's field and mine, when my heart has made no division between our interests; but shares all his joys and sorrows with the same force and vivacity as if originally my own? Every man, upon this supposition, being a second self to another, would trust all his interests to the discretion of every man; without jealousy, without partition, without distinction. And the whole human race would form only one family; where all would lie in common, and be used freely, without regard to property; but cautiously too, with as entire regard to the necessities of each individual, as if our own interests were most intimately concerned.

In the present disposition of the human heart, it would, perhaps, be difficult to find complete instances of such enlarged affections; but still we may observe, that the case of families approaches towards it; and the stronger the mutual benevolence is among the individuals, the nearer it approaches; till all distinction of property be, in a great measure, lost and confounded among them. Between married persons, the cement of friendship is by the laws supposed so strong as to abolish all division of possessions; and has often, in reality, the force ascribed to it. And it is observable, that, during the ardour of new enthusiasms, when every principle is inflamed into extravagance, the community of goods has frequently been attempted; and nothing but experience of its inconveniences, from the returning or disguised selfishness of men, could make the imprudent fanatics adopt anew the ideas of justice and of separate property. So true is it, that this virtue derives its existence entirely from its necessary *use* to the intercourse and social state of mankind.

To make this truth more evident, let us reverse the foregoing suppositions; and carrying everything to the opposite extreme, consider what would be the effect of these new situations. Suppose a society to fall into such want of all common necessaries, that the utmost frugality and industry cannot preserve the greater number from perishing, and the whole from extreme misery; it will readily, I believe, be admitted, that the strict laws of justice are suspended, in such a pressing emergence, and give place to the stronger motives of necessity and self-preservation. Is it any crime, after a shipwreck, to seize whatever means or instrument of safety one can lay hold of, without regard to former limitations of property? Or if a city besieged were perishing with hunger; can we imagine, that men will see any means of preservation before them, and lose their lives, from a scrupulous regard to what, in other situations, would be the rules of equity and justice? The use and tendency of that virtue is to procure happiness and security, by preserving order in society: but where the society is ready to perish from extreme necessity, no greater evil can be dreaded from violence and injustice; and every man may now provide for himself by all the means which prudence can dictate, or humanity permit. The public, even in less urgent necessities, opens granaries, without the consent of proprietors; as justly supposing, that the authority of magistracy may, consistent with equity, extend so far: but were any number of men to assemble, without the tie of laws or civil jurisdiction; would an equal partition of bread in a famine, though effected by power and even violence, be regarded as criminal or injurious?

Suppose likewise, that it should be a virtuous man's fate to fall into the society of ruffians, remote from the protection of laws and government; what conduct must he embrace in that melancholy situation? He sees such a desperate rapaciousness prevail; such a disregard to equity, such contempt of order, such stupid blindness to future consequences, as must immediately have the most tragical conclusion, and must terminate in destruction to the greater number, and in a total dissolution of society to the rest. He, meanwhile, can have no other expedient than to arm himself, to whomever the sword he seizes, or the buckler, may belong: To make provision of all means of defence and security: And his particular regard to justice being no longer of use to his own safety or that of others, he must consult the dictates of self-preservation alone, without concern for those who no longer merit his care and attention.

When any man, even in political society, renders himself by his crimes, obnoxious to the public, he is punished by the laws in his goods and person; that is, the ordinary rules of justice are, with regard to him, suspended for a moment, and it becomes equitable to inflict on him, for the *benefit* of society, what otherwise he could not suffer without wrong or injury.

The rage and violence of public war; what is it but a suspension of justice among the warring parties, who perceive, that this virtue is now no longer of any *use* or advantage to them? The laws of war, which then succeed to those of equity and justice, are rules calculated for the *advantage* and *utility* of that particular state, in which men are now placed. And were a civilized nation engaged with barbarians, who observed no rules even of war, the former must also suspend their observance of them, where they no longer serve to any purpose; and must render every action or encounter as bloody and pernicious as possible to the first aggressors.

Thus, the rules of equity or justice depend entirely on the particular state and condition in which men are placed, and owe their origin and existence to that utility, which results to the public from their strict and regular observance. Reverse, in any considerable circumstance, the condition of men: Produce extreme abundance or extreme necessity: Implant in the human breast perfect moderation and humanity, or perfect rapaciousness and malice: By rendering justice totally *useless*, you thereby totally destroy its essence, and suspend its obligation upon mankind.

The common situation of society is a medium amidst all these extremes. We are naturally partial to ourselves, and to our friends; but are capable of learning the advantage resulting from a more equitable conduct. Few enjoyments are given us from the open and liberal hand of nature; but by art, labour, and industry, we can extract them in great abundance. Hence the ideas of property become necessary in all civil society: Hence justice derives its usefulness to the public: And hence alone arises its merit and moral obligation.

These conclusions are so natural and obvious, that they have not escaped even the poets, in their descriptions of the felicity attending the golden age or the reign of Saturn. The seasons, in that first period of nature, were so temperate, if we credit these agreeable fictions, that there was no necessity for men to provide themselves with clothes and houses, as a security against the violence of heat and cold: The rivers flowed with wine and milk: The oaks yielded honey; and nature spontaneously produced her greatest delicacies. Nor were these the chief advantages of that happy age. Tempests were not alone removed from nature; but those more furious tempests were unknown to human breasts, which now cause such uproar, and engender such confusion. Avarice, ambition, cruelty, selfishness, were never heard of: Cordial affection, compassion, sympathy, were the only movements with which the mind was yet acquainted. Even the punctilious distinction of *mine* and *thine* was banished from among that happy race of mortals, and carried with it the very notion of property and obligation, justice and injustice.

This *poetical* fiction of the *golden age* is, in some respects, of a piece with the *philosophical* fiction of the *state of nature*; only that the former is represented as the most charming and most peaceable condition, which can possibly be imagined; whereas the latter is painted out as a state of mutual war and violence, attended with the most extreme necessity. On the first origin of mankind, we are told, their ignorance and savage nature were so prevalent, that they could give no mutual trust, but must each depend upon himself and his own force or cunning for protection and security. No law was heard of: No rule of justice known: No distinction of property regarded: Power was the only measure of right; and a perpetual war of all against all was the result of men's untamed selfishness and barbarity.

Whether such a condition of human nature could ever exist, or if it did, could continue so long as to merit the appellation of a *state*, may justly be doubted. Men are necessarily born in a family-society, at least; and are trained up by their parents to some rule of conduct and behaviour. But this must be admitted, that, if such a state of mutual war and violence was ever real, the suspension of all laws of justice, from their absolute inutility, is a necessary and infallible consequence.

The more we vary our views of human life, and the newer and more unusual the lights are in which we survey it, the more shall we be convinced, that the origin here assigned for the virtue of justice is real and satisfactory.

Were there a species of creatures intermingled with men, which, though rational, were possessed of such inferior strength, both of body and mind, that they were incapable of all resistance, and could never, upon the highest provocation, make us feel the effects of their resentment; the necessary consequence, I think, is that we should be bound by the laws of humanity to give gentle usage to these creatures, but should not, properly speaking, lie under any restraint of justice with regard to them, nor could they possess any right or property, exclusive of such arbitrary lords. Our intercourse with them could not be called society, which supposes a degree of equality; but absolute command on the one side, and servile obedience on the other. Whatever we covet, they must instantly resign: Our permission is the only tenure, by which they hold their possessions: Our compassion and kindness the only check, by which they curb our lawless will: And as no inconvenience ever results from the exercise of a power, so firmly established in nature, the restraints of justice and property, being totally *useless*, would never have place in so unequal a confederacy.

This is plainly the situation of men, with regard to animals; and how far these may be said to possess reason, I leave it to others to determine. The great superiority of civilized Europeans above barbarous Indians, tempted us to imagine ourselves on the same footing with regard to them, and made us throw off all restraints of justice, and even of humanity, in our treatment of them. In many nations, the female sex are reduced to like slavery, and are rendered incapable of all property, in opposition to their lordly masters. But though the males, when united, have in all countries bodily force sufficient to maintain this severe tyranny, yet such are the insinuation, address, and charms of their fair companions, that women are commonly able to break the confederacy, and share with the other sex in all the rights and privileges of society.

Were the human species so framed by nature as that each individual possessed within himself every faculty, requisite both for his own preservation and for the propagation of his kind: Were all society and intercourse cut off between man and man, by the primary intention of the supreme Creator: It seems evident, that so solitary a being would be as much incapable of justice, as of social discourse and conversation. Where mutual regards and forbearance serve to no manner of purpose, they would never direct the conduct of any reasonable man. The headlong course of the passions would be checked by no reflection on future consequences. And as each man is here supposed to love himself alone, and to depend only on himself and his own activity for safety and happiness, he would, on every occasion, to the utmost of his power, challenge the preference above every other being, to none of which he is bound by any ties, either of nature or of interest.

But suppose the conjunction of the sexes to be established in nature, a family immediately arises; and particular rules being found requisite for its subsistence, these are immediately embraced; though without comprehending the rest of mankind within their prescriptions. Suppose that several families unite together into one society, which is totally disjoined from all others, the rules, which preserve peace and order, enlarge themselves to the utmost extent of that society; but becoming then entirely useless, lose their force when carried one step farther. But again suppose, that several distinct societies maintain a kind of intercourse for mutual convenience and advantage, the boundaries of justice still grow larger, in proportion to the largeness of men's views, and the force of their mutual connexions. History, experience, reason sufficiently instruct us in this natural progress of human sentiments, and in the gradual enlargement of our regards to justice, in proportion as we become acquainted with the extensive utility of that virtue.

PART II. JUSTICE IS NECESSARY FOR THE EXISTENCE OF SOCIETY

If we examine the *particular* laws, by which justice is directed, and property determined; we shall still be presented with the same conclusion. The good of mankind is the only object of all these laws and regulations. Not only it is requisite, for the peace and interest of society, that men's possessions should be separated; but the rules, which we follow, in making the separation, are such as can best be contrived to serve farther the interests of society.

We shall suppose that a creature, possessed of reason, but unacquainted with human nature, deliberates with himself what rules of justice or property would best promote public interest, and establish peace and security among mankind: His most obvious thought would be, to assign the largest possessions to the most extensive virtue, and give every one the power of doing good, proportioned to his inclination. In a perfect theocracy, where a being, infinitely intelligent, governs by particular volitions, this rule would certainly have place, and might serve to the wisest purposes: But were mankind to execute such a law; so great is the uncertainty of merit, both from its natural obscurity, and from the self-conceit of each individual, that no determinate rule of conduct would ever result from it; and the total dissolution of society must be the immediate consequence. Fanatics may suppose, *that dominion is founded on grace*, and *that saints alone inherit the earth*; but the civil magistrate very justly puts these sublime theorists on the same footing with common robbers, and teaches them by the severest discipline, that a rule, which, in speculation, may seem the most advantageous to society, may yet be found, in practice, totally pernicious and destructive.

That there were *religious* fanatics of this kind in England, during the civil wars, we learn from history; though it is probable, that the obvious *tendency* of these principles excited such horror in mankind, as soon obliged the dangerous enthusiasts to renounce, or at least conceal their tenets. Perhaps the *levellers*, who claimed an equal distribution of property, were a kind of *political* fanatics, which arose from the religious species, and more openly avowed their pretensions; as carrying a more plausible appearance, of being practicable in themselves, as well as useful to human society.

It must, indeed, be confessed, that nature is so liberal to mankind, that, were all her presents equally divided among the species, and improved by art and industry, every individual would enjoy all the necessaries, and even most of the comforts of life; nor would ever be liable to any ills, but such as might accidentally arise from the sickly frame and constitution of his body. It must also be confessed, that, wherever we depart from this equality, we rob the poor of more satisfaction than we add to the rich, and that the slight gratification of a frivolous vanity, in one individual, frequently costs more than bread to many families, and even provinces. It may appear withal, that the rule of equality, as it would be highly *useful*, is not altogether *impracticable*; but has taken place, at least in an imperfect degree, in some republics; particularly that of Sparta; where it was attended, it is said, with the most beneficial consequences. Not to mention that the Agrarian laws, so frequently claimed in Rome, and carried into execution in many Greek cities, proceeded, all of them, from a general idea of the utility of this principle.

But historians, and even common sense, may inform us, that, however specious these ideas of *perfect* equality may seem, they are really, at bottom, *impracticable*; and were they not so, would be extremely *pernicious* to human society. Render possessions ever so equal, men's different degrees of art, care, and industry will immediately break that equality. Or if you check these virtues, you reduce society to the most extreme indigence; and instead of preventing want and beggary in a few, render it unavoidable to the whole community. The most rigorous inquisition too is requisite to watch every inequality on its first appearance; and the most severe jurisdiction, to punish and redress it. But besides, that so much authority must soon degenerate into tyranny, and be exerted with great partialities; who can possibly be possessed of it, in such a situation as is here supposed? Perfect equality of possessions, destroying all subordination, weakens extremely the authority of magistracy, and must reduce all power nearly to a level, as well as property.

We may conclude, therefore, that, in order to establish laws for the regulation of property, we must be acquainted with the nature and situation of man; must reject appearances, which may be false, though specious; and must search for those rules, which are, on the whole, most *useful* and *beneficial.* Vulgar sense and slight experience are sufficient for this purpose; where men give not way to too selfish avidity, or too extensive enthusiasm.

Who sees not, for instance, that whatever is produced or improved by a man's art or industry ought, for ever, to be secured to him, in order to give encouragement to such *useful* habits and accomplishments? That the property ought also to descend to children and relations, for the same *useful* purpose? That it may be alienated by consent, in order to beget that commerce and intercourse, which is so *beneficial* to human society? And that all contracts and promises ought carefully to be fulfilled, in order to secure mutual trust and confidence, by which the general *interest* of mankind is so much promoted?

Examine the writers on the laws of nature; and you will always find, that, whatever principles they set out with, they are sure to terminate here at last, and to assign, as the ultimate reason for every rule which they establish, the convenience and necessities of mankind. A concession thus extorted, in opposition to systems, has more authority than if it had been made in prosecution of them.

What other reason, indeed, could writers ever give, why this must be *mine* and that *yours*; since uninstructed nature surely never made any such distinction? The objects which receive those appellations are, of themselves, foreign to us; they are totally disjoined and separated from us; and nothing but the general interests of society can form the connexion.

Sometimes the interests of society may require a rule of justice in a particular case; but may not determine any particular rule, among several, which are all equally beneficial. In that case, the slightest *analogies* are laid hold of, in order to prevent that indifference and ambiguity, which would be the source of perpetual dissension. Thus possession alone, and first possession, is supposed to convey property, where no body else has any preceding claim and pretension. Many of the reasonings of lawyers are of this analogical nature, and depend on very slight connexions of the imagination.

Does any one scruple, in extraordinary cases, to violate all regard to the private property of individuals, and sacrifice to public interest a distinction, which had been established for the sake of that interest? The safety of the people is the supreme law: All other particular laws are subordinate to it, and dependent on it: And if, in the *common* course of things, they be followed and regarded; it is only because the public safety and interest *commonly* demand so equal and impartial an administration.

Sometimes both *utility* and *analogy* fail, and leave the laws of justice in total uncertainty. Thus, it is highly requisite, that prescription or long possession should convey property; but what number of days or months or years should be sufficient for that purpose, it is impossible for reason alone to determine. *Civil laws* here supply the place of the natural *code*, and assign different terms for prescription, according to the different *utilities*, proposed by the legislator. Bills of exchange and promissory notes, by the laws of most countries, prescribe sooner than bonds, and mortgages, and contracts of a more formal nature.

In general we may observe that all questions of property are subordinate to the authority of civil laws, which extend, restrain, modify, and alter the rules of natural justice, according to the particular *convenience* of each community. The laws have, or ought to have, a constant reference to the constitution of government, the manners, the climate, the religion, the commerce, the situation of each society. A late author of genius, as well as learning, has prosecuted this subject at large, and has established, from these principles, a system of political knowledge, which abounds in ingenious and brilliant thoughts, and is not wanting in solidity. [*The Spirit of the Laws* by Montesquieu]

What is a man's property? Anything which it is lawful for him, and for him alone, to use. *But what rule have we, by which we can distinguish these objects?* Here we must have recourse to statutes, customs, precedents, analogies, and a hundred other circumstances; some of which are constant and inflexible, some variable and arbitrary. But the ultimate point, in which they all professedly terminate, is the interest and happiness of human society. Where this enters not into consideration, nothing can appear more whimsical, unnatural, and even superstitious, than all or most of the laws of justice and of property.

Those who ridicule vulgar superstitions, and expose the folly of particular regards to meats, days, places, postures, apparel, have an easy task; while they consider all the qualities and relations of the objects, and discover no adequate cause for that affection or antipathy, veneration or horror, which have so mighty an influence over a considerable part of mankind. A Syrian would have starved rather than taste pigeon; an Egyptian would not have approached bacon: But if these species of food be examined by the senses of sight, smell, or taste, or scrutinized by the sciences of chemistry, medicine, or physics, no difference is ever found between them and any other species, nor can that precise circumstance be pitched on, which may afford a just foundation for the religious passion. A fowl on Thursday is lawful food; on Friday abominable: Eggs in this house and in this diocese, are permitted during Lent; a hundred paces farther, to eat them is a damnable sin. This earth or building, yesterday was profane; to-day, by the muttering of certain words, it has become holy and sacred. Such reflections as these, in the mouth of a philosopher, one may safely say, are too obvious to have any influence; because they must always, to every man, occur at first sight; and where they prevail not, of themselves, they are surely obstructed by education, prejudice, and passion, not by ignorance or mistake.

It may appear to a careless view, or rather a too abstracted reflection, that there enters a like superstition into all the sentiments of justice; and that, if a man expose its object, or what we call property, to the same scrutiny of sense and science, he will not, by the most accurate enquiry, find any foundation for the difference made by moral sentiment. I may lawfully nourish myself from this tree; but the fruit of another of the same species, ten paces off, it is criminal for me to touch. Had I worn this apparel an hour ago, I had merited the severest punishment; but a man, by pronouncing a few magical syllables, has now rendered it fit for my use and service. Were this house placed in the neighbouring territory, it had been immoral for me to dwell in it; but being built on this side the river, it is subject to a different municipal law, and by its becoming mine I incur no blame or censure. The same species of reasoning it may be thought, which so successfully exposes superstition, is also applicable to justice; nor is it possible, in the one case more than in the other, to point out, in the object, that precise quality or circumstance, which is the foundation of the sentiment.

But there is this material difference between *superstition* and *justice*, that the former is frivolous, useless, and burdensome; the latter is absolutely requisite to the well-being of mankind and existence of society. When we abstract from this circumstance (for it is too apparent ever to be overlooked) it must be confessed, that all regards to right and property, seem entirely without foundation, as much as the grossest and most vulgar superstition. Were the interests of society nowise concerned, it is as unintelligible why another's articulating certain sounds implying consent, should change the nature of my actions with regard to a particular object, as why the reciting of a liturgy by a priest, in a certain habit and posture, should dedicate a heap of brick and timber, and render it, thenceforth and for ever, sacred.[1]

These reflections are far from weakening the obligations of justice, or diminishing anything from the most sacred attention to property. On the contrary, such sentiments must acquire new force from the present reasoning. For what stronger foundation can be desired or conceived for any duty, than to observe, that human society, or even human nature, could not subsist without the establishment of it; and will still arrive at greater degrees of

---

[1]It is evident, that the will or consent alone never transfers property, nor causes the obligation of a promise (for the same reasoning extends to both) but the will must be expressed by words or signs, in order to impose a tie upon any man. The expression being once brought in as subservient to the will, soon becomes the principal part of the promise; nor will a man be less bound by his word, though he secretly gives a different direction to his intention, and withhold the assent of his mind. But though the expression makes, on most occasions, the whole of the promise, yet it does not always so; and one who should make use of any expression, of which he knows not the meaning, and which he uses without any sense of the consequences, would not certainly be bound by it. Nay, though he know its meaning, yet if he use it in jest only, and with such signs as evidently show, that he has no serious intention of binding himself, he would not lie under any obligation of performance; but it is necessary, that the words be a perfect expression of the will, without any contrary signs. Nay, even this we must not carry so far as to imagine, that one, whom, by our quickness of understanding, we conjecture, from certain signs, to have an intention of deceiving us, is not bound by his expression or verbal promise, if we accept of it; but must limit this conclusion to those cases where the signs are of a different nature from those of deceit. All these contradictions are easily accounted for, if justice arise entirely from its usefulness to society; but will never be explained on any other hypothesis. . . .

happiness and perfection, the more inviolable the regard is, which is paid to that duty?

The dilemma seems obvious: As justice evidently tends to promote public utility and to support civil society, the sentiment of justice is either derived from our reflecting on that tendency, or like hunger, thirst, and other appetites, resentment, love of life, attachment to offspring, and other passions, arises from a simple original instinct in the human breast, which nature has implanted for like salutary purposes. If the latter be the case, it follows, that property, which is the object of justice, is also distinguished by a simple original instinct, and is not ascertained by any argument or reflection. But who is there that ever heard of such an instinct? Or is this a subject in which new discoveries can be made? We may as well expect to discover, in the body, new senses, which had before escaped the observation of all mankind.

But farther, though it seems a very simple proposition to say, that nature, by an instinctive sentiment, distinguishes property, yet in reality we shall find, that there are required for that purpose ten thousand different instincts, and these employed about objects of the greatest intricacy and nicest discernment. For when a definition of *property* is required, that relation is found to resolve itself into any possession acquired by occupation, by industry, by prescription, by inheritance, by contract, etc. Can we think that nature, by an original instinct, instructs us in all these methods of acquisition?

These words too, inheritance and contract, stand for ideas infinitely complicated; and to define them exactly, a hundred volumes of laws, and a thousand volumes of commentators, have not been found sufficient. Does nature, whose instincts in men are all simple, embrace such complicated and artificial objects, and create a rational creature, without trusting anything to the operation of his reason?

But even though all this were admitted, it would not be satisfactory. Positive laws can certainly transfer property. Is it by another original instinct, that we recognize the authority of kings and senates, and mark all the boundaries of their jurisdiction? Judges too, even though their sentence be erroneous and illegal, must be allowed, for the sake of peace and order, to have decisive authority, and ultimately to determine property. Have we original innate ideas of praetors and chancellors and juries? Who sees not, that all these institutions arise merely from the necessities of human society?

All birds of the same species in every age and country, build their nests alike: In this we see the force of instinct. Men, in different times and places, frame their houses differently: Here we perceive the influence of reason and custom. A like inference may be drawn from comparing the instinct of generation and the institution of property.

How great soever the variety of municipal laws, it must be confessed, that their chief out-lines pretty regularly concur; because the purposes, to which they tend, are everywhere exactly similar. In like manner, all houses have a roof and walls, windows and chimneys; though diversified in their shape, figure, and materials. The purposes of the latter, directed to the conveniences of human life, discover not more plainly their origin from reason and reflection, than do those of the former, which point all to a like end.

I need not mention the variations, which all the rules of property receive from the finer turns and connexions of the imagination, and from the subtilties and abstractions of law-topics and reasonings. There is no possibility of reconciling this observation to the notion of original instincts.

What alone will beget a doubt concerning the theory, on which I insist, is the influence of education and acquired habits, by which we are so accustomed to blame injustice, that we are not, in every instance, conscious of any immediate reflection on the pernicious consequences of it. The views the most familiar to us are apt, for that very reason, to escape us; and what we have very frequently performed from certain motives, we are apt likewise to continue mechanically, without recalling, on every occasion, the reflections, which first determined us. The convenience, or rather necessity, which leads to justice is so universal, and everywhere points so much to the same rules, that the habit takes place in all societies; and it is not without some scrutiny, that we are able to ascertain its true origin. The matter, however, is not so obscure, but that even in common life we have every moment recourse to the principle of public utility, and ask, *What must become of the world, if such practices prevail? How could society subsist under such disorders?* Were the distinction or separation of possessions entirely useless, can any one conceive, that it ever should have obtained in society?

Thus we seem, upon the whole, to have attained a knowledge of the force of that principle here insisted on, and can determine what degree of esteem or moral approbation may result from reflections on public interest and utility. The necessity of justice to the support of society is the sole foundation of that virtue; and since no moral excellence is more highly esteemed, we may conclude that this circumstance of usefulness has, in general, the strongest energy, and most entire command over our sentiments. It must, therefore, be the source of a considerable part of the merit ascribed to humanity, benevolence, friendship, public spirit, and other social virtues of that stamp; as it is the sole source of the moral approbation paid to fidelity, justice, veracity, integrity, and those other estimable and useful qualities and principles. It is entirely agreeable to the rules of philosophy, and even of common reason; where any principle has been found to have a great force and energy in one instance, to ascribe to it a like energy in all similar instances. This indeed is Newton's chief rule of philosophizing.

JEAN-JACQUES ROUSSEAU

1 7 1 2 – 1 7 7 8

INTRODUCTION

It is difficult to think of a greater contrast than that between the placid, well-organized, and prudential David Hume and the turbulent, impulsive, disorganized, and self-accusatory Rousseau. Yet they were acquaintances, and have left a record of Hume's unsuccessful attempt to provide a refuge in England for the exiled Rousseau when he was being harassed by French and Swiss authorities and persecuted by his own paranoiac fears. There is a similar contrast between the modesty displayed in the seven-page autobiography that Hume left to be published after his death and the self-indulgent narcissism in the 600 pages of Rousseau's autobiographical *Confessions*, also published posthumously.

The second son of a Protestant watchmaker in Geneva, Rousseau lost his mother shortly after his birth and was reared by an erratic father who offered him no education except access to the books of his dead mother. At the age of 15 Rousseau left his apprenticeship as an engraver because of his master's brutality, was converted to Catholicism in Turin, and supported himself for a number of years as a music teacher, civil servant, and tutor. Throughout this period he was given help and shelter by Madame de Warens, his wealthy surrogate mother, patron, and sometime mistress. In 1741 he moved to Paris where he became known to a circle of artists, writers, and philosophers, worked as a journalist, and formed a permanent liaison with a servant girl, Thérèse Lavasseur. Each of their five children was sent to a foundlings' home.

Rousseau's public career as a social philosopher did not begin until he was almost middle aged. In 1749 he won a prize for his *Discourse on the Arts and Sciences*, an essay that criticized the moral corruption produced by social institutions and defended the view that people are naturally good. This success was followed by that of his opera, *The Village Fortune-teller*, which brought him substantial returns, and in 1755 by his long discourse on the *Origin and Foundation of the Inequality of Mankind*. He also contributed articles on music and political economy to the great *Encyclopedia* being edited by d'Alembert and Diderot.

From 1755 until 1762 Rousseau worked on his novel *Julie*, or *Emile*, his tract concerning human nature and its education, and on the *Social Contract*. All three were condemned in Geneva and Paris as religiously unorthodox and he fled for protection to the Swiss territory held by Frederick the Great of Prussia, renouncing for the third time his Genevan citizenship. Feeling insecure there and elsewhere in the area and having quarrelled with most of his friends, he went briefly and unhappily to England on Hume's invitation. By then his persecutory beliefs gave him no rest and he returned to France highly disturbed, marrying Thérèse the next year, and remaining in and near Paris for the next 8 years until his death from a stroke. Despite his psychological condition during these last years, he was active as a creative writer and thinker to the very end of his life.

A Dissertation on the Origin and Foundation of the Inequality of Mankind, published in Paris, 1755, was a prize essay on the question, set by the Academy of Dijon, "What is the origin of inequality among men, and is it authorized by natural law?" Rousseau did not answer the second part of the question. *The Social Contract or Principles of Political Right* appeared in 1762. The selections from both books have been taken from the translation entitled *The Social Contract and Discourses* by G. D. H. Cole, revised and augmented by J. H. Brumfitt and John C. Hall, published by J. M. Dent & Sons, London, 1973, and are used here by permission. The selection from the *Origin of Inequality* is taken from pp. 64–72 and 83–90.

SELECTIONS FROM
A Dissertation on the Origin and Foundation of the Inequality of Mankind

The First Part: Man in A State of Nature

. . . It appears, at first view, that men in a state of nature, having no moral relations or determinate obligations one with another, could not be either good or bad, virtuous or vicious; unless we take these terms in a physical sense, and call, in an individual, those qualities vices which may be injurious to his preservation, and those virtues which contribute to it; in which case, he would have to be accounted most virtuous, who put least check on the pure impulses of nature. But without deviating from the ordinary sense of the words, it will be proper to suspend the judgment we might be led to form on such a state, and be on our guard against our prejudices, till we have weighed the matter in the scales of impartiality, and seen whether virtues or vices preponderate among civilized men: and whether their virtues do them more good than their vices do harm; till we have discovered whether the progress of the sciences sufficiently indemnifies them for the mischiefs they do one another, in proportion as they are better informed of the good they ought to do; or whether they would not be, on the whole, in a much happier condition if they had nothing to fear or to hope from any one, than as they are, subjected to universal dependence, and obliged to take everything from those who engage to give them nothing in return.

Above all, let us not conclude, with Hobbes, that because man has no idea of goodness, he must be naturally wicked; that he is vicious because he does not know virtue; that he always refuses to do his fellow-creatures services which he does not think they have a right to demand; or that by virtue of the right he justly claims to all he needs, he foolishly imagines himself the sole proprietor of the whole universe. Hobbes had seen clearly the defects of all the modern definitions of natural right: but the consequences which he deduces from his own show that he understands it in an equally false sense. In reasoning on the principles he lays down, he ought to have said that the state of nature, being that in which the care for our own preservation is the least prejudicial to that of others, was consequently the best calculated to promote peace, and the most suitable for mankind. He does say the exact opposite, in consequence of having improperly admitted, as a part of savage man's care for self-preservation, the gratification of a multitude of passions which are the work of society, and have made laws necessary. A bad man, he says, is a robust child. But it remains to be proved whether man in a state of nature is this robust child: and, should we grant that he is, what would he infer? Why truly, that if this man, when robust and strong, were dependent on others as he is when feeble, there is no extravagance he would not be guilty of; that he would beat his mother when she was too slow in giving him her breast; that he would strangle one of his younger brothers, if he should be troublesome to him, or bite the leg of another, if he put him to any inconvenience. But that man in the state of nature is both strong and dependent involves two contrary suppositions. Man is weak when he is dependent, and is his own master before he comes to be strong. Hobbes did not reflect that the same cause, which prevents a savage from making use of his reason, as our jurists hold, prevents him also from abusing his faculties, as Hobbes himself allows: so that it may be justly said that savages are not bad merely because they do not know what it is to be good: for it is neither the development of the understanding nor the restraint of law that hinders them from doing ill; but the peacefulness of their passions, and their ignorance of vice. . . . There is another principle which has escaped Hobbes; which, having been bestowed on mankind, to moderate, on certain occasions, the impetuosity of *amour-propre*, or, before its birth, the desire of self-preservation, tempers the ardour with which he pursues his own welfare, by an innate repugnance at seeing a fellow-creature suffer. I think I need not fear contradiction in holding man to be possessed of the only natural virtue, which could not be denied him by the most violent detractor of human virtue. I am speaking of compassion, which is a disposition suitable to creatures so weak and subject to so many evils as we certainly are: by so much the more universal and useful to mankind, as it comes before any kind of reflection; and at the same time so natural, that the very brutes themselves sometimes give evident proofs of it. Not to mention the tenderness of mothers for their offspring and the perils they encounter to save them from danger, it is well known that horses show a reluctance to trample on living bodies. One animal never passes by the dead body of another of its species without disquiet: some even give their fellows a sort of burial; while the mournful lowings of the cattle when they enter the slaughter-house show the impressions made on them by the horrible spectacle which meets them. We find, with pleasure, the author of *The Fable of the Bees* obliged to own that man is a compassionate and sensible being, and laying aside his cold subtlety of style, in the example he gives, to present us with the pathetic description of a man who, from a place of confinement, is compelled to behold a wild beast tear a child from the arms of its mother, grinding its tender limbs with its murderous teeth, and tearing its palpitating entrails with its claws. What horrid agitation must not the eye-witness of such a scene experience, although he would not be personally concerned! What anguish would he not suffer at not being able to give any assistance to the fainting mother and the dying infant!

Such is the pure emotion of nature, prior to all kinds of reflection! Such is the force of natural compassion, which the greatest depravity of morals has as yet hardly been able to destroy! for we daily find at our theatres men affected, nay, shedding tears at the sufferings of a wretch who, were he in the tyrant's place, would probably even add to the torments of his enemies; like the bloodthirsty Sulla, who was so sensitive to ills he had not caused, or that Alexander of Pheros who did not dare to go and see any tragedy acted, for fear of being seen weeping with Andromache and Priam, though he could listen without emotion to the cries of all the citizens who were daily strangled at his command. . . . Mandeville well knew that, in spite of all their morality, men would have never been better than monsters, had not nature bestowed on them a sense of compassion, to aid their reason: but he did not see that from this quality alone flow all those social virtues, of which he denied man the possession. But what is generosity, clemency, or humanity but compassion applied to the weak, to the guilty, or to mankind in general? Even benevolence and friendship are, if we judge rightly, only the effects of compassion, constantly set upon a particular object: for how is it different to wish that another person may not suffer pain and uneasiness and to wish him happy? Were it even true that pity is no more than a feeling, which puts us in the place of the sufferer, a feeling obscure yet lively in a savage, developed yet feeble in civilized man; this truth would have no other consequence than to confirm my argument. Compassion must, in fact, be the stronger, the more the animal beholding any kind of distress identifies himself with the animal that suffers. Now, it is plain that such identification must have been much more perfect in a state of nature than it is in a state of reason. It is reason that engenders *amour-propre*, and reflection that confirms it: it is reason which turns man's mind back upon itself, and divides him from everything that could disturb or afflict him. It is philosophy that isolates him, and bids him say, at sight of the misfortunes of others: 'Perish if you will, I am secure.' Nothing but such general evils as threaten the whole community can disturb the tranquil sleep of the philosopher, or tear him from his bed. A murder may with impunity be committed under his window; he has only to put his hands to his ears and argue a little with himself, to prevent nature, which is shocked within him, from identifying itself with the unfortunate sufferer. Uncivilized man has not this admirable talent; and for want of reason and wisdom, is always foolishly ready to obey the first promptings of humanity. It is the populace that flocks together at riots and street brawls, while the wise man prudently makes off. It is the mob and the market-women, who part the combatants, and stop decent people from cutting one another's throats.

It is then certain that compassion is a natural feeling, which, by moderating the activity of love of self in each individual, contributes to the preservation of the whole species. It is this compassion that hurries us without reflection to the relief of those who are in distress: it is this which in a state of nature supplies the place of laws, morals, and virtues, with the advantage that none are tempted to disobey its gentle voice: it is this which will always prevent a sturdy savage from robbing a weak child or a feeble old man of the sustenance they may have with pain and difficulty acquired, if he sees a possibility of providing for himself by other means: it is this which, instead of inculcating that sublime maxim of rational justice, *Do to others as you would have them do unto you,* inspires all men with that other maxim of natural goodness, much less perfect indeed, but perhaps more useful; *Do good to yourself with as little evil as possible to others.* In a word, it is rather in this natural feeling than in any subtle arguments that we must look for the cause of that repugnance, which every man would experience in doing evil, even independently of the maxims of education. Although it might belong to Socrates and other minds of the like craft to acquire virtue by reason, the human race would long since have ceased to be, had its preservation depended only on the reasonings of the individuals composing it.

With passions so little active, and so good a curb, men, being rather wild than wicked, and more intent to guard themselves against the mischief that might be done them, than to do mischief to others, were by no means subject to very perilous dissensions. They maintained no kind of intercourse with one another, and were consequently strangers to vanity, deference, esteem, and contempt; they had not the least idea of 'mine' and 'thine', and no true conception of justice; they looked upon every violence to which they were subjected, rather as an injury that might easily be repaired than as a crime that ought to be punished; and they never thought of taking revenge, unless perhaps mechanically and on the spot, as a dog will sometimes bite the stone which is thrown at him. Their quarrels therefore would seldom have very bloody consequences; for the subject of them would be merely the question of subsistence. But I am aware of one greater danger, which remains to be noticed.

Of the passions that stir the heart of man, there is one which makes the sexes necessary to each other, and is extremely ardent and impetuous; a terrible passion that braves danger, surmounts all obstacles, and in its transports seems calculated to bring destruction on the human race which it is really destined to preserve. What must become of men who are left to this brutal and boundless rage, without modesty, without shame, and daily upholding their amours at the price of their blood?

It must, in the first place, be allowed that, the more violent the passions are, the more are laws necessary to keep them under restraint. But, setting aside the inadequacy of laws to effect this purpose, which is evident from the crimes and disorders to which these passions daily give rise among us, we should do well to inquire if these evils did not spring up with the laws themselves; for in this case, even if the laws were capable of repressing such evils, it is the least that could be expected from them, that they should check a mischief which would not have arisen without them.

Let us begin by distinguishing between the physical and moral ingredients in the feeling of love. The physical part of love is that general desire which urges the sexes to union with each other. The moral part is that which determines and fixes this desire exclusively upon one particular object; or at least gives it a greater degree of energy toward the object thus preferred. It is easy to see that the moral part of love is a factitious feeling, born of social usage, and enhanced by the women with much care and cleverness, to establish their empire, and put in power the sex which ought to obey. This feeling, being founded on certain ideas of beauty and merit which a savage is not in a position to acquire, and on comparisons which he is incapable of making, must be for him almost non-existent; for, as his mind cannot form abstract ideas of proportion and regularity, so his heart is not susceptible of the feelings of love and admiration, which are even insensibly produced by the application of these ideas. He follows solely the character nature has implanted in him, and not tastes which he could never have acquired; so that every woman equally answers his purpose.

Men in a state of nature being confined merely to what is physical in love, and fortunate enough to be ignorant of those excellences, which whet the appetite while they increase the difficulty of gratifying it, must be subject to fewer and less violent fits of passion, and consequently fall into fewer and less violent disputes. The imagination, which causes such ravages among us, never speaks to the heart of savages, who quietly await the impulses of nature, yield to them involuntarily, with more pleasure than ardour, and, their wants once satisfied, lose the desire. It is therefore incontestable that love, as well as all other passions, must have acquired in society that glowing impetuosity, which makes it so often fatal to mankind. And it is the more absurd to represent savages as continually cutting one another's throats to indulge their brutality, because this opinion is directly contrary to experience; the Caribbeans, who have as yet least of all deviated from the state of nature, being in fact the most peaceable of people in their amours, and the least subject to jealousy, though they live in a hot climate which seems always to inflame the passions.

With regard to the inferences that might be drawn, in the case of several species of animals, the males of which fill our poultry-yards with blood and slaughter, or in spring make the forests resound with their quarrels over their females; we must begin by excluding all those species, in which nature has plainly established, in the comparative power of the sexes, relations different from those which exist among us: thus we can base no conclusion about men on the habits of fighting cocks. In those species where the proportion is better observed, these battles must be entirely due to the scarcity of females in comparison with males; or, what amounts to the same thing, to the intervals during which the female constantly refuses the advances of the male: for if each female admits the male but during two months in the year, it is the same as if the number of females were five-sixths less. Now, neither of these two cases is applicable to the human species, in which the number of females usually exceeds that of males, and among whom it has never been observed, even among savages, that the females have, like those of other animals, their stated times of passion and indifference. Moreover, in several of these species, the individuals all take fire at once, and there comes a fearful moment of universal passion, tumult, and disorder among them; a scene which is never beheld in the human species, whose love is not thus seasonal. We must not then conclude from the combats of such animals for the enjoyment of the females, that the case would be the same with mankind in a state of nature: and, even if we drew such a conclusion, we see that such contests do not exterminate other kinds of animals, and we have no reason to think they would be more fatal to ours. It is indeed clear that they would do still less mischief than is the case in a state of society; especially in those countries in which, morals being still held in some repute, the jealousy of lovers and the vengeance of husbands are the daily cause of duels, murders, and even worse crimes; where the obligation of eternal fidelity only occasions adultery, and the very laws of honour and continence necessarily increase debauchery and lead to the multiplication of abortions.

Let us conclude then that man in a state of nature, wandering up and down the forests, without industry, without speech, and without home, an equal stranger to war and to all ties, neither standing in need of his fellow-creatures nor having any desire to hurt them, and perhaps even not distinguishing them one from another; let us conclude that, being self-sufficient and subject to so few passions, he could have no feelings or knowledge but such as befitted his situation; that he felt only his actual necessities, and disregarded everything he did not think himself immediately concerned to notice, and that his understanding made no greater progress than his vanity. If by accident he made any discovery, he was the less able to communicate it to others, as he did not know even his own children. Every art would necessarily perish with its inventor, where there was no kind of education among men, and generations succeeded generations without the least advance; when, all setting out from the same point, centuries must have elapsed in the barbarism of the first ages; when the race was already old, and man remained a child. . . .

The Second Part: The Inequalities of Civilization

. . . So long as men remained content with their rustic huts, so long as they were satisfied with clothes made of the skins of animals and sewn together with thorns and fish-bones, adorned themselves only with feathers and shells, and continued to paint their bodies different colours, to improve and beautify their bows and arrows, and to make with sharp-edged stones fishing boats or clumsy musical instruments; in a word, so long as they undertook only what a single person could accomplish, and confined themselves to such arts as did not require the joint labour of several hands, they lived free, healthy, honest, and happy lives, in so far as their nature allowed, and they continued to enjoy the pleasures of mutual and independent intercourse. But from the moment one man began to stand in need of the help of another; from the moment it appeared advantageous to any one man to have enough provisions for two, equality disappeared, property was introduced, work became indispensable, and vast forests became smiling fields, which man had to water with the sweat of his brow, and where slavery and misery were soon seen to germinate and grow up with the crops.

Metallurgy and agriculture were the two arts which produced this great revolution. The poets tell us it was gold and silver, but, for the philosophers, it was iron and corn, which first civilized men, and ruined humanity. Thus both were unknown to the savages of America, who for that reason are still savage: the other nations also seem to have continued in a state of barbarism while they practised only one of these arts. One of the best reasons, perhaps, why Europe has been, if not longer, at least more constantly and highly civilized than the rest of the world, is that it is at once the most abundant in iron and the most fertile in corn.

It is difficult to conjecture how men first came to know and use iron; for it is impossible to suppose they would of themselves think of digging the ore out of the mine, and preparing it for smelting, before they knew what would be the result. On the other hand, we have the less reason to suppose this discovery the effect of any accidental fire, as mines are only formed in barren places, bare of trees and plants; so that it looks as if nature had taken pains to keep the fatal secret from us. There remains, therefore, only the extraordinary accident of some volcano which, by ejecting metallic substances already in fusion, suggested to the spectators the idea of imitating the natural operation. And we must further conceive them as possessed of uncommon courage and foresight, to undertake so laborious a work, with so distant a prospect of drawing advantage from it; yet these qualities are united only in minds more advanced than we can suppose those of these first discoverers to have been.

With regard to agriculture, the principles of it were known long before they were put in practice; and it is indeed hardly possible that men, constantly employed in drawing their subsistence from plants and trees, should not readily acquire a knowledge of the means made use of by nature for the propagation of vegetables. It was in all probability very long, however, before their industry took that turn, either because trees, which together with hunting and fishing afforded them food, did not require their attention; or because they were ignorant of the use of corn, or without instruments to cultivate it; or because they lacked foresight to future needs; or lastly, because they were without means of preventing others from robbing them of the fruit of their labour.

When they grew more industrious, it is natural to believe that they began, with the help of sharp stones and pointed sticks, to cultivate a few vegetables or roots around their huts; though it was long before they knew how to prepare corn, or were provided with the implements necessary for raising it in any large quantity; not to mention how essential it is, for husbandry, to consent to immediate loss, in order to reap a future gain — a precaution very foreign to the turn of a savage's mind; for, as I have said, he hardly foresees in the morning what he will need at night.

The invention of the other arts must therefore have been necessary to compel mankind to apply themselves to agriculture. No sooner were artificers wanted to smelt and forge iron, than others were required to maintain them; the more hands that were employed in manufactures, the fewer were left to provide for the common subsistence, though the number of mouths to be furnished with food remained the same: and as some required commodities in exchange for their iron, the rest at length discovered the method of making iron serve for the multiplication of commodities. By this means the arts of husbandry and agriculture were established on the one hand, and the art of working metals and multiplying their uses on the other.

The cultivation of the earth necessarily brought about its distribution; and property, once recognized, gave rise to the first rules of justice; for, to secure each man his own, it had to be possible for each to have something. Besides, as men began to look forward to the future, and all had something to lose, every one had reason to apprehend that reprisals would follow any injury he might do to another. This origin is so much the more natural, as it is impossible to conceive how property can come from anything but manual labour: for what else can a man add to things which he does not originally create, so as to make them his own property? It is the husbandman's labour alone that, giving him a title to the produce of the ground he has tilled, gives him a claim also to the land itself, at least till harvest; and so, from year to year, a constant possession which is easily transformed into property. When the ancients, says Grotius, gave to Ceres the title of Legislatrix, and to a festival celebrated in her honour the name of Thesmophoria, they meant by that that the distribution of lands had produced a new kind of right: that is to say, the right of property, which is different from the right deducible from the law of nature.

In this state of affairs, equality might have been sustained, had the talents of individuals been equal, and had, for example, the use of iron and the consumption of commodities always exactly balanced each other; but, as there was nothing to preserve this balance, it was soon disturbed; the strongest did most work; the most skilful turned his labour to best account; the most ingenious devised methods of diminishing his labour: the husbandman wanted more iron, or the smith more corn, and, while both laboured equally, the one gained a great deal by his work, while the other could hardly support himself. Thus natural inequality unfolds itself insensibly with that of combination, and the difference between men, developed by their different circumstances, becomes more sensible and permanent in its effects, and begins to have an influence, in the same proportion, over the lot of individuals.

Matters once at this pitch, it is easy to imagine the rest, I shall not detain the reader with a description of the successive invention of other arts, the development of language, the trial and utilization of talents, the inequality of fortunes, the use and abuse of riches, and all the details connected with them which the reader can easily supply for himself. I shall confine myself to a glance at mankind in this new situation.

Behold then all human faculties developed, memory and imagination in full play, *amour-propre* interested, reason active, and the mind almost at the highest point of its perfection. Behold all the natural qualities in action, the rank and condition of every man assigned him; not merely his share of property and his power to serve or injure others, but also his wit, beauty, strength or skill, merits or talents: and these being the only qualities capable of commanding respect, it soon became necessary to possess or to affect them.

It now became the interest of men to appear what they really were not. To be and to seem became two totally different things; and from this distinction sprang insolent pomp and cheating trickery, with all the numerous vices that go in their train. On the other hand, free and independent as men were before, they were now, in consequence of a multiplicity of new wants, brought into subjection, as it were, to all nature, and particularly to one another; and each became in some degree a slave even in becoming the master of other men: if rich, they stood in need of the services of others; if poor, of their assistance; and even a middle condition did not enable them to do without one another. Man must now, therefore, have been perpetually employed in getting others to interest themselves in his lot, and in making them, apparently at least, if not really, find their advantage in promoting his own. Thus he must have been sly and artful in his behaviour to some, and imperious and cruel to others; being under a kind of necessity to ill-use all the persons of whom he stood in need, when he could not frighten them into compliance, and did not judge it his interest to be useful to them. Insatiable ambition, the thirst of raising their respective fortunes, not so much from real want as from the desire to surpass others, inspired all men with a vile propensity to injure one another, and with a secret jealousy, which is the more dangerous, as it puts on the mask of benevolence, to carry its point with greater security. In a word, there arose rivalry and competition on the one hand, and conflicting interests on the other, together with a secret desire on both of profiting at the expense of others. All these evils were the first effects of property, and the inseparable attendants of growing inequality.

Before the invention of signs to represent riches, wealth could hardly consist in anything but lands and cattle, the only real possessions men can have. But, when inheritances so increased in number and extent as to occupy the whole of the land, and to border on one another, one man could aggrandize himself only at the expense of another; at the same time the supernumeraries, who had been too weak or too indolent to make such acquisitions, and had grown poor without sustaining any loss, because, while they saw everything change around them, they remained still the same, were obliged to receive their subsistence, or steal it, from the rich; and this soon bred, according to their different characters, dominion and slavery, or violence and rapine. The wealthy, on their part, had no sooner begun to taste the pleasure of command, than they disdained all others, and, using their old slaves to acquire new, thought of nothing but subduing and enslaving their neighbours; like ravenous wolves, which, having once tasted human flesh, despise every other food and thenceforth seek only men to devour.

Thus, as the most powerful or the most miserable considered their might or misery as a kind of right to the possessions of others, equivalent, in their opinion, to that of property, the destruction of equality was attended by the most terrible disorders. Usurpations by the rich, robbery by the poor, and the unbridled passions of both, suppressed the cries of natural compassion and the still feeble voice of justice, and filled men with avarice, ambition, and vice. Between the title of the strongest and that of the first occupier, there arose perpetual conflicts, which never ended but in battles and bloodshed. The new-born state of society thus gave rise to a horrible state of war; men thus harassed and depraved were no longer capable of retracing their steps or renouncing the fatal acquisitions they had made, but, labouring by the abuse of the faculties which do them honour, merely to their own confusion, brought themselves to the brink of ruin. . . .

It is impossible that men should not at length have reflected on so wretched a situation, and on the calamities that overwhelmed them. The rich, in particular, must have felt how much they suffered by a constant state of war, of which they bore all the expense; and in which, though all risked their lives, they alone risked their property. Besides, however speciously they might disguise their usurpations, they knew that they were founded on precarious and false titles; so that, if others took from them by force what they themselves had gained by force, they would have no reason to complain. Even those who had been enriched by their own industry, could hardly base their proprietorship on better claims. It was in vain to repeat: 'I built this well; I gained this spot by my industry.' Who gave you your standing, it might be answered, and what right have you to demand payment of us for doing what we never asked you to do? Do you not know that numbers of your fellow-creatures are starving, for want of what you have too much of? You ought to have had the express and universal consent of mankind, before appropriating more of the common subsistence than you needed for your own mainte-nance. Destitute of valid reasons to justify and sufficient strength to defend himself, able to crush individuals with ease, but easily crushed himself by a troop of bandits, one against all, and incapable, on account of mutual jeal-ousy, of joining with his equals against numerous enemies united by the common hope of plunder, the rich man, thus urged by necessity, conceived at length the profoundest plan that ever entered the mind of man: this was to employ in his favour the forces of those who attacked him, to make allies of his adversaries, to inspire them with different maxims, and to give them other institutions as favourable to himself as the law of nature was unfavourable.

With this view, after having represented to his neighbours the horror of a situation which armed every man against the rest, and made their possessions as burdensome to them as their wants, and in which no safety could be expected either in riches or in poverty, he readily devised plausible arguments to make them close with his design. 'Let us join,' said he, 'to guard the weak from oppression, to restrain the ambitious, and secure to every man the possession of what belongs to him: let us institute rules of justice and peace, to which all without exception may be obliged to conform; rules that may in some measure make amends for the caprices of fortune, by subjecting equally the powerful and the weak to the observance of reciprocal obligations. Let us, in a word, instead of turning our forces against ourselves, collect them in a supreme power which may govern us by wise laws, protect and defend all the members of the association, repulse their common enemies, and maintain eternal harmony among us.'

Far fewer words to this purpose would have been enough to impose on men so barbarous and easily seduced; especially as they had too many disputes among themselves to do without arbitrators, and too much ambition and avarice to go long without masters. All ran headlong to their chains, in hopes of securing their liberty; for they had just wit enough to perceive the advantages of political institutions, without experience enough to enable them to foresee the dangers. The most capable of foreseeing the dangers were the very persons who expected to benefit by them; and even the most prudent judged it not inexpedient to sacrifice one part of their freedom to ensure the rest; as a wounded man has his arm cut off to save the rest of his body.

Such was, or may well have been, the origin of society and law, which bound new fetters on the poor, and gave new powers to the rich; which irretrievably destroyed natural liberty, eternally fixed the law of property and inequality, converted clever usurpation into unalterable right, and, for the advantage of a few ambitious individuals, subjected all mankind to perpetual labour, slavery, and wretchedness. It is easy to see how the establishment of one community made that of all the rest necessary, and how, in order to make head against united forces, the rest of mankind had to unite in turn. Societies soon multiplied and spread over the face of the earth, till hardly a corner of the world was left in which a man could escape the yoke, and withdraw his head from beneath the sword which he saw perpetually hanging over him by a thread. Civil right having thus become the common rule among the members of each community, the law of nature maintained its place only between different communities, where, under the name of the right of nations, it was qualified by certain tacit conventions, in order to make commerce practicable, and serve as a substitute for natural compassion, which lost, when applied to societies, almost all the influence it had over individuals, and survived no longer except in some great cosmopolitan spirits, who, breaking down the imaginary barriers that separate different peoples, follow the example of our Sovereign Creator, and include the whole human race in their benevolence.

But bodies politic, remaining thus in a state of nature among themselves, presently experienced the inconveniences which had obliged individuals to forsake it; for this state became still more fatal to these great bodies than it had been to the individuals of whom they were composed. Hence arose national wars, battles, murders, and reprisals, which shock nature and outrage reason; together with all those horrible prejudices which class among the virtues the honour of shedding human blood. The most distinguished men hence learned to consider cutting each other's throats a duty; at length men massacred their fellow-creatures by thousands without so much as knowing why, and committed more murders in a single day's fighting, and more violent outrages in the sack of a single town, than were committed in the state of nature during whole ages over the whole earth. Such were the first effects which we can see to have followed the division of mankind into different communities. But let us return to their institution.

SELECTIONS FROM
The Social Contract or Principles of Political Right

Foederis aequas
Dicamus leges. (Vergil, *Aeneid XI*)

Book I, Chapter VI The Social Compact

I SUPPOSE men to have reached the point at which the obstacles in the way of their preservation in the state of nature show their power of resistance to be greater than the resources at the disposal of each individual for his mainte-nance in that state. That primitive condition can then subsist no longer; and the human race would perish unless it changed its manner of existence.

But, as men cannot engender new forces, but only unite and direct existing ones, they have no other means of preserving themselves than the formation, by aggregation, of a sum of forces great enough to overcome the resistance. These they have to bring into play by means of a single motive power, and cause to act in concert.

This sum of forces can arise only where several persons come together: but, as the force and liberty of each man are the chief instruments of his self-preservation, how can he pledge them without harming his own interests, and neglecting the care he owes to himself? This difficulty, in its bearing on my present subject, may be stated in the following terms:

'The problem is to find a form of association which will defend and protect with the whole common force the person and goods of each asso-ciate, and in which each, while uniting himself with all, may still obey himself alone, and remain as free as before.' This is the fundamental problem of which the social contract provides the solution.

The clauses of this contract are so determined by the nature of the act that the slightest modification would make them vain and ineffective; so that, although they have perhaps never been formally set forth, they are every-where the same and everywhere tacitly admitted and recognized, until, on the violation of the social compact, each regains his original rights and resumes his natural liberty, while losing the conventional liberty in favour of which he renounced it.

These clauses, properly understood, may be reduced to one — the total alienation of each associate, together with all his rights, to the whole commu-nity; for, in the first place, as each gives himself absolutely, the conditions are the same for all; and, this being so, no one has any interest in making them burdensome to others.

Moreover, the alienation being without reserve, the union is as perfect as it can be, and no associate has anything more to demand: for, if the individuals retained certain rights, as there would be no common superior to decide between them and the public, each, being on one point his own judge, would ask to be so on all; the state of nature would thus continue, and the association would necessarily become inoperative or tyrannical.

Finally, each man, in giving himself to all, gives himself to nobody; and as there is no associate over which he does not acquire the same right as he yields others over himself, he gains an equivalent for everything he loses, and an increase of force for the preservation of what he has.

If then we discard from the social compact what is not of its essence, we shall find that it reduces itself to the following terms:

'*Each of us puts his person and all his power in common under the supreme direction of the general will, and, in our corporate capacity, we receive each member as an indivisible part of the whole.*'

At once, in place of the individual personality of each contracting party, this act of association creates a corporate and collective body, composed of as many members as the assembly contains voters, and receiving from this act its unity, its common identity, its life, and its will. This public person, so formed by the union of all other persons, formerly took the name of *city*, and now takes that of *Republic* or *body politic*; it is called by its members *State* when passive, *Sovereign* when active, and *Power* when compared with others like itself. Those who are associated in it take collectively the name of *people*, and severally are called *citizens*, as sharing in the sovereign authority, and *subjects*, as being under the laws of the State. But these terms are often confused and taken one for another: it is enough to know how to distinguish them when they are being used with precision.

Chapter VII The Sovereign

This formula shows us that the act of association comprises a mutual undertaking between the public and the individuals, and that each individual, in making a contract, as we may say, with himself, is bound in a double relation; as a member of the Sovereign he is bound to the individuals, and as a member of the State to the Sovereign. But the maxim of civil right, that no one is bound by undertakings made to himself, does not apply in this case; for there is a great difference between incurring an obligation to yourself and incurring one to a whole of which you form a part.

Attention must further be called to the fact that public deliberation, while competent to bind all the subjects to the Sovereign, because of the two different capacities in which each of them may be regarded, cannot, for the opposite reason, bind the Sovereign to itself; and that it is consequently against the nature of the body politic for the Sovereign to impose on itself a law which it cannot infringe. Being able to regard itself in only one capacity, it is in the position of an individual who makes a contract with himself; and this makes it clear that there neither is nor can be any kind of fundamental law binding on the body of the people — not even the social contract itself. This does not mean that the body politic cannot enter into undertakings with others, provided the contract is not infringed by them; for in relation to the foreigner, it becomes a simple being, an individual.

But the body politic or the Sovereign, drawing its being wholly from the sanctity of the contract, can never bind itself, even to an outsider, to do anything derogatory to the original act, for instance, to alienate any part of itself, or to submit to another Sovereign. Violation of the act by which it exists would be self-annihilation; and that which is itself nothing can create nothing.

As soon as this multitude is so united in one body, it is impossible to offend against one of the members without attacking the body, and still more to offend against the body without the members resenting it. Duty and interest therefore equally oblige the two contracting parties to give each other help; and the same men should seek to combine, in their double capacity, all the advantages dependent upon that capacity.

Again, the Sovereign, being formed wholly of the individuals who compose it, neither has nor can have any interest contrary to theirs; and consequently the sovereign power need give no guarantee to its subjects, because it is impossible for the body to wish to hurt all its members. We shall also see later on that it cannot hurt any in particular. The Sovereign, merely by virtue of what it is, is always what it should be.

This, however, is not the case with the relation of the subjects to the Sovereign, which, despite the common interest, would have no security that they would fulfil their undertakings, unless it found means to assure itself of their fidelity.

In fact, each individual, as a man, may have a particular will contrary or dissimilar to the general will which he has as a citizen. His particular interest may speak to him quite differently from the common interest: his absolute and naturally independent existence may make him look upon what he owes to the common cause as a gratuitous contribution, the loss of which will do less harm to others than the payment of it is burdensome to himself; and, regarding the corporate person which constitutes the State as a *persona ficta*, because not a man, he may wish to enjoy the rights of citizenship without being ready to fulfil the duties of a subject. The continuance of such an injustice could not but prove the undoing of the body politic.

In order then that the social compact may not be an empty formula, it tacitly includes the undertaking, which alone can give force to the rest, that whoever refuses to obey the general will shall be compelled to do so by the whole body. This means nothing less than that he will be forced to be free; for this is the condition which, by giving each citizen to his country, secures him against all personal dependence. In this lies the key to the working of the political machine; this alone legitimizes civil undertakings, which, without it, would be absurd, tyrannical and liable to the most frightful abuses.

Chapter VIII The Civil State

The passage from the state of nature to the civil state produces a very remarkable change in man, by substituting justice for instinct in his conduct, and giving his actions the morality they had formerly lacked. Then only, when the voice of duty takes the place of physical impulses and right of appetite, does man, who so far had considered only himself, find that he is forced to act on different principles, and to consult his reason before listening to his inclinations. Although, in this state, he deprives himself of some advantages which he got from nature, he gains in return others so great, his faculties are so stimulated and developed, his ideas so extended, his feelings so ennobled, and his whole soul so uplifted, that, did not the abuses of this new condition often degrade him below that which he left, he would be bound to bless continually the happy moment which took him from it for ever, and, instead of a stupid and unimaginative animal, made him an intelligent being and a man.

Let us draw up the whole account in terms easily commensurable. What man loses by the social contract is his natural liberty and an unlimited right to everything he tries to get and succeeds in getting; what he gains in civil liberty and the proprietorship of all he possesses. If we are to avoid mistake in weighing one against the other, we must clearly distinguish natural liberty, which is bounded only by the strength of the individual, from civil liberty, which is limited by the general will; and possession, which is merely the effect of force or the right of the first occupier, from property, which can be founded only on a positive title.

We might, over and above all this, add, to what man acquires in the civil state, moral liberty, which alone makes him truly master of himself; for the mere impulse of appetite is slavery, while obedience to a law which we prescribe to ourselves is liberty. But I have already said too much on this head, and the philosophical meaning of the word liberty is now what concerns us here.

Chapter IX Real Property

Each member of the community gives himself to it, at the moment of its foundation, just as he is, with all the resources at his command, including the goods he possesses. This act does not make possession, in changing hands, change its nature, and become property in the hands of the Sovereign; but, as the forces of the city are incomparably greater than those of an individual, public possession is also, in fact, stronger and more irrevocable, without being any more legitimate, at any rate from the point of view of foreigners. For the State, in relation to its members, is master of all their goods by the social contract, which, within the State, is the basis of all rights; but, in relation to other powers, it is so only by the right of the first occupier, which it holds from its members.

The right of the first occupier, though more real than the right of the strongest, becomes a real right only when the right of property has already been established. Every man has naturally a right to everything he needs; but the positive act which makes him proprietor of one thing excludes him from everything else. Having his share, he ought to keep to it, and can have no further right against the community. This is why the right of the first occupier, which in the state of nature is so weak, claims the respect of every man in civil society. In this right we are respecting not so much what belongs to another as what does not belong to ourselves.

In general, to establish the right of the first occupier over a plot of ground, the following conditions are necessary: first, the land must not yet be inhabited; secondly, a man must occupy only the amount he needs for his subsistence; and, in the third place, possession must be taken, not by an empty ceremony, but by labour and cultivation, the only sign of proprietorship that should be respected by others, in default of a legal title.

In granting the right of first occupancy to necessity and labour, are we not really stretching it as far as it can go? Is it possible to leave such a right unlimited? Is it to be enough to set foot on a plot of common ground, in order to be able to call yourself at once the master of it? Is it to be enough that a man has the strength to expel others for a moment, in order to establish his right to prevent them from ever returning? How can a man or a people seize an immense territory and keep it from the rest of the world except by a punishable usurpation, since all others are being robbed, by such an act, of the place of habitation and the means of subsistence which nature gave them in common? When Nuñez Balbao, standing on the seashore, took possession of the South Seas and the whole of South America in the name of the crown of Castille, was that enough to dispossess all their actual inhabitants, and to shut out from them all the princes of the world? If this was the case, it was quite unnecessary to multiply these ceremonies, and all the King of Spain had to do was, from his apartment, to take possession all at once of the whole universe, allowing himself subsequently to exclude from his empire what had formerly been possessed by other princes.

We can imagine how the lands of individuals, where they were contiguous and came to be united, became the public territory, and how the right of Sovereignty, extending from the subjects over the lands they held, became at once real and personal. The possessors were thus made more dependent, and the forces at their command used to guarantee their fidelity. The advantage of this does not seem to have been felt by ancient monarchs, who called themselves King of the Persians, Scythians, or Macedonians, and seemed to regard themselves more as rulers of men than as masters of a country. Those of the present day more cleverly call themselves Kings of France, Spain, England, etc.: thus holding the land, they are quite confident of holding the inhabitants.

The peculiar fact about this alienation is that, in taking over the goods of individuals, the community, so far from despoiling them, only assures them legitimate possession, and changes usurpation into a true right and enjoyment into proprietorship. Thus the possessors, being regarded as depositaries of public property, and having their rights respected by all the members of the State and maintained against foreign aggression by all its forces, have, by a cession which benefits both the public and still more themselves, acquired, so to speak, all that they gave up. This paradox may easily be explained by the distinction between the rights which the Sovereign and the proprietor have over the same estate, as we shall see later on.

It may also happen that men begin to unite one with another before they possess anything, and that, subsequently occupying a tract of country which is enough for all, they enjoy it in common, or share it out among themselves, either equally or according to a scale fixed by the Sovereign. However the acquisition be made, the right which each individual has to his own estate is always subordinate to the right which the community has over all: without this, there would be neither stability in the social tie, nor real force in the exercise of Sovereignty.

I shall end this chapter and this book by remarking on a fact on which the whole social system should rest: i.e. that, instead of destroying natural equality, the fundamental compact substitutes, for such physical inequality as nature may have set up between men, an equality that is moral and legitimate, and that men, who may be unequal in strength or intelligence, become every one equal by convention and legal right.

Book II, Chapter I That Sovereignty Is Inalienable

The first and most important deduction from the principles we have so far laid down is that the general will alone can direct the State according to the object for which it was instituted, i.e. the common good: for if the clashing of particular interests made the establishment of societies necessary, the agreement of these very interests made it possible. The common element in these different interests is what forms the social tie; and, were there no point of agreement between them all, no society could exist. It is solely on the basis of this common interest that every society should be governed.

I hold then that Sovereignty, being nothing less than the exercise of the general will, can never be alienated, and that the Sovereign, who is no less than a collective being, cannot be represented except by himself: the power indeed may be transmitted, but not the will.

In reality, if it is not impossible for a particular will to agree on some point with the general will, it is at least impossible for the agreement to be lasting and constant; for the particular will tends, by its very nature, to partiality, while the general will tends to equality. It is even more impossible to have any guarantee of this agreement; for even if it should always exist, it would be the effect not of art, but of chance. The Sovereign may indeed say: 'I now will actually what this man wills, or at least what he says he wills'; but it cannot say: 'What he wills to-morrow, I too shall will' because it is absurd for the will to bind itself for the future, nor is it incumbent on any will to consent to anything that is not for the good of the being who wills. If then the people promises simply to obey, by that very act it dissolves itself and loses what makes it a people; the moment a master exists, there is no longer a Sovereign, and from that moment the body politic has ceased to exist.

This does not mean that the commands of the rulers cannot pass for general wills, so long as the Sovereign, being free to oppose them, offers no opposition. In such a case, universal silence is taken to imply the consent of the people. This will be explained later on.

Chapter II That Sovereignty Is Indivisible

Sovereignty, for the same reason as makes it inalienable, is indivisible; for will either is, or is not, general; it is the will either of the body of the people, or only of a part of it. In the first case, the will, when declared, is an act of Sovereignty and constitutes law: in the second, it is merely a particular will, or act of magistracy—at the most a decree.

But our political theorists, unable to divide Sovereignty in its principle, divide it according to its object; into force and will; into legislative power and executive power; into rights of taxation, justice, and war; into internal administration and power of foreign treaty. Sometimes they confuse all these sections, and sometimes they distinguish them; they turn the Sovereign into a fantastic being composed of several connected pieces; it is as if they were making man of several bodies, one with eyes, one with arms, another with feet, and each with nothing besides. We were told that the jugglers of Japan dismember a child before the eyes of the spectators; then they throw all the members into the air one after another, and the child falls down alive and whole. The conjuring tricks of our political theorists are very like that; they first dismember the body politic by an illusion worthy of a fair, and then join it together again we know not how.

This error is due to a lack of exact notions concerning the Sovereign authority, and to taking for parts of it what are only emanations from it. Thus, for example, the acts of declaring war and making peace have been regarded as acts of Sovereignty; but this is not the case, as these acts do not constitute law, but merely the application of a law, a particular act which decides how the law applies, as we shall see clearly when the idea attached to the word 'law' has been defined.

If we examined the other divisions in the same manner, we should find that, whenever Sovereignty seems to be divided, there is an illusion: the rights which are taken as being part of Sovereignty are really all subordinate, and always imply supreme wills of which they only sanction the execution.

It would be impossible to estimate the obscurity this lack of exactness has thrown over the decisions of writers who have dealt with political right, when they have used the principles laid down by them to pass judgment on the respective rights of kings and peoples. Every one can see, in Chapters III and IV of the first book of Grotius, how the learned man and his translator, Barbeyrac, entangle and tie themselves up in their own sophistries, for fear of saying too little or too much of what they think, and so offending the interests they have to conciliate. Grotius, a refugee in France, ill content with his own country, and desirous of paying his court to Louis XIII, to whom his book is dedicated, spares no pains to rob the peoples of all their rights and invest kings with them by every conceivable artifice. This would also have been much to the taste of Barbeyrac, who dedicated his translation to George I of England. But unfortunately the expulsion of James II, which he called his 'abdication," compelled him to use all reserve, to shuffle and to tergiversate, in order to avoid making William out a usurper. If these two writers had adopted the true principles, all difficulties would have been removed, and they would have been always consistent; but it would have been a sad truth for them to tell, and would have paid court for them to no one save the people. Moreover, truth is no road to fortune, and the people dispenses neither ambassadorships, nor professorships, nor pensions.

Chapter III Whether the General Will Is Fallible

It follows from what has gone before that the general will is always upright and always tends to the public advantage; but it does not follow that the deliberations of the people always have the same rectitude. Our will is always for our own good, but we do not always see what that is; the people is never corrupted, but it is often deceived, and on such occasions only does it seem to will what is bad.

There is often a great deal of difference between the will of all and the general will; the latter considers only the common interest, while the former takes private interest into account, and is no more than a sum of particular wills: but take away from these same wills the pluses and minuses that cancel one another, and the general will remains as the sum of the differences.

If, when the people, being furnished with adequate information, held its deliberations, the citizens had no communication one with another, the grand total of the small differences would always give the general will, and the decision would always be good. But when intrigues arise, and partial associations are formed at the expense of the great association, the will of each of these associations becomes general in relation to its members, while it remains particular in relation to the State: it may then be said that there are no longer as many votes as there are men, but only as many as there are associations. The differences become less numerous and give a less general result. Lastly, when one of these associations is so great as to prevail over all the rest, the result is no longer a sum of small differences, but a single difference; in this case there is no longer a general will, and the opinion which prevails is purely particular.

It is therefore essential, if the general will is to be able to make itself known, that there should be no partial society in the State and that each citizen should express only his own opinion: which was indeed the sublime and unique system established by the great Lycurgus. But if there are partial societies, it is best to have as many as possible and to prevent them from being unequal, as was done by Solon, Numa, and Servius. These precautions are the only ones that can guarantee that the general will shall be always enlightened, and that the people shall in no way deceive itself.

EDMUND BURKE

1 7 2 9 - 1 7 9 7

INTRODUCTION

"Much to admire, and nothing to agree with" was the verdict of the leader of Burke's own party in the British Parliament when Burke advocated armed intervention in the French Revolution. Many later critics have thought this judgment applicable to much of Burke's writings and speeches. What they have admired is Burke's command of language, his passion, knowledge, conviction, and consistency of principle. What they have disagreed with is the conservative and pessimistic content of his views. But set against this was his support for the American colonists in the prelude to the American Revolution — a support that led to his two speeches of 1774 – 1775, one on American taxation and the other on conciliation with America, being widely studied in American high schools until quite recently.

Born in Dublin, Burke was the son of a Protestant lawyer and a Catholic mother. Educated in classical languages at a Quaker boarding school and at Trinity College, Dublin, he remained an intensely religious Anglican all his life, and made a national established church one of his requirements for a sound government. In 1750 he went to London to study law but soon gave it up. Little is known of the next 5 years of his life. In 1756 he published anonymously his first book, *A Vindication of Natural Society*, a satire on the view that the rise of civilization produces unhappiness and distress. A year later he published the *Origin of Our Ideas on the Sublime and Beautiful*, his most philosophical work, but once again anonymous, and became editor of *The Annual Register*, a record of current political events. After serving as private secretary to several senior parliamentarians, Burke was given a seat himself in 1765 and remained in Parliament until his retirement almost 30 years later. His success as an orator, political writer, and party member was immediate and great, although he was never given especially high office by his party when it took government.

During Burke's political career he campaigned ceaselessly, but in the short term unsuccessfully, for a number of policies. He advocated administrative reform of the royal household and of the power of the Crown to reward its supporters and elimination of the anti-Catholic laws and of the severe controls on trade with Ireland; he was for generous treatment of the American colonists; he favored strong state support for the established Anglican Church and for the landed gentry; he fought for restriction of the powers of the East India Company in its administration of India; and he agitated both for military action against the French for executing their king and for tighter control of the civil liberties of their supporters in Britain. All these causes were lost, but Burke's advocacy made them burning issues and made him famous. He died a disappointed man 3 years after his retirement and the death of his son to whom he was greatly attached.

Reflections on the Revolution in France was written and published in 1790, a year or so after the Revolution began and 2 years before Louis XVI went to the guillotine. The book and Burke's parliamentary speeches cost him the favor of his party leader, Charles James Fox, whose policy of peace with France was opposed by Burke. The *Reflections* has been reprinted many times. The present selection is taken from the Clarendon Press edition, Oxford, 1877, pp. 34–39, 65–73.

SELECTIONS FROM
Reflections on the Revolution in France

Kings, in one sense, are undoubtedly the servants of the people, because their power has no other rational end than that of the general advantage; but it is not true that they are, in the ordinary sense (by our constitution, at least) any thing like servants; the essence of whose situation is to obey the commands of some other, and to be removeable at pleasure. But the king of Great Britain obeys no other person; all other persons are individually, and collectively too, under him, and owe to him a legal obedience. The law, which knows neither to flatter nor to insult, calls this high magistrate, not our servant, as this humble Divine calls him, but '*our sovereign Lord the King*,' and we, on our parts, have learned to speak only the primitive language of the law, and not the confused jargon of their Babylonian pulpits.

As he is not to obey us, but as we are to obey the law in him, our constitution has made no sort of provision towards rendering him, as a servant, in any degree responsible. Our constitution knows nothing of a magistrate like the *Justicia* of Arragon; nor of any court legally appointed, nor of any process legally settled for submitting the king to the responsibility belonging to all servants. In this he is not distinguished from the commons and the lords; who, in their several public capacities, can never be called to an account for their conduct; although the Revolution Society chooses to assert, in direct opposition to one of the wisest and most beautiful parts of our constitution, that 'a king is no more than the first servant of the public, created by it, *and responsible to it.*'

Ill would our ancestors at the Revolution have deserved their fame for wisdom, if they had found no security for their freedom, but in rendering their government feeble in its operations, and precarious in its tenure; if they had been able to contrive no better remedy against arbitrary power than civil confusion. Let these gentlemen state who that *representative* public is to whom they will affirm the king, as a servant, to be responsible. It will be then time enough for me to produce to them the positive statute law which affirms that he is not.

The ceremony of cashiering kings, of which these gentlemen talk so much at their ease, can rarely, if ever, be performed without force. It then becomes a case of war, and not of constitution. Laws are commanded to hold their tongues amongst arms; and tribunals fall to the ground with the peace they are no longer able to uphold. The Revolution of 1688 was obtained by a just war, in the only case in which any war, and much more a civil war, can be just. 'Justa bella quibus *necessaria*.' The question of dethroning, or, if these gentlemen like the phrase better, 'cashiering' kings, will always be, as it has always been, an extraordinary question of state, and wholly out of the law; a question (like all other questions of state) of dispositions, and of means, and of probable consequences, rather than of positive rights. As it was not made for common abuses, so it is not to be agitated by common minds. The speculative line of demarcation, where obedience ought to end, and resistance must begin, is faint, obscure, and not easily definable. It is not a single act, or a single event, which determines it. Governments must be abused and deranged indeed, before it can be thought of; and the prospect of the future must be as bad as the experience of the past. When things are in that lamentable condition, the nature of the disease is to indicate the remedy to those whom nature has qualified to administer in extremities this critical, ambiguous, bitter potion to a distempered state. Times and occasions, and provocations, will teach their own lessons. The wise will determine from the gravity of the case; the irritable from sensibility to oppression; the high-minded from disdain and indignation at abusive power in unworthy hands; the brave and bold from the love of honourable danger in a generous cause: but, with or without right, a revolution will be the very last resource of the thinking and the good.

THE third head of right, asserted by the pulpit of the Old Jewry, namely, the 'right to form a government for ourselves,' has, at least, as little countenance from any thing done at the Revolution, either in precedent or principle, as the two first of their claims. The Revolution was made to preserve our *antient* indisputable laws and liberties, and that *antient* constitution of government which is our only security for law and liberty. If you are desirous of knowing the spirit of our constitution, and the policy which predominated in that great period which has secured it to this hour, pray look for both in our histories, in our records, in our acts of parliament, and journals of parliament, and not in the sermons of the Old Jewry, and the after-dinner toasts of the Revolution Society. In the former you will find other ideas and another language. Such a claim is as ill-suited to our temper and wishes as it is unsupported by any appearance of authority. The very idea of the fabrication of a new government is enough to fill us with disgust and horror. We wished at the period of the Revolution, and do now wish, to derive all we possess as *an inheritance from our forefathers.* Upon that body and stock of inheritance we have taken care not to inoculate any cyon alien to the nature of the original plant. All the reformations we have hitherto made, have proceeded upon the principle of reference to antiquity; and I hope, nay I am persuaded, that all those which possibly may be made hereafter, will be carefully formed upon analogical precedent, authority, and example.

Our oldest reformation is that of Magna Charta. You will see that Sir Edward Coke, that great oracle of our law, and indeed all the great men who follow him, to Blackstone, are industrious to prove the pedigree of our liberties. They endeavour to prove, that the antient charter, the Magna Charta of King John, was connected with another positive charter from Henry I. and that both the one and the other were nothing more than a re-affirmance of the still more antient standing law of the kingdom. In the matter of fact, for the greater part, these authors appear to be in the right; perhaps not always: but if the lawyers mistake in some particulars, it proves my position still the more strongly; because it demonstrates the powerful prepossession towards antiquity, with which the minds of all our lawyers and legislators, and of all the people whom they wish to influence, have been always filled; and the stationary policy of this kingdom in considering their most sacred rights and franchises as an *inheritance.*

In the famous law of the 3rd of Charles I. called the *Petition of Right,* the parliament says to the king, 'Your subjects have *inherited* this freedom,' claiming their franchises, not on abstract principles as the 'rights of men,' but as the rights of Englishmen, and as a patrimony derived from their forefathers. Selden, and the other profoundly learned men, who drew this petition of right, were as well acquainted, at least, with all the general theories concerning the 'rights of men,' as any of the discoursers in our pulpits, or on your tribune; full as well as Dr. Price, or as the Abbé Sieyes. But, for reasons worthy of that practical wisdom which superseded their theoretic science, they preferred this positive, recorded, *hereditary* title to all which can be dear to the man and the citizen, to that vague speculative right, which exposed their sure inheritance to be scrambled for and torn to pieces by every wild litigious spirit.

The same policy pervades all the laws which have since been made for the preservation of our liberties. In the 1st of William and Mary, in the famous statute, called the Declaration of Right, the two houses utter not a syllable of 'a right to frame a government for themselves.' You will see, that their whole care was to secure the religion, laws, and liberties, that has been long possessed, and had been lately endangered. 'Taking into their most serious consideration the *best* means for making such an establishment, that their religion, laws, and liberties might not be in danger of being again subverted,' they auspicate all their proceedings, by stating as some of those *best* means, 'in the *first place*' to do 'as their *ancestors in like cases have usually* done for vindicating their *antient* rights and liberties, to *declare;*' — and then they pray the king and queen, 'that it may be *declared* and enacted, that *all and singular* the rights and liberties *asserted and declared* are the true *antient* and indubitable rights and liberties of the people of this kingdom.'

You will observe, that from Magna Charta to the Declaration of Right, it has been the uniform policy of our constitution to claim and assert our liberties, as an *entailed inheritance* derived to us from our forefathers, and to be transmitted to our posterity; as an estate specially belonging to the people of this kingdom without any reference whatever to any other more general or prior right. By this means our constitution preserves an unity in so great a diversity of its parts. We have an inheritable crown; an inheritable peerage; and an house of commons and a people inheriting privileges, franchises, and liberties, from a long line of ancestors.

This policy appears to me to be the result of profound reflection; or rather the happy effect of following nature, which is wisdom without reflection, and above it. A spirit of innovation is generally the result of a selfish temper and confined views. People will not look forward to posterity, who never look backward to their ancestors. Besides, the people of England well know, that the idea of inheritance furnishes a sure principle of conservation, and a sure principle of transmission; without at all excluding a principle of improvement. It leaves acquisition free; but it secures what it acquires. Whatever advantages are obtained by a state proceeding on these maxims, are locked fast as in a sort of family settlement; grasped as in a kind of mortmain for ever. By a constitutional policy, working after the pattern of nature, we receive, we hold, we transmit our government and our privileges, in the same manner in which we enjoy and transmit our property and our lives. The institutions of policy, the goods of fortune, the gifts of Providence, are handed down, to us and from us, in the same course and order. Our political system is placed in a just correspondence and symmetry with the order of the world, and with the mode of existence decreed to a permanent body composed of transitory parts; wherein, by the disposition of a stupendous wisdom, moulding together the great mysterious incorporation of the human race, the whole, at one time, is never old, or middle-aged, or young, but in a condition of unchangeable constancy, moves on through the varied tenour of perpetual decay, fall, renovation, and progression. Thus, by preserving the method of nature in the conduct of the state, in what we improve, we are never wholly new; in what we retain we are never wholly obsolete. . . .

The Revolution Society has discovered that the English nation is not free. They are convinced that the inequality in our representation is a 'defect in our constitution so *gross and palpable*, as to make it excellent chiefly in *form* and *theory.*' That a representation in the legislature of a kingdom is not only the basis of all constitutional liberty in it, but of '*all legitimate government*; that without it a *government* is nothing but an *usurpation*;'—that 'when the representation is *partial*, the kingdom possesses liberty only *partially*; and if extremely partial it gives only a *semblance*; and if not only extremely partial, but corruptly chosen, it becomes a *nuisance.*' Dr. Price considers this inadequacy of representation as our *fundamental grievance*; and though, as to the corruption of this semblance of representation, he hopes it is not yet arrived to its full perfection of depravity; he fears that 'nothing will be done towards gaining for us this *essential blessing*, until some *great abuse of power* again provokes our resentment, or some *great calamity* again alarms our fears, or perhaps till the acquisition of a *pure and equal representation by other countries*, whilst we are *mocked* with the *shadow*, kindles our shame.' To this he subjoins a note in these words. 'A representation, chosen chiefly by the Treasury, and a *few* thousands of the *dregs* of the people, who are generally paid for their votes.'

. . . It would require a long discourse to point out to you the many fallacies that lurk in the generality and equivocal nature of the terms 'inadequate representation.' I shall only say here, in justice to that old-fashioned constitution, under which we have long prospered, that our representation has been found perfectly adequate to all the purposes for which a representation of the people can be desired or devised. I defy the enemies of our constitution to show the contrary. To detail the particulars in which it is found so well to promote its ends, would demand a treatise on our practical constitution. I state here the doctrine of the Revolutionists, only that you and others may see, what an opinion these gentlemen entertain of the constitution of their country, and why they seem to think that some great abuse of power, or some great calamity, as giving a chance for the blessing of a constitution according to their ideas, would be much palliated to their feelings; you see why they are so much enamoured of your fair and equal representation, which being once obtained, the same effects might follow. You see they consider our house of commons as only 'a semblance,' 'a form,' 'a theory,' 'a shadow,' 'a mockery,' perhaps 'a nuisance.'

These gentlemen value themselves on being systematic; and not without reason. They must therefore look on this gross and palpable defect of representation, this fundamental grievance (so they call it), as a thing not only vicious in itself, but as rendering our whole government absolutely *illegitimate*, and not at all bettter than a downright *usurpation*. Another revolution, to get rid of this illegitimate and usurped government, would of course be perfectly justifiable, if not absolutely necessary. Indeed their principle, if you observe it with any attention, goes much further than to an alteration in the election of the house of commons; for, if popular representation, or choice, is necessary to the *legitimacy* of all government, the house of lords is, at one stroke, bastardized and corrupted in blood. That house is not representative of the people at all, even in 'semblance' or in 'form.' The case of the crown is altogether as bad. In vain the crown may endeavour to screen itself against these gentlemen by the authority of the establishment made on the Revolution. The Revolution which is resorted to for a title, on their system, wants a title itself. The Revolution is built, according to their theory, upon a basis not more solid than our present formalities, as it was made by an house of lords not representing any one but themselves; and by an house of commons exactly such as the present, that is, as they term it, by a mere 'shadow and mockery' of representation. . . .

Far am I from denying in theory; full as far is my heart from withholding in practice, (if I were of power to give or to withhold,) the *real* rights of men. In denying their false claims of right, I do not mean to injure those which are real, and are such as their pretended rights would totally destroy. If civil society be made for the advantage of man, all the advantages for which it is made become his right. It is an institution of beneficence; and law itself is only beneficence acting by a rule. Men have a right to live by that rule; they have a right to justice; as between their fellows, whether their fellows are in politic function or in ordinary occupation. They have a right to the fruits of their industry; and to the means of making their industry fruitful. They have a right to the acquisitions of their parents; to the nourishment and improvement of their offspring; to instruction in life, and to consolation in death. Whatever each man can separately do, without trespassing upon others, he has a right to do for himself; and he has a right to a fair portion of all which society, with all its combinations of skill and force, can do in his favour. In this partnership all men have equal rights; but not to equal things. He that has but five shillings in the partnership, has as good a right to it, as he that has five hundred pound has to his larger proportion. But he has not a right to an equal dividend in the product of the joint stock; and as to the share of power, authority, and direction which each individual ought to have in the management of the state, that I must deny to be amongst the direct original rights of man in civil society; for I have in my contemplation the civil social man, and no other. It is a thing to be settled by convention.

If civil society be the offspring of convention, that convention must be its law. That convention must limit and modify all the descriptions of constitution which are formed under it. Every sort of legislative, judicial, or executory power are its creatures. They can have no being in any other state of things; and how can any man claim, under the conventions of civil society, rights which do not so much as suppose its existence? Rights which are absolutely repugnant to it? One of the first motives to civil society, and which becomes one of its fundamental rules, is, *that no man should be judge in his own cause.* By this each person has at once divested himself of the first fundamental right of uncovenanted man, that is, to judge for himself, and to assert his own cause. He abdicates all right to be his own governor. He inclusively, in a great measure, abandons the right of self-defence, the first law of nature. Men cannot enjoy the rights of an uncivil and of a civil state together. That he may obtain justice he gives up his right of determining what it is in points the most essential to him. That he may secure some liberty, he makes a surrender in trust of the whole of it.

Government is not made in virtue of natural rights, which may and do exist in total independence of it; and exist in much greater clearness, and in a much greater degree of abstract perfection: but their abstract perfection is their practical defect. By having a right to every thing they want every thing. Government is a contrivance of human wisdom to provide for human *wants.* Men have a right that these wants should be provided for by this wisdom. Among these wants is to be reckoned the want, out of civil society, of a sufficient restraint upon their passions. Society requires not only that the passions of individuals should be subjected, but that even in the mass and body as well as in the individuals, the inclinations of men should frequently be thwarted, their will controlled, and their passions brought into subjection. This can only be done *by a power out of themselves*; and not, in the exercise of its function, subject to that will and to those passions which it is its office to bridle and subdue. In this sense the restraints on men, as well as their liberties, are to be reckoned among their rights. But as the liberties and the restrictions vary with times and circumstances, and admit of infinite modifications, they cannot be settled upon any abstract rule; and nothing is so foolish as to discuss them upon that principle.

The moment you abate any thing from the full rights of men, each to govern himself, and suffer any artificial positive limitation upon those rights, from that moment the whole organization of government becomes a consideration of convenience. This it is which makes the constitution of a state, and the due distribution of its powers, a matter of the most delicate and complicated skill. It requires a deep knowledge of human nature and human necessities, and of the things which facilitate or obstruct the various ends which are to be pursued by the mechanism of civil institutions. The state is to have recruits to its strength, and remedies to its distempers. What is the use of discussing a man's abstract right to food or to medicine? The question is upon the method of procuring and administering them. In that deliberation I shall always advise to call in the aid of the farmer and the physician, rather than the professor of metaphysics.

The science of constructing a commonwealth, or renovating it, or reforming it, is, like every other experimental science, not to be taught à priori. Nor is it a short experience that can instruct us in that practical science; because the real effects of moral causes are not always immediate; but that which in the first instance is prejudicial may be excellent in its remoter operation; and its excellence may arise even from the ill effects it produces in the beginning. The reverse also happens; and very plausible schemes, with very pleasing commencements, have often shameful and lamentable conclusions. In states there are often some obscure and almost latent causes, things which appear at first view of little moment, on which a very great part of its prosperity or adversity may most essentially depend. The science of government being therefore so practical in itself, and intended for such practical purposes, a matter which requires experience, and even more experience than any person can gain in his whole life, however sagacious and observing he may be, it is with infinite caution that any man ought to venture upon pulling down an edifice which has answered in any tolerable degree for ages the common purposes of society, or on building it up again, without having models and patterns of approved utility before his eyes.

These metaphysic rights entering into common life, like rays of light which pierce into a dense medium, are, by the laws of nature, refracted from their straight line. Indeed in the gross and complicated mass of human passions and concerns, the primitive rights of men undergo such a variety of refractions and reflections, that it becomes absurd to talk of them as if they continued in the simplicity of their original direction. The nature of man is intricate; the objects of society are of the greatest possible complexity; and therefore no simple disposition or direction of power can be suitable either to man's nature, or to the quality of his affairs. When I hear the simplicity of contrivance aimed at and boasted of in any new political constitutions, I am at no loss to decide that the artificers are grossly ignorant of their trade, or totally negligent of their duty. The simple governments are fundamentally defective, to say no worse of them. If you were to contemplate society in but one point of view, all these simple modes of polity are infinitely captivating. In effect each would answer its single end much more perfectly than the more complex is able to attain all its complex purposes. But it is better that the whole should be imperfectly and anomalously answered, than that, while some parts are provided for with great exactness, others might be totally neglected, or perhaps materially injured, by the overcare of a favourite member.

The pretended rights of these theorists are all extremes; and in proportion as they are metaphysically true, they are morally and politically false. The rights of men are in a sort of *middle*, incapable of definition, but not impossible to be discerned. The rights of men in governments are their advantages; and these are often in balances between differences of good; in compromises sometimes between good and evil, and sometimes, between evil and evil. Political reason is a computing principle; adding, subtracting, multiplying, and dividing, morally and not metaphysically or mathematically, true moral denominations.

By these theorists the right of the people is almost always sophistically confounded with their power. The body of the community, whenever it can come to act, can meet with no effectual resistance; but till power and right are the same, the whole body of them has no right inconsistent with virtue, and the first of all virtues, prudence. Men have no right to what is not reasonable, and to what is not for their benefit. . . .

THOMAS PAINE

1 7 3 7 – 1 8 0 9

INTRODUCTION

An active supporter of both the American War of Independence and the French Revolution, Paine was the first writer to call for American independence from Britain and the first to defend the French revolutionary government against Burke's attack on it. His pamphlet *Common Sense* (1776) making the case for independence was highly influential, and his reply to Burke, in *The Rights of Man* (1791–1792), was equally important in persuading democrats everywhere to welcome the overthrow of the French monarchy. His third important work, *The Age of Reason* (1794–1795), a religious criticism of the Old Testament as the word of God and the New Testament as the revelation of Jesus Christ, was mistaken for atheism and lost him many friends and admirers, especially in the United States. A citizen of his native Britain and of his two adopted countries, Paine was the best known and most popular political writer of his time, the inventor of an iron bridge, the friend or enemy of most of the important public figures in two continents, an economist, and an indefatigable proposer of social reforms, many of which have since been adopted without acknowledgment.

Paine was the only son of a Quaker corsetmaker and an older Anglican woman. He left school at age 13 to become an apprentice in his father's business at Thetford in the south of England, and he then practiced his trade in various towns until he became a customs officer in 1764. Dismissed a year later for collusion, he taught school before being reinstated in the service in 1768. His pay was so poor that by 1772 he was bankrupt, and his first published work entitled *Case of the Officers of Excise* was a vigorously written pamphlet designed to persuade Parliament to raise the officers' salaries. It failed and was perhaps the cause of his second dismissal from the Excise service. Within a year and a half Paine had been introduced to

Benjamin Franklin in London, obtained letters of introduction from him as "an ingenious, worthy young man" — although Paine was then aged 37 — and had emigrated to Philadelphia to found an academy. Instead, he became the energetic editor of *The Pennsylvania Magazine* and published anonymously *Common Sense*, a pamphlet that was a great and immediate success in advocating self-rule for the American colonists, and was later influential in preparing the way for the French Revolution.

Pursuing his career as an American supporter and journalist, Paine went to Paris in 1781 to help raise money for the American cause. Having been successful, he returned to America to work on his plan for a single-arch bridge and remained there until going to Paris in 1787. The following year in England he was still on friendly terms with Edmund Burke while traveling constantly between Paris and London. But with the publication of Burke's *Reflections* and Paine's answer to it the two men became political enemies. By 1792 Paine was back in Paris helping to draft a constitution for the newly made republic. His views led him into conflict with Robespierre's party and Paine was imprisoned for the greater part of 1794, but was lucky enough to escape being executed. In prison he wrote the first volume of *The Age of Reason*. After Robespierre's fall from power and execution, Paine was released and honored once again by the French government. Barred from returning to England because of his attacks on the British monarchy, he remained active in French–American diplomacy until finally leaving for the United States in 1802. When he died in poverty 7 years later in New York, his many services to America and France had largely been forgotten.

Burke's speech in Parliament attacking the French revolutionaries early in 1790 was followed by his announcement of a forthcoming publication on the subject. Alerted by this announcement, Paine began preparing a reply whose first part he published in February, 1791, with the second part appearing the next year. The passages given here are from Moncure Conway's edition for G. P. Putnam's Sons, 1894, pp. 275–279, 283–286, 306–309, 385–387, 406–409.

SELECTIONS FROM
The Rights of Man

Part I

Among the incivilities by which nations or individuals provoke and irritate each other, Mr. Burke's pamphlet on the French Revolution is an extraordinary instance. Neither the People of France, nor the National Assembly, were troubling themselves about the affairs of England, or the English Parliament; and that Mr. Burke should commence an unprovoked attack upon them, both in Parliament and in public, is a conduct that cannot be pardoned on the score of manners, nor justified on that of policy. . . .

Dr. Price had preached a sermon on the 4th of November, 1789, being the anniversary of what is called in England the Revolution, which took place in 1688. Mr. Burke, speaking of this sermon, says: "The political Divine proceeds dogmatically to assert, that by the principles of the Revolution, the people of England have acquired three fundamental rights.

1. To choose our own governors.
2. To cashier them for misconduct.
3. To frame a government for ourselves."

Dr. Price does not say that the right to do these things exists in this or in that person, or in this or in that description of persons, but that it exists in the *whole*; that it is a right resident in the nation. Mr. Burke, on the contrary, denies that such a right exists in the nation, either in whole or in part, or that it exists anywhere; and, what is still more strange and marvellous, he says: "that the people of England utterly disclaim such a right, and that they will resist the practical assertion of it with their lives and fortunes." That men should take up arms and spend their lives and fortunes, *not* to maintain their rights, but to maintain they have *not* rights, is an entirely new species of discovery, and suited to the paradoxical genius of Mr. Burke.

The method which Mr. Burke takes to prove that the people of England have no such rights, and that such rights do not now exist in the nation, either in whole or in part, or anywhere at all, is of the same marvellous and monstrous kind with what he has already said; for his arguments are that the persons, or the generation of persons, in whom they did exist, are dead, and with them the right is dead also. To prove this, he quotes a declaration made by Parliament about a hundred years ago, to William and Mary, in these words: "The Lords Spiritual and Temporal, and Commons, do, in the name of the people aforesaid" (meaning the people of England then living) "most humbly and faithfully *submit* themselves, their *heirs* and *posterities*, for EVER." He quotes a clause of another Act of Parliament made in the same reign, the terms of which he says, "bind us" (meaning the people of their day), "our *heirs* and our *posterity*, to *them*, their *heirs* and *posterity*, to the end of time."

Mr. Burke conceives his point sufficiently established by producing those clauses, which he enforces by saying that they exclude the right of the nation for *ever*. And not yet content with making such declarations, repeated over and over again, he farther says, "that if the people of England possessed such a right before the Revolution" (which he acknowledges to have been the case, not only in England, but throughout Europe, at an early period), "yet that the *English Nation* did, at the time of the Revolution, most solemnly renounce and abdicate it, for themselves, and for *all their posterity, for ever.*"

As Mr. Burke occasionally applies the poison drawn from his horrid principles, not only to the English nation, but to the French Revolution and the National Assembly, and charges that august, illuminated and illuminating body of men with the epithet of *usurpers*, I shall, *sans cérémonie*, place another system of principles in opposition to his.

The English Parliament of 1688 did a certain thing, which, for themselves and their constituents, they had a right to do, and which it appeared right should be done. But, in addition to this right, which they possessed by delegation, *they set up another right by assumption*, that of binding and controlling posterity to the end of time. The case, therefore, divides itself into two parts; the right which they possessed by delegation, and the right which they set up by assumption. The first is admitted; but with respect to the second, I reply—

There never did, there never will, and there never can, exist a Parliament, or any description of men, or any generation of men, in any country, possessed of the right or the power of binding and controuling posterity to the *"end of time,"* or of commanding for ever how the world shall be governed, or who shall govern it; and therefore all such clauses, acts or declarations by which the makers of them attempt to do what they have neither the right nor the power to do, nor the power to execute, are in themselves null and void. Every age and generation must be as free to act for itself *in all cases* as the age and generations which preceded it. The vanity and presumption of governing beyond the grave is the most ridiculous and insolent of all tyrannies. Man has no property in man; neither has any generation a property in the generations which are to follow. The Parliament or the people of 1688, or of any other period, had no more right to dispose of the people of the present day, or to bind or to control them *in any shape whatever*, than the parliament or the people of the present day have to dispose of, bind or control those who are to live a hundred or a thousand years hence. Every generation is, and must be, competent to all the purposes which its occasions require. It is the living, and not the dead, that are to be accommodated. When man ceases to be, his power and his wants cease with him; and having no longer any participation in the concerns of this world, he has no longer any authority in directing who shall be its governors, or how its government shall be organised, or how administered.

I am not contending for nor against any form of government, nor for nor against any party, here or elsewhere. That which a whole nation chooses to do it has a right to do. Mr. Burke says, No. Where, then, does the right exist? I am contending for the rights of the *living*, and against their being willed away and controuled and contracted for by the manuscript assumed authority of the dead, and Mr. Burke is contending for the authority of the dead over the rights and freedom of the living. There was a time when kings disposed of their crowns by will upon their death-beds, and consigned the people, like beasts of the field, to whatever successor they appointed. This is now so exploded as scarcely to be remembered, and so monstrous as hardly to be believed. But the Parliamentary clauses upon which Mr. Burke builds his political church are of the same nature.

The laws of every country must be analogous to some common principle. In England no parent or master, nor all the authority of Parliament, omnipotent as it has called itself, can bind or control the personal freedom even of an individual beyond the age of twenty-one years. On what ground of right, then, could the Parliament of 1688, or any other Parliament, bind all posterity for ever?

Those who have quitted the world, and those who have not yet arrived at it, are as remote from each other as the utmost stretch of mortal imagination can conceive. What possible obligation, then, can exist between them — what rule or principle can be laid down that of two nonentities, the one out of existence and the other not in, and who never can meet in this world, the one should controul the other to the end of time? . . .

. . . "We have seen," says Mr. Burke, "the French rebel against a mild and lawful monarch, with more fury, outrage, and insult, than any people has been known to rise against the most illegal usurper, or the most sanguinary tyrant." This is one among a thousand other instances, in which Mr. Burke shows that he is ignorant of the springs and principles of the French Revolution.

It was not against Louis XVIth but against the despotic principles of the Government, that the nation revolted. These principles had not their origin in him, but in the original establishment, many centuries back: and they were become too deeply rooted to be removed, and the Augean stables of parasites and plunderers too abominably filthy to be cleansed by anything short of a complete and universal Revolution. When it becomes necessary to do anything, the whole heart and soul should go into the measure, or not attempt it. That crisis was then arrived, and there remained no choice but to act with determined vigor, or not to act at all. The king was known to be the friend of the nation, and this circumstance was favorable to the enterprise. Perhaps no man bred up in the style of an absolute king, ever possessed a heart so little disposed to the exercise of that species of power as the present King of

France. But the principles of the Government itself still remained the same. The Monarch and the Monarchy were distinct and separate things; and it was against the established despotism of the latter, and not against the person or principles of the former, that the revolt commenced, and the Revolution has been carried.

Mr. Burke does not attend to the distinction between men and principles, and, therefore, he does not see that a revolt may take place against the despotism of the latter, while there lies no charge of despotism against the former.

The natural moderation of Louis XVIth contributed nothing to alter the hereditary despotism of the monarchy. All the tyrannies of former reigns, acted under that hereditary despotism, were still liable to be revived in the hands of a successor. It was not the respite of a reign that would satisfy France, enlightened as she was then become. A casual discontinuance of the *practice* of despotism, is not a discontinuance of its *principles*: the former depends on the virtue of the individual who is in immediate possession of the power; the latter, on the virtue and fortitude of the nation. In the case of Charles Ist and James IInd of England, the revolt was against the personal despotism of the men; whereas in France, it was against the hereditary despotism of the established Government. But men who can consign over the rights of posterity for ever on the authority of a mouldy parchment, like Mr. Burke, are not qualified to judge of this Revolution. It takes in a field too vast for their views to explore, and proceeds with a mightiness of reason they cannot keep pace with.

But there are many points of view in which this Revolution may be considered. When despotism has established itself for ages in a country, as in France, it is not in the person of the king only that it resides. It has the appearance of being so in show, and in nominal authority; but it is not so in practice and in fact. It has its standard everywhere. Every office and department has its despotism, founded upon custom and usage. Every place has its Bastille, and every Bastille its despot. The original hereditary despotism resident in the person of the king, divides and sub-divides itself into a thousand shapes and forms, till at last the whole of it is acted by deputation. This was the case in France; and against this species of despotism, proceeding on through an endless labyrinth of office till the source of it is scarcely perceptible, there is no mode of redress. It strengthens itself by assuming the appearance of duty, and tyrannises under the pretence of obeying.

When a man reflects on the condition which France was in from the nature of her government, he will see other causes for revolt than those which immediately connect themselves with the person or character of Louis XVI. There were, if I may so express it, a thousand despotisms to be reformed in France, which had grown up under the hereditary despotism of the monarchy, and became so rooted as to be in a great measure independent of it. Between the Monarchy, the Parliament, and the Church there was a *rivalship* of despotism; besides the feudal despotism operating locally, and the ministerial despotism operating everywhere. But Mr. Burke, by considering the king as the only possible object of a revolt, speaks as if France was a village, in which everything that passed must be known to its commanding officer, and no oppression could be acted but what he could immediately controul. Mr. Burke might have been in the Bastille his whole life, as well under Louis XVI as Louis XIV., and neither the one nor the other have known that such a man as Burke existed. The despotic principles of the government were the same in both reigns, though the dispositions of the men were as remote as tyranny and benevolence.

What Mr. Burke considers as a reproach to the French Revolution (that of bringing it forward under a reign more mild than the preceding ones) is one of its highest honors. The Revolutions that have taken place in other European countries, have been excited by personal hatred. The rage was against the man, and he became the victim. But, in the instance of France we see a Revolution generated in the rational contemplation of the Rights of Man, and distinguishing from the beginning between persons and principles.

But Mr. Burke appears to have no idea of principles when he is contemplating Governments. "Ten years ago," says he, "I could have felicitated France on her having a Government, without inquiring what the nature of that Government was, or how it was administered." Is this the language of a rational man? Is it the language of a heart feeling as it ought to feel for the rights and happiness of the human race? On this ground, Mr. Burke must compliment all the Governments in the world, while the victims who suffer under them, whether sold into slavery, or tortured out of existence, are wholly forgotten. It is power, and not principles, that Mr. Burke venerates; and under this abominable depravity he is disqualified to judge between them. . . .

. . . Hitherto we have spoken only (and that but in part) of the natural rights of man. We have now to consider the civil rights of man, and to show how the one originates from the other. Man did not enter into society to become *worse* than he was before, not to have fewer rights than he had before, but to have those rights better secured. His natural rights are the foundation of all his civil rights. But in order to pursue this distinction with more precision, it will be necessary to mark the different qualities of natural and civil rights.

A few words will explain this. Natural rights are those which appertain to man in right of his existence. Of this kind are all the intellectual rights, or rights of the mind, and also all those rights of acting as an individual for his own comfort and happiness, which are not injurious to the natural rights of others. Civil rights are those which appertain to man in right of his being a member of society. Every civil right has for its foundation some natural right pre-existing in the individual, but to the enjoyment of which his individual power is not, in all cases, sufficiently competent. Of this kind are all those which relate to security and protection.

From this short review it will be easy to distinguish between that class of natural rights which man retains after entering into society and those which he throws into the common stock as a member of society.

The natural rights which he retains are all those in which the *power* to execute is as perfect in the individual as the right itself. Among this class, as is before mentioned, are all the intellectual rights, or rights of the mind; consequently religion is one of those rights. The natural rights which are not retained, are all those in which, though the right is perfect in the individual, the power to execute them is defective. They answer not his purpose. A man, by natural right, has a right to judge in his own cause; and so far as the right of the mind is concerned, he never surrenders it. But what availeth it him to judge, if he has not power to redress? He therefore deposits this right in the common stock of society, and takes the arm of society, of which he is a part, in preference and in addition to his own. Society *grants* him nothing. Every man is a proprietor in society, and draws on the capital as a matter of right.

From these premisses two or three certain conclusions will follow:

First, That every civil right grows out of a natural right; or, in other words, is a natural right exchanged.

Secondly, That civil power properly considered as such is made up of the aggregate of that class of the natural rights of man, which becomes defective in the individual in point of power, and answers not his purpose, but when collected to a focus becomes competent to the purpose of every one.

Thirdly, That the power produced from the aggregate of natural rights, imperfect in power in the individual, cannot be applied to invade the natural rights which are retained in the individual, and in which the power to execute is as perfect as the right itself.

We have now, in a few words, traced man from a natural individual to a member of society, and shewn, or endeavoured to shew, the quality of the natural rights retained, and of those which are exchanged for civil rights. Let us now apply these principles to governments.

In casting our eyes over the world, it is extremely easy to distinguish the governments which have arisen out of society, or out of the social compact, from those which have not; but to place this in a clearer light than what a single glance may afford, it will be proper to take a review of the several sources from which governments have arisen and on which they have been founded.

They may be all comprehended under three heads. First, Superstition. Secondly, Power. Thirdly, the common interest of society and the common rights of man.

The first was a government of priestcraft, the second of conquerors, and the third of reason.

When a set of artful men pretended, through the medium of oracles, to hold intercourse with the Deity, as familiarly as they now march up the back-stairs in European courts, the world was completely under the government of superstition. The oracles were consulted, and whatever they were made to say became the law; and this sort of government lasted as long as this sort of superstition lasted.

After these a race of conquerors arose, whose government, like that of William the Conqueror, was founded in power, and the sword assumed the name of a sceptre. Governments thus established last as long as the power to support them lasts; but that they might avail themselves of every engine in their favor, they united fraud to force, and set up an idol which they called *Divine Right*, and which, in imitation of the Pope, who affects to be spiritual and temporal, and in contradiction to the Founder of the Christian religion, twisted itself afterwards into an idol of another shape, called *Church and State*. The key of St. Peter and the key of the Treasury became quartered on one another, and the wondering cheated multitude worshipped the invention.

When I contemplate the natural dignity of man, when I feel (for Nature has not been kind enough to me to blunt my feelings) for the honour and happiness of its character, I become irritated at the attempt to govern mankind by force and fraud, as if they were all knaves and fools, and can scarcely avoid disgust at those who are thus imposed upon.

We have now to review the governments which arise out of society, in contradistinction to those which arose out of superstition and conquest.

It has been thought a considerable advance towards establishing the principles of Freedom to say that Government is a compact between those who govern and those who are governed; but this cannot be true, because it is putting the effect before the cause; for as man must have existed before governments existed, there necessarily was a time when governments did not exist, and consequently there could originally exist no governors to form such a compact with.

The fact therefore must be that the *individuals themselves*, each in his own personal and sovereign right, *entered into a compact with each other* to produce a government: and this is the only mode in which governments have a right to arise, and the only principle on which they have a right to exist. . . .

. . . When we survey the wretched condition of man, under the monarchical and hereditary systems of Government, dragged from his home by one power, or driven by another, and impoverished by taxes more than by enemies, it becomes evident that those systems are bad, and that a general revolution in the principle and construction of Governments is necessary.

What is government more than the management of the affairs of a Nation? It is not, and from its nature cannot be, the property of any particular man or family, but of the whole community, at whose expence it is supported; and though by force and contrivance it has been usurped into an inheritance, the usurpation cannot alter the right of things. Sovereignty, as a matter of right, appertains to the Nation only, and not to any individual; and a Nation has at all times an inherent indefeasible right to abolish any form of Government it finds inconvenient, and to establish such as accords with its interest, disposition and happiness. The romantic and barbarous distinction of men into Kings and subjects, though it may suit the condition of courtiers, cannot that of citizens; and is exploded by the principle upon which Governments are now founded. Every citizen is a member of the Sovereignty, and, as such, can acknowledge no personal subjection; and his obedience can be only to the laws. . . .

. . . What were formerly called Revolutions, were little more than a change of persons, or an alteration of local circumstances. They rose and fell like things of course, and had nothing in their existence or their fate that could influence beyond the spot that produced them. But what we now see in the world, from the Revolutions of America and France, are a renovation of the natural order of things, a system of principles as universal as truth and the existence of man, and combining moral with political happiness and national prosperity.

"I. *Men are born, and always continue, free and equal in respect of their rights. Civil distinctions, therefore, can be founded only on public utility.*

"II. *The end of all political associations is the preservation of the natural and imprescriptible rights of man; and these rights are liberty, property, security, and resistance of oppression.*

"III. *The nation is essentially the source of all sovereignty; nor can any* INDIVIDUAL, *or* ANY BODY OF MEN, *be entitled to any authority which is not expressly derived from it.*"

In these principles, there is nothing to throw a Nation into confusion by inflaming ambition. They are calculated to call forth wisdom and abilities, and to exercise them for the public good, and not for the emolument or aggrandisement of particular descriptions of men or families. Monarchical sovereignty, the enemy of mankind, and the source of misery, is abolished; and the sovereignty itself is restored to its natural and original place, the Nation. Were this the case throughout Europe, the cause of wars would be taken away. . . .

Part II
Chapter I.
Of Society and Civilisation

. . . To understand the nature and quantity of government proper for man, it is necessary to attend to his character. As Nature created him for social life, she fitted him for the station she intended. In all cases she made his natural wants greater than his individual powers. No one man is capable, without the aid of society, of supplying his own wants; and those wants, acting upon every individual, impel the whole of them into society, as naturally as gravitation acts to a centre.

But she has gone further. She has not only forced man into society by a diversity of wants which the reciprocal aid of each other can supply, but she has implanted in him a system of social affections, which, though not necessary to his existence, are essential to his happiness. There is no period in life when this love for society ceases to act. It begins and ends with our being.

If we examine with attention into the composition and constitution of man, the diversity of his wants, and the diversity of talents in different men for reciprocally accommodating the wants of each other, his propensity to society, and consequently to preserve the advantages resulting from it, we shall easily discover, that a great part of what is called government is mere imposition.

Government is no farther necessary than to supply the few cases to which society and civilisation are not conveniently competent; and instances are not wanting to show, that everything which government can usefully add thereto, has been performed by the common consent of society, without government.

For upwards of two years from the commencement of the American War, and to a longer period in several of the American States, there were no established forms of government. The old governments had been abolished, and the country was too much occupied in defence to employ its attention in establishing new governments; yet during this interval order and harmony were preserved as inviolate as in any country in Europe. There is a natural aptness in man, and more so in society, because it embraces a greater variety of abilities and resource, to accommodate itself to whatever situation it is in. The instant formal government is abolished, society begins to act: a general association takes place, and common interest produces common security.

So far is it from being true, as has been pretended, that the abolition of any formal government is the dissolution of society, that it acts by a contrary impulse, and brings the latter the closer together. All that part of its organisation which it had committed to its government, devolves again upon itself, and acts through its medium. When men, as well from natural instinct as from reciprocal benefits, have habituated themselves to social and civilised life, there is always enough of its principles in practice to carry them through any changes they may find necessary or convenient to make in their government. In short, man is so naturally a creature of society that it is almost impossible to put him out of it.

Formal government makes but a small part of civilised life; and when even the best that human wisdom can devise is established, it is a thing more in name and idea than in fact. It is to the great and fundamental principles of society and civilisation — to the common usage universally consented to, and mutually and reciprocally maintained — to the unceasing circulation of interest, which, passing through its million channels, invigorates the whole mass of civilised man — it is to these things, infinitely more than to anything which even the best instituted government can perform, that the safety and prosperity of the individual and of the whole depends. . . .

. . . If we look back to the riots and tumults which at various times have happened in England, we shall find that they did not proceed from the want of a government, but that government was itself the generating cause; instead of consolidating society it divided it; it deprived it of its natural cohesion, and engendered discontents and disorders which otherwise would not have existed. In those associations which men promiscuously form for the purpose of trade, or of any concern in which government is totally out of the question, and in which they act merely on the principles of society, we see how naturally the various parties unite; and this shews, by comparison, that governments, so far from being always the cause or means of order, are often the destruction of it. . . .

Georg W. F. Hegel

1 7 7 0 - 1 8 3 1

INTRODUCTION

Known during most of his lifetime as the very model of a purely academic philosopher, Hegel, by the last decade of his life, was to exert considerable influence on the educated public of Germany, although he never sought to do so. He was born in Stuttgart, the oldest son of a Protestant revenue officer employed by the Duke of Württemberg. His mother must have been educated, for he learned elementary Latin from her before he entered the Stuttgart grammar school. He left there in 1788 at the age of 18, with a good classical education, and enrolled in the theological seminary at Tübingen, remaining there for 5 years. He obtained a degree in philosophy with a dissertation entitled "On the Limits of Human Duties, Assuming That the Soul Is Immortal," was qualified for clerical orders, but did not otherwise make his mark. During the next 7 years he acted as private tutor in Berne and Frankfurt, using his ample free time to read the Greek and Roman classics, and other authors such as Gibbon, Montesquieu, and Kant. During this period he became preoccupied with two of his enduring interests — the origins of Christianity and the pattern of history. Hegel tried to relate these to each other and then to use the results as a means of criticizing Kant's views on the limits of human knowledge.

In 1801 Hegel became a lecturer in logic and metaphysics at the University in Jena, and for the next 4 years worked on a philosophical system that although not especially attractive to most of his students, won him a professorship. He lost this when Napoleon invaded Jena. He became a newspaper editor for a year, and then for the following 8 years Rector of the high school at Nürnberg. In 1807 Hegel published his first important work, *The Phenomenology of Mind*. His second major volume, *The Science of Logic* (part one, 1807; part two, 1816), helped to earn him a professorship at Heidelberg, a position he occupied for only a year before accepting the chair of philosophy in Berlin. There he published the *Philosophy of Right (or Law)* in 1821, devoted himself to his young wife and three sons, and through his many students became well known for his lectures on religion, history, and aesthetics. These lectures were published from student notes after his sudden death in the cholera epidemic that was sweeping across western Europe in 1831. He died having been Rector of the university, decorated by the king, a close friend of the minister of education, and through him an important influence in the development of higher education in Prussia.

Lectures on the Philosophy of History was first edited and published in 1837, 6 years after Hegel's death, and first published in English translation 20 years later by J. Sibree. The present text is taken from one of the several reprints of that translation.

SELECTIONS FROM
Lectures on the Philosophy of History

Introduction

The subject of this course of Lectures is the Philosophical History of the World. And by this must be understood, not a collection of general observations respecting it, suggested by the study of its records, and proposed to be illustrated by its facts, but Universal History itself. To gain a clear idea, at the outset, of the nature of our task, it seems necessary to begin with an examination of the other methods of treating History. The various methods may be ranged under three heads:

I. Original History.
II. Reflective History.
III. Philosophical History.

I. Of the first kind, the mention of one or two distinguished names will furnish a definite type. To this category belong *Herodotus, Thucydides,* and other historians of the same order, whose descriptions are for the most part limited to deeds, events, and states of society, which they had before their eyes, and whose spirit they shared. They simply transferred what was passing in the world around them, to the realm of re-presentative intellect. An external phenomenon is thus translated into an internal conception. In the same way the *poet* operates upon the material supplied him by his emotions; projecting it into an image for the conceptive faculty. These original historians did, it is true, find statements and narratives of other men ready to hand. One person cannot be an eye or ear witness of everything. But they make use of such aids only as the poet does of that heritage of an already-formed language, to which he owes so much; merely as an ingredient. Historiographers bind together the fleeting elements of story, and treasure them up for immortality in the Temple of Mnemosyne. Legends, Ballad-stories, Traditions, must be excluded from such original history. These are but dim and hazy forms of historical apprehension, and therefore belong to nations whose intelligence is but half awakened. Here, on the contrary, we have to do with people fully conscious of what they were and what they were about. The domain of reality — actually seen, or capable of being so — affords a very different basis in point of firmness from that fugitive and shadowy element, in which were engendered those legends and poetic dreams whose historical prestige vanishes, as soon as nations have attained a mature individuality.

Such original historians, then, change the events, the deeds, and the states of society with which they are conversant, into an object for the conceptive faculty. The narratives they leave us cannot, therefore, be very comprehensive in their range. Herodotus, Thucydides, Guicciardini, may be taken as fair samples of the class in this respect. What is present and living in their environment is their proper material. The influences that have formed the writer are identical with those which have moulded the events that constitute the matter of his story. The author's spirit, and that of the actions he narrates, is one and the same. He describes scenes in which he himself has been an actor, or at any rate an interested spectator. It is short periods of time, individual shapes of persons and occurrences, single, unreflected traits, of which he makes his picture. And his aim is nothing more than the presentation to posterity of an image of events as clear as that which he himself possessed in virtue of personal observation, or life-like descriptions. Reflections are none of his business, for he lives in the spirit of his subject; he has not attained an elevation above it. If, as in Cæsar's case, he belongs to the exalted rank of generals or statesmen, it is the prosecution of *his own aims* that constitutes the history.

Such speeches as we find in Thucydides (for example) of which we can positively assert that they are not *bonâ fide* reports, would seem to make against our statement that a historian of his class presents us no reflected picture; that persons and people appear in his works in *propriâ personâ*. Speeches, it must be allowed, are veritable transactions in the human commonwealth; in fact, very gravely influential transactions. It is, indeed, often said, "Such and such things are only talk;" by way of demonstrating their harmlessness. That for which this excuse is brought may be mere "talk"; and talk enjoys the important privilege of being harmless. But addresses of peoples to peoples, or orations directed to nations and to princes, are integrant constituents of history. Granted that such orations as those of Pericles — that most profoundly accomplished, genuine, noble statesman — were elaborated by Thucydides, it must yet be maintained that they were not foreign to the character of the speaker. In the orations in question, these men proclaim the maxims adopted by their countrymen, and which formed their own character; they record their views of their political relations, and of their moral and spiritual nature; and the principles of their designs and conduct. What the historian puts into their mouths is no supposititious system of ideas, but an uncorrupted transcript of their intellectual and moral habitudes.

Of these historians, whom we must make thoroughly our own, with whom we must linger long, if we would live with their respective nations, and enter deeply into their spirit: of these historians, to whose pages we may turn not for the purposes of erudition merely, but with a view to deep and genuine enjoyment, there are fewer than might be imagined. Herodotus the *Father*, i.e., the *Founder* of History, and Thucydides have been already mentioned. Xenophon's *Retreat of the Ten Thousand*, is a work equally original. Cæsar's *Commentaries* are the simple masterpiece of a mighty spirit. Among the ancients, these annalists were necessarily great captains and statesmen. In the Middle Ages, if we except the Bishops, who were placed in the very centre of the political world, the Monks monopolize this category as näive chroniclers who were as decidedly *isolated* from active life as those elder annalists had been connected with it. In modern times the relations are entirely altered. Our culture is essentially comprehensive, and immediately changes all events into historical representations. Belonging to the class in question, we have vivid, simple, clear narrations — especially of military transactions — which might fairly take their place with those of Cæsar. In richness of matter and fulness of detail as regards strategic appliances, and attendant circumstances, they are even more instructive. The French "Memoires," also, fall under this category. In many cases these are written by men of mark, though relating to affairs of little note. They not unfrequently contain a large proportion of anecdotal matter, so that the ground they occupy is narrow and trivial. Yet they are often veritable masterpieces in history; as those of Cardinal Retz, which in fact trench on a larger historical field. In Germany such masters are rare. Frederick the Great ("Histoire de Mon Temps") is an illustrious exception. Writers of this order must occupy an elevated position. Only from such a position is it possible to take an extensive view of affairs — to see everything. This is out of the question for him, who from below merely gets a glimpse of the great world through a miserable cranny.

II. The second kind of history we may call the *reflective*. It is history whose mode of representation is not really confined by the limits of the time to which it relates, but whose spirit transcends the present. In this second order a strongly marked variety of species may be distinguished.

1. It is the aim of the investigator to gain a view of the entire history of a people or a country, or of the world, in short, what we call *Universal History*. In this case the working up of the historical material is the main point. The workman approaches his task with *his own* spirit; a spirit distinct from that of the element he is to manipulate. Here a very important consideration will be the principles to which the author refers the bearing and motives of the actions and events which he describes, and those which determine the form of his narrative. Among us Germans this reflective treatment and the display of ingenuity which it occasions assume a manifold variety of phases. Every writer of history proposes to himself an original method. The English and French confess to general principles of historical composition. Their standpoint is more that of cosmopolitan or of national culture. Among us each labors to invent a purely individual point of view. Instead of writing history, we are always beating our brains to discover how history ought to be written. This first kind of Reflective History is most nearly akin to the preceding, when it has no farther aim than to present the annals of a country complete. Such compilations (among which may be reckoned the works of Livy, Diodorus Siculus, Johannes von Müller's History of Switzerland) are, if well performed, highly meritorious. Among the best of the kind may be reckoned such annalists as approach those of the first class; who give so vivid a transcript of events that the reader may well fancy himself listening to contemporaries and eye-witnesses. But it often happens that the individuality of tone which must characterize a writer belonging to a different culture, is not modified in

accordance with the periods such a record must traverse. The spirit of the writer is quite other than that of the times of which he treats. Thus Livy puts into the mouths of the old Roman kings, consuls, and generals, such orations as would be delivered by an accomplished advocate of the Livian era, and which strikingly contrast with the genuine traditions of Roman antiquity (*e.g.* the fable of Menenius Agrippa). In the same way he gives us descriptions of battles, as if he had been an actual spectator; but whose features would serve well enough for battles in any period, and whose distinctness contrasts on the other hand with the want of connection and the inconsistency that prevail elsewhere, even in his treatment of chief points of interest. The difference between such a compiler and an original historian may be best seen by comparing Polybius himself with the style in which Livy uses, expands, and abridges his annals in those periods of which Polybius's account has been preserved. Johannes von Müller has given a stiff, formal, pedantic aspect to his history, in the endeavor to remain faithful in his portraiture to the times he describes. We much prefer the narratives we find in old Tschudy. All is more naïve and natural than it appears in the garb of a fictitious and affected archaism.

A history which aspires to traverse long periods of time, or to be universal, must indeed forego the attempt to give individual representations of the past as it actually existed. It must foreshorten its pictures by abstractions; and this includes not merely the omission of events and deeds, but whatever is involved in the fact that Thought is, after all, the most trenchant epitomist. A battle, a great victory, a siege, no longer maintains its original proportions, but is put off with a bare mention. When Livy *e.g.* tell us of the wars with the Volsci, we sometimes have the brief announcement: "This year war was carried on with the Volsci."

2. A second species of Reflective History is what we may call the *Pragmatical.* When we have to deal with the Past, and occupy ourselves with a remote world, a Present rises into being for the mind — produced by its own activity, as the reward of its labor. The occurrences are, indeed, various; but the idea which pervades them — their deeper import and connection — is *one*. This takes the occurrence out of the category of the Past and makes it virtually Present. Pragmatical (didactic) reflections, though in their nature decidedly abstract, are truly and indefeasibly of the Present, and quicken the annals of the dead Past with the life of to-day. Whether, indeed, such reflections are truly interesting and enlivening, depends on the writer's own spirit. Moral reflections must here be specially noticed — the moral teaching expected from history; which latter has not infrequently been treated with a direct view to the former. It may be allowed that examples of virtue elevate the soul, and are applicable in the moral instruction of children for impressing excellence upon their minds. But the destinies of peoples and states, their interests, relations, and the complicated tissue of their affairs, present quite another field. Rulers, Statesmen, Nations, are wont to be emphatically commended to the teaching which experience offers in history. But what experi-

ence and history teach is this—that peoples and governments never have learned anything from history, or acted on principles deduced from it. Each period is involved in such peculiar circumstances, exhibits a condition of things so strictly idiosyncratic, that its conduct must be regulated by considerations connected with itself, and itself alone. Amid the pressure of great events, a general principle gives no help. It is useless to revert to similar circumstances in the Past. The pallid shades of memory struggle in vain with the life and freedom of the Present. Looked at in this light, nothing can be shallower than the oft-repeated appeal to Greek and Roman examples during the French Revolution. Nothing is more diverse than the genius of those nations and that of our times. Johannes v. Müller, in his "Universal History" as also in his "History of Switzerland," had such moral aims in view. He designed to prepare a body of political doctrines for the instruction of princes, governments, and peoples (he formed a special collection of doctrines and reflections—frequently giving us in his correspondence the exact number of apophthegms which he had compiled in a week); but he cannot reckon this part of his labor as among the best that he accomplished. It is only a thorough, liberal, comprehensive view of historical relations (such *e.g.* as we find in Montesquieu's "Esprit des Loix"), that can give truth and interest to reflections of this order. One Reflective History, therefore, supersedes another. The materials are patent to every writer: each is likely enough to believe himself capable of arranging and manipulating them; and we may expect that each will insist upon his own spirit as that of the age in question. Disgusted by such reflective histories, readers have often returned with pleasure to a narrative adopting no particular point of view. These certainly have their value; but for the most part they offer only material for history. We Germans are content with such. The French, on the other hand, display great genius in reanimating bygone times, and in bringing the past to bear upon the present condition of things.

3. The third form of Reflective History is the *Critical*. This deserves mention as pre-eminently the mode of treating history, now current in Germany. It is not history itself that is here presented. We might more properly designate it as a History of History; a criticism of historical narratives and an investigation of their truth and credibility. Its peculiarity in point of fact and of intention, consists in the acuteness with which the writer extorts something from the records which was not in the matters recorded. The French have given us much that is profound and judicious in this class of composition. But they have not endeavored to pass a merely critical procedure for substantial history. They have duly presented their judgments in the form of critical treatises. Among us, the so-called "higher criticism," which reigns supreme in the domain of philology, has also taken possession of our historical literature. This "higher criticism" has been the pretext for introducing all the anti-historical monstrosities that a vain imagination could suggest. Here we have the other method of making the past a living reality; putting subjective fancies in the place of historical data; fancies whose merit is measured by their bold-

ness, that is, the scantiness of the particulars on which they are based, and the peremptoriness with which they contravene the best established facts of history.

4. The last species of Reflective History announces its fragmentary character on the very face of it. It adopts an abstract position; yet, since it takes general points of view (*e.g.* as the History of Art, of Law, of Religion), it forms a transition to the Philosophical History of the World. In our time this form of the history of ideas has been more developed and brought into notice. Such branches of national life stand in close relation to the entire complex of a people's annals; and the question of chief importance in relation to our subject is, whether the connection of the whole is exhibited in its truth and reality, or referred to merely external relations. In the latter case, these important phenomena (Art, Law, Religion, etc.) appear as purely accidental national peculiarities. It must be remarked that, when Reflective History has advanced to the adoption of general points of view, if the position taken is a true one, these are found to constitute — not a merely external thread, a superficial series — but are the inward guiding soul of the occurrences and actions that occupy a nation's annals. For, like the soul-conductor Mercury, the Idea is in truth, the leader of peoples and of the World; and Spirit, the rational and necessitated will of that conductor, is and has been the director of the events of the World's History. To become acquainted with Spirit in this its office of guidance, is the object of our present undertaking. This brings us to

III. The third kind of history — the *Philosophical.* No explanation was needed of the two previous classes; their nature was self-evident. It is otherwise with this last, which certainly seems to require an exposition or justification. The most general definition that can be given, is, that the Philosophy of History means nothing but the *thoughtful consideration of it.* Thought is, indeed, essential to humanity. It is this that distinguishes us from the brutes. In sensation, cognition, and intellection; in our instincts and volitions, as far as they are truly human, Thought is an invariable element. To insist upon Thought in this connection with history may, however, appear unsatisfactory. In this science it would seem as if Thought must be subordinate to what is given, to the realities of fact; that this is its basis and guide: while Philosophy dwells in the region of self-produced ideas, without reference to actuality. Approaching history thus prepossessed, Speculation might be expected to treat it as a mere passive material; and, so far from leaving it in its native truth, to force it into conformity with a tyrannous idea, and to construe it, as the phrase is, "*à priori.*" But as it is the business of history simply to adopt into its records what is and has been, actual occurrences and transactions; and since it remains true to its character in proportion as it strictly adheres to its data, we seem to have in Philosophy, a process diametrically opposed to that of the historiographer. This contradiction, and the charge consequently brought against speculation, shall be explained and confuted. We do not, however, propose to correct the innumerable special misrepresentations, trite or novel, that are current respecting the aims, the interests, and the modes of treating history, and its relation to Philosophy.

The only Thought which Philosophy brings with it to the contemplation of History, is the simple conception of *Reason*; that Reason is the Sovereign of the World; that the history of the world, therefore, presents us with a rational process. This conviction and intuition is a hypothesis in the domain of history as such. In that of Philosophy it is no hypothesis. It is there proved by speculative cognition, that Reason — and this term may here suffice us, without investigating the relation sustained by the Universe to the Divine Being — is *Substance*, as well as *Infinite Power*, its own *Infinite Material* underlying all the natural and spiritual life which it originates, as also the *Infinite Form* — that which sets this Material in motion. On the one hand, Reason is the *substance* of the Universe; viz., that by which and in which all reality has its being and subsistence. On the other hand, it is the *Infinite Energy* of the Universe; since Reason is not so powerless as to be incapable of producing anything but a mere ideal, a mere intention — having its place outside reality, nobody knows where; something separate and abstract, in the heads of certain human beings. It is *the infinite complex of things*, their entire Essence and Truth. It is its own material which it commits to its own Active Energy to work up; not needing, as finite action does, the conditions of an external material of given means from which it may obtain its support, and the objects of its activity. It supplies its own nourishment, and is the object of its own operations. While it is exclusively its own basis of existence, and absolute final aim, it is also the energizing power realizing this aim; developing it not only in the phenomena of the Natural, but also of the Spiritual Universe — the History of the World. That this "Idea" or "Reason" is the *True*, the *Eternal*, the absolutely *powerful* essence; that it reveals itself in the World, and that in that World nothing else is revealed but this and its honor and glory — is the thesis which, as we have said, has been proved in Philosophy, and is here regarded as demonstrated.

In those of my hearers who are not acquainted with Philosophy, I may fairly presume, at least, the existence of a *belief* in Reason, a desire, a thirst for acquaintance with it, in entering upon this course of Lectures. It is, in fact, the wish for rational insight, not the ambition to amass a mere heap of acquirements, that should be presupposed in every case as possessing the mind of the learner in the study of science. If the clear idea of Reason is not already developed in our minds, in beginning the study of Universal History, we should at least have the firm, unconquerable faith that Reason *does* exist there; and that the World of intelligence and conscious volition is not abandoned to chance, but must show itself in the light of the self-cognizant Idea. Yet I am not obliged to make any such preliminary demand upon your faith. What I have said thus provisionally, and what I shall have further to say, is, even in reference to *our* branch of science, not to be regarded as hypothetical, but as a summary view of the whole; the *result of the investigation* we are about to pursue; a result which happens to be known to *me*, because I have traversed the entire field. It is only an inference from the history of the World, that its development has been a rational process; that the history in question has constituted the rational necessary course of the World-Spirit — that Spirit whose nature is always one and the same, but which unfolds this its one nature in the phenomena of the World's existence. This must, as before stated, present itself as the ultimate *result* of History. But we have to take the latter as it is. We must proceed historically — empirically. Among other precautions we must take care not to be misled by professed historians who (especially among the Germans, and enjoying a considerable authority), are chargeable with the very procedure of which they accuse the Philosopher — introducing *à priori* inventions of their own into the records of the Past. It is, for example, a widely current fiction, that there was an original primeval people, taught immediately by God, endowed with perfect insight and wisdom, possessing a thorough knowledge of all natural laws and spiritual truth; that there have been such or such sacerdotal peoples; or, to mention a more specific averment, that there was a Roman Epos, from which the Roman historians derived the early annals of their city, etc. Authorities of this kind we leave to those talented historians by profession, among whom (in Germany at least) their use is not uncommon. — We might then announce it as the first condition to be observed, that we should faithfully adopt all that is historical. But in such general expressions themselves, as "faithfully" and "adopt," lies the ambiguity. Even the ordinary, the "impartial" historiographer, who believes and professes that he maintains a simply receptive attitude; surrendering himself only to the data supplied him — is by no means passive as regards the exercise of his thinking powers. He brings his categories with him, and sees the phenomena presented to his mental vision, exclusively through these media. And, especially in all that pretends to the name of science, it is indispensable that Reason should not sleep — that reflection should be in full play. To him who looks upon the world rationally, the world in its turn presents a rational aspect. The relation is mutual. But the various exercises of reflection — the different points of view — the modes of deciding the simple question of the relative importance of events (the first category that occupies the attention of the historian), do not belong to this place.

I will only mention two phases and points of view that concern the generally diffused conviction that Reason has ruled, and is still ruling in the world, and consequently in the world's history; because they give us, at the same time, an opportunity for more closely investigating the question that presents the greatest difficulty, and for indicating a branch of the subject, which will have to be enlarged on in the sequel.

I. One of these points is, that passage in history, which informs us that the Greek Anaxagoras was the first to enunciate the doctrine that νοῦς, Understanding generally, or Reason, governs the world. It is not intelligence as self-conscious Reason — not a Spirit as such that is meant; and we must clearly distinguish these from each other. The movement of the solar system takes place according to unchangeable laws. These laws are Reason, implicit in the phenomena in question. But neither the sun nor the planets, which revolve around it according to these laws, can be said to have any consciousness of them.

A thought of this kind — that Nature is an embodiment of Reason; that it is unchangeably subordinate to universal laws, appears nowise striking or strange to us. We are accustomed to such conceptions, and find nothing extraordinary in them. And I have mentioned this extraordinary occurrence, partly to show how history teaches, that ideas of this kind, which may seem trivial to us, have not always been in the world; that, on the contrary, such a thought makes an epoch in the annals of human intelligence. Aristotle says of Anaxagoras, as the originator of the thought in question, that he appeared as a sober man among the drunken. Socrates adopted the doctrine from Anaxagoras, and it forthwith became the ruling idea in Philosophy — except in the school of Epicurus, who ascribed all events to chance. "I was delighted with the sentiment" — Plato makes Socrates say — "and hoped I had found a teacher who would show me Nature in harmony with Reason, who would demonstrate in each particular phenomenon its specific aim, and in the whole, the grand object of the Universe. I would not have surrendered this hope for a great deal. But how very much was I disappointed, when, having zealously applied myself to the writings of Anaxagoras, I found that he adduces only external causes, such as Atmosphere, Ether, Water, and the like." It is evident that the defect which Socrates complains of respecting Anaxagoras's doctrine, does not concern the principle itself, but the shortcoming of the propounder in applying it to Nature in the concrete. Nature is not deduced from that principle: the latter remains in fact a mere abstraction, inasmuch as the former is not comprehended and exhibited as a development of it — an organization produced by and from Reason. I wish, at the very outset, to call your attention to the important difference between a conception, a principle, a truth limited to an *abstract* form and its determinate application, and concrete development. This distinction affects the whole fabric of philosophy; and among other bearings of it there is one to which we shall have to revert at the close of our view of Universal History, in investigating the aspect of political affairs in the most recent period.

We have next to notice the rise of this idea — that Reason directs the World — in connection with a further application of it, well known to us — in the form, viz., of the *religious truth*, that the world is not abandoned to chance and external contingent causes, but that a *Providence* controls it. I stated above, that I would not make a demand on your faith, in regard to the principle announced. Yet I might appeal to your belief in it, *in this religious aspect*, if, as a general rule, the nature of philosophical science allowed it to attach authority to presuppositions. To put it in another shape — this appeal is forbidden, because the science of which we have to treat, proposes itself to furnish the proof (not indeed of the abstract *Truth* of the doctrine, but) of its correctness as compared with facts. The truth, then, that a Providence (that of God) presides over the events of the World — consorts with the proposition in question; for *Divine* Providence is Wisdom, endowed with an infinite Power, which realizes its aim, viz., the absolute rational design of the World. Reason is Thought conditioning itself with perfect freedom. But a difference — rather a contradiction — will manifest itself, between this belief and our principle, just as was the case in reference to the demand made by Socrates in the case of Anaxagoras's dictum. For that belief is similarly indefinite; it is what is called a belief in a general Providence, and is not followed out into definite application, or displayed in its bearing on the grand total — the entire course of human history. But to *explain* History is to depict the passions of mankind, the genius, the active powers, that play their part on the great stage; and the providentially determined process which these exhibit, constitutes what is generally called the "plan" of Providence. Yet it is this very plan which is supposed to be concealed from our view: which it is deemed presumption, even to wish to recognize. The ignorance of Anaxagoras, as to how intelligence reveals itself in actual existence, was ingenuous. Neither in his consciousness, nor in that of Greece at large, had that thought been farther expanded. He had not attained the power to apply his general principle to the concrete, so as to deduce the latter from the former. It was Socrates who took the first step in comprehending the union of the Concrete with the Universal. Anaxagoras, then, did not take up a *hostile* position toward such an application. The common belief in Providence *does*; at least it opposes the use of the principle on the large scale, and denies the possibility of discerning the plan of Providence. In isolated cases this plan is supposed to be manifest. Pious persons are encouraged to recognize in particular circumstances, something more than mere chance; to acknowledge the guiding hand of God; *e.g.*, when help has unexpectedly come to an individual in great perplexity and need. But these instances of providential design are of a limited kind, and concern the accomplishment of nothing more than the desires of the individual in question. But in the history of the World, the *Individuals* we have to do with are *Peoples;* Totalities that are States. We cannot, therefore, be satisfied with what we may call this "peddling" view of Providence, to which the belief alluded to limits itself. Equally unsatisfactory is the merely abstract, undefined belief in a Providence, when that belief is not brought to bear upon the details of the process which it conducts. On the contrary our earnest endeavor must be directed to the recognition of the ways of Providence, the means it uses, and the historical phenomena in which it manifests itself; and we must show their connection with the general principle above mentioned. But in noticing the recognition of the plan of Divine Providence generally, I have implicitly touched upon a prominent question of the day; viz., that of the possibility of knowing God: or rather — since public opinion has ceased to allow it to be a matter of *question* — the *doctrine* that it is impossible to know God. In direct contravention of what is commanded in holy Scripture as the highest duty — that we should not merely love, but *know* God — the prevalent dogma involves the denial of what is there said; viz., that it is the Spirit (der Geist) that leads into Truth, knows all things, penetrates even into the deep things of the

Godhead. While the Divine Being is thus placed beyond our knowledge, and outside the limit of all human things, we have the convenient license of wandering as far as we list, in the direction of our own fancies. We are freed from the obligation to refer our knowledge to the Divine and True. On the other hand, the vanity and egotism which characterize it, find, in this false position, ample justification; and the pious modesty which puts far from it the knowledge of God, can well estimate how much furtherance thereby accrues to its own wayward and vain strivings. I have been unwilling to leave out of sight the connection between our thesis — that Reason governs and has governed the World — and the question of the possibility of a knowledge of God, chiefly that I might not lose the opportunity of mentioning the imputation against Philosophy of being shy of noticing religious truths, or of having occasion to be so; in which is insinuated the suspicion that it has anything but a clear conscience in the presence of these truths. So far from this being the case, the fact is, that in recent times Philosophy has been obliged to defend the domain of religion against the attacks of several theological systems. In the Christian religion God has revealed Himself — that is, he has given us to understand what He is; so that He is no longer a concealed or secret existence. And this possibility of knowing Him, thus afforded us, renders such knowledge a duty. God wishes no narrow-hearted souls or empty heads for his children; but those whose spirit is of itself indeed, poor, but rich in the knowledge of Him; and who regard this knowledge of God as the only valuable possession. That development of the thinking spirit, which has resulted from the revelation of the Divine Being as its original basis, must ultimately advance to the *intellectual* comprehension of what was presented in the first instance, to *feeling* and *imagination*. The time must eventually come for understanding that rich product of active Reason, which the History of the World offers to us. It was for awhile the fashion to profess admiration for the wisdom of God, as displayed in animals, plants, and isolated occurrences. But, if it be allowed that Providence manifests itself in such objects and forms of existence, why not also in Universal History? This is deemed too great a matter to be thus regarded. But Divine Wisdom, *i.e.*, Reason, is one and the same in the great as in the little; and we must not imagine God to be too weak to exercise his wisdom on the grand scale. Our intellectual striving aims at realizing the conviction that what was *intended* by eternal wisdom, is actually *accomplished* in the domain of existent, active Spirit, as well as in that of mere Nature. Our mode of treating the subject is, in this aspect, a Theodicaea — a justification of the ways of God — which Leibnitz attempted metaphysically, in his method, *i.e.*, in indefinite abstract categories — so that the ill that is found in the World may be comprehended, and the thinking Spirit reconciled with the fact of the existence of evil. Indeed, nowhere is such a harmonizing view more pressingly demanded than in Universal History; and it can be attained only by recognizing the *positive* existence, in which that negative element is a subordinate, and vanquished nullity. On the one hand, the ultimate design of the World must be perceived; and, on the other hand, the fact that this design has been actually realized in it, and that evil has not been able permanently to assert a competing position. But this superintending νοῦς, or in "Providence." "Reason," whose sovereignty over the World has been maintained, is as indefinite a term as "Providence," supposing the term to be used by those who are unable to characterize it distinctly—to show wherein it consists, so as to enable us to decide whether a thing is rational or irrational. An adequate definition of Reason is the first desideratum; and whatever boast may be made of strict adherence to it in explaining phenomena—without such a definition we get no farther than mere words. With these observations we may proceed to the second point of view that has to be considered in this Introduction.

II. The inquiry into the *essential destiny* of Reason—as far as it is considered in reference to the World—is identical with the question, *what is the ultimate design of the World?* And the expression implies that that design is destined to be realized. Two points of consideration suggest themselves; first, the *import* of this design—its abstract definition; and secondly, its *realization*.

It must be observed at the outset, that the phenomenon we investigate—Universal History—belongs to the realm of *Spirit*. The term "*World*," includes both physical and psychical Nature. Physical Nature also plays its part in the World's History, and attention will have to be paid to the fundamental natural relations thus involved. But Spirit, and the course of its development, is our substantial object. Our task does not require us to contemplate Nature as a Rational System in itself—though in its own proper domain it proves itself such—but simply in its relation to *Spirit*. On the stage on which we are observing it—Universal History—Spirit displays itself in its most concrete reality. Notwithstanding this (or rather for the very purpose of comprehending the *general* principles which this, its form of *concrete reality*, embodies) we must premise some abstract characteristics of the *nature of Spirit*. Such an explanation, however, cannot be given here under any other form than that of bare assertion. The present is not the occasion for unfolding the idea of Spirit speculatively; for whatever has a place in an Introduction, must, as already observed, be taken as simply historical; something assumed as having been explained and proved elsewhere; or whose demonstration awaits the sequel of the Science of History itself.

We have therefore to mention here:

(1) The abstract characteristics of the nature of Spirit.

(2) What means Spirit uses in order to realize its Idea.

(3) Lastly, we must consider the shape which the perfect embodiment of Spirit assumes—the State.

(1) The nature of Spirit may be understood by a glance at its direct opposite—*Matter*. As the essence of Matter is Gravity, so, on the other hand, we may affirm that the substance, the essence of spirit is Freedom. All will readily assent to the doctrine that Spirit, among other properties, is also

endowed with Freedom; but philosophy teaches that all the qualities of Spirit exist only through Freedom; that all are but means for attaining Freedom; that all seek and produce this and this alone. It is a result of speculative Philosophy, that Freedom is the sole truth of Spirit. Matter possesses gravity in virtue of its tendency toward a central point. It is essentially composite; consisting of parts that *exclude* each other. It seeks its Unity; and therefore exhibits itself as self-destructive, as verging toward its opposite [an indivisible point]. If it could attain this, it would be Matter no longer, it would have perished. It strives after the realization of its Idea; for in Unity it exists *ideally*. Spirit, on the contrary, may be defined as that which has its centre in itself. It has not a unity outside itself, but has already found it; it exists *in* and *with itself*. Matter has its essence out of itself; Spirit is *self-contained existence* (Bei-sich-selbst-seyn). Now this is Freedom, exactly. For if I am dependent, my being is referred to something else which I am not; I cannot exist independently of something external. I am free, on the contrary, when my existence depends upon myself. This self-contained existence of Spirit is none other than self-consciousness — consciousness of one's own being. Two things must be distinguished in consciousness; first, the fact *that I know*; secondly, *what I know*. In *self* consciousness these are merged in one; for Spirit *knows itself*. It involves an appreciation of its own nature, as also an energy enabling it to realize itself; to make itself *actually* that which it is *potentially*. According to this abstract definition it may be said of Universal History, that it is the exhibition of Spirit in the process of working out the knowledge of that which it is potentially. And as the germ bears in itself the whole nature of the tree, and the taste and form of its fruits, so do the first traces of Spirit virtually contain the whole of that History. The Orientals have not attained the knowledge that Spirit — Man *as such* — is free; and because they do not know this, they are not free. They only know that *one is free*. But on this very account, the freedom of that one is only caprice; ferocity — brutal recklessness of passion, or a mildness and tameness of the desires, which is itself only an accident of Nature — mere caprice like the former. — That *one* is therefore only a Despot; not a *free man*. The consciousness of Freedom first arose among the Greeks, and therefore they were free; but they, and the Romans likewise, knew only that *some* are free — not man as such. Even Plato and Aristotle did not know this. The Greeks, therefore, had slaves; and their whole life and the maintenance of their splendid liberty, was implicated with the institution of slavery: a fact moreover, which made that liberty on the one hand only an accidental, transient and limited growth; on the other hand, constituted it a rigorous thraldom of our common nature — of the Human. The German nations, under the influence of Christianity, were the first to attain the consciousness, that man, as man, is free: that it is the *freedom* of Spirit which constitutes its essence. This consciousness arose first in religion, the inmost region of Spirit; but to introduce the principle into the various relations of the actual world, involves a more extensive problem than its simple implantation; a problem whose solution and application require a severe and lengthened process of culture. In proof of this, we may note that slavery did not cease immediately on the reception of Christianity. Still less did liberty predominate in States; or Governments and Constitutions adopt a rational organization, or recognize freedom as their basis. That application of the principle to political relations; the thorough moulding and interpenetration of the constitution of society by it, is a process identical with history itself. I have already directed attention to the distinction here involved, between a principle as such, and its *application*; *i.e.*, its introduction and carrying out in the actual phenomena of Spirit and Life. This is a point of fundamental importance in our science, and one which must be constantly respected as essential. And in the same way as this distinction has attracted attention in view of the *Christian* principle of self-consciousness—Freedom; it also shows itself as an essential one, in view of the principle of Freedom *generally*. The History of the world is none other than the progress of the consciousness of Freedom; a progress whose development according to the necessity of its nature, it is our business to investigate.

The general statement given above, of the various grades in the consciousness of Freedom—and which we applied in the first instance to the fact that the Eastern nations knew only that *one* is free; the Greek and Roman world only that *some* are free; while *we* know that all men absolutely (man *as man*) are free—supplies us with the natural division of Universal History, and suggests the mode of its discussion. This is remarked, however, only incidentally and anticipatively; some other ideas must be first explained.

The destiny of the spiritual World, and—since this is the *substantial World*, while the physical remains subordinate to it, or, in the language of speculation, has no truth *as against* the spiritual—*the final cause of the World at large*, we allege to be the *consciousness* of its own freedom on the part of Spirit, and *ipso facto*, the *reality* of that freedom. But that this term "Freedom," without further qualification, is an indefinite, and incalculable ambiguous term; and that while that which it represents is the *ne plus ultra* of attainment, it is liable to an infinity of misunderstandings, confusions and errors, and to become the occasion for all imaginable excesses—has never been more clearly known and felt than in modern times. Yet, for the present, we must content ourselves with the term itself without farther definition. Attention was also directed to the importance of the infinite difference between a principle in the abstract, and its realization in the concrete. In the process before us, the essential nature of freedom—which involves in it absolute necessity—is to be displayed as coming to a consciousness of itself (for it is in its very nature, self-consciousness) and thereby realizing its existence. Itself is its own object of attainment, and the sole aim of Spirit. This result it is, at which the process of the World's History has been continually aiming; and to which the sacrifices that have ever and anon been laid on the vast altar of the earth, through the long lapse of ages, have been offered. This is the only aim that sees itself realized and fulfilled; the only pole of repose amid the ceaseless change of events and conditions, and the sole efficient principle that pervades them. This final aim is God's purpose with the world; but God is the absolutely perfect Being, and can, therefore, will nothing other than himself — his own Will. The Nature of His Will — that is, His Nature itself — is what we here call the Idea of Freedom; translating the language of Religion into that of Thought. The question, then, which we may next put, is: What means does this principle of Freedom use for its realization? This is the second point we have to consider.

(2) The question of the *means* by which Freedom develops itself to a World, conducts us to the phenomenon of History itself. Although Freedom is, primarily, an undeveloped idea, the means it uses are external and phenomenal; presenting themselves in History to our sensuous vision. The first glance at History convinces us that the actions of men proceed from their needs, their passions, their characters and talents; and impresses us with the belief that such needs, passions and interests are the sole springs of action — the efficient agents in this scene of activity. Among these may, perhaps, be found aims of a liberal or universal kind — benevolence it may be, or noble patriotism; but such virtues and general views are but insignificant as compared with the World and its doings. We may perhaps see the Ideal of Reason actualized in those who adopt such aims, and within the sphere of their influence; but they bear only a trifling proportion to the mass of the human race; and the extent of that influence is limited accordingly. Passions, private aims, and the satisfaction of selfish desires, are on the other hand, most effective springs of action. Their power lies in the fact that they respect none of the limitations which justice and morality would impose on them; and that these natural impulses have a more direct influence over man than the artificial and tedious discipline that tends to order and self-restraint, law and morality. When we look at this display of passions, and the consequences of their violence; the Un-reason which is associated not only with them, but even (rather we might say *especially*) with *good* designs and righteous aims; when we see the evil, the vice, the ruin that has befallen the most flourishing kingdoms which the mind of man ever created; we can scarce avoid being filled with sorrow at this universal taint of corruption: and, since this decay is not the work of mere Nature, but of the Human Will — a moral embitterment —a revolt of the Good Spirit (if it have a place within us) may well be the result of our reflections. Without rhetorical exaggeration, a simply truthful combination of the miseries that have overwhelmed the noblest of nations and polities, and the finest exemplars of private virtue — forms a picture of most fearful aspect, and excites emotions of the profoundest and most hopeless sadness, counterbalanced by no consolatory result. We endure in beholding it a mental torture, allowing no defence or escape but the consideration that what has happened could not be otherwise; that it is a fatality which no intervention could alter. And at last we draw back from the intolerable disgust with which these sorrowful reflections threaten us, into the more agreeable environment of our individual life — the Present formed by our private aims and interests. In short we retreat into the selfishness that stands

on the quiet shore, and thence enjoys in safety the distant spectacle of "wrecks confusedly hurled." But even regarding History as the slaughter-bench at which the happiness of peoples, the wisdom of States, and the virtue of individuals have been victimized — the question involuntarily arises — to what principle, to what final aim these enormous sacrifices have been offered. From this point the investigation usually proceeds to that which we have made the general commencement of our inquiry. Starting from this we pointed out those phenomena which made up a picture so suggestive of gloomy emotions and thoughtful reflections — as *the very field* which we, for our part, regard as exhibiting only the means for realizing what we assert to be the essential destiny — the absolute aim, or — which comes to the same thing — the true *result* of the World's History. We have all along purposely eschewed "moral reflections" as a method of rising from the scene of historical specialties to the general principles which they embody. Besides, it is not the interest of such sentimentalities, really to rise above those depressing emotions; and to solve the enigmas of Providence which the considerations that occasioned them, present. It is essential to their character to find a gloomy satisfaction in the empty and fruitless sublimities of that negative result. We return them to the point of view which we have adopted; observing that the successive steps (Momente) of the analysis to which it will lead us, will also evolve the conditions requisite for answering the inquiries suggested by the panorama of sin and suffering that history unfolds.

The *first* remark we have to make, and which — though already presented more than once — cannot be too often repeated when the occasion seems to call for it — is that what we call *principle, aim, destiny*, or the nature and idea of Spirit, is something merely general and abstract. Principle — Plan of Existence — Law — is a hidden, undeveloped essence, which *as such* — however true in itself — is not completely real. Aims, principles, etc., have a place in our thoughts, in our subjective design only; but not yet in the sphere of reality. That which exists for itself only, is a possibility, a potentiality; but has not yet emerged into Existence. A *second* element must be introduced in order to produce actuality — viz., actuation, realization; and whose motive power is the Will — the activity of man in the widest sense. It is only by this activity that that Idea as well as abstract characteristics generally, are realized, actualized; for of themselves they are powerless. The motive power that puts them in operation, and gives them determinate existence, is the need, instinct, inclination, and passion of man. That some conception of mine should be developed into act and existence, is my earnest desire: I wish to assert my personality in connection with it: I wish to be satisfied by its execution. If I am to exert myself for any object, it must in some way or other be *my* object. In the accomplishment of such or such designs I must at the same time find *my* satisfaction; although the purpose for which I exert myself includes a complication of results, many of which have no interest for me. This is the absolute right of personal existence — to find *itself* satisfied in its activity and labor. If men are to interest themselves for anything, they must (so to speak) have part of their existence involved in it; find their individuality gratified by its attainment. Here a mistake must be avoided. We intend blame, and justly impute it as a fault, when we say of an individual, that he is "interested" (in taking part in such or such transactions), that is, seeks only his private advantage. In reprehending this we find fault with him for furthering his personal aims without any regard to a more comprehensive design; of which he takes advantage to promote his own interest, or which he even sacrifices with this view. But he who is active in *promoting an object*, is not simply "interested," but interested in that object itself. Language faithfully expresses this distinction. — Nothing therefore happens, nothing is accomplished, unless the individuals concerned, seek their own satisfaction in the issue. They are particular units of society; *i.e.*, they have special needs, instincts, and interests generally, peculiar to themselves. Among these needs are not only such as we usually call necessities — the stimuli of individual desire and volition — but also those connected with individual views and convictions; or — to use a term expressing less decision — leanings of opinion; supposing the impulses of reflection, understanding, and reason, to have been awakened. In these cases people demand, if they are to exert themselves in any direction, that the object should commend itself to them; that in point of opinion — whether as to its goodness, justice, advantage, profit — they should be able to "enter into it" (dabei seyn). This is a consideration of especial importance in our age, when people are less than formerly influenced by reliance on others, and by authority; when, on the contrary, they devote their activities to a cause on the ground of their own understanding, their independent conviction and opinion.

We assert then that nothing has been accomplished without interest on the part of the actors; and — if interest be called passion, inasmuch as the whole individuality, to the neglect of all other actual or possible interests and claims, is devoted to an object with every fibre of volition, concentrating all its desires and powers upon it — we may affirm absolutely that *nothing great in the World* has been accomplished without *passion*. Two elements, therefore, enter into the object of our investigation; the first the Idea, the second the complex of human passions; the one the warp, the other the woof of the vast arras-web of Universal History. The concrete mean and union of the two is Liberty, under the conditions of morality in a State. We have spoken of the Idea of Freedom as the nature of Spirit, and the absolute goal of History. Passion is regarded as a thing of sinister aspect, as more or less immoral. Man is required to have no passions. Passion, it is true, is not quite the suitable word for what I wish to express. I mean here nothing more than the human activity as resulting from private interests — special, or if you will, self-seeking designs — with this qualification, that the whole energy of will and character is devoted to their attainment; that other interests (which would in themselves constitute attractive aims) or rather all things else, are sacrificed to them. The object in question is so bound up with the man's will, that it entirely and alone determines the "hue of resolution," and is inseparable from it. It has become the very essence of his volition. For a person is a specific existence; not man in general (a term to which no real existence corresponds) but a particular human being. The term "character" likewise expresses this idiosyncrasy of Will and Intelligence. But *Character* comprehends all peculiarities whatever; the way in which a person conducts himself in private relations, etc., and is not limited to his idiosyncrasy in its practical and active phase. I shall, therefore, use the term "passions"; understanding thereby the particular bent of character, as far as the peculiarities of volition are not limited to private interest, but supply the impelling and actuating force for accomplishing deeds shared in by the community at large. Passion is in the first instance the *subjective*, and therefore the *formal* side of energy, will, and activity—leaving the object or aim still undetermined. And there is a similar relation of formality to reality in merely individual conviction, individual views, individual conscience. It is always a question of essential importance, what is the purport of my conviction, what the object of my passion, in deciding whether the one or the other is of a true and substantial nature. Conversely, if it is so, it will inevitably attain actual existence—be realized.

From this comment on the second essential element in the historical embodiment of an aim, we infer—glancing at the institution of the State in passing—that a State is then well constituted and internally powerful, when the private interest of its citizens is one with the common interest of the State; when the one finds its gratification and realization in the other—a proposition in itself very important. But in a State many institutions must be adopted, much political machinery invented, accompanied by appropriate political arrangements—necessitating long struggles of the understanding before what is really appropriate can be discovered—involving, moreover, contentions with private interest and passions, and a tedious discipline of these latter, in order to bring about the desired harmony. The epoch when a State attains this harmonious condition, marks the period of its bloom, its virtue, its vigor, and its prosperity. But the history of mankind does not begin with a *conscious* aim of any kind, as it is the case with the particular circles into which men form themselves of set purpose. The mere social instinct implies a conscious purpose of security for life and property; and when society has been constituted, this purpose becomes more comprehensive. The History of the World begins with its general aim—the realization of the Idea of Spirit—only in an *implicit* form (*an sich*) that is, as Nature; a hidden, most profoundly hidden, unconscious instinct; and the whole process of History (as already observed), is directed to rendering this unconscious impulse a conscious one. Thus appearing in the form of merely natural existence, natural will—that which has been called the subjective side—physical craving, instinct, passion, private interest, as also opinion and subjective conception—spontaneously present themselves at the very commencement. This vast congeries of volitions, interests and activities constitute the instruments and means of the World-Spirit for attaining its object; bringing it to consciousness, and realizing it. And this aim is none other than finding itself—coming to

itself — and contemplating itself in concrete actuality. But that those manifestations of vitality on the part of individuals and peoples, in which they seek
and satisfy their own purposes, are, at the same time, the means and instruments of a higher and broader purpose of which they know nothing — which
they realize unconsciously — might be made a matter of question; rather has
been questioned, and in every variety of form negatived, decried and con-
temned as mere dreaming and "Philosophy." But on this point I announced
my view at the very outset, and asserted our hypothesis — which, however,
will appear in the sequel, in the form of a legitimate inference — and our
belief, that Reason governs the world, and has consequently governed its
history. In relation to this independently universal and substantial existence
—all else is subordinate, subservient to it, and the means for its
development. — The Union of Universal Abstract Existence generally with the
Individual — the Subjective — that this alone is Truth, belongs to the department of speculation, and is treated in this general form in Logic. — But in the
process of the World's History itself — as still incomplete — the abstract final
aim of history is not yet made the distinct object of desire and interest. While
these limited sentiments are still unconscious of the purpose they are fulfilling, the universal principle is implicit in them, and is realizing itself through
them. The question also assumes the form of the union of *Freedom* and
Necessity; the latent abstract process of Spirit being regarded as *Necessity*,
while that which exhibits itself in the conscious will of men, as their interest,
belongs to the domain of *Freedom*. As the metaphysical connection (*i.e.,* the
connection in the Idea) of these forms of thought, belongs to Logic, it would
be out of place to analyze it here. . . .

Part IV
The German World, Section III

Chapter III
The Enlightenment and Revolution

Protestantism had introduced the *principle* of Subjectivity, importing religious
emancipation and inward harmony, but accompanying this with the *belief* in
Subjectivity as Evil, and in a power [adverse to man's highest interests] whose
embodiment is "the World." Within the Catholic pale also, the casuistry of the
Jesuits brought into vogue interminable investigations, as tedious and wire-
drawn as those in which the scholastic theology delighted, respecting the
subjective spring of the Will and the motives that affect it. This Dialectic,
which unsettles all particular judgments and opinions, transmuting the Evil
into Good and Good into Evil, left at last nothing remaining but the mere
action of subjectivity itself, the Abstractum of Spirit — *Thought*. Thought
contemplates everything under the form of Universality, and is consequently

the impulsion towards and production of the Universal. In that elder scholastic theology the real subject-matter of investigation — the doctrine of the Church, remained an ultramundane affair; in the Protestant theology also Spirit still sustained a relation to the Ultramundane; for on the one side we have the will of the individual — the Spirit of Man — I myself, and on the other the Grace of God, the Holy Ghost; and so in the Wicked, the Devil. But in Thought, Self moves within the limits of its own sphere; that with which it is occupied — its objects are as absolutely present to it [as they were distinct and separate in the intellectual grade above mentioned]; for in thinking I must elevate the object to Universality. This is utter and absolute Freedom, for the pure Ego, like pure Light, is with itself alone [is not involved with any alien principle]; thus that which is diverse from itself, sensuous or spiritual, no longer presents an object of dread, for in contemplating such diversity it is inwardly free and can freely confront it. A practical interest makes use of, consumes the objects offered to it: a theoretical interest calmly contemplates them, assured that in themselves they present no alien element. — Consequently, the *ne plus ultra* of Inwardness, of Subjectiveness, is Thought. Man is not free, when he is not thinking; for except when thus engaged he sustains a relation to the world around him as to another, an alien form of being. This comprehension — the penetration of the Ego into and beyond other forms of being with the most profound self-certainty [the identity of subjective and objective Reason being recognized], directly involves the harmonization of Being: for it must be observed that the unity of Thought with its Object is already *implicitly* present [*i.e.* in the fundamental constitution of the Universe], for Reason is the substantial basis of Consciousness as well as of the External and Natural. Thus that which presents itself as the Object of Thought is no longer an absolutely distinct form of existence [ein Jenseits], not of an alien and grossly substantial [as opposed to intelligible] nature.

Thought is the grade to which Spirit has now advanced. It involves the Harmony of Being in its purest essence, challenging the external world to exhibit the same Reason which Subject [the Ego] possesses. Spirit perceives that Nature — the World — must also be an embodiment of Reason, for God created it on principles of Reason. An interest in the contemplation and comprehension of the present world became universal. Nature embodies Universality, inasmuch as it is nothing other than Sorts, Genera, Power, Gravitation, etc., phenomenally presented. Thus *Experimental Science* became the science of the World; for experimental science involves on the one hand the observation of phenomena, on the other hand also the discovery of the Law, the essential being, the hidden force that causes those phenomena —thus reducing the data supplied by observation to their simple principles. Intellectual consciousness was first extricated from that sophistry of thought, which unsettles everything, by *Descartes*. As it was the purely German nations among whom the principle of *Spirit* first manifested itself, so it was by the Romanic nations that the *abstract idea* (to which the character assigned them above—viz., that of internal schism, more readily conducted them) was first comprehended. Experimental science therefore very soon made its way among them (in common with the Protestant English), but especially among the Italians. It seemed to men as if God had but just created the moon and stars, plants and animals, as if the laws of the universe were now established for the first time; for only then did they feel a real interest in the universe, when they recognized their own Reason in the Reason which pervades it. The human eye became *clear*, perception quick, thought active and interpretative. The discovery of the laws of Nature enabled men to contend against the monstrous superstition of the time, as also against all notions of mighty alien powers which magic alone could conquer. The assertion was even ventured on, and that by Catholics not less than by Protestants, that the External [and Material], with which the Church insisted upon associating superhuman virtue, was external and material, and nothing more—that the Host was simply *dough*, the relics of the Saints mere *bones*. The independent authority of Subjectivity was maintained against belief founded on authority, and the Laws of Nature were recognized as the only bond connecting phenomena with phenomena. Thus all miracles were disallowed: for Nature is a system of known and recognized Laws; Man is at home in it, and that only passes for truth in which he finds himself at home; he is free through the acquaintance he has gained with Nature. Nor was thought less vigorously directed to the Spiritual side of things: Right and [Social] Morality came to be looked upon as having their foundation in the actual present Will of man, whereas formerly it was referred only to the command of God enjoined *ab extra*, written in the Old and New Testament, or appearing in the form of particular Right [as opposed to that based on general principles] in old parchments, as *privilegia*, or in international compacts. What the nations acknowledge as international Right was deduced empirically from observation (as in the work of Grotius); then the source of the existing civil and political law was looked for, after Cicero's fashion, in those instincts of men which Nature has planted in their hearts— *e.g.*, the social instinct; next the principle of security for the person and property of the citizens, and of the advantage of the commonwealth— that which belongs to the class of "reasons of State." On these principles private rights were on the one hand despotically contravened, but on the other hand such contravention was the instrument of carrying out the general objects of the State in opposition to mere positive or prescriptive claims. Frederick II may be mentioned as the ruler who inaugurated the new epoch in the sphere of practical life—that epoch in which practical *political interest* attains Universality [is recognized as an abstract principle], and receives an absolute sanction. Frederick II merits especial notive as having compre- hended the general object of the State, and as having been the first sovereign who kept the general interest of the State steadily in view, ceasing to pay any respect to particular interests when they stood in the way of the common weal. His immortal work is a domestic code—the Prussian municipal law.

How the head of a household energetically provides and governs with a view to the weal of that household and of his dependents—of this he has given a unique specimen.

These general conceptions, deduced from actual and present consciousness—the Laws of Nature and the substance of what is right and good—have received the name of *Reason*. The recognition of the validity of these laws was designated by the term *Eclaircissement* (Aufklärung). From France it passed over into Germany, and created a new world of ideas. The absolute criterion—taking the place of all authority based on religious belief and positive laws of Right (especially political Right)—is the verdict passed by Spirit itself on the character of that which is to be believed or obeyed. After a free investigation in open day, Luther had secured to mankind Spiritual Freedom and the Reconciliation [of the Objective and Subjective] in the concrete: he triumphantly established the position that man's eternal destiny [his spiritual and moral position] must be wrought out *in himself* [cannot be an *opus operatum*, a work performed *for him*]. But the *import* of that which is to take place in him—what truth is to become vital in him, was taken for granted by Luther as something already given, something revealed by religion. *Now*, the principle was set up that this import must be capable of actual investigation—something of which I [in this modern time] can gain an inward conviction—and that to this basis of inward demonstration every dogma must be referred.

This principle of thought makes its appearance in the first instance in a general and abstract form; and is based on the axiom of Contradiction and Identity. The results of thought are thus posited as finite, and the eclaircissement utterly banished and extirpated all that was speculative from things human and divine. Although it is of incalculable importance that the multiform complex of things should be reduced to its simplest conditions, and brought into the form of Universality, yet this still abstract principle does not satisfy the living Spirit, the concrete human soul.

This formally absolute principle brings us to *the last stage in History, our world, our own time*.

Secular life is the positive and definite embodiment of the Spiritual Kingdom—the Kingdom of the *Will* manifesting itself in outward existence. Mere impulses are also forms in which the inner life realizes itself; but these are transient and disconnected; they are the ever-changing applications of volition. But that which is just and moral belongs to the essential, independent, intrinsically universal Will; and if we would know what Right really is, we must abstract from inclination, impulse and desire as the particular; *i.e.*, we must know what the Will is in itself. For benevolent, charitable, social impulses are nothing more than impulses—to which others of a different class are opposed. What the Will is in itself can be known only when these specific and contradictory forms of volition have been eliminated. Then Will appears as Will, in its abstract essence. The Will is Free only when it does not will anything alien, extrinsic, foreign to itself (for as long as it does so, it is dependent), but wills itself alone — wills the Will. This is absolute Will — the volition to be free. Will making itself its own object is the basis of all Right and Obligation — consequently of all statutory determinations of Right, categorical imperatives, and enjoined obligations. The Freedom of the Will *per se*, is the principle and substantial basis of all Right — is itself absolute, inherently eternal Right, and the Supreme Right in comparison with other specific Rights; nay, it is even that by which Man becomes Man, and is therefore the fundamental principle of Spirit. But the next question is: How does Will assume a definite form? For in willing itself, it is nothing but an identical reference to itself; but, in point of fact, it wills something specific: there *are*, we know, distinct and special Duties and Rights. A particular application, a definite form of Will, is desiderated; for pure Will is its own object, its own application, which, as far as this showing goes, is no object, no application. In fact, in this form it is nothing more than *formal* Will. But the metaphysical process by which this abstract Will develops itself, so as to attain a definite form of Freedom, and how Rights and Duties are evolved therefrom, this is not the place to discuss. It may however be remarked that the same principle obtained speculative recognition in Germany, in the *Kantian* Philosophy. According to it the simple unity of Self-consciousness, the Ego, constitutes the absolutely independent Freedom, and is the fountain of all general conceptions — *i.e.* all conceptions elaborated by Thought — Theoretical Reason; and likewise of the highest of all practical determinations [or conceptions] — Practical Reason, as free and pure Will; and Rationality of Will is none other than the maintaining one's self in pure Freedom — willing this and this alone — Right purely for the sake of Right, Duty purely for the sake of Duty. Among the Germans this view assumed no other form than that of tranquil theory; but the French wished to give it practical effect. Two questions, therefore, suggest themselves: Why did this principle of Freedom remain merely formal? and why did the French alone, and not the Germans, set about realizing it?

With the formal principle more significant categories were indeed connected: one of the chief of these (for instance) was Society, and that which is advantageous for Society: but the aim of Society is itself political — that of the State (vid. "Droits de l'homme et du citoyen," 1791) — the conservation of *Natural* Rights; but Natural Right is Freedom, and, as further determined, it is *Equality* of Rights before the Law. A direct connection is manifest here, for Equality, *Parity*, is the result of the comparison of many; the "Many" in question being human beings, whose essential characteristic is the same, viz. Freedom. That principle remains formal, because it originated with abstract Thought — with the Understanding, which is primarily the self-consciousness of Pure Reason, and as direct [unreflected, undeveloped] is abstract. As yet, nothing further is developed from it, for it still maintains an adverse position to Religion, *i.e.* to the concrete absolute substance of the Universe.

As respects the second question — why the French immediately passed over from the theoretical to the practical, while the Germans contented themselves with theoretical abstraction, it might be said: the French are hot-headed [ils ont la tête près du bonnet]; but this is a superficial solution: the fact is that the formal principle of philosophy in Germany encounters a concrete real World in which Spirit finds inward satisfaction and in which conscience is at rest. For on the one hand it was the *Protestant World* itself which advanced so far in Thought as to realize the absolute culmination of Self-Consciousness; on the other hand, Protestantism enjoys, with respect to the moral and legal relations of the real world, a tranquil confidence in the [Honorable] Disposition of men—a sentiment, which, [in the Protestant World,] constituting one and the same thing with Religion, is the fountain of all the equitable arrangements that prevail with regard to private right and the constitution of the State. In Germany the eclaircissement was conducted in the interest of theology: in France it immediately took up a position of hostility to the Church. In Germany the entire compass of secular relations had already undergone a change for the better; those pernicious ecclesiastical institutes of celibacy, voluntary pauperism, and laziness, had been already done away with; there was no dead weight of enormous wealth attached to the Church, and no constraint put upon Morality—a constraint which is the source and occasion of vices; there was not that unspeakably hurtful form of iniquity which arises from the interference of spiritual power with secular law, nor that other of the Divine Right of Kings, *i.e.* the doctrine that the arbitrary will of princes, in virtue of their being "the Lord's Anointed," is divine and holy: on the contrary their will is regarded as deserving of respect only so far as in association with reason, it wisely contemplates Right, Justice, and the weal of the community. The principle of Thought, therefore, had been so far conciliated already; moreover the Protestant World had a conviction that in the Harmonization which had previously been evolved [in the sphere of Religion] the principle which would result in a further development of equity in the political sphere was already present.

Consciousness that has received an abstract culture, and whose sphere is the Understanding [Verstand] can be indifferent to Religion, but Religion is the general form in which Truth exists for *non-abstract* consciousness. And the Protestant Religion does not admit of two kinds of consciences, while in the Catholic world the Holy stands on the one side and on the other side abstraction opposed to Religion, that is to its superstition and its truth. That formal, individual Will is in virtue of the abstract position just mentioned made the basis of political theories; Right in Society is that which the Law wills, and the Will in question appears as an isolated *individual* will; thus the State, as an aggregate of many individuals, is not an independently substantial Unity, and the truth and essence of Right in and for itself—to which the will of its individual members ought to be conformed in order to be true, free Will; but the volitional atoms [the individual wills of the members of the State] are made the starting point, and each will is represented as absolute.

An *intellectual principle* was thus discovered to serve as a basis for the State—one which does not, like previous principles, belong to the sphere of opinion, such as the social impulse, the desire of security for property, etc. nor owe its origin to the religious sentiment, as does that of the Divine appointment of the governing power — but the principle of Certainty, which is identity with my self-consciousness, stopping short however of that of Truth, which needs to be distinguished from it. This is a vast discovery in regard to the profoundest depths of being and Freedom. The consciousness of the Spiritual is now the essential basis of the political fabric, and *Philosophy* has thereby become dominant. It has been said, that the *French Revolution* resulted from Philosophy, and it is not without reason that Philosophy has been called "Weltweisheit" [World Wisdom;] for it is not only Truth in and for itself, as the pure essence of things, but also Truth in its living form as exhibited in the affairs of the world. We should not, therefore, contradict the assertion that the Revolution received its first impulse from Philosophy. But this philosophy is in the first instance only abstract Thought, not the concrete comprehension of absolute Truth — intellectual positions between which there is an immeasurable chasm.

The principle of the Freedom of the Will, therefore, asserted itself against existing Right. Before the French Revolution, it must be allowed, the power of the grandees had been diminished by Richelieu, and they had been deprived of privileges; but, like the clergy, they retained all the prerogatives which gave them an advantage over the lower class. The political condition of France at that time presents nothing but a confused mass of privileges altogether contravening Thought and Reason — an utterly irrational state of things, and one with which the greatest corruption of morals, of Spirit was associated — an empire characterized by Destitution of Right, and which, when its real state begins to be recognized, becomes shameless destitution of Right. The fearfully heavy burdens that pressed upon the people, the embarrassment of the government to procure for the Court the means of supporting luxury and extravagance, gave the first impulse to discontent. The new Spirit began to agitate men's minds: oppression drove men to investigation. It was perceived that the sums extorted from the people were not expended in furthering the objects of the State, but were lavished in the most unreasonable fashion. The entire political system appeared one mass of injustice. The change was necessarily violent, because the work of transformation was not undertaken by the government. And the reason why the government did not undertake it was that the Court, the Clergy, the Nobility, the Parliaments themselves, were unwilling to surrender the privileges they possessed, either for the sake of expediency or that of abstract Right; moreover, because the government as the concrete centre of the power of the State, could not adopt as its principle abstract individual wills, and reconstruct the State on this basis; lastly, because it was Catholic, and therefore the Idea of Freedom — Reason embodied in Laws — did not pass for the final absolute obligation, since the Holy and the religious conscience are separated from them. The conception, the idea of Right asserted its authority *all at once*, and the old framework of injustice could offer no resistance to its onslaught. A constitution, therefore, was established in harmony with the conception of Right, and on this foundation all future legislation was to be based. Never since the sun had stood in the firmament and the planets revolved around him had it been perceived that man's existence centres in his head, *i.e.* in Thought, inspired by which he builds up the world of reality. Anaxagoras had been the first to say that νοῦς governs the World; but not until now had man advanced to the recognition of the principle that Thought ought to govern spiritual reality. This was accordingly a glorious mental dawn. All thinking beings shared in the jubilation of this epoch. Emotions of a lofty character stirred men's minds at that time; a spiritual enthusiasm thrilled through the world, as if the reconciliation between the Divine and the Secular was now first accomplished.

The two following points must now occupy our attention: 1st. The course which the Revolution in France took; 2d. How that Revolution became World-Historical.

1. Freedom presents two aspects: the one concerns its substance and purport — its objectivity — the thing itself — [that which is performed as a free act]; the other relates to the Form of Freedom, involving the consciousness of his activity on the part of the individual; for Freedom demands that the individual recognize himself in such acts, that they should be veritably his, it being his interest that the result in question should be attained. The three elements and powers of the State in actual working must be contemplated according to the above analysis, their examination in detail being referred to the Lectures on the Philosophy of Right.

(1.) *Laws* of Rationality — of intrinsic Right — Objective or Real Freedom: to this category belong Freedom of Property and Freedom of Person. Those relics of that condition of servitude which the feudal relation had introduced are hereby swept away, and all those fiscal ordinances which were the bequest of the feudal law — its tithes and dues, are abrogated. Real [practical] Liberty requires moreover freedom in regard to trades and professions — the permission to every one to use his abilities without restriction — and the free admission to all offices of State. This is a summary of the elements of real Freedom, and which are not based on feeling — for feeling allows of the continuance even of serfdom and slavery — but on the thought and self-consciousness of man recognizing the spiritual character of his existence.

(2.) But the agency which gives the laws practical effect is the *Government* generally. Government is primarily the formal execution of the laws and the maintenance of their authority: in respect to foreign relations it prosecutes the interest of the State; that is, it assists the independence of the nation as an individuality against other nations; lastly, it has to provide for the internal weal of the State and all its classes — what is called administration: for it is not enough that the citizen is allowed to pursue a trade or calling, it must also be a source of gain to him; it is not enough that men are permitted to use their powers, they must also find an opportunity of applying them to purpose. Thus the State involves a body of abstract principles and a practical application of them. This application must be the work of a subjective will, a will which resolves and decides. Legislation itself — the invention and positive enactment of these statutory arrangements, is an application of such general principles. The next step, then, consists in [specific] determination and execution. Here then the question presents itself: what is the decisive will to be? The ultimate decision is the prerogative of the monarch: but if the State is based on Liberty, the many wills of individuals also desire to have a share in political decisions. But the *Many* are *All*; and it seems but a poor expedient, rather a monstrous inconsistency, to allow only a few to take part in those decisions, since each wishes that his volition should have a share in determining what is to be law for him. The Few assume to be the *deputies*, but they are often only the *despoilers* of the Many. Nor is the sway of the Majority over the Minority a less palpable inconsistency.

(3.) This collision of subjective wills leads therefore to the consideration of a third point, that of *Disposition* — an *ex animo* acquiescence in the laws; nor the mere customary observance of them, but the cordial recognition of laws and the Constitution as in principle fixed and immutable, and of the supreme obligation of individuals to subject their particular wills to them. There may be various opinions and views respecting laws, constitution and government, but there must be a disposition on the part of the citizens to regard all these opinions as subordinate to the substantial interest of the State, and to insist upon them no further than that interest will allow; moreover nothing must be considered higher and more sacred than good will towards the State; or, if Religion be looked upon as higher and more sacred, it must involve nothing really alien or opposed to the Constitution. It is, indeed, regarded as a maxim of the profoundest wisdom entirely to separate the laws and constitution of the State from Religion, since bigotry and hypocrisy are to be feared as the results of a State Religion. But although the aspects of Religion and the State are different, they are radically *one*; and the laws find their highest confirmation in Religion.

Here it must be frankly stated, that with the Catholic Religion no rational constitution is possible; for Government and People must reciprocate that final guarantee of Disposition, and can have it only in a Religion that is not opposed to a rational political constitution.

Plato in his Republic makes everything depend upon the Government, and makes Disposition the principle of the State; on which account he lays the chief stress on Education. The modern theory is diametrically opposed to this, referring everything to the individual will. But here we have no guarantee that the will in question has that right disposition which is essential to the stability of the State.

In view then of these leading considerations we have to trace the course of the *French Revolution* and the remodelling of the State in accordance with the Idea of Right. In the first instance purely abstract philosophical principles were set up: Disposition and Religion were not taken into account. The first Constitutional form of Government in France was one which recognized

Royalty; the monarch was to stand at the head of the State, and on him in conjunction with his Ministers was to devolve the executive power; the legislative body on the other hand were to make the laws. But this constitution involved from the very first an internal contradiction; for the legislature absorbed the whole power of the administration: the budget, affairs of war and peace, and the levying of the armed force were in the hands of the Legislative Chamber. Everything was brought under the head of Law. The budget however is in its nature something diverse from law, for it is annually renewed, and the power to which it properly belongs is that of the Government. With this moreover is connected the indirect nomination of the ministry and officers of state, etc. The government was thus transferred to the Legislative Chamber, as in England to the Parliament. This constitution was also vitiated by the existence of absolute mistrust; the dynasty lay under suspicion, because it had lost the power it formerly enjoyed, and the priests refused the oath. Neither government nor constitution could be maintained on this footing, and the ruin of both was the result. A government of some kind however is always in existence. The question presents itself then, Whence did it emanate? Theoretically, it proceeded from the people; really and truly from the National Convention and its Committees. The forces now dominant are the abstract principles — Freedom, and, as it exists within the limits of the Subjective Will — Virtue. This Virtue has now to conduct the government in opposition to the Many, whom their corruption and attachment to old interests, or a liberty that has degenerated into license, and the violence of their passions, render unfaithful to virtue. Virtue is here a simple abstract principle and distinguishes the citizens into two classes only — those who are favorably disposed and those who are not. But disposition can only be recognized and judged of by disposition. *Suspicion* therefore is in the ascendant; but virtue, as soon as it becomes liable to suspicion, is already condemned. Suspicion attained a terrible power and brought to the scaffold the Monarch, whose subjective will was in fact the religious conscience of a Catholic. Robespierre set up the principle of Virtue as supreme, and it may be said that with this man Virtue was an earnest matter. *Virtue* and *Terror* are the order of the day; for Subjective Virtue, whose sway is based on disposition only, brings with it the most fearful tyranny. It exercises its power without legal formalities, and the punishment it inflicts is equally simple — *Death*. This tyranny could not last; for all inclinations, all interests, reason itself revolted against this terribly consistent Liberty, which in its concentrated intensity exhibited so fanatical a shape. An organized government is introduced, analogous to the one that had been displaced; only that its chief and monarch is now a mutable Directory of Five, who may form a moral, but have not an individual unity; under them also suspicion was in the ascendant, and the government was in the hands of the legislative assemblies; this constitution therefore experienced the same fate as its predecessor, for it had proved to itself the absolute necessity of a governmental *power*. *Napoleon* restored it as a military power, and followed up this step by establishing himself as an individual will at the head of the State: he knew how to rule, and soon settled the internal affairs of France. The *avocats*, idealogues and abstract-principle men who ventured to show themselves he sent "to the right about," and the sway of mistrust was exchanged for that of respect and fear. He then, with the vast might of his character turned his attention to foreign relations, subjected all Europe, and diffused his liberal institutions in every quarter. Greater victories were never gained, expeditions displaying greater genius were never conducted: but never was the powerlessness of Victory exhibited in a clearer light than then. The disposition of the peoples, *i.e.* their religious disposition and that of their nationality, ultimately precipitated this colossus; and in France constitutional monarchy, with the "Charte" as its basis, was restored. But here again the antithesis of Disposition [good feeling] and Mistrust made its appearance. The French stood in a mendacious position to each other, when they issued addresses full of devotion and love to the monarchy, and loading it with benediction. A fifteen years' farce was played. For although the *Charte* was the standard under which all were enrolled, and though both parties had sworn to it, yet on the one side the ruling disposition was a Catholic one, which regarded it as a matter of conscience to destroy the existing institutions. Another breach, therefore, took place, and the Government was overturned. At length, after forty years of war and confusion indescribable, a weary heart might fain congratulate itself on seeing a termination and tranquillization of all these disturbances. But although one main point is set at rest, there remains on the one hand that rupture which the Catholic principle inevitably occasions, on the other hand that which has to do with men's subjective will. In regard to the latter, the main feature of incompatibility still presents itself, in the requirement that the ideal general will should also be the *empirically* general — *i.e.* that the units of the State, in their individual capacity, should rule, or at any rate take part in the government. Not satisfied with the establishment of rational rights, with freedom of person and property, with the existence of a political organization in which are to be found various circles of civil life each having its own functions to perform, and with that influence over the people which is exercised by the intelligent members of the community, and the confidence that is felt in them, *"Liberalism"* sets up in opposition to all this the atomistic principle, that which insists upon the sway of individual wills; maintaining that all government should emanate from their express power, and have their express sanction. Asserting this formal side of Freedom — this abstraction — the party in question allows no political organization to be firmly established. The particular arrangements of the government are forthwith opposed by the advocates of liberty as the mandates of a particular will, and branded as displays of arbitrary power. The will of the Many expels the Ministry from power, and those who had formed the Opposition fill the vacant places; but the latter having now become the Government, meet with hostility from the Many, and share the same fate. Thus agitation and unrest are perpetuated. This collision, this nodus, this problem is that with which history is now occupied, and whose solution it has to work out in the future.

2. We have now to consider the French Revolution in its organic con-

nection with the *History of the World;* for in its substantial import that event is World-Historical, and that contest of Formalism which we discussed in the last paragraph must be properly distinguished from its wider bearings. As regards outward diffusion its principle gained access to almost all modern states, either through conquest or by express introduction into their political life. Particularly all the Romanic nations, and the Roman Catholic World in special — *France, Italy, Spain* — were subjected to the dominion of Liberalism. But it became bankrupt everywhere; first, the grand firm in France, then its branches in Spain and Italy; twice, in fact, in the states into which it had been introduced. This was the case in Spain, where it was first brought in by the Napoleonic Constitution, then by that which the Cortes adopted — in Piedmont, first when it was incorporated with the French Empire, and a second time as the result of internal insurrection; so in Rome and in Naples it was twice set up. Thus Liberalism as an abstraction, emanating from France, traversed the Roman World; but Religious slavery held that world in the fetters of political servitude. For it is a false principle that the fetters which bind Right and Freedom can be broken without the emancipation of conscience — that there can be a Revolution without a Reformation. — These countries, therefore, sank back into their old condition — in Italy with some modifications of the outward political condition. Venice and Genoa, those ancient aristocracies, which could at least boast of legitimacy, vanished as rotten despotisms. Material superiority in power can achieve no enduring results: Napoleon could not coerce Spain into freedom any more than Philip II could force Holland into slavery.

Contrasted with these Romanic nations we observe the other powers of Europe, and especially the Protestant nations. *Austria* and *England* were not drawn within the vortex of internal agitation, and exhibited great, immense proofs of their internal solidity. *Austria* is not a Kingdom, but an Empire, *i.e.* an aggregate of many political organizations. The inhabitants of its chief provinces are not German in origin and character, and have remained unaffected by "ideas." Elevated neither by education nor religion, the lower classes in some districts have remained in a condition of serfdom, and the nobility have been kept down, as in Bohemia; in other quarters, while the former have continued the same, the barons have maintained their despotism, as in Hungary. Austria has surrendered that more intimate connection with Germany which was derived from the imperial dignity, and renounced its numerous possessions and rights in Germany and the Netherlands. It now takes its place in Europe as a distinct power, involved with no other. *England,* with great exertions, maintained itself on its old foundations; the English *Constitution* kept its ground amid the general convulsion, though it seemed so much the more liable to be affected by it, as a public Parliament, that habit of assembling in public meeting which was common to all orders of the state, and a free press, offered singular facilities for introducing the French principles of Liberty and Equality among all classes of the people. Was the English nation too backward in point of culture to apprehend these general principles? Yet in no country has the question of Liberty been more frequently a subject of reflection and public discussion. Or was the English constitution so entirely a Free Constitution—had those principles been already so completely realized in it, that they could no longer excite opposition or even interest? The English nation may be said to have approved of the emancipation of France; but it was proudly reliant on its own constitution and freedom, and instead of imitating the example of the foreigner, it displayed its ancient hostility to its rival, and was soon involved in a popular war with France.

The Constitution of England is a complex of mere *particular Rights* and particular privileges: the Government is essentially administrative—that is, conservative of the interests of all particular orders and classes; and each particular Church, parochial district, county, society, takes care of itself, so that the Government, strictly speaking, has nowhere less to do than in England. This is the leading feature of what Englishmen call their Liberty, and is the very antithesis of such a centralized administration as exists in France, where down to the least village the Maire is named by the Ministry or their agents. Nowhere can people less tolerate free action on the part of others than in France: there the Ministry combines in itself all administrative power, to which, on the other hand, the Chamber of Deputies lays claim. In England, on the contrary, every parish, every subordinate division and association has a part of its own to perform. Thus the common interest is concrete, and particular interests are taken cognizance of and determined in view of that common interest. These arrangements, based on particular interests, render a general system impossible. Consequently, abstract and general principles have no attraction for Englishmen—are addressed in their case to inattentive ears.—The particular interests above referred to have positive rights attached to them, which date from the antique times of Feudal Law, and have been preserved in England more than in any other country. By an inconsistency of the most startling kind, we find them contravening equity most grossly; and of institutions characterized by real freedom there are nowhere fewer than in England. In point of private right and freedom of possession they present an incredible deficiency: sufficient proof of which is afforded in the rights of primogeniture, involving the necessity of purchasing or otherwise providing military or ecclesiastical appointments for the younger sons of the aristocracy.

The *Parliament governs*, although Englishmen are unwilling to allow that such is the case. It is worthy of remark, that what has been always regarded as the period of the corruption of a republican people, presents itself here; viz. election to seats in parliament by means of bribery. But this also they call freedom—the power to sell one's vote, and to purchase a seat in parliament.

But this utterly inconsistent and corrupt state of things has nevertheless one advantage, that it provides for the possibility of a government—that it introduces a majority of men into parliament who are statesmen, who from their very youth have devoted themselves to political business and have worked and lived in it. And the nation has the correct conviction and perception that there must be a government, and is therefore willing to give its confidence to a body of men who have had experience in governing; for a general sense of particularity involves also a recognition of that form of particularity which is a distinguishing feature of one class of the community —that knowledge, experience, and facility acquired by practice, which the aristocracy who devote themselves to such interests exclusively possess. This is quite opposed to the appreciation of principles and abstract views which everyone can understand at once, and which are besides to be found in all Constitutions and Charters. It is a question whether the Reform in Parliament now on the tapis, consistently carried out, will leave the possibility of a Government.

The material existence of England is based on commerce and industry, and the English have undertaken the weighty responsibility of being the missionaries of civilization to the world; for their commercial spirit urges them to traverse every sea and land, to form connections with barbarous peoples, to create wants and stimulate industry, and first and foremost to establish among them the conditions necessary to commerce, viz. the relinquishment of a life of lawless violence, respect for property, and civility to strangers.

Germany was traversed by the victorious French hosts, but German nationality delivered it from this yoke. One of the leading features in the political condition of Germany is that code of Rights which was certainly occasioned by French oppression, since this was the especial means of bringing to light the deficiencies of the old system. The fiction of an Empire has utterly vanished. It is broken up into sovereign states. Feudal obligations are abolished, for freedom of property and of person have been recognized as fundamental principles. Offices of State are open to every citizen, talent and adaptation being of course the necessary conditions. The government rests with the official world, and the personal decision of the monarch constitutes its apex; for a final decision is, as was remarked above, absolutely necessary. Yet with firmly established laws, and a settled organization of the State, what is left to the sole arbitrament of the monarch is, in point of substance, no great matter. It is certainly a very fortunate circumstance for a nation, when a sovereign of noble character falls to its lot; yet in a great state even this is of small moment, since its strength lies in the Reason incorporated in it. Minor states have their existence and tranquillity secured to them more or less by their neighbors: they are therefore, properly speaking, not independent, and have not the fiery trial of war to endure. As has been remarked, a share in the government may be obtained by every one who has a competent knowledge, experience, and a morally regulated will. Those who know ought to govern—οι ἄριστοι, not ignorance and the presumptuous conceit of "knowing better." Lastly, as to Disposition, we have already remarked that in the Protestant Church the reconciliation of Religion with Legal Right has taken place. In the Protestant world there is no sacred, no religious conscience in a state of separation from, or perhaps even hostility to Secular Right.

This is the point which consciousness has attained, and these are the principal phases of that form in which the principle of Freedom has realized itself; — for the History of the World is nothing but the development of the Idea of Freedom. But Objective Freedom — the laws of *real* Freedom — demand the subjugation of the mere contingent Will — for this is in its nature formal. If the Objective is in itself Rational, human insight and conviction must correspond with the Reason which it embodies, and then we have the other essential element — Subjective Freedom — also realized. We have confined ourselves to the consideration of that progress of the Idea [which has led to this consummation], and have been obliged to forego the pleasure of giving a detailed picture of the prosperity, the periods of glory that have distinguished the career of peoples, the beauty and grandeur of the character of individuals, and the interest attaching to their fate in weal or woe. Philosophy concerns itself only with the glory of the Idea mirroring itself in the History of the World. Philosophy escapes from the weary strife of passions that agitate the surface of society into the calm region of contemplation; that which interests it is the recognition of the process of development which the Idea has passed through in realizing itself — *i.e.* the Idea of Freedom, whose reality is the consciousness of Freedom and nothing short of it.

That the History of the World, with all the changing scenes which its annals present, is this process of development and the realization of Spirit — this is the true *Theodicœa*, the justification of God in History. Only *this* insight can reconcile Spirit with the History of the World — viz., that what has happened, and is happening every day, is not only not "without God," but is essentially His Work.

JOHN STUART MILL

1 8 0 6 – 1 8 7 3

INTRODUCTION

Almost all that Rousseau and Mill have in common is the great volume of information about themselves that each left behind. Mill's *Autobiography* begins by recording the details of the forbiddingly advanced education that his father, James Mill, a Scottish writer, political reformer, and philosopher, provided for him at their home in London. By the age of 9 Mill had been learning arithmetic, geometry, algebra, Greek, and Latin for some years. By the age of 13 he had read a good deal of the chief Greek and Latin authors, helped to correct proofs of the three volumes of his father's *History of India*, and begun the study of logic and political economy. His education continued in this way until he was 17. Then he began work in the East India Company of which his father was by then a senior officer. From this point on John Stuart Mill was immersed in the regular discussions and meetings held by the various intellectual clubs and political societies that he helped to organize, in writing many articles for *The Westminster Review*, a journal devoted to the views of the Philosophical Radicals, and in agitating for birth control.

In 1826 Mill underwent a period of deep depression and reacted against the severely rational theories and policies of his father and the circle of people to which both the Mills belonged. He developed an interest in literature and moral questions, which was strengthened by his permanent attachment, after 1830, to Harriet Taylor, a married woman and mother whom he was eventually to marry 20 years later when she became a widow. This unconventional relationship estranged Mill from his family and most of his friends. A parallel difference of an intellectual kind became clear with the publication of Mill's first important book, *A System of Logic*, in 1843, for it criticized some of his father's philosophical views just as *On Liberty* was to criticize, many years afterward, his father's moral beliefs. The *Logic* made Mill famous and *Principles of Political Economy*, published 5 years later, consolidated Mill's position as the foremost British philosopher and economist of the period. These works were followed by a stream of essays and several shorter books that made his name known to an even wider public: *On Liberty* in 1859, *Representative Government* and *Utilitarianism* in 1861, *August Comte and Positivism* in 1865, and *The Subjection of Women* in 1869. Mill's *Autobiography* and his essays on socialism and on religion were published after his death.

Mill's writings were produced in the free time left to him from his position as a senior official of the East India Company until 1858, and as a member of Parliament, 1865–1868. His wife died in the seventh year of their marriage, and for the next 15 years Mill continued their practice of living much of the time in the south of France. Weakened by long standing tuberculosis, he died there in the cottage he had shared with his stepdaughter since his wife's death from the same disease, probably contracted from him.

In his autobiography Mill said that *On Liberty* was written in close collaboration with his wife, and that since it was as much her work as his no alteration to it would ever be made by him. It was published in London, 1859, 4 months after the death of Harriet Mill and was dedicated to her. *The Subjection of Women* was published in London in 1869 as part of Mill's campaign for women's rights, although the book itself was written in 1861.

SELECTIONS FROM
On Liberty

Chapter I   Introductory: The Nature of Civil Liberty

The subject of this Essay is not the so-called Liberty of the Will, so unfortunately opposed to the misnamed doctrine of Philosophical Necessity; but Civil, or Social Liberty: the nature and limits of the power which can be legitimately exercised by society over the individual. A question seldom stated, and hardly ever discussed, in general terms, but which profoundly influences the practical controversies of the age by its latent presence, and is likely soon to make itself recognized as the vital question of the future. It is so far from being new, that, in a certain sense, it has divided mankind, almost from the remotest ages; but in the stage of progress into which the more civilized portions of the species have now entered, it presents itself under new conditions, and requires a different and more fundamental treatment.

The struggle between Liberty and Authority is the most conspicuous feature in the portions of history with which we are earliest familiar, particularly in that of Greece, Rome, and England. But in old times this contest was between subjects, or some classes of subjects, and the Government. By liberty, was meant protection against the tyranny of the political rulers. The rulers were conceived (except in some of the popular governments of Greece) as in a necessarily antagonistic position to the people whom they ruled. They consisted of a governing One, or a governing tribe or caste, who derived their authority from inheritance or conquest, who, at all events, did not hold it at the pleasure of the governed, and whose supremacy men did not venture, perhaps did not desire, to contest, whatever precautions might be taken against its oppressive exercise. Their power was regarded as necessary, but also as highly dangerous; as a weapon which they would attempt to use against their subjects, no less than against external enemies. To prevent the weaker members of the community from being preyed upon by innumerable vultures, it was needful that there should be an animal of prey stronger than the rest, commissioned to keep them down. But as the king of the vultures would be no less bent upon preying on the flock than any of the minor harpies, it was indispensable to be in a perpetual attitude of defence against his beak and claws. The aim, therefore, of patriots was to set limits to the power which the ruler should be suffered to exercise over the community; and this limitation was what they meant by liberty. It was attempted in two ways. First, by obtaining a recognition of certain immunities, called political liberties or rights, which it was to be regarded as a breach of duty in the ruler to infringe, and which, if he did infringe, specific resistance, or general rebellion, was held to be justifiable. A second, and generally a later expedient, was the establishment of constitutional checks, by which the consent of the community, or of a body of some sort, supposed to represent its interests, was made a necessary condition to some of the more important acts of the governing power. To the first of these modes of limitation, the ruling power, in most European countries, was compelled, more or less, to submit. It was not so with the second; and, to attain this, or when already in some degree possessed, to attain it more completely, became everywhere the principal object of the lovers of liberty. And so long as mankind were content to combat one enemy by another, and to be ruled by a master, on condition of being guaranteed more or less efficaciously against his tyranny, they did not carry their aspirations beyond this point.

A time, however, came, in the progress of human affairs, when men ceased to think it a necessity of nature that their governors should be an independent power, opposed in interest to themselves. It appeared to them much better that the various magistrates of the State should be their tenants or delegates, revocable at their pleasure. In that way alone, it seemed, could they have complete security that the powers of government would never be abused to their disadvantage. By degrees this new demand for elective and temporary rulers became the prominent object of the exertions of the popular party, wherever any such party existed; and superseded, to a considerable extent, the previous efforts to limit the power of rulers. As the struggle proceeded for making the ruling power emanate from the periodical choice of the ruled, some persons began to think that too much importance had been attached to the limitation of the power itself. *That* (it might seem) was a resource against rulers whose interests were habitually opposed to those of the people. What was now wanted was, that the rulers should be identified with the people; that their interest and will should be the interest and will of the nation. The nation did not need to be protected against its own will. There was no fear of its tyrannizing over itself. Let the rulers be effectually responsible to it, promptly removable by it, and it could afford to trust them with power of which it could itself dictate the use to be made. Their power was but the nation's own power, concentrated, and in a form convenient for exercise. This mode of thought, or rather perhaps of feeling, was common among the last generation of European liberalism, in the Continental section of which it still apparently predominates. Those who admit any limit to what a government may do, except in the case of such governments as they think ought not to exist, stand out as brilliant exceptions among the political thinkers of the Continent. A similar tone of sentiment might by this time have been prevalent in our own country, if the circumstances which for a time encouraged it, had continued unaltered.

But, in political and philosophical theories, as well as in persons, success discloses faults and infirmities which failure might have concealed from observation. The notion, that the people have no need to limit their power over themselves, might seem axiomatic, when popular government was a thing only dreamed about, or read of as having existed at some distant period of the past. Neither was that notion necessarily disturbed by such temporary aberrations as those of the French Revolution, the worst of which were the work of an usurping few, and which, in any case, belonged, not to the permanent working of popular institutions, but to a sudden and convulsive outbreak against monarchical and aristocratic despotism. In time, however, a democratic republic came to occupy a large portion of the earth's surface, and made itself felt as one of the most powerful members of the community of nations; and elective and responsible government became subject to the observations and criticisms which wait upon a great existing fact. It was now perceived that such phrases as 'self-government', and 'the power of the people over themselves', do not express the true state of the case. The 'people' who exercise the power are not always the same people with those over whom it is exercised; and the 'self-government' spoken of is not the government of each by himself, but of each by all the rest. The will of the people, moreover, practically means the will of the most numerous or the most active *part* of the people; the majority, or those who succeed in making themselves accepted as the majority; the people, consequently, *may* desire to oppress a part of their number; and precautions are as much needed against this as against any other abuse of power. The limitation, therefore, of the power of government over individuals loses none of its importance when the holders of power are regularly accountable to the community, that is, to the strongest party therein. This view of things, recommending itself equally to the intelligence of thinkers and to the inclination of those important classes in European society to whose real or supposed interests democracy is adverse, has had no difficulty in establishing itself; and in political speculations 'the tyranny of the majority' is now generally included among the evils against which society requires to be on its guard.

Like other tyrannies, the tyranny of the majority was at first, and is still vulgarly, held in dread, chiefly as operating through the acts of the public authorities. But reflecting persons perceived that when society is itself the tyrant — society collectively, over the separate individuals who compose it — its means of tyrannizing are not restricted to the acts which it may do by the hands of its political functionaries. Society can and does execute its own mandates: and if it issues wrong mandates instead of right, or any mandates at all in things with which it ought not to meddle, it practises a social tyranny more formidable than many kinds of political oppression, since, though not usually upheld by such extreme penalties, it leaves fewer means of escape, penetrating much more deeply into the details of life, and enslaving the soul itself. Protection, therefore, against the tyranny of the magistrate is not enough: there needs protection also against the tyranny of the prevailing opinion and feeling; against the tendency of society to impose, by other means than civil penalties, its own ideas and practices as rules of conduct on those who dissent from them; to fetter the development, and, if possible, prevent the formation, of any individuality not in harmony with its ways, and compel all characters to fashion themselves upon the model of its own. There is a limit to the legitimate interference of collective opinion with individual independence: and to find that limit, and maintain it against encroachment, is as indispensable to a good condition of human affairs, as protection against political despotism.

But though this proposition is not likely to be contested in general terms, the practical question, where to place the limit—how to make the fitting adjustment between individual independence and social control—is a subject on which nearly everything remains to be done. All that makes existence valuable to any one, depends on the enforcement of restraints upon the actions of other people. Some rules of conduct, therefore, must be imposed, by law in the first place, and by opinion on many things which are not fit subjects for the operation of law. What these rules should be, is the principal question in human affairs; but if we except a few of the most obvious cases, it is one of those which least progress has been made in resolving. No two ages, and scarcely any two countries, have decided it alike; and the decision of one age or country is a wonder to another. Yet the people of any given age and country no more suspect any difficulty in it, than if it were a subject on which mankind had always been agreed. The rules which obtain among themselves appear to them self-evident and self-justifying. This all but universal illusion is one of the examples of the magical influence of custom, which is not only, as the proverb says, a second nature, but is continually mistaken for the first. The effect of custom, in preventing any misgiving respecting the rules of conduct which mankind impose on one another, is all the more complete because the subject is one on which it is not generally considered necessary that reasons should be given, either by one person to others, or by each to himself. People are accustomed to believe, and have been encouraged in the belief by some who aspire to the character of philosophers, that their feelings, on subjects of this nature, are better than reasons, and render reasons unnecessary. The practical principle which guides them to their opinions on the regulation of human conduct, is the feeling in each person's mind that everybody should be required to act as he, and those with whom he sympathizes, would like them to act. No one, indeed, acknowledges to himself that his standard of judgement is his own liking; but an opinion on a point of conduct, not supported by reasons, can only count as one person's preference; and if the reasons, when given, are a mere appeal to a similar preference felt by other people, it is still only many people's liking instead of one. To an ordinary man, however, his own preference, thus supported, is not only a perfectly satisfactory reason, but the only one he generally has for any of his notions of morality, taste, or propriety, which are not expressly written in his religious creed; and his chief guide in the interpretation even of that. Men's opinions, accordingly, on what is laudable or blameable, are affected by all the multifarious causes which influence their wishes in regard to the conduct of others, and which are as numerous as those which determine their wishes on any other subject. Sometimes their reason—at other times their prejudices or superstitions: often their social affections, not seldom their antisocial ones, their envy or jealousy, their arrogance or contemptuousness: but most commonly, their desires or fears for themselves — their legitimate or illegitimate self-interest. Wherever there is an ascendant class, a large portion of the morality of the country emanates from its class interests, and its feelings of class superiority. The morality between Spartans and Helots, between planters and negroes, between princes and subjects, between nobles and roturiers, between men and women, has been for the most part the creation of these class interests and feelings: and the sentiments thus generated, react in turn upon the moral feelings of the members of the ascendant class, in their relations among themselves. Where, on the other hand, a class, formerly ascendant, has lost its ascendancy, or where its ascendancy is unpopular, the prevailing moral sentiments frequently bear the impress of an impatient dislike of superiority. Another grand determining principle of the rules of conduct, both in act and forbearance, which have been enforced by law or opinion, has been the servility of mankind towards the supposed preferences or aversions of their temporal masters, or of their gods. This servility, though essentially selfish, is not hypocrisy; it gives rise to perfectly genuine sentiments of abhorrence; it made men burn magicians and heretics. Among so many baser influences, the general and obvious interests of society have of course had a share, and a large one, in the direction of the moral sentiments: less, however, as a matter of reason, and on their own account, than as a consequence of the sympathies and antipathies which grew out of them: and sympathies and antipathies which had little or nothing to do with the interests of society, have made themselves felt in the establishment of moralities with quite as great force.

The likings and dislikings of society, or of some powerful portion of it, are thus the main thing which has practically determined the rules laid down for general observance, under the penalties of law or opinion. And in general, those who have been in advance of society in thought and feeling, have left this condition of things unassailed in principle, however they may have come into conflict with it in some of its details. They have occupied themselves rather in inquiring what things society ought to like or dislike, than in questioning whether its likings or dislikings should be a law to individuals. They preferred endeavouring to alter the feelings of mankind on the particular points on which they were themselves heretical, rather than make common cause in defence of freedom, with heretics generally. The only case in which the higher ground has been taken on principle and maintained with consistency, by any but an individual here and there, is that of religious belief: a case instructive in many ways, and not least so as forming a most striking instance of the fallibility of which is called the moral sense: for the *odium theologicum*, in a sincere bigot, is one of the most unequivocal cases of moral feeling. Those who first broke the yoke of what called itself the Universal Church, were in general as little willing to permit difference of religious opinion as that church itself. But when the heat of the conflict was over, without giving a complete victory to any party, and each church or sect was reduced to limit its hopes to retaining possession of the ground it already occupied; minorities, seeing that they had no chance of becoming majorities, were under the necessity of pleading to those whom they could not convert, for permission to differ. It is accordingly on this battle-field, almost solely, that the rights of the individual against society have been asserted on broad grounds of principle, and the claim of society to exercise authority over dissentients, openly controverted. The great writers to whom the world owes what religious liberty it possesses, have mostly asserted freedom of conscience as an indefeasible right, and denied absolutely that a human being is accountable to others for his religious belief. Yet so natural to mankind is intolerance in whatever they really care about, that religious freedom has hardly anywhere been practically realized, except where religious indifference, which dislikes to have its peace disturbed by theological quarrels, has added its weight to the scale. In the minds of almost all religious persons, even in the most tolerant countries, the duty of toleration is admitted with tacit reserves. One person will bear with dissent in matters of church government, but not of dogma; another can tolerate everybody, short of a Papist or a Unitarian; another, every one who believes in revealed religion; a few extend their charity a little further, but stop at the belief in a God and in a future state. Wherever the sentiment of the majority is still genuine and intense, it is found to have abated little of its claim to be obeyed.

In England, from the peculiar circumstances of our political history, though the yoke of opinion is perhaps heavier, that of law is lighter, than in most other countries of Europe; and there is considerable jealousy of direct interference, by the legislative or the executive power, with private conduct; not so much from any just regard for the independence of the individual, as from the still subsisting habit of looking on the government as representing an opposite interest to the public. The majority have not yet learnt to feel the power of the government their power, or its opinions their opinions. When they do so, individual liberty will probably be as much exposed to invasion from the government, as it already is from public opinion. But, as yet, there is a considerable amount of feeling ready to be called forth against any attempt of the law to control individuals in things in which they have not hitherto been accustomed to be controlled by it; and this with very little discrimination as to whether the matter is, or is not, within the legitimate sphere of legal control; insomuch that the feeling, highly salutary on the whole, is perhaps quite as often misplaced as well grounded in the particular instances of its application. There is, in fact, no recognized principle by which the propriety or impropriety of government interference is customarily tested. People decide according to their personal preferences. Some, whenever they see any good to be done, or evil to be remedied, would willingly instigate the government to undertake the business; while others prefer to bear almost any amount of social evil, rather than add one to the departments of human interests amenable to governmental control. And men range themselves on one or the other side in any particular case, according to this general direction of their senti-

CLASSICAL POLITICAL THEORIES

ments; or according to the degree of interest which they feel in the particular thing which it is proposed that the government should do, or according to the belief they entertain that the government would, or would not, do it in the manner they prefer; but very rarely on account of any opinion to which they consistently adhere, as to what things are fit to be done by a government. And it seems to me that in consequence of this absence of rule or principle, one side is at present as often wrong as the other; the interference of government is, with about equal frequency, improperly invoked and improperly condemned.

The object of this Essay is to assert one very simple principle, as entitled to govern absolutely the dealings of society with the individual in the way of compulsion and control, whether the means used be physical force in the form of legal penalties, or the moral coercion of public opinion. That principle is, that the sole end for which mankind are warranted, individually or collectively, in interfering with the liberty of action of any of their number, is self-protection. That the only purpose for which power can be rightfully exercised over any member of a civilized community, against his will, is to prevent harm to others. His own good, either physical or moral, is not a sufficient warrant. He cannot rightfully be compelled to do or forbear because it will be better for him to do so, because it will make him happier, because, in the opinions of others, to do so would be wise, or even right. These are good reasons for remonstrating with him, or reasoning with him, or persuading him, or entreating him, but not for compelling him, or visiting him with any evil in case he do otherwise. To justify that, the conduct from which it is desired to deter him, must be calculated to produce evil to some one else. The only part of the conduct of any one, for which he is amenable to society, is that which concerns others. In the part which merely concerns himself, his independence is, of right, absolute. Over himself, over his own body and mind, the individual is sovereign.

It is, perhaps, hardly necessary to say that this doctrine is meant to apply only to human beings in the maturity of their faculties. We are not speaking of children, or of young persons below the age which the law may fix as that of manhood or womanhood. Those who are still in a state to require being taken care of by others, must be protected against their own actions as well as against external injury. For the same reason, we may leave out of consideration those backward states of society in which the race itself may be considered as in its nonage. The early difficulties in the way of spontaneous progress are so great, that there is seldom any choice of means for overcoming them; and a ruler full of the spirit of improvement is warranted in the use of any expedients that will attain an end, perhaps otherwise unattainable. Despotism is a legitimate mode of government in dealing with barbarians, provided the end be their improvement, and the means justified by actually effecting that end. Liberty, as a principle, has no application to any state of things anterior to the time when mankind have become capable of being improved by free and equal discussion. Until then, there is nothing for them but implicit obedience to an Akbar or a Charlemagne, if they are so fortunate as to find one. But as soon as mankind have attained the capacity of being guided to their own improvement by conviction or persuasion (a period long since reached in all nations with whom we need here concern ourselves), compulsion, either in the direct form or in that of pains and penalties for non-compliance, is no longer admissible as a means to their own good, and justifiable only for the security of others.

It is proper to state that I forgo any advantage which could be derived to my argument from the idea of abstract right, as a thing independent of utility. I regard utility as the ultimate appeal on all ethical questions; but it must be utility in the largest sense, grounded on the permanent interests of man as a progressive being. Those interests, I contend, authorize the subjection of individual spontaneity to external control, only in respect to those actions of each, which concern the interest of other people. If any one does an act hurtful to others, there is a prima facie case for punishing him, by law, or, where legal penalties are not safely applicable, by general disapprobation. There are also many positive acts for the benefit of others, which he may rightfully be compelled to perform; such as, to give evidence in a court of justice; to bear his fair share in the common defence, or in any other joint work necessary to the interest of the society of which he enjoys the protection; and to perform certain acts of individual beneficence, such as saving a fellow creature's life, or interposing to protect the defenceless against ill-usage, things which whenever it is obviously a man's duty to do, he may rightfully be made responsible to society for not doing. A person may cause evil to others not only by his actions but by his inaction, and in either case he is justly accountable to them for the injury. The latter case, it is true, requires a much more cautious exercise of compulsion than the former. To make any one answerable for doing evil to others, is the rule; to make him answerable for not preventing evil, is, comparatively speaking, the exception. Yet there are many cases clear enough and grave enough to justify that exception. In all things which regard the external relations of the individual, he is *de jure* amenable to those whose interests are concerned, and if need be, to society as their protector. There are often good reasons for not holding him to the responsibility; but these reasons must arise from the special expediencies of the case: either because it is a kind of case in which he is on the whole likely to act better, when left to his own discretion, than when controlled in any way in which society have it in their power to control him; or because the attempt to exercise control would produce other evils, greater than those which it would prevent. When such reasons as these preclude the enforcement of responsibility, the conscience of the agent himself should step into the vacant judgement-seat, and protect those interests of others which have no external protection; judging himself all the more rigidly, because the case does not admit of his being made accountable to the judgement of his fellow creatures.

But there is a sphere of action in which society, as distinguished from the individual, has, if any, only an indirect interest; comprehending all that portion of a person's life and conduct which affects only himself, or if it also affects others, only with their free, voluntary, and undeceived consent and participation. When I say only himself, I mean directly, and in the first instance: for whatever affects himself, may affect others through himself; and the objection which may be grounded on this contingency will receive consideration in the sequel. This, then, is the appropriate region of human liberty. It comprises, first, the inward domain of consciousness; demanding liberty of conscience, in the most comprehensive sense; liberty of thought and feeling; absolute freedom of opinion and sentiment on all subjects, practical or speculative, scientific, moral, or theological. The liberty of expressing and publishing opinions may seem to fall under a different principle, since it belongs to that part of the conduct of an individual which concerns other people; but, being almost of as much importance as the liberty of thought itself, and resting in great part on the same reasons, is practically inseparable from it. Secondly, the principle requires liberty of tastes and pursuits; of framing the plan of our life to suit our own character; of doing as we like, subject to such consequences as may follow: without impediment from our fellow creatures, so long as what we do does not harm them, even though they should think our conduct foolish, perverse, or wrong. Thirdly, from this liberty of each individual, follows the liberty, within the same limits, of combination among individuals; freedom to unite, for any purpose not involving harm to others: the persons combining being supposed to be of full age, and not forced or deceived.

No society in which these liberties are not, on the whole, respected, is free, whatever may be its form of government; and none is completely free in which they do not exist absolute and unqualified. The only freedom which deserves the name, is that of pursuing our own good in our own way, so long as we do not attempt to deprive others of theirs, or impede their efforts to obtain it. Each is the proper guardian of his own health, whether bodily, or mental and spiritual. Mankind are greater gainers by suffering each other to live as seems good to themselves, than by compelling each to live as seems good to the rest.

Though this doctrine is anything but new, and, to some persons, may have the air of a truism, there is no doctrine which stands more directly opposed to the general tendency of existing opinion and practice. Society has expended fully as much effort in the attempt (according to its lights) to compel people to conform to its notions of personal, as of social excellence. The ancient commonwealths thought themselves entitled to practise, and the ancient philosophers countenanced, the regulation of every part of private conduct by public authority, on the ground that the State had a deep interest in the whole bodily and mental discipline of every one of its citizens; a mode of thinking which may have been admissible in small republics surrounded by powerful enemies, in constant peril of being subverted by foreign attack or internal commotion, and to which even a short interval of relaxed energy and self-command might so easily be fatal, that they could not afford to wait for the salutary permanent effects of freedom. In the modern world, the greater size of political communities, and, above all, the separation between spiritual and temporal authority (which placed the direction of men's consciences in other hands than those which controlled their worldly affairs), prevented so great an interference by law in the details of private life; but the engines of moral repression have been wielded more strenuously against divergence from the reigning opinion in self-regarding, than even in social matters; religion, the most powerful of the elements which have entered into the formation of moral feeling, having almost always been governed either by the ambition of a hierarchy, seeking control over every department of human conduct, or by the spirit of Puritanism. And some of those modern reformers who have placed themselves in strongest opposition to the religions of the past, have been no way behind either churches or sects in their assertion of the right of spiritual domination: M. Comte, in particular, whose social system, as unfolded in his *Système de Politique Positive*, aims at establishing (though by moral more than by legal appliances) a despotism of society over the individual, surpassing anything contemplated in the political ideal of the most rigid disciplinarian among the ancient philosophers.

Apart from the peculiar tenets of individual thinkers, there is also in the world at large an increasing inclination to stretch unduly the powers of society over the individual, both by the force of opinion and even by that of legislation: and as the tendency of all the changes taking place in the world is to strengthen society, and diminish the power of the individual, this encroachment is not one of the evils which tend spontaneously to disappear, but, on the contrary, to grow more and more formidable. The disposition of mankind, whether as rulers or as fellow citizens, to impose their own opinions and inclinations as a rule of conduct on others, is so energetically supported by some of the best and by some of the worst feelings incident to human nature, that it is hardly ever kept under restraint by anything but want of power; and as the power is not declining, but growing, unless a strong barrier of moral conviction can be raised against the mischief, we must expect, in the present circumstances of the world, to see it increase.

It will be convenient for the argument, if, instead of at once entering upon the general thesis, we confine ourselves in the first instance to a single branch of it, on which the principle here stated is, if not fully, yet to a certain point, recognized by the current opinions. This one branch is the Liberty of Thought: from which it is impossible to separate the cognate liberty of speaking and of writing. Although these liberties, to some considerable amount, form part of the political morality of all countries which profess religious toleration and free institutions, the grounds, both philosophical and practical, on which they rest, are perhaps not so familiar to the general mind, nor so thoroughly appreciated by many even of the leaders of opinion, as might have been expected. Those grounds, when rightly understood, are of much wider application than to only one division of the subject, and a thorough consideration of this part of the question will be found the best introduction to the remainder. Those to whom nothing which I am about to say will be new, may therefore, I hope, excuse me, if on a subject which for now three centuries has been so often discussed, I venture on one discussion more.

Chapter II   On Liberty of Thought and Discussion

. . . It still remains to speak of one of the principal causes which make diversity of opinion advantageous, and will continue to do so until mankind shall have entered a stage of intellectual advancement which at present seems at an incalculable distance. We have hitherto considered only two possibilities: that the received opinion may be false, and some other opinion, consequently, true; or that, the received opinion being true, a conflict with the opposite error is essential to a clear apprehension and deep feeling of its truth. But there is a commoner case than either of these; when the conflicting doctrines, instead of being one true and the other false, share the truth between them; and the nonconforming opinion is needed to supply the remainder of the truth, of which the received doctrine embodies only a part. Popular opinions, on subjects not palpable to sense, are often true, but seldom or never the whole truth. They are a part of the truth; sometimes a greater, sometimes a smaller part, but exaggerated, distorted, and disjoined from the truths by which they ought to be accompanied and limited. Heretical opinions, on the other hand, are generally some of these suppressed and neglected truths, bursting the bonds which kept them down, and either seeking reconciliation with the truth contained in the common opinion, or fronting it as enemies, and setting themselves up, with similar exclusiveness, as the whole truth. The latter case is hitherto the most frequent, as, in the human mind, one-sidedness has always been the rule, and many-sidedness the exception. Hence, even in revolutions of opinion, one part of the truth usually sets while another rises. Even progress, which ought to superadd, for the most part only substitutes, one partial and incomplete truth for another; improvement consisting chiefly in this, that the new fragment of truth is more wanted, more adapted to the needs of the time, than that which it displaces. Such being the partial character of prevailing opinions, even when resting on a true foundation, every opinion which embodies somewhat of the portion of truth which the common opinion omits, ought to be considered precious, with whatever amount of error and confusion that truth may be blended. No sober judge of human affairs will feel bound to be indignant because those who force on our notice truths which we should otherwise have overlooked, overlook some of those which we see. Rather, he will think that so long as popular truth is one-sided, it is more desirable than otherwise that unpopular truth should have one-sided asserters too; such being usually the most energetic, and the most likely to compel reluctant attention to the fragment of wisdom which they proclaim as if it were the whole.

Thus, in the eighteenth century, when nearly all the instructed, and all those of the uninstructed who were led by them, were lost in admiration of what is called civilization, and of the marvels of modern science, literature, and philosophy, and while greatly overrating the amount of unlikeness between the men of modern and those of ancient times, indulged the belief that the whole of the difference was in their own favour; with what a salutary shock did the paradoxes of Rousseau explode like bombshells in the midst, dislocating the compact mass of one-sided opinion, and forcing its elements to recombine in a better form and with additional ingredients. Not that the current opinions were on the whole farther from the truth than Rousseau's were; on the contrary, they were nearer to it; they contained more of positive truth, and very much less of error. Nevertheless there lay in Rousseau's doctrine, and has floated down the stream of opinion along with it, a considerable amount of exactly those truths which the popular opinion wanted; and these are the deposit which was left behind when the flood subsided. The superior worth of simplicity of life, the enervating and demoralizing effect of the trammels and hypocrisies of artificial society, are ideas which have never been entirely absent from cultivated minds since Rousseau wrote; and they will in time produce their due effect, though at present needing to be asserted as much as ever, and to be asserted by deeds, for words, on this subject, have nearly exhausted their power.

In politics, again, it is almost a commonplace, that a party of order or stability, and a party of progress or reform, are both necessary elements of a healthy state of political life; until the one or the other shall have so enlarged its mental grasp as to be a party equally of order and of progress, knowing and distinguishing what is fit to be preserved from what ought to be swept away. Each of these modes of thinking derives its utility from the deficiencies of the other; but it is in a great measure the opposition of the other that keeps each within the limits of reason and sanity. Unless opinions favourable to democracy and to aristocracy, to property and to equality, to co-operation and to competition, to luxury and to abstinence, to sociality and individuality, to liberty and discipline, and all the other standing antagonisms of practical life, are expressed with equal freedom, and enforced and defended with equal talent and energy, there is no chance of both elements obtaining their due; one scale is sure to go up, and the other down. Truth, in the great practical concerns of life, is so much a question of the reconciling and combining of opposites, that very few have minds sufficiently capacious and impartial to make the adjustment with an approach to correctness, and it has to be made by the rough process of a struggle between combatants fighting under hostile banners. On any of the great open questions just enumerated, if either of the two opinions has a better claim than the other, not merely to be tolerated, but to be encouraged and countenanced, it is the one which happens at the particular time and place to be in a minority. That is the opinion which, for the time being, represents the neglected interests, the side of human well-being which is in danger of obtaining less than its share. I am aware that there is not, in this country, any intolerance of differences of opinion on most of these topics. They are adduced to show, by admitted and multiplied examples, the universality of the fact, that only through diversity of opinion is there, in the existing state of human intellect, a chance of fair play to all sides of the truth. When there are persons to be found, who form an exception to the apparent unanimity of the world on any subject, even if the world is in the right, it is always probable that dissentients have something worth hearing to say for themselves, and that truth would lose something by their silence.

It may be objected, 'But *some* received principles, especially on the highest and most vital subjects, are more than half-truths. The Christian morality, for instance, is the whole truth on that subject, and if any one teaches a morality which varies from it, he is wholly in error.' As this is of all cases the most important in practice, none can be fitter to test the general maxim. But before pronouncing what Christian morality is or is not, it would be desirable to decide what is meant by Christian morality. If it means the morality of the New Testament, I wonder that any one who derives his knowledge of this from the book itself, can suppose that it was announced, or intended, as a complete doctrine of morals. The Gospel always refers to a pre-existing morality, and confines its precepts to the particulars in which that morality was to be corrected, or superseded by a wider and higher; express-ing itself, moreover, in terms most general, often impossible to be interpreted literally, and possessing rather the impressiveness of poetry or eloquence than the precision of legislation. To extract from it a body of ethical doctrine, has never been possible without eking it out from the Old Testament, that is, from a system elaborate indeed, but in many respects barbarous, and in-tended only for a barbarous people. St. Paul, a declared enemy to this Judaical mode of interpreting the doctrine and filling up the scheme of his Master, equally assumes a pre-existing morality, namely that of the Greeks and Romans; and his advice to Christians is in a great measure a system of accommodation to that; even to the extent of giving an apparent sanction to slavery. What is called Christian, but should rather be termed theological, morality, was not the work of Christ or the Apostles, but is of much later origin, having been gradually built up by the Catholic church of the first five centuries, and though not implicitly adopted by moderns and Protestants, has been much less modified by them than might have been expected. For the most part, indeed, they have contented themselves with cutting off the additions which had been made to it in the middle ages, each sect supplying the place by fresh additions, adapted to its own character and tendencies. That mankind owe a great debt to this morality, and to its early teachers, I should be the last person to deny; but I do not scruple to say of it, that it is, in many important points, incomplete and one-sided, and that unless ideas and feelings, not sanctioned by it, had contributed to the formation of European life and character, human affairs would have been in a worse condition than they now are. Christian morality (so called) has all the characters of a reaction; it is, in great part, a protest against Paganism. Its ideal is negative rather than positive; passive rather than active; Innocence rather than Nobleness; Abstinence from Evil, rather than energetic Pursuit of Good: in its precepts (as has been well said) 'thou shalt not' predominates unduly over 'thou shalt'. In its horror of sensuality, it made an idol of asceticism, which has been gradually compromised away into one of legality. It holds out the hope of heaven and the threat of hell, as the appointed and appropriate motives to a virtuous life: in this falling far below the best of the ancients, and doing what lies in it to give to human morality an essentially selfish character, by disconnecting each man's feelings of duty from the interests of his fellow-creatures, except so far as a self-interested inducement is offered to him for consulting them. It is essentially a doctrine of passive obedience; it inculcates submission to all authorities found established; who indeed are not to be actively obeyed when they command what religion forbids, but who are not to be resisted, far less rebelled against, for any amount of wrong to ourselves. And while, in the morality of the best Pagan nations, duty to the State holds even a disproportionate place, infringing on the just liberty of the individual; in purely Christian ethics, that grand department of duty is scarcely noticed or acknowledged. It is in the Koran, not the New Testament, that we read the maxim — 'A ruler who appoints any man to an office, when there is in his dominions another man better qualified for it, sins against God and against the State.' What little recognition the idea of obligation to the public obtains in modern morality, is derived from Greek and Roman sources, not from Christian; as, even in the morality of private life, whatever exists of magnanimity, highmindedness, personal dignity, even the sense of honour, is derived from the purely human, not the religious part of our education, and never could have grown out of a standard of ethics in which the only worth, professedly recognized, is that of obedience.

I am as far as any one from pretending that these defects are necessarily inherent in the Christian ethics, in every manner in which it can be conceived, or that the many requisites of a complete moral doctrine which it does not contain, do not admit of being reconciled with it. Far less would I insinuate this of the doctrines and precepts of Christ himself. I believe that the sayings of Christ are all, that I can see any evidence of their having been intended to be; that they are irreconcilable with nothing which a comprehensive morality requires; that everything which is excellent in ethics may be brought within them, with no greater violence to their language than has been done to it by all who have attempted to deduce from them any practical system of conduct whatever. But it is quite consistent with this, to believe that they contain, and were meant to contain, only a part of the truth; that many essential elements of the highest morality are among the things which are not provided for, nor intended to be provided for, in the recorded deliverances of the Founder of Christianity, and which have been entirely thrown aside in the system of ethics erected on the basis of those deliverances by the Christian Church. And this being so, I think it a great error to persist in attempting to find in the Christian doctrine that complete rule for our guidance, which its author intended it to sanction and enforce, but only partially to provide. I believe, too, that this narrow theory is becoming a grave practical evil, detracting greatly from the value of the moral training and instruction, which so many well-meaning persons are now at length exerting themselves to promote. I much fear that by attempting to form the mind and feelings on an exclusively religious type, and discarding those secular standards (as for want of a better name they may be called) which heretofore co-existed with and supplemented the Christian ethics, receiving some of its spirit, and infusing into it some of theirs, there will result, and is even now resulting, a low, abject, servile type of character, which, submit itself as it may to what it deems the Supreme Will, is incapable of rising to or sympathizing in the conception of Supreme Goodness. I believe that other ethics than any which can be evolved from exclusively Christian sources, must exist side by side with Christian ethics to produce the moral regeneration of mankind; and that the Christian system is no exception to the rule, that in an imperfect state of the human mind, the interests of truth require a diversity of opinions. It is not necessary that in ceasing to ignore the moral truths not contained in Christianity, men should ignore any of those which it does contain. Such prejudice, or oversight, when it occurs, is altogether an evil; but it is one from which we cannot hope to be always exempt, and must be regarded as the price paid for an inestimable good. The exclusive pretension made by a part of the truth to be the whole, must and ought to be protested against; and if a reactionary impulse should make the protestors unjust in their turn, this one-sidedness, like the other, may be lamented, but must be tolerated. If Christians would teach infidels to be just to Christianity, they should themselves be just to infidelity. It can do truth no service to blink the fact, known to all who have the most ordinary acquaintance with literary history, that a large portion of the noblest and most valuable moral teaching has been the work, not only of men who did not know, but of men who knew and rejected, the Christian faith.

I do not pretend that the most unlimited use of the freedom of enunciating all possible opinions would put an end to the evils of religious or philosophical sectarianism. Every truth which men of narrow capacity are in earnest about, is sure to be asserted, inculcated, and in many ways even acted on, as if no other truth existed in the world, or at all events none that could limit or qualify the first. I acknowledge that the tendency of all opinions to become sectarian is not cured by the freest discussion, but is often heightened and exacerbated thereby; the truth which ought to have been, but was not, seen, being rejected all the more violently because proclaimed by persons regarded as opponents. But it is not on the impassioned partisan, it is on the calmer and more disinterested bystander, that this collision of opinions works its salutary effect. Not the violent conflict between parts of the truth, but the quiet suppression of half of it, is the formidable evil; there is always hope when people are forced to listen to both sides; it is when they attend only to one that errors harden into prejudices, and truth itself ceases to have the effect of truth, by being exaggerated into falsehood. And since there are few mental attributes more rare than that judicial faculty which can sit in intelligent judgement between two sides of a question, of which only one is represented by an advocate before it, truth has no chance but in proportion as every side of it, every opinion which embodies any fraction of the truth, not only finds advocates, but is so advocated as to be listened to.

We have now recognized the necessity to the mental well-being of mankind (on which all their other well-being depends) of freedom of opinion, and freedom of the expression of opinion, on four distinct grounds; which we will now briefly recapitulate.

First, if any opinion is compelled to silence, that opinion may, for aught we can certainly know, be true. To deny this is to assume our own infallibility.

Secondly, though the silenced opinion be an error, it may, and very commonly does, contain a portion of truth; and since the general or prevailing opinion on any subject is rarely or never the whole truth, it is only by the collision of adverse opinions that the remainder of the truth has any chance of being supplied.

Thirdly, even if the received opinion be not only true, but the whole truth; unless it is suffered to be, and actually is, vigorously and earnestly contested, it will, by most of those who receive it, be held in the manner of a prejudice, with little comprehension or feeling of its rational grounds. And not only this, but, fourthly, the meaning of the doctrine itself will be in danger of being lost, or enfeebled, and deprived of its vital effect on the character and conduct: the dogma becoming a mere formal profession, inefficacious for good, but cumbering the ground, and preventing the growth of any real and heartfelt conviction, from reason or personal experience.

Before quitting the subject of freedom of opinion, it is fit to take some notice of those who say, that the free expression of all opinions should be permitted, on condition that the manner be temperate, and do not pass the bounds of fair discussion. Much might be said on the impossibility of fixing where these supposed bounds are to be placed; for if the test be offence to those whose opinion is attacked, I think experience testifies that this offence is given whenever the attack is telling and powerful, and that every opponent who pushes them hard, and whom they find it difficult to answer, appears to them, if he shows any strong feeling on the subject, an intemperate opponent. But this, though an important consideration in a practical point of view, merges in a more fundamental objection. Undoubtedly the manner of asserting an opinion, even though it be a true one, may be very objectionable, and may justly incur severe censure. But the principal offences of the kind are such as it is mostly impossible, unless by accidental self-betrayal, to bring home to conviction. The gravest of them is, to argue sophistically, to suppress facts or arguments, to misstate the elements of the case, or misrepresent the opposite opinion. But all this, even to the most aggravated degree, is so continually done in perfect good faith, by persons who are not considered, and in many other respects may not deserve to be considered, ignorant or incompetent, that it is rarely possible on adequate grounds conscientiously to stamp the misrepresentation as morally culpable; and still less could law presume to interfere with this kind of controversial misconduct. With regard to what is commonly meant by intemperate discussion, namely invective, sarcasm, personality, and the like, the denunciation of these weapons would deserve more sympathy if it were ever proposed to interdict them equally to both sides; but it is only desired to restrain the employment of them against the prevailing opinion: against the unprevailing they may not only be used without general disapproval, but will be likely to obtain for him who uses them the praise of honest zeal and righteous indignation. Yet whatever mischief arises from their use, is greatest when they are employed against the comparatively defenceless; and whatever unfair advantage can be derived by any opinion from this mode of asserting it, accrues almost exclusively to received opinions. The worst offence of this kind which can be committed by a polemic, is to stigmatize those who hold the contrary opinion as bad and immoral men. To calumny of this sort, those who hold any unpopular opinion are peculiarly exposed, because they are in general few and uninfluential, and nobody but themselves feels much interested in seeing justice done them; but this weapon is, from the nature of the case, denied to those who attack a prevailing opinion: they can neither use it with safety to themselves, nor, if they could, would it do anything but recoil on their own cause. In general, opinions contrary to those commonly received can only obtain a hearing by studied moderation of language, and the most cautious avoidance of unnecessary offence, from which they hardly ever deviate even in a slight degree without losing ground: while unmeasured vituperation employed on the side of the prevailing opinion, really does deter people from professing contrary opinions, and from listening to those who profess them. For the interest, therefore, of truth and justice, it is far more important to restrain this employment of vituperative language than the other; and, for example, if it were necessary to choose, there would be much more need to discourage offensive attacks on infidelity, than on religion. It is, however, obvious that law and authority have no business with restraining either, while opinion ought, in every instance, to determine its verdict by the circumstances of the individual case; condemning every one, on whichever side of the argument he places himself, in whose mode of advocacy either want of candour, or malignity, bigotry, or intolerance of feeling manifest themselves; but not inferring these vices from the side which a person takes, though it be the contrary side of the question to our own: and given merited honour to every one, whatever opinion he may hold, who has calmness to see and honesty to state what his opponents and their opinions really are, exaggerating nothing to their discredit, keeping nothing back which tells, or can be supposed to tell, in their favour. This is the real morality of public discussion: and if often violated, I am happy to think that there are many controversialists who to a great extent observe it, and a still greater number who conscientiously strive towards it.

Chapter IV   Of the Limits to the Authority of Society
Over the Individual

What, then, is the rightful limit to the sovereignty of the individual over himself? Where does the authority of society begin? How much of human life should be assigned to individuality, and how much to society?

Each will receive its proper share, if each has that which more particularly concerns it. To individuality should belong the part of life in which it is chiefly the individual that is interested; to society, the part which chiefly interests society.

Though society is not founded on a contract, and though no good purpose is answered by inventing a contract in order to deduce social obligations from it, every one who receives the protection of society owes a return for the benefit, and the fact of living in society renders it indispensable that each should be bound to observe a certain line of conduct towards the rest. This conduct consists, first, in not injuring the interests of one another; or rather certain interests, which, either by express legal provision or by tacit understanding, ought to be considered as rights; and secondly, in each person's bearing his share (to be fixed on some equitable principle) of the labours and sacrifices incurred for defending the society or its members from injury and molestation. These conditions society is justified in enforcing at all costs to those who endeavour to withhold fulfilment. Nor is this all that society may do. The acts of an individual may be hurtful to others, or wanting in due consideration for their welfare, without going the length of violating any of their constituted rights. The offender may then be justly punished by opinion, though not by law. As soon as any part of a person's conduct affects prejudicially the interests of others, society has jurisdiction over it, and the question whether the general welfare will or will not be promoted by interfering with it, becomes open to discussion. But there is no room for entertaining any such question when a person's conduct affects the interests of no persons besides himself, or needs not affect them unless they like (all the persons concerned being of full age, and the ordinary amount of understanding). In all such cases there should be perfect freedom, legal and social, to do the action and stand the consequences.

It would be a great misunderstanding of this doctrine to suppose that it is one of selfish indifference, which pretends that human beings have no business with each other's conduct in life, and that they should not concern themselves about the well-doing or well-being of one another, unless their own interest is involved. Instead of any diminution, there is need of a great increase of disinterested exertion to promote the good of others. But disinterested benevolence can find other instruments to persuade people to their good, than whips and scourges, either of the literal or the metaphorical sort. I am the last person to undervalue the self-regarding virtues; they are only second in importance, if even second, to the social. It is equally the business of education to cultivate both. But even education works by conviction and persuasion as well as by compulsion, and it is by the former only that, when the period of education is past, the self-regarding virtues should be inculcated. Human beings owe to each other help to distinguish the better from the worse, and encouragement to choose the former and avoid the latter. They should be for ever stimulating each other to increased exercise of their higher faculties, and increased direction of their feelings and aims towards wise instead of foolish, elevating instead of degrading, objects and contemplations. But neither one person, nor any number of persons, is warranted in saying to another human creature of ripe years, that he shall not do with his life for his own benefit what he chooses to do with it. He is the person most interested in his own well-being: the interest which any other person, except in cases of strong personal attachment, can have in it, is trifling, compared with that which he himself has; the interest which society has in him individually (except as to his conduct to others) is fractional, and altogether indirect: while, with respect to his own feelings and circumstances, the most ordinary man or woman has means of knowledge immeasurably surpassing those that can be possessed by any one else. The interference of society to overrule his judgement and purposes in what only regards himself, must be grounded on general presumptions; which may be altogether wrong, and even if right, are as likely as not to be misapplied to individual cases, by persons no better acquainted with the circumstances of such cases than those are who look at them merely from without. In this department, therefore, of human affairs, individuality has its proper field of action. In the conduct of human beings towards one another, it is necessary that general rules should for the most part be observed, in order that people may know what they have to expect; but in each person's own concerns, his individual spontaneity is entitled to free exercise. Considerations to aid his judgement, exhortations to strengthen his will, may be offered to him, even obtruded on him, by others; but he himself is the final judge. All errors which he is likely to commit against advice and warning, are far outweighed by the evil of allowing others to constrain him to what they deem his good.

I do not mean that the feelings with which a person is regarded by others, ought not to be in any way affected by his self-regarding qualities or deficiencies. This is neither possible nor desirable. If he is eminent in any of the qualities which conduce to his own good, he is, so far, a proper object of admiration. He is so much the nearer to the ideal perfection of human nature. If he is grossly deficient in those qualities, a sentiment the opposite of admiration will follow. There is a degree of folly, and a degree of what may be called (though the phrase is not unobjectionable) lowness or depravation of taste, which, though it cannot justify doing harm to the person who manifests it, renders him necessarily and properly a subject of distaste, or, in extreme cases, even of contempt: a person could not have the opposite qualities in due strength without entertaining these feelings. Though doing no wrong to any one, a person may so act as to compel us to judge him, and feel to him, as a fool, or as a being of an inferior order: and since this judgement and feeling are a fact which he would prefer to avoid, it is doing him a service to warn him of it beforehand, as of any other disagreeable consequence to which he exposes himself. It would be well, indeed, if this good office were much more freely rendered than the common notions of politeness at present permit, and if one person could honestly point out to another that he thinks him in fault, without being considered unmannerly or presuming. We have a right, also, in various ways, to act upon our unfavourable opinion of any one, not to the oppression of his individuality, but in the exercise of ours. We are not bound, for example, to seek his society; we have a right to avoid it (though not to parade the avoidance), for we have a right to choose the society most acceptable to us. We have a right, and it may be our duty, to caution others against him, if we think his example or conversation likely to have a pernicious effect on those with whom he associates. We may give others a preference over him in optional good offices, except those which tend to his improvement. In these various modes a person may suffer very severe penalties at the hands of others, for faults which directly concern only himself; but he suffers these penalties only in so far as they are the natural, and, as it were, the spontaneous consequences of the faults themselves, not because they are purposely inflicted on him for the sake of punishment. A person who shows rashness, obstinacy, self-conceit — who cannot live within moderate means — who cannot restrain himself from hurtful indulgences — who pursues animal pleasures at the expense of those of feeling and intellect — must expect to be lowered in the opinion of others, and to have a less share of their favourable sentiments; but of this he has no right to complain, unless he has merited their favour by special excellence in his social relations, and has thus established a title to their good offices, which is not affected by his demerits towards himself.

What I contend for is, that the inconveniences which are strictly inseparable from the unfavourable judgement of others, are the only ones to which a person should ever be subjected for that portion of his conduct and character which concerns his own good, but which does not affect the interests of others in their relations with him. Acts injurious to others require a totally different treatment. Encroachment on their rights; infliction on them of any loss or damage not justified by his own rights; falsehood or duplicity in dealing with them; unfair or ungenerous use of advantages over them; even selfish abstinence from defending them against injury — these are fit objects of moral reprobation, and, in grave cases, of moral retribution and punishment. And not only these acts, but the dispositions which lead to them, are properly immoral, and fit subjects of disapprobation which may rise to abhorrence. Cruelty of disposition; malice and ill nature; that most anti-social and odious of all passions, envy; dissimulation and insincerity; irascibility on insufficient cause, and resentment disproportioned to the provocation; the love of domineering over others; the desire to engross more than one's share of advantages (the πλεονεξία of the Greeks); the pride which derives gratification from the abasement of others; the egotism which thinks self and its concerns more important than everything else, and decides all doubtful questions in its own favour; — these are moral vices, and constitute a bad and odious moral character: unlike the self-regarding faults previously mentioned, which are not properly immoralities, and to whatever pitch they may be carried, do not constitute wickedness. They may be proofs of any amount of folly, or want of personal dignity and self-respect; but they are only a subject of moral reprobation when they involve a breach of duty to others, for whose sake the individual is bound to have care for himself. What are called duties to ourselves are not socially obligatory, unless circumstances render them at the same time duties to others. The term duty to oneself, when it means anything more than prudence, means self-respect or self-development; and for none of these is any one accountable to his fellow creatures, because for none of them is it for the good of mankind that he be held accountable to them.

The distinction between the loss of consideration which a person may rightly incur by defect of prudence or of personal dignity, and the reprobation which is due to him for an offence against the rights of others, is not a merely nominal distinction. It makes a vast difference both in our feelings and in our conduct towards him, whether he displeases us in things in which we think we have a right to control him, or in things in which we know that we have not. If he displeases us, we may express our distaste, and we may stand aloof from a person as well as from a thing that displeases us; but we shall not therefore feel called on to make his life uncomfortable. We shall reflect that he already bears, or will bear, the whole penalty of his error; if he spoils his life by mismanagement, we shall not, for that reason, desire to spoil it still further: instead of wishing to punish him, we shall rather endeavour to alleviate his punishment, by showing him how he may avoid or cure the evils his conduct tends to bring upon him. He may be to us an object of pity, perhaps of dislike, but not of anger or resentment; we shall not treat him like an enemy of society: the worst we shall think ourselves justified in doing is leaving him to himself, if we do not interfere benevolently by showing interest or concern for him. It is far otherwise if he has infringed the rules necessary for the protection of his fellow creatures, individually or collectively. The evil consequences of his acts do not then fall on himself, but on others; and society, as the protector of all its members, must retaliate on him; must inflict pain on him for the express purpose of punishment, and must take care that it be sufficiently severe. In the one case, he is an offender at our bar, and we are called on not only to sit in judgement on him, but, in one shape or another, to execute our own sentence; in the other case, it is not our part to inflict any suffering on him, except what may incidentally follow from our using the same liberty in the regulation of our own affairs, which we allow to him in his.

The distinction here pointed out between the part of a person's life which concerns only himself, and that which concerns others, many persons will refuse to admit. How (it may be asked) can any part of the conduct of a member of society be a matter of indifference to the other members? No person is an entirely isolated being; it is impossible for a person to do anything seriously or permanently hurtful to himself, without mischief reaching at least to his near connexions, and often far beyond them. If he injures his property, he does harm to those who directly or indirectly derived support from it, and usually diminishes, by a greater or less amount, the general resources of the community. If he deteriorates his bodily or mental faculties, he not only brings evil upon all who depended on him for any portion of their happiness, but disqualifies himself for rendering the services which he owes to his fellow creatures generally; perhaps becomes a burthen on their affection or benevolence; and if such conduct were very frequent, hardly any offence that is committed would detract more from the general sum of good. Finally, if by his vices or follies a person does no direct harm to others, he is nevertheless (it may be said) injurious by his example; and ought to be compelled to control himself, for the sake of those whom the sight or knowledge of his conduct might corrupt or mislead.

And even (it will be added) if the consequences of misconduct could be confined to the vicious or thoughtless individual, ought society to abandon to their own guidance those who are manifestly unfit for it? If protection against themselves is confessedly due to children and persons under age, is not society equally bound to afford it to persons of mature years who are equally incapable of self-government? If gambling, or drunkenness, or incontinence, or idleness, or uncleanliness, are as injurious to happiness, and as great a hindrance to improvement, as many or most of the acts prohibited by law, why (it may be asked) should not law, so far as is consistent with practicability and social convenience, endeavour to repress these also? And as a supplement to the unavoidable imperfections of law, ought not opinion at least to organize a powerful police against these vices, and visit rigidly with social penalties those who are known to practise them? There is no question here (it may be said) about restricting individuality, or impeding the trial of new and original experiments in living. The only things it is sought to prevent are things which have been tried and condemned from the beginning of the world until now; things which experience has shown not to be useful or suitable to any person's individuality. There must be some length of time and amount of experience, after which a moral or prudential truth may be regarded as established: and it is merely desired to prevent generation after generation from falling over the same precipice which has been fatal to their predecessors.

I fully admit that the mischief which a person does to himself may seriously affect, both through their sympathies and their interests, those nearly connected with him, and in a minor degree, society at large. When, by conduct of this sort, a person is led to violate a distinct and assignable obligation to any other person or persons, the case is taken out of the self-regarding class, and becomes amenable to moral disapprobation in the proper sense of the term. If, for example, a man, through intemperance or extravagance, becomes unable to pay his debts, or, having undertaken the moral responsibility of a family, becomes from the same cause incapable of supporting or educating them, he is deservedly reprobated, and might be justly punished; but it is for the breach of duty to his family or creditors, not for the extravagance. If the resources which ought to have been devoted to them, had been diverted from them for the most prudent investment, the moral culpability would have been the same. George Barnwell murdered his uncle to get money for his mistress, but if he had done it to set himself up in business, he would equally have been hanged. Again, in the frequent case of a man who causes grief to his family by addiction to bad habits, he deserves reproach for his unkindness or ingratitude; but so he may for cultivating habits not in themselves vicious, if they are painful to those with whom he passes his life, or who from personal ties are dependent on him for their comfort. Whoever fails in the consideration generally due to the interests and feelings of others, not being compelled by some more imperative duty, or justified by allowable self-preference, is a subject of moral disapprobation for that failure, but not for the cause of it, nor for the errors, merely personal to himself, which may have remotely led to it. In like manner, when a person disables himself, by conduct purely self-regarding, from the performance of some definite duty incumbent on him to the public, he is guilty of a social offence. No person ought to be punished simply for being drunk; but a soldier or a policeman should be punished for being drunk on duty. Whenever, in short, there is a definite damage, or a definite risk of damage, either to an individual or to the public, the case is taken out of the province of liberty, and placed in that of morality or law.

But with regard to the merely contingent, or, as it may be called, constructive injury which a person causes to society, by conduct which neither violates any specific duty to the public, nor occasions perceptible hurt to any assignable individual except himself; the inconvenience is one which society can afford to bear, for the sake of the greater good of human freedom. If grown persons are to be punished for not taking proper care of themselves, I would rather it were for their own sake, than under pretence of preventing them from impairing their capacity of rendering to society benefits which society does not pretend it has a right to exact. But I cannot consent to argue the point as if society had no means of bringing its weaker members up to its ordinary standard of rational conduct, except waiting till they do something irrational, and then punishing them, legally or morally, for it. Society has had absolute power over them during all the early portion of their existence: it has had the whole period of childhood and nonage in which to try whether it could make them capable of rational conduct in life. The existing generation is master both of the training and the entire circumstances of the generation to come; it cannot indeed make them perfectly wise and good, because it is itself so lamentably deficient in goodness and wisdom; and its best efforts are not always, in individual cases, its most successful ones; but it is perfectly well able to make the rising generation, as a whole, as good as, and a little better than, itself. If society lets any considerable number of its members grow up mere children, incapable of being acted on by rational consideration of distant motives, society has itself to blame for the consequences. Armed not only with all the powers of education, but with the ascendancy which the authority of a received opinion always exercises over the minds who are least fitted to judge for themselves; and aided by the *natural* penalties which cannot be prevented from falling on those who incur the distaste or the contempt of those who know them; let not society pretend that it needs, besides all this, the power to issue commands and enforce obedience in the personal concerns of individuals, in which, on all principles of justice and policy, the decision ought to rest with those who are to abide the consequences. Nor is there anything which tends more to discredit and frustrate the better means of influencing conduct, than a resort to the worse. If there be among those whom it is attempted to coerce into prudence or temperance, any of the material of which vigorous and independent characters are made, they will infallibly rebel against the yoke. No such person will ever feel that others have a right to control him in his concerns, such as they have to prevent him from injuring them in theirs; and it easily comes to be considered a mark of spirit and courage to fly in the face of such usurped authority, and do with ostentation the exact opposite of what it enjoins; as in the fashion of grossness which succeeded, in the time of Charles II, to the fanatical moral intolerance of the Puritans. With respect to what is said of the necessity of protecting society from the bad example set to others by the vicious or the self-indulgent; it is true that bad example may have a pernicious effect, especially the example of doing wrong to others with impunity to the wrong-doer. But we are now speaking of conduct which, while it does no wrong to others, is supposed to do great harm to the agent himself: and I do not see how those who believe this, can think otherwise than that the example, on the whole, must be more salutary than hurtful, since, if it displays the misconduct, it displays also the painful or degrading consequences which, if the conduct is justly censured, must be supposed to be in all or most cases attendant on it.

But the strongest of all the arguments against the interference of the public with purely personal conduct, is that when it does interfere, the odds are that it interferes wrongly, and in the wrong place. On questions of social morality, of duty to others, the opinion of the public, that is, of an overruling majority, though often wrong, is likely to be still oftener right; because on such questions they are only required to judge of their own interests; of the manner in which some mode of conduct, if allowed to be practised, would affect themselves. But the opinion of a similar majority, imposed as a law on the minority, on questions of self-regarding conduct, is quite as likely to be wrong as right; for in these cases public opinion means, at the best, some people's opinion of what is good or bad for other people; while very often it does not even mean that; the public, with the most perfect indifference, passing over the pleasure or convenience of those whose conduct they censure, and considering only their own preference. There are many who consider as an injury to themselves any conduct which they have a distaste for, and resent it as an outrage to their feelings; as a religious bigot, when charged with disregarding the religious feelings of others, has been known to retort that they disregard his feelings, by persisting in their abominable worship or creed. But there is no parity between the feeling of a person for his own opinion, and the feeling of another who is offended at his holding it; no more than between the desire of a thief to take a purse, and the desire of the right owner to keep it. And a person's taste is as much his own peculiar concern as his opinion or his purse. It is easy for any one to imagine an ideal public, which leaves the freedom and choice of individuals in all uncertain matters undisturbed, and only requires them to abstain from modes of conduct which universal experience has condemned. But where has there been seen a public which set any such limit to its censorship? or when does the public trouble itself about universal experience? In its interferences with personal conduct it is seldom thinking of anything but the enormity of acting or feeling differently from itself; and this standard of judgement, thinly disguised, is held up to mankind as the dictate of religion and philosophy, by nine-tenths of all moralists and speculative writers. These teach that things are right because they are right; because we feel them to be so. They tell us to search in our own minds and hearts for laws of conduct binding on ourselves and on all others. What can the poor public do but apply these instructions, and make their own personal feelings of good and evil, if they are tolerably unanimous in them, obligatory on all the world?

The evil here pointed out is not one which exists only in theory; and it may perhaps be expected that I should specify the instances in which the public of this age and country improperly invests its own preferences with the character of moral laws. I am not writing an essay on the aberrations of existing moral feeling. That is too weighty a subject to be discussed parenthetically, and by way of illustration. Yet examples are necessary, to show that the principle I maintain is of serious and practical moment, and that I am not endeavouring to erect a barrier against imaginary evils. And it is not difficult to show, by abundant instances, that to extend the bounds of what may be called moral police, until it encroaches on the most unquestionably legitimate liberty of the individual, is one of the most universal of all human propensities.

As a first instance, consider the antipathies which men cherish on no better grounds than that persons whose religious opinions are different from theirs, do not practise their religious observances, especially their religious abstinences. To cite a rather trivial example, nothing in the creed or practice of Christians does more to envenom the hatred of Mohammedans against them, than the fact of their eating pork. There are few acts which Christians and Europeans regard with more unaffected disgust, than Mussulmans regard this particular mode of satisfying hunger. It is, in the first place, an offence against their religion; but this circumstance by no means explains either the degree or the kind of their repugnance; for wine also is forbidden by their religion, and to partake of it is by all Mussulmans accounted wrong, but not disgusting. Their aversion to the flesh of the 'unclean beast' is, on the contrary, of that peculiar character, resembling an instinctive antipathy, which the idea of uncleanness, when once it thoroughly sinks into the feelings, seems always to excite even in those whose personal habits are anything but scrupulously cleanly, and of which the sentiment of religious impurity, so intense in the Hindoos, is a remarkable example. Suppose now that in a people, of whom the majority were Mussulmans, that majority should insist upon not permitting pork to be eaten within the limits of the country. This would be nothing new in Mohammedan countries. Would it be a legitimate exercise of the moral authority of public opinion? and if not, why not? The practice is really revolting to such a public. They also sincerely think that it is forbidden and abhorred by the Deity. Neither could the prohibition be censured as religious persecution. It might be religious in its origin, but it would not be persecution for religion, since nobody's religion makes it a duty to eat pork. The only tenable ground of condemnation would be, that with the personal tastes and self-regarding concerns of individuals the public has no business to interfere.

To come somewhat nearer home: the majority of Spaniards consider it a gross impiety, offensive in the highest degree to the Supreme Being, to worship him in any other manner than the Roman Catholic; and no other public worship is lawful on Spanish soil. The people of all Southern Europe look upon a married clergy as not only irreligious, but unchaste, indecent, gross, disgusting. What do Protestants think of these perfectly sincere feelings, and of the attempt to enforce them against non-Catholics? Yet, if mankind are justified in interfering with each other's liberty in things which do not concern the interests of others, on what principle is it possible consistently to exclude these cases? or who can blame people for desiring to suppress what they regard as a scandal in the sight of God and man? No stronger case can be shown for prohibiting anything which is regarded as a personal immorality, than is made out for suppressing these practices in the eyes of those who regard them as impieties; and unless we are willing to adopt the logic of persecutors, and to say that we may persecute others because we are right, and that they must not persecute us because they are wrong, we must beware of admitting a principle of which we should resent as a gross injustice the application to ourselves.

The preceding instances may be objected to, although unreasonably, as drawn from contingencies impossible among us: opinion, in this country, not being likely to enforce abstinence from meats, or to interfere with people for worshipping, and for either marrying or not marrying, according to their creed or inclination. The next example, however, shall be taken from an interference with liberty which we have by no means passed all danger of. Wherever the Puritans have been sufficiently powerful, as in New England, and in Great Britain at the time of the Commonwealth, they have endeavoured, with considerable success, to put down all public, and nearly all private, amusements: especially music, dancing, public games, or other assemblages for purposes of diversion, and the theatre. There are still in this country large bodies of persons by whose notions of morality and religion these recreations are condemned; and those persons belonging chiefly to the middle class, who are the ascendant power in the present social and political condition of the kingdom, it is by no means impossible that persons of these sentiments may at some time or other command a majority in Parliament. How will the remaining portion of the community like to have the amusements that shall be permitted to them regulated by the religious and moral sentiments of the stricter Calvinists and Methodists? Would they not, with considerable peremptoriness, desire these intrusively pious members of society to mind their own business? This is precisely what should be said to every government and every public, who have the pretension that no person shall enjoy any pleasure which they think wrong. But if the principle of the pretension be admitted, no one can reasonably object to its being acted on in the sense of the majority, or other preponderating power in the country; and all persons must be ready to conform to the idea of a Christian commonwealth, as understood by the early settlers in New England, if a religious profession similar to theirs should ever succeed in regaining its lost ground, as religions supposed to be declining have so often been known to do.

To imagine another contingency, perhaps more likely to be realized than the one last mentioned. There is confessedly a strong tendency in the modern world towards a democratic constitution of society, accompanied or not by popular political institutions. It is affirmed that in the country where this tendency is most completely realized — where both society and the government are most democratic — the United States — the feeling of the majority, to whom any appearance of a more showy or costly style of living than they can hope to rival is disagreeable, operates as a tolerably effectual sumptuary law, and that in many parts of the Union it is really difficult for a person possessing a very large income, to find any mode of spending it, which will not incur popular disapprobation. Though such statements as these are doubtless much exaggerated as a representation of existing facts, the state of things they describe is not only a conceivable and possible, but a probable result of democratic feeling, combined with the notion that the public has a right to a veto on the manner in which individuals shall spend their incomes. We have only further to suppose a considerable diffusion of Socialist opinions, and it may become infamous in the eyes of the majority to possess more property than some very small amount, or any income not earned by manual labour. Opinions similar in principle to these, already prevail widely among the artisan class, and weigh oppressively on those who are amenable to the opinion chiefly of that class, namely, its own members. It is known that the bad workmen who form the majority of the operatives in many branches of industry, are decidedly of opinion that bad workmen ought to receive the same wages as good, and that no one ought to be allowed, through piece-work or otherwise, to earn by superior skill or industry more than others can without it. And they employ a moral police, which occasionally becomes a physical one, to deter skilful workmen from receiving, and employers from giving, a larger remuneration for a more useful service. If the public have any jurisdiction over private concerns, I cannot see that these people are in fault, or that any individual's particular public can be blamed for asserting the same authority over his individual conduct, which the general public asserts over people in general.

But, without dwelling upon supposititious cases, there are, in our own day, gross usurpations upon the liberty of private life actually practised, and still greater ones threatened with some expectation of success, and opinions propounded which assert an unlimited right in the public not only to prohibit by law everything which it thinks wrong, but in order to get at what it thinks wrong, to prohibit any number of things which it admits to be innocent.

Under the name of preventing intemperance, the people of one English colony, and of nearly half the United States, have been interdicted by law from making any use whatever of fermented drinks, except for medical purposes: for prohibition of their sale is in fact, as it is intended to be, prohibition of their use. And though the impracticability of executing the law has caused its repeal in several of the States which had adopted it, including the one from which it derives its name, an attempt has notwithstanding been commenced, and is prosecuted with considerable zeal by many of the professed philanthropists, to agitate for a similar law in this country. The association, or 'Alliance' as it terms itself, which has been formed for this purpose, has acquired some notoriety through the publicity given to a correspondence between its Secretary and one of the very few English public men who hold that a politician's opinions ought to be founded on principles. Lord Stanley's share in this correspondence is calculated to strengthen the hopes already built on him, by those who know how rare such qualities as are manifested in some of his public appearances, unhappily are among those who figure in political life. The organ of the Alliance, who would 'deeply deplore the recognition of any principle which could be wrested to justify bigotry and persecution', undertakes to point out the 'broad and impassable barrier' which divides such principles from those of the association. 'All matters relating to thought, opinion, conscience, appear to me,' he says, 'to be without the sphere of legislation; all pertaining to social act, habit, relation, subject only to a discretionary power vested in the State itself, and not in the individual, to be within it.' No mention is made of a third class, different from either of these, viz. acts and habits which are not social, but individual; although it is to this class, surely, that the act of drinking fermented liquors belongs. Selling fermented liquors, however, is trading, and trading is a social act. But the infringement complained of is not on the liberty of the seller, but on that of the buyer and consumer; since the State might just as well forbid him to drink wine, as purposely make it impossible for him to obtain it. The Secretary, however, says, 'I claim, as a citizen, a right to legislate whenever my social rights are invaded by the social act of another.' And now for the definition of these 'social rights'. 'If anything invades my social rights, certainly the traffic in strong drink does. It destroys my primary right of security, by constantly creating and stimulating social disorder. It invades my right of equality, by deriving a profit from the creation of a misery I am taxed to support. It impedes my right to free moral and intellectual development, by surrounding my path with dangers, and by weakening and demoralizing society, from which I have a right to claim mutual aid and intercourse.' A theory of 'social rights', the like of which probably never before found its way into distinct language: being nothing short of this—that it is the absolute social right of every individual, that every other individual shall act in every respect exactly as he ought; that whosoever fails thereof in the smallest particular, violates my social right, and entitles me to demand from the legislature the removal of the grievance. So monstrous a principle is far more dangerous than any single interference with liberty; there is no violation of liberty which it would not justify; it acknowledges no right to any freedom whatever, except perhaps to that of holding opinions in secret, without ever disclosing them; for, the moment an opinion which I consider noxious passes any one's lips, it invades all the 'social rights' attributed to me by the Alliance. The doctrine ascribes to all mankind a vested interest in each other's moral, intellectual, and even physical perfection, to be defined by each claimant according to his own standard.

Another important example of illegitimate interference with the rightful liberty of the individual, not simply threatened, but long since carried into triumphant effect, is Sabbatarian legislation. Without doubt, abstinence on one day in the week, so far as the exigencies of life permit, from the usual daily occupation, though in no respect religiously binding on any except Jews, is a highly beneficial custom. And inasmuch as this custom cannot be observed without a general consent to that effect among the industrious classes, therefore, in so far as some persons by working may impose the same necessity on others, it may be allowable and right that the law should guarantee to each the observance by others of the custom, by suspending the greater operations of industry on a particular day. But this justification, grounded on the direct interest which others have in each individual's observ-ance of the practice, does not apply to the self-chosen occupations in which a person may think fit to employ his leisure; nor does it hold good, in the smallest degree, for legal restrictions on amusements. It is true that the amusement of some is the day's work of others; but the pleasure, not to say the useful recreation, of many, is worth the labour of a few, provided the occupation is freely chosen, and can be freely resigned. The operatives are perfectly right in thinking that if all worked on Sunday, seven days' work would have to be given for six days' wages: but so long as the great mass of employments are suspended, the small number who for the enjoyment of others must still work, obtain a proportional increase of earnings; and they are not obliged to follow those occupations, if they prefer leisure to emolu-ment. If a further remedy is sought, it might be found in the establishment by custom of a holiday on some other day of the week for those particular classes of persons. The only ground, therefore, on which restrictions on Sunday amusements can be defended, must be that they are religiously wrong; a motive of legislation which never can be too earnestly protested against. 'Deorum injuriae Diis curae.' It remains to be proved that society or any of its officers holds a commission from on high to avenge any supposed offence to Omnipotence, which is not also a wrong to our fellow creatures. The notion that it is one man's duty that another should be religious, was the foundation of all the religious persecutions ever perpetrated, and if admitted, would fully justify them. Though the feeling which breaks out in the repeated attempts to stop railway travelling on Sunday, in the resistance to the opening of Museums, and the like, has not the cruelty of the old persecutors, the state of mind indicated by it is fundamentally the same. It is a determination not to tolerate others in doing what is permitted by their religion, because it is not permitted by the persecutor's religion. It is a belief that God not only abominates the act of the misbeliever, but will not hold us guiltless if we leave him unmolested.

I cannot refrain from adding to these examples of the little account commonly made of human liberty, the language of downright persecution which breaks out from the press of this country, whenever it feels called on to notice the remarkable phenomenon of Mormonism. Much might be said on the unexpected and instructive fact, that an alleged new revelation, and a religion founded on it, the product of palpable imposture, not even supported by the *prestige* of extra-ordinary qualities in its founder, is believed by hundreds of thousands, and has been made the foundation of a society, in the age of newspapers, railways, and the electric telegraph. What here concerns us is, that this religion, like other and better religions, has its martyrs; that its prophet and founder was, for his teaching, put to death by a mob; that others of its adherents lost their lives by the same lawless violence; that they were forcibly expelled, in a body, from the country in which they first grew up; while, now that they have been chased into a solitary recess in the midst of a desert, many in this country openly declare that it would be right (only that it is not convenient) to send an expedition against them, and compel them by force to conform to the opinions of other people. The article of the Mormonite doctrine which is the chief provocative to the antipathy which thus breaks through the ordinary restraints of religious tolerance, is its sanction of polygamy; which, though permitted to Mohammedans, and Hindoos, and Chinese, seems to excite unquenchable animosity when practised by persons who speak English, and profess to be a kind of Christians. No one has a deeper disapprobation than I have of this Mormon institution; both for other reasons, and because, far from being in any way countenanced by the principle of liberty, it is a direct infraction of that principle, being a mere riveting of the chains of one-half of the community, and an emancipation of the other from reciprocity of obligation towards them. Still, it must be remembered that this relation is as much voluntary on the part of the women concerned in it, and who may be deemed the sufferers by it, as is the case with any other form of the marriage institution; and however surprising this fact may appear, it has its explanation in the common ideas and customs of the world, which teaching women to think marriage the one thing needful, make it intelligible that many a woman should prefer being one of several wives, to not being a wife at all. Other countries are not asked to recognize such unions, or release any portion of their inhabitants from their own laws on the score of Mormonite opinions. But when the dissentients have conceded to the hostile sentiments of others, far more than could justly be demanded; when they have left the countries to which their doctrines were unacceptable, and established themselves in a remote corner of the earth, which they have been the first to render habitable to human beings; it is difficult to see on what principles but those of tyranny they can be prevented from living there under what laws they please, provided they commit no aggression on other nations, and allow perfect freedom of departure to those who are dissatisfied with their ways. A recent writer, in some respects of considerable merit, proposes (to use his own words) not a crusade, but a *civilizade*, against this polygamous community, to put an end to what seems to him a retrograde step in civilization. It also appears so to me, but I am not aware that any community has a right to force another to be civilized. So long as the sufferers by the bad law do not invoke assistance from other communities, I cannot admit that persons entirely unconnected with them ought to step in and require that a condition of things with which all who are directly interested appear to be satisfied, should be put an end to because it is a scandal to persons some thousands of miles distant, who have no part or concern in it. Let them send missionaries, if they please, to preach against it; and let them, by any fair means (of which silencing the teachers is not one), oppose the progress of similar doctrines among their own people. If civilization has got the better of barbarism when barbarism had the world to itself, it is too much to profess to be afraid lest barbarism, after having been fairly got under, should revive and conquer civilization. A civilization that can thus succumb to its vanquished enemy, must first have become so degenerate, that neither its appointed priests and teachers, nor anybody else, has the capacity, or will take the trouble, to stand up for it. If this be so, the sooner such a civilization receives notice to quit, the better. It can only go on from bad to worse, until destroyed and regenerated (like the Western Empire) by energetic barbarians.

SELECTIONS FROM
The Subjection of Women

Chapter I   Arguments Against Present Inequalities

The object of this Essay is to explain, as clearly as I am able, the grounds of an opinion which I have held from the very earliest period when I had formed any opinions at all on social or political matters, and which, instead of being weakened or modified, has been constantly growing stronger by the progress of reflection and the experience of life: That the principle which regulates the existing social relations between the two sexes—the legal subordination of one sex to the other—is wrong in itself, and now one of the chief hindrances to human improvement; and that it ought to be replaced by a principle of perfect equality, admitting no power or privilege on the one side, nor disability on the other.

The very words necessary to express the task I have undertaken, show how arduous it is. But it would be a mistake to suppose that the difficulty of the case must lie in the insufficiency or obscurity of the grounds of reason on which my conviction rests. The difficulty is that which exists in all cases in which there is a mass of feeling to be contended against. So long as an opinion is strongly rooted in the feelings, it gains rather than loses in stability by having a preponderating weight of argument against it. For if it were accepted as a result of argument, the refutation of the argument might shake the solidity of the conviction; but when it rests solely on feeling, the worse it fares in argumentative contest, the more persuaded its adherents are that their feeling must have some deeper ground, which the arguments do not reach; and while the feeling remains, it is always throwing up fresh entrenchments of argument to repair any breach made in the old. . . .

The generality of a practice is in some cases a strong presumption that it is, or at all events once was, conducive to laudable ends. This is the case, when the practice was first adopted, or afterwards kept up, as a means to such ends, and was grounded on experience of the mode in which they could be most effectually attained. If the authority of men over women, when first established, had been the result of a conscientious comparison between different modes of constituting the government of society; if, after trying various other modes of social organization—the government of women over men, equality between the two, and such mixed and divided modes of government as might be invented—it had been decided, on the testimony of experience, that the mode in which women are wholly under the rule of men, having no share at all in public concerns, and each in private being under the legal obligation of obedience to the man with whom she has associated her destiny, was the arrangement most conducive to the happiness and well-being of both; its general adoption might then be fairly thought to be some evidence that, at the time when it was adopted, it was the best: though even then the considerations which recommended it may, like so many other primeval social facts of the greatest importance, have subsequently, in the course of ages, ceased to exist. But the state of the case is in every respect the reverse of this. In the first place, the opinion in favour of the present system, which entirely subordinates the weaker sex to the stronger, rests upon theory only; for there never has been trial made of any other: so that experience, in the sense in which it is vulgarly opposed to theory, cannot be pretended to have pronounced any verdict. And in the second place, the adoption of this system of inequality never was the result of deliberation, or forethought, or any social ideas, or any notion whatever of what conduced to the benefit of humanity or the good order of society. It arose simply from the fact that from the very earliest twilight of human society, every woman (owing to the value attached to her by men, combined with her inferiority in muscular strength) was found in a state of bondage to some man. Laws and systems of polity always begin by recognizing the relations they find already existing between individuals. They convert what was a mere physical fact into a legal right, give it the sanction of society, and principally aim at the substitution of public and organized means of asserting and protecting these rights, instead of the irregular and lawless conflict of physical strength. Those who had already been compelled to obedience became in this manner legally bound to it. Slavery, from being a mere affair of force between the master and the slave, became regularized and a matter of compact among the masters, who, binding themselves to one another for common protection, guaranteed by their collective strength the private possessions of each, including his slaves. In early times, the great majority of the male sex were slaves, as well as the whole of the female. And many ages elapsed, some of them ages of high cultivation, before any thinker was bold enough to question the rightfulness, and the absolute social necessity, either of the one slavery or of the other. By degrees such thinkers did arise: and (the general progress of society assisting) the slavery of the male sex has, in all the countries of Christian Europe at least (though, in one of them, only within the last few years) been at length abolished, and that of the female sex has been gradually changed into a milder form of dependence. But this dependence, as it exists at present, is not an original institution, taking a fresh start from considerations of justice and social expediency — it is the primitive state of slavery lasting on, through successive mitigations and modifications occasioned by the same causes which have softened the general manners, and brought all human relations more under the control of justice and the influence of humanity. It has not lost the taint of its brutal origin. No presumption in its favour, therefore, can be drawn from the fact of its existence. The only such presumption which it could be supposed to have, must be grounded on its having lasted till now, when so many other things which came down from the same odious source have been done away with. And this, indeed, is what makes it strange to ordinary ears, to hear it asserted that the inequality of rights between men and women has no other source than the law of the strongest. . . .

. . . Whatever gratification of pride there is in the possession of power, and whatever personal interest in its exercise, is in this case not confined to a limited class, but common to the whole male sex. Instead of being, to most of its supporters, a thing desirable chiefly in the abstract, or, like the political ends usually contended for by factions, of little private importance to any but the leaders; it comes home to the person and hearth of every male head of a family, and of every one who looks forward to being so. The clodhopper exercises, or is to exercise, his share of the power equally with the highest nobleman. And the case is that in which the desire of power is the strongest: for every one who desires power, desires it most over those who are nearest to him, with whom his life is passed, with whom he has most concerns in common, and in whom any independence of his authority is oftenest likely to interfere with his individual preferences. If, in the other cases specified, powers manifestly grounded only on force, and having so much less to support them, are so slowly and with so much difficulty got rid of, much more must it be so with this, even if it rests on no better foundation than those. We must consider, too, that the possessors of the power have facilities in this case, greater than in any other, to prevent any uprising against it. Every one of the subjects lives under the very eye, and almost it may be said, in the hands, of one of the masters — in closer intimacy with him than with any of her fellow subjects; with no means of combining against him, no power of even locally overmastering him, and, on the other hand, with the strongest motives for seeking his favour and avoiding to give him offence. In struggles for political emancipation, everybody knows how often its champions are bought off by bribes, or daunted by terrors. In the case of women, each individual of the subject-class is in a chronic state of bribery and intimidation combined. In setting up the standard of resistance, a large number of the leaders, and still more of the followers, must make an almost complete sacrifice of the pleasures or the alleviations of their own individual lot. If ever any system of privilege and enforced subjection had its yoke tightly riveted on the necks of those who are kept down by it, this has. I have not yet shown that it is a wrong system: but every one who is capable of thinking on the subject must see that even if it is, it was certain to outlast all other forms of unjust authority. And when some of the grossest of the other forms still exist in many civilized countries, and have only recently been got rid of in others, it would be strange if that which is so much the deepest-rooted had yet been perceptibly shaken anywhere. There is more reason to wonder that the protests and testimonies against it should have been so numerous and so weighty as they are. . . .

. . . The subjection of women to men being a universal custom, any departure from it quite naturally appears unnatural. But how entirely, even in this case, the feeling is dependent on custom, appears by ample experience. Nothing so much astonishes the people of distant parts of the world, when they first learn anything about England, as to be told that it is under a queen: the thing seems to them so unnatural as to be almost incredible. To Englishmen this does not seem in the least degree unnatural, because they are used to it; but they do feel it unnatural that women should be soldiers or members of Parliament. In the feudal ages, on the contrary, war and politics were not thought unnatural to women, because not unusual; it seemed natural that women of the privileged classes should be of manly character, inferior in nothing but bodily strength to their husbands and fathers. The independence of women seemed rather less unnatural to the Greeks than to other ancients, on account of the fabulous Amazons (whom they believed to be historical), and the partial example afforded by the Spartan women; who, though no less subordinate by law than in other Greek states, were more free in fact, and being trained to bodily exercises in the same manner with men, gave ample proof that they were not naturally disqualified for them. There can be little doubt that Spartan experience suggested to Plato, among many other of his doctrines, that of the social and political equality of the two sexes.

But, it will be said, the rule of men over women differs from all these others in not being a rule of force: it is accepted voluntarily; women make no complaint, and are consenting parties to it. In the first place, a great number of women do not accept it. Ever since there have been women able to make their sentiments known by their writings (the only mode of publicity which society permits to them), an increasing number of them have recorded protests against their present social condition: and recently many thousands of them, headed by the most eminent women known to the public, have petitioned Parliament for their admission to the Parliamentary Suffrage. The claim of women to be educated as solidly, and in the same branches of knowledge, as men, is urged with growing intensity, and with a great prospect of success; while the demand for their admission into professions and occupations hitherto closed against them, becomes every year more urgent. Though there are not in this country, as there are in the United States, periodical Conventions and an organized party to agitate for the Rights of Women, there is a numerous and active Society organized and managed by women, for the more limited object of obtaining the political franchise. Nor is it only in our own country and in America that women are beginning to protest, more or less collectively, against the disabilities under which they labour. France, and Italy, and Switzerland, and Russia now afford examples of the same thing. How many more women there are who silently cherish similar aspirations, no one can possibly know; but there are abundant tokens how many *would* cherish them, were they not so strenuously taught to repress them as contrary to the proprieties of their sex. It must be remembered, also, that no enslaved class ever asked for complete liberty at once. . . . It is a political law of nature that those who are under any power of ancient origin never begin by complaining of the power itself, but only of its oppressive exercise. There is never any want of women who complain of ill usage by their husbands. There would be infinitely more, if complaint were not the greatest of all provocatives to a repetition and increase of the ill usage. It is this which frustrates all attempts to maintain the power but protect the woman against its abuses. In no other case (except that of a child) is the person who has been proved judicially to have suffered an injury, replaced under the physical power of the culprit who inflicted it. Accordingly wives, even in the most extreme and protracted cases of bodily ill usage, hardly ever dare avail themselves of the laws made for their protection: and if, in a moment of irrepressible indignation, or by the interference of neighbours, they are induced to do so, their whole effort afterwards is to disclose as little as they can, and to beg off their tyrant from his merited chastisement.

All causes, social and natural, combine to make it unlikely that women should be collectively rebellious to the power of men. They are so far in a position different from all other subject classes, that their masters require something more from them than actual service. Men do not want solely the obedience of women, they want their sentiments. All men, except the most brutish, desire to have, in the woman most nearly connected with them, not a forced slave but a willing one; not a slave merely, but a favourite. They have therefore put everything in practice to enslave their minds. The masters of all other slaves rely, for maintaining obedience, on fear; either fear of themselves, or religious fears. The masters of women wanted more than simple obedience, and they turned the whole force of education to effect their purpose. All women are brought up from the very earliest years in the belief that their ideal of character is the very opposite to that of men; not self-will, and government by self-control, but submission, and yielding to the control of others. All the moralities tell them that it is the duty of women, and all the current sentimentalities that it is their nature, to live for others; to make complete abnegation of themselves, and to have no life but in their affections. And by their affections are meant the only ones they are allowed to have — those to the men with whom they are connected, or to the children who constitute an additional and indefeasible tie between them and a man. When we put together three things — first, the natural attraction between opposite sexes; secondly, the wife's entire dependence on the husband, every privilege or pleasure she has being either his gift, or depending entirely on his will; and lastly, that the principal object of human pursuit, consideration, and all objects of social ambition, can in general be sought or obtained by her only through him — it would be a miracle if the object of being attractive to men had not become the polar star of feminine education and formation of character. And, this great means of influence over the minds of women having been acquired, an instinct of selfishness made men avail themselves of it to the utmost as a means of holding women in subjection, by representing to them meekness, submissiveness, and resignation of all individual will into the hands of a man, as an essential part of sexual attractiveness. Can it be doubted that any of the other yokes which mankind have succeeded in breaking, would have subsisted till now if the same means had existed, and had been as sedulously used, to bow down their minds to it? If it had been made the object of the life of every young plebeian to find personal favour in the eyes of some patrician, of every young serf with some seigneur; if domestication with him, and a share of his personal affections, had been held out as the prize which they all should look out for, the most gifted and aspiring being able to reckon on the most desirable prizes; and if, when this prize had been obtained, they had been shut out by a wall of brass from all interests not centring in him, all feelings and desires but those which he shared or inculcated; would not serfs and seigneurs, plebeians and patricians, have been as broadly distinguished at this day as men and women are? and would not all but a thinker here and there have believed the distinction to be a fundamental and unalterable fact in human nature? . . .

Neither does it avail anything to say that the *nature* of the two sexes adapts them to their present functions and position, and renders these appropriate to them. Standing on the ground of common sense and the constitution of the human mind, I deny that any one knows, or can know, the nature of the two sexes, as long as they have only been seen in their present relation to one another. If men had ever been found in society without women, or women without men, or if there had been a society of men and women in which the women were not under the control of the men, something might have been positively known about the mental and moral differences which may be inherent in the nature of each. What is now called the nature of women is an eminently artificial thing — the result of forced repression in some directions, unnatural stimulation in others. It may be asserted without scruple, that no other class of dependents have had their character so entirely distorted from its natural proportions by their relation with their masters; for, if conquered and slave races have been, in some respects, more forcibly repressed, whatever in them has not been crushed down by an iron heel has generally been let alone, and if left with any liberty of development, it has developed itself according to its own laws; but in the case of women, a hot-house and stove cultivation has always been carried on of some of the capabilities of their nature, for the benefit and pleasure of their masters. Then, because certain products of the general vital force sprout luxuriantly and reach a great development in this heated atmosphere and under this active nurture and watering, while other shoots from the same root, which are left outside in the wintry air, with ice purposely heaped all round them, have a stunted growth, and some are burnt off with fire and disappear; men, with that inability to recognize their own work which distinguishes the unanalytic mind, indolently believe that the tree grows of itself in the way they have made it grow, and that it would die if one half of it were not kept in a vapour bath and the other half in the snow.

Of all difficulties which impede the progress of thought, and the formation of well-grounded opinions on life and social arrangements, the greatest is now the unspeakable ignorance and inattention of mankind in respect to the influences which form human character. Whatever any portion of the human species now are, or seem to be, such, it is supposed, they have a natural tendency to be: even when the most elementary knowledge of the circumstances in which they have been placed, clearly points out the causes that made them what they are. Because a cottier deeply in arrears to his landlord is not industrious, there are people who think that the Irish are naturally idle. Because constitutions can be overthrown when the authorities appointed to execute them turn their arms against them, there are people who think the French incapable of free government. Because the Greeks cheated the Turks, and the Turks only plundered the Greeks, there are persons who think that the Turks are naturally more sincere: and because women, as is often said, care nothing about politics except their personalities, it is supposed that the general good is naturally less interesting to women than to men. History, which is now so much better understood than formerly, teaches another lesson: if only by showing the extraordinary susceptibility of human nature to external influences, and the extreme variableness of those of its manifestations which are supposed to be most universal and uniform. But in history, as in travelling, men usually see only what they already had in their own minds; and few learn much from history, who do not bring much with them to its study.

Hence, in regard to that most difficult question, what are the natural differences between the two sexes — a subject on which it is impossible in the present state of society to obtain complete and correct knowledge — while almost everybody dogmatizes upon it, almost all neglect and make light of the only means by which any partial insight can be obtained into it. This is, an analytic study of the most important department of psychology, the laws of the influence of circumstances on character. For, however great and apparently ineradicable the moral and intellectual differences between men and women might be, the evidence of their being natural differences could only be negative. Those only could be inferred to be natural which could not possibly be artificial — the residuum, after deducing every characteristic of either sex which can admit of being explained from education or external circumstances. The profoundest knowledge of the laws of the formation of character is indispensable to entitle any one to affirm even that there is any difference, much more what the difference is, between the two sexes considered as moral and rational beings; and since no one, as yet, has that knowledge (for there is hardly any subject which, in proportion to its importance, has been so little studied), no one is thus far entitled to any positive opinion on the subject. Conjectures are all that can at present be made; conjectures more or less probable, according as more or less authorized by such knowledge as we yet have of the laws of psychology, as applied to the formation of character.

Even the preliminary knowledge, what the differences between the sexes now are, apart from all question as to how they are made what they are, is still in the crudest and most incomplete state. Medical practitioners and physiologists have ascertained, to some extent, the differences in bodily constitution; and this is an important element to the psychologist: but hardly any medical practitioner is a psychologist. Respecting the mental characteristics of women; their observations are of no more worth than those of common men. It is a subject on which nothing final can be known, so long as those who alone can really know it, women themselves, have given but little testimony, and that little, mostly suborned. It is easy to know stupid women. Stupidity is much the same all the world over. A stupid person's notions and feelings may confidently be inferred from those which prevail in the circle by which the person is surrounded. Not so with those whose opinions and feelings are an emanation from their own nature and faculties. It is only a man here and there who has any tolerable knowledge of the character even of the women of his own family. I do not mean, of their capabilities; these nobody knows, not even themselves, because most of them have never been called out. I mean their actually existing thoughts and feelings. Many a man thinks he perfectly understands women, because he has had amatory relations with several, perhaps with many of them. If he is a good observer, and his experience extends to quality as well as quantity, he may have learnt something of one narrow department of their nature — an important department, no doubt. But of all the rest of it, few persons are generally more ignorant, because there are few from whom it is so carefully hidden. The most favourable case which a man can generally have for studying the character of a woman, is that of his own wife: for the opportunities are greater, and the cases of complete sympathy not so unspeakably rare. And in fact, this is the source from which any knowledge worth having on the subject has, I believe, generally come. But most men have not had the opportunity of studying in this way more than a single case: accordingly one can, to an almost laughable degree, infer what a man's wife is like, from his opinions about women in general. To make even this one case yield any result, the woman must be worth knowing, and the man not only a competent judge, but of a character so sympathetic in itself, and so well adapted to hers, that he can either read her mind by sympathetic intuition, or has nothing in himself which makes her shy of disclosing it. Hardly anything, I believe, can be more rare than this conjunction. It often happens that there is the most complete unity of feeling and community of interests as to all external things, yet the one has as little admission into the internal life of the other as if they were common acquaintance. Even with true affection, authority on the one side and subordination on the other prevent perfect confidence. Though nothing may be intentionally withheld, much is not shown. In the analogous relation of parent and child, the corresponding phenomenon must have been in the observation of every one. As between father and son, how many are the cases in which the father, in spite of real affection on both sides, obviously to all the world does not know, nor suspect, parts of the son's character familiar to his companions and equals. The truth is, that the position of looking up to another is extremely unpropitious to complete sincerity and openness with him. The fear of losing ground in his opinion or in his feelings is so strong, that even in an upright character, there is an unconscious tendency to show only the best side, or the side which, though not the best, is that which he most likes to see: and it may be confidently said that thorough knowledge of one another hardly ever exists, but between persons who, besides being intimates, are equals. How much more true, then, must all this be, when the one is not only under the authority of the other, but has it inculcated on her as a duty to reckon everything else subordinate to his comfort and pleasure, and to let him neither see nor feel anything coming from her, except what is agreeable to him. All these difficulties stand in the way of a man's obtaining any thorough knowledge even of the one woman whom alone, in general, he has sufficient opportunity of studying. When we further consider that to understand one woman is not necessarily to understand any other woman; that even if he could study many women of one rank, or of one country, he would not thereby understand women of other ranks or countries; and even if he did, they are still only the women of a single period of history; we may safely assert that the knowledge which men can acquire of women, even as they have been and are, without reference to what they might be, is wretchedly imperfect and superficial, and always will be so, until women themselves have told all that they have to tell. . . .

One thing we may be certain of — that what is contrary to women's nature to do, they never will be made to do by simply giving their nature free play. The anxiety of mankind to interfere in behalf of nature, for fear lest nature should not succeed in effecting its purpose, is an altogether unnecessary solicitude. What women by nature cannot do, it is quite superfluous to forbid them from doing. What they can do, but not so well as the men who are their competitors, competition suffices to exclude them from; since nobody asks for protective duties and bounties in favour of women; it is only asked that the present bounties and protective duties in favour of men should be recalled. If women have a greater natural inclination for some things than for others, there is no need of laws or social inculcation to make the majority of them do the former in preference to the latter. Whatever women's services are most wanted for, the free play of competition will hold out the strongest inducements to them to undertake. And, as the words imply, they are most wanted for the things for which they are most fit; by the apportionment of which to them, the collective faculties of the two sexes can be applied on the whole with the greatest sum of valuable result.

The general opinion of men is supposed to be, that the natural vocation of a woman is that of a wife and mother. I say, is supposed to be, because, judging from acts — from the whole of the present constitution of society — one might infer that their opinion was the direct contrary. They might be supposed to think that the alleged natural vocation of women was of all things the most repugnant to their nature; insomuch that if they are free to do anything else — if any other means of living, or occupation of their time and faculties, is open, which has any chance of appearing desirable to them — there will not be enough of them who will be willing to accept the condition said to be natural to them. If this is the real opinion of men in general, it would be well that it should be spoken out. I should like to hear somebody openly enunciating the doctrine (it is already implied in much that is written on the subject) — 'It is necessary to society that women should marry and produce children. They will not do so unless they are compelled. Therefore it is necessary to compel them.' The merits of the case would then be clearly defined. It would be exactly that of the slaveholders of South Carolina and Louisiana. 'It is necessary that cotton and sugar should be grown. White men cannot produce them. Negroes will not, for any wages which we choose to give. *Ergo* they must be compelled.' An illustration still closer to the point is that of impressment. Sailors must absolutely be had to defend the country. It often happens that they will not voluntarily enlist. Therefore there must be the power of forcing them. How often has this logic been used! and, but for one flaw in it, without doubt it would have been successful up to this day. But it is open to the retort — First pay the sailors the honest value of their labour. When you have made it as well worth their while to serve you, as to work for other employers, you will have no more difficulty than others have in obtaining their services. To this there is no logical answer except 'I will not': and as people are now not only ashamed, but are not desirous, to rob the labourer of his hire, impressment is no longer advocated. Those who attempt to force women into marriage by closing all other doors against them, lay themselves open to a similar retort. If they mean what they say, their opinion must evidently be, that men do not render the married condition so desirable to women, as to induce them to accept it for its own recommendations. It is not a sign of one's thinking the boon one offers very attractive, when one allows only Hobson's choice, 'that or none.' And here, I believe, is the clue to the feelings of those men, who have a real antipathy to the equal freedom of women. I believe they are afraid, not lest women should be unwilling to marry, for I do not think that any one in reality has that apprehension; but lest they should insist that marriage should be on equal conditions; lest all women of spirit and capacity should prefer doing almost anything else, not in their own eyes degrading, rather than marry, when marrying is giving themselves a master, and a master too of all their earthly possessions., And truly, if this consequence were necessarily incident to marriage, I think that the apprehension would be very well founded. I agree in thinking it probable that few women, capable of anything else, would, unless under an irresistible *entraîn-ement*, rendering them for the time insensible to anything but itself, choose such a lot, when any other means were open to them of filling a conventionally honourable place in life: and if men are determined that the law of marriage shall be a law of despotism, they are quite right, in point of mere policy, in leaving to women only Hobson's choice. But, in that case, all that has been done in the modern world to relax the chain on the minds of women, has been a mistake. They never should have been allowed to receive a literary education. Women who read, much more women who write, are, in the existing constitution of things, a contradiction and a disturbing element: and it was wrong to bring women up with any acquirements but those of an odalisque, or of a domestic servant.

Chapter III   The Supposed Incapacity of Women

On the other point which is involved in the just equality of women, their admissibility to all the functions and occupations hitherto retained as the monopoly of the stronger sex, I should anticipate no difficulty in convincing any one who has gone with me on the subject of the equality of women in the family. I believe that their disabilities elsewhere are only clung to in order to maintain their subordination in domestic life; because the generality of the male sex cannot yet tolerate the idea of living with an equal. Were it not for that, I think that almost every one, in the existing state of opinion in politics and political economy, would admit the injustice of excluding half the human race from the greater number of lucrative occupations, and from almost all high social functions; ordaining from their birth either that they are not, and cannot by any possibility become, fit for employments which are legally open to the stupidest and basest of the other sex, or else that however fit they may be, those employments shall be interdicted to them, in order to be preserved for the exclusive benefit of males. In the last two centuries, when (which was seldom the case) any reason beyond the mere existence of the fact was thought to be required to justify the disabilities of women, people seldom assigned as a reason their inferior mental capacity; which, in times when there was a real trial of personal faculties (from which all women were not excluded) in the struggles of public life, no one really believed in. The reason given in those days was not women's unfitness, but the interest of society, by which was meant the interest of men: just as the *raison d'état*, meaning the convenience of the government, and the support of existing authority, was deemed a sufficient explanation and excuse for the most flagitious crimes. In the present day, power holds a smoother language, and whomsoever it oppresses, always pretends to do so for their own good: accordingly, when anything is forbidden to women, it is thought necessary to say, and desirable to believe, that they are incapable of doing it, and that they depart from their real path of success and happiness when they aspire to it. But to make this reason plausible (I do not say valid), those by whom it is urged must be prepared to carry it to a much greater length than any one ventures to do in the face of present experience. It is not sufficient to maintain that women on the average are less gifted than men on the average, with certain of the higher mental faculties, or that a smaller number of women than of men are fit for occupations and functions of the highest intellectual character. It is necessary to maintain that no women at all are fit for them, and that the most eminent women are inferior in mental faculties to the most mediocre of the men on whom those functions at present devolve. For if the performance of the function is decided either by competition, or by any mode of choice which secures regard to the public interest, there needs be no apprehension that any important employments will fall into the hands of women inferior to average men, or to the average of their male competitors. The only result would be that there would be fewer women than men in such employments; a result certain to happen in any case, if only from the preference always likely to be felt by the majority of women for the one vocation in which there is nobody to compete with them. Now, the most determined depreciator of women will not venture to deny, that when we add the experience of recent times to that of ages past, women, and not a few merely, but many women, have proved themselves capable of everything, perhaps without a single exception, which is done by men, and of doing it successfully and creditably. The utmost that can be said is, that there are many things which none of them have succeeded in doing as well as they have been done by some men — many in which they have not reached the very highest rank. But there are extremely few, dependent only on mental faculties, in which they have not attained the rank next to the highest. Is not this enough, and much more than enough, to make it a tyranny to them, and a detriment to society, that they should not be allowed to compete with men for the exercise of these functions? Is it not a mere truism to say, that such functions are often filled by men far less fit for them than numbers of women, and who would be beaten by women in any fair field of competition? What difference does it make that there may be men somewhere, fully employed about other things, who may be still better qualified for the things in question than these women? Does not this take place in all competitions? Is there so great a superfluity of men fit for high duties, that society can afford to reject the service of any competent person? Are we so certain of always finding a man made to our hands for any duty or function of social importance which falls vacant, that we lose nothing by putting a ban upon one-half of mankind, and refusing beforehand to make their faculties available, however distinguished they may be? And even if we could do without them, would it be consistent with justice to refuse to them their fair share of honour and distinction, or to deny to them the equal moral right of all human beings to choose their occupation (short of injury to others) according to their own preferences, at their own risk? Nor is the injustice confined to them: it is shared by those who are in a position to benefit by their services. To ordain that any kind of persons shall not be physicians, or shall not be advocates, or shall not be members of parliament, is to injure not them only, but all who employ physicians or advocates, or elect members of parliament, and who are deprived of the stimulating effect of greater competition on the exertions of the competitors, as well as restricted to a narrower range of individual choice.

It will perhaps be sufficient if I confine myself, in the details of my argument, to functions of a public nature: since, if I am successful as to those, it probably will be readily granted that women should be admissible to all other occupations to which it is at all material whether they are admitted or not. And here let me begin by marking out one function, broadly distinguished from all others, their right to which is entirely independent of any question which can be raised concerning their faculties. I mean the suffrage, both parliamentary and municipal. The right to share in the choice of those who are to exercise a public trust, is altogether a distinct thing from that of competing for the trust itself. If no one could vote for a member of parliament who was not fit to be a candidate, the government would be a narrow oligarchy indeed. To have a voice in choosing those by whom one is to be governed, is a means of self-protection due to every one, though he were to remain for ever excluded from the function of governing: and that women are considered fit to have such a choice, may be presumed from the fact, that the law already gives it to women in the most important of all cases to themselves: for the choice of the man who is to govern a woman to the end of life, is always supposed to be voluntarily made by herself. In the case of election to public trusts, it is the business of constitutional law to surround the right of suffrage with all needful securities and limitations; but whatever securities are sufficient in the case of the male sex, no others need be required in the case of women. Under whatever conditions, and within whatever limits, men are admitted to the suffrage, there is not a shadow of justification for not admitting women under the same. The majority of the women of any class are not likely to differ in political opinion from the majority of the men of the same class, unless the question be one in which the interests of women, as such, are in some way involved; and if they are so, women require the suffrage, as their guarantee of just and equal consideration. This ought to be obvious even to those who coincide in no other of the doctrines for which I contend. Even if every woman were a wife, and if every wife ought to be a slave, all the more would these slaves stand in need of legal protection: and we know what legal protection the slaves have, where the laws are made by their masters. . . .

KARL MARX

1818 – 1883

INTRODUCTION

Although Marx and Mill were contemporaries and lived in London for many of the same years, they never met. Mill does not seem to have read Marx, but in the first volume of *Capital* (1867) Marx makes frequent reference to Mill's economic writings, especially the *Principles of Political Economy* (1848). Marx's estimate of Mill as an economist is summarized in the remark that "On a level plain, mere mounds look like hills. We can measure the imbecile flatness of the modern bourgeoisie by the altitudes its 'great intellects' can reach." This mixture of sarcasm and abuse, so characteristic of Marx's treatment of those with whom he disagreed, is in striking contrast to the gentility that Mill's critical writing usually displays.

Born in the city of Trier in the German Rhineland, Marx was the son of a successful and well-educated Jewish lawyer who, shortly before Karl's birth, accepted Christian baptism in order to retain his government post. Karl Marx obtained good but not outstanding results at his graduation from academic high school and then became secretly engaged to his future wife, Jenny von Westphalen, the daughter of a leading lawyer who, though a liberal aristocrat, was opposed to their relationship. Marx began the study of law at the University of Bonn, transferred to Berlin, and 5 years later received from the University of Jena a doctorate for his thesis on ancient Greek philosophies of nature.

Barred from a university career by his liberal political views, Marx became, for a brief period, the editor of a newspaper in Cologne that was soon threatened by the Prussian censors. In 1843 Marx married, moved to Paris where he began his lifelong partnership with Frederick Engels, and was then expelled successively from Paris, Brussels, and Cologne for his editorial and organizational work, on behalf of revolutionary democracy, both before and during the European uprisings of 1848. By the next year Marx and his family were in permanent exile in London and had begun two decades of poverty, ill health, financial incompetence, and reliance upon friends, especially Engels, for aid and support. Despite these crushing burdens, Marx managed to produce in this period not only a stream of serious political journalism— including *The Class Struggles in France*, *The Eighteenth Brumaire*, and the articles for *The New York Tribune*— but also the theoretical study, *A Contribution to the Critique of Political Economy*, and in 1867 the first volume of *Capital*. This sold well in various translations, and from this point on Marx's reputation rose steadily throughout the world, although *Capital* did not appear in English until 1887. Marx's health deteriorated badly in 1873, and during the last 10 years of his life he suffered from the lung ailments from which he eventually died and was unable to put into final form the last two volumes of *Capital*. They, and a number of his early writings of the 1840s, were published posthumously. The latter, appearing long after his death, have strongly influenced recent discussions of Marx's thought.

The *Economic and Philosophic Manuscripts of 1844* were written as a set of essays early in 1844 before Marx met Engels. They were first published in Berlin in 1932. The present selections from the volume of that title are from the English translation by Martin Milligan, edited by Dirk J. Struik, published by International Publishers, New York, 1964, and reprinted here with their permission. *The German Idealogy* was written jointly by Marx and Engels in 1845–1846 but was not published, with the exception of one chapter, until 1932. The present selection was translated by W. Lough, revised and published in *The German Idealogy*, Progress Publishers, Moscow, 1968. It is used here with permission of International Publishers, New York. The *Manifesto of the Communist Party* was written and published in London early in 1848 to put forward the policy of the Communist League, then a German Workers' secret society. A French translation appeared in Paris a few months later, but the first English translation did not come out until 2 years later. The first two sections of the *Manifesto* reprinted here have been taken from the translation by Samuel Moore, first published in London, 1888.

SELECTIONS FROM
Economic and Philosophic Manuscripts of 1844

I. Estranged Labor

We have proceeded from the premises of political economy. We have accepted its language and its laws. We presupposed private property, the separation of labor, capital and land, and of wages, profit of capital and rent of land — likewise division of labor, competition, the concept of exchange-value, etc. On the basis of political economy itself, in its own words, we have shown that the worker sinks to the level of a commodity and becomes indeed the most wretched of commodities; that the wretchedness of the worker is in inverse proportion to the power and magnitude of his production; that the necessary result of competition is the accumulation of capital in a few hands, and thus the restoration of monopoly in a more terrible form; and that finally the distinction between capitalist and land rentier, like that between the tiller of the soil and the factory worker, disappears and that the whole of society must fall apart into the two classes — the property *owners* and the property-less *workers*.

Political economy starts with the fact of private property, but it does not explain it to us. It expresses in general, abstract formulas the *material* process through which private property actually passes, and these formulas it then takes for *laws*. It does not *comprehend* these laws, i.e., it does not demonstrate how they arise from the very nature of private property. Political economy does not disclose the source of the division between labor and capital, and between capital and land. When, for example, it defines the relationship of wages to profit, it takes the interest of the capitalists to be the ultimate cause, i.e., it takes for granted what it is supposed to explain. Similarly, competition comes in everywhere. It is explained from external circumstances. As to how far these external and apparently accidental circumstances are but the expression of a necessary course of development, political economy teaches us nothing. We have seen how exchange itself appears to it as an accidental fact. The only wheels which political economy sets in motion are *greed* and the war *amongst the greedy — competition.*

Precisely because political economy does not grasp the way the movement is connected, it was possible to oppose, for instance, the doctrine of competition to the doctrine of monopoly, the doctrine of the freedom of the crafts to the doctrine of the guild, the doctrine of the division of landed property to the doctrine of the big estate — for competition, freedom of the crafts and the division of landed property were explained and comprehended only as accidental, premeditated and violent consequences of monopoly, of the guild system, and of feudal property, not as their necessary, inevitable and natural consequences.

Now, therefore, we have to grasp the essential connection between private property, greed, and the separation of labor, capital and landed property; between exchange and competition, value and the devaluation of men, monopoly and competition, etc. — the connection between this whole estrangement and the *money* system.

Do not let us go back to a fictitious primordial condition as the political economist does, when he tries to explain. Such a primordial condition explains nothing; it merely pushes the question away into a gray nebulous distance. It assumes in the form of a fact, of an event, what the economist is supposed to deduce — namely, the necessary relationship between two things — between, for example, division of labor and exchange. Theology in the same way explains the origin of evil by the fall of man; that is, it assumes as a fact, in historical form, what has to be explained.

We proceed from an economic fact *of the present.* The worker becomes all the poorer the more wealth he produces, the more his production increases in power and size. The worker becomes an ever cheaper commodity the more commodities he creates. With the *increasing value* of the world of things proceeds in direct proportion the *devaluation* of the world of men. Labor produces not only commodities: it produces itself and the worker as a *commodity* — and this in the same general proportion in which it produces commodities.

This fact expresses merely that the object which labor produces — labor's product — confronts it as *something alien,* as a *power independent* of the producer. The product of labor is labor which has been embodied in an object, which has become material: it is the *objectification* of labor. Labor's realization is its objectification. In the sphere of political economy this realization of labor appears as *loss of realization* for the workers; objectification as *loss of the object* and *bondage to it;* appropriation as *estrangement,* as *alienation.*

So much does labor's realization appear as loss of realization that the worker loses realization to the point of starving to death. So much does objectification appear as loss of the object that the worker is robbed of the objects most necessary not only for his life but for his work. Indeed, labor itself becomes an object which he can obtain only with the greatest effort and with the most irregular interruptions. So much does the appropriation of the object appear as estrangement that the more objects the worker produces the less he can possess and the more he falls under the sway of his product, capital.

All these consequences result from the fact that the worker is related to the *product of his labor* as to an *alien* object. For on this premise it is clear that the more the worker spends himself, the more powerful becomes the alien world of objects which he creates over and against himself, the poorer he himself — his inner world — becomes, the less belongs to him as his own. It is the same in religion. The more man puts into God, the less he retains in himself. The worker puts his life into the object; but now his life no longer belongs to him but to the object. Hence, the greater this activity, the greater is the worker's lack of objects. Whatever the product of his labor is, he is not. Therefore the greater this product, the less is he himself. The *alienation* of the worker in his product means not only that his labor becomes an object, an *external* existence, but that it exists *outside him*, independently, as something alien to him, and that it becomes a power on its own confronting him. It means that the life which he has conferred on the object confronts him as something hostile and alien.

Let us now look more closely at the *objectification*, at the production of the worker; and in it at the *estrangement*, the *loss* of the object, of his product.

The worker can create nothing without *nature*, without the *sensuous external world*. It is the material on which his labor is realized, in which it is active, from which and by means of which it produces.

But just as nature provides labor with the *means of life* in the sense that labor cannot *live* without objects on which to operate, on the other hand, it also provides the *means of life* in the more restricted sense, i.e., the means for the physical subsistence of the *worker* himself.

Thus the more the worker by his labor *appropriates* the external world, hence sensuous nature, the more he deprives himself of *means of life* in a double manner: first, in that sensuous external world more and more ceases to be an object belonging to his labor — to be his labor's *means of life;* and secondly, in that it more and more ceases to be *means of life* in the immediate sense, means for the physical subsistence of the worker.

In both respects, therefore, the worker becomes a slave of his object, first, in that he receives an *object of labor*, i.e., in that he receives *work;* and secondly, in that he receives *means of subsistence*. Therefore, it enables him to exist, first, as a *worker;* and, second as a *physical subject*. The height of this bondage is that it is only as a *worker* that he continues to maintain himself as a *physical subject*, and that it is only as a *physical subject* that he is a worker.

(The laws of political economy express the estrangement of the worker in his object thus: the more the worker produces, the less he has to consume; the more values he creates, the more valueless, the more unworthy he becomes; the better formed his product, the more deformed becomes the worker; the more civilized his object, the more barbarous becomes the worker; the more powerful labor becomes, the more powerless becomes the worker; the more ingenious labor becomes, the less ingenious becomes the worker and the more he becomes nature's bondsman.)

Political economy conceals the estrangement inherent in the nature of labor by not considering the direct relationship between the worker (labor) *and production.* It is true that labor produces for the rich wonderful things — but for the worker it produces privation. It produces palaces — but for the worker, hovels. It produces beauty — but for the worker, deformity. It replaces labor by machines, but it throws a section of the workers back to a barbarous type of labor, and it turns the other workers into machines. It produces intelligence — but for the worker stupidity, cretinism.

The direct relationship of labor to its products is the relationship of the worker to the objects of his production. The relationship of the man of means to the objects of production and to production itself is only a *consequence* of this first relationship — and confirms it. We shall consider this other aspect later.

When we ask, then, what is the essential relationship of labor we are asking about the relationship of the *worker* to production.

Till now we have been considering the estrangement, the alienation of the worker only in one of its aspects, i.e., the worker's *relationship to the products of his labor.* But the estrangement is manifested not only in the result but in the *act of production,* within the *producing activity,* itself. How could the worker come to face the product of his activity as a stranger, were it not that in the very act of production he was estranging himself from himself? The product is after all but the summary of the activity, of production. If then the product of labor is alienation, production itself must be active alienation, the alienation of activity, the activity of alienation. In the estrangement of the object of labor is merely summarized the estrangement, the alienation, in the activity of labor itself.

What, then, constitutes the alienation of labor?

First, the fact that labor is *external* to the worker, i.e., it does not belong to his essential being; that in his work, therefore, he does not affirm himself but denies himself, does not feel content but unhappy, does not develop freely his physical and mental energy but mortifies his body and ruins his mind. The worker therefore only feels himself outside his work, and in his work feels outside himself. He is at home when he is not working, and when he is working he is not at home. His labor is therefore not voluntary, but coerced; it is *forced labor.* It is therefore not the satisfaction of a need; it is merely a *means* to satisfy needs external to it. Its alien character emerges clearly in the fact that as soon as no physical or other compulsion exists, labor is shunned like the plague. External labor, labor in which man alienates himself, is a labor of self-sacrifice, of mortification. Lastly, the external character of labor for the worker appears in the fact that it is not his own, but someone else's, that it does not belong to him, that in it he belongs, not to himself, but to another. Just as in religion the spontaneous activity of the human imagination, of the human brain and the human heart, operates independently of the individual — that is, operates on him as an alien, divine or diabolical activity — so is the worker's activity not his spontaneous activity. It belongs to another; it is the loss of his self.

As a result, therefore, man (the worker) only feels himself freely active in his animal functions — eating, drinking, procreating, or at most in his dwelling and in dressing-up, etc.; and in his human functions he no longer feels himself to be anything but an animal. What is animal becomes human and what is human becomes animal.

Certainly eating, drinking, procreating, etc., are also genuinely human functions. But abstractly taken, separated from the sphere of all other human activity and turned into sole and ultimate ends, they are animal functions.

We have considered the act of estranging practical human activity, labor, in two of its aspects. (1) The relation of the worker to the *product of labor* as an alien object exercising power over him. This relation is at the same time the relation to the sensuous external world, to the objects of nature, as an alien world inimically opposed to him. (2) The relation of labor to the *act of production* within the *labor* process. This relation is the relation of the worker to his own activity as an alien activity not belonging to him; it is activity as suffering, strength as weakness, begetting as emasculating, the workers' *own* physical and mental energy, his personal life indeed, what is life but activity? —as an activity which is turned against him, independent of him and not belonging to him. Here we have *self-estrangement*, as previously we had the estrangement of the *thing*.

We have still a third aspect of *estranged labor* to deduce from the two already considered.

Man is a species being, not only because in practice and in theory he adopts the species as his object (his own as well as those of other things), but—and this is only another way of expressing it—also because he treats himself as the actual, living species; because he treats himself as a *universal* and therefore a free being.

The life of the species, both in man and in animals, consists physically in the fact that man (like the animal) lives on inorganic nature; and the more universal man is compared with an animal, the more universal is the sphere of inorganic nature on which he lives. Just as plants, animals, stones, air, light, etc., constitute theoretically a part of human consciousness, partly as objects of natural science, partly as objects of art—his spiritual inorganic nature, spiritual nourishment which he must first prepare to make palatable and digestible—so also in the realm of practice they constitute a part of human life and human activity. Physically man lives only on these products of nature, whether they appear in the form of food, heating, clothes, a dwelling, etc. The universality of man appears in practice precisely in the universality which makes all nature his *inorganic* body—both inasmuch as nature is (1) his direct means of life, and (2) the material, the object, and the instrument of his life activity. Nature is man's *inorganic body*—nature, that is, in so far as it is not itself the human body. Man *lives* on nature—means that nature is his *body*, with which he must remain in continuous interchange if he is not to die. That man's physical and spiritual life is linked to nature means simply that nature is linked to itself, for man is a part of nature.

In estranging from man (1) nature, and (2) himself, his own active functions, his life activity, estranged labor estranges the *species* from man. It changes for him the *life of the species* into a means of individual life. First it estranges the life of the species and individual life, and secondly it makes individual life in its abstract form the purpose of the life of the species, likewise in its abstract and estranged form.

Indeed, labor, *life-activity, productive life* itself, appears in the first place merely as a *means* of satisfying a need—the need to maintain physical

existence. Yet the productive life is the life of the species. It is life-engender-
ing life. The whole character of a species — its species character — is contained in the character of its life activity; and free, conscious activity is man's
species character. Life itself appears only as a *means to life*.

The animal is immediately one with its life activity. It does not distinguish
itself from it. It is *its life activity*. Man makes his life activity itself the object of
his will and of his consciousness. He has conscious life activity. It is not a
determination with which he directly merges. Conscious life activity distinguishes man immediately from animal life activity. It is just because of this that
he is a species being. Or rather, it is only because he is a species being that he
is a conscious being, i.e., that his own life is an object for him. Only because
of that is his activity free activity. Estranged labor reverses this relationship, so
that it is just because man is a conscious being that he makes his life activity,
his *essential* being, a mere means to his *existence*.

In creating a *world of objects* by his practical activity, in *his work upon*
inorganic nature, man proves himself a conscious species being, i.e., as a
being that treats the species as its own essential being, or that treats itself as a
species being. Admittedly animals also produce. They build themselves nests,
dwellings, like the bees, beavers, ants, etc. But an animal only produces what
it immediately needs for itself or its young. It produces one-sidedly, whilst
man produces universally. It produces only under the dominion of immediate
physical need, whilst man produces even when he is free from physical need
and only truly produces in freedom therefrom. An animal produces only itself,
whilst man reproduces the whole of nature. An animal's product belongs
immediately to its physical body, whilst man freely confronts his product. An
animal forms things in accordance with the standard and the need of the
species to which it belongs, whilst man knows how to produce in accordance
with the standard of every species, and knows how to apply everywhere the
inherent standard to the object. Man therefore also forms things in accordance with the laws of beauty.

It is just in his work upon the objective world, therefore, that man first
really proves himself to be a *species being*. This production is his active
species life. Through and because of this production, nature appears as *his*
work and his reality. The object of labor is, therefore, the *objectification of
man's species life:* for he duplicates himself not only, as in consciousness,
intellectually, but also actively, in reality, and therefore he contemplates
himself in a world that he has created. In tearing away from man the object of
his production, therefore, estranged labor tears from him his *species life*, his
real objectivity as a member of the species and transforms his advantage over
animals into the disadvantage that his inorganic body, nature, is taken away
from him.

Similarly, in degrading spontaneous, free, activity, to a means, estranged
labor makes man's species life a means to his physical existence.

The consciousness which man has of his species is thus transformed by
estrangement in such a way that species life becomes for him a means.

Estranged labor turns thus:

(3) *Man's species being*, both nature and his spiritual species property, into a being *alien* to him, into a *means* to his *individual existence.* It estranges from man his own body, as well as external nature and his spiritual essence, his *human* being.

(4) An immediate consequence of the fact that man is estranged from the product of his labor, from his life activity, from his species being is the *estrangement* of *man* from *man.* When man confronts himself, he confronts the *other* man. What applies to a man's relation to his work, to the product of his labor and to himself, also holds of a man's relation to the other man, and to the other man's labor and object of labor.

In fact, the proposition that man's species nature is estranged from him means that one man is estranged from the other, as each of them is from man's essential nature.

The estrangement of man, and in fact every relationship in which man stands to himself, is first realized and expressed in the relationship in which a man stands to other men.

Hence within the relationship of estranged labor each man views the other in accordance with the standard and the relationship in which he finds himself as a worker.

We took our departure from a fact of political economy — the estrangement of the worker and his production. We have formulated this fact in conceptual terms of *estranged, alienated* labor. We have analyzed this concept — hence analyzing merely a fact of political economy.

Let us now see, further, how the concept of estranged, alienated labor must express and present itself in real life.

If the product of labor is alien to me, if it confronts me as an alien power, to whom, then, does it belong?

If my own activity does not belong to me, if it is an alien, a coerced activity, to whom, then, does it belong?

To a being *other* than myself.

Who is this being?

The *gods*? To be sure, in the earliest times the principal production (for example, the building of temples, etc., in Egypt, India and Mexico) appears to be in the service of the gods, and the product belongs to the gods. However, the gods on their own were never the lords of labor. No more was *nature*. And what a contradiction it would be if, the more man subjugated nature by his labor and the more the miracles of the gods were rendered superfluous by the miracles of industry, the more man were to renounce the joy of production and the enjoyment of the product in favor of these powers.

The *alien* being, to whom labor and the product of labor belongs, in whose service labor is done and for whose benefit the product of labor is provided, can only be *man* himself.

If the product of labor does not belong to the worker, if it confronts him as an alien power, then this can only be because it belongs to some *other man than the worker.* If the worker's activity is a torment to him, to another it must be *delight* and his life's joy. Not the gods, not nature, but only man himself can be this alien power over man.

We must bear in mind the previous proposition that man's relation to himself only becomes for him *objective* and *actual* through his relation to the other man. Thus, if the product of his labor, his labor *objectified*, is for him an *alien*, hostile, powerful object independent of him, then his position towards it is such that someone else is master of this object, someone who is alien, hostile, powerful, and independent of him. If his own activity is to him related as an unfree activity, then he is related to it as an activity performed in the service, under the dominion, the coercion, and the yoke of another man.

Every self-estrangement of man, from himself and from nature, appears in the relation in which he places himself and nature to men other than and differentiated from himself. For this reason religious self-estrangement necessarily appears in the relationship of the layman to the priest, or again to a mediator, etc., since we are here dealing with the intellectual world. In the real practical world self-estrangement can only become manifest through the real practical relationship to other men. The medium through which estrangement takes place is itself *practical.* Thus through estranged labor man not only creates his relationship to the object and to the act of production as to men that are alien and hostile to him; he also creates the relationship in which other men stand to his production and to his product, and the relationship in which he stands to these other men. Just as he creates his own production as the loss of his reality, as his punishment; his own product as a loss, as a product not belonging to him; so he creates the domination of the person who does not produce over production and over the product. Just as he estranges his own activity from himself, so he confers to the stranger an activity which is not his own.

We have until now only considered this relationship from the standpoint of the worker and later we shall be considering it also from the standpoint of the non-worker.

Through *estranged, alienated labor,* then, the worker produces the relationship to this labor of a man alien to labor and standing outside it. The relationship of the worker to labor creates the relation to it of the capitalist (or whatever one chooses to call the master of labor). *Private property* is thus the product, the result, the necessary consequence, of *alienated labor,* of the external relation of the worker to nature and to himself.

Private property thus results by analysis from the concept of *alienated labor,* i.e., of *alienated man,* of estranged labor, of estranged life, of *estranged* man.

True, it is as a result of the *movement of private property* that we have obtained the concept of *alienated labor* (*of alienated life*) from political economy. But on analysis of this concept it becomes clear that though private property appears to be the source, the cause of alienated labor, it is rather its consequence, just as the gods are *originally* not the cause but the effect of man's intellectual confusion. Later this relationship becomes reciprocal.

Only at the last culmination of the development of private property does this, its secret, appear again, namely, that on the one hand it is the *product* of alienated labor, and that on the other it is the *means* by which labor alienates itself, the *realization of this alienation.*

This exposition immediately sheds light on various hitherto unsolved conflicts.

(1) Political economy starts from labor as the real soul of production; yet to labor it gives nothing, and to private property everything. Confronting this contradiction, Proudhon has decided in favor of labor against private property. We understand, however, that this apparent contradiction is the contradiction of *estranged labor* with itself, and that political economy has merely formulated the laws of estranged labor.

We also understand, therefore, that *wages* and *private property* are identical: since the product, as the object of labor pays for labor itself, therefore the wage is but a necessary consequence of labor's estrangement. After all, in the wage of labor, labor does not appear as an end in itself but as the servant of the wage. We shall develop this point later, and meanwhile will only derive some conclusions.

An enforced increase of wages (disregarding all other difficulties, including the fact that it would only be by force, too, that higher wages, being an anomaly, could be maintained) would therefore be nothing but *better payment for the slave,* and would not win either for the worker or for labor their human status and dignity.

Indeed, even the *equality of wages* demanded by Proudhon only transforms the relationship of the present-day worker to his labor into the relationship of all men to labor. Society is then conceived as an abstract capitalist.

Wages are a direct consequence of estranged labor, and estranged labor is the direct cause of private property. The downfall of the one must involve the downfall of the other.

(2) From the relationship of estranged labor to private property it follows further that the emancipation of society from private property, etc., from servitude, is expressed in the *political* form of the *emancipation of the workers;* not that *their* emancipation alone is at stake, but because the emancipation of the workers contains universal human emancipation — and it contains this, because the whole of human servitude is involved in the relation of the worker to production, and every relation of servitude is but a modification and consequence of this relation.

Just as we have derived the concept of *private property* from the concept of *estranged, alienated labor* by *analysis,* so we can develop every *category* of political economy with the help of these two factors; and we shall find again in each category, e.g., trade, competition, capital, money, only a *definite* and *developed expression* of these first elements.

Before considering this aspect, however, let us try to solve two problems. (1) To define the general *nature of private property*, as it has arisen as a result of estranged labor, in its relation to *truly human* and *social property*. (2) We have accepted the *estrangement of labor*, its *alienation*, as a fact, and we have analyzed this fact. How, we now ask, does *man* come to *alienate*, to estrange, *his labor?* How is this estrangement rooted in the nature of human development? We have already gone a long way to the solution of this problem by *transforming* the question of the *origin of private property* into the question of the relation of *alienated labor* to the course of humanity's development. For when one speaks of *private property*, one thinks of dealing with something external to man. When one speaks of labor, one is directly dealing with man himself. This new formulation of the question already contains its solution.

As to (1): The general nature of private property and its relation to truly human property.

Alienated labor has resolved itself for us into two elements which mutually condition one another, or which are but different expressions of one and the same relationship. *Appropriation* appears as *estrangement*, as *alienation;* and *alienation* appears as *appropriation, estrangement* as true introduction into society.

We have considered the one side — *alienated* labor in relation to the *worker* himself, i.e., the *relation of alienated labor to itself.* The *property relation of the non-worker to the worker and to labor* we have found as the product, the necessary outcome of this relationship. *Private property*, as the material, summary expression of alienated labor, embraces both relations — the *relation of the worker to work and to the product of his labor and to the non-worker*, and the relation of the *non-worker to the worker and to the product of his labor.*

Having seen that in relation to the worker who *appropriates* nature by means of his labor, this appropriation appears as estrangement, his own spontaneous activity as activity for another and as activity of another, vitality as a sacrifice of life, production of the object as loss of the object to an alien power, to an *alien* person — we shall now consider the relation to the worker, to labor and its object of this person who is *alien* to labor and the worker.

First it has to be noted that everything which appears in the worker as an *activity of alienation, of estrangement,* appears in the non-worker as a *state of alienation, of estrangement.*

Secondly, that the worker's *real, practical attitude* in production and to the product (as a state of mind) appears in the non-worker confronting him as a *theoretical* attitude.

Thirdly, the non-worker does everything against the worker which the worker does against himself; but he does not do against himself what he does against the worker.

Let us look more closely at these three relations.

[*At this point the first manuscript breaks off unfinished.*]

II. Private Property and Communism

The antithesis between *lack of property* and *property*, so long as it is not comprehended as the antithesis of *labor* and *capital*, still remains an indifferent antithesis, not grasped in its *active connection*, with its *internal* relation —an antithesis not yet grasped as a *contradiction*. It can find expression in this *first* form even without the advanced development of private property (as in ancient Rome, Turkey, etc.). It does not yet *appear* as having been established by private property itself. But labor, the subjective essence of private property as exclusion of property, and capital, objective labor as exclusion of labor, constitute *private property* as its developed state of contradiction—hence a dynamic relationship moving to its resolution.

The transcendence of self-estrangement follows the same course as self-estrangement. *Private property* is first considered only in its objective aspect—but nevertheless with labor as its essence. Its form of existence is therefore *capital*, which is to be annulled "as such" (Proudhon). Or a *particular form* of labor—labor leveled down, parceled, and therefore unfree—is conceived as the source of private property's *perniciousness* and of its existence in estrangement from men. For instance, *Fourier*, who, like the physiocrats, also conceived *agricultural labor* to be at least the *exemplary* type, whilst *Saint-Simon* declares in contrast that *industrial labor* as such is the essence, and only aspires to the *exclusive* rule of the industrialists and the improvement of the workers' condition. Finally, *communism* is the *positive* expression of annulled private property—at first as *universal* private property. By embracing this relation as a *whole*, communism is:

(1) In its first form only a *generalization* and *consummation* of this relationship. As such it appears in a twofold form: on the one hand, the dominion of *material* property bulks so large that it wants to destroy *everything* which is not capable of being possessed by all as *private property*. It wants to do away *by force* with talent, etc. For it the sole purpose of life and existence is direct, physical *possession*. The task of the laborer is not done away with, but extended to all men. The relationship of private property persists as the relationship of the community to the world of things.

Finally, this movement of opposing universal private property to private property finds expression in the animal form of opposing to *marriage* (certainly a *form of exclusive private property*) the *community of women*, in which a woman becomes a piece of *communal* and *common* property. It may be said that this idea of the *community of women* gives away the *secret* of this as yet completely crude and thoughtless communism. Just as woman passes from marriage to general prostitution, so the entire world of wealth (that is, of man's objective substance) passes from the relationship of exclusive marriage with the owner of private property to a state of universal prostitution with the community. In negating the *personality* of man in every sphere, this type of communism is really nothing but the logical expression of private property, which is its negation. General *envy* constituting itself as a power is the disguise in which *greed* reestablishes itself and satisfies itself, only in *another* way. The thought of every piece of private property — inherent in each piece as such — is *at least* turned against all *wealthier* private property in the form of envy and the urge to reduce things to a common level, so that this envy and urge even constitute the essence of competition. The crude communism is only the culmination of this envy and of this leveling-down proceeding from the *preconceived* minimum. It has a *definite, limited* standard. How little this annulment of private property is really an appropriation is in fact proved by the abstract negation of the entire world of culture and civilization, the regression to the *unnatural* simplicity of the *poor and undemanding* man who has not only failed to go beyond private property, but has not yet even reached it.

The community is only a community of *labor,* and of equality of *wages* paid out by communal capital — the *community* as the universal capitalist. Both sides of the relationship are raised to an *imagined* universality — *labor* as a state in which every person is placed, and *capital* as the acknowledged universality and power of the community.

In the approach to *woman* as the spoil and handmaid of communal lust is expressed the infinite degradation in which man exists for himself, for the secret of this approach has its *unambiguous,* decisive, *plain* and undisguised expression in the relation of *man* to *woman* and in the manner in which the *direct* and *natural* species relationship is conceived. This direct, natural, and necessary relation of person to person is the *relation of man to woman.* In this *natural* species relationship man's relation to nature is immediately his relation to man, just as his relation to man is immediately his relation to nature — his own *natural* destination. In this relationship, therefore, is *sensuously manifested,* reduced to an observable *fact,* the extent to which the human essence has become nature to man, or to which nature to him has become the human essence of man. From this relationship one can therefore judge man's whole level of development. From the character of this relationship follows how much *man* as a *species being,* as *man,* has come to be himself and to comprehend himself; the relation of man to woman is *the most natural* relation of human being to human being. It therefore reveals the extent to which man's *natural* behavior has become *human,* or the extent to which the *human* essence in him has become a *natural* essence — the extent to which his *human nature* has come to be *nature to him.* In this relationship is revealed, too, the extent to which man's *need* has become a *human* need; the extent to which, therefore, the *other* person as a person has become for him a need — the extent to which he in his individual existence is at the same time a social being.

The first positive annulment of private property — *crude* communism — is thus merely one *form* in which the vileness of private property, which wants to set itself up as the *positive community, comes to the surface.*

(2) Communism (*a*) still political in nature — democratic or despotic; (*b*)

with the abolition of the state, yet still incomplete, and being still affected by private property (i.e., by the estrangement of man). In both forms communism already is aware of being reintegration or return of man to himself, the transcendence of human self-estrangement; but since it has not yet grasped the positive essence of private property, and just as little the *human* nature of need, it remains captive to it and infected by it. It has, indeed, grasped its concept, but not its essence.

(3) *Communism* as the *positive* transcendence of *private property*, as *human self-estrangement*, and therefore as the real *appropriation of the human* essence by and for man; communism therefore as the complete return of man to himself as a *social* (i.e., human) being—a return become conscious, and accomplished within the entire wealth of previous development. This communism, as fully developed naturalism, equals humanism, and as fully developed humanism equals naturalism; it is the *genuine* resolution of the conflict between man and nature and between man and man—the true resolution of the strife between existence and essence, between objectification and self-confirmation, between freedom and necessity, between the individual and the species. Communism is the riddle of history solved, and it knows itself to be this solution.

The entire movement of history is, therefore, both its *actual* act of genesis (the birth act of its empirical existence) and also for its thinking consciousness the *comprehended* and *known* process of its *becoming*. That other, still immature communism, meanwhile, seeks an *historical* proof for itself—a proof in the realm of what already exists—among disconnected historical phenomena opposed to private property, tearing single phases from the historical process and focusing attention on them as proofs of its historical pedigree (a hobbyhorse ridden hard especially by Cabet, Villegardelle, etc.). By so doing it simply makes clear that by far the greater part of this process contradicts its own claim, and that, if it has ever existed, precisely its being in the past refutes its pretension to being *essential being*.

It is easy to see that the entire revolutionary movement necessarily finds both its empirical and its theoretical basis in the movement of *private property*—more precisely, in that of the economy.

This *material*, immediately perceptible private property is the material perceptible expression of *estranged human* life. Its movement—production and consumption—is the *perceptible* revelation of the movement of all production until now, i.e., the realization or the reality of man. Religion, family, state, law, morality, science, art, etc., are only *particular* modes of production, and fall under its general law. The positive transcendence of *private property*, as the appropriation of *human* life, is therefore the positive transcendence of all estrangement—that is to say, the return of man from religion, family, state, etc., to his *human*, i.e., *social* existence. Religious estrangement as such occurs only in the realm of *consciousness*, of man's inner life, but economic estrangement is that of *real life*; its transcendence therefore embraces both aspects. It is evident that the *initial* stage of the movement amongst the various peoples depends on whether the true and *authentic* life of the people manifests itself more in consciousness or in the external world — is more ideal or real. Communism begins from the outset (*Owen*) with atheism; but atheism is at first far from being *communism*; indeed, it is still mostly an abstraction.

The philanthropy of atheism is therefore at first only *philosophical*, abstract, philanthropy, and that of communism is at once *real* and directly bent on *action*.

We have seen how on the assumption of positively annulled private property man produces man — himself and the other man; how the object, being the direct embodiment of his individuality, is simultaneously his own existence for the other man, the existence of the other man, and that existence for him. Likewise, however, both the material of labor and man as the subject, are the point of departure as well as the result of the movement (and precisely in this fact, that they must constitute the *point of departure*, lies the historical *necessity* of private property). Thus the *social* character is the general character of the whole movement: *just as* society itself produces *man as man*, so is society *produced* by him. Activity and mind, both in their content and in their *mode of existence*, are *social*: *social* activity and *social* mind. The *human* essence of nature first exists only for *social* man; for only here does nature exist for him as a *bond* with *man* — as his existence for the other and the other's existence for him — as the life-element of human reality. Only here does nature exist as the *foundation* of his own *human* existence. Only here has what is to him his *natural* existence become his *human* existence, and nature become man for him. Thus *society* is the unity of being of man with nature — the true resurrection of nature — the naturalism of man and the humanism of nature both brought to fulfillment.

Social activity and social mind exist by no means *only* in the form of some *directly* communal activity and directly *communal* mind, although *communal* activity and *communal* mind — i.e., activity and mind which are manifested and directly revealed in *real association* with other men — will occur wherever such a *direct* expression of sociability stems from the true character of the activity's content and is adequate to its nature.

But also when I am active *scientifically*, etc. — when I am engaged in activity which I can seldom perform in direct community with others — then I am *social*, because I am active as a *man*. Not only is the material of my activity given to me as a social product (as is even the language in which the thinker is active): my *own* existence is social activity, and therefore that which I make of myself, I make of myself for society and with the consciousness of myself as a social being.

My *general* consciousness is only the *theoretical* shape of that which the *living* shape is the *real* community, the social fabric, although at the present day *general* consciousness is an abstraction from real life and as such confronts it with hostility. The *activity* of my general consciousness, as an activity, is therefore also my *theoretical* existence as a social being.

Above all we must avoid postulating "Society" again as an abstraction *vis-à-vis* the individual. The individual *is the social being*. His life, even if it may not appear in the direct form of a *communal* life in association with others—is therefore an expression and confirmation of *social life*. Man's individual and species life are not *different*, however much—and this is inevitable—the mode of existence of the individual is a more *particular*, or more *general* mode of the life of the species, or the life of the species is a more *particular* or more *general* individual life.

In his *consciousness of species* man confirms his real *social life* and simply repeats his real existence in thought, just as conversely the being of the species confirms itself in species-consciousness and exists for *itself* in its generality as a thinking being.

Man, much as he may therefore be a *particular* individual (and it is precisely his particularity which makes him an individual, and a real *individual* social being), is just as much the *totality*—the ideal totality—the subjective existence of thought and experienced society for itself; just as he exists also in the real world as the awareness and the real mind of social existence, and as a totality of human manifestation of life.

Thinking and being are thus no doubt *distinct*, but at the same time they are in *unity* with each other.

Death seems to be a harsh victory of the species over the *definite* individual and to contradict their unity. But the particular individual is only a *particular species being*, and as such mortal.

(4) Just as *private property* is only the perceptible expression of the fact that man becomes *objective* for himself and at the same time becomes to himself a strange and inhuman object; just as it expresses the fact that the assertion of his life is the alienation of his life, that his realization is his loss of reality, is an *alien* reality: so, the positive transcendence of private property —i.e., the *perceptible* appropriation for and by man of the human essence and of human life, of objective man, of human *achievements*—should not to be conceived merely in the sense of *immediate*, one-sided *gratification*— merely in the sense of *possessing*, of *having*. Man appropriates his total essence in a total manner, that is to say, as a whole man. Each of his *human* relations to the world—seeing, hearing, smelling, tasting, feeling, thinking, observing, experiencing, wanting, acting, loving—in short, all the organs of his individual being, like those organs which are directly social in their form, are in their *objective* orientation or in their *orientation to the object*, the appropriation of that object. The appropriation of *human* reality; its orientation to the object is the *manifestation of the human reality*, it is human *activity* and human *suffering*, for suffering, humanly considered, is a self-indulgence of man.

Private property has made us so stupid and one-sided that an object is only *ours* when we have it—when it exists for us as capital, or when it is directly possessed, eaten, drunk, worn, inhabited, etc.,—in short, when it is *used* by us. Although private property itself again conceives all these direct realizations of possession only as *means of life*, and the life which they serve as means is the *life of private property*—labor and conversion into capital. *All* these physical and mental senses have therefore—the sheer estrangement of *all* these senses—the sense of *having*. The human being had to be reduced to this absolute poverty in order that he might yield his inner wealth to the outer world. (On the category of "*having*," see Hess in the *Twenty-One Sheets*.)

The transcendence of private property is therefore the complete *emancipation* of all human senses and qualities, but it is this emancipation precisely because these senses and attributes have become, subjectively and objectively, *human*. The eye has become a *human* eye, just as its *object* has become a social, *human* object—an object made by man for man. The *senses* have therefore become directly in their practice *theoreticians*. They relate themselves to the *thing* for the sake of the thing, but the thing itself is an *objective human* relation to itself and to man, and vice versa. Need or enjoyment have consequently lost the *egotistical* nature, and nature has lost its mere *utility* by use becoming *human* use. . . .

SELECTIONS FROM
The German Ideology

I. Feuerbach. Opposition of the Materialistic and Idealistic Outlook
   A. Ideology in General, German Ideology in Particular

The premises from which we begin are not arbitrary ones, not dogmas, but real premises from which abstraction can only be made in the imagination. They are the real individuals, their activity and the material conditions under which they live, both those which they find already existing and those produced by their activity. These premises can thus be verified in a purely empirical way.

The first premise of all human history is, of course, the existence of living human individuals. Thus the first fact to be established is the physical organisation of these individuals and their consequent relation to the rest of nature. Of course, we cannot here go either into the actual physical nature of man, or into the natural conditions in which man finds himself — geological, orohydrographical, climatic and so on. The writing of history must always set out from these natural bases and their modification in the course of history through the action of men.

Men can be distinguished from animals by consciousness, by religion or anything else you like. They themselves begin to distinguish themselves from animals as soon as they begin to *produce* their means of subsistence, a step which is conditioned by their physical organisation. By producing their means of subsistence men are indirectly producing their actual material life.

The way in which men produce their means of subsistence depends first of all on the nature of the actual means of subsistence they find in existence and have to reproduce. This mode of production must not be considered simply as being the reproduction of the physical existence of the individuals. Rather it is a definite form of activity of these individuals, a definite form of expressing their life, a definite *mode of life* on their part. As individuals express their life, so they are. What they are, therefore, coincides with their production, both with *what* they produce and with *how* they produce. The nature of individuals thus depends on the material conditions determining their production.

This production only makes its appearance with the *increase of population*. In its turn this presupposes the *intercourse* of individuals with one another. The form of this intercourse is again determined by production.

The relations of different nations among themselves depend upon the extent to which each has developed its productive forces, the division of labour and internal intercourse. This statement is generally recognised. But not only the relation of one nation to others, but also the whole internal structure of the nation itself depends on the stage of development reached by its production and its internal and external intercourse. How far the productive forces of a nation are developed is shown most manifestly by the degree to which the division of labour has been carried. Each new productive force, insofar as it is not merely a quantitative extension of productive forces already known (for instance the bringing into cultivation of fresh land), causes a further development of the division of labour.

The division of labour inside a nation leads at first to the separation of industrial and commercial from agricultural labour, and hence to the separation of *town* and *country* and to the conflict of their interests. Its further development leads to the separation of commercial from industrial labour. At the same time through the division of labour inside these various branches there develop various divisions among the individuals co-operating in definite kinds of labour. The relative position of these individual groups is determined by the methods employed in agriculture, industry and commerce (patriarchalism, slavery, estates, classes). These same conditions are to be seen (given a more developed intercourse) in the relations of different nations to one another.

The various stages of development in the division of labour are just so many different forms of ownership, i.e., the existing stage in the division of labour determines also the relations of individuals to one another with reference to the material, instrument, and product of labour.

The first form of ownership is tribal (*Stammeigentum*) ownership. It corresponds to the undeveloped stage of production, at which a people lives by hunting and fishing, by the rearing of beasts or, in the highest stage, agriculture. In the latter case it presupposes a great mass of uncultivated stretches of land. The division of labour is at this stage still very elementary and is confined to a further extension of the natural division of labour existing in the family. The social structure is, therefore, limited to an extension of the family; patriarchal family chieftains, below them the members of the tribe, finally slaves. The slavery latent in the family only develops gradually with the increase of population, the growth of wants, and with the extension of external relations, both of war and of barter.

The second form is the ancient communal and State ownership which proceeds especially from the union of several tribes into a *city* by agreement or by conquest, and which is still accompanied by slavery. Beside communal ownership we already find movable, and later also immovable, private property developing, but as an abnormal form subordinate to communal ownership. The citizens hold power over their labouring slaves only in their community, and on this account alone, therefore, they are bound to the form of communal ownership. It is the communal private property which compels the active citizens to remain in this spontaneously derived form of association over against their slaves. For this reason the whole structure of society based on this communal ownership, and with it the power of the people, decays in the same measure as, in particular, immovable private property evolves. The division of labour is already more developed. We already find the antagonism of town and country; later the antagonism between those states which represent town interests and those which represent country interests, and inside the towns themselves the antagonism between industry and maritime commerce. The class relation between citizens and slaves is now completely developed.

This whole interpretation of history appears to be contradicted by the fact of conquest. Up till now violence, war, pillage, murder and robbery, etc., have been accepted as the driving force of history. Here we must limit ourselves to the chief points and take, therefore, only the most striking example — the destruction of an old civilisation by a barbarous people and the resulting formation of an entirely new organisation of society. (Rome and the barbarians; feudalism and Gaul; the Byzantine Empire and the Turks.) With the conquering barbarian people war itself is still, as indicated above, a regular form of intercourse, which is the more eagerly exploited as the increase in population together with the traditional and, for it, the only possible, crude mode of production gives rise to the need for new means of production. In Italy, on the other hand, the concentration of landed property (caused not only by buying-up and indebtedness but also by inheritance, since loose living being rife and marriage rare, the old families gradually died out and their possessions fell into the hands of a few) and its conversion into grazing-land (caused not only by the usual economic forces still operative today but by the importation of plundered and tribute-corn and the resultant lack of demand for Italian corn) brought about the almost total disappearance of the free population. The very slaves died out again and again, and had constantly to be replaced by new ones. Slavery remained the basis of the whole productive system. The plebeians, midway between freemen and slaves, never succeeded in becoming more than a proletarian rabble. Rome indeed never became more than a city; its connection with the provinces was almost exclusively political and could, therefore, easily be broken again by political events.

With the development of private property, we find here for the first time the same conditions which we shall find again, only on a more extensive scale, with modern private property. On the one hand, the concentration of private property, which began very early in Rome (as the Licinian agrarian law proves) and proceeded very rapidly from the time of the civil wars and especially under the Emperors; on the other hand, coupled with this, the transformation of the plebeian small peasantry into a proletariat, which, however, owing to its intermediate position between propertied citizens and slaves, never achieved an independent development.

The third form of ownership is feudal or estate property. If antiquity started out from the *town* and its little territory, the Middle Ages started out from the *country*. This different starting-point was determined by the sparseness of the population at that time, which was scattered over a large area and which received no large increase from the conquerors. In contrast to Greece and Rome, feudal development at the outset, therefore, extends over a much wider territory, prepared by the Roman conquests and the spread of agriculture at first associated with them. The last centuries of the declining Roman Empire and its conquest by the barbarians destroyed a number of productive forces; agriculture had declined, industry had decayed for want of a market, trade had died out or been violently suspended, the rural and urban population had decreased. From these conditions and the mode of organisation of the conquest determined by them, feudal property developed under the influence of the Germanic military constitution. Like tribal and communal ownership, it is based again on a community; but the directly producing class standing over against it is not, as in the case of the ancient community, the slaves, but the enserfed small peasantry. As soon as feudalism is fully developed, there also arises antagonism to the towns. The hierarchical structure of landownership, and the armed bodies of retainers associated with it, gave the nobility power over the serfs. This feudal organisation was, just as much as the ancient communal ownership, an association against a subjected producing class; but the form of association and the relation to the direct producers were different because of the different conditions of production.

This feudal system of landownership had its counterpart in the *towns* in the shape of corporative property, the feudal organisation of trades. Here property consisted chiefly in the labour of each individual person. The necessity for association against the organised robber-nobility, the need for communal covered markets in an age when the industrialist was at the same time a merchant, the growing competition of the escaped serfs swarming into the rising towns, the feudal structure of the whole country: these combined to bring about the *guilds*. The gradually accumulated small capital of individual craftsmen and their stable numbers, as against the growing population, evolved the relation of journeyman and apprentice, which brought into being in the towns a hierarchy similar to that in the country.

Thus the chief form of property during the feudal epoch consisted on the one hand of landed property with serf labour chained to it, and on the other of the labour of the individual with small capital commanding the labour of journeymen. The organisation of both was determined by the restricted conditions of production — the small-scale and primitive cultivation of the land, and the craft type of industry. There was little division of labour in the heyday of feudalism. Each country bore in itself the antithesis of town and country; the division into estates was certainly strongly marked; but apart from the differentiation of princes, nobility, clergy and peasants in the country, and masters, journeymen, apprentices and soon also the rabble of casual labourers in the towns, no division of importance took place. In agriculture it was rendered difficult by the strip-system, beside which the cottage industry of the peasants themselves emerged. In industry there was no division of labour at all in the individual trades themselves, and very little between them. The separation of industry and commerce was found already in existence in older towns; in the newer it only developed later, when the towns entered into mutual relations.

The grouping of larger territories into feudal kingdoms was a necessity for the landed nobility as for the towns. The organisation of the ruling class, the nobility, had, therefore, everywhere a monarch at its head.

The fact is, therefore, that definite individuals who are productively active in a definite way enter into these definite social and political relations. Empirical observation must in each separate instance bring out empirically, and without any mystification and speculation, the connection of the social and political structure with production. The social structure and the State are continually evolving out of the life-process of definite individuals, but of individuals, not as they may appear in their own or other people's imagination, but as they *really* are; i.e., as they operate, produce materially, and hence as they work under definite material limits, presuppositions and conditions independent of their will.

The production of ideas, of conceptions, of consciousness, is at first directly interwoven with the material activity and the material intercourse of men, the language of real life. Conceiving, thinking, the mental intercourse of men, appear at this stage as the direct efflux of their material behaviour. The same applies to mental production as expressed in the language of politics, laws, morality, religion, metaphysics, etc., of a people. Men are the producers of their conceptions, ideas, etc. — real, active men, as they are conditioned by a definite development of their productive forces and of the intercourse corresponding to these, up to its furthest forms. Consciousness can never be anything else than conscious existence, and the existence of men is their actual life-process. If in all ideology men and their circumstances appear upside-down as in a *camera obscura*, this phenomenon arises just as much from their historical life-process as the inversion of objects on the retina does from their physical life-process.

In direct contrast to german philosophy which descends from heaven to earth, here we ascend from earth to heaven. That is to say, we do not set out from what men say, imagine, conceive, nor from men as narrated, thought of, imagined, conceived, in order to arrive at men in the flesh. We set out from real, active men, and on the basis of their real life-process we demonstrate the development of the ideological reflexes and echoes of this life-process. The phantoms formed in the human brain are also, necessarily, sublimates of their material life-process, which is empirically verifiable and bound to material premises. Morality, religion, metaphysics, all the rest of ideology and their corresponding forms of consciousness, thus no longer retain the semblance of independence. They have no history, no development; but men, developing their material production and their material intercourse, alter, along with this their real existence, their thinking and the products of their thinking. Life is not determined by consciousness, but consciousness by life. In the first method of approach the starting-point is consciousness taken as the living individual; in the second method, which conforms to real life, it is the real living individuals themselves, and consciousness is considered solely as *their* consciousness.

This method of approach is not devoid of premises. It starts out from the real premises and does not abandon them for a moment. Its premises are men, not in any fantastic isolation and rigidity, but in their actual, empirically perceptible process of development under definite conditions. As soon as this active life-process is described, history ceases to be a collection of dead facts as it is with the empiricists (themselves still abstract), or an imagined activity of imagined subjects, as with the idealists.

Where speculation ends — in real life — there real, positive science begins: the representation of the practical activity, of the practical process of development of men. Empty talk about consciousness ceases, and real knowledge has to take its place. When reality is depicted, philosophy as an independent branch of knowledge loses its medium of existence. At the best its place can only be taken by a summing-up of the most general results, abstractions which arise from the observation of the historical development of men. Viewed apart from real history, these abstractions have in themselves no value whatsoever. They can only serve to facilitate the arrangement of historical material, to indicate the sequence of its separate strata. But they by no means afford a recipe or schema, as does philosophy, for neatly trimming the epochs of history. On the contrary, our difficulties begin only when we set about the observation and the arrangement — the real depiction — of our historical material, whether of a past epoch or of the present. The removal of these difficulties is governed by premises which it is quite impossible to state here, but which only the study of the actual life-process and the activity of the individuals of each epoch will make evident. We shall select here some of these abstractions, which we use in contradistinction to the ideologists, and shall illustrate them by historical examples.

(1.) History

Since we are dealing with the Germans, who are devoid of premises, we must begin by stating the first premise of all human existence and, therefore, of all history, the premise, namely, that men must be in a position to live in order to be able to "make history". But life involves before everything else eating and drinking, a habitation, clothing and many other things. The first historical act is thus the production of the means to satisfy these needs, the production of material life itself. And indeed this is an historical act, a fundamental condition of all history, which today, as thousands of years ago, must daily and hourly be fulfilled merely in order to sustain human life. Even when the sensuous world is reduced to a minimum, to a stick as with Saint Bruno, it presupposes the action of producing the stick. Therefore in any interpretation of history one has first of all to observe this fundamental fact in all its significance and all its implications and to accord it its due importance. It is well known that the Germans have never done this, and they have never, therefore, had an *earthly* basis for history and consequently never a historian.

The French and the English, even if they have conceived the relation of this fact with so-called history only in an extremely one-sided fashion, particularly as long as they remained in the toils of political ideology, have nevertheless made the first attempts to give the writing of history a materialistic basis by being the first to write histories of civil society, of commerce and industry.

The second point is that the satisfaction of the first need (the action of satisfying, and the instrument of satisfaction which has been acquired) leads to new needs; and this production of new needs is the first historical act. Here we recognise immediately the spiritual ancestry of the great historical wisdom of the Germans who, when they run out of positive material and when they can serve up neither theological nor political nor literary rubbish, assert that this is not history at all, but the "prehistoric era". They do not, however, enlighten us as to how we proceed from this nonsensical "prehistory" to history proper; although, on the other hand, in their historical speculation they seize upon this "prehistory" with especial eagerness because they imagine themselves safe there from interference on the part of "crude facts", and, at the same time, because there they can give full rein to their speculative impulse and set up and knock down hypotheses by the thousand.

The third circumstance which, from the very outset, enters into historical development, is that men, who daily remake their own life, begin to make other men, to propagate their kind: the relation between man and woman, parents and children, the *family*. The family, which to begin with is the only social relationship, becomes later, when increased needs create new social relations and the increased population new needs, a subordinate one (except in Germany), and must then be treated and analysed according to the existing empirical data, not according to "the concept of the family", as is the custom in Germany. These three aspects of social activity are not of course to be taken as three different stages, but just as three aspects or, to make it clear to the Germans, three "moments", which have existed simultaneously since the dawn of history and the first men, and which still assert themselves in history today.

The production of life, both of one's own in labour and of fresh life in procreation, now appears as a double relationship: on the one hand as a natural, on the other as a social relationship. By social we understand the co-operation of several individuals, no matter under what conditions, in what manner and to what end. It follows from this that a certain mode of production, or industrial stage, is always combined with a certain mode of co-operation, or social stage, and this mode of co-operation is itself a "productive force". Further, that the multitude of productive forces accessible to men determines the nature of society, hence, that the "history of humanity" must always be studied and treated in relation to the history of industry and exchange. But it is also clear how in Germany it is impossible to write this sort of history, because the Germans lack not only the necessary power of comprehension and the material but also the "evidence of their senses", for across the Rhine you cannot have any experience of these things since history has stopped happening. Thus it is quite obvious from the start that there exists a materialistic connection of men with one another, which is determined by their needs and their mode of production, and which is as old as men themselves. This connection is ever taking on new forms, and thus presents a "history" independently of the existence of any political or religious nonsense which would especially hold men together.

Only now, after having considered four moments, four aspects of the primary historical relationships, do we find that man also possesses "consciousness"; but, even so, not inherent, not "pure" consciousness. From the start the "spirit" is afflicted with the curse of being "burdened" with matter, which here makes its appearance in the form of agitated layers of air, sounds, in short, of language. Language is as old as consciousness, language is practical consciousness that exists also for other men, and for that reason alone it really exists for me personally as well; language, like consciousness, only arises from the need, the necessity, of intercourse with other men. Where there exists a relationship, it exists for me: the animal does not enter into "*relations*" with anything, it does not enter into any relation at all. For the animal, its relation to others does not exist as a relation. Consciousness is, therefore, from the very beginning a social product, and remains so as long as men exist at all. Consciousness is at first, of course, merely consciousness concerning the *immediate* sensuous environment and consciousness of the limited connection with other persons and things outside the individual who is growing self-conscious. At the same time it is consciousness of nature, which first appears to men as a completely alien, all-powerful and unassailable force, with which men's relations are purely animal and by which they are overawed like beasts; it is thus a purely animal consciousness of nature (natural religion).

We see here immediately: this natural religion or this particular relation of men to nature is determined by the form of society and vice versa. Here, as everywhere, the identity of nature and man appears in such a way that the restricted relation of men to nature determines their restricted relation to one another, and their restricted relation to one another determines men's restricted relation to nature, just because nature is as yet hardly modified historically; and, on the other hand, man's consciousness of the necessity of associating with the individuals around him is the beginning of the consciousness that he is living in society at all. This beginning is as animal as social life itself at this stage. It is mere herd-consciousness, and at this point man is only distinguished from sheep by the fact that with him consciousness takes the place of instinct or that his instinct is a conscious one. This sheep-like or tribal consciousness receives its further development and extension through increased productivity, the increase of needs, and, what is fundamental to both of these, the increase of population. With these there develops the division of labour, which was originally nothing but the division of labour in the sexual act, then that division of labour which develops spontaneously or "naturally" by virtue of natural predisposition (e.g., physical strength), needs, accidents, etc., etc. Division of labour only becomes truly such from the moment when a division of material and mental labour appears. From this moment onwards consciousness can really flatter itself that it is something other than consciousness of existing practice, that it *really* represents something without representing something real; from now on consciousness is in a position to emancipate itself from the world and to proceed to the formation of "pure" theory, theology, philosophy, ethics, etc. But even if this theory, theology, philosophy, ethics, etc., comes into contradiction with the existing relations, this can only occur because existing social relations have come into contradiction with existing forces of production; this, moreover, can also occur in a particular national sphere of relations through the appearance of the contradiction, not within the national orbit, but between this national consciousness and the practice of other nations, i.e., between the national and the general consciousness of a nation (as we see it now in Germany).

Moreover, it is quite immaterial what consciousness starts to do on its own: out of all such muck we get only the one inference that these three moments, the forces of production, the state of society, and consciousness, can and must come into contradiction with one another, because the *division of labour* implies the possibility, nay the fact that intellectual and material activity—enjoyment and labour, production and consumption—devolve on different individuals, and that the only possibility of their not coming into contradiction lies in the negation in its turn of the division of labour. It is self-evident, moreover, that "spectres", "bonds", "the higher being", "concept", "scruple", are merely the idealistic, spiritual expression, the conception apparently of the isolated individual, the image of very empirical fetters and limitations, within which the mode of production of life and the form of intercourse coupled with it move.

With the division of labour, in which all these contradictions are implicit, and which in its turn is based on the natural division of labour in the family and the separation of society into individual families opposed to one another, is given simultaneously the *distribution*, and indeed the unequal distribution, both quantitative and qualitative, of labour and its products, hence property: the nucleus, the first form, of which lies in the family, where wife and children are the slaves of the husband. This latent slavery in the family, though still very crude, is the first property, but even at this early stage it corresponds perfectly to the definition of modern economists who call it the power of disposing of the labour-power of others. Division of labour and private property are, moreover, identical expressions: in the one the same thing is affirmed with reference to activity as is affirmed in the other with reference to the product of the activity.

Further, the division of labour implies the contradiction between the interest of the separate individual or the individual family and the communal interest of all individuals who have intercourse with one another. And indeed, this communal interest does not exist merely in the imagination, as the "general interest", but first of all in reality, as the mutual interdependence of the individuals among whom the labour is divided. And finally, the division of labour offers us the first example of how, as long as man remains in natural society, that is, as long as a cleavage exists between the particular and the common interest, as long, therefore, as activity is not voluntarily, but naturally, divided, man's own deed becomes an alien power opposed to him, which enslaves him instead of being controlled by him. For as soon as the distribution of labour comes into being, each man has a particular, exclusive sphere of activity, which is forced upon him and from which he cannot escape. He is a hunter, a fisherman, a shepherd, or a critical critic, and must remain so if he does not want to lose his means of livelihood; while in communist society, where nobody has one exclusive sphere of activity but each can become accomplished in any branch he wishes, society regulates the general production and thus makes it possible for me to do one thing today and another tomorrow, to hunt in the morning, fish in the afternoon, rear cattle in the evening, criticise after dinner, just as I have a mind, without ever becoming hunter, fisherman, shepherd or critic. This fixation of social activity, this consolidation of what we ourselves produce into an objective power above us, growing out of our control, thwarting our expectations, bringing to naught our calculations, is one of the chief factors in historical development up till now.

And out of this very contradiction between the interest of the individual and that of the community the latter takes an independent form as the *State*, divorced from the real interests of individual and community, and at the same time as an illusory communal life, always based, however, on the real ties existing in every family and tribal conglomeration — such as flesh and blood, language, division of labour on a larger scale, and other interests — and especially, as we shall enlarge upon later, on the classes, already determined by the division of labour, which in every such mass of men separate out, and of which one dominates all the others. It follows from this that all struggles within the State, the struggle between democracy, aristocracy, and monarchy, the struggle for the franchise, etc., etc., are merely the illusory forms in which the real struggles of the different classes are fought out among one another (of this the German theoreticians have not the faintest inkling, although they have received a sufficient introduction to the subject in the *Deutsch-Französische Jahrbücher* and *Die heilige Familie*). Further, it follows that every class which is struggling for mastery, even when its domination, as is the case with the proletariat, postulates the abolition of the old form of society in its entirety and of domination itself, must first conquer for itself political power in order to represent its interest in turn as the general interest, which in the first moment it is forced to do. Just because individuals seek *only* their particular interest, which for them does not coincide with their communal interest (in fact the general is the illusory form of communal life), the latter will be imposed on them as an interest "alien" to them, and "independent" of them, as in its turn a particular, peculiar "general" interest; or they themselves must remain within this discord, as in democracy. On the other hand, too, the *practical* struggle of these particular interests, which constantly *really* run counter to the communal and illusory communal interests, makes *practical* intervention and control necessary through the illusory "general" interest in the form of the State. The social power, i.e., the multiplied productive force, which arises through the co-operation of different individuals as it is determined by the division of labour, appears to these individuals, since their co-operation is not voluntary but has come about naturally, not as their own united power, but as an alien force existing outside them, of the origin and goal of which they are ignorant, which they thus cannot control, which on the contrary passes through a peculiar series of phases and stages independent of the will of the action of man, nay even being the prime governor of these.

This *"estrangement"* (to use a term which will be comprehensible to the philosophers) can, of course, only be abolished given two *practical* premises. For it to become an "intolerable" power, i.e., a power against which men make a revolution, it must necessarily have rendered the great mass of humanity "propertyless", and produced, at the same time, the contradiction of an existing world of wealth and culture, both of which conditions presuppose a great increase in productive power, a high degree of its development. And, on the other hand, this development of productive forces (which itself implies the actual empirical existence of men in their *world-historical*, instead of local, being) is an absolutely necessary practical premise because without it *want* is merely made general, and with *destitution* the struggle for necessities and all the old filthy business would necessarily be reproduced; and furthermore, because only with this universal development of productive forces is a *universal* intercourse between men established, which produces in all nations simultaneously the phenomenon of the "propertyless" mass (universal competition), makes each nation dependent on the revolutions of the others, and finally has put *world-historical*, empirically universal individuals in place of local ones. Without this, (1) communism could only exist as a local event; (2) the *forces* of intercourse themselves could not have developed as *universal*, hence intolerable powers; they would have remained home-bred conditions surrounded by superstition; and (3) each extension of intercourse would abolish local communism. Empirically, communism is only possible as the act of the dominant peoples "all at once" and simultaneously, which presupposes the universal development of productive forces and the world intercourse bound up with communism. How otherwise could for instance property have had a history at all, have taken on different forms, and landed property, for example, according to the different premises given, have proceeded in France from parcellation to centralisation in the hands of a few, in England from centralisation in the hands of a few to parcellation, as is actually the case today? Or how does it happen that trade, which after all is nothing more than the exchange of products of various individuals and countries, rules the whole world through the relation of supply and demand —a relation which, as an English economist says, hovers over the earth like the fate of the ancients, and with invisible hand allots fortune and misfortune to men, sets up empires and overthrows empires, causes nations to rise and to disappear — while with the abolition of the basis of private property, with the communistic regulation of production (and, implicit in this, the destruction of the alien relation between men and what they themselves produce), the power of the relation of supply and demand is dissolved into nothing, and men get exchange, production, the mode of their mutual relation, under their own control again?

Communism is for us not a *state of affairs* which is to be established, an *ideal* to which reality (will) have to adjust itself. We call communism the *real* movement which abolishes the present state of things. The conditions of this movement result from the premises now in existence. Moreover, the mass of *propertyless workers* — the utterly precarious position of labour-power on a mass scale cut off from capital or from even a limited satisfaction and, therefore, no longer merely temporarily deprived of work itself as a secure source of life — presupposes the *world market* through competition. The proletariat can thus only exist *world-historically*, just as communism, its activity, can only have a "world-historical" existence. World-historical existence of individuals, i.e., existence of individuals which is directly linked up with world history.

The form of intercourse determined by the existing productive forces at all previous historical stages, and in its turn determining these, is *civil society*. The latter, as is clear from what we have said above, has as its premises and basis the simple family and the multiple, the so-called tribe, and the more precise determinants of this society are enumerated in our remarks above. Already here we see how this civil society is the true source and theatre of all history, and how absurd is the conception of history held hitherto, which neglects the real relationships and confines itself to high-sounding dramas of princes and states.

Civil society embraces the whole material intercourse of individuals within a definite stage of the development of productive forces. It embraces the whole commercial and industrial life of a given stage and, insofar, transcends the State and the nation, though, on the other hand again, it must assert itself in its foreign relations as nationality, and inwardly must organise itself as State. The term "civil society" emerged in the eighteenth century, when property relationships had already extricated themselves from the ancient and medieval communal society. Civil society as such only develops with the bourgeoisie; the social organisation evolving directly out of production and commerce, which in all ages forms the basis of the State and of the rest of the idealistic superstructure, has, however, always been designated by the same name.

(2.) Concerning the Production of Consciousness

In history up to the present it is certainly an empirical fact that separate individuals have, with the broadening of their activity into world-historical activity, become more and more enslaved under a power alien to them (a pressure which they have conceived of as a dirty trick on the part of the so-called universal spirit, etc.), a power which has become more and more enormous and, in the last instance, turns out to be the *world market*. But it is just as empirically established that, by the overthrow of the existing state of society by the communist revolution (of which more below) and the abolition of private property which is identical with it, this power, which so baffles the German theoreticians, will be dissolved; and that then the liberation of each single individual will be accomplished in the measure in which history becomes transformed into world history. From the above it is clear that the real intellectual wealth of the individual depends entirely on the wealth of his real connections. Only then will the separate individuals be liberated from the various national and local barriers, be brought into practical connection with the material and intellectual production of the whole world and be put in a position to acquire the capacity to enjoy this all-sided production of the whole earth (the creations of man). *All-round* dependence, this natural form of the *world-historical* co-operation of individuals, will be transformed by this communist revolution into the control and conscious mastery of these powers, which, born of the action of men on one another, have till now overawed and governed men as powers completely alien to them. Now this view can be expressed again in speculative-idealistic, i.e., fantastic, terms as "self-generation of the species" ("society as the subject"), and thereby the consecutive series of interrelated individuals connected with each other can be conceived as a single individual, which accomplishes the mystery of generating itself. It is clear here that individuals certainly make *one another*, physically and mentally, but do not make themselves either in the nonsense of Saint Bruno, or in the sense of the "Unique", of the "made" man.

This conception of history depends on our ability to expound the real process of production, starting out from the material production of life itself, and to comprehend the form of intercourse connected with this and created by this mode of production (i.e., civil society in its various stages), as the basis of all history; and to show it in its action as State, to explain all the different theoretical products and forms of consciousness, religion, philosophy, ethics, etc., etc., and trace their origins and growth from that basis; by which means, of course, the whole thing can be depicted in its totality (and therefore, too, the reciprocal action of these various sides on one another). It has not, like the idealistic view of history, in every period to look for a category, but remains constantly on the real *ground* of history; it does not explain practice from the idea but explains the formation of ideas from material practice; and accordingly it comes to the conclusion that all forms and products of consciousness cannot be dissolved by mental criticism, by resolution into "self-consciousness" or transformation into "apparitions", "spectres", "fancies", etc., but only by the practical overthrow of the actual social relations which gave rise to this idealistic humbug; that not criticism but revolution is the driving force of history, also of religion, of philosophy and all other types of theory. It shows that history does not end by being resolved into "self-consciousness" as "spirit of the spirit", but that in it at each stage there is found a material result: a sum of productive forces, a historically created relation of individuals to nature and to one another, which is handed down to each generation from its predecessor; a mass of productive forces, capital funds and conditions, which, on the one hand, is indeed modified by the new generation, but also on the other prescribes for it its conditions of life and gives it a definite development, a special character. It shows that circumstances make men just as much as men make circumstances. This sum of productive forces, capital funds and social forms of intercourse, which every individual and generation finds in existence as something given, is the real basis of what the philosophers have conceived as "substance" and "essence of man", and what they have deified and attacked: a real basis which is not in the least disturbed, in its effect and influence on the development of men, by the fact that these philosophers revolt against it as "self-consciousness" and the "Unique". These conditions of life, which different generations find in existence, decide also whether or not the periodically recurring revolutionary convulsion will be strong enough to overthrow the basis of the entire existing system. And if these material elements of a complete revolution are not present (namely, on the one hand the existing productive forces, on the other the formation of a revolutionary mass, which revolts not only against separate conditions of society up till then, but against the very "production of life" till then, the "total activity" on which it was based), then, as far as practical development is concerned, it is absolutely immaterial whether the *idea* of this revolution has been expressed a hundred times already, as the history of communism proves. . . .

SELECTIONS FROM
Manifesto of the Communist Party

A spectre is haunting Europe—the spectre of Communism. All the Powers of old Europe have entered into a holy alliance to exorcise this spectre: Pope and Tsar, Metternich and Guizot, French Radicals and German police-spies.

Where is the party in opposition that has not been decried as Communistic by its opponents in power? Where the Opposition that has not hurled back the branding reproach of Communism, against the more advanced opposition parties, as well as against its reactionary adversaries?

Two things result from this fact.

I. Communism is already acknowledged by all European Powers to be itself a Power.

II. It is high time that Communists should openly, in the face of the whole world, publish their views, their aims, their tendencies, and meet this nursery tale of the Spectre of Communism with a Manifesto of the party itself.

To this end, Communists of various nationalities have assembled in London, and sketched the following Manifesto, to be published in the English, French, German, Italian, Flemish, and Danish languages.

I
Bourgeois and Proletarians

The history of all hitherto existing society is the history of class struggles.

Freeman and slave, patrician and plebeian, lord and serf, guild-master and journeyman—in a word, oppressor and oppressed, stood in constant opposition to one another, carried on an uninterrupted, now hidden, now open fight, a fight that each time ended either in a revolutionary re-constitution of society at large or in the common ruin of the contending classes.

In the earlier epochs of history, we find almost everywhere a complicated arrangement of society into various orders, a manifold gradation of social rank. In ancient Rome we have patricians, knights, plebeians, slaves; in the Middle Ages, feudal lords, vassals, guild-masters, journeymen, apprentices, serfs; in almost all of these classes, again, subordinate gradations.

The modern bourgeois society that has sprouted from the ruins of feudal society has not done away with class antagonisms. It has but established new classes, new conditions of oppression, new forms of struggle in place of the old ones.

Our epoch, the epoch of the bourgeoisie, possesses, however, this distinctive feature: it has simplified the class antagonisms. Society as a whole is more and more splitting up into two great hostile camps, into two great classes directly facing each other: Bourgeoisie and Proletariat.

From the serfs of the Middle Ages sprang the chartered burghers of the earliest towns. From these burgesses the first elements of the bourgeoisie were developed.

The discovery of America, the rounding of the Cape, opened up fresh ground for the rising bourgeoisie. The East Indian and Chinese markets, the colonization of America, trade with the colonies, the increase in the means of exchange and in commodities generally, gave to commerce, to navigation, to industry, an impulse never before known, and thereby, to the revolutionary element in the tottering feudal society, a rapid development.

The feudal system of industry, under which industrial production was monopolized by closed guilds, now no longer sufficed for the growing wants of the new markets. The manufacturing system took its place. The guild-masters were pushed on one side by the manufacturing middle class; division of labour between the different corporate guilds vanished in the face of division of labour in each single workshop.

Meantime the markets kept ever growing, the demand ever rising. Even manufacture no longer sufficed. Thereupon, steam and machinery revolutionized industrial production. The place of manufacture was taken by the giant, Modern Industry, the place of the industrial middle class, by industrial millionaires, the leaders of whole industrial armies, the modern bourgeois.

Modern industry has established the world-market, for which the discovery of America paved the way. This market has given an immense development to commerce, to navigation, to communication by land. This development has, in its turn, reacted on the extension of industry; and in proportion as industry, commerce, navigation, railways extended, in the same proportion the bourgeoisie developed, increased its capital, and pushed into the background every class handed down from the Middle Ages.

We see, therefore, how the modern bourgeoisie is itself the product of a long course of development, of a series of revolutions in the modes of production and of exchange.

Each step in the development of the bourgeoisie was accompanied by a corresponding political advance of that class. An oppressed class under the sway of the feudal nobility, an armed and self-governing association in the medieval commune; here independent urban republic (as in Italy and Germany), there taxable 'third estate' of the monarchy (as in France), after wards, in the period of manufacture proper, serving either the semi-feudal or the absolute monarchy as a counterpoise against the nobility, and, in fact, corner-stone of the great monarchies in general, the bourgeoisie has at last, since the establishment of Modern Industry and of the world-market, conquered for itself, in the modern representative State, exclusive political sway. The executive of the modern State is but a committee for managing the common affairs of the whole bourgeoisie.

The bourgeoisie, historically, has played a most revolutionary part.

The bourgeoisie, wherever it has got the upper hand, has put an end to all feudal, patriarchal, idyllic relations. It has pitilessly torn asunder the motley feudal ties that bound man to his 'natural superiors', and has left remaining no other nexus between man and man than naked self-interest, than callous 'cash payment'. It has drowned the most heavenly ecstasies of religious fervour, of chivalrous enthusiasm, of philistine sentimentalism, in the icy water of egotistical calculation. It has resolved personal worth into exchange value, and in place of the numberless indefeasible chartered freedoms, has set up that single, unconscionable freedom — Free Trade. In one word, for exploitation, veiled by religious and political illusions, it has substituted naked, shameless, direct, brutal exploitation.

The bourgeoisie has stripped of its halo every occupation hitherto honoured and looked up to with reverent awe. It has converted the physician, the lawyer, the priest, the poet, the man of science into its paid wage-labourers.

The bourgeoisie has torn away from the family its sentimental veil, and has reduced the family relation to a mere money relation.

The bourgeoisie has disclosed how it came to pass that the brutal display of vigour in the Middle Ages, which Reactionists so much admire, found its fitting complement in the most slothful indolence. It has been the first to show what man's activity can bring about. It has accomplished wonders far surpassing Egyptian pyramids, Roman aqueducts, and Gothic cathedrals; it has conducted expeditions that put in the shade all former Exoduses of nations and crusades.

The bourgeoisie cannot exist without constantly revolutionizing the instruments of production, and thereby the relations of production, and with them the whole relations of society. Conservation of the old modes of production in unaltered form, was, on the contrary, the first condition of existence for all earlier industrial classes. Constant revolutionizing of production, uninterrupted disturbance of all social conditions, everlasting uncertainty and agitation distinguish the bourgeois epoch from all earlier ones. All fixed, fast-frozen relations, with their train of ancient and venerable prejudices and opinions, are swept away, all new-formed ones become antiquated before they can ossify. All that is solid melts into air, all that is holy is profaned, and man is at last compelled to face with sober senses, his real conditions of life, and his relations with his kind.

The need of a constantly expanding market for its products chases the bourgeoisie over the whole surface of the globe. It must nestle everywhere, settle everywhere, establish connections everywhere.

The bourgeoisie has through its exploitation of the world-market given a cosmopolitan character to production and consumption in every country. To the great chagrin of Reactionists, it has drawn from under the feet of industry the national ground on which it stood. All old-established national industries have been destroyed or are daily being destroyed. They are dislodged by new industries, whose introduction becomes a life-and-death question for all civilized nations, by industries that no longer work up indigenous raw material, but raw material drawn from the remotest zones; industries whose products are consumed, not only at home, but in every quarter of the globe. In place of the old wants, satisfied by the productions of the country, we find new wants, requiring for their satisfaction the products of distant lands and climes. In place of the old local and national seclusion and self-sufficiency, we have intercourse in every direction, universal interdependence of nations. And as in material, so also in intellectual production. The intellectual creations of individual nations become common property. National one-sidedness and narrow-mindedness become more and more impossible, and from the numerous national and local literatures, there arises a world literature.

The bourgeoisie, by the rapid improvement of all instruments of production, by the immensely facilitated means of communication, draws all, even the most barbarian, nations into civilization. The cheap prices of its commodities are the heavy artillery with which it batters down all Chinese walls, with which it forces the barbarians' intensely obstinate hatred of foreigners to capitulate. It compels all nations, on pain of extinction, to adopt the bourgeois mode of production; it compels them to introduce what it calls civilization into their midst, i.e., to become bourgeois themselves. In one word, it creates a world after its own image.

The bourgeoisie has subjected the country to the rule of the towns. It has created enormous cities, has greatly increased the urban population as compared with the rural, and has thus rescued a considerable part of the population from the idiocy of rural life. Just as it has made the country dependent on the towns, so it has made barbarian and semi-barbarian countries dependent on the civilized ones, nations of peasants on nations of bourgeois, the East on the West.

The bourgeoisie keeps more and more doing away with the scattered state of the population, of the means of production, and of property. It has agglomerated population, centralized means of production, and has concentrated property in a few hands. The necessary consequence of this was political centralization. Independent or but loosely connected provinces, with separate interests, laws, governments, and systems of taxation, became lumped together into one nation, with one government, one code of laws, one national class-interest, one frontier, and one customs-tariff.

The bourgeoisie, during its rule of scarcely one hundred years, has created more massive and more colossal productive forces than have all preceding generations together. Subjection of Nature's forces to man, machinery, application of chemistry to industry and agriculture, steam-navigation, railways, electric telegraphs, clearing of whole continents for cultivation, canalization of rivers, whole populations conjured out of the ground—what earlier century had even a presentiment that such productive forces slumbered in the lap of social labour?

We see then that the means of production and of exchange, on whose foundation the bourgeoisie built itself up, were generated in feudal society. At a certain stage in the development of these means of production and of exchange, the conditions under which feudal society produced and exchanged, the feudal organization of agriculture and manufacturing industry, in one word, the feudal relations of property become no longer compatible with the already developed productive forces; they became so many fetters. They had to be burst asunder; they were burst asunder.

Into their place stepped free competition, accompanied by a social and political constitution adapted to it, and by the economical and political sway of the bourgeois class.

A similar movement is going on before our own eyes. Modern bourgeois society with its relations of production, of exchange and of property, a society that has conjured up such gigantic means of production and of exchange, is like the sorcerer, who is no longer able to control the powers of the nether world which he has called up by his spells. The history of industry and commerce for many a decade past is but the history of the revolt of modern productive forces against modern conditions of production, against the property relations that are the conditions for the existence of the bourgeoisie and of its rule. It is enough to mention the commercial crises that by their periodical return put on trial, each time more threateningly, the existence of the entire bourgeois society. In these crises a great part not only of the existing products, but also of the previously created productive forces, are periodically destroyed. In these crises there breaks out an epidemic that, in all earlier epochs, would have seemed an absurdity — the epidemic of overproduction. Society suddenly finds itself put back into a state of momentary barbarism; it appears as if a famine, a universal war of devastation, has cut off the supply of every means of subsistence; industry and commerce seem to be destroyed; and why? Because there is too much civilization, too much means of subsistence, too much industry, too much commerce. The productive forces at the disposal of society no longer tend to further the development of the conditions of bourgeois property; on the contrary, they have become too powerful for these conditions, by which they are fettered, and so soon as they overcome these fetters, they bring disorder into the whole of bourgeois society, endanger the existence of bourgeois property. The conditions of bourgeois society are too narrow to comprise the wealth created by them. And how does the bourgeoisie get over these crises? On the one hand by enforced destruction of a mass of productive forces; on the other, by the conquest of new markets, and by the more thorough exploitation of the old ones. That is to say, by paving the way for more extensive and more destructive crises, and by diminishing the means whereby crises are prevented.

The weapons with which the bourgeoisie felled feudalism to the ground are now turned against the bourgeoisie itself.

But not only has the bourgeoisie forged the weapons that bring death to itself; it has also called into existence the men who are to wield those weapons — the modern working class — the proletarians.

In proportion as the bourgeoisie, i.e., capital, is developed, in the same proportion is the proletariat, the modern working class, developed — a class of labourers, who live only so long as they find work, and who find work only so long as their labour increases capital. These labourers, who must sell themselves piecemeal, are a commodity, like every other article of commerce, and are consequently exposed to all the vicissitudes of competition, to all the fluctuations of the market.

Owing to the extensive use of machinery and to division of labour, the work of the proletarians has lost all individual character, and, consequently, all charm for the workman. He becomes an appendage of the machine, and it is only the most simple, most monotonous, and most easily acquired knack, that is required of him. Hence, the cost of production of a workman is restricted, almost entirely, to the means of subsistence that he requires for his maintenance, and for the propagation of his race. But the price of a commodity, and therefore also of labour, is equal to its cost of production. In proportion, therefore, as the repulsiveness of the work increases, the wage decreases. Nay more, in proportion as the use of machinery and division of labour increases, in the same proportion the burden of toil also increases, whether by prolongation of the working hours, by increase of the work exacted in a given time or by increased speed of the machinery, etc.

Modern industry has converted the little workshop of the patriarchal master into the great factory of the industrial capitalist. Masses of labourers, crowded into the factory, are organized like soldiers. As privates of the industrial army they are placed under the command of a perfect hierarchy of officers and sergeants. Not only are they slaves of the bourgeois class, and of the bourgeois State; they are daily and hourly enslaved by the machine, by the overlooker, and, above all, by the individual bourgeois manufacturer himself. The more openly this despotism proclaims gain to be its end and aim, the more petty, the more hateful, and the more embittering it is.

The less the skill and exertion of strength implied in manual labour, in other words, the more modern industry becomes developed, the more is the labour of men superseded by that of women. Differences of age and sex have no longer any distinctive social validity for the working class. All are instruments of labour, more or less expensive to use, according to their age and sex.

No sooner is the exploitation of the labourer by the manufacturer, so far, at an end, and he receives his wages in cash, than he is set upon by the other portions of the bourgeoisie, the landlord, the shopkeeper, the pawnbroker, etc.

The lower strata of the middle class — the small tradespeople, shopkeepers, and retired tradesmen generally, the handicraftsmen and peasants — all these sink gradually into the proletariat, partly because their diminutive capital does not suffice for the scale on which Modern Industry is carried on, and is swamped in the competition with the large capitalists, partly because their specialized skill is rendered worthless by new methods of production. Thus the proletariat is recruited from all classes of the population.

The proletariat goes through various stages of development. With its birth begins its struggle with the bourgeoisie. At first the contest is carried on by individual labourers, then by the workpeople of a factory, then by the operatives of one trade, in one locality, against the individual bourgeois who directly exploits them. They direct their attacks not against the bourgeois conditions of production, but against the instruments of production themselves; they destroy imported wares that compete with their labour, they smash to pieces machinery, they set factories ablaze, they seek to restore by force the vanished status of the workman of the Middle Ages.

At this stage the labourers still form an incoherent mass scattered over the whole country, and broken up by their mutual competition. If anywhere they unite to form more compact bodies, this is not yet the consequence of their own active union, but of the union of the bourgeoisie, which class, in order to attain its own political ends, is compelled to set the whole proletariat in motion, and is moreover yet, for a time, able to do so. At this stage, therefore, the proletarians do not fight their enemies, but the enemies of their enemies, the remnants of absolute monarchy, the landowners, the non-industrial bourgeois, the petty bourgeoisie. Thus the whole historical movement is concentrated in the hands of the bourgeoisie; every victory so obtained is a victory for the bourgeoisie.

But with the development of industry the proletariat not only increases in number; it becomes concentrated in greater masses, its strength grows, and it feels that strength more. The various interests and conditions of life within the ranks of the proletariat are more and more equalized, in proportion as machinery obliterates all distinctions of labour, and nearly everywhere reduces wages to the same low level. The growing competition among the bourgeois, and the resulting commercial crises, make the wages of the workers ever more fluctuating. The unceasing improvement of machinery, ever more rapidly developing, makes their livelihood more and more precarious; the collisions between individual workmen and individual bourgeois take more and more the character of collisions between two classes. Thereupon the workers begin to form combinations (Trades' Unions) against the bourgeois; they club together in order to keep up the rate of wages; they found permanent associations in order to make provision beforehand for these occasional revolts. Here and there the contest breaks out into riots.

Now and then the workers are victorious, but only for a time. The real fruit of their battles lies, not in the immediate result, but in the ever-expanding union of the workers. This union is helped on by the improved means of communication that are created by modern industry and that place the workers of different localities in contact with one another. It was just this contact that was needed to centralize the numerous local struggles, all of the same character, into one national struggle between classes. But every class struggle is a political struggle. And that union, to attain which the burghers of the Middle Ages, with their miserable highways, required centuries, the modern proletarians, thanks to railways, achieve in a few years.

This organization of the proletarians into a class, and consequently into a political party, is continually being upset again by the competition between the workers themselves. But it ever rises up again, stronger, firmer, mightier. It compels legislative recognition of particular interests of the workers, by taking advantage of the divisions among the bourgeoisie itself. Thus the ten-hours' bill in England was carried.

Altogether, collisions between the classes of the old society further in many ways the course of development of the proletariat. The bourgeoisie finds itself involved in a constant battle. At first with the aristocracy; later on, with those portions of the bourgeoisie itself whose interests have become antagonistic to the progress of industry; at all times, with the bourgeoisie of foreign countries. In all these battles it sees itself compelled to appeal to the proletariat, to ask for its help, and thus to drag it into the political arena. The bourgeoisie itself, therefore, supplies the proletariat with its own elements of political and general education, in other words, it furnishes the proletariat with weapons for fighting the bourgeoisie.

Further, as we have already seen, entire sections of the ruling classes are, by the advance of industry, precipitated into the proletariat, or are at least threatened in their conditions of existence. These also supply the proletariat with fresh elements of enlightenment and progress.

Finally, in times when the class struggle nears the decisive hour, the process of dissolution going on within the ruling class, in fact within the whole range of old society, assumes such a violent, glaring character, that a small section of the ruling class cuts itself adrift, and joins the revolutionary class, the class that holds the future in its hands. Just as, therefore, at an earlier period, a section of the nobility went over to the bourgeoisie, so now a portion of the bourgeoisie goes over to the proletariat, and in particular, a portion of the bourgeois ideologists, who have raised themselves to the level of comprehending theoretically the historical movement as a whole.

Of all the classes that stand face to face with the bourgeoisie today, the proletariat alone is a really revolutionary class. The other classes decay and finally disappear in the face of Modern Industry; the proletariat is its special and essential product.

The lower middle class, the small manufacturer, the shopkeeper, the artisan, the peasant, all these fight against the bourgeoisie, to save from extinction their existence as fractions of the middle class. They are therefore not revolutionary, but conservative. Nay more, they are reactionary, for they try to roll back the wheel of history. If by chance they are revolutionary, they are so only in view of their impending transfer into the proletariat; they thus defend not their present, but their future interests, they desert their own standpoint to place themselves at that of the proletariat.

The 'dangerous class', the social scum, that passively rotting mass thrown off by the lowest layers of old society, may, here and there, be swept into the movement by a proletarian revolution; its conditions of life, however, prepare it far more for the part of a bribed tool of reactionary intrigue.

In the conditions of the proletariat, those of old society at large are already virtually swamped. The proletarian is without property; his relation to his wife and children has no longer anything in common with the bourgeois family relations; modern industrial labour, modern subjection to capital, the same in England as in France, in America as in Germany, has stripped him of every trace of national character. Law, morality, religion are to him so many bourgeois prejudices, behind which lurk in ambush just as many bourgeois interests.

All the preceding classes that got the upper hand, sought to fortify their already acquired status by subjecting society at large to their conditions of appropriation. The proletarians cannot become masters of the productive forces of society, except by abolishing their own previous mode of appropriation, and thereby also every other previous mode of appropriation. They have nothing of their own to secure and to fortify; their mission is to destroy all previous securities for, and insurances of, individual property.

All previous historical movements were movements of minorities, or in the interests of minorities. The proletarian movement is the self-conscious, independent movement of the immense majority, in the interests of the immense majority. The proletariat, the lowest stratum of our present society, cannot stir, cannot raise itself up, without the whole superincumbent strata of official society being sprung into the air.

Though not in substance, yet in form, the struggle of the proletariat with the bourgeoisie is at first a national struggle. The proletariat of each country must, of course, first of all settle matters with its own bourgeoisie.

In depicting the most general phases of the development of the proletariat, we traced the more or less veiled civil war, raging within existing society, up to the point where that war breaks out into open revolution, and where the violent overthrow of the bourgeoisie lays the foundation for the sway of the proletariat.

Hitherto, every form of society has been based, as we have already seen, on the antagonism of oppressing and oppressed classes. But in order to oppress a class, certain conditions must be assured to it under which it can, at least, continue its slavish existence. The serf, in the period of serfdom, raised himself to membership in the commune, just as the petty bourgeois, under the yoke of feudal absolutism, managed to develop into a bourgeois. The modern labourer, on the contrary, instead of rising with the progress of industry, sinks deeper and deeper below the conditions of existence of his own class. He becomes a pauper, and pauperism develops more rapidly than population and wealth. And here it becomes evident, that the bourgeoisie is unfit any longer to be the ruling class in society, and to impose its conditions of existence upon society as an overriding law. It is unfit to rule because it is incompetent to assure an existence to its slave within his slavery, because it cannot help letting him sink into such a state, that it has to feed him, instead of being fed by him. Society can no longer live under this bourgeoisie, in other words, its existence is no longer compatible with society.

The essential condition for the existence, and for the sway of the bourgeois class, is the formation and augmentation of capital; the condition for capital is wage-labour. Wage-labour rests exclusively on competition between the labourers. The advance of industry, whose involuntary promoter is the bourgeoisie, replaces the isolation of the labourers, due to competition, by their revolutionary combination, due to association. The development of Modern Industry, therefore, cuts from under its feet the very foundation on which the bourgeoisie produces and appropriates products. What the bourgeoisie, therefore, produces, above all, is its own grave-diggers. Its fall and the victory of the proletariat are equally inevitable.

II
Proletarians and Communists

In what relation do the Communists stand to the proletarians, as a whole?

The Communists do not form a separate party opposed to other working-class parties.

They have no interests separate and apart from those of the proletariat as a whole.

They do not set up any sectarian principles of their own, by which to shape and mould the proletarian movement.

The Communists are distinguished from the other working-class parties by this only: 1. In the national struggles of the proletarians of the different countries, they point out and bring to the front the common interests of the entire proletariat, independently of all nationality. 2. In the various stages of development which the struggle of the working class against the bourgeoisie has to pass through, they always and everywhere represent the interests of the movement as a whole.

The Communists, therefore, are on the one hand, practically, the most advanced and resolute section of the working-class parties of every country, that section which pushes forward all others; on the other hand, theoretically, they have over the great mass of the proletariat the advantage of clearly understanding the line of march, the conditions, and the ultimate general results of the proletarian movement.

The immediate aim of the Communists is the same as that of all the other proletarian parties: formation of the proletariat into a class, overthrow of the bourgeois supremacy, conquest of political power by the proletariat.

The theoretical conclusions of the Communists are in no way based on ideas or principles that have been invented, or discovered, by this or that would-be universal reformer.

They merely express, in general terms, actual relations springing from an existing class struggle, from a historical movement going on under our very eyes. The abolition of existing property relations is not at all a distinctive feature of Communism.

All property relations in the past have continually been subject to historical change consequent upon the change in historical conditions.

The French Revolution, for example, abolished feudal property in favour of bourgeois property.

The distinguishing feature of Communism is not the abolition of property generally, but the abolition of bourgeois property. But modern bourgeois private property is the final and most complete expression of the system of producing and appropriating products, that is based on class antagonisms, on the exploitation of the many by the few.

In this sense, the theory of the Communists may be summed up in the single sentence: Abolition of private property.

We Communists have been reproached with the desire of abolishing the right of personally acquiring property as the fruit of a man's own labour, which property is alleged to be the groundwork of all personal freedom, activity, and independence.

Hard-won, self-acquired, self-earned property! Do you mean the property of the petty artisan and of the small peasant, a form of property that preceded the bourgeois form? There is no need to abolish that; the development of industry has to a great extent already destroyed it, and is still destroying it daily.

Or do you mean modern bourgeois private property?

But does wage-labour create any property for the labourer? Not a bit. It creates capital, i.e., that kind of property which exploits wage-labour, and which cannot increase except upon condition of begetting a new supply of wage-labour for fresh exploitation. Property, in its present form, is based on the antagonism of capital and wage-labour. Let us examine both sides of this antagonism.

To be a capitalist, is to have not only a purely personal, but a social, status in production. Capital is a collective product, and only by the united action of many members, nay, in the last resort, only by the united action of all members of society, can it be set in motion.

Capital is, therefore, not a personal, it is a social power.

When, therefore, capital is converted into common property, into the property of all members of society, personal property is not thereby transformed into social property. It is only the social character of the property that is changed. It loses its class-character.

Let us now take wage-labour.

The average price of wage-labour is the minimum wage, i.e., that quantum of the means of subsistence which is absolutely requisite to keep the labourer in bare existence as a labourer. What, therefore, the wage-labourer appropriates by means of his labour merely suffices to prolong and reproduce a bare existence. We by no means intend to abolish this personal appropriation of the products of labour, an appropriation that is made for the maintenance and reproduction of human life, and that leaves no surplus wherewith to command the labour of others. All that we want to do away with is the miserable character of this appropriation, under which the labourer lives merely to increase capital, and is allowed to live only in so far as the interest of the ruling class requires it.

In bourgeois society, living labour is but a means to increase accumulated labour. In Communist society, accumulated labour is but a means to widen, to enrich, to promote the existence of the labourer.

In bourgeois society, therefore, the past dominates the present; in Communist society, the present dominates the past. In bourgeois society capital is independent and has individuality, while the living person is dependent and has no individuality.

And the abolition of this state of things is called by the bourgeois abolition of individuality and freedom! And rightly so. The abolition of bourgeois individuality, bourgeois independence, and bourgeois freedom is undoubtedly aimed at.

By freedom is meant, under the present bourgeois conditions of production, free trade, free selling and buying.

But if selling and buying disappears, free selling and buying disappears also. This talk about free selling and buying, and all the other 'brave words' of our bourgeoisie about freedom in general, have a meaning, if any, only in contrast with restricted selling and buying, with the fettered traders of the Middle Ages, but have no meaning when opposed to the Communistic abolition of buying and selling, of the bourgeois conditions of production, and of the bourgeoisie itself.

You are horrified at our intending to do away with private property. But in your existing society, private property is already done away with for nine-tenths of the population; its existence for the few is solely due to its non-existence in the hands of those nine-tenths. You reproach us, therefore, with intending to do away with a form of property, the necessary condition for whose existence is the non-existence of any property for the immense majority of society.

In one word, you reproach us with intending to do away with your property. Precisely so; that is just what we intend.

From the moment when labour can no longer be converted into capital, money, or rent, into a social power capable of being monopolized, i.e., from the moment when individual property can no longer be transformed into bourgeois property, into capital, from that moment, you say, individuality vanishes.

You must, therefore, confess that by 'individual' you mean no other person than the bourgeois, than the middle-class owner of property. This person must, indeed, be swept out of the way, and made impossible.

Communism deprives no man of the power to appropriate the products of society; all that it does is to deprive him of the power to subjugate the labour of others by means of such appropriation.

It has been objected that upon the abolition of private property all work will cease, and universal laziness will overtake us.

According to this, bourgeois society ought long ago to have gone to the dogs through sheer idleness; for those of its members who work acquire nothing, and those who acquire anything do not work. The whole of this objection is but another expression of the tautology: that there can no longer be any wage-labour when there is no longer any capital.

All objections urged against the Communistic mode of producing and appropriating material products have, in the same way, been urged against the Communistic modes of producing and appropriating intellectual products. Just as, to the bourgeois, the disappearance of class property is the disappearance of production itself, so the disappearance of class culture is to him identical with the disappearance of all culture.

That culture, the loss of which he laments, is, for the enormous majority, a mere training to act as a machine.

But don't wrangle with us so long as you apply, to our intended abolition of bourgeois property, the standard of your bourgeois notions of freedom, culture, law, etc. Your very ideas are but the outgrowth of the conditions of your bourgeois production and bourgeois property, just as your jurisprudence is but the will of your class made into a law for all, a will whose essential character and direction are determined by the economical conditions of existence of your class.

The selfish misconception that induces you to transform into eternal laws of nature and of reason the social forms springing from your present mode of production and form of property—historical relations that rise and disappear in the progress of production—this misconception you share with every ruling class that has preceded you. What you see clearly in the case of ancient property, what you admit in the case of feudal property, you are of course forbidden to admit in the case of your own bourgeois form of property.

Abolition of the family! Even the most radical flare up at this infamous proposal of the Communists.

On what foundation is the present family, the bourgeois family, based? On capital, on private gain. In its completely developed form this family exists only among the bourgeoisie. But this state of things finds its complement in the practical absence of the family among the proletarians, and in public prostitution.

The bourgeois family will vanish as a matter of course when its complement vanishes, and both will vanish with the vanishing of capital.

Do you charge us with wanting to stop the exploitation of children by their parents? To this crime we plead guilty.

But, you will say, we destroy the most hallowed of relations, when we replace home education by social.

And your education! Is not that also social, and determined by the social conditions under which you educate, by the intervention, direct or indirect, of society, by means of schools, etc.? The Communists have not invented the intervention of society in education; they do but seek to alter the character of that intervention, and to rescue education from the influence of the ruling class.

The bourgeois clap-trap about the family and education, about the hallowed co-relation of parent and child, becomes all the more disgusting, the more, by the action of Modern Industry, all family ties among the proletarians are torn asunder, and their children transformed into simple articles of commerce and instruments of labour.

But you Communists would introduce community of women, screams the whole bourgeoisie in chorus.

The bourgeois sees in his wife a mere instrument of production. He hears that the instruments of production are to be exploited in common, and, naturally, can come to no other conclusion than that the lot of being common to all will likewise fall to the women.

He has not even a suspicion that the real point aimed at is to do away with the status of women as mere instruments of production.

For the rest, nothing is more ridiculous than the virtuous indignation of our bourgeois at the community of women which, they pretend, is to be openly and officially established by the Communists. The Communists have no need to introduce community of women; it has existed almost from time immemorial.

Our bourgeois, not content with having the wives and daughters of their proletarians at their disposal, not to speak of common prostitutes, take the greatest pleasure in seducing each other's wives.

Bourgeois marriage is in reality a system of wives in common and thus, at the most, what the Communists might possibly be reproached with, is that they desire to introduce, in substitution for a hypocritically concealed, an openly legalized community of women. For the rest, it is self-evident that the abolition of the present system of production must bring with it the abolition of the community of women springing from that system, i.e., of prostitution both public and private.

The Communists are further reproached with desiring to abolish countries and nationality.

The working men have no country. We cannot take from them what they have not got. Since the proletariat must first of all acquire political supremacy, must rise to be the leading class of the nation, must constitute itself *the* nation, it is, so far, itself national, though not in the bourgeois sense of the world.

National differences and antagonisms between peoples are daily more and more vanishing, owing to the development of the bourgeoisie, to freedom of commerce, to the world-market, to uniformity in the mode of production and in the conditions of life corresponding thereto.

The supremacy of the proletariat will cause them to vanish still faster. United action, of the leading civilized countries at least, is one of the first conditions for the emancipation of the proletariat.

In proportion as the exploitation of one individual by another is put an end to, the exploitation of one nation by another will also be put an end to. In proportion as the antagonism between classes within the nation vanishes, the hostility of one nation to another will come to an end.

The charges against Communism made from a religious, a philosophical, and, generally, from an ideological standpoint are not deserving of serious examination.

Does it require deep intuition to comprehend that man's ideas, views, and conceptions, in one word, man's consciousness, changes with every change in the conditions of his material existence, in his social relation, and in his social life?

What else does the history of ideas prove, than that intellectual production changes its character in proportion as material production is changed? The ruling ideas of each age have ever been the ideas of its ruling class.

When people speak of ideas that revolutionize society, they do but express the fact, that within the old society, the elements of a new one have been created, and that the dissolution of the old ideas keeps even pace with the dissolution of the old conditions of existence.

When the ancient world was in its last throes, the ancient religions were overcome by Christianity. When Christian ideas succumbed in the eighteenth century to rationalist ideas, feudal society fought its death battle with the then revolutionary bourgeoisie. The ideas of religious liberty and freedom of conscience merely gave expression to the sway of free competition within the domain of knowledge.

'Undoubtedly,' it will be said, 'religious, moral, philosophical, and juridical ideas have been modified in the course of historical development. But religion, morality, philosophy, political science, and law constantly survived this change.'

'There are, besides, eternal truths, such as Freedom, Justice, etc., that are common to all states of society. But Communism abolishes eternal truths, it abolishes all religion and all morality, instead of constituting them on a new basis; it therefore acts in contradiction to all past historical experience.'

What does this accusation reduce itself to? The history of all past society has consisted in the development of class antagonisms, antagonisms that assumed different forms at different epochs.

But whatever form they may have taken, one fact is common to all past ages, viz., the exploitation of one part of society by the other. No wonder, then, that the social consciousness of past ages, despite all the multiplicity and variety it displays, moves within certain common forms, or general ideas, which cannot completely vanish except with the total disappearance of class antagonisms.

The Communist revolution is the most radical rupture with traditional property relations; no wonder that its development involves the most radical rupture with traditional ideas.

But let us have done with the bourgeois objections to Communism.

We have seen above, that the first step in the revolution by the working class is to raise the proletariat to the position of ruling class, to win the battle of democracy.

The proletariat will use its political supremacy to wrest, by degrees, all capital from the bourgeoisie, to centralize all instruments of production in the hands of the State, i.e., of the proletariat organized as the ruling class; and to increase the total of productive forces as rapidly as possible.

Of course, in the beginning this cannot be effected except by means of despotic inroads on the rights of property, and on the conditions of bourgeois production; by means of measures, therefore, which appear economically insufficient and untenable, but which, in the course of the movement, outstrip themselves, necessitate further inroads upon the old social order, and are unavoidable as a means of entirely revolutionizing the mode of production.

These measures will of course be different in different countries.

Nevertheless, in the most advanced countries, the following will be pretty generally applicable.

1. Abolition of property in land and application of all rents of land to public purposes.
2. A heavy progressive or graduated income tax.
3. Abolition of all right of inheritance.
4. Confiscation of the property of all emigrants and rebels.
5. Centralization of credit in the hands of the State, by means of a national bank with State capital and an exclusive monopoly.
6. Centralization of the means of communication and transport in the hands of the State.
7. Extension of factories and instruments of production owned by the State; the bringing into cultivation of wastelands, and the improvement of the soil generally in accordance with a common plan.
8. Equal liability of all to labour. Establishment of industrial armies, especially for agriculture.
9. Combination of agriculture with manufacturing industries; gradual abolition of the distinction between town and country, by a more equable distribution of the population over the country.
10. Free education for all children in public schools. Abolition of children's factory labour in its present form. Combination of education with industrial production, etc., etc.

When, in the course of development, class distinctions have disappeared, and all production has been concentrated in the hands of associated individuals, the public power will lose its political character. Political power, properly so called, is merely the organized power of one class for oppressing another. If the proletariat during its contest with the bourgeoisie is compelled, by the force of circumstances, to organize itself as a class, if, by means of a revolution, it makes itself the ruling class, and, as such, sweeps away by force the old conditions of production, then it will, along with these conditions, have swept away the conditions for the existence of class antagonisms and of classes generally, and will thereby have abolished its own supremacy as a class.

In place of the old bourgeois society, with its classes and class antagonisms, we shall have an association, in which the free development of each is the condition for the free development of all.

BIBLIOGRAPHY

PLATO

Ernest Barker: *The Political Theory of Plato and Aristotle.* New York, Dover, 1959.
Frederick Copleston: *A History of Philosophy,* Vol. I, Part III. New York, Doubleday, 1962.
R. C. Cross and A. D. Woosley: *Plato's Republic.* London, Macmillan, and New York, St. Martin's Press, 1964.
W. K. C. Guthrie: *A History of Greek Philosophy,* Vol. IV. Cambridge, Cambridge University Press, 1975.
R. L. Nettleship: *Lectures on the Republic of Plato.* London and New York, Macmillan, 1906.
K. R. Popper: *The Open Society and its Enemies,* Vol. I. London, Routledge, 1945.
J. E. Raven: *Plato's Thought in the Making.* Cambridge, Cambridge University Press, 1965.
Gilbert Ryle: "Plato," *The Encyclopedia of Philosophy.* New York, Macmillan, 1967.
Paul Shorey: *What Plato Said.* Chicago, University of Chicago Press, 1933.
Gregory Vlastos (ed.): *Plato, A Collection of Critical Essays,* Vol. II. New York, Doubleday, 1971.

ARISTOTLE

D. J. Allan: *The Philosophy of Aristotle.* London and New York, Oxford University Press, 1952.
Renford Bambrough (ed.): *New Essays on Plato and Aristotle.* London, Routledge, and New York, Humanities Press, 1965.
Ernest Barker: *The Politics of Aristotle.* Oxford, Clarendon Press, 1946.
Theodor Gomperz: *Greek Thinkers,* Vol. 4. London, John Murray, 1912.
W. K. C. Guthrie: *A History of Greek Philosophy,* Vol. VI. Cambridge, Cambridge University Press, 1981.
W. von Leyden: *Aristotle on Equality and Justice.* London, Macmillan, 1985.
G. E. R. Lloyd: *Aristotle: The Growth and Structure of His Thought.* Cambridge, Cambridge University Press, 1968.
J. B. Morrall: *Aristotle.* London and Boston, Allen & Unwin, 1977.
R. G. Mulgan: *Aristotle's Political Theory.* Oxford, Clarendon Press, 1977.
George H. Sabine: *A History of Political Theory.* New York, Henry Holt, 1938.

CICERO

R. W. Carlyle and A. J. Carlyle: *A History of Medieval Political Theory in the West,* Vol. 1. New York, Putnam's, 1903.
F. R. Cowell: *Cicero and the Roman Republic.* London, Pitman, 1948.
C. J. Friedrich: *The Philosophy of Law in Historical Perspective.* Chicago, University of Chicago Press, 1958.

Mason Hammond: *City State and World State.* Cambridge, Harvard University Press, 1951.

George H. Sabine: *A History of Political Theory.* New York, Henry Holt, 1938.

George H. Sabine and S. B. Smith: *Cicero, On the Commonwealth.* Indianapolis, Bobbs-Merrill, n.d.

AQUINAS

Dino Bigongiari: *The Political Ideas of St. Thomas Aquinas.* New York, Hafner, 1953.

R. W. Carlyle and A. J. Carlyle: *A History of Medieval Political Theory in the West,* Vol. V. Edinburgh, Blackwood, 1928.

F. C. Copleston: *Aquinas.* Harmondsworth, Penguin, 1955.

A. P. d'Entrèves: *The Medieval Contribution to Political Thought.* London, Oxford University Press, 1939.

Thomas Gilby: *The Political Thought of Thomas Aquinas.* Chicago, University of Chicago Press, 1958.

Anthony Kenny (ed.): *Aquinas, A Collection of Critical Essays.* London, Macmillan, 1969.

D. J. O'Connor: *Aquinas and Natural Law.* London, Macmillan, 1967.

George H. Sabine: *A History of Political Theory.* New York, Henry Holt, 1938.

Ernst Troeltsch: *The Social Teaching of the Christian Churches,* Vol. I. New York, Allen & Unwin, 1931.

Walter Ullman: *Medieval Political Thought.* Harmondsworth, Penguin, 1975.

Walter Ullman: *Principles of Government and Politics in the Middle Ages,* 2nd ed. London, Methuen, 1966.

MACHIAVELLI

Federico Chabod: *Machiavelli and the Renaissance.* London, Harper, 1965.

Bernard Crick (ed.): *The Discourses of Machiavelli.* Harmondsworth, Penguin, 1974.

M. Fleisher (ed.): *Machiavelli and the Nature of Political Thought.* New York, Atheneum, 1972.

Alan Gilbert (trans.): *Machiavelli, The Prince.* New York, Farrar, Straus, n.d.

J. G. A. Pocock: *The Machiavellian Moment.* New Jersey, Princeton University Press, 1975.

Quentin Skinner: *Machiavelli.* London and New York, Oxford University Press, 1981.

L. J. Walker (trans.): *The Discourses of Niccolo Machiavelli.* London and Boston, Routledge, 1975.

J. H. Whitfield: *Discourses on Machiavelli.* London, Cambridge University Press, 1969.

BODIN

J. W. Allen: *A History of Political Thought in the Sixteenth Century.* London, Methuen, 1928.

J. H. Franklin: *Jean Bodin and the Rise of Absolutist Theory.* Cambridge, Harvard University Press, 1973.

J. H. Franklin: *Jean Bodin and the Sixteenth Century Revolution in the Methodology of Law and History.* New York, Columbia University Press, 1963.

N. O. Keohane: *Philosophy and the State in France.* New Jersey, Princeton University Press, 1980.

K. D. McRae (ed.): *Jean Bodin, The Six Books of a Commonweale.* Cambridge, Harvard University Press, 1962.
John Plamenatz: *Man and Society,* Vol. I. London, Longman's, 1963.
George H. Sabine: *A History of Political Theory.* New York, Henry Holt, 1938.

HOBBES
M. Cranston and R. S. Peters: *Hobbes and Rousseau, A Collection of Critical Essays.* New York, Doubleday, 1972.
C. B. Macpherson: *The Political Theory of Possessive Individualism.* London, Oxford University Press, 1962.
Michael Oakeshott (ed.): *Leviathan by Thomas Hobbes.* New York, Macmillan, 1947.
Richard Peters: *Hobbes.* Harmondsworth, Penguin, 1956.
John Plamenatz: *Man and Society,* Vol. I. London, Longman's, 1963.
D. D. Raphael: *Hobbes: Morals and Politics.* London and Boston, Allen & Unwin, 1977.
Leslie Stephen: *Hobbes.* 1904; reprint: Ann Arbor, University of Michigan Press, 1961.
Leo Strauss: *The Political Philosophy of Hobbes.* Oxford, Clarendon Press, 1936.
Howard Warrender: *The Political Philosophy of Hobbes.* Oxford, Oxford University Press, 1957.

PUFENDORF
Duncan Forbes: *Hume's Philosophical Politics.* Cambridge, Cambridge University Press, 1975.
C. J. Friedrich: *The Philosophy of Law in Historical Perspective,* 2nd ed. Chicago, University of Chicago Press, 1963.
Istvan Hont: "The language of sociability and commerce: Samuel Pufendorf and the theoretical foundations of the 'Four-Stages Theory.'" In *The Languages of Political Theory in Early Modern Europe,* Anthony Pagden (ed.). Cambridge, Cambridge University Press, 1987.
Leonard Krieger: *The Politics of Discretion.* Chicago, University of Chicago Press, 1965.
Patrick Riley (ed.): *The Political Writings of Leibniz.* Cambridge, Cambridge University Press, 1972.
J. B. Schneewind: "Pufendorf's Place in the History of Ethics." *Synthese 72,* 123—155, 1987.
Richard Tuck: *Natural Rights Theories, Their Origin and Development.* Cambridge, Cambridge University Press, 1979.
James Tully: *A Discourse on Property.* Cambridge, Cambridge University Press, 1980.

LOCKE
Richard Ashcraft: *Locke's "Two Treatises of Government."* London and Boston, Allen & Unwin, 1987.
Richard Ashcraft: *Revolutionary Politics and Locke's "Two Treatises of Government."* New Jersey, Princeton University Press, 1986.
John Dunn: *The Political Thought of John Locke.* Cambridge, Cambridge University Press, 1969.
J. H. Franklin: *John Locke and the Theory of Sovereignty.* Cambridge, Cambridge University Press, 1978.

J. W. Gough: *John Locke's Political Philosophy*, 2nd ed. Oxford, Clarendon Press, 1973.

Peter Laslett (ed.): *Locke, Two Treatises of Government*. Cambridge, Cambridge University Press, 1970.

C. B. Martin and D. M. Armstrong (eds.): *Locke and Berkeley, A Collection of Critical Essays*. New York, Doubleday, 1968.

D. J. O'Connor: *John Locke*. Harmondsworth, Penguin, 1952.

Gordon Schochet (ed.): *Life, Liberty and Property: Essays on Locke's Political Ideas*. Belmont, California, Wadsworth, 1971.

James Tully: *A Discourse on Property*. Cambridge, Cambridge University Press, 1980.

J. W. Yolton, (ed.): *John Locke: Problems and Perspectives*. Cambridge, Cambridge University Press, 1969.

MONTESQUIEU
Isaiah Berlin: *Against the Current*. London, Hogarth Press, 1979.

C. P. Courtney: *Montesquieu and Burke*. Oxford, Basil Blackwell, 1963.

F. T. H. Fletcher: *Montesquieu and English Politics*. London, Edward Arnold & Co., 1939.

Norman Hampson: *Will and Circumstance. Montesquieu, Rousseau and the French Revolution*. London, Duckworth, 1983.

T. L. Pangle: *Montesquieu's Philosophy of Liberalism*. Chicago, University of Chicago Press, 1973.

Melvin Richter: *The Political Theory of Montesquieu*. Cambridge, Cambridge University Press, 1977.

Patrick Riley: *The General Will before Rousseau*. New Jersey, Princeton University Press, 1986.

Robert Shakelton: *Montesquieu, A Critical Biography*. Oxford, Oxford University Press, 1961.

J. N. Shklar: *Montesquieu*. Oxford, Oxford University Press, 1987.

W. Stark: *Montesquieu, Pioneer of the Sociology of Knowledge*. London, Routledge, 1960.

M. H. Waddicor: *Montesquieu and The Philosophy of Natural Law*. The Hague, Nijhoff, 1970.

HUME
Duncan Forbes: *Hume's Philosophical Politics*. Cambridge, Cambridge University Press, 1975.

Knud Haakonssen: *The Science of a Legislator: The Natural Jurisprudence of David Hume & Adam Smith*. Cambridge, Cambridge University Press, 1981.

D. W. Livingston and J. T. King (eds.): *Hume: A Re-valuation*. New York, Fordham University Press, 1976.

David Miller: *Philosophy and Ideology in Hume's Political Thought*. Oxford, Clarendon Press, 1981.

James Moore: "Hume's Theory of Justice and Property." *Political Studies XXIV*, 103–119, 1976.

G. P. Morice (ed.): *Hume: Bicentenary Papers*. Edinburgh, Edinburgh University Press, 1977.

John Plamenatz: *Man and Society*, Vol I. London, Longman's, 1963.

J. B. Stewart: *The Moral and Political Philosophy of David Hume.* New York, Columbia University Press, 1963.
Barry Stroud: *Hume.* London and Boston, Routledge, 1977.
Frederick Whelan: *Order and Artifice in Hume's Political Philosophy.* New Jersey, Princeton University Press, 1985.

ROUSSEAU
A. Cobban: *Rousseau and the Modern State,* 2nd rev. ed. London, Allen & Unwin, 1964.
M. Cranston and R. S. Peters (eds.): *Hobbes and Rousseau, A Collection of Critical Essays.* New York, Doubleday, 1972.
Ronald Grimsley: *The Philosophy of Rousseau.* London, Oxford University Press, 1973.
J. C. Hall: *Rousseau.* London, Macmillan, 1973.
C. W. Hendel: *Jean-Jacques Rousseau: Moralist.* Indianapolis, Bobbs-Merrill, 1934.
R. D. Masters: *The Political Philosophy of Rousseau.* New Jersey, Princeton University Press, 1968.
John Plamenatz: *Man and Society,* Vol. I. London, Longman's, 1963.
J. N. Shklar: *Men and Citizens: A Study of Rousseau's Social Theory.* Cambridge, Harvard University Press, 1969.

BURKE
G. W. Chapman: *Edmund Burke: the Practical Imagination.* Cambridge, Harvard University Press, 1967.
C. B. Cone: *Burke and the Nature of Politics,* 2 Vols. Lexington, University of Kentucky Press, 1957–64.
T. W. Copeland: *Edmund Burke: Six Essays.* London, Jonathan Cape, 1950.
H. J. Laski: *Political Thought in England, Locke to Bentham.* New York, Oxford University Press, 1920.
C. B. Macpherson: *Burke.* Oxford, Oxford University Press, 1980.
H. C. Mansfield: *Statesmanship and Party Government.* Chicago, University of Chicago Press, 1965.
Charles Parkin: *The Moral Basis of Burke's Political Thoughts.* Cambridge, Cambridge University Press, 1956.
John Plamenatz: *Man and Society,* Vol. I. London, Longman's, 1963.
P. J. Stanlis: *Edmund Burke and the Natural Law.* Ann Arbor, University of Michigan Press, 1958.
B. T. Wilkins: *The Problem of Burke's Political Philosophy.* Oxford, Clarendon Press, 1967.

PAINE
A. O. Aldridge: *Thomas Paine's American Ideology.* Newark, University of Delaware Press, 1984.
A. J. Ayer, *Thomas Paine.* London, Secker & Warburg, 1988.
J. T. Boulton: *The Language of Politics in the Age of Wilkes and Burke.* London, Routledge, 1963.
M. D. Conway: *The Life of Thomas Paine,* 2 Vols. New York, G. P. Putnam's Sons, 1892.

R. R. Fennessy: *Burke, Paine and the Rights of Man.* The Hague, Nijhoff, 1963.
Eric Foner: *Tom Paine and Revolutionary America.* Oxford, Oxford University Press, 1976.
D. F. Hawke: *Paine.* New York, Harper & Row, 1974.
Audrey Williamson: *Thomas Paine, His Life, Work, and Times.* New York, St. Martin's Press, 1973.

HEGEL

H. B. Acton: "Hegel", *The Encyclopedia of Philosophy.* New York, Macmillan, 1967.
Shlomo Aveneri: *Hegel's Theory of the Modern State.* Cambridge, Cambridge University Press, 1972.
C. J. Friedrich: *The Philosophy of History, G.W.F. Hegel.* New York, Dover, 1956.
C. J. Friedrich: *The Philosophy of Law in Historical Perspective.* Chicago, University of Chicago Press, 1958.
Sidney Hook: *From Hegel to Marx.* New York, Humanities Press, 1950.
Michael Inwood (ed.): *Hegel.* London, Oxford University Press, 1985.
Walter Kaufmann (ed.): *Hegel's Political Philosophy.* New York, Atherton Press, 1970.
T. M. Knox (trans.): *Hegel's Philosophy of Right.* Oxford, Clarendon Press, 1945.
Herbert Marcuse: *Reason and Revolution.* New York, Oxford University Press, 1941.
G. D. O'Brien: *Hegel on Reason and History.* Chicago, University of Chicago Press, 1975.
J. O'Malley (ed.): *Karl Marx: Critique of Hegel's Philosophy of Right.* Cambridge, Cambridge University Press, 1970.
Z. A. Pelczynski (ed.): *Hegel's Political Philosophy.* Cambridge, Cambridge University Press, 1971.
Z. A. Pelczynski: *The State and Civil Society: Studies in Hegel's Political Philosophy.* Cambridge, Cambridge University Press, 1984.
Raymond Plant: *Hegel.* London, Allen & Unwin, 1973.
K. R. Popper: *The Open Society and Its Enemies,* Vol. II. London, Routledge, 1945.
Stanley Rosen: *Hegel.* New Haven, Yale University Press, 1974.
Charles Taylor: *Hegel.* Cambridge, Cambridge University Press, 1975.
Charles Taylor: *Hegel and Modern Society.* Cambridge, Cambridge University Press, 1979.
W. H. Walsh: *Hegelian Ethics.* New York, St. Martin's Press, 1969.

MILL

R. P. Anschutz: *The Philosophy of J.S. Mill.* Oxford, Clarendon Press, 1953.
Isaiah Berlin: *Four Essays on Liberty.* London, Oxford University Press, 1969.
Karl Brittain: *John Stuart Mill.* Harmondsworth, Penguin, 1953.
Graeme Duncan: *Marx and Mill.* Cambridge, Cambridge University Press, 1973.
Gertrude Himmelfarb (ed.): *On Liberty.* Harmondsworth, Penguin, 1974.
S. R. Letwyn: *The Pursuit of Certainty.* Cambridge, Cambridge University Press, 1965.
H. J. McCloskey: *John Stuart Mill: A Critical Study.* New York, St. Martin's Press, 1971.
John Plamenatz: *The English Utilitarians.* Oxford, Blackwell, 1949.
Peter Radcliff (ed.): *Limits of Liberty.* Belmont, California, Wadsworth, 1966.
J. M. Robson: *The Improvement of Mankind.* Toronto, University of Toronto Press, 1968.

Alan Ryan: *J. S. Mill.* London, Routledge, 1975.

J. B. Schneewind (ed.): *Mill: A Collection of Critical Essays.* New York, Doubleday, 1968.

David Spitz (ed.): *On Liberty: John Stuart Mill.* New York, Norton, 1975.

Leslie Stephen: *The English Utilitarians,* Vol. 3. London, Duckworth, 1900.

C. L. Ten: *Mill on Liberty.* London, Oxford University Press, 1980.

MARX

Shlomo Aveneri: *The Social and Political Thought of Karl Marx.* Cambridge, Cambridge University Press, 1968.

Tom Bottomore (ed.): *Karl Marx.* Oxford, Blackwell, 1979.

Eugene Kamenka: *Marxism and Ethics.* New York, St. Martin's Press, 1969.

Eugene Kamenka (ed.): *The Portable Karl Marx.* New York, Penguin, 1983.

Henri Lefebre: *The Sociology of Karl Marx.* Harmondsworth, Penguin, 1968.

George Lichtheim: *Marxism.* London, Routledge, 1967.

D. McLellan: *Karl Marx: His Life and Thought.* London, Macmillan, 1973.

Bertell Ollman: *Alienation.* Cambridge, Cambridge University Press, 1971.

John Plamenatz: *Man and Society,* Vol. II. London, Longman's, 1963.

Melvin Rader: *Marx's Interpretation of History.* New York, Oxford University Press, 1979.

R. C. Tucker: *The Marxian Revolutionary Idea.* London, Allen & Unwin, 1970.

Allen Wood: *Karl Marx.* London, Routledge, 1981.